SO-CEC-860

URBAN RENEWAL: PEOPLE, POLITICS, AND PLANNING

JEWEL BELLUSH received her B.A. from the University of Wisconsin and the M.A. and Ph.D. from Columbia University. She is an Associate Professor of Political Science at Hunter College in New York City.

She has contributed articles to several journals, among them the *New England Quarterly* and the *National Civic Review*.

Professor Bellush has worked in California as executive assistant to Governor Brown's Commission on Metropolitan Area Problems, and is actively interested in the planning problems of New York City. She lives, with her husband and their two children, in Pelham, New York.

MURRAY HAUSKNECHT received his Bachelor of Social Science from the City College of New York, and the M.A. and Ph.D. from Columbia University. He is an Assistant Professor of Sociology at Hunter College in New York.

Professor Hausknecht is the author of *The Joiners: A Sociological Description of Voluntary Association Membership in the United States,* and numerous papers and articles which have appeared in such publications as *Dissent, The Journal of the American Institute of Planners,* and *The American Journal of Economics and Sociology*.

Professor Hausknecht, his wife, and two children live in New York City.

Urban Renewal: People, Politics, and Planning

EDITED BY JEWEL BELLUSH AND
MURRAY HAUSKNECHT

ANCHOR BOOKS
DOUBLEDAY & COMPANY, INC.
GARDEN CITY, NEW YORK

The Anchor Books edition is the first publication
of *Urban Renewal: People, Politics, and Planning*

Anchor Books edition: 1967

Library of Congress Catalog Card Number 67–10410
Copyright © 1967 by Jewel Bellush and Murray Hausknecht
All Rights Reserved
Printed in the United States of America

Grateful acknowledgment is made for the use of the following
material:

"The Political Side of Urban Development and Redevelopment"
by Scott Greer and David W. Minar, from *The Annals of the
American Academy of Political and Social Science,* March 1964.
Reprinted by permission of The American Academy of Political
and Social Science and the authors.

Selected portions of "The Myths of Housing Reform" by John P.
Dean, from *American Sociological Review.* Reprinted by permission of The American Sociological Association and Lois R. Dean.

Excerpt from *Urban Renewal and American Cities* by Scott
Greer. Copyright © 1965 by The Bobbs-Merrill Company, Inc.
Reprinted by permission of the publishers.

Selected portions of "NHA: The Strategy of Slum Clearance"
from *Urban Renewal Politics* by Harold Kaplan. Copyright © 1963
by Columbia University Press. Reprinted by permission of the
publisher.

"Some Sources of Residential Satisfaction in an Urban Slum"
by Marc Fried and Peggy Gleicher, from Volume XXVII, No. 4
(November 1961), *Journal of the American Institute of Planners;*
"The Slum: Its Nature, Use, and Users" by John R. Seeley, from
Volume XXV, No. 1 (February 1959), *Journal of the American
Institute of Planners;* "Planning and Politics: Citizen Participation
in Urban Renewal" by James Q. Wilson, from Volume XXIX, No.
4 (November 1963), *Journal of the American Institute of Plan-
ners;* selected portions of "The Housing of Relocated Families" by
Chester W. Hartman, from Volume XXX, No. 4 (November 1964),
Journal of the American Institute of Planners; selected portions of
"Fear and the House-as-Haven in the Lower Class" by Lee Rain-
water, from Volume XXXII, No. 1 (January 1966), *Journal of the
American Institute of Planners;* and selected portions of "Plan
Reviews: New York City's Renewal Strategy, 1965" by Richard

May, Jr. and Walter Thabit, from Volume XXXII, March 1966, *Journal of the American Institute of Planners.* All reprinted by permission of the American Institute of Planners and the authors.

"The Failure of Urban Renewal: a Critique and Some Proposals" by Herbert J. Gans; and selected portions of "Urban Renewal: Controversy" by George M. Raymond, Malcolm D. Rivkin, and Herbert Gans. Copyright © 1965 by the American Jewish Committee. Reprinted by permission of *Commentary,* in which the articles first appeared, and the authors.

"Lincoln Center, Emporium of the Arts" by Percival Goodman, from *Dissent,* Summer 1961, Volume VIII, No. 3. Reprinted by permission of *Dissent.*

Excerpt from *Politics, Planning and the Public Interest* by Martin Meyerson and Edward Banfield. Copyright 1955 by The Free Press, a Corporation. Reprinted by permission of the publisher.

Excerpts from *The Future of Housing* by Charles Abrams, copyright 1946 by Harper & Brothers; and "Some Blessings of Urban Renewal" from *The City is the Frontier* by Charles Abrams, copyright © 1965 by Charles Abrams. Reprinted by permission of Harper & Row, Publishers.

Excerpt from *Myth and Reality of Our Urban Problems* by Raymond Vernon. Copyright 1962, by the President and Fellows of Harvard College. Reprinted by permission of Harvard University Press.

Selected portions of "Alcoa Looks at Urban Redevelopment," a speech delivered by Leon E. Hickman at the National Mortgage Banking Conference, February 17, 1964. Reprinted by permission of Leon E. Hickman.

Selected portions of "The Relation of Local Government Structure to Urban Renewal" by George S. Duggar, from *Law and Contemporary Problems* (Vol. 26, No. 1, Winter 1961), copyright 1961 by Duke University; an adaptation of "The Sophistry that Made Urban Renewal Possible" by Martin Anderson and selected portions of "Urban Renewal Realistically Reappraised" by Robert Groberg, from *Law and Contemporary Problems* (Vol. 30, No. 1, Winter 1965), copyright 1965 by Duke University. Reprinted by permission of *Law and Contemporary Problems* and the authors.

Excerpts from *Manchild in the Promised Land* by Claude Brown. Copyright © Claude Brown 1965. Reprinted by permission of The Macmillan Company.

Excerpt from *The Federal Bulldozer* by Martin Anderson. Copyright © 1964 by the Massachusetts Institute of Technology and the President and Fellows of Harvard College. Reprinted by permission of The M.I.T. Press.

Abridgment of "Omissions in evaluating relocation effectiveness cited" by Chester W. Hartman and selected portions of " 'New Towns' Role in Urban Growth Explored" by Robert Gladstone, from Vol. 23, No. 2, January 1966, *Journal of Housing.* Reprinted by permission of the National Association of Housing and Redevelopment Officials and the authors.

Excerpts from *The Progressives and the Slums* by Roy Lubove. Reprinted by permission of the University of Pittsburgh Press.

Excerpt from *The Death and Life of Great American Cities* by Jane Jacobs. Copyright © 1961 by Jane Jacobs. Reprinted by permission of Random House, Inc., and Jonathan Cape, Ltd.

Selected portions from "Rental Assistance for Large Families: An Interim Report" by Joel Cogen and Kathryn Feidelson, from *Pratt Planning Papers*, June 1964. Reprinted by permission of George M. Raymond.

Excerpts from *Who Governs?* by Robert Dahl. Reprinted by permission of the Yale University Press.

Excerpts from *The Urban Complex* by Robert C. Weaver. Copyright © 1960, 1961, 1963, 1964 by Robert C. Weaver. Reprinted by permission of Doubleday & Company, Inc.

Excerpt from *The Shook-up Generation* by Harrison E. Salisbury. Copyright © 1958 by Harrison E. Salisbury. Reprinted by permission of Harper & Row, Publishers, and Curtis Brown, Ltd., New York.

For Gerry and Debbi
and
David and Gina

ACKNOWLEDGMENTS

Our chief debt of gratitude is to the authors of the papers in this volume for their cooperation. We are also greatly indebted to Denise Rathbun for initially encouraging our project, and for her many invaluable suggestions and criticisms. Murray N. Wortzel of Hunter College in the Bronx Library was of great help in calmly dealing with our often importunate requests, and without Diane Feld's efficient clerical aid we would have drowned in a sea of paper. This book is an offshoot of a research on urban renewal that has been aided by grants from The George N. Shuster Fund of Hunter College, The Center for Education in Politics, as well as assistance from The Urban Research Center of Hunter College. Finally, thanks are due to the patience and forbearance of our families who have their own unique reason for ambivalence about urban renewal.

CONTENTS

IV. EXECUTION

V. OVERVIEW: SUCCESS OR FAILURE?

VI. NEW DIRECTIONS

INTRODUCTION

The American city is a universe expanding at a rapid rate along several axes. In 1880 about 28 per cent of all Americans lived in urban communities; in 1960 the Census Bureau reported that this figure had grown to 70 per cent. The growth in the size of the urban population is linked to changes in the social and economic structure of the society, and as a result the conventional definitions of the city have become obsolete. The city of concern to urban planners, scholars, and men of affairs is the "metropolitan area" that includes the suburbs and smaller cities in the counties surrounding a large central city. Some even talk of "Megalopolis," the contiguous metropolitan areas stretching from Washington, D.C. to Boston, as a model for thinking about the city and the urban society of the future. Matching this lateral expansion is a vertical growth; today the office skyscraper and the residential tower substitute for the medieval wall as the dominant symbols of the city. From these offices, the corporate headquarters of the large manufacturing, financial, and communication industries issue the decisions that affect the life of the entire society; the American city as never before has become the center of power and influence. Yet growth by itself is not an unequivocal sign that all is well.

The American city grew in a more or less uncontrolled fashion, for it developed in a political and social climate of *laissez-faire* liberalism. Consequently, the contemporary city as a physical entity inherits a catalogue of problems that are among the stable clichés of the society: substandard and deteriorating housing; air and water pollution; urban sprawl; monstrous traffic jams. But the city is also a community, and it too has been affected by a history of, as it were, absent-minded growth. Weaving through the preoccupations with the physical problems of the city is a consciousness of the social ills besetting the community: crime, delinquency, addiction, racial conflict, the flight of the middle classes. These concerns have given rise to discussions, arguments, denunciations, and sermons. But amidst all the public and private talk and the exhortations of the professional Pollyannas and Jeremiahs, one thing remains constant: An almost universal agreement that "something must be done." One response to this consensus has been urban renewal.

But the response itself is now as problematic as the phenomena it is designed to remedy. Like all policies relevant to the fundamental problems of a society and civilization, urban renewal emerged from a fierce debate that cut across the usual political and ideological categories. Now that it has been in existence for some time the debate continues, and, if anything, grows in shrillness and intensity. Whether the focus is on its goals, procedures, or achievements, there is little agreement. As with all such controversies in our society the ratio of heat to light steadily increases; people lose sight of what the argument is all about; and, as the fog of words becomes thicker, more and more people may decide the whole issue is not worth bothering about. But this last is surely the ultimate disaster. Urban renewal may or may not be an adequate response to the problems of the city, but we must grapple with the questions it raises if the cities and indeed the society itself are to retain their vitality.

It is too much to expect of one book that it dissipate all the heat, and shine the light of rationality over the scene so that all the issues and problems stand forth in unambiguous clarity. Nor, for that matter, should one desire to eliminate all the heat, for passion is a valuable, if dangerous, stimulus to thought. Nor, again, should one *want* to achieve unambiguous clarity, for that would seriously misrepresent the inherent nature of the problems of the city and urban renewal; these are human problems that, by definition, are surrounded by a penumbra of ambiguity. Our objectives in this volume, therefore, have been scaled accordingly.

The issues and questions we have elected to concentrate on are those we feel are fundamental to the problems of the city and urban renewal as a public policy. They also have, we hope, a broader and more general pertinence. No discussion of renewal can long avoid a cluster of related themes: planning; bureaucracy; the allocation of resources and the political process; the proper limits of government power; poverty; class interests; etc. But can these themes be avoided in the discussion of any public policy? To explore urban renewal, then, is also to explore fundamental problems of the society. To retain the smell and feel of the real world we try to recapture the clamor of controversy by matching opposing points of view in our selections whenever possible. In addition to helping one remember the realities of life, this device should also be a reminder that it is only out of continuing controversy and discussion that adequate public policies are forged in a democratic society.

Part I of the volume is devoted to examining the history of the early roots of renewal and some basic constitutional issues it raises. In Part II questions about the objectives of urban renewal are raised, and one major goal, slum clearance, is examined in greater detail. Part III revolves about renewal as a political process with the emphasis on institutional structure, problems of leadership and organization, and citizen participation. The progress or lack of progress of renewal is examined in Part IV, with problems of relocation and public housing receiving special attention. Part V is an "overview," an attempt to assess renewal as a whole. Finally, in Part VI some innovations and new ideas are described and tentatively assessed.

Urban Renewal: People, Politics, and Planning

I. ANTECEDENTS

HOUSING AND THE NEW DEAL

Before one plunges into the many facets of urban renewal it is worthwhile to have some of its historical background in mind as well as a brief overview of the entire program from its inception to its present state. This is the task of the first essay. The major portion concentrates on the period of the Roosevelt and Truman administrations for two reasons: First, the subsequent legislation of the Eisenhower, Kennedy, and Johnson administrations is either an extension or an elaboration of the basic legislation enacted between 1932 and 1949. Second, the later legislation and its consequences are the subjects of various selections throughout the rest of the volume.

Despite what many contemporaries thought, the New Deal did not spring fully formed from the fevered imagination of Franklin D. Roosevelt. The spirit and sentiments of the New Deal that captured the imagination of the great mass of working class people can be traced back to many ideas of the Progressive Era. To the extent that the New Deal legislation was animated by a concern with the "one-third of a nation ill-housed, ill-clothed, and ill-fed," this concern was stimulated in significant measure by the ideas and work of such people as Jane Addams, Lillian Wald, and Jacob Riis. In the selection from Roy Lubove's book on the Progressives and housing reform we can see their conceptions of the nature of the city, the problems of the poor, and the role housing reform was to play in ameliorating the conditions they deplored. Their most important legacy, perhaps, was the notion that better housing was the best way to solve all social problems of an urban community—their "environmental determinism," as Lubove puts it. This legacy is still part of our current intellectual coin, but John Dean, writing in the mid-forties with the benefit of social research findings, demonstrates the "mythical" nature of these beliefs. In the concluding section of his paper he makes some suggestions that, by implication, cast doubt on the validity of the thinking behind some renewal programs of the fifties and sixties.

But the New Deal, while concerned with the "one-third of a nation," was a highly pragmatic series of programs that were far from being subversive of established social and economic institutions. Charles Abrams shows how its housing programs were based on the assumption that housing needs had to be provided by private enterprise, and how this undermined efforts to deal effectively with the ill-housed urban poor.

If housing reform has suffered from the intellectual and ideological confusions of its friends, it has suffered more from the power of its enemies. The excerpt from the Congressional Hearings on the Housing Bill of 1945 illustrates the sentiments and attitudes of the powerful real estate lobbies. Their arguments were faithfully repeated year after year until the Housing Act of 1949 was finally approved by Congress. As subsequent events made clear, it is still an open question as to who won and who lost in that final battle.

URBAN RENEWAL: AN HISTORICAL OVERVIEW

Jewel Bellush and Murray Hausknecht

In 1890 the United States Census Bureau officially declared the frontier closed, and reported that about one-third of the population was "urban." For the prescient this meant that in the future the urbanized, industrial areas of the nation would determine essential characteristics of the society; that the social, economic, and political institutions of the past would have to be modified and adapted to meet the new exigencies. Not much foresight was needed, on the other hand, to recognize that already the forces of industrialization and mass immigration to the land of opportunity had created new problems and intensified old ones. Most people, however, grasped neither the meaning of the present nor the portents for the future.

Yet there were some whose attention and interest were caught by the problems of the urban community, and who were to lay the groundwork for programs that were to be influential for many years to come. Between 1890 and World War I the settlement house movement headed by such figures as Jane Addams in Chicago and Lillian Wald in New York brought the problems of immigrants in slum neighborhoods into focus. During the same period Jacob Riis gained fame by his reporting on the problems of assimilation and the conditions in the slums. As a result of his efforts and those of Lawrence Veiller, New York and other states passed Tenement Laws that were the initial, faltering steps in achieving decent housing for the poor. Aside from their concrete achievements, these urban reforms, along with others in the Progressive Movement, succeeded in raising the social level of awareness about problems of poverty and housing. Unfortunately, the twenties saw little progress. There were some philanthropists who financed small-scale "model" housing projects for slum dwellers, but these were no more than mere experiments. New York State passed a Limited Dividend Housing Law designed to stimulate non-profit housing, but what little housing was built under its provisions mainly benefited the lower middle class and skilled workers. In the New York metropolitan area as well as a scattering of other places around the country some planned communities were built. Among the best-known of these were Radburn, New Jersey and Sunnyside Gardens in New York City, but they too were more appropriate to the needs of the middle class who moved into them than to the needs of those living in substandard tenements. In reality, it was not until the first Roosevelt administration that the problem of housing began to occupy something like the center of the stage for public policy.

PROSPERITY AND DEPRESSION: 1929–33

At the height of prosperity in 1929 eighteen million families, roughly 50 per cent of all families, were living at minimum subsistence income. A government inventory of real property in sixty-four cities revealed that 2.3 per cent of all dwellings were unfit for human habitation; 15.6 per cent needed major structural repairs; and only 37.7 per cent were in "good" condition. Much of the nation's housing was described as obsolete; many units lacked an interior water supply, were without private toilets, and a third still had only wood- or coal-burning stoves. One expert summarized the situation by estimating that about ten million people lived under conditions that endangered their "health, safety, and morals." It was against this background of need and absence of social initiative in coping with the need that the country entered the Great Depression.

The Hoover administration responded to the crisis by an attempt to stimulate the economy through increasing the supply of capital. In order to cut down the rate of mortgage foreclosure the Home Loan Board, established by the Federal Home Loan Act of 1932, was empowered to advance money to lending institutions to secure first mortgages, and the Emergency Relief and Reconstruction Act allowed the Reconstruction Finance Administration to lend money to limited dividend housing corporations. However, these measures were insufficient to stem the growing economic crisis or the continuing deterioration of the housing situation. Between 1928 and 1933 construction of residential property fell 95 per cent; expenditures for home repairs dropped half a billion to fifty million dollars; and in 1932 alone 273,000 homeowners lost their property through foreclosures.

The prevailing mood of the time, a combination of traditional definitions of the situation and an uneasy awareness that new approaches might be necessary, are apparent in the conclusions of a housing conference called by President Hoover:

> The committee has taken into account the housing experience of European countries. Their governments have been forced to participate in low-cost housing . . . to a much greater degree than we hope will be necessary in the United States. This committee is firmly of the opinion that private initiative taken by private capital is essential, at the present time, for the successful planning and operation of large-scale projects. Still, if we do not accept this challenge, the alternative may have to be government housing.[1]

HOLC

The measures adopted by the Hoover administration to cut the rate of mortgage foreclosure were ineffective; by 1933 mortgages were being foreclosed at the rate of a thousand a day. The Home Owners Loan Corporation, established by the new Roosevelt administration, was designed to alleviate this situation by providing money to refinance existing mortgages at lower interest rates and longer repayment periods. Within three years HOLC loaned three billion dollars to refinance the mortgages of over a million homeowners. Although this New Deal measure was designed to help banks weather the financial crisis, it also saved thousands of small homeowners. It also paid an unexpected dividend to the Administration. Thus, while there is considerable justice to Charles Abrams' description of the program as a windfall which helped "bail out the lenders," the small homeowner saw it as a program that helped save his home, and he was duly grateful to the Administration.[2] If the HOLC was beneficial for banks and homeowners, there can be no doubt that the ill-housed "one-third of a nation" were excluded from its benefits.

[1] "Large-Scale Housing," in John M. Gries and James Ford (eds.), *Final Report on the Committee on Large-Scale Operations.* The President's Conference on Home Building and Home Ownership (Washington, D.C., 1932), p. 24.

The statistics of housing conditions are based on United States Department of Commerce, *Real Property Inventory* (Washington, D.C.: Government Printing Office, 1934), and United States Federal Emergency Administration of Public Works *Urban Housing: The Story of PWA* (Housing Division, 1933–36, Bulletin No. 2, Washington, D.C., 1936).

[2] Abrams, Charles, *The Future of Housing* (New York: Harper & Brothers, 1946), Chapter 18.

FHA

In 1934 steps were taken to stimulate the building industry with the establishment of the Federal Housing Administration under the terms of the National Housing Act. FHA was to encourage home building by insuring new home mortgages and loans for repair and construction at low interest rates and for long repayment periods. Established early in the New Deal as a measure to cope with an economic emergency, FHA has remained a permanent fixture of the economy. No matter what the formal ideologies of the administrations in power have been, none has seen fit to do away with a system which allows the government to assume the risks that in a "free enterprise" system are supposed to be assumed by the entrepreneur.

During the thirties the FHA program did little or nothing to alleviate the housing situation of blue-collar people or the lower middle class, because FHA regulations discouraged the issuance of mortgages on low-priced homes and rental properties. It was not until after World War II, under the stimulus of the housing shortage, that FHA became a significant factor in the housing problems of these two strata. Like HOLC, then, this new measure still did not come to grips with the problems of housing as a distinct issue in its own right.

PWA and Housing

However, there was one early New Deal Program that began to take a few tentative, timid steps in this direction. In 1933 the Public Works Administration was established by the National Industrial Recovery Act (NIRA) to administer public works programs, another means of stimulating the economy and employment. As part of the over-all PWA program the government for the first time sponsored slum clearance projects and public low-rent housing.

The Housing Division of PWA was authorized to:

1. lend money to any limited-dividend corporation financing slum clearance projects, or engaged in construction or rehabilitation of low-rent housing;
2. make grants and loans to public bodies for the same purposes;
3. buy, condemn, sell, or lease property in developing new projects itself.

Originally, PWA attempted to interest private capital by means of limited dividend projects. Unfortunately, this resulted in a concerted effort by real estate operators to unload on the government, at excessive valuations, land for which they could find no other buyers. The Housing Division then entered on a program of lending money and awarding grants to cover the entire cost of the housing projects, thus assuming responsibility for construction. Under this program the PWA cleared some of the country's most widely publicized slum areas, and replaced them with fifty low-rent developments that provided dwellings for some twenty-two thousand families in over thirty cities.[3]

Toward the end of the program Harold Ickes outlined its principal objectives:

> First, to deal with the unemployment situation by giving employment to workers. . . . Second, to furnish decent, sanitary dwellings to those whose incomes are so low that private capital is unable to provide adequate housing within their means. Third, to eradicate and rehabilitate slum areas. Fourth, to demonstrate to private builders, planners, and the public at large the practicability of large-scale community planning. Fifth, to encourage the enactment of necessary state-enabling housing legislation so as to make possible an early decentralization of the construction and operation of public-housing projects.[4]

This is a paradigmatic statement not only of the New Deal's approach to the problems of an urban society but of every subsequent administration. It also contains clues to the difficulties which this and later programs experienced.

First, there is an oblique recognition that a problem exists: a significant portion of the population is "ill-housed" and will continue to remain so because it is poor. Second, the economic system is functioning so badly that it cannot meet the needs of the poor, but, nonetheless, it assumed that the economic institutions of the society *can* meet those needs. The function of government is to do nothing more than to "demonstrate" how these needs can be met and to encourage "private enterprise" to the task—with judicious subsidies.

[3] Beyer, Glenn, *Housing: A Factual Analysis* (New York: The Macmillan Company, 1958), p. 247.

[4] Quoted in Swanson, Bert, "The Public Policy of Urban Renewal: Its Goals, Trends and Conditions in New York City." Paper delivered at American Political Science Association, New York City, September 7, 1963, p. 10.

Clearly, the focus is not on dealing with the problems of urban dwellers as such, but on stimulating the economy. In addition, we can see the ambivalence about the responsibility of the federal government in the field of housing and slums; an ambivalence reflecting the era's "climate of opinion."

Indeed, in many ways the program was far ahead of many segments of public opinion. Thus, in 1935 a Federal Court ruled that the Housing Division could not condemn property for housing, since this did not constitute a public use. This circumscribed the slum clearance program, because the Division was restricted to sites whose owners were willing to sell. Within most local communities there was noticeable lack of enthusiasm for slum clearance and public housing, and this too circumscribed the extent of the program. There were some notable exceptions: Experimental projects in Chicago, Memphis, Atlanta, and Cleveland were brick monuments symbolic of the New Deal's willingness to respond to the needs of the working class slum dweller. Unfortunately, many of these monuments were too expensive for the working class to live in. Located on expensive land, rents averaged twenty-six dollars a month—too high for the average slum dweller. Knickerbocker Village, for example, in New York's Lower East Side charged $12.50 a room per month, although the rents in the area before clearance ranged from three to six dollars a room per month. Langdon Post, Chairman of the New York City Housing Authority in the early thirties, acknowledged that it was impossible to construct new buildings that would rent for less than between ten to twelve dollars a room. This situation in which the slum dweller does not reap the benefits of slum clearance remains a perennial feature of such programs.[5]

Another major problem was related to the long-standing issue of federal versus local control. Ickes, highly sensitive to the possibilities of corruption at the local community level, maintained tight control over funds, and local administrators complained that it interfered with the proper planning of projects.[6] There were others who favored even stronger federal intervention: Some felt it would be instrumental in the setting of standards, while others lacked confidence in the technical competence of local officials. Among those who

[5] Post, Langdon W., *The Challenge of Housing* (New York: Farrar and Rinehart, 1938).

[6] Ickes, Harold, *The Secret Diary of Harold Ickes* (New York: Simon and Schuster, 1954, pp. 662, 665–69; Abrams, pp. 251 ff.).

favored a strong federal role was Robert Weaver, later to become the government's chief housing official under Presidents Kennedy and Johnson. Weaver's argument was that federal control made for a more equitable distribution of dwellings to Negroes. His position, of course, points up which is usually involved in the conflict over which level of government should exercise control; it is less a matter of ideological conviction than a matter of one's specific interests.

Despite the severe limitations of the PWA housing program, in conception and actuality, it did serve some valuable functions. By creating the first government-subsidized housing projects for low-income groups, it established an important precedent for future policy. In doing this it focused public attention on housing needs, and thus helped gain support for future programs. The experience gained in these initial ventures by officials at all levels of government facilitated the implementation of future programs. In short, the PWA housing program was a dress rehearsal for the programs to be authorized in the last half of the decade.

THE HOUSING ACT OF 1937

If the PWA experience helped gain support for stronger slum clearance and public housing legislation, it did not overcome resistance to it. The basis of a substantial core of this resistance was typified by a congressman who declared that the poor "are living in shacks and hovels because God made them unable to earn more." However, after the Roosevelt landslide of 1936 and the inaugural address which included the famous "one-third of a nation" theme, the opponents of public housing could not completely block new legislation. In 1937 Congress passed the Wagner-Steagall Low Rent Housing Bill which created the United States Housing Authority (USHA).

The stated objectives of the bill were: ". . . to alleviate present and recurring unemployment . . . to remedy the unsafe and unsanitary housing conditions and the acute shortage of decent, safe and sanitary dwelling for families of low income." Under the new law the Federal Government was restricted to lending money to local public housing agencies; once federal approval of sites, plans, costs, and rents was secured, site acquisition, development, administration, and ownership was in the hands of these local agencies.

Adherents of public housing hailed the law as the government's final recognition that large segments of the population could not find decent housing through the free market:

> In providing this money the government finally accepts housing on its own merits, recognizes it to be a problem by itself, and frankly states that it no longer intends to make housing merely an excuse for something else.

This, obviously, was entirely too sanguine a view. The measure's first objective was no different from the one Ickes had specified years before: housing construction was a means of dealing with an economic crisis. Moreover, the initial appropriation to carry out the provisions of the bill was a mere half billion dollars for a three-year period, a mere pittance in terms of the needs of the time. But perhaps the central deficiency was one that became apparent once the program got under way. The USHA put its emphasis on slum clearance and that, as useful as it may be, always results in fewer dwelling units within the high-density area. That is, clearance without a simultaneous large-scale building program leaves many slum dwellers worse off than before. In their enthusiasm for slum clearance government officials and advocates of public housing overlooked the fundamental problem, the lack of adequate housing.[7]

THE HOUSING ACT OF 1949

It was not until 1949 that the next major development appeared. The twelve-year delay in attention to the nation's housing problems was a result of a number of factors. By 1937 the New Deal for all intents and purposes had run its course; in Roosevelt's third term his administration became increasingly preoccupied with international rather than domestic affairs. With the outbreak of war in Europe the United States was converted into the "arsenal for democracy," and the grip of the Depression was finally broken. Since the pump priming functions of the housing program had always been its main justification, its saliency was blunted once the economy showed signs of rejuvenation. By 1941 any housing program was a practical impossibility as all the productive energies of the nation were channeled into the war effort. In the

---

[7] Bauer, Catherine, "Redevelopment: A Misfit in the Fifties," Coleman Woodbury (ed.), *The Future of Cities and Urban Redevelopment* (Chicago: University of Chicago Press, 1953, pp. 8–18; Abrams, pp. 268–69).

immediate postwar years the economy continued to run in high gear, and the primary problem was the control of inflation. It was not until after the elections of 1948, which conclusively demonstrated the electorate's acceptance of the innovations introduced by the New Deal, that the Administration in Washington proposed new, major housing legislation.

The housing needs were, of course, acute. According to the 1940 housing census, of the approximately thirty million non-farm dwelling units the typical unit was twenty-five years old. In urban communities 40 per cent of the housing was found to be seriously defective in some respect: 14 per cent needed major repairs; 11 per cent more lacked running water and plumbing; and an additional 13 per cent lacked private bathrooms and flush toilets. While the supply of decent housing had decreased, the demand for such housing was going up.[8] In Chicago, for example, the Housing Authority reported in 1949 that while 1,178,000 families required housing there were only 906,000 "standard" units available.[9] President Truman's State of the Union message in the same year stated that "five million families were still living in slums and fire-traps, [and] three million families shared their homes with others."

Although the situation was a critical one for millions of American families it still was not serious enough to significantly affect opposition to the public housing provisions of the 1949 program. The legislative hearings saw the usual parade of witnesses representing the traditional forces opposed to public housing engaging its enthusiastic proponents. But this time there was another dimension to the conflict. The bill, sponsored by the unlikely trio of Senators Robert Taft, Allen Ellender, and Robert F. Wagner, Sr., also contained an urban redevelopment program supported by many of the same groups opposed to its public housing provisions. It seems likely that without the latter the bill would have passed with little or no difficulty, and that the redevelopment sections helped overcome opposition to the public housing titles.

It is easy to see why the urban redevelopment section of

[8] Lasch, Robert, *Breaking the Building Blockade* (Chicago: University of Chicago Press, 1946, Chapter 2); United States, National Housing Agency, *Housing Needs: A Preliminary Estimate,* National Housing Bulletin 1 (Washington, D.C., November 1944).

[9] Meyerson, Martin and Edward Banfield, *Politics, Planning and the Public Interest* (Glencoe: The Free Press, 1955), pp. 29–30.

the act, Title I, gained support from those opposed to public housing. A brief outline of an actual Title I project will illustrate the working of the law: Just south of Washington Square in New York in the late nineteen forties was an area of deteriorated industrial and commercial loft buildings interspersed with a handful of sound residential structures. This blighted area, adjacent to a Washington Square that had not yet had its charming brownstones razed by the university sharing the Square with them, was designated as a redevelopment area. Under Title I the costs incidental to planning the redevelopment of the area were defrayed by a federal loan to the city out of a fund specially set up for this purpose. After the plan was approved by the federal government the city purchased this valuable land for forty-one million dollars, and then resold it to private interests for twenty million dollars. Two-thirds of the twenty-one-million-dollar difference between what the city paid and the price it received for the land, the "write-down," was recovered in the form of a federal grant to the city. The other third, or seven million dollars of the costs, were borne by the city. In other words, Title I subsidized the purchase of prime land by private entrepreneurs, with the federal government paying the lion's share of the subsidy.

Land acquired for redevelopment under Title I could be used for a wide variety of purposes: luxury housing; low-rent private housing; commercial or industrial use; public parks, etc. All these projects had to meet some broad conditions: the plan for an area had to conform to some over-all plan for the development of the locality; the purchaser of the land had to utilize it as specified in the plan within a "reasonable time"; and the developer had to assume responsibility for relocating site residents in "decent, safe, and sanitary housing" at rents they could afford.

If Title I was something of an innovation, the public housing sections were the mixture as before. The provisions for loans and subsidies for locally built low-rent housing found in the 1937 law were continued, and 135,000 new housing starts a year for a six-year period were authorized. The President was empowered to increase this figure to two hundred thousand units or to reduce it to fifty thousand units a year upon recommendation of his Council of Economic Advisers. To prevent competition between private and public housing the law also provided that the upper limit of rents in public housing had to be 20 per cent below the rents in standard units of private housing. In addition, some general criteria for eligibility for public housing were set.

The public housing title of the new law was also a continuation of the 1937 law in the sense that they embodied the same assumptions. Public housing was still defined as a mechanism for dealing with the economic cycle. Indeed, as one housing expert noted,

> The Housing Act of 1949 contained more specific provisions bearing on the possible use of public housing as a contracyclical measure. In the legislation, Congress declared that sufficient housing production "is necessary to enable the housing industry to make its full contribution toward an economy of maximum employment, production, and purchasing power."

In the 1949 Act particular emphasis was placed on the role of private enterprise; it was encouraged to provide as large a part of the total housing need as possible. Communities could be assisted in slum clearance programs only after it was demonstrated that their "needs are not being met through reliance solely upon private enterprise." There is apparent in the law a not-too-subtle shift to concern with private enterprise rather than the very real housing need of the society. Thus, Title I helps clear slums by helping private entrepreneurs, but Title I does nothing about the reverse side of the coin—standard housing for the displaced slum dweller.[10] In 1937 public housing was seen, in part at least, as a means of alleviating the distress of the slum dweller. In 1949 such housing is seen as a prerequisite for private redevelopment projects; that is, public housing is justified to a larger extent for those displaced by private projects who cannot find housing at rents they can afford. In sum, the emphasis shifts from the social and economic situation of the slum resident to the needs of private enterprise.

Finally, one should note that the Housing Act of 1949 was totally irrelevant to the needs of the three million families who were sharing homes with others. Virtually no new housing had been built during the war, and now thousands of new families started by returning veterans found themselves without any place to live. Nothing in the new law was designed to deal with this situation.

---

[10] Beyer, pp. 237–39; Bauer, pp. 8 ff.; Fisher, Robert M., *Twenty Years of Public Housing* (New York: Harper & Brothers, 1959).

However, for the next five years the law was the basis of slum clearance programs, public housing construction, and redevelopment projects in urban communities.

CONTINUITY WITHOUT PROGRESS

The 1949 Act did not introduce any innovations into the slum clearance policies of the federal government; it was largely a continuation of the policies of PWA and the 1937 Housing Law. In the twenty-year period, 1934 to 1954, the program eliminated four hundred thousand substandard units, but this was only a little more than 7 per cent of 5.6 million substandard units existing in metropolitan areas in 1950. In 1953 a Presidential Committee, composed largely of businessmen, reported, "If we continue only at the present rate of clearance and rely on demolition alone to eliminate slums, it will take us something over two hundred years to do the job."[11] Clearly, the 1949 Act had not accelerated the pace of slum clearance.

The critical housing shortage was a complicating factor in the clearance program during this period. If the clearance rate had been accelerated the basic problem, adequate housing, still would not have been solved for the seventeen million families living in substandard dwellings in 1950. Given the shortage of standard public and private housing, slum clearance actually represented the transfer of families from one slum area to another. Competition for standard housing within the financial means of low-income families was intensified by families displaced by other urban construction programs and the flow of migrants from rural to urban areas.

The housing shortage had another consequence for clearance programs. Ownership of slum dwellings has always been a profitable enterprise, but during periods of extreme shortage it becomes even more profitable. Those who were profiting from the ownership of slum properties—"the ugly business of slum racketeering," as President Eisenhower's conservative Advisory Committee on Housing put it—were not particularly enthusiastic about clearance programs, and this was reflected in a lack of zealousness in City Halls from one end of the country to the other.

[11] *Report of the President's Advisory Committee on Government Housing Policies and Programs* (Washington, D.C.: Government Printing Office, December 1953).

THE HOUSING ACT OF 1954 AND SUBSEQUENT CHANGES

In 1954 some important changes were introduced but without significantly changing the basic structure of redevelopment. An Advisory Committee on Housing created by President Eisenhower urged that cities face up to the "process of urban decay" and the need for a "broader" and more "comprehensive" approach to prevent the growth of slums. What cities needed, the Committee said, introducing a new term, were programs of "urban renewal." Its recommendations were incorporated in the Housing Act of 1954.

The new emphasis was on the rehabilitation of houses and the conservation of neighborhoods as alternatives to the bulldozer. Federal grants were authorized for cities that wished to revise their housing codes and study new ways of code enforcement. Since banks and other lending institutions were notoriously loath to invest money in precisely those areas that could be rehabilitated and conserved, funds were made available to guarantee bank loans made for the purposes of rehabilitation and conservation. Before a city could become eligible for federal funds it had to demonstrate it had a "workable program" of urban renewal. A "workable program" had to contain such things as a plan for relocating those displaced from clearance and redevelopment sites; a housing code setting minimal standards for dwellings; and a program for citizen participation in the renewal process. These innovations were greeted with great enthusiasm; many people thought the changes represented significant progress.[12] However, the experience with rehabilitation and conservation since 1954 indicates that, as usual, the initial response was overoptimistic. The programs are very costly, and the need to resolve many conflicting neighborhood interests makes it extremely difficult to get a conservation program under way. Consequently, there have been relatively few programs successfully completed.[13]

The 1954 law also signaled a shift from the emphasis on housing in Title I of the 1949 Act. Originally, redevelopment projects had to be predominantly residential, but in 1954 10

---

[12] *Ibid.;* Swanson, pp. 14 ff. Beyer, Chapter 9.
[13] Nash, William, *Residential Rehabilitation: Private Profits and Public Purposes* (New York: McGraw-Hill Book Company, 1959); Meyerson, Martin, Barbara Terrett, and William Wheaton, *Housing, People and Cities* (New York: McGraw-Hill, 1962, Chapter 11).

per cent (later increased to 30 per cent) of the total federal funds available for redevelopment could be used for projects that were not predominantly residential. This means, of course, that fewer dollars are available for projects that result in an increased supply of housing.

From 1949 onward a persistent problem renewal faced was the relocation of those displaced from clearance sites. Any financial aid a community gave to families and businessmen forced to move had to come out of local community funds. But in 1956 federal money became available for this purpose.

Despite all the calls for a "comprehensive" approach to renewal few cities responded; each community seemed content to "plan" project by project. Therefore, in 1959 the federal government announced that it was prepared to help any city that drew up a comprehensive Community Renewal Program. Such a program would map out all the redevelopment and housing needs of a city; inventory its resources; and list priorities in terms of needs and resources available. The Community Renewal Program is nothing more than an extension of the ideas embodied in the "workable program" concept, but once the carrot of federal funds appeared on the horizon some cities immediately began work on a CRP.

THE PROGRESSIVES AND THE SLUMS*

Roy Lubove

For all his social consciousness, Riis was squarely in the American entrepreneurial tradition. His basic economic and social creed was individualism, but tempered by justice, moral responsibility and Christian love—the kind of restraints upon individual assertiveness presumably found in the primary-group. The nation did not need socialism, communism, or any other form of collectivism to cure its social ills so much as the creation of an environment which insured the individual a chance to realize his potentialities; an environment that did not, like the tenement, stifle his moral sensibilities and choke off his ambitions. Riis believed fervently in all the contemporary entrepreneurial, individualistic cliches: "Nothing is more certain, humanly speaking, than this, that what a man wills himself to be, that he will be"; "Luck is lassoed by the masterful man, by the man who knows and who can"; "All the little defeats are just to test . . . grit. It is a question of grit, that is all."[1] Here was the spirit which was to find its most elaborate expression in Wilson's New Freedom.

Individualism and love of nature were two basic components of Riis's moral *Weltanschauung*. They were closely related. "For hating the slum what credit belongs to me?" Riis asked. "When it comes to that, perhaps it was the open, the woods, the freedom of my Danish fields I loved, the contrast that was hateful." Despite a lifetime spent in New York, Riis never reconciled himself to the complexity and impersonality of city life. The city, generally, and the tenement slum in particular, he equated with physical and spiritual decay. The city hindered the individual from growing into a moral and sensitive human being. Too often, it elicited the worst instead of the best in his nature. The child, especially, suffered damnation in the urban wilderness. Any "plan of rescue for the boy in

* Pittsburgh: University of Pittsburgh Press, 1962, pp. 58–62 (selected portions) and 245–52 (selected portions).

[1] Jacob A. Riis, *Theodore Roosevelt the Citizen* (New York, 1904), 15, 63–64, 125.

which the appeal to the soil has no place" was false in principle and in practice.[2]

For Riis, the real America most resembled Ribe. It was in the countryside that the values which best exemplified America were born and nourished. Here tightly-knit family life insured the individual's proper moral development; respect for hard work and the dignity of labor was taught; and love of God and nature inculcated respect for human life and all living things. By contrast the city was a babel of moral confusion.

. . .

We can begin to understand now why Riis's star shone so brightly in the reform firmament of the 1890's. He himself was part of a great drama of human transplantation, and he expressed the deepest sentiments of his less vocal immigrant contemporaries. In a period of doubt and social unrest in this country, he reaffirmed those values which Americans had always believed were the foundation of national greatness. And Riis intensified his affirmations, his tributes to individualism and the countryside, with all the zeal and uncompromising dedication of the convert. In an era of pervasive nativism and troubled questioning of the free immigration policy, the former Danish immigrant stood out as an American among Americans. Riis's nationalism, his loyalty to his adopted country, were as deeply rooted in his character as his rural bias and his individualism. In a sense, Riis's Americanism was the keystone of his entire moral philosophy. Any man who pledged allegiance to God, whose life's work was directed by the code of rural virtues, and who took advantage of his country's freedom and opportunities to realize his maximum potentialities as an individual was simply being a good American.

. . . Riis's predecessors had emphasized the dual purpose of housing reform. Better housing would, in the first place, contribute to the physical safety of both the poor and the community as a whole. There can be no quarrel with this assumption. The overcrowding, filth, and inferior sanitary facilities in the tenement obviously had an unfavorable effect upon health. Science and common sense confirmed this. But the housing reformer had also considered better housing as an instrument of social control. He observed that tenement neighborhoods, populated often by foreigners and their chil-

[2] Riis, *The Making of an American,* 423; Jacob A. Riis, "One Way Out," *Century Magazine,* LI (1895–96), 308.

dren, seemed to abound in vice, crime, and pauperism. He assumed, therefore, that the physical environment was at fault. The tenement must cause a deterioration of character, making the individual more susceptible to vice than he would have been in a different environment. Improve his housing, it followed, and you would influence his character for the better.

It is true that a statistical correlation could be drawn between poor housing on the one hand, and a resistance to Americanization or a low individual and neighborhood moral tone, on the other. It did not necessarily follow, however, that improved housing, in and of itself, would have socially desirable effects. The housing reformer never subjected to rigorous analysis his assumption that housing influenced character. He applied a crude environmental determinism to the problem, underestimating the tenacious persistence in the individual of set habits and values.

Riis did not, in any clear and systematic fashion, analyze the relationship between housing and social structure. He accepted without much reflection the assumption that better housing would result in various social blessings. Often, however, Riis broke loose from this simple determinism. Almost unconsciously, he expanded the usual scope of housing reform to include the neighborhood in which the tenement was situated. Like the settlement worker, Riis realized that the tenement neighborhood contained many objectionable features which needed to be eliminated. More than previous housing reformers, he sensed that the tenement, the slum, was a way of life and not simply a problem of sub-standard housing. . . .

In the Progressive era, the settlement was the profoundest embodiment of the ideal which inspired Riis, the ideal of community and human brotherhood expressed in a common Americanism. It concentrated, like Riis, upon the neighborhood as the unit of social reconstruction. The neighborhood ideal, as Riis observed, was "the heart of the settlement movement." The convictions which led Jane Addams to Halsted Street in Chicago and Lillian Wald to Henry Street in New York were exactly those which inspired Riis to declare war on the tenement and the slum.[3]

[3] Riis, *How the Other Half Lives,* 159, 163; Jacob A. Riis, *The Peril and Preservation of the Home* (Philadelphia, 1903), 187. Riis was highly conscious of the similarity of ideals and purposes between the settlements and himself. See *The Making of an American,* 316, and his personal tribute to the settlement movement, "What Settlements Stand For," *Outlook,* LXXXIX (1908), 69–72.

Everywhere in the tenement neighborhood, Riis saw the saloon, the poor man's social club. Its brightness and relaxed atmosphere contrasted sharply with the squalor and dinginess of the tenement. But if the saloon satisfied the worker's gregarious instinct, his need for companionship and sociability, it also encouraged him to squander his earnings on liquor while his family went without necessities. The saloon thus contributed to the decline of family life, a process presumably set in motion by the tenement. . . .

As ubiquitous as the saloon in the tenement neighborhood was the street gang, the refuge of children who lacked any sense of identity and turned to their similarly confused peers for protection, security, and a code of values. Every corner had its gang of toughs, hostile to each other but united in their defiance of society.[4] What was the use of improving the tenement child's housing if the street gang waited outside, ready to initiate him into the jungle code of the pack. Riis realized that boys would form into gangs. His object was to direct this gregarious instinct into socially productive channels. Instead of an instigator of mischief and crime and the promoter of a distorted code of values, the street gang could be revamped into an organized force for good. But reform depended upon the alternatives to the saloon or the street, which were all society offered in the tenement neighborhood, and upon the interest taken in the moral development of the tenement child.

The East Side in the 1890's was in New York's great red light district.[5] Prostitution downtown was unabashedly open. An army of prostitutes, pimps, and madams plied their trade unmolested by the Tammany-ruled police: "On sunshiny days the whores sat on chairs along the sidewalks. They sprawled indolently, their legs taking up half the pavements. People stumbled over a gauntlet of whores' meaty legs," the novelist Michael Gold recalled. "The girls gossiped and chirped like a jungle of parrots. Some knitted shawls and stockings. Others hummed. Others chewed Russian sunflower seeds and monotonously spat out the shells."[6] . . .

Equally important, critics of tenement evils had not always

---

[4] Riis, *How the Other Half Lives*, 164.

[5] It was unmolested except for the necessary protection money paid to politicians and police officers. Two state investigations in the 1890's, the Lexow Committee in 1894 and the Mazet Committee in 1899, documented the deeply-rooted police corruption in New York City.

[6] Gold, *Jews Without Money*, 15.

considered alternatives to the vices they struggled to suppress. Riis, however, understood that the saloon and street gang served a functional purpose; they satisfied social needs and desires. The reformer could not abolish them unless he devised wholesome substitutes capable of fulfilling these same needs. In concrete terms, Riis's answer to the street gang was not the policeman's nightstick or the reform school, but rather the playground, boy's club, and public school. . . .

Improved housing and the establishment of a neighborhood in which such institutions as the saloon, the house of prostitution, and the street gang were less influential would surely benefit immigrant parents as well as their children. But for all his optimism, for all his faith in the power of environment to shape individual habits and values, Riis realized that the adult was sometimes beyond redemption. . . .

By transmitting to the tenement child and adult a meaningful life-organization which would facilitate their acceptance of middle-class American values, Riis was striving, in the final analysis, to create a new system of primary group ties in the tenement neighborhood. The confusion of nationalities, religions, and cultural standards in tenement districts had discouraged, he believed, the birth of any sense of community. There was little to nurture social unity and cohesiveness. Apart from individual moral standards and the voluntary submission of the individual to the social norms of his ethnic group, there was no effective instrument of social control except for the law and policeman's club. . . .

The social implications of the tenement slum received increasing attention after 1880. The city, it seemed, had become a world characterized by physical proximity and social distance, divided by class, race and nationality. Immigrant working-class ghettos had formed in which foreign speech, customs, and culture prevailed, where crime and vice abounded. Such a development, in the eyes of reformers, threatened the social and political stability of the entire community. The tenement slum was a potential volcano, its inhabitants the willing recruits of the demagogue and revolutionist. . . .

As a housing reformer Riis promoted the three traditional methods of amelioration: restrictive legislation, model tenements, and the Octavia Hill plan. Riis was both a prophet and the child of his time. He adhered very often to the simple environmental faith of his contemporaries, assuming that a change in material condition such as housing would result in immeasurable social and moral improvement. Yet he had the insight to transcend his own environmental determinism. For one thing, Riis paid great attention to the tenement child, admitting that the adult was often beyond redemption, despite the quality of his housing. Thus he sensed that a modification of the environment did not automatically insure a change in individual character or social structure. More important, Riis stressed the necessity of reconstructing the total environment of the poor, not simply their housing. He viewed the tenement neighborhood in all its complexity as the basic unit of social control, in which environmental changes must be accompanied by every form of moral influence which the reformer could exert. Riis recognized that the tenement was a way of life, whose social and moral tone was determined by the process of immigrant adaptation to a total environment. The problem of social control, Riis intuitively grasped, was more difficult than earlier generations of housing reformers had assumed. . . .

The significance of Progressive housing reform, in perspective, is threefold. First, the ideal of neighborhood reconstruction identified with Jacob Riis and the social settlement retains significant contemporary implications. Relocation difficulties and the disruption of established neighborhood social patterns connected with wholesale demolition in public housing and urban renewal projects have emphasized the fact that housing, good or bad, is inseparable from a broader neighborhood and community environment. It is likely that in terms of social control Riis overestimated the potency of parks, playgrounds, supervised club activity, and the public school. He did, however, realize that for purposes of public social policy, housing could not be isolated from other influences which affected personal behavior and family and neighborhood life.

Lawrence Veiller's emphasis upon effective restrictive legislation and a technically proficient, well-organized housing reform movement is a second useful legacy of the Progressive era. No one interested in housing problems today can fail to profit from a perusal of Veiller's model housing laws or his handbook on housing reform, in which he outlined his philosophy of reform and the characteristics of good housing legislation. If Veiller was too narrowly concerned with minimum standards legislation, this does not make such legislation less indispensable to any rounded housing, planning or urban renewal program.

Finally, Progressive housing reform is significant for its af-

filiation with the early planning movement. Both housing reformers and planners undoubtedly exaggerated the possibilities of creating a satisfactory urban residential environment
through zoning and garden city schemes. Hoping to lower
housing costs and rents by stabilizing or reducing land values,
they favored measures designed to relieve and prevent con-
gestion and encourage migration from high density areas. If
a program organized around the prospect of urban decentrali-
zation or dispersion is subject to criticism as the product of
men who disliked or feared the city of their time, it is equally
true that these reformers of the Progressive era launched a
continuing search for principles of efficient urban development and control, relating housing to industrial and commercial location, land and tax policy, transportation, population
density, zoning, and similar fundamentals.

Any balanced appraisal of Progressive housing reform must
consider two important limitations. The first of these, already
mentioned, is that restrictive legislation may prevent the worst
housing from being erected, but cannot guarantee a sufficient
supply of good housing at rents (or costs) suited to low-
income or even middle-income groups. Without necessarily
endorsing an elaborate and expensive public housing program,
it seems essential for reformers to devise some means of providing housing for those whom private enterprise cannot
profitably accommodate. Glancing at Europe the rebels
against Veiller's exclusive emphasis upon restrictive legislation
stressed the need for state loans, municipal land purchase, and
other devices to reduce housing costs. New Deal housing reformers, of course, developed a program of federal mortgage
insurance and subsidized public housing. Whatever the
method, the problem of insuring good housing for those whom
private builders cannot profitably accommodate must be
faced.

Progressive housing reformers, in the second place, including those who participated in labor, recreation, and other reform movements, did not devote much thought to the elusive
relationship between housing, on the one hand, and personality, family life, and social structure, on the other. The relationship seemed so obvious that they did not even consider
it an issue. They were sure that better housing would operate
to transmit the values and cultural norms of middle-class
America to immigrants and workers. Good housing would
help in re-establishing the primary group controls of the

peasant village or small town which had disintegrated in the modern industrial city.

This question of the social value of housing reform is not mere academic whimsy, but is crucial in relation to the formulation of public policy. Let us admit that certain minimum standards in housing are essential to the health, and probably to the social well-being of any community. For most people it is a serious handicap to grow up and live amidst filth and dilapidation. It is possible, however, that beyond a certain point the social benefits anticipated from improved housing can be achieved more quickly, cheaply, or effectively by alternative methods. Can an apartment in a mammoth public housing project, for example, assist the multiproblem family as much as a supply of trained social workers? Perhaps both are necessary, but to what degree? The crucial point is that the resources of a society are limited; they should be allocated in order to accomplish the most good at the least cost.

THE MYTHS OF HOUSING REFORM*

John P. Dean

The story of housing reform is shot through with controversy, emotion, and pseudo-science. The smoke generated out of this controversy has concealed the economic and political manipulations of various groups seeking to maneuver the situation. The private housing industry has its folklore in terms of "Own-Your-Own-Homes," and "Filtering Down"; the chief medicine men of housing reform have now developed their own folklore; both groups make all the necessary passes and incantations before the public. In the meantime, the patient continues to sicken.

This situation arises from the recurrent dilemma of social reform movements: a set of conditions widely condemned is brought to public attention—in this case unhealthful and unsafe housing. But to remove these conditions would be to change established ways of doing things. L. K. Frank pointed out as far back as 1925: "The crux of the problem is to find some way of avoiding the undesirable consequences of established laws, institutions, and social practices, without changing those established laws, etc."[1]

Social reformers have long realized that restrictive municipal codes clinging to the margin where health and safety are threatened can change operating practices barely enough to achieve minimum protection for the family. To achieve broader social objectives, reformers embody these objectives in housing standards that would require considerable change in existing institutions.

Once codified, such housing standards give a point of leverage from which to pry at existing housing regulations. Much of the fight for better housing revolves around the battle to narrow the gap between currently enforced regulations and reformers' standards of social welfare. Any achievement results mainly in a reformulation of the welfare standards to give a new margin for "progress." In a double sense the re-

* FROM *American Sociological Review*, XIV (April 1949), pp. 281–88 (selected portions).

[1] Frank, L. K., "Social Problems," *American Journal of Sociology*, January, 1925, p. 467.

formers are the "standard bearers" in the battle of the slums.

Frequently, however, reformers are hard pressed to justify these higher standards, since they represent debatable value-judgments and difficult scientific analyses. Therefore, the fight for social welfare through housing reform appeals to science and business realities where it can, but readily falls back on emotional appeals and myth where its defenses are weak.

By and large, these non-rational defenses of housing reform are of four kinds: (a) appeals to the subjective evaluational roots of housing standards, (b) myths surrounding the complex relationship of slums to social disorder, (c) myths about the social effects of rehousing and (d) myths about the financial liability of slums to the municipality.

(a) *Appeals to the subjective evaluational roots of housing standards*. Beyond considerations of health and safety, a housing standard embodying social objectives is likely to represent some personal yardstick or subjective judgment among the professional and technical people who fight for better housing. A subjective criterion is of little help in justifying legislation in the political arena. So, to bolster their position, housing reformers naturally appeal to the sympathies of good-hearted people by devices such as dramatic photographs of the squalor of slum dwellings. These techniques frequently pull a few heart and purse strings. Photographs of this sort, statistics on the lack of plumbing, spot maps of social disorders, and other similar trappings have become institutionalized as standard paraphernalia of housing reports.

(b) *The myths surrounding complex relationship of slums to social disorder*. But since it is often considered "emotional" to dramatize the unpleasantness of the slums, attention is devoted to "proving" that slums impair other social values by causing crime and delinquency, ill health, or exorbitant municipal expenditures. These studies grew rapidly in the 1930's and helped to rally support for local housing reforms; they were quoted by high federal officials in the halls of Congress in support of legislation to implement slum clearance; they achieved a currency that entitled them to be quoted by the best authorities.

Most housing reformers probably believe that the effect of substandard housing on social welfare has been determined. But even with workable criteria for discriminating standard from substandard housing, an enormous amount of research time and effort would be needed to untangle the complicated causal relations. And one could probably never say "sub-standard housing contributes this much to delinquency, that much to poor health."

A number of commonly-used indices of social conditions and social pathology correlate with slum or blighted areas. By one or another study, the areas of most substandard housing have been found linked with:

—high population density
—high death rates
—high proportion of families dependent on social assistance
—high proportion of illiteracy
—high proportion of women employed
—high juvenile delinquency rates
—high rate of sex offenses
—high rate of gambling arrests
—more multi-family dwellings
—large average family size
—high proportion of males to females
—small proportion of owner-occupied homes
—high proportion of relief cases
—more unemployment
—more poverty
—high rates of divorce
—high rates of non-support cases
—high rates of illegitimacy
—high rates of venereal disease
—high rates of alcoholism
—low proportion of males married
—high proportion of foreign born
—high suicide rate
—high rates for various mental disorders
—low marriage rates
—high residential mobility
—more restaurants per 1,000 population
—low average educational level
—low proportion of radio ownership
—high rates of mental deficiency
—low proportion of telephones

In city after city—Buffalo, Birmingham, Cleveland, Denver, Detroit, Hartford, Indianapolis, Los Angeles, Milwaukee, Newark, Washington, and others—slum areas have been shown to be the areas of poorest health and the greatest personal and social disorder.[2] The implication is: "Remove the slums and you remove the social ills!" But it would be just as illogical to say that ills of slum areas are caused not by substandard housing conditions, but by the absence of telephone service, which also correlates with indexes of social disorder. Scientifically, we should not attribute causation to one or a few factors in an *area* which happens to be correlated with an overall *rate* of disorder. This blend of correlation does not explain why many families living in substandard conditions do *not* experience divorce, or delinquency, or alcoholism. It fails, further, to explain why in a given family in substandard housing one boy may be delinquent, or mentally deficient, or unhealthy, while his brother has remained free of these maladies. Beyond these few expected relationships between slum dwellings and health, the effect of poor housing becomes quite difficult to determine, especially where *social* behavior is involved. Goldfeld's study[3] tested one relationship with greater care than most studies. In the East Harlem slum area he held social factors constant where possible and compared the delinquency rates among families that lived in the superior structures with the rates among families that lived in inferior structures. He stated after careful statistical manipulation: "The one unmistakable conclusion that emerges from the study is that there is no relationship between bad housing in its physical aspects and juvenile delinquency as revealed by court records."

(c) *Myths surrounding Social Effects of Rehousing.* In their eagerness to get slum clearance legislation, housing reformers fought against the idea that slum conditions were the fault of the families that lived in the slums: How could the tenants be responsible for housing deficiencies such as lack of air, light, toilet, bath, or central heating? The reformers argued further that ill-health, uncleanliness, and delinquency are not *innate* characteristics, but are the result of life in the slum

[2] A good summary of these studies appears in Part III of the *Cost of Slums,* a pamphlet prepared for the Housing Authority of the City of Newark by Dr. Jay Rumney and Sara Shuman (Newark, 1946, pp. 32 ff.). Also see: Mowrer, E. R., *Disorganization: Personal and Social,* Phila., 1942; Faris, R. E. L. and Dunham, H. W. *Mental Disorders in Urban Areas,* Chicago, 1939; Shaw, C. L. and McKay, *Juvenile Delinquency and Urban Areas,* Chicago 1942; Ford, James, *Slums-Housing,* Cambridge, 1936, 2 vol.

[3] Goldfeld, Abraham, "Substandard Housing as a Potential Factor in Juvenile Delinquency in a Local Area in New York City," abstract of Ph.D. Thesis, N.Y. University, 1937 (reprint).

environment. Their conception of slum environment emphasized primarily the inadequate *physical* environment of the slums. It understressed the connection between the *social* environment of the slums and the disorders they wanted to cure. So it was easy to jump to the conclusion that slum clearance would remove the social ills—and the public housing program has been sold with that assumption.

Social reformers hoped that the USHA would introduce a new way of life for the slum family. They believed that many personal and social maladjustments would wither away in the new life of the housing community. But they failed to appreciate the problems of rehousing. Public housing developments, once completed, have provided a laboratory for testing out the housing gospel that "decent housing instead of slums means less crime, less juvenile delinquency, lower costs for police and fire protection; it also means better health, lower death rates, and lower costs of medical care."[4]

Studies in Gary, Newark, Philadelphia, and Pittsburgh[5] have shown that rehoused slum families have relatively low rates of tuberculosis, infant mortality, adult criminal offenses, juvenile delinquency, fires, home accidents, and communicable childhood diseases. But we cannot tell whether or not the families admitted to the projects were different in personal and social characteristics that would account for the lower rates. Low-rent public housing projects (where these studies took place) admit only families from substandard dwellings who are citizens of the United States, have low incomes, and no substantial assets. Single persons and oversized families are not accommodated. Tenant selection procedures draw proportionately more families with children or about to have them, more of the reliable or steadily employed and fewer trouble makers. Public assistance cases are accepted but kept to a limited proportion. Families that apply for admission are also "self-selected" according to their knowledge of available

[4] Myer, Dillon S., Commissioner of the Federal Public Housing Authority, at the *Hearings* before the Committee on Banking and Currency, U. S. Senate, 80th Congress, on S. 866, Gov't. Printing Office, Washington, 1947, p. 118.

[5] Housing Authority of the City of Gary (Indiana), *A Report,* Gary, 1945; Housing Authority of the City of Newark (N.J.) *The Social Effects of Public Housing,* Newark, 1944; Phila. Housing Authority, *Homes for War Workers and Families of Low Income,* Phila., 1943, and Bureau of Social Research, Federation of Social Agencies of Pittsburgh and Allegheny Counties. *Juvenile Delinquency in Public Housing,* 1944, and *Vital Statistics of Public Housing Residents,* 1945.

public housing and their willingness to move in, if approved. Some families are undoubtedly deterred by such considerations as: home ownership, satisfaction with present quarters, unwillingness to leave their present neighborhood, their preference for a store-dwelling combination, or misconceptions or prejudices against "Government housing."

The extent of self-selection in determining the "effective" public housing market is indicated in the results of a pilot survey in deteriorated areas of Aliquippa, Beaver Falls, and several other small steel towns in Beaver County, Pennsylvania, in May 1946. The 1,194 interviews revealed that the families eligible and willing to move in amounted to only six per cent of the families interviewed, only 14 per cent of the families in substandard housing conditions. Only 31 per cent of all *eligible* families said they were willing to move in. This willingness of families to move into public housing varies sharply with condition of dwelling, tenure, and income. Compared with an equivalent number of dwellings in slum or blighted areas, public housing developments undoubtedly include fewer aged indigents, transients, single men and women, hobos, crackpots, criminals, panhandlers, prostitutes, alcoholics, bohemians, taxi-dancers, and other social misfits. Little wonder that indexes of social-welfare favor public housing.

A few studies have made thoughtful attempts to discover whether families transplanted from the slums to public housing developments improve in health and social life:

(1) Full medical data were secured for seventeen tuberculous families admitted to public housing in New Haven and resident there for three to seven years. They were matched with seventeen parallel families on the date of primary diagnosis, the status of the disease at the time of diagnosis, and, so far as possible, on age, sex, and racial characteristics. While only nine of the control group showed favorable progress, fifteen of the rehoused families progressed.[6]

(2) For 317 families resident in a public housing development in New Haven for 2½ to 4½ years, the rate of juvenile delinquency per 100 children per year was only 1.64 as compared with a rate of 3.18 for those same families during the seventeen years before entrance to the project.[7]

(3) Forty-four families about to be admitted to public

[6] Barer, Naomi, "A Note on Tuberculosis Among Residents of a Housing Project," *Public Housing,* August 1945, p. 133.

[7] Barer, Naomi, "Delinquency Before, After Admission to New Haven Housing Development," *Journal of Housing,* Dec. 1945–Jan. 1946, p. 27.

housing were matched on ten characteristics with 38 families who were on the waiting list to be admitted and both groups were given tests on sociometric scales on morale, general adjustment, social participation, and social status before the experimental families moved in in 1939 and a year later in 1940 after the experimental families moved in. The results showed no significant change in morale for either group. Both groups gained in social participation, but the rehoused group gained twice as much. Both groups gained in social status, but the rehoused group showed a greater gain. The scores on condition of living room showed a striking gain for the rehoused group, but a loss for the control group. Both groups improved in percentage "use crowded," but the rehoused group improved three times as much.[8]

(d) *Myths surrounding the dollars-and-cents costs of slum dwellings to the municipality.* In all, about a dozen studies have been made to show that slums are a financial liability to the city. The methods for showing the deficit vary widely, but in every case (1) municipal expenditures must be allocated to substandard areas, and (2) assumptions must be made about the relation of bad housing to those expenditures. The cost of public baths may be counted against dwellings where bath facilities are lacking, but it may be impossible to tell how much was spent on patrons from a given area. Other costs, such as arrests for burglary or prostitution, are usually assigned against the slums where the offenders live, thus ignoring arbitrarily that this protection may benefit the people in better residential areas. Most studies assign to slum areas costs that might be attributed to the population composition of those areas. The well known "Cost of the Slums in Newark" study, for example, assumes that the cost of educating a child is the same for a slum as for a good residential area. It then assigns to the slum area a per capita cost for education that is double the per capita cost for education in the good residential area on the grounds that in the slum area "20 per cent of the population consisted of children attending public schools whereas only 10 per cent of the population of (the good residential area) were in that category." Before assessing the costs of these additional school children against the slums, the Newark Housing Authority might have reflected on the figures in its earlier study showing that (1)

[8] Chapin, F. Stuart, "An Experiment on the Social Effects of Good Housing," *American Sociological Review*, December 1940, pp. 868–79.

the proportion of school age children and (2) the birth-rates per 1,000 women 15–44 years of age are *both* substantially higher in its public housing projects than in substandard areas it compared these projects to.

If studies of the costs of slums were to throw out all expenditures that either are not allocable by area or are related to population composition rather than to substandard housing, much of the so-called financial deficit of the slums would disappear. And surely, any municipal contribution to the cost of rehousing (which in 1944 ran over $5.00 per unit per month in public housing nationwide) would overbalance any municipal expenditures chargeable directly to the substandardness of the dwellings.

With these myths, the humanitarian fight for housing reform has opposed the traditional mores that maintain "business-as-usual" attitudes toward the slums. Public housing, as a new reform institution, represents a sharp and unconventional departure in operation of residential real estate: "Government" on both local and federal levels becomes directly concerned with the construction, financing, ownership, and operation of housing. But even though public housing has spread from community to community, it is clear that the battle for social welfare through housing is far from won. Without question, public housing has provided rehoused families with structures more comfortable and decent (Standard I) and more healthful and safe (Standard II) to live in; but the anticipated improvements in social welfare (Standard III) have failed to materialize. Studies that show striking gains in social welfare have generally fallen into some unwarranted manipulation of the facts; they are inconclusive at best.

This failure should not surprise us: public housing operations have been hedged in and hampered in the pursuit of social welfare objectives by several traditions: (a) the heritage of laissez-faire individualism, (b) the current practices of real estate, of local government, and of federal government, (c) housing reformers' confusion about the social effects of rehousing.

a. *The Heritage of Laissez-faire Individualism.* Public housing reflects the conditioning atmosphere of those aspects of protestant ethic and the spirit of capitalism that underwrite (1) the sanctity of private enterprise, (2) the debilitating effect of "charity," and (3) the moral qualifications for public aid. Each of these is reflected in the operation of public housing:

(1) The American faith in the sanctity of private enterprise is reflected in the increasing clarity with which public housing formulates its sphere of activity as non-competitive with private enterprise. Public housing permits occupancy only by families of low-income who are unable to afford decent available private quarters. "Low-income" has frequently been interpreted at levels well below the minimum budgetary requirements for working class families (as defined in welfare assistance budgets). In New York City, the admission limits for veterans to a post-war project were originally set so low that many of the young families admitted found that without the assistance of the in-laws they had been doubled-up with, they were quite unable to make ends meet. A family that exceeds the income limits in public housing is expected to vacate even though the increase in income is unlikely to continue. The breaking of local friendships and community ties makes stable community life an objective hard to achieve.

(2) Public housing has operated under the stress of the American folk belief that "any individual worth his salt can get ahead and raise his family out of the slums." By this reasoning a slum family is morally inadequate and must not be pauperized by public assistance which makes things too easy. This belief in "minimum charity" is translated into accommodations that are often pared to the bone in room size, equipment, noise insulation, cupboards, and floor covering. A government study reported that many units required about $85 to bring the dwelling up to tenants' standards.

(3) Public housing reflects the widespread American attitude that help should be given only to the "deserving." Thus benefits are limited to citizens and to families of more than one person. Since slum children, forced to live in the slums through no fault of their own, deserve a better break, tenant selection procedures generally cater to families *with* children. Few accommodations are provided for the aged and the proportion of public assistance cases is limited. And since those who help themselves are more "deserving" of help, the steadier, more reliable, less troublesome families are generally favored.

b. *The current practices of real estate, local and federal government.* (1) Public housing operation reflects, too, private real estate customs. The rent in private dwellings is determined by the size and "quality" of the accommodations; public housing emphasizes that families should pay according to their ability. Many rent schedules in current operation in public housing are a curious amalgam of these two points of view; in some schedules the rent is determined by both *income* (ability to pay) and *number of bedrooms* (size of accommodations). Furthermore, the private landlord concerns himself only with property maintenance and rent collection; public housing following the example of private practice has concentrated on these as its primary duties and left social considerations in the background.

(2) Public housing operation reflects its status as an adjunct of the local government. Local housing authorities were set up as organizations separate from the city administration proper to avoid political interference. And for the most part, graft or favoritism have been negligible in land acquisition, contract awards, tenant selection, and job-filling. Occasionally, the services for a project (such as utility contracts or orders for management supplies) have been manipulated in favor of one local son rather than another. Sometimes the top positions have been filled by political favorites, but sometimes, too, this guaranteed needed political support. But when local political connections have been emphasized at the expense of contacts with local social service organizations, the long-run social welfare objectives of public housing have been hampered. In dealing with these problems the supervising Federal agency has walked a tightrope between local autonomy and a too-close supervision of—or "interference" in—local affairs.

(3) Public housing must gear itself to the practices of federal politics (and in New York, state politics). Since legislators are often under attack for over-spending and since their housing attitudes have usually been derived from private real estate practices, political experience has encouraged local housing authorities to emphasize the efficiency of its real estate operation rather than the extension of its achievements in social welfare.

c. *Housing reformers' confusion about the social effects of rehousing.* The housing reformers themselves have frequently been taken in by their own myth: "Clear the slums and you remove the social ills." Those who are well trained in community organization and leadership have never thought of clearing the slums and providing in their place decent, safe and sanitary homes as the whole public housing job. But the vast bulk of housing officials are not well trained in the arts of organization and leadership. Faced with the concrete realities of rent collection, property maintenance, and budget balancing, they have not been in a position to make the most of the opportunity rehousing offers to inaugurate social relationships, to help families to participate in community life, to encourage the use of social services infrequently or never used, and to create leisure time satisfactions which exceed anything previously experienced. Until housing officials frankly face the rehousing of families as a *social* experiment in relocation and adjust policies and procedures accordingly, large-scale rehousing operations will frequently be accompanied by conditions falling far short of current objectives of social welfare.

Fortunately, a few scattered housing research studies point in this direction: both R. K. Merton's Studies of Craftown and Hilltown and M.I.T.'s Group Dynamics' Study of a Veteran's Housing Development for Students[9] approached housing developments as unusual opportunities to study social organization. The New School's Research Center for Human Relations has underway a study of intergroup relations in several housing developments with varying patterns of Negro-White occupancy. If a few studies such as these can demonstrate the decisive impact of haphazard architectural decisions and of operating policies and practices arrived at by loose judgment, then perhaps we can look forward to a widening circle of housing reformers who argue their case *not* in terms of myth but in terms of housing's real possibilities for social reform and sociological experiment.

[9] Both studies are still in manuscript, as yet unavailable.

THE FUTURE OF HOUSING*

Charles Abrams

FEDERAL ENLIGHTENMENT

The New Deal venture into realty operations was a striking departure from traditional boundaries of Federal power. Even the legality of Federal expenditures for social welfare, which had gradually won a place in Federal policy, was in 1935 still being questioned by the lawyers. Few persons have envisioned real estate as within the domain of Federal power, nor were real estate's dislocations sufficiently social to warrant intervention for the national welfare.

Real estate, mortgage lending, and home construction were still viewed as local matters for state and city jurisdiction. The slum was a local problem, as were housing shortages, community planning and zoning, home foreclosures, and all the other elements of the housing problem.

The occasional exceptions, such as those involving public lands, agricultural problems,[1] war housing, and the work of the Bureau of Standards, were rationalized as being within the traditional Federal framework. But it was otherwise with the other ramifications of housing and real estate generally.

The prevailing American attitude after the First World War, when England launched a government-subsidized housing program, was that private initiative was not only to play first fiddle but call the tune and pull all the strings. That attitude crystallized in 1920 in the report of a United States Senate Committee headed by Senator Calder which had sought methods to free the building industry from paralysis so that the housing shortage could be eased. Relief, said the senators, lay with private initiative exclusively. All the government could or might do was furnish a little elbow grease in the form of easier credit. British public housing was viewed as a form of "benevolent paternalism" which would lower the

* New York: Harper & Brothers, 1946, pp. 210–20 (selected portions).
[1] The Federal government in 1916 set up machinery under the Federal Farm Loan Act to provide buildings and for the improvement of farm land. A small proportion of the loans was actually used to build farm homes. E. E. Wood, *Recent Trends in American Housing*, New York, The Macmillan Company, 1931, p. 20.

moral and economic standard of the country. "It is an insult to the ingenuity and enterprise of the American people to assume that structural and material costs can not be satisfactorily reduced. If there is anything in which the American people have confidence, it is in their ingenuity and low-cost quantity production." . . .

President Hoover in 1931 summoned housing experts to report on home ownership. They produced a twelve-volume report instead of a two-page appropriation bill which might have accomplished something constructive. The conference adjourned after making the expected generalizations, which included recommendations that each community develop a building program to meet its social needs; that each have a master plan; that cities be zoned; that houses be of good design and sound construction, available to every thrifty family. The recommended mechanism was a system of credit to finance homes which eventuated into the Home Loan Bank System. All the experts agreed that old homes should be brought up to standard, slums eliminated, large-scale housing facilitated, tax reform initiated. "Beauty as well as utility should be made available" and the same conveniences enjoyed by city dwellers should be extended to the residents of rural districts.[2] The final dictum was that "the promotion of home ownership and better homes is the prerogative of all civic leaders and of citizens." . . .

There was a rumbling in the distance, echoing the need of more comprehensive measures to put the building industry back on its feet. An Emergency Relief and Construction Act of 1932 was enacted, providing for housing loans by the Reconstruction Finance Corporation to limited dividend corporations. As might be expected, little came of that. The act was hardly more than the usual attempt to stimulate private enterprise into functioning without rectifying or even examining into the underlying defects that lay at the root of private building operations.

REAL ESTATE AND THE NEW DEAL

The government economists who diagnosed the depression in 1933 saw factory employment in that year shrink from the

---

[2] The President's Conference on Home Building and Home Ownership, *op. cit.*, Vol. XI, 1932, p. 12.

1929 index of 104.8 per cent to 62.6 per cent.[3] The estimated number of unemployed jumped during the same period from 1,864,000 to 15,653,000.[4] Relief in 1932 required $307,000,-000, more than 7 times the requirements in 1929.[5] By July, 1933, 13 per cent of the population was getting relief from public funds.[6] The revenues of cities dried up just when the need for local financial aid was greatest.

Once again, the building industry was expected to be the inspirational force for a return to the good old days. But the expected revival in building operations simply did not arrive. Precisely why was a current mystery. There was a need for dwellings and repairs. Building costs were low. Labor and materials were available. Everything seemed set for the sequence of boom following depression, a sequence always believed to be as inevitable as the backward swing of the pendulum. The pendulum did not swing back because the real estate business had received a stunning blow and its paralysis in turn crippled the building industry.

In 1926 there were only 70,000 foreclosures against urban homes. For both 1932 and 1933 there were about 250,000. The collapse of real estate values increased tax delinquency and foreclosures, forced assessed valuations downward, and pushed tax rates upward. New construction ceased almost completely by February, 1933. There were as many as 3250 governmental bodies in simultaneous default.[7]

During the first quarter of 1933 the value of construction contracts awarded in 37 states was 90 per cent less than during the corresponding period of 1928. Taking the yearly average from 1921 to 1929 inclusive as 100, building activity for the 3 years 1930–32 in 16 representative cities in Illinois stood at 6.4; in Chicago it was 4.2.[8] Throughout the United States,

[3] "Trend of Employment in 1935: Revised Figures," *Monthly Labor Review*, May, 1935, p. 1339.

[4] American Federation of Labor, "The Federation's Revised Unemployment Estimate," *The American Federationist*, January 1936. It was estimated by the Alexander Hamilton Institute that more than 17,000,-000 were unemployed at that time (*Business Conditions Weekly*, September 1, 1934).

[5] *Monthly Bulletin on Social Statistics*, Children's Bureau, Dept. of Labor, July, 1934.

[6] Report of the Federal Emergency Relief Administrator to the Chairman of the Senate Committee on Appropriations. Sen. Doc. 56, 74th Cong., 1st Sess.

[7] Albert G. Hart, *Debt and Recovery*, New York, Twentieth Century Fund, 1938, p. 224.

[8] Final Report of the Illinois Housing Commission, April, 1935, p. 10.

employment in the building industry had fallen between August, 1929, and March, 1933, by more than 63 per cent. In August, 1929, a total of 2,325,689 persons were directly or indirectly employed in this industry, and in March, 1933, the number had dwindled to 850,414.[9]

The relation of real estate and home building to the depression was at first not clearly seen by the New Deal economists. Public works were favored as the way to prime a general recovery, which in turn would inspire a renewal of other activities.

Although the Federal recovery measures were aimed primarily at resuscitating the credit structure and promoting reemployment, they seemed to be driven, as by destiny, toward correcting maladjustments in the real estate economy. Encouragement of new construction, bolstering of homeownership, aid to mortgagees, and incidentally (almost accidentally) the elimination of slums became part of the recovery program.

The broad social objectives of slum clearance were, of course, subordinate to the main purpose: lubricating construction. But social reform intruded itself into the picture. By the very nature of a public works program, activity is limited to work that does not compete with private enterprise. Aside from public works, the projects that best met the requirement were those with social significance.

The recovery formula dictated wholesale construction of roads, bridges, tunnels, airports, army housing, public buildings, and similar noncompetitive ventures. But not enough of these projects could be scheduled, and all of them took months to plan. Bridges and similar projects, used too large a proportion of materials, too little of direct labor. Finally, any formula requiring cash contributions by the debt-ridden cities was useless. Public works on a debtor-creditor basis, even though sweetened by a small Federal subsidy, would get nowhere. . . .

But social objectives steadily gained in stature and emphasis, and soon became a featured part of New Deal pronouncements. President Roosevelt cited the "one third of a nation" that was "ill-nourished, ill-clothed, and ill-housed." A Federal Theater Project production took up the cry in "One Third of a Nation," a Broadway success that heightened the demand for action on slums. Public interest was further stimulated

---

[9] *American Federationist, op. cit.,* p. 72. This figure covers those employed directly and indirectly by building contractors, by builders on their own accounts, and by road construction companies.

by the lecture tour of Sir Raymond Unwin and others, who told of England's successful experience with public housing. Langdon W. Post in New York put slums and housing on the front pages of the newspapers. The need for business by the order-starved materials industries and the general feeling that everything must be done to stimulate employment supplied the additional impetus required to translate public sympathy into legislation.

The ultimate result was establishment of the United States Housing Authority in 1937 and the authorization of a total of $800,000,000 in loans to local housing authorities, plus $28,-000,000 in subsidies.

The initial appropriation for public housing had slipped through the Congress in the deep deflationary days largely because opposition had not yet fully crystallized. Building materials industries in particular saw benefits in housing construction and since these manufacturers were allied with the larger business pressure organizations in Washington, there was no concerted opposition in 1937 when the United States Housing Act was passed; there was even some positive support.[10] Real estate pressure groups and building and loan associations were still too depression-shocked to offer any effective opposition.

Soon, however, public housing met tougher opposition. Social objectives faded in the dawn of recovery. The National Association of Real Estate Boards and the building and loan associations began organized attacks against public housing. Further appropriations were blocked. Home builders saw in the Federal Housing Administration an opportunity to perform the social function themselves at a profit. The building and loan associations, benefiting from the new home loan bank system and the Home Owners' Loan Corporation windfall, began to view the Federal government not as a threat to enterprise but as a convenient utensil in which to season profit with honor. Private enterprise, it was felt, was still the traditional vehicle for correcting the social abuses private enterprise had created. Government should, therefore, stimulate private enterprise, rather than spend money for social betterment.

[10] General Hugh S. Johnson, anxious to write a column on the United States Housing Bill, told the writer that his reading public was interested not in who was for a program or what its merits were so much as it was in the villains opposed to it. Were there any? There were simply no villains to be identified at the time.

Thus, although the preambles of recovery bills expressed purposes noble enough in the verbiage, whatever help was given the homeowner had also to be lucrative to the entrepreneurs and lenders involved. The effort to halt deflation of home equities and stave off foreclosures was diverted primarily to buying up mortgages from lending institutions and only secondarily to helping the owners. Though mortgage moratoria in 28 states checked inconsiderate action by lending institutions, national policy was aimed to bail out the sour and frozen mortgages from the overloaded institutional portfolios. The formula for providing new homes was fashioned so that builders needed no investment to venture and lenders assumed no risk in lending. A conflict of pressures had developed between those who favored government intervention to aid the people at the base of the economic pyramid and those who saw in government intervention a handy means of assuring private profits and absorbing private losses. . . .

THE FEDERAL APPROACH TO REAL ESTATE

The government's excursion into the moribund real estate and home-building fields after 1933 was well intentioned but random and undirected. There was no basic plan to correlate the scattered efforts. A variety of remedies was offered, all predicated upon the common diagnosis that spending in all directions was necessary for the recovery. A leaning toward fortuitous experimentation resulted in a series of demonstrations in real estate and building which embodied the pet ideas of administrators or their assistants. Though vamped up with brave language and promise of reanimation of enterprise, they were incapable in practice of effecting a stabilization of the disorderly real estate business.

A main goal was to create jobs by reviving the construction industry. Its recovery was thought to be held back by (a) the dearth of loan funds for building; (b) the absence of equity venture capital; and (c) the inability of local governments to finance public improvements. The solutions seemed simple. Make loan funds available, make less venture capital necessary for speculative undertakings, and subsidize local public building to supplement Federal works.

The Federal adventure into real estate inevitably fanned out into a multitude of unrelated directions. RFC set up a mortgage company to supply loans which private lenders were eschewing. FHA would underwrite the safety of mortgage loan funds. HOLC, while staving off foreclosures, would also release institutional funds frozen in home mortgages so these funds could be used for fresh mortgages. The Federal Home Loan Bank System would provide a permanent credit reserve to keep urban home mortgages liquid. A Federal Savings and Loan Insurance Corporation would insure accounts up to $5000 in Federal savings and loan associations and local thrift associations. The Farm Credit Administration and the Farm Security Administration would make farm loans, and other loans would be facilitated for household appliances, electric equipment, and the purchase and improvement of farm lands and buildings. So much for lending operations.

While lending operations thus seemed to cover almost every conceivable need, the problem of venture capital was tougher. It was well enough to advance money to public agencies but a loan was considered safe only when cushioned by somebody's equity investment or secured by satisfactory collateral. The cities could supply none. The solution was roughly as follows:

Loans for "self-liquidating" improvements would be made to public agencies with a simultaneous cancellation of part of the indebtedness (30 per cent of the cost of labor and materials). This would create the equity brace necessary to shore up the loan.

So far as private building was concerned, FHA would diminish the amount of money needed for equities on new homes by guaranteeing principal and interest to lending institutions if they made loans at 90 per cent of the value. This narrowed to 10 per cent the equity margin needed to build or buy a home. All the builders needed to invest would be their organizing ability and the little turnover capital required to get the venture under way and to offset any charge of a complete bail-out at government expense. Larger scale rental housing would be encouraged too by requiring only a 20 per cent equity investment by the builders. FHA was also authorized to make loans to owners for repair and modernization.

Since these remedies were not of themselves sufficient to stimulate recovery, the government also undertook direct construction operations. The Tennessee Valley Authority dammed the Tennessee River, built homes and power lines. The Civil Works Administration and the Works Progress Administration built roads, sewers, airports, playgrounds and other works. Miscellaneous agencies built camps for migrants, greenbelt towns, subsistence homesteads, and so on.

Yet the multifold efforts at pump-priming did not operate

with the anticipated efficiency. In some cases the formula was basically unworkable; in others administration was faulty, in still others the purpose was corrupted by groups seeking private advantage by blocking social programs or diverting them toward their own benefit.

RFC Mortgage Company and the Public Works Administration assumed a traditional banking view in their dealings with public borrowers. RFC made loans only on the best security at interest rates often higher than those of private lenders. PWA, though many of its operations were effective, refused to decentralize and entrust authority to local public bodies which might have, in such undertakings as public housing, been vastly more efficient. Its grants were often too modest to induce construction by the beleaguered public agencies.

FHA operations, begun haltingly, were welcomed by most institutions but regarded by some of the larger lending institutions as a competitive threat to their own business. HOLC delighted the building and loan associations, insurance companies and other lending institutions whose mortgages it had lifted from their bulging portfolios without requiring more than nominal concession of principal. Failure to stipulate that the unfrozen funds be lent again resulted in their being refrozen into bank reserves which grew large enough to be an additional check upon a recovery.

Poor administration and the lack of a guiding policy produced many incompatibilities and conflicts. Sometimes each agency operated as a competitor in what might be described as a laissez-faire bureaucracy. USHA, for example, would approve the clearance and rebuilding of a slum area, only to find that FHA had made loans for the modernization and repair of some of the obsolete buildings, while HOLC had propped up values by buying mortgages in the area at par. USHA, naturally, wanted land prices low to facilitate site assemblage, while HOLC wanted them high so that the increased equities would make its mortgages safer. The policy of the Home Loan Bank was to keep interest rates up in the interests of its member institutions, thus checking any sentiment in the FHA organization to force a lower interest rate on its insured mortgages. FHA policy, not integrated with USHA policy, encouraged developments in peripheral areas thus drawing the population from the central areas and accelerating blight. . . .

HOLC aided some owners who were being put out of their homes and got some delinquent real estate taxes into the hands of cities, though mainly it served as a handy method for helping out lending institutions whether they needed help or not. FHA assisted many home buyers, stimulated home building, and effected some reforms in the mortgage system. But finally, it became a permanent prop in the mortgage setup and was welcomed into the entrepreneurial family as a new vehicle for removing risk from mortgage lending and building operations.

As recovery set in, appropriations for social programs were curtailed but the parts of the program which benefited business and finance, though intended to be temporary, stood fast. The Federal expenditures and commitments in real estate and mortgage operations (including FHA insurance) exceeded $15,000,000,000 by 1944. Yet, they had accomplished little in the stabilizing of the real estate structure and mortgage lending economy. Benefit to special groups was the inevitable result of a program which had failed to envision the basic disabilities of the real estate pattern. None of the Federal operations, with the occasional exception of public works and those conducted by local housing authorities, was related even remotely to the general city plan or to its reform but represented efforts to deal with individual owners as though each enterprise were a separate isolated transaction.

By 1945 no modification of this curious pattern had been made. It was ratified by President Truman in his message to Congress, though he expressed interest in further public housing appropriations. The agencies and remedies which benefited private enterprise continued to function and flourish. In 1946, with mortgage funds more abundant than ever before, FHA and the Home Loan Bank System were still insuring mortgage lenders. Public housing, which private enterprise charged was competitive, was having tough sledding, despite the pressing need for it and its proved accomplishments. Fresh blight and peripheral mushrooming of developments continued without abatement. Home ownership, which seemed safer as real estate conditions improved, remained in the long run as insecure as ever as a new crop of victims bought into homes often at twice their values.

HEARINGS ON GENERAL HOUSING ACT OF 1945*

United States Senate Committee on Banking and Currency

STATEMENT OF NEWTON C. FARR, CHICAGO, ILL., REPRE-
SENTING THE NATIONAL ASSOCIATION OF REAL ESTATE BOARDS

The National Association of Real Estate Boards cannot en-
dorse this measure. We in the real-estate business, whose job
it is to provide the commodity of housing—to plan it, finance
it, build it, and operate it—are keenly aware of the multiplicity
of problems involved in the subject of shelter. We have ever
been hopeful that answers could be found to the complex and
difficult questions revolving around the rescue of our cities
from slums and blight, and in the provision of more good
housing to more of our families at lower costs. We would like
to see every family in this country well housed. We would
like to see the blight that is eating out the heart of our municipalities stopped. We would like to see every returning veteran
coming back to a home of his own, where he can shelter his
family and raise his children. We would like to see every other
family that needs a dwelling find it. But we do not think that
this bill can accomplish these things. I realize that it was the
hope of the sponsors of this legislation that the programs proposed in the measure would accomplish these objectives. I
am afraid, however, that these hopes would not materialize.

In general, we feel that with the Nation facing the most
critical housing shortage in our history every possible effort
ought to be concentrated by the Federal Government on
clearing the way for production of houses and apartments.
By that I mean it should direct intensive effort to eliminating
the bottlenecks in production of materials, in price and wage
disputes, in manpower, in ceilings, and similar matters. Every
element necessary for opening up a truly big-scale home-
building program to meet the extraordinary need is present
and available except abundant materials and labor. Both of
those things are complicated by various problems that demand coordinated action that can be given only by the Federal Government. The Government could encourage the

* 79th Congress, 1st Session, S. 1592, Part I, November 27–30, December 4–5, 1945 (Government Printing Office, 1946), pp. 436–37, 440,
444–45, 451 (selected portions).

building of vast numbers of dwellings by stimulating the faster production of materials; by settling labor disputes; by helping recruit manpower; by encouraging cities to put their building codes and zoning requirements on a reasonable basis; by crystallizing its attitude toward the construction industry so that industry will know where it stands and with what it must contend, and by holding consistently to a helpful policy. It would even restrict its own construction activities to only such public works or health projects as are absolutely essential, so that more materials could be channeled to the building of houses. In that way we could speed the production of housing. That is the real job that ought to be done.

Even the most helpful provisions that have been included in this bill with respect to lower cost financing, for aid to rental projects, the streamlining amendments for the Federal Housing Administration and the Home Loan Bank Board will be absolutely meaningless unless the preceding things I have mentioned are done. The most favorable financing in the world will not of itself build housing if bottlenecks exist in labor, prices, and materials. All agencies must cooperate in helping the builder get under way. . . .

Senator ELLENDER. If your statement includes a question that I am about to ask, forget about it. If we are to strike out from this bill the title dealing with public housing, what would your association's attitude be as to the bill?

Mr. FARR. We would be very much happier about the bill.

Senator ELLENDER. Happier, or would you be for it, killing yourselves to pass it?

Mr. FARR. No. I'll say there are certain other features in the bill that we are not satisfied with. I think, perhaps, the statement will clarify that as I go on.

Senator ELLENDER. All right.

Mr. FARR. I want to assure you that I am here because I think that both you and I——

Senator ELLENDER. Yes.

Mr. FARR. Are interested in trying to do something about the housing shortage. I am trying to do so on my part, and I am sure you are on your part.

Senator ELLENDER. Yes. Well, the thing is this, and you might bear this in mind as you go along—you say, "We are trying to do the job."

Mr. FARR. That is right.

Senator ELLENDER. "To give decent housing to everybody." You are for that, aren't you?

Mr. FARR. That is right. And we are trying to do it now just as fast as we can.

Senator ELLENDER. All right. And you realize that slums should be cleared?

Mr. FARR. That is correct.

Senator ELLENDER. Yes. Now, we have offered in this bill what we think is a solution to the problem, or something that will aid in solving the problem; and what this committee, I am sure, would like to have from you, since you agree with us that it ought to be done, give us your plan as to how it can be done.

Mr. FARR. I think some of them will be pointed out here, and I will be glad to expand on that later. . . .

Mr. FARR. . . . I am trying to make it clear why we are against the bill.

Certain provisions of the bill we are heartily in accord with.

Senator ELLENDER. Did I understand you to state a while ago that you were in favor of that part of the bill in respect to slum clearance?

Mr. FARR. That is right.

Senator ELLENDER. Why should you favor that and not public housing along with slum clearance?

Mr. FARR. We believe that some clearance can be achieved best by local groups of people, or local groups of builders and others interested in the community who will finance the reconstruction of those areas.

Senator ELLENDER. Has that been done in the past?

Mr. FARR. I am involved in that very thing myself at the present time.

Senator ELLENDER. Where?

Mr. FARR. In Chicago.

Senator ELLENDER. How much of it have you done?

Mr. FARR. I am personally active in two areas of Chicago. One is on the South Side in the vicinity of Thirty-third and State Streets where we have in process a reconstruction program covering an area of about a half square mile.

I am also actively interested in an area on the West Side known as the Medical Center area, where we have about a square mile.

Senator ELLENDER. How are you financing that—privately?

Mr. FARR. The work in the Medical Center area is being done through money supplied by the State of Illinois.

Senator ELLENDER. The State of Illinois?

Mr. FARR. And some through institutions that are in that

area. That is confined to land assembly. We have a group, of which I am a member, that is prepared now to go in and actually finance the construction of housing in areas near those centers that I speak of.

Senator ELLENDER. To what extent does the State of Illinois help you?

Mr. FARR. The State of Illinois is helping in the Medical Center area in two ways. They are providing funds for the University of Illinois for its medical school which is located there, which has been acquiring additional land and wrecking slum buildings. They have also appropriated a million dollars for land assembly in that area by the Medical Center Commission. The Medical Center Commission is made up of a group, part of whom are appointed by the Governor and part by the mayor of Chicago. The Medical Center Commission is now actively in process of starting a land assembly job.

Frankly, this is the first money they have had to spend in slum clearance, and they are just starting their program.

Senator ELLENDER. Would you be able, or would you undertake this job in Illinois except that you receive money from the State?

Mr. FARR. It is my belief that this program of land assembly —and I am talking now about land assembly rather than reconstruction—is primarily a local problem. I think that local communities, however, should have all the aid they can get from their State government, and also from the Federal Government.

I am happy about the provisions of your slum clearance title which provides supplementary money from the Federal Government to augment that of local communities in doing this job.

Senator MURDOCK. You want the control of the expenditures in local hands?

Mr. FARR. Yes. . . .

Mr. FARR. Remember that the slum-clearance program has been one also of the ability to finance redevelopment in those areas.

Senator ELLENDER. Of course, that is why private capital has not ventured, because it is not profitable enough, and that is why we are offering a method here whereby it can be done. I am really disappointed that you folks should be willing to accept aid from the Federal Government to clear the slums and get this real estate back at a very large mark-down price and not be willing to utilize money in the same way to aid and assist the people that you have never been able to assist up to now. I cannot understand it.

Mr. FARR. Don't you want to encourage investment of this large mass of capital that is represented by the banks and insurance companies and other institutions?

Senator ELLENDER. Yes. The bill sets forth unmistakably that the local community decides its housing needs, the local community decides the extent to which private enterprise will do the job, and if a time comes when private enterprise cannot do it, then what happens? You don't come to Washington immediately, but you have got to get your municipal government to investigate, and the municipal government itself must make the determination that private enterprise cannot do it.

Until that is done, under this bill, you cannot come to Washington and get a dime for public housing. All the other requirements we added to make it certain that private enterprise would have the opportunity to do the job at home.

Mr. FARR. I think you should give private enterprise the opportunity to do that, and they have not had that opportunity up to now.

Senator ELLENDER. But the bill does it.

Mr. FARR. The bill is not enacted yet, and the opportunity we would like to have——

Senator ELLENDER. In other words, you would want to set the bill aside and give you a chance to try to do it for another 40 years, and maybe fail.

Mr. FARR. We all want to make progress, don't we? We don't want to spend all of our time arguing and disputing as to just how this should be done. We believe that things should be done that can be done now. We are much distressed at the obstacles that have been in the way of the private builder during the past few years, but the war is over now, and we think those obstacles should be eliminated.

Senator ELLENDER. If this bill is enacted into law, the Federal Government would not have to put up a dime of money for public housing if the local community can ascertain that private enterprise can do the whole job.

Mr. FARR. Why not give the local community that opportunity then?

Senator ELLENDER. I say, what difference does it make if the local community is prohibited from doing it until it is established that you cannot do the job. You have elected officials there who are put into office by the voters. . . .

THE CONSTITUTIONAL QUESTION

All urban renewal programs rest on the power of the government to condemn private property for public use, the right of eminent domain. What constitutes the legitimate use of this power has been a question the courts have been deciding since the earliest days of the Republic, and renewal too has had its day in court. The substantive issues in *Berman v. Parker* revolved around a Title I project in the District of Columbia, the Southwest Washington Project in an area that once, in the shadow of the White House, contained one of the worst slums in the nation. Because it involved the only community in the country over which Congress has direct jurisdiction, the Supreme Court's finding was based on the general welfare powers of Congress. These powers (the equivalent of the police powers of the state legislatures) make it permissible to use eminent domain to remedy conditions injurious to health, safety, and morals; a definition that accurately described the slums of Washington. Martin Anderson reviews the basis of the Court's reasoning in *Berman v. Parker,* and at the same time attempts to rebut the principles on which the decision is based. He makes at least one telling point: While it is quite legitimate for a government to condemn private property to erect schools, build highways, etc., is it equally legitimate to condemn one person's property and then resell it to another private person?

As might be expected, John Groberg, Assistant Director of the National Association of Housing and Redevelopment Officials, strongly disagrees with Anderson. If the latter views urban renewal from a highly "conservative" position, Groberg's rejoinder, with its emphasis on the necessity for a broad interpretation of the concept of "public use," can be taken as the typical "liberal" viewpoint.

While Charles Abrams, now head of the Department of City Planning, Columbia University, does not deal directly with the constitutional issue, what he has to say puts it, in effect, into a more general context that is increasingly salient.

Slum clearance and housing, Abrams argues, are part of a planning process, and planning means more government intervention and interference with traditional property rights. For Abrams a key problem is the maintainance of democratic controls over the planning process. Seen from this perspective, Anderson's position may not be as pertinent or relevant as it is when thought of in context of the traditional free market and private enterprise. Abrams' perspective suggests still another consideration: We are, as a society, dedicated to the ideology of private enterprise while the imperatives of a complex industrial social and economic order drive us to increased planning and government intervention. May not *Berman v. Parker* represent our attempt to ride both horses at once?

THE SOPHISTRY THAT MADE URBAN
RENEWAL POSSIBLE*

Martin Anderson†

This member of government was at first considered as the
most harmless and helpless of all its organs. But it has proved
that the power of declaring what the law is, *ad libitum*, by
sapping and mining, slyly, and without alarm, the foundations
of the Constitution, can do what open force would not dare to
attempt.

— Thomas Jefferson: *Letter to Edward Livingston,* 1825

For over fifteen years government agencies throughout the
United States have been taking private property by eminent
domain for the private use of some person other than the
original owner. Why? To carry out the federal urban renewal
program (FURP). How? Because such action was apparently
deemed constitutional by the Supreme Court in 1954.[1]

Passed in 1949 by Congress, the essential purpose and clear
intent of the FURP was to "help" our economic system of
free enterprise achieve better housing conditions for all Americans. The decision made by the Supreme Court in 1954 appeared to sanction the constitutionality of the program. Since
then the FURP has grown rapidly and it has been endorsed
enthusiastically by many well-known, influential people.

Today many people seem to feel that (1) the program is
absolutely necessary, and, except for a few setbacks here and
there, is making significant progress, and (2) in spite of some
uneasiness over the idea of taking private property by eminent
domain for private use, it "must" be all right because the
Supreme Court has indicated that it is constitutional.

* FROM *Law and Contemporary Problems,* XXX (Winter 1965), parts
of pp. 198 and 201–11 as revised by the author.

† A.B. 1957, *summa cum laude,* Dartmouth College; M.S. in Engineering and Business Administration, 1958, Thayer School of Engineering
and the Tuck School of Business Administration; Ph.D. in Industrial
Management, 1962, Massachusetts Institute of Technology. Research
Fellow, Joint Center for Urban Studies, Massachusetts Institute of Technology and Harvard University, 1961–62. Associate Professor of Business, Columbia University Graduate School of Business. Author, THE
FEDERAL BULLDOZER: A CRITICAL ANALYSIS OF URBAN RENEWAL, 1949–
62, M.I.T. Press (1964).

[1] Berman v. Parker, 348 U.S. 26 (1954).

I disagree. In my judgment the FURP is not necessary, it is not working, and it is unconstitutional.

The FURP has been a failure. Contrary to the widely publicized claims of the proponents of federally aided and directed urban renewal, the program has worsened the housing situation that it set out to help; it has not revitalized a single city; and its costs—both in dollars and personal liberty—have been great.[2]

. . .

Is the FURP Constitutional?

This article deals basically with one simple, clear issue— *the issue of whether or not any government agency in the United States should have the right to take private property by eminent domain for private use.*

The basic idea of forcibly seizing the private property of one man, compensating him for it at the appraised value, and then conveying this property to someone else is, I am convinced, considered illegal and immoral by the great majority of the people in the United States—particularly when this abstract principle becomes concrete and people are faced with the prospect of having their own homes seized.

In 1954 the constitutionality of the FURP was challenged. At this time the nine men who were then the Justices of the Supreme Court had the opportunity to stop this program in its infancy before it had a chance to grow into the firmly entrenched giant that it is today, reaching into over 750 cities and embracing over 1500 projects. But they did not; in effect they released the FURP to interfere with the property rights and lives of millions of city dwellers in the United States.

While the *Berman v. Parker* case only applies to the use of the power of eminent domain in connection with urban renewal projects in the District of Columbia, it is vitally important, for it clearly shows the thinking of the Court on the basic issues involved in the FURP, and thus has influenced the thinking of lawyers and judges across the country.

The opinion was written by Justice Douglas and concurred in by the rest of the Court. Since then, the composition of the Court has changed significantly—only four of the Justices remain who participated in this decision. They include Justice Douglas, the author, Chief Justice Warren, and Justices Black

[2] Martin Anderson, The Federal Bulldozer, M.I.T. Press (1964).

and Clark. The five present Justices who did not participate in *Berman v. Parker* are Harlan, Brennan, Stewart, White, and Goldberg.

It is my contention that the opinion handed down in 1954 is illogical and contains sophistic reasoning. On a quick, superficial reading it may appear plausible, but a careful, detailed reading will reveal basic errors. Following is the complete text of *Berman v. Parker*.[3] Interspersed through it are my comments on what I consider to be the crucial elements of the opinion.

This is an appeal (28 U.S.C. § 1253) from the judgment of a three-judge District Court which dismissed a complaint seeking to enjoin the condemnation of appellants' property under the District of Columbia Redevelopment Act of 1945, 60 Stat. 790, D.C. Code 1951, §§ 5-701–5-719. The challenge was to the constitutionality of the Act, particularly as applied to the taking of appellants' property. The District Court sustained the constitutionality of the Act. 117 F. Supp. 705.

Here the Court clearly identifies the main issue to be decided upon—"the constitutionality of the Act, particularly as applied to the taking of the appellants' property."

By § 2 of the Act, Congress made a "legislative determination" that "owing to technological and sociological changes, obsolete lay-out, and other factors, conditions existing in the District of Columbia with respect to substandard housing and blighted areas, including the use of buildings in alleys as dwellings for human habitation, are injurious to the public health, safety, morals, and welfare, and it is hereby declared to be the policy of the United States to protect and promote the welfare of the inhabitants of the seat of the Government by eliminating all such injurious conditions by employing all means necessary and appropriate for the purpose."[1]

[1] The Act does not define either "slums" or "blighted areas." Sec. 3(r), however, states: " 'Substandard housing conditions' means the conditions obtaining in connection with the existence of any dwelling, or dwellings, or housing accommodations for human beings, which because of lack of sanitary facilities, ventilation, or light, or because of dilapidation, overcrowding, faulty interior arrangement, or any combinations of these factors, is in the opinion of the Commissioners detrimental to the safety, health, morals, or welfare of the inhabitants of the District of Columbia." [Footnote, Berman v. Parker, 348 U.S. 26 (1954)].

Section 2 goes on to declare that acquisition of property is necessary to eliminate these housing conditions.

[3] *Supra* note 1.

Congress further finds in § 2 that these ends cannot be attained "by the ordinary operations of private enterprise alone without public participation"; that "the sound replanning and redevelopment of an obsolescent or obsolescing portion" of the District "cannot be accomplished unless it be done in the light of comprehensive and coordinated planning of the whole of the territory of the District of Columbia and its environs"; and "that the acquisition and the assembly of real property and the leasing or sale thereof for redevelopment pursuant to a project area redevelopment plan . . . is hereby declared to be a public use."

The main issue is clarified further here. Congress declares that it must use "all means necessary" and then goes on to declare "that acquisition of property is necessary" and further that this is a "public use." Because Congress declares something to be a "public use" does not necessarily mean that it is, in fact, a public use. Approximately seventy per cent of all new construction in federal urban renewal areas is privately owned—and this is a private use as anyone may easily verify by attempting to use these homes or places of business as he would use a public park or a highway.

Section 4 creates the District of Columbia Redevelopment Land Agency (hereinafter called the Agency), composed of five members, which is granted power by § 5(a) to acquire and assemble, by eminent domain and otherwise, real property for "the redevelopment of blighted territory in the District of Columbia and the prevention, reduction, or elimination of blighting factors or causes of blight."

Section 6(a) of the Act directs the National Capital Planning Commission (hereinafter called the Planning Commission) to make and develop "a comprehensive or general plan" of the District, including "a land-use plan" which designates land for use for "housing, business, industry, recreation, education, public buildings, public reservations, and other general categories of public and private uses of the land." Section 6(b) authorizes the Planning Commission to adopt redevelopment plans for specific project areas. These plans are subject to the approval of the District Commissioners after a public hearing; and they prescribe the various public and private land uses for the respective areas, the "standards of population density and building intensity," and "the amount or character or class of any low-rent housing."

This section shows that there is a contradiction in the Act itself. Earlier the process of federal urban renewal was "declared to be a public use." Here they specify (twice) that there will be both "public *and private* uses of the land." Unless one attempts to maintain the intellectually indefensible position that a private use can be construed to be a public use (this is a contradiction in terms), then the only conclusion one can draw is that the wording of the Act itself is illogical and contradictory.

Once the Planning Commission adopts a plan and that plan is approved by the Commissioners, the Planning Commission certifies it to the Agency. § 6(d). At that point, the Agency is authorized to acquire and assemble the real property in the area. *Ibid.*

After the real estate has been assembled, the Agency is authorized to transfer to public agencies the land to be devoted to such public purposes as streets, utilities, recreational facilities, and schools, § 7(a), and to lease or sell the remainder as an entirety or in parts to a redevelopment company, individual, or partnership. § 7(b), (f). The leases or sales must provide that the lessees or purchasers will carry out the redevelopment plan and that "no use shall be made of any land or real property included in the lease or sale nor any building or structure erected thereon" which does not conform to the plan. §§ 7(d), 11. Preference is to be given to private enterprise over public agencies in executing the redevelopment plan. § 7(g).

This brief description of how the process of federal urban renewal will work implies that private use is involved. For example, it is stated that land can be sold or leased to an *individual*. By no distortion of the thinking process can this be construed to be a public use.

The first project undertaken under the Act relates to Project Area B in Southwest Washington, D.C. In 1950 the Planning Commission prepared and published a comprehensive plan for the District. Surveys revealed that in Area B, 64.3% of the dwellings were beyond repair, 18.4% needed major repairs, only 17.3% were satisfactory; 57.8% of the dwellings had outside toilets, 60.3% had no baths, 29.3% lacked electricity, 82.2% had no wash basins or laundry tubs, 83.8% lacked central heating. In the judgment of the District's Director of Health it was necessary to redevelop Area B in the interests of public health. The population of Area B amounted to 5,012 persons, of whom 97.5% were Negroes.

The plan for Area B specifies the boundaries and allocates the use of the land for various purposes. It makes detailed provisions for types of dwelling units and provides that at least one-third of them are to be low-rent housing with a maximum rental of $17 per room per month.

After a public hearing, the Commissioners approved the

plan and the Planning Commission certified it to the Agency for execution. The Agency undertook the preliminary steps for redevelopment of the area when this suit was brought.

Appellants own property in Area B at 712 Fourth Street, S.W. It is not used as a dwelling or place of habitation. A department store is located on it. Appellants object to the appropriation of this property for the purposes of the project. They claim that their property may not be taken constitutionally for this project. It is commercial, not residential property; it is not slum housing; it will be put into the project under the management of a private, not a public, agency and redeveloped for private, not public, use. That is the argument; and the contention is that appellants' private property is being taken contrary to two mandates of the Fifth Amendment—(1) "No person shall . . . be deprived of . . . property, without due process of law"; (2) "nor shall private property be taken for public use, without just compensation." To take for the purpose of ridding the area of slums is one thing; it is quite another, the argument goes, to take a man's property merely to develop a better balanced, more attractive community. The District Court, while agreeing in general with that argument, saved the Act by construing it to mean that the Agency could condemn property only for the reasonable necessities of slum clearance and prevention, its concept of "slum" being the existence of conditions "injurious to the public health, safety, morals and welfare." 117 F. Supp. 705, 724–25.

The power of Congress over the District of Columbia includes all the legislative powers which a state may exercise over its affairs. See *District of Columbia v. John R. Thompson Co.,* 346 U.S. 100, 108.

This summarizes the situation that was presented to the Justices of the Supreme Court. Now Justice Douglas begins with the analysis and the conclusion derived therefrom, in which the rest of the Justices concurred.

We deal, in other words, with what traditionally has been known as the police power. An attempt to define its reach or trace its outer limits is fruitless, for each case must turn on its own facts. The definition is essentially the product of legislative determinations addressed to the purposes of government, purposes neither abstractly nor historically capable of complete definition. Subject to specific constitutional limitations, when the legislature has spoken, the public interest has been declared in terms well-nigh conclusive.

But the main point here is *"subject to specific constitutional limitations"*—and no matter what the *purpose* of the legislature, no matter how well-meaning, no matter how plausible the reasons, it is the responsibility of the Supreme Court to analyze logically the totality of the law—not only to see if the primary purposes of the law are unconstitutional, but also to see if anything incidental, but necessary, to the law is also unconstitutional.

For example, if Congress passed a law whose purpose was to eliminate slums, but which contained a proviso stating that the government could conscript labor for the actual physical work, the mere fact that the *good* of eliminating slums is desirable would not therefore justify the re-institution of slavery.

The fact that an action necessary to implement a law is incidental to the main purpose of the law does not mean that the "incidental" action is immune from scrutiny as to its constitutionality.

> In such cases the legislature, not the judiciary, is the main guardian of the public needs to be served by social legislation, whether it be Congress legislating concerning the District of Columbia or the States legislating concerning local affairs.
> This principle admits of no exception merely because the power of eminent domain is involved. The role of the judiciary in determining whether that power is being exercised for a public purpose is an extremely narrow one.[4]

The Court states that its role "in determining whether that power is being exercised for a public purpose is an extremely narrow one." The critical word here is *"purpose."* But the issue is not whether eminent domain is being used for a public purpose, but rather whether the use of the land seized will be *public* or *private.*

The appellants claim—in the Court's own words—that their property, after it has been taken, "will be put into the project under the management of a private, not a public, agency and redeveloped for private, not public, use." The critical word here is *"use."*

According to the *American College Dictionary* the legal definition of "use" is "the enjoyment of property, as by the employment, occupation, or exercise of it." "Purpose," on

---

[4] Defenders of the FURP point out that in the past there have been a number of instances where the power of eminent domain has been exercised to acquire property for private use, but these previous isolated lapses do not justify the current widespread seizure of the homes and land of some for the eventual private use of others in urban renewal areas; past errors never justify current ones.

the other hand, is "the object for which anything exists or is done, made, *used*, etc."

Use refers to the actual employment of material objects—to their occupation or to their exercise. *Purpose* refers to the object or goal *for which* any particular material object is used. Purpose and use do not mean the same thing.

The elementary point that should be decided by the Court is whether or not private property is being taken for *public* use or for *private* use. The question of whether or not it is for a public *purpose* is irrelevant here.

The word "public" pertains to the people as a whole—and thus the concept embraces every single individual within the community, state or nation that the context of its use implies. The word "private" means belonging to some *particular* person or persons.

It appears that early in its analysis the Court has made a serious error. They have construed their role as one of determining whether the police power is being used for a public purpose. This is not the crucial issue. The crucial issue is whether or not private property can be taken for private *use* if the legislature decrees this taking to be for a public purpose. Whether or not the taking is for a public purpose is irrelevant to the question of whether or not the means employed to achieve this purpose result in an action that is clearly unconstitutional.

> Public safety, public health, morality, peace and quiet, law and order—these are some of the more conspicuous examples of the traditional application of the police power to municipal affairs. Yet they merely illustrate the scope of the power and do not delimit it.

It may be true that the traditional application of the police power to municipal affairs only illustrates the scope of its power and does not delimit it, but it does not follow from this that Supreme Court Justices have a carte blanche for deciding the desirable limits. The Court has no right to condone the extension of police power if this extension involves actions that are unconstitutional.

> Miserable and disreputable housing conditions may do more than spread disease and crime and immorality. They may also suffocate the spirit by reducing the people who live there to the status of cattle. They may indeed make living an almost insufferable burden. They may also be an ugly sore, a blight on the community which robs it of charm, which makes it a

place from which men turn. The misery of housing may despoil a community as an open sewer may ruin a river.

This highly emotional statement, while dealing with an important problem, does not pertain to the main point of constitutionality at issue here.

We do not sit to determine whether a particular housing project is or is not desirable. The concept of the public welfare is broad and inclusive. The values it represents are spiritual as well as physical, aesthetic as well as monetary. It is within the power of the legislature to determine that the community should be beautiful as well as healthy, spacious as well as clean, well-balanced as well as carefully patrolled. In the present case, the Congress and its authorized agencies have made determinations that take into account a wide variety of values. It is not for us to reappraise them. If those who govern the District of Columbia decide that the Nation's Capital should be beautiful as well as sanitary, there is nothing in the Fifth Amendment that stands in the way.

The clear statement that it is within the power of the legislature to determine that the community should be beautiful, spacious and well-balanced has far reaching implications. In effect they are saying that Congress may dictate to the individual citizens of the United States what style of architecture they may build (because what is beautiful to one may not be to another), how much space should be between buildings, and what they must do to make the community "well-balanced." "Well-balanced" puzzles me. Do they mean it should be racially balanced, and, if so, what ratio? Do they mean that it should be culturally balanced, and, if so, to what cultural activities are they referring?

Once the object is within the authority of Congress, the right to realize it through the exercise of eminent domain is clear. For the power of eminent domain is merely the means to the end. Once the object is within the authority of Congress, the means by which it will be attained is also for Congress to determine.

In simple terms, this says that *the end justifies the means.* This is an appalling philosophy to be upheld by any court, let alone the Supreme Court. Here the Court has stated that if the Court agrees that the object of a law passed by Congress is within its authority, then it has no concern about the means used to acquire this object.

This is an illogical and immoral position. Clearly the means by which the legislature attempts to gain its ends must be moral and just—and when legislation is challenged, it is the responsibility of the Court to see to it that the means are constitutional, not to dismiss the issue.

What if Congress were to pass a law which had as its goal the elimination of poverty (clearly within the terms of "public welfare" as defined by the Court) and had as its means gas chambers to liquidate the poor who after all may be "a blight on the community which robs it of charm"? Would the Court declare that, "Once the object is within the authority of Congress, the means by which it will be attained is also for Congress to determine"? Of course not. The reasoning used by the Court here is illogical. The result of this error is to lead the Court into the untenable position where it implicitly adopts the principle that the means are irrelevant if the end is "good."

> Here one of the means chosen is the use of private enterprise for redevelopment of the area. Appellants argue that this makes the project a taking from one businessman for the benefit of another businessman.

Taking from one businessman by force for the benefit of another businessman is *not* private enterprise. Private enterprise is based solely on *voluntary* trade—the use of physical force is prohibited. This is clearly government action with private individuals and firms engaged to carry out part of the work.

> But the means of executing the project are for Congress and Congress alone to determine, once the public purpose has been established. The public end may be as well or better served through an agency of private enterprise than through a department of government—or so the Congress might conclude. We cannot say that public ownership is the sole method of promoting the public purposes of community redevelopment projects. What we have said also disposes of any contention concerning the fact that certain property owners in the area may be permitted to repurchase their properties for redevelopment in harmony with the overall plan. That, too, is a legitimate means which Congress and its agencies may adopt, if they choose.

This clinches their position—the end justifies the means.

> In the present case, Congress and its authorized agencies attack the problem of the blighted parts of the community on an area rather than on a structure-by-structure basis. That,

too, is opposed by appellants. They maintain that since their
building does not imperil health or safety nor contribute to
the making of a slum or a blighted area, it cannot be swept
into a redevelopment plan by the mere dictum of the Planning
Commission or the Commissioners. The particular uses to be
made of the land in the project were determined with regard
to the needs of the particular community.

This last sentence is not quite accurate. It should read:
"The particular uses to be made of the land in the project
were determined with regard to the needs *of particular people*
in the community." What happened to the "needs" of those
living in the community whose property is to be seized? Why
do the "needs" of some take precedence over the "needs" of
others?

The experts concluded that if the community were to be
healthy, if it were not to revert again to a blighted or slum
area, as though possessed of a congenital disease, the area
must be planned as a whole. It was not enough, they believed,
to remove existing buildings that were insanitary or unsightly.
It was important to redesign the whole area so as to eliminate
the conditions that cause slums—the overcrowding of dwellings, the lack of parks, the lack of adequate streets and alleys,
the absence of recreational areas, the lack of light and air,
the presence of outmoded street patterns. It was believed that
the piecemeal approach, the removal of individual structures
that were offensive, would be only a palliative. The entire
area needed redesigning so that a balanced, integrated plan
could be developed for the region, including not only new
homes but also schools, churches, parks, streets, and shopping centers. In this way it was hoped that the cycle of decay
of the area could be controlled and the birth of future slums
prevented. Such diversification in future use is plainly relevant
to the maintenance of the desired housing standards and therefore within congressional power.

The implication of this whole section is that if the "experts"
say it is so, it *is* so, and therefore is desirable, lawful and just.
I find it quite incredible that Justices of the Supreme Court
could ascribe such knowledge and wisdom to city planning
experts. The profession of city planning is in its intellectual
infancy—and there are few generally accepted standards or
criteria by which these people operate.

The District Court below suggested that, if such a broad
scope were intended for the statute, the standards contained
in the Act would not be sufficiently definite to sustain the

delegation of authority. We do not agree. We think the standards prescribed were adequate for executing the plan to eliminate not only slums as narrowly defined by the District Court but also the blighted areas that tend to produce slums.

At this point I can only refer to the footnote that the Court itself appended to its opinion. In the footnote the Court states, "The Act does not define either 'slums' or 'blighted area,'" and now, a few pages later in the same opinion, they say, "We think the standards prescribed were adequate. . . ." The logic here is impeccably false. Standards that do not exist cannot be adequate.

Property may of course be taken for this redevelopment which, standing by itself, is innocuous and unoffending. But we have said enough to indicate that it is the need of the area as a whole which Congress and its agencies are evaluating. If owner after owner were permitted to resist these redevelopment programs on the ground that his particular property was not being used against the public interest, integrated plans for redevelopment would suffer greatly. The argument pressed on us is, indeed, a plea to substitute the landowner's standard of the public need for the standard prescribed by Congress. But as we have already stated, community redevelopment programs need not, by force of the Constitution, be on a piecemeal basis—lot by lot, building by building.

It is not for the courts to oversee the choice of the boundary line nor to sit in review on the size of a particular project area. Once the question of the public purpose has been decided, the amount and character of land to be taken for the project and the need for a particular tract to complete the integrated plan rests in the discretion of the legislative branch.

For the third time—the end justifies the means.

The District Court indicated grave doubts concerning the Agency's right to take full title to the land as distinguished from the objectionable buildings located on it. We do not share those doubts. If the Agency considers it necessary in carrying out the redevelopment project to take full title to the real property involved, it may do so. It is not for the courts to determine whether it is necessary for successful consummation of the project that unsafe, unsightly, or insanitary building alone be taken or whether title to the land be included, any more than it is the function of the courts to sort and choose among the various parcels selected for condemnation.

The Supreme Court Justices do not seem to share anyone's

doubts with regard to any areas concerning this case. Now they say that "if the Agency (not the legislature) considers it necessary . . . to take full title to the real property, it may do so." Does this also imply that the Court would support anything the "Agency" wished to do as long as the "Agency" considered it necessary?

> The rights of these property owners are satisfied when they receive that just compensation which the Fifth Amendment exacts as the price of the taking.

There are many property owners and others that do not agree that their rights are satisfied simply by receiving what someone else thinks their seized property is worth.

> The judgment of the District Court, as modified by this opinion, is *affirmed*.

CONCLUSION

In essence the Supreme Court was presented with the established fact that a law had been passed by Congress which involved, as part of the means of implementation, the taking of private property by eminent domain for private use. This is proven by the fact that approximately seventy per cent of the new construction in urban renewal areas is privately owned, and also by the intent and wording of the act itself.

The Constitution is unequivocal on this question. A specific reference clearly states, "nor shall private property be taken for public use, without just compensation." And "for public use" is *not* the same as "for public purpose."

Faced with this problem the Justices appear to have found themselves in something of a dilemma. They had three alternatives: (1) They could decide that the Constitution meant what it said, and thus end the FURP. (2) They could declare that private property could be taken by eminent domain for private use, or (3) they could somehow attempt to evade the issue and simply declare that the FURP was constitutional because it was "within the power of the legislature to determine that the community should be beautiful as well as healthy, spacious as well as clean, well-balanced as well as beautiful" and then go on to say that "the power of eminent domain is merely the means to the end."

By not taking the first alternative, which, in my judgment, is the only logical conclusion, they were left with two untenable choices. To accept the second alternative would put them clearly on record in favor of allowing private property to be seized by eminent domain for private use. The enormous implications of a clear, unqualified acceptance of this principle probably deterred them from this course. Thus, they were left with only one alternative: to somehow allow eminent domain to be used as a tool in the FURP, and to evade any clear endorsement of the principle involved.

This is the course they followed by concurring in the opinion drafted by Justice Douglas. If we take this opinion literally, the Court has upheld the general principle that the end can justify the means, and that once the legislature has determined the end, the means are incidental to it, thus implying that the crucial issue of whether or not a law is constitutional is irrelevant when the law deals only with the means employed to gain some particular end.

But it is obvious that the means of any legislation must lie within the specific limitations of the Constitution. To declare otherwise is to revert in history to the rule of men, and to abandon the rule of law and the concept of human rights. An evasive decision of this type simply allows government seizure of private property by eminent domain for private use without openly endorsing it.

On the other hand, it might be that the Court simply did not address itself to the main issue raised in *Berman v. Parker:* Is it constitutional to seize private property by eminent domain for private use? The Justices are human, and thus fallible, and it is certainly reasonable to expect some errors in the decisions they make, particularly when one considers the tremendous time pressures under which they operate.

If this is the case, then they should rule on this crucial issue at some time in the future, and steer clear of expounding on what they feel is in the best interests of the community. When, and if, they do face this issue squarely, they will have to choose between the following alternatives:

1. Rule that private property *cannot* be taken by eminent domain for private use, and thus eliminate the FURP.

2. Rule that private property *can* be taken by eminent domain for private use, and thus cause the FURP to continue. Of course, the adoption of this principle has far-reaching implications. It means that no man's property would be absolutely safe from seizure by a government official, if

that government official maintained that the seizure was for a "public purpose" and could show this to the satisfaction of the Court.

In my judgment, the first alternative is the only logical and moral course to follow.

URBAN RENEWAL REALISTICALLY REAPPRAISED*

Robert P. Groberg†

Recent—and often misguided—critical outpourings against urban renewal justify an effort to determine realistically the actual and potential contribution of government to the solution of urban problems. Broadly defined, urban renewal can encompass all public and private efforts to improve city form and life. Realism requires recognition at the outset that there are no panaceas for every problem a city may possess and that some "solutions" create or emphasize other problems. Equally, realism requires careful consideration of the genesis and purposes of government programs with limited objectives so that criticism of them relates to their efforts and not to the broader notion of urban renewal goals. One recent attempt at major analysis[1] has gone astray partly because its author failed to see clearly the historical perspective and the limits of federal aid for slum clearance and redevelopment authorized by Congress under the Housing Act of 1949 and its amendments.[2]

The author of *The Federal Bulldozer* views this urban redevelopment assistance as though it had been expected by the Congress to solve *all* national housing problems. He cites the 1949 Declaration of National Housing Policy, preface to a comprehensive housing act with six separate titles, as though

* FROM *Law and Contemporary Problems*, XXX (Winter 1965), pp. 212–16 (selected portions).

† B.A. Syracuse, 1951; L.L.B. Columbia, 1954; Member New York State Bar; M.P.A. New York University, 1962; Assistant Director, National Association of Housing and Redevelopment Officials.

[1] MARTIN ANDERSON, THE FEDERAL BULLDOZER (1964) [hereinafter cited as ANDERSON].

[2] Note that the 1949 Act authorized federal loans and grants for what was defined as "slum clearance and redevelopment" and is now often cited as "urban redevelopment." The term "urban renewal" did not come into use until the Housing Act of 1954 amended and broadened the 1949 program to encompass a city-wide program—including renewal of commercial and industrial areas—rather than individual projects. With new emphasis on code enforcement, structural rehabilitation and neighborhood conservation, the objectives were extended to slum prevention as well as slum clearance. Amendments since then have sought to improve the assistance and provide better tools to achieve the program's goals.

that declaration pertained only to title I. He then proceeds to condemn urban renewal for not achieving (its) aims . . . , and other national housing efforts. *The Federal Bulldozer* is based on the assumption that federal assistance for local slum clearance and redevelopment projects was meant to achieve the housing aims of such other programs as low-rent public housing and FHA mortgage insurance. By incorporating these and other myths in his analysis, he began with unrealistic expectations for urban renewal efforts undertaken with federal assistance.

I. URBAN RENEWAL IS A LOCAL PROGRAM

Another myth incorporated into *The Federal Bulldozer* is that there is a separate, monolithic "federal urban renewal program" run from Washington by decree. The author completely misunderstands that urban renewal is a local program. He makes it appear that the power to plan, acquire, and prepare project sites for redevelopment or rehabilitation is vested in the federal government and based on an opinion of the United States Supreme Court. He does not recognize that the federal government cannot initiate any project. He does not mention that there can be no urban renewal project anywhere unless:

—a state legislature has first adopted an enabling law to give cities the governmental power for urban renewal, and some forty-eight states have;

—an elected city council has first organized an operating local renewal agency, and some 800 cities have;

—the same city council has first approved the project, and some 1600 projects have been so approved;

—the local government has first authorized local public expenditures to supplement federal funds, and more than one billion dollars in local public funds have been so approved to back the program;

—local citizens are participating in the urban renewal process, as required by law, and citizens everywhere are so doing.

By ignoring these facts, he never explains that the program depends completely on active local political support, given through the established system of representative government. The author does not state that the federal government neither operates any bulldozer, nor acquires any property for any urban renewal project. Instead, he alleges that "the federal urban renewal program is a firmly entrenched giant, reaching into virtually every important city in the United States . . ."[3] and falsely claims that "the federal government . . . will forcibly displace . . . American citizens . . ."[4] and that "the Urban Renewal Administration reported . . . that . . . businesses had already been acquired by them [*i.e.*, the URA] in urban renewal projects throughout the United States. . . ."[5] The federal government cannot select a project area, cannot prepare a plan, cannot acquire property, cannot demolish dilapidated structures, cannot sell the land or install the public improvements. Yet these are the critical steps in urban renewal projects. This misleading emphasis on the "federal" role in urban renewal programs all but obscures the fact that the powers to carry out urban renewal derive from state enabling legislation.[6]

In fact, some twenty-five states had slum clearance and redevelopment legislation of some kind prior to the Housing Act of 1949. New York state, for example, passed a constitutional amendment in 1938 and enacted legislation in 1942 authorizing slum clearance and redevelopment projects. State enabling acts have withstood constitutional attacks based on state and federal constitutional provisions beginning in 1947 in Pennsylvania.[7] By 1954 (when the U.S. Supreme Court upheld redevelopment legislation for the District of Columbia),[8] the courts in twenty-one states had reviewed such legislation, and in all but two states had upheld the constitutionality of urban redevelopment. At present urban renewal legislation has been tested and upheld in the highest courts of thirty-three states. Only in South Carolina, Georgia, and Florida has such legislation successfully been assailed. In Georgia a later constitutional amendment authorized the undertaking of urban renewal, while in Florida the position originally taken has been modified substantially by the state's highest court. In short, the author of *The Federal Bulldozer* seems to have been quite unaware, as are many opponents of urban renewal, that

[3] ANDERSON 33.
[4] *Id.* at 55.
[5] *Id.* at 68.
[6] For a summary and citations to state enabling acts, see HOUSING AND HOME FINANCE AGENCY, LIST OF CITATIONS TO STATUTES, CONSTITUTIONAL PROVISIONS, AND COURT DECISIONS (1962).
[7] Belovsky v. Redevelopment Authority of the City of Philadelphia, 357 Pa. 329, 54 A.2d 277 (1947).
[8] Berman v. Parker, 358 U.S. 269 (1954).

if his suggestion for "repeal" of the "federal" urban renewal program were adopted (cf. chapter fourteen), the program's authority would not be impaired at all because, with constitutional powers derived from the states, it is locally run.

II. THE USE OF THE POWER OF EMINENT DOMAIN IN URBAN RENEWAL RESTS ON A LONG TRADITION OF STATE COURT DECISIONS

At this late date complaints concerning the constitutional basis of urban renewal would seem ill-timed.[9] They may arise from those who ignore or misread the historical basis for government action to solve the problems of society. Foes of urban renewal have attempted to create a mythology with respect to the "inviolate" right of private property in support of their contention that government should not have the power to act in removing slums, and they have focused their attacks on the Supreme Court of the United States: "The federal urban renewal program has drastically altered the traditional concept of eminent domain; it is doubtful if any of the founding fathers could recognize it in its present form."[10] Instead of citing "the founding fathers," they cite Pitt and Blackstone, the latter in a classic example of tearing statements from context: "Regard of the law for private property is so great that it will not authorize the least violation of it, not even for the general good of the whole community; for it would be dangerous to allow any private man, or even any public tribunal, to be the judge of this common good. . . ." The preceding lines are the full text of a quote from *The Federal Bulldozer*.[11] The identical passage is also cited in a book published in 1962.[12] Both books ignored what came before and what followed in Blackstone's *Commentaries*. The quoted passage is preceded in Blackstone by the phrase "save only by the laws of the land" and is followed by: "In this and similar cases the legislature alone can, and indeed frequently does, interpose, and compel the individual to acquiesce . . .

[9] For a well-reasoned discussion of these issues, see COLEMAN WOODBURY (ED.), URBAN REDEVELOPMENT: PROBLEMS AND PRACTICES, pt. VI, "Eminent Domain in Acquiring Subdivision and Open Land in Redevelopment Programs: A Question of Public Use" (1953).

[10] ANDERSON 188.

[11] *Id.* at 185.

[12] THOMAS F. JOHNSON, JAMES R. MORRIS & JOSEPH G. BUTTS, RENEWING AMERICA'S CITIES, ch. III, at 46 (The Institute for Social Science Research, 1962).

by giving him a full indemnification and equivalent for the injury thereby sustained."[13] Thus, while Blackstone recognized the importance of private property, he also acknowledged that the legislature could authorize the taking of property for proper purposes upon payment of just compensation to the owner. This view was incorporated in the fifth amendment to the United States Constitution: ". . . nor shall private property be taken for public use without just compensation." It was written into some, but not all state constitutions.[14] But its incorporation in the federal and state constitutions still left to the legislatures the determination of what were proper purposes for the use of eminent domain.

In some states from the very start it was clear that private uses served public purposes. For instance, Idaho's constitution of 1890, cited by Professor Haar:[15]

> The necessary use of lands for the construction of reservoirs or storage basins, for the purpose of irrigation, or for rights of way for the construction of canals, ditches . . . or for the drainage of mines . . . or any other use necessary to the complete development of the material resources of the state, or the preservation of the health of its inhabitants, is hereby declared to be a public use and subject to the regulation and control of the state.

Such state constitutional provisions or amendments were adopted over a period from 1780 (Massachusetts) to 1938 (New York).

The courts of most states have ruled that "public use," as it appears in state constitutional provisions authorizing takings of private property by eminent domain, is equivalent to "public benefit." As one leading text puts it:[16]

> Anything that tends to enlarge the resources, increase the industrial advantages and promote the productive power of any considerable number of the inhabitants of a section of a state, or which leads to the growth of towns and the creation of new resources for the employment of capital prosperity of

---

[13] 1 WILLIAM BLACKSTONE, COMMENTARIES ON THE LAWS OF ENGLAND 138 (Sharswood ed. 1895).

[14] Professor Charles M. Haar of the Harvard Law School observes that: "The constitutions of most of the thirteen original states did not require compensation upon the condemnation of land. . . . But with the establishment of roads, limitations began to appear. . . ." CHARLES M. HAAR, LAND USE PLANNING 470 (1959).

[15] *Id.* at 411.

[16] PHILIP NICHOLS, THE LAW OF EMINENT DOMAIN § 7.2 (Sackman & Van Brunt, 3d ed. rev., 1963).

the whole community and, giving the constitution a broad and comprehensive interpretation, constitutes a public use. Under this view it has been held that the scope of eminent domain has been made as broad as the powers under the police and tax provisions of the constitution.

In accord with this view innumerable state legislatures and courts have authorized eminent domain proceedings in behalf of mills, railroads, power companies, private universities, and for other private concerns whose operations were considered to involve "public benefit." In these instances the property was taken by a *private* enterprise through a judicial proceeding which assured the payment of just compensation to the property owner; the title was not acquired by a public body or agency.

On the other hand, in urban renewal programs the property is acquired by a local *public* agency pursuant to the provisions and safeguards of an urban renewal plan adopted by a city council or other local governing body, after public hearings. Although most courts consider the elimination of the slum to be the public purpose for which the power of eminent domain may be employed, they also recognize that the prevention of future slums is a related public purpose. The existence of an official urban renewal plan is considered by these courts to be necessary to assure that this public purpose is served.

Thus, there is a tradition of broad interpretation of the term "public use" which would justify the use of eminent domain for urban redevelopment despite the fact that the property might eventually end up in private ownership. But in line with the finding that slum clearance and prevention are the public purposes which justify the employment of eminent domain in urban renewal, most courts have held that the disposition of the land is *incidental*, and the fact that it may be sold to private parties for private use does not vitiate the public purpose of slum clearance.

There is a minority view which holds in South Carolina where the sale of such land must be to public bodies. The foes of urban renewal hold fast to this narrow position, and they interpret the language of the fifth amendment of the United States Constitution literally. Not only does this fly in the face of the tradition described above, it flies in the face of what is now thoroughly understood to constitute the general well-being of society in the twentieth century. The following quote from a California court opinion which upheld an urban renewal project on predominantly vacant land sums it up:[17]

It might be pointed out that as our community life becomes more complex, our cities grow and become overcrowded, and the need to use for the benefit of the public areas which are not adapted to the pressing needs of the public becomes more imperative, a broader concept of what is a public use is necessitated. Fifty years ago no court would have interpreted, under the eminent domain statutes, slum clearance even for public housing as a public use, and yet, it is now so recognized. To hold that clearance of blighted areas as characterized by the [California] act and as shown in this case and the redevelopment of such areas as contemplated here are not public uses, is to view present day conditions under the myopic eyes of years now gone.

. . .

[17] Redevelopment Agency of City and County of San Francisco et al. v. Hayes et al., 122 Cal. A.2d 777, 802–3, 266 P.2d 105, 122 (1954).

THE FUTURE OF HOUSING*

Charles Abrams

Housing is only a single phase of city planning and city planning a single phase of the general planning process. Before we can deal with specific proposals for a housing program, the meaning of planning, and of city planning in particular, must be stated.

CITY PLANNING IN A DEMOCRACY

City planning in a totalitarian state meets little or no opposition from public opinion or private ownership, no curb by courts; there, eminent domain can be confiscatory, police power incontestable.

City planning in a democracy has a wider horizon. It involves more than the plotting of houses, parks, and utilities on an architect's blueprint or the planning of public works. Here, it demands a knowledge of the national aims, political habitudes, and public folkways. It operates within a complex of vested rights and deep-rooted fears against infringement of liberties. It entails the improvement of the living patterns of the greater number without confiscating the established rights of the smaller.

Before city planning can function in a democracy, it must hurdle at least four obstacles: (a) win the approval of the public to its proposal; (b) be sufficiently influential to obtain the authorizing legislation; (c) gain co-operation as to policy, plan, and detail of the necessary officials, or official agencies; and (d) survive the scrutiny of the courts as to the reasonableness of the plan in its effect on property rights.

These tests will demand more than the simple technical skill of the average city planner. It is one thing to plan a neighborhood in which the property rights affected are minor or where the plan is only experimental or when the benefits accruing to the property exceed the value of the rights taken away. It is another thing to reorder a community where vast incomes have already been capitalized into value. If city planning en-

* New York: Harper & Brothers, 1946, pp. 339–42 (selected portions).

tailed solely the esthetic and technical considerations usually assigned to it by the planning books, the job would be easier. But in a propertied society clashes of interest arise between groups of citizens. The city strives on the one hand to serve the social welfare of its people as people, without too radically undermining the financial welfare of its people as taxpayers. A conflict of interests usually results in a stalemate. It is not surprising that with the many hundreds of official planning agencies, relatively little planning has been accomplished by them.

The planner's job in the American democracy has been made more difficult by the prejudice against economic planning in a country that has thrived under the fullest form of economic liberalism. With economic planning now an ugly word in Congressional circles, an agency like the National Resources Planning Board will be ruthlessly struck down largely because it ventures into economic planning. Lesser local planning agencies have changed their names to civic development associations, while still other planning bodies have stopped functioning altogether owing to the unpopularity of "planning."

One reason for this is that the planners have failed to fit the architectural aspects of planning into the architecture of the political system. The public often confuses economic planning with a planned economy. Because Communist Russia planned, many think all economic planning communistic. Yet business plans, and without planning business would fail. Adam Smith's "Wealth of Nations," the most influential argument for economic liberalism, was a plan. The Constitution was a plan. While economic planning may imply the substitution for the profit system of a scheme of socialized production and distribution, it may also denote the regulation of that segment of private enterprise operating to the detriment of the public welfare and the traditional entry of government into non-competitive and limited spheres of essential enterprise. Such planning should offer no threat to democracy, yet the scope and the limitations of government intervention must be plotted, else it will be ineffectual, fall short of its purpose, or go beyond the bounds intended.

While planning operates to a greater or lesser degree in almost every phase of activity, public planning is its application to the sphere of public purposes and policy. Democratic planning operates within accepted institutional patterns, and attempts to provide for the resolution of the diverse group interests in the society. The business of the city planner is to employ the means that are efficient, lawful and politically palatable, to achieve the ends generally accepted as socially desirable. Part of his job is public education, and in this connection he must accept not only the technical but the social and political responsibilities the job entails.

In the exploration of the means, the planner is confronted with the peculiarities of the private enterprise society in which we live. Our government acts in relation to economic activities by encouraging those activities, restricting them or taking them over. The most palatable politically of the processes is encouragement of private enterprise, accomplished either by non-interference with enterprise, subsidy, tariff or other aid. The least popular is restriction, while direct operation may cause mixed feelings depending upon the interests affected and the benefits attained. The mechanisms used to carry out these processes are the tax power and its concomitant the spending power; the police power; and eminent domain. Within this complicated framework lies the planner's role in housing—to bring about better housing conditions and environments, while building upon the public attitudes which, as was said at the outset, fortify the private enterprise formula. It is with this aim in mind that the program set forth in the succeeding chapters was framed.

PLANNING AND GOVERNMENT POWER

Sometimes more effective planning requires more governmental "interference." But this does not mean that government interference always brings rational city planning. We have already had a great deal of government interference in the real estate and building enterprise and have achieved no satisfactory planning. We have had more government exercise of the restrictive powers in these spheres than in any other phase of the economy. Yet no solution has been achieved.

It is not that we have had insufficient government intervention, but that we have not had the right kind of intervention. This is so partly because we have done little planning in advance, and partly from our failure to understand the meaning and importance of planning. Opposition to planning today more often reflects the fear of change than the logic of change, just as it did in the early opposition to public education.

City planning in action may entail an interference with private rights. So do other exercises of the police power—dwelling legislation, zoning, building codes, penal laws, usury legislation. But all property is held subject to the public right to interfere with its use when it threatens the people's welfare. No precise lines can be drawn, usually, to show where reasonable regulation ends and confiscation begins. The issue is continually fluid, and like the exercise of the tax power reduces itself to one of degree. Where the limits of the police power should end and the eminent domain power begin are matters over which the courts stand guard. If the regulation goes too far, they will allow public interference only through processes entailing the award of compensation. In that respect, the checks on the city planning process are greater than upon taxation, the rights of private property more secured. While the power to tax may be said to contain the power to destroy, the planning power does not. It is more restricted, more guarded by the courts. One of its main functions, in fact, is to improve the long term security of real estate by assuring the long term soundness of homes and communities.

II. EXPECTATIONS AND GOALS

GOALS FOR RENEWAL

Legislation in a democratic society is subject to the pressures of contending parties, and any bill that becomes an Act of Congress is a product of the arts of compromise. The compromise is often effected by stating the goals of the law in broad, general terms that will allow each party to feel his interests have not been overlooked or damaged. Consequently, the actual objectives of a law are inherent in the decisions made by those who administer it, and to discover the ends one must look at the law in action. Urban renewal legislation is a classic example of the need to look at what is actually being done rather than formal statements of purpose.

Scott Greer, Professor of Government and Sociology at Northwestern University, has done just this, and reports the goals and expectations of the local officials who make the important decisions about urban redevelopment. Since the law may be used for a variety of ends—the federal government merely approves or disapproves a proposed plan—the local decisions are the strategic ones. Ultimately, Greer concludes, the goals and expectations of renewal are the ends local communities themselves choose to pursue.

The wide range of available ends is less a result of the wisdom of Congress than of assumptions Americans make about the proper way of doing things. In the selection by the editors we point out that renewal legislation makes few demands, if any, for over-all city planning, and thus leaves the way open for a series of small projects unrelated to the development of the community as a whole. Beyond this, renewal legislation assumes that private enterprise must be the central force in development. Thus, if "good is what cities want to make themselves," their self-images will, to a large extent, be finally shaped by the leverage the law puts into the hands of private enterprise.

When President Kennedy appointed Robert Weaver as head of the Housing & Home Finance Agency (HHFA), for the first time in a long while, the White House had an acknowledged expert as its principal adviser on housing. In addition to expertise Weaver had a favorable attitude toward public housing and a sensitivity to the problems of urban communities. Weaver, now Secretary of the Department of Housing and Urban Development, shows his grasp of the realities of urban development by pinpointing its segmental approach and the many gaps between its theory and practice. But he is confident that all the necessary tools for meaningful renewal are present, and that the total effort can be administratively redesigned toward this end. This is certainly the faith and optimism that one may expect of a member of the Johnson administration. But is faith and the will to overcome obstacles sufficient to conquer the "localism" described by Greer and the persistent apathy to city planning?

URBAN RENEWAL AND AMERICAN CITIES*

Scott Greer

OFFICIALS TALK OF GOALS

Urban renewal is a tool that can be used for a wide variety of tasks. It can be used to renew banks, to build tall buildings in the CBD where only pawnshops and tattoo parlors stood before. It can be used to keep Negroes out of threatened neighborhoods. It can also be used to rehabilitate mixed neighborhoods, leaving them clean, standard, and still ethnically "integrated." It can be used for various purposes, public and private.

Some programs are being used for public improvements in the slums:

"All the same, I'd like to show the critics some of these small southern cities. These places are really using urban renewal money to pave and sewer the Negro quarters, to start improving their physical plant *for the first time in history*."

And some LPA officials are primarily oriented to providing alternatives to slums for the citizens of their towns. When one was asked what he thought the program should do, his answer was short: "Produce more low-cost housing." Such answers were rare, however. As a Negro official in a city with thousands of Negroes on the waiting list for public housing said: "No, sir. It's aimed at central city build-up. You can't sell it here as housing."

And this was the common focus of attention: the "central city build-up."

Q: "Do you really need urban renewal? Why?
A: "Yes sir. For instance, this street here should be the central business district. It once was. But now look at it. One man can't redevelop one building and make sense—it has to be a community project. So instead, they move away, leasing us this property. The guy across the street demolished one old building; he makes more on the space as a parking lot. Urban renewal in this area would be justified by your tax increase alone."

* Indianapolis: The Bobbs-Merrill Company, Inc., 1965, pp. 113–23.

And:

"Our CBD project is cheek by jowl with the central financial
and administrative area. It will be redeveloped with a complex of high- and low-rise residential structures. It will also
provide five commercial blocks as a reserve for the central
financial district—2,000,000 square feet of office space!"

And:

"I think there are great possibilities for residential renewal
for the inner city. You see it going on in Philadelphia and you
see it in Los Angeles. I suppose it's a question of how you
buffer areas, change codes for conversion—how you deal with
accusations that are thrown about for corraling certain minority groups."

The open-ended definition of the program leads to some
truly global aims. Starting with the slum clearance program
of 1937, modest and limited, the urban renewal program
today represents a general attack on everything to some of its
protagonists:

"It should do whatever is necessary in the local community
to overcome problems that, without it, wouldn't be overcome.
    Q: "How do you decide what is necessary?
    A: "Different communities have different problems. There
could be a city that needs most of all a monument. In another
city the most important thing may be to clean out something
so terrible that cleaning it out—even to open land if there's no
other need—is still worth doing. I don't object to getting away
from a housing program. The more flexible we are the more
effective we'll be in tackling the individual problems of the
community. Every problem we uncover has ganglions into
many corners of the community. This is why so many things
have been tacked on."

For those who are still concerned with residential blight, or
slums, the program opens up indefinitely:

"The project allowed us to take an inventory of housing. In
the process we took an inventory of all the social problems of
slums. People often blamed us for the social problems! We
had to say, 'Look, we didn't do it.' In one household we found
two generations of unwed mothers, with twenty-one children
altogether.

Q: "What did you do?

A: "We put them in a house and watched them for a year —but we were too easy on them. We ended up having a hell of a time getting rid of them—and they'd do nothing to improve their position. Now we're talking about the experimental segregation of all the problem families [i.e., from public housing] in housing especially administered."

Such concern is logical, if slums result from poverty and if poverty results from "social problems." Two "housers" were asked why they were concerned with housing:

"Next time I hear the phrase, 'our American way of life,' I'll scream. What is it? And 'private enterprise'? They're all for government subsidy to the fast buck. You're inviting Communism when a fourteen-year-old girl, like one in my neighborhood last week, is taken to a hospital for severe malnutrition.

"I have an old-fashioned ideal. Democracy should work for everybody. I'm not going to change it either; I'm going to try to make it work. I want us to say there *is* an American way of life. I see people living in a condition that doesn't support the dignity of a human life and I don't believe in it and I'm trying to do something about it."

And:

"Well, we argue this and that. Because people are interested in the payoff for them, I tell them, I tell an assessor—he isn't interested in anything except there'll be a lot of assessment business.

"But when you get down to it, we want to get people into better shape, so they can live better lives."

The more broadly the program is conceived, the more vague and general become the terms in which it is described. In one city, with projects ranging from slum clearance to downtown renovation, university campus expansion to public housing, an official put it this way:

"Fundamentally, I think renewal ought to be used as the device by which you seek to mobilize every available resource in the community from a political and economic and social standpoint to do whatever may be required to provide a better urban climate.

"The local public authority is, hopefully, a catalyst to bring this about. You can't take on one job at a time—it's a hopeless strategy. Your dynamics will overtake you. You've also got to take the curse off—that urban renewal is done only when something is bad. You've got to try to get something for everyone.

"If only there could be acceptance that the urban renewal approach is in effect never-ending, not just a concentrated initial task but a means of constantly updating, looking at promise and practice in the program, continually adjusting."

Another official agreed with the last point, but differed sharply in the range of ambitions an urban renewal program should espouse:

"You don't aim at rehabilitation—it's a fixation. Instead, we want constant maintenance. We're experimenting with the proportion of public investment that will spark a given amount of private investment in a given place, used to maintain the plant at a given level. Urban renewal should be a way of programing public capital investment for areas that need renewal, conservation, rehabilitation, and the like.

"You can't get at everything. You must focus. Otherwise your studies end up as a pile of crap, or a massive pile of data on the community in general which the community doesn't understand.

"These programs, as they age, add factors that seem relevant, factor after factor, until you end up with efforts to handle the whole damned universe and you just can't do it!"

The urban renewal program may also be seen as a series of experiments in community development and redevelopment.

"I think you've got to start with the assumption that you've got dozens of different situations. Each LPA is struggling to handle its problems in its situation, and they differ. St. Louis, Little Rock, Milwaukee, all are different. I think each may work out a good method, but different. Maybe in another decade or so we'll have a really dependable and effective tool to build our cities with. Maybe by the year 2,000 we'll have licked the slums."

Another, more cynical observer, put the same proposition in a different way:

"Look, your community is whatever your political structure will let you get done. The community makes up its mind. It's like your wife when she buys a new dress. How does she do it? I don't know, but the main thing is she did it. Maybe it's a lousy decision, but—so she made a mistake! Whatever mechanism you've got to make a decision the community makes up its mind and you have to work with it.

Q: "What do you mean by a 'lousy decision'?

A: "Good is what cities want to make themselves into; some cities are shallow in their notion of what's good—some just want to grow. This is the way most people think. They're not very smart about it. They just want to make a buck.

Q: "What is the long-run possibility that urban renewal *can* work for the city as a whole?

A: "We have actually got to start planning for new metropolitan areas. You just can't make L.A. or Chicago an effective city. It isn't possible. We're lucky that, in our infinite unreason, we didn't make another Tokyo.

"Why, you drive on that [express highway] at rush hour and it's almost more than your nerves can stand. You can't just go on, adding more and more to it. We've got to think about planning some new metropolitan areas."

SUMMARY: URBAN RENEWAL AS SOCIAL ORGANIZATION

The urban renewal program has accumulated, over the twenty-five years since the Housing Act of 1937, three different sets of aims. First, and hallowed by age if not by effectiveness, is the goal of a "decent home and a suitable environment" for every American family; that is, replacement of slums by standard housing. Second is the goal of redeveloping the central city and, particularly, the central business district. Finally, as a result of deep uncertainty concerning the effects of spot redevelopment and rehabilitation, the program has developed the general goal of the planned city based upon a community renewal program.

Such goals are not necessarily contradictory. In fact, the last is supposed to integrate the other two. However, they are not identical. As we have noted earlier, *blight* may be so defined as to leave *slums* extant, and vice versa. And either commercial blight removal in the CBD or slum elimination in the gray areas may progress without any general community renewal plan. Thus the LPA has a wide range of alternatives in its choice of project sites and goals. In trying to understand how it is that particular buildings are destroyed in some areas of a city, it is useful to look at the LPA as a social organization, deeply committed to the local community on one hand, to URA on the other.

Because of the widespread American belief that local autonomy is sacred, that local agents know better "what is two in this town," and that local commitment is therefore necessary, the projects are locally initiated. This is of basic importance to the entire program, for it is the localities that propose; the URA can only dispose. Its disposal is frequently late in the game, after a complex chain of events has developed a tentative consensus in the local polity. Thus the decision may be between *this* project and *no* project. The federal agency, however, has no very dependable guide for evaluating proposed projects anyway; it may suspect that a given project will not "work" in terms of short-run financial considerations, but there is no theory of slum causation and CBD withering away that would allow evaluation beyond such suspicions. Thus the agency falls back upon its Workable Program requirements and accepts a wide variety of local efforts. But it should be reemphasized that the program, as written in the law, simply *does not offer clear priorities*.

When two or more widely differing aims are allocated to the same social organization, particularly if the basic logic of these aims is not congruent, that organization appears opportunistic and lacking in integrity. The LPA suffers from this condition. This is accentuated by the weakness of our theory about urban social change, and the confusion of two kinds of propositions: (1) those that have to do with the "goodness" or "badness" of given conditions, and, (2) those that have to do with fact and cause. Many of the basic decisions made in the LPAs are based upon the first kind of judgment: Where is the "blighted" area to be redeveloped, which "slum" is to be cleared?

These are pejorative judgments, of land use and of housing conditions. We have noted their essentially administrative nature—they are facts by fiat. Codified in standards, they reflect the norms and values of the standard-makers and not necessarily any broad consensus in the community, certainly not the opinions of those who work or live there. Housing codes have no necessary relationship to the norms held by those who live in neighborhoods judged substandard; their neighborhood norms are internally produced and validated among their equals. The Negroes of Hyde Park-Kenwood felt, with justification, that the neighborhoods were excellent, relative to their alternative choices. But, since the LPA has no theory that would direct action to Hyde Park-Kenwood on the basis of maximal social benefits as compared to alternative action, its decisions are produced by the grounds of consensus in the larger, political, community.

The *effective* grounds of consensus in any community are the decisions of those groups whose support is necessary for the LPA to stay in business. Therefore the "local community" is heavily biased toward those who control political power and community approval, on the one hand, and those who control credit and building development on the other. The LPA needs a market for its cleared land; it needs capital for the local contribution; it needs political support for the authoritative actions the local governors must take. (In one city, sixty-two separate council actions were necessary for one small project.) To aggregate consent among these scattered groups requires a program tailored to their needs and norms.

As a result, the residents of the declining neighborhoods have very little weight in the decisions. Banfield and Wilson note that, "Only rarely, if ever, has the opposition of slum dwellers prevented a redevelopment project anywhere once it has been seriously proposed."[1] These are usually neighborhoods of the bottom dogs; they lack expertise, organizational skills, and association with the powerful. The local interests represented are usually quite alien to those people most immediately affected.

Pointing out the lack of information, as well as lack of organizational competence among the Boston West Enders, Gans finally concludes:

> The truth was, that for a group unaccustomed to organizational activity, saving the West End was an overwhelming, and perhaps impossible, task. Indeed, there was relatively little the Committee could do. The decision had been made early in the decade, and it had received the blessings of the city's decisive business leaders and politicians. The West End's local politicians all opposed the redevelopment, but were powerless against the unanimity of those who favored it.[2]

Burd details the long and unsuccessful struggle of Mrs. Scala, a leader of the Harrison-Halstead area, to prevent its demolition; again, she was utterly ineffectual against the coalition of Chicago leaders who found the area the solution to their problems. Referring to the final shape of the Hyde Park-

---

[1] In *City Politics in America*, Chap. XX (in manuscript).
[2] Gans, *The Urban Villagers*, p. 298.

Kenwood redevelopment plan, Rossi and Dentler observe the coerciveness of the chain of events:

> . . . the administrative machinery surrounding urban renewal did not provide means for the participation of metropolitan groups until the very last stages. . . . Furthermore, the City Council was not empowered to do more than give blanket endorsement or rejection of the Plan. [235] [And], The effect of such last minute opposition is to draw together the former antagonists into a solid front and to arouse suspicions about the motives of the late-comer. [238][3]

In Newark, as in Chicago, Kaplan observed the development (through private negotiations) of a "non-amendable package" that was presented as a *fait accompli* to the residents in areas to be cleared, as well as the remainder of the citizenry.

Then the three relevant components of the "local community" are the LPA, the local governing body, and the business interests concerned with redevelopment. There is intense interaction among the three classes, over a long period of time, when the settlement is under negotiation. The LPA is usually weakest, since it is overwhelmingly committed to action, while such action may be only marginally attractive to political, financial, or civic leaders. As a consequence, the LPA director becomes, willy-nilly, a public entrepreneur, an operator who makes the public business of urban renewal his private business. Aided by local civic leaders and, in the more successful programs, by a powerful elected political leader, he defines his program, but only in terms acceptable to his supporters.[4] These are a relatively small proportion of the organized and powerful groups in the city. In fact, the city can be divided into (1) those who want renewal, (2) those who do not care about renewal but do care about protecting other interests that may be affected, (3) those who do not know *or* care at all (most citizens), and (4) those who will care most but have the least say.

The consequence is a program that rewards the strong and punishes the weak. Accepting support where it is available, the LPA also tailors its program to the desires of those with an interest in "reviving downtown," the central business dis-

[3] *The Politics of Urban Renewal,* pp. indicated in actual quotations. For the Harrison-Halstead opposition, see Burd, "Press Coverage."

[4] Cf., for many case studies, George Duggar and others, *Local Organization for Urban Renewal in the United States* (Berkeley: University of California Bureau of Public Administration, preliminary reading copy, n.d.).

trict. These turn out to be mayors concerned with increasing the central city tax base, civic leaders with a patriotic desire to "make our city center beautiful," businessmen with deep commitments to downtown real estate, and those who believe government should innovate in the public interest. For:

> The urban renewal slogan has proved to be a clarion call to everyone within hearing distance, and an omnibus for all wayfarers, night crawlers, social workers, and city planners. Its sex appeal is simple: It has allowed a new start.[5]

The "new start" represents a summing up of the interests of this heterogeneous group, weighted by their independent power and their commitment to showing accomplishment in a tangible form. Thus there is very little that is new about the start. The radical proposal that housing be brought up to a certain standard by the use of the police power is ignored; the older order, wherein the CBD should be the center and symbolic hub of the metropolitan community, is shored up with public funds and the right of eminent domain.

Nor is this surprising. The local programs reflect the city as it is, a loose congeries of organized and segmented groups. Each LPA is concerned with its own interests—to attain funds, change land use, and thereby show cause for existence. In the process, it reinforces the existing system. Discussing the net loss of low-cost housing in Hyde Park-Kenwood, Rossi and Dentler concluded:

> . . . as proponents worked to build widespread support for the plan, the most controversial features of the program had to be eliminated. The program had to become big enough, but *bland* enough, to attract powerful supporters.[6]

Or, as the informant quoted earlier would have it, "Your community is whatever your political structure will let you get done."

[5] Dean Swartzel, as quoted by George S. Duggar, "The Politics of Urban Renewal: Suggestions for a Conceptual Scheme" (St. Louis: American Political Science Association, paper, September 1961).

[6] Rossi and Dentler, *Politics of Urban Renewal*, p. 64.

THE URBAN COMPLEX*

Robert Weaver

AN EARLY APPRAISAL

It is perhaps indicative of a significant trend in American governmental policy that by the mid-1950s discussions of housing and slum clearance in central cities dealt for the most part with privately-financed construction. This was in striking contrast to earlier concern with public housing and its problems. There was, however, no less need for low-cost housing than there had been in the past, and much of what is termed privately-financed construction enjoys some form of public assistance. One of the great apprehensions I had at that time was the tendency of advocates of various programs to imply or state that one special tool or one identified approach offered the answer to the housing problem of America.

The housing requirements of the Nation are so complex and so vast in magnitude that they cannot be conceived of in terms of public housing versus private housing or urban renewal versus construction in the suburbs. Of necessity, any successful approach must be a synthesis of these various devices. This synthesis had become difficult to effect in the post-World War II period since each element had already become identified with its own proponents and the principal champions of each were often the most deadly foes of some of the others.

No doubt, the then prevalent segmented-approach orientation reflected failure to outline clearly and categorically the goals of a housing program for America. It seems obvious, however, that certain elements must be involved. First and foremost, housing is for people, and it is adequate housing only when and if it meets the needs and suits the paying ability of the population. Secondly, a sound housing program must be developed within a concept of effective city planning. Of course, in 1954 most professionals in the field gave lip service to the importance of planning. However, there was far from complete agreement as to what good city planning involved, although progress had been made in realizing that it must be

* Garden City: Doubleday & Company, 1964, pp. 46–49, 51–53, 54–56, 81–87 (selected portions).

concerned with land use and the provision of those services and institutions which are needed in a modern community.

Discussions of slums and blight at that time reminded me of the general condemnation of sin. Few, if any, were in favor of these social ills, but there was, and is, a vast difference between being against sin and knowing what to do to eradicate it. Similarly, opposition to slums was, and is, far from commitment for their eradication or realization of the painful and slow process that is involved in effecting this objective.

There was one significant contribution which had been made by emphasis upon urban renewal. We had for the first time thought and spoken in terms of preventing blight as well as wiping out and controlling substandard housing. This had its advantages and its disadvantages. Among the former was the obvious one that more than a piecemeal job was implied, while the stage was set for demonstrating the need for a combination of the various tools and approaches to achieve the announced goal. By the same token, a tremendous potential of public support was created since the more comprehensive approach inspired and aroused local pride in its achievement. Finally, there were possibilities in this program for securing the maximum cooperation between local, state, and federal governments in carrying out urban renewal. Theoretically, at least, there should also have been a favorable climate for cooperation between public and private housing.

Among the disadvantages, the major one was already apparent by 1954. Because of the very magnitude of this undertaking, it could, and often did, bog down in execution. We were, therefore, faced with the possibility that urban renewal might be talked about rather than executed; that it could become the subject of a tremendous promotional program which would excite the imagination of the people without simultaneously providing effective vehicles for its execution. Actually, our horizons had been lifted and our concepts had been broadened. At the same time initial results had not been commensurate with the thinking, the planning, and the hopes which had brought urban renewal into the foreground as a program for housing in American cities.

In my analysis of residential segregation, published in the late 1940s,[1] I devoted a chapter to "Urban Redevelopment— A Threat or an Opportunity." The situation in the mid-1950s

[1] Robert C. Weaver, *The Negro Ghetto* (New York: Harcourt, Brace and Co., 1948), 404 pp.

could have been summarized by substituting "Urban Renewal" for the term "Urban Redevelopment." Then, even more than in 1948, the threat in urban renewal loomed large and had been documented by experience. On the other hand, the opportunities under this program remained as a possibility and a challenge to those concerned with good housing and sound human relations.

Such progress as had been made in urban renewal raised serious questions and created serious problems for the disadvantaged. As one would expect, the displacement of the low-income recipients, the aged, and the non-whites under the program of slum clearance and rehabilitation had been disproportionately high. While this was almost an inevitable consequence, it had been accentuated because of the basic law and the administrative policies adopted by the Federal Government and by local authorities. We were developing a program which reduced the supply of low-cost housing at a time when there was an existing shortage of shelter of this type.

The idea of slum clearance germinated during the depression when there were many vacancies, so that substandard properties could be torn down and families relocated with a minimum of difficulty. That concept was carried over and still persisted in the mid-1950s, despite the fact that the Defense Production Program, World War II, and their aftermath occasioned large-scale migrations to urban centers and created an entirely different housing supply situation, a situation typified by a tight housing market. . . .

Slums and blight are not the lone reflections of physical decay. Occupancy patterns and standards are equally important. As a matter of fact, they often precede and forecast the physical deterioration. The type of overcrowding and improvised living which follows in the wake of the geographic expansion of the racial ghetto into surrounding areas of housing ill-designed to meet the pocketbooks of low-income families has been and remains a principal factor in the spread of blight and generation of slums.

This, too, was in part a reflection of administrative inadequacies in the early execution of urban renewal. A program which in theory would expose the need for, and require the creation of, additional housing units for displaced families had, in practice, proceeded without occasioning the prescribed increase in dwelling accommodations.

There is also another basic consideration which must be kept in mind. It is the fact that in most instances urban renewal has involved a major change in cost of housing. Slum clearance and rebuilding by private enterprise on the land made available through urban renewal usually produced much higher-priced housing. Thus, urban renewal generated two major problems: it created the need for relocation housing for those families which were initially displaced, and it involved permanent displacement of a large class of families formerly living in the areas affected by the new program.

From the beginning of the urban renewal program relocation has been a major issue. Problems of large dimensions developed in cities like Chicago, Detroit, and New York, where low-income families were either forced out by economic and political pressures, required to purchase secondhand properties at inflated prices, or were further overcrowded in contiguous areas already substandard or in the process of becoming substandard due, primarily, to overoccupancy. With the exception of those families which qualified for the available public housing (in which they had priority), the relocation experience could be, and was often, unfortunate and fraught with extreme hardship for many of those involved.

Occasionally areas subjected to renewal were occupied either by families which had created socially viable, if physically blighted, neighborhoods, or by a large number of homeowners, or both. Clearly, relocation of those who had been long identified with an area, who were attached to their neighborhood, and who had long utilized its institutions, created real psychological problems. For homeowners, both psychological and economic problems were involved. The former are obvious—the threat to security incident to displacement from a home that was owned by a family. The second was more complex—loss of real or imputed value incident to leaving an area which had sentimental and imputed great economic worth. This, too, was complicated by the difficulty of acquiring, in a tight housing market, a comparable dwelling with the equity derived from the old house.

Of course, as real as these costs were to some families, there was, and continues to be, a false assumption that every renewal area was a tightly integrated and socially stable neighborhood and that all relocation extracted, and extracts, major psychological and economic costs from those affected. While any forced displacement occasions inconvenience and a feeling of outrage incident to being forced to move on the part of many involved, especially the older residents, the areas selected for renewal in the larger cities were occupied predominantly by renters, most of whom move frequently. These were basically the same people who had been dislocated by public housing. There was little written about the latter's displacement, perhaps because the new housing was for low-income occupancy and because the loose housing market facilitated relocation.

At the same time, priority for displaced families in public housing projects, when combined with concentration of urban renewal areas on sites inhabited largely by non-whites, increased the proportion of colored tenants in subsidized projects. As a consequence, many racially integrated public housing projects in the North became predominantly or exclusively Negro developments largely as a result of the pressures created by the displacement incident to urban renewal. . . .

There was still another development which had social implications. It was the result of selecting for urban renewal those sites in which whites and non-whites formerly lived side by side under substandard conditions. In some instances, especially in Southern and border cities and some small cities outside the South, it was planned to redevelop these areas for the exclusive occupancy of white families. Even when this was not clearly indicated in the local plans, it would sometimes become a *de facto* situation due to elimination of minority groups on economic rather than racial grounds. Where, in a few Southern cities, there had been a protest against this, a compromise was sometimes reached involving a proposed re-use for other than residential purposes. Thus, a slum area formerly housing both Negro and white families was proposed as the location for industry or a public institution. Urban renewal too often seemed to be an instrument for wiping out racially integrated living in one area at the same time that it failed to provide for an equal degree of racial integration on the site or in another section of the city.

In a situation where relocation was often poorly done and human suffering frequently occasioned, the other defects of renewal became magnified out of proportion to their true incidence. This, too, was a function of the fact that renewal, at best, is a slow process. As a new program, it was subject to mistakes and faulty execution. Thus one of the principal criticisms of it in the mid-1950s was the amount of vacant land that lay unused.

As pessimistic as this picture may have been, there were several rays of hope as early as the mid-1950s. One arose from the fact that a real job of urban renewal cannot be effected unless the defects which have been outlined above are corrected. It is significant that in Washington, D.C., where a total program had been envisioned and outlined, redevelopers were committed to open occupancy in the new housing which was to be built in renewal areas. This meant that white and non-white families would be living together in a limited amount of public housing adjacent to the redevelopment and in privately-financed, upper middle-income housing in the redevelopment. Actually, with the exception of the public housing developments in the area, the degree of non-white participation was expected to be relatively small, due to income distribution among non-whites. It was contemplated to be significant, however, insofar as it represented the stamp of governmental approval on open-occupancy housing at the higher income ranges where prestige values are important. By the same token, there was every reason to believe that elsewhere in the city the concentration of lower-income non-whites in racial ghettos would probably increase under the new program. This, of course, was facilitated and accelerated by the movement of white families from the city to the suburban areas outside the limits of the Nation's capital at the same time that the non-white population was increasing.

By 1954 there were unmistakable evidences that urban renewal, while failing to solve the housing problems of minorities, was forcing public officials and private redevelopers to face up to the issue. A few involved in urban renewal were realizing the impediment to their objectives inherent in residential segregation and its restrictions upon maximum utilization of the housing supply. Others were talking and thinking in terms of more and better Negro housing. All, or almost all, had come to realize that something had to be done in the realm of housing for minorities and for low- and moderate-income households as a whole.

The earlier mistakes in relocation had also aroused public anger and political pressure. Consequently, there was evidence that many local agencies, particularly those in large cities, were attempting to do a better job. All involved in the program came to realize that valuable time was lost and many problems were created when sites remained vacant. Related to this, of course, were the difficulties in securing competent redevelopers. However, out of the mistakes and experience came greater understanding of this new effort.

Even more important from the point of view of public acceptance of urban renewal was the fact that a few developments were moving into the execution stage. They were tangible evidences of the potential of the program, indicating its capacity for revitalizing core areas, restoring economic health in the heart of the city, and affording an effective vehicle for advanced city and site planning. As an instrument for clearing slums, arresting physical decay, and providing attractive housing in the central city, urban renewal had evidenced real promise. . . .

THE PROGRESS OF URBAN RENEWAL

Discussions of urban problems evoke many points of view. There are those who question whether cities should or can be revitalized. At the other extreme are the uncritical proponents of urban renewal who attach magic significance to a phrase. They seem to believe that we have in that concept the final and inflexible answer to all the problems of the city. There is no one established and proven road to revitalizing our cities. Although we do not know all we should about how to accomplish this objective, we are learning how to do so through study, analysis, evaluation, and by doing.

One thing that needs to be done is to demonstrate how false are those who, under the guise of "individual initiative," "free enterprise," and "government economy," would let us drift into apathy. For freedom has never been reached through indifference. It can only be achieved with responsibility. In our desire to see more American cities accept their responsibilities, however, we must avoid dishonesty about the difficulties which have beset us in the past.

It is only a dozen or so years since urban renewal became a program of the Federal Government. In the history of our cities that is no more than a moment. In that period there have been some real accomplishments and some tragic failures. Too often those who are the advocates of bigger and better urban renewal talk only of the achievements; the new housing, the inspiring cultural facilities, the thousands who were moved from slums to better homes, the increased tax revenues. Just as often those who are the apostles of drift and do-nothing point only to the failures; the haphazard planning, the irresponsible or unsuccessful developers, the high rents, the destruction of housing which could have been saved, the indifference toward relocation, and the augmentation of ghetto patterns.

One of the most unfortunate mistakes which has been made in the past was simply a disregard for democracy. Planners and public officials have occasionally acquiesced in urban renewal projects to serve particular interests, without regard for the interests of the community as a whole. This particular mistake has attracted not only wrath but ridicule: witness the simulated greeting cards which have been circulated. On the cover they read: "Urban Renewal Is Good for You," and inside they say, "So Shut Up."

Since 1954 the Federal Government has required localities to have what is called a Workable Program for Community Improvement before they can receive urban renewal assistance.

Such a program has seven elements and they are as follows:

(a) Codes and ordinances establishing adequate standards of health and safety for a community's housing.

(b) A comprehensive plan for the community's future development.

(c) Analyses of the neighborhoods in the community to identify those where something should be done about blight.

(d) Administrative organization capable of coordinating and carrying out a community program.

(e) Financial resources to support the localities' share of an urban renewal program.

(f) Housing resources to meet the needs of those displaced by urban renewal.

(g) Assurance that the community as a whole is fully informed and has the fullest opportunity to take part in developing and executing an urban renewal program.

Critics of urban renewal have accused, with ample basis, the Federal Government of being lax in enforcing these requirements. The Kennedy administration resolved to correct the situation. For President Kennedy declared in his housing message to Congress that "only when the citizens of a community have participated in selecting the goals which will shape their environment can they be expected to support the actions necessary to accomplish those goals." In accordance with this statement of purpose, those who assumed responsibility for the Federal Government's housing programs initiated a review and re-evaluation of the Workable Program so as to determine its adequacy and the efficacy of its administration. Since it is the basic tool available to the Federal Government for establishing minimum standards for urban renewal, it must constantly be challenged and refined.

Relocation had become a dirty word in America. We took action to see that this was changed, resolving that relocation must no longer be the tragedy it has too often been, but the opportunity it should always have been. It can become, and in many instances it has become, a positive rehousing program for those now living in substandard homes.

William Slayton, the current Commissioner of the Urban Renewal Administration, reorganized the machinery for supervising relocation. In this connection he said: "I intend to look carefully at a community's relocation activities—that is, at its actual relocation operation, to make sure that the job is being done well before we permit a community to undertake new renewal activities." To implement this statement, he created within his agency a new position, Assistant Commissioner for Relocation. To fill this crucial post he recruited the man who had directed the successful relocation program in Washington, D.C.

During the early years urban renewal demolished a significant amount of good housing because it was intermingled with bad housing. The housing resources of our country are far too valuable to be indiscriminately destroyed if they can be rehabilitated satisfactorily. In the past, however, rehabilitation often had been financially impossible. The owners of buildings in declining areas lacked the resources to finance rehabilitation themselves, and financial institutions were reluctant to lend money on buildings in such areas.

The Kennedy administration attempted to develop and perfect programs to encourage and facilitate rehabilitation of our existing stock of housing. With these tools, we hoped to be able to salvage a large number of dwellings. This will enable our cities to blend the old with the new, minimize the bulldozer approach, and reduce the volume of economic and ethnic displacement incident to urban renewal. But one thing must be made clear. The fact that many existing structures which lend themselves to rehabilitation can and will be preserved does not mean that local programs should or will preserve all of them. Where there are some sound buildings in a sea of hopeless ones, it is not feasible or desirable to preserve the occasional structures at the cost of destroying a redevelopment plan through inflexible application of a sound principle.

Urban renewal has been denounced because of the high rentals for apartments in its redevelopments. We cannot indefinitely go on redeveloping areas with housing which can be afforded only by families of substantial means. We must redevelop more of our slums and blighted areas in such a way as to provide accommodations for families of modest means as well.

The Housing Act of 1961, in Section 221(d)(3), permits the Federal Housing Administration and the Federal National Mortgage Association, popularly known as Fannie Mae, to join in a program of mortgage insurance and purchase to make more moderate rentals possible. Under this proposal, long-term loans below the market interest rates can be made to non-profit organizations and cooperatives, certain public agencies, or limited-dividend corporations to build housing which would be limited to those of moderate incomes. This makes possible rentals well below those formerly available in renewal areas. In order to facilitate the most reasonable rents or carrying charges, FHA waives its usual ½ per cent insurance premiums and insures loans for as long as forty years. The exact amount of rental or carrying charge reduction possible will, of course, vary with the size of accommodations, cost of construction, and duration of the loan, and would be materially augmented by partial tax exemption. State laws in Delaware, Massachusetts, Missouri, New Jersey, and New York provide for tax exemption or partial tax exemption for non-profit or limited dividend cooperatives. In Hawaii non-profit housing can be tax-exempt, and in Illinois the same is true of non-profit "old peoples' homes."

On the basis of 7586 dwelling units of Section 221(d)(3) housing in thirty-seven localities for which cost figures were available in October, 1963, the average monthly rental per unit was $87.78. This was 57 per cent less than the average figure achieved in the regular FHA multi-family housing program. It reflected, of course, wide geographic variations—from $74.13 in the Southeast to $102.61 in the Northeast. The maximum incomes permitted at time of admission to the new moderate-income housing varied for a three- or four-person family from $4150 to $8400 in the continental United States.

The concept of economic diversity in urban renewal is a long-range, community-wide objective. It does not imply that each and every project must be multi-income, but that the city-wide approach must achieve such diversity. The economic realities and current consumer preferences, related as they are to prestige considerations, limit the tempo and extensiveness of economic mixing, especially in areas which have lost their attractiveness in the process of decline. (The previous section of this chapter dealt with this matter in greater detail.)

We have developed goals, and we shall pursue them without being so unrealistic and doctrinaire as to lose both the immediate objective and unduly complicate and endanger urban renewal. Nor have we ignored the economic realities of land use. There are some sites which, because of their location and value, should be used for housing that will produce high rents and correspondingly high taxes. But a local program composed exclusively of such sites is, in my opinion, unsatisfactory.

Another charge frequently leveled against urban renewal is that it suffers from "projectitis," a vision which does not extend beyond the limits of a single development. The Federal Government already provides assistance for planning comprehensive community renewal programs. These are programs in which urban renewal activities and capital improvements can be coordinated (to be delineated more fully in the next chapter). From the start we encouraged as many cities as possible to take part in this planning, because in order to be successful with urban renewal a city must know where it is going. A Community Renewal Program enables it to determine this, and associated, objectives.

The role of the Federal Government in all aspects of urban renewal, however, is a secondary one. It is the cities themselves which must take the initiative and must do the work. The Federal Government can only advise, assist, and offer financial aid. Each city has as its urban renewal program only what it deserves. Some take the easy path, and do nothing. As a result they have nothing, and for them the Federal Government does nothing. Others take the high road, but make the program, by their own ineptness, far more difficult than it need be. We hope, with advice and assistance, to make their way easier in the future. Happily there are cities which have always had wide vision, great vigor, and the wholehearted support of their citizens. They are the only ones that really know to what heights the road marked "urban renewal" can lead. There are, however, phases of urban renewal, like the Workable Program and relocation, where the Federal Government is directed to establish and secure compliance with minimum standards. We are resolved to accept these responsibilities.

Ours is a concept of a flow of change, the cadence of which

will be determined primarily by the aptness of administration. We have our objectives, but we realize that we must pace our activity in terms of community understanding and community acceptance. Nor do we think of the central city as separate and distinct from the metropolitan complex of which it is the heart. The suburbs and the core areas are interdependent. Our responsibility is to articulate and emphasize this fact at the same time that we encourage, to the maximum degree, programs and approaches which assure metropolis-wide activities.

THE AMBIGUOUS SLUM

All interests affected by public housing and redevelopment legislation agree, no matter what their other differences are, that slums are evil and slum clearance is good. The unanimity is testimony to the lasting influence of the early urban reformers. Recently, however, many social scientists have gone back, as it were, to the slum, and returned with a portrait at odds with the cultural stereotype. The conflicting images call into question the goal of slum clearance. In effect, they seem to imply that the problem is not slum clearance but which "slums" ought to be cleared, and what criteria should be used in making the decision.

The old view of the slum defines it as the source of social problems, but the sociologist, John Seeley, asks, "Are the slums also useful?" He points out that some people "need" the slum—those who for social or psychological reasons cannot adapt to life elsewhere in the city. There are others who find the slum a place of "opportunities" not offered in the rest of the community. Is clearance or redevelopment, then, an unalloyed benefit?

A slum is popularly thought to be "socially disorganized," but Marc Fried and Peggy Gleicher, sociological researchers at the Joint Center for Urban Studies, find few symptoms of disorganization. On the contrary, a slum neighborhood can be the site of strong relationships among individuals and families, and the styles of life it harbors may be highly satisfying to its inhabitants. Other researchers here and in England have reported similar findings. Jane Jacobs is not, of course, a trained social scientist and does not attempt to bring systematic methods to bear on the phenomenon of the slum. Her strength lies in the fact that she lives in an area formerly dubbed a slum and is a keen and lively observer. Miss Jacobs believes that slum clearance may not be necessary. Pointing to her own neighborhood and others like Boston's North End, she says these areas have the ability to reconstruct themselves, to perform a bootstrap operation. Even granting what

some may consider an exaggerated optimism about the resources and capacities of a slum population, she does make
problematic what conventional wisdom takes for granted—
always a welcome contribution.

The usual image of the slum is inaccurate, but is it wholly
false? Claude Brown, a young Negro, tells us what it is like to
grow up in Harlem. His Harlem is a place of violence, thiev-
ery, drugs, alcohol, prostitution, psychosis . . . a nightmare
of all the terrible things that can afflict a community. It is a
significant reminder that there are many different kinds of
slums, and some are horrors that brutalize human existence.

THE SLUM: ITS NATURE, USE, AND USERS*

John R. Seeley

To cling to a dream or a vision may be heroic—or merely
pathetic. Slum-clearance, slum renewal, or, more grandiosely,
the extirpation of the slum, is for many planners just such a
dream: brightly imagined, cherished, fought for, often seem-
ing—but for stupidity here or cupidity or malice there—at very
finger-tip's reach. To ask how realistic this orientation is, what
is possible at what costs and to whose benefit, is almost as
idle-seeming an enterprise to many as it would be to raise
doubts about the sanctity of American motherhood or the
soundness of the American home. If a direct challenge to the
orthodox view seems too bold, let us tease at the fabric of the
dream only a little, to see how it appears—and perhaps still
shimmers—in the cooler light of moderately disinterested
curiosity as against the warm glow of programmatic commitment.

I

The very notion of a "slum" depends on a number of more
primitive notions. We must invoke at least—(and I believe
only)—the notions of

Space
Population
A value-position defining "goods" and "ills"
Dispersion in the distribution of any good (or ill) among
the population so that, in that respect, all men are not equal
Correlation[1] among goods (or ills) so that one good tends
to be attended by another, rather than offset by an ill
Concentration (in space) of those who have the most (and
also those who have the least) of what there is to get

Any alteration in any of the realities that lie behind these
six terms changes what "the slum problem" is; the elimination
of any corresponding reality eliminates slums; and anything

* FROM *Journal of the American Institute of Planners*, XXV, No. 1
(February 1959), pp. 7–14 (selected portions).
[1] "Positive correlation," of course.

short of that guarantees the slum's survival. It cannot be over-emphasized that no change in the plane of living—as for example, the doubling of all real incomes—would remove the problem. It is not a matter of absolutes. In a society where nearly everyone walks, the man with a horse is a rich man, and the man without is a poor man; in a society where nearly everyone has (or could have) a car, the man who can only afford a bicycle is *by that much* disadvantaged, and, potentially, a slum dweller. The criteria for what is a slum—as a social *fact*—are subjective and relative: for one brand of mystic this world is a slum (relative to the next) and for another there *is* no slum, because the proper objects of desire are as available in one area as another.

Since, for the planner, space is an eternal datum and population is also given, at least in the moderately long run, any attempt to "deal with" the slum must turn on affecting in some way one of the other factors. Since, commonly, the value-position from which goods or ills are to be defined is uncritically received from the culture or projected by the individual planner, this too appears as something given—although this unexamined acceptance undoubtedly leads to much of the defeat and frustration which the planner encounters and manufactures. We shall have to return to this question of values later, but for the moment we may ask, what is possible if indeed a single value-scheme—the value-scheme of middle-class materialism—is applicable? The answer, if the analysis is correct so far, is obvious: we can attempt an attack on any one or on all of the remaining factors: dispersion, correlation, and concentration. These are discussed in decreasing order of difficulty.

To attempt to diminish the dispersion in the distribution of any one good—say, money—is actually a matter of high politics rather than "planning" in the customary sense. Two courses are classically open politically: the periodic redistribution of goods gained; and the blocking of opportunities to gain them. An example of the first is the combination of income taxation or succession-duties with "equalizing" distribution of the proceeds—as, for instance, by differential "social security benefits." An example of the second—insofar as it is effective at all—lies in antitrust or antimonopoly proceedings, more particularly in the form which they have taken in recent years, that is, the prevention of particularly blatant potential concentrations before they actually occur. Not only is this whole route attended by vexing ethical and political problems, but also limits are set for it by the culture and, in the ultimate analysis, by economics itself. We may or may not be anywhere near those limits in North America, but it is obvious that dispersion-reduction beyond a certain point may, in fact, reduce the total of what there is to distribute—may, in fact, reduce it to the point where the least advantaged are in absolute, though not relative, terms more disadvantaged than before. We may discover limits and optimum points by trial-and-error or experiment in the course of history, but this clearly falls outside the planning procedure. This leaves us with correlation and concentration to examine.

An attack upon the correlation of goods with goods and ills with ills, in the life of any person or group, is notoriously difficult. Nothing multiplies like misfortune or succeeds like success. As the work of Bradley Buell[2] so unequivocally demonstrated for the whole range of problems with which social work deals, disaster is so wedded to further disaster in the lives of families that the combined case-load of innumerable separate agencies in a city is very largely represented by only a small core of "multi-problem families," families in which economic dependency may be the child of poor nutrition and poor physical health and the father of overcrowding and desperate family relations and poor mental health—and so, in a new and horrible incest, in turn the father of its own father, more economic dependency . . . and so on. And what Buell finds for social work problems is not restricted to that field. Within single problem-fields themselves, diseases tend to follow diseases in the field of medicine, just as one bungled social relation generally follows another, as students of society observe, and one psychological catastrophe is the ancestor of the next in the case history of almost any psychiatric patient. Every social agency, every "caretaker institution,"[3] is concerned to break up or diminish these correlations or to palliate their effects; but the whole apparatus can deal with only the few, worst cases; and nothing short of a society quite different from any yet seriously contemplated is likely to make sensible inroads upon the fact of correlation itself. In any case, this too falls outside the domain of local, or even regional, planning. So we are left with geographic concentration as our last point, seemingly, of promising attack. And it

[2] See Bradley Buell, *Community Planning for Human Services* (New York: Columbia University Press, 1952).

[3] To use the phrase of Erich Lindemann.

is at this point, if I am not mistaken, that the weight of the planners' planning has so far largely fallen.

The problem of "deconcentration" may be seen as the problem of moving from the present state of a heterogeneity of neighborhoods each homogeneous within itself to a homogeneity of neighborhoods each heterogeneous within itself. Upon succeeding, we should no longer be able to write of *The Gold Coast and the Slum*[4] but only, perhaps, of the gold coast within the slum and the slum within the gold coast. It is hard to doubt that—if we are willing to pay the price—here we *can* be successful. And it is equally hard to doubt that some increases in positive goods and some diminutions in positive evils would follow upon such a geographic transfer of the "variance" in fortune from the "between communities" label to the "within communities" one.

No one, perhaps, has put the case for the positive benefits so well as Catherine Bauer who brings knowledge, experience, vision, and passion to her task.[5] She argues, in reality, from the full depth of her feelings but, in form at least, from primitive democratic principles against the one-class, one-occupation, one-economic-level community and for the broad-spectrum neighborhood where a child may at least encounter the aged, the ethnically strange, the poorer, the richer, the better, the worse, the different, and, therefore, the educative and exciting. The essence of her argument, I think, is that since the efficacy of our type of democracy depends on the achievement of consensus even in a highly differentiated society, whatever militates against "understanding" diminishes the national welfare. This is a telling point, especially if lack of direct exposure does militate against "understanding," and if increased exposure promotes it.

Another argument for "deconcentration" can be made, I believe, on negative grounds; and for some it may have considerable force. The argument is that the very concentration of evils or ills is itself an additional ill or evil—quite separate from the mere sum of the evils concentrated. I think this is a valid point. Anyone who has watched a child checking quite equably his separate bruises and scratches before bedtime, only to be suddenly overborne emotionally as their totality

[4] See Harvey Zorbaugh, *The Gold Coast and the Slum* (Chicago: University of Chicago Press, 1937).

[5] See, e.g., Catherine Bauer, "Good Neighborhoods," *The Annals of the American Academy of Political and Social Science,* Vol. 242 (1945), pp. 104–15.

dawns upon him, will know what is meant at an individual level.[6] The pervasive air of squalor of a Tobacco Road or any of its innumerable counterparts is, I think, differentiable from the separately existent miseries that otherwise go to make it up.

However, even at this level of analysis, things are not so simple as they seem. If it is true that the concentration of the defeated and despairing casts a pall, a psychological smog, of defeatism and despair, it is also true that "misery loves company" and that support to bear the hurt comes chiefly from the hurt. Beyond this, awareness of one's disabilities and disasters is heightened if they must be borne in the presence of the able and successful; and this awareness—unless it can lead to a remedy—is itself an additional, and perhaps disabling, disaster. It is also to be noted that to the extent that compresent misery adds to misery at one end of the scale, the "slum," compresent abundance adds to the sense of abundance and security at the other end, the elite community or "gold coast." Thus, at the very least, "deconcentration" is not likely to be an unmixed good to anyone or even a mixed good to everyone.

Things are much less simple again if we are willing to be realistic and to recall for re-examination one of the premises accepted for the sake of argument earlier: that the question may properly be examined at all in the light of the planner's value-system, or the one he assumes to represent the society at large. The first possibility we shall not even examine; few would argue seriously that an urban plan should rest ultimately purely on the private preferences of the urban planner who plans to please himself. The second is worth some study.

It is a persistent illusion characterizing, I believe, only the middle-class meliorist, and only the middle-class meliorist in America—where it is least true!—that there is some particular case-applicable value-system that may be ascribed to the society at large. I do not doubt that *at a very high level of abstraction* consensus around value-statements can be obtained: America believes in justice; it simply divides on segregation. America believes in due process; it divides, however, on the propriety of what happens at many a Congressional investigation. What is at issue regarding the slum is a case and not an abstraction, and around it Americans divide, not simply in

[6] Cf. Bruno Bettelheim, *Love is Not Enough* (Glencoe: Free Press, 1950).

terms of slum-dwellers versus non-slum-dwellers, but within as well as between both groups.

It must be recognized at the outset, I believe, that the slum is almost as much a "social necessity" for some sizable segment of the elite as is, say, an adequate, centralized, and appropriately located medical center. I do not mean this only in the relatively trivial sense, referred to earlier, in which those who enjoy the greater proportion of social goods also desire protection against the debris entailed in their production. I mean it in the quite literal sense that, like the supermarket in its locus, or the central business district in its locus, the slum provides on an appropriate site a set of services called out by, produced for, delivered to, and paid for by the self-same elite whose wives are likely to adorn with their names the letterheads of committees to wipe out or "clean up" the slum. Many of the services provided by the slum are not within the monetary reach of slum people: the bulk of the bootlegging, the call-girl services, a great part of what some feel able to call "vice," the greater part of the gambling, and the whole set of connections that connect the underworld with the over-world serve the latter rather than the former, and are as much a response to effective (that is, money-backed) demand as is the price of a share of A.T.&T. or General Motors.

Given this "effective demand," taking it for granted that such demand will indeed call out "supply" somewhere, the question for the planner—at least in the moderately long run—must not be *whether?* but *where?* To the degree that the services are highly specialized, as many of them are,[7] there seems no economically appropriate locus for them too far from the core of the central city proper. To the degree that the services are not so specialized, they will generally have already found their way—by a combination of economic logic with police pressure—to the ring of satellite municipalities immediately outside the city itself.

If these services, and a whole chain of other "opportunities" that the slum presents, were solely of interest and profit to an

---

[7] Compare, for instance, the (twelve at least) institutionalized sets of provisions for sex satisfaction demanded and supplied in a large mid-Western metropolis simply out of the changes to be rung on gender, race, and activity as against passivity. Omitting further variations and refinements, and using an obvious code, we have: (*MNA–MNP*), (*MNA–MWP*), (*MNP–MWA*), (*MWA–MWP*), (*FNA–FNP*), (*FNA–FWP*), (*FNP–FWA*), (*FWA–FWP*), (*MN–FN*), (*MN–FW*), (*MW–FN*) and (*MW–FW*).

elite group who already had most of what there was to get, a case might be made out for the abolition of the slum (if possible) as being in the public interest. (There is a sense in which this is true just as, no doubt, sinlessness or prohibition are in the public interest.) But this view of a one-sided exploitative interest in the maintenance of the slum by *outside* landlords or "service" users simply will not fit the facts. The facts are that the slum-dwellers also have sizable investments, of interest, of sentiment, and of opportunity, both in the site of these services and its appurtenances and in the way of life that goes on there.

Slums differ, of course, and I have lived intensively only in one, Back-of-the-Yards, Chicago, in the early 'forties, and, together with others,[8] have studied another, "Relocation Area A" in Indianapolis. I do not intend to give in detail any account of the former, especially as the main features of a somewhat similar area were sketched in William Foote Whyte's *Street Corner Society*.[9] Something of the intensity, excitement, rewardingness, and color of the slum that I experienced is missing from his account of his slum, either because his *was* different or because sociological reporting militates against vibrancy of description (or, perhaps, because we cut into the material of our participant-observer experience in different ways). In any case, I would have to say, for what it is worth, that no society I have lived in before or since, seemed to me to present to so many of its members so many possibilities and actualities of fulfillment of a number at least of basic human demands: for an outlet for aggressiveness, for adventure, for a sense of effectiveness, for deep feelings of belonging without undue sacrifice of uniqueness or identity, for sex satisfaction, for strong if not fierce loyalties, for a sense of independence from the pervasive, omnicompetent, omniscient authority-in-general, which at that time still overwhelmed the middle-class child to a greater degree than it now does. These things had their prices, of course—not all values can be simultaneously maximized. But few of the inhabitants whom I reciprocally took "slumming" into middle-class life understood it, or, where they did, were at all envious of it. And, be it asserted, this was not a matter of "ignorance" or incapacity to "appreciate finer things." It was merely an inability to see one moderately coherent and sense-making

[8] Mr. Donald A. Saltzman and Dr. B. H. Junker.
[9] Second edition (Chicago: University of Chicago Press, 1958).

satisfaction-system which they didn't know, as preferable to the quite coherent and sense-making satisfaction-system they did know. This is not analogous to Beethoven versus boogie-woogie, but more nearly to the choice between English and French as a vehicle of expression. (I will not even say which is which.)

Possibly I can give a clearer impression of the variety of dwellers in one slum and the variety of uses they make of it by quoting at length from the published report of the Indianapolis area that we studied. Section II of this paper is accordingly taken from that report.[10]

II. Types of Slum-Dwellers

There are always, of course, innumerable ways of classifying a population so immensely various as that of the slum, or, perhaps, of any urban area. We were struck again and again (both when we examined the way in which these people thought about themselves and when we examined behavior objectively) by two major differences: the difference between necessity and opportunity, and the difference between permanence and change.

Quite obviously, for many the slum constitutes a set of opportunities for behavior which they want (at least at the conscious level) to indulge in or to be permitted. For others, equally obviously, the slum constitutes a set of necessities to which, despite their wants, they have been reduced.

Similarly—though changes are *possible*—some are in the slum and feel they are in the slum on a temporary basis only, and others are there and feel they are there to stay. These distinctions establish four major types:

1. The "permanent necessitarians"
2. The "temporary necessitarians"
3. The "permanent opportunists"
4. The "temporary opportunists"

The meaning of these terms[11] will become clear as we proceed. . . .

[10] *Redevelopment: Some Human Gains and Losses* (Indianapolis: Community Surveys, 1956), pp. 48–59. Field work by Mr. Donald A. Saltzman and others; report by Mr. Saltzman, Dr. B. H. Junker, and the author in collaboration.

[11] The distinction—like other human distinctions—must not be "overworked." The difference between necessity and opportunity is largely subjective—a necessity welcomed with joy is often regarded as an opportunity; an opportunity accepted only with regret may be construed

1. *The Permanent Necessitarians.* Those in the slum per-
manently and by necessity evidently include at least three subtypes: the "indolent," the "adjusted poor," and the "social
outcasts." In Area "A," these three subtypes seem to constitute the greater part of that "hard and unmovable core,"
which in turn constitutes about half of the population still
living in Redevelopment Commission property. These are the
people who feel they "cannot" leave the area, and who will
or can do nothing to find alternative housing.

The "indolent" are those whose most striking characteristic[12] is a general apathy or immobility. Whether from inherited characteristics, disease, maleducation, malnutrition,
the experience of perennial defeat, religiously founded "resignation," or mere valuation of other things—these are the do-
nothings, those who "have no get up and go," those whose
immobility is grounded now in their very physique or character.

Whatever the cause for the "indolence," and no matter
what miracles feeding, better care, or therapy (physical or
psychological) could accomplish for such people in the very
long run, at least in the short run no plan looking to them for
even moderate effort or initiative is a feasible one. "Care"
and "custody" are the only public-policy alternatives to neglect;[13] rehabilitation, if possible at all, would be a long, hard,
slow process of uncertain outcome or economy.

The *"adjusted poor"* represent similarly, though likely less
immovably, a population living in the slum by necessity but
adapted by deep-seated habit (and now almost by preference)
to its ways. This group represents the concentration in the
area of the destitute, or nearly destitute, whose adaptation
consists in "acceptance" of the nearly unfit-for-human-habita-
tion shacks and shanties, holes and cellars of the area—provided only they be available at "that low rent." Among them
are many of those who value independence fiercely enough

---

as a necessity. Even "permanent" and "temporary" refer largely subjectively to expectations and intentions, though they also partly (on that
account) refer objectively to probabilities of later behavior.

[12] It should not be overlooked that we have classified only by the
most obvious characteristic. Many people have several characteristics,
e.g., one could find examples of the "indolent-adjusted poor" or the
"adjusted poor and trapped."

[13] "Neglect," as used here, means "leaving them alone" or "not inter-
fering" with the "natural" process by which these people are able to
get along and to subsist.

that they would rather cling to this most marginal physical existence in independence than accept relative comfort in dependency—even supposing they could have the latter. (At least this is their first and habitual reaction. Some few who were persuaded later to move into Lockefield Gardens are now glad they made the exchange of relative independence for relative comfort.) In this group are many of the very old, the "single" women with many dependents, and other persons prevented in one way or another from working continuously enough or at pay high enough to qualify for a more respectable poverty. Many, if not most of these, are still in the area in Redevelopment Commission property, "unable to move" and unlikely, in the absence of harder necessity than they yet know, to do so.

The last subgroup among the "permanent necessitarians" are the *"social outcasts."*[14] Police evidence, tradition, and common gossip have it that these people were relatively prominent in Area "A" at one time, but left when redevelopment became imminent or even earlier. These people included the "winoes," the drug addicts, peddlers and pushers, the "hustlers," prostitutes and pimps, and others whose marginal, counter-legal, or "shady" activities both excluded them from better-organized neighborhoods and made the slum a more receptive or less rejecting habitat.

In any case, by 1955 these had largely disappeared from the area. By that date, all that was left of this group seemed to be those living in common-law relationships, a handful of "winoes," and a few others living habitually in unconventional ways, for whom the slum provided escape, refuge, sympathy, tolerance, and even some stimulation by the very fact of their being together.

2. *The Temporary Necessitarians.* The *"respectable poor,"* who are in the slum by necessity but whose residence there is or may be more temporary, usually spend a good part of their lives in it—now in and now out, although mostly in. Though slum-dwellers, and often as poor financially as the "adjusted poor," these people are unadjusted or unreconciled to the slum in the sense that all their values and identifications

---

[14] They are so classified although some of them belong no doubt among the permanent opportunists (those who feel they *chose* the slum as a place of operation rather than that they were excluded from better areas) and some (those few who find their way to "respectable" roles) among the "temporary necessitarians."

and most of their associations are outside it. They pay their bills, mind their own business, remain well inside the law, hold the aspirations and, within their means, practice the life-ways of a socially higher class, most of whose members far outrank them economically.

Some of these wind up in public housing, but more often than not they resist such a solution, hoping that "things will take a turn for the better," a turn that will permit them to live more nearly where they feel they belong and how they feel they should. For many of these, redevelopment provided either the money (if they owned their homes) or the incentive or both that made that "turn for the better" reality rather than wish.

The *"trapped"* are people who, having bought a home (or had one left to them by a parent or relative) at a time when the area was not so run down, one day find themselves living right in the middle of a slum. Blight filters insensibly in and around them, destroying the value of their property. Though many remain, through a program such as redevelopment many more are induced finally to get out.

3. *The Permanent Opportunists.* Those who are in the slum to stay, primarily because of the opportunities it affords, are the fugitives, the unfindables, the "models" and the "sporting crowd."

The *fugitives* are really of two types: those whose encounters with the law or the credit agency have led them into a life of subterfuge and flight, more or less permanent; and those whose nature or experience has decided them to flee the exigencies of rigorous competition in a better area in their own business or profession.

The former, probably not numerous, are really using the possibility of anonymity which the slum offers. To them it offers literal sanctuary or asylum, a cover or protection from the too-pressing inquiries of the more respectable world. These people, poorly circumstanced for the most part, had also left Area "A" in large numbers before our study began.

The latter, seeking escape from the status struggles of the world outside, or looking for a more easily maintained economic niche, occupied some of the best property within the area, and when catapulted out by redevelopment, found successful ways to maintain themselves and even to enhance their position outside the area. Many of them were merchants, doctors, lawyers, or other professionals who had served that part of the population that was later to migrate to the "better neighborhoods" with them. (They resembled the "climbers" discussed below, except that they did not want or expect to escape from their refuge in the slums.)

Somewhat like the first group of fugitives are the *"unfindables."* By definition, we had no contact with them, although we did have contact with those who had had contact. From their descriptions, there is suggested the presence in the population (before the advent of redevelopment) of a sizable "floating population," who could not readily be located, rarely got counted in any census, and lived a shadowy kind of existence both in terms of location and social identity. These were not so much people in flight as people whose individualism of outlook and whose detachment from urban ways led them to seek no clear social identity (or to operate under many). Some could be found by laboriously following a chain of vague touch-and-go relationships, some only by sorting out and tracing down a variety of "names" and nicknames under which each had serially or simultaneously lived. Most could not be found at all—with our resources or the census-taker's. These, too, had mostly disappeared from the area by the time we came, although some were left, and the memory of others was still green.

The *"models"* constitute a rare but interesting type. These are people who have somehow become, or conceived of themselves as, social or religious missionaries. They are people who stay in the slum (actually, or as they interpret their own behavior) primarily in order to "furnish an example" or "bring a message" to "the others," the "less cultured," or the "unsaved." Some of them are people who were first among "the trapped," but who have adapted further by finding a satisfying permanent life in the slum; the satisfaction consists in bringing culture or religious light to "those still less fortunate." Some of them patently find some martyr-like satisfaction in such "service," but others more soberly find genuine relatedness and utility in this adaptation.

Some of these remained in Area "A"; some went early. Those who went seemed shortly to find themselves cast in the same role in their new neighborhoods.

Finally among the (relatively) permanent opportunists are the members of the *"sporting crowd."* This term, in local use, evidently connotes a range of characters noted primarily for their jollity and informality—perhaps a certain breezy offhandedness is their distinguishing characteristic—rather than for any necessary preference for illegal or marginal activities as such. They live in the slum for a complex of reasons. First, living in the slum leaves them more money to spend on "other things"; second, having spent a large share of their incomes on those "other things," what is left is only enough for slum rents; third, the slum is the place to meet others similarly situated; fourth, the slum itself provides (or, rather, in the case of Area "A," did provide once) facilities for their pursuits, such as taverns, bookmaking and other betting facilities, and so on. Marginal to this type are those who have been described to us as ranging from "the roughnecks who make it unsafe for others to be in the area" to the less violent types who just create nuisances, which, as one woman explains, ". . . cause you to be afraid to have a friend visit, because you never know whether someone is going to walk in on you without any clothes on." The informality, rather than roughness or nudity as such, is the hallmark of this group.

These, too, by now have mostly fled the area.

4. *The Temporary Opportunists.* It remains to describe the temporary opportunists, a most important group both because of their numbers and because the slum of these people is a way—perhaps the only way—to the pursuit of those things that American culture has taught them are worth pursuing: "self-improvement," independence, property, a savings account, and so on. It may be only for this group that the general reader will feel fully sympathetic, and it may be only here that he will ask himself, "How are these people to get where we want them to get, if we systematically destroy the slums which are the traditional, if unspoken-of, way of getting there?" The question is a good one, and the study leaves its answering to the wisdom of the agencies, public and private, charged or self-charged with such responsibility.

We find that in this group there are three subtypes: the "beginners," the "climbers," and the "entrepreneurs."

The *"beginners"* are mostly the unattached immigrants to the city who have neither helpful kin nor access to powerful agencies of assimilation, such as churches and ethnic associations. The slum is simply their "area of first settlement" where they rest on arrival in the city not for "the pause that refreshes" so much as for the pause that instructs, the pause that permits them a precarious period in which to "get oriented," find a first job, and learn the elements of urban living. Many of these are young married couples, some with first children, trying to learn simultaneously to be citizens, husbands and wives, and parents in the urban manner. Their slim resources, financial, educational, and psychological, necessitate a place to stay that will not strain these resources much further; the slum furnishes an opportunity to rest, to gather fresh forces, and to prepare for moving on as soon as may be—if disease, misfortune, or the fortune of more children does not exert more "drag" than can be overcome. From this source the city replenishes its labor force at the lower economic levels, and its "respectable poor" and other types at the lower social rungs.

The *"climbers"* are somewhat similar to the beginners except that they may have been in the city for some time and that their plans are somewhat more long-term and ambitious. These are the ones who live in the slum in what amounts to a period of apprenticeship, self-denial and self-sacrifice with a view to accumulating enough goods, money, and know-how to leap later into a much "better" area, a considerably higher standard of living, and a much more "respectable" way of life. They are "saving"—out of the very stuff of their own lives—the material and nonmaterial means of achieving better housing, greater status, "success," and homeownership.

For many of these, the period of stay becomes protracted because the dream tends to become embellished even as savings accumulate, and the time to move seems always "a little later, when we have a little more." Redevelopment, for many of these, helped toward a settlement with reality by putting period to an unduly prolonged stay in the slums or overextended plans; for a few, it cut off the possibility of any great "improvement" at all, insofar as it caught them in the initial phases of their plans. Some of those thus "caught" simply moved into neighboring slums to begin again. Some abandoned plans for ownership and became renters outside the area.

Last are the *"entrepreneurs,"* a special class of climbers, oriented similarly to the climbers, mostly more ambitious, but saving out of businesslike enterprises—rather than their own miseries—the wherewithal to escape misery in due time. Beginning usually as people of small financial means, they establish a small business or, more frequently, make the slum itself their business. They somehow (frequently by a kind of financial skin-of-your-teeth operation) get hold of a duplex or house that can be "subdivided." That part of it in which they do not themselves reside must, if possible, pay the costs of the whole, and moreover, yield "a little something" so that more property can be bought as time goes by. Often they purchase property, first, in the slum and, later, in better neighborhoods. In the case of at least one person in the area, a drug store was eventually purchased out of the money thus saved by living in the slums.

This kind of person lives a large part of his life in the slum, but usually leaves about the time he reaches fifty. He may by then own enough slum property to live very comfortably in a better neighborhood; or he may, out of his small-scale slum business operation, develop a larger business in a different area, becoming thus an undifferentiable element of the respectable business community.

III

If the earlier part of this paper made—or even labored—the point that in no way within reach of local planning could the slum be "wiped out," and if the second part drew attention via a particular case to the general situation of a vast variety of people coexisting in the slum's complex fastnesses, what, it may be asked, happens when planned steps are nevertheless taken to "do something" about an area, in this case to "redevelop" it. No general answer can be given—it depends on the steps and the people—except that the greater part of what happens is a redistribution of phenomena in space. We say "the greater part of what happens" because, as is evident from the original report,[15] this is not all that happens: in the very act of relocation *some* "positive" potentialities that were formerly only latent are released or actualized. As far as the redistribution in space is concerned, it is hard to say whether it should be viewed as "deconcentration": it is rather like a resifting and resorting, a speeding up of the city's "natural" ecological processes, with results both "good" and "bad," certainly unintended as well as intended. In this process, opportunities are created for some and destroyed for others, or very often for the same person; certainly, lifelong adjustments or habituations, comfortable and uncomfortable, productive

[15] *Ibid,* pp. 67–143.

and nonproductive, are overset, disturbed, interrupted, or destroyed. Moreover, in most cases one population is advantaged and another further disadvantaged, and it is not at all clear that the balance is tipped in favor of those who initially had least—perhaps, rather, the contrary.

SOME SOURCES OF RESIDENTIAL SATISFACTION IN AN URBAN SLUM*

Marc Fried and Peggy Gleicher

Since the most common foci of urban renewal are areas which have been designated as slums, it is particularly important to obtain a clearer picture of so-called slum areas and their populations. Slum areas undoubtedly show much variation, both variation from one slum to another and heterogeneity within urban slum areas. However, certain consistencies from one slum area to another have begun to show up in the growing body of literature. It is quite notable that the available systematic studies of slum areas indicate a very broad working-class composition in slums, ranging from highly skilled workers to the nonworking and sporadically working members of the "working" class. Moreover, even in our worst residential slums it is likely that only a minority of the inhabitants (although sometimes a fairly large and visible minority) are afflicted with one or another form of social pathology. Certainly the idea that social pathology in any form is decreased by slum clearance finds little support in the available data. The belief that poverty, delinquency, prostitution, and alcoholism magically inhere in the buildings of slums and will die with the demolition of the slum has a curious persistence . . . but can hardly provide adequate justification for the vast enterprise of renewal planning.

In a larger social sense, beyond the political and economic issues involved, planning for urban renewal has important human objectives. Through such planning we wish to make available to a larger proportion of the population some of the advantages of modern urban facilities, ranging from better plumbing and decreased fire hazards to improved utilization of local space and better neighborhood resources. These values are all on the side of the greater good for the greatest number. Yet it is all too apparent that we know little enough about the meaning and consequences of differences in physical environment either generally or for specific groups. Urban renewal may lead, directly and indirectly, to improved hous-

* FROM *Journal of the American Institute of Planners*, XXVII, No. 4 (November 1961), pp. 305–15 (selected portions).

ing for slum residents. But we cannot evaluate the larger effects of relocation or its appropriateness without a more basic understanding than we now have of the meaning of the slum's physical and social environment. This report is an initial essay toward understanding the issue. We shall consider some of the factors that give meaning to the residential environment of the slum dweller. Although the meaning of the environment to the resident of a slum touches only one part of the larger problem, it is critical that we understand this if we are to achieve a more effectively planned and designed urban environment.[1]

II. THE SIGNIFICANCE OF THE SLUM ENVIRONMENT

People do not like to be dispossessed from their dwellings, and every renewal project that involves relocation can anticipate considerable resistance, despite the best efforts to insure community support.[2] It is never quite clear whether most people object mainly to being forced to do something they have not voluntarily elected to do; or whether they simply object to relocation, voluntary or involuntary. There is, of course, considerable evidence for the commitment of slum residents to their habitat. Why this should be so is less clear and quite incomprehensible in the face of all middle-class residential values. In order to evaluate the issue more closely we shall consider the problem of the meaning and functional significance of residence in a slum area. Although we are primarily concerned with a few broadly applicable generalizations, a complete analysis will take better account of the diversities in the composition of slum populations.

The fact that more than half the respondents in our sample[3] have a long-standing experience of familiarity with the

[1] This is one of a series of reports on the meaning and significance of various aspects of working-class life. This group of studies will provide a basis for a subsequent analysis of the impact of relocation through a comparison of the pre-relocation and the post-relocation situation. The population of the original area was predominantly white, of mixed ethnic composition (mainly Italian, Polish, and Jewish). The many ethnic differences do not vitiate the larger generalizations of this study.

[2] This does not seem limited to contemporary relocation situations. Firey reports a similar phenomenon in Boston during the nineteenth century. Walter Firey, *Land Use in Central Boston* (Cambridge: Harvard University Press, 1947).

[3] These data are based on a probability sample of residents from the West End of Boston interviewed during 1958–59. The sampling criteria

area in which they lived before relocation suggests a very basic residential stability. Fifty-five per cent of the sample first moved to or were born in the West End approximately 20 years ago or more. Almost one-fourth of the entire sample was born in the West End. Not only is there marked residential stability within the larger area of the West End, but the total rate of movement from one dwelling unit to another has been exceedingly low. . . . It is readily evident that the largest proportion of the sample has made very few moves indeed. In fact, a disproportionate share of the frequent moves is made by a small group of relatively high-status people, largely professional and semiprofessional people who were living in the West End only temporarily. Regardless of which criterion we use, these data indicate that we cannot readily accept those impressions of a slum which suggest a highly transient population. An extremely large proportion shows unusual residential stability, and this is quite evenly distributed among the several levels of working-class occupational groups.

The Slum Environment as Home

What are the sources of this residential stability? Undoubtedly they are many and variable, and we could not hope to extricate the precise contribution of each factor. Rents were certainly low. If we add individually expended heating costs to the rental figures reported we find that 25 per cent were paying $34 a month or less, and 85 per cent paying $54 a month or less. But though this undoubtedly played a role as a background factor, it can hardly account for the larger findings. Low rental costs are rarely mentioned in discussing aspects of the West End or of the apartment that were sources of satisfaction. And references to the low West End rents are infrequent in discussing the sources of difficulty which people expected in the course of moving. In giving reasons for having moved to the last apartment they occupied before relocation, only 12 per cent gave any type of economic reason (including decreased transportation costs as well as low rents). Thus, regardless of the practical importance that low rents must

included only households in which there was a female household member between the ages of 20 and 65. The present analysis is based on the pre-relocation data from the female respondents. Less systematic pre-relocation data on the husbands are also available, as well as systematic post-relocation data for both wives and husbands and women without husbands.

have had for a relatively low income population, they were not among the most salient aspects of the perceived issues in living in the West End.

On the other hand, there is considerable evidence to indicate that living in the West End had particular meaning for a vast majority of West End residents. . . . The distribution in response to the question, "How do you feel about living in the West End?", clearly indicated how the West End was a focus for very positive sentiments.

That the majority of West Enders do not remain in or come back to the West End simply because it is practical (inexpensive, close to facilities) is further documented by the responses of the question, "Which neighborhood, this one or any other place, do you think of as your real home, that is where you feel you really belong?" It is quite striking that fully 71 per cent of the people named the West End as their real home, only slightly less than the proportion who specify liking the West End or liking it very much. Although there is a strong relationship between liking the West End and viewing it as home, 14 per cent of those who view the West End as home have moderately or markedly negative feelings about the area. On the other hand, 50 per cent of those who do not regard the West End as home have moderately or markedly positive feelings about the area. Thus, liking the West End is not contingent on experiencing the area as that place in which one most belongs. However, the responses to this item give us an even more basic and global sense of the meaning the West End had for a very large proportion of its inhabitants.

· · ·

These responses merely summarize a group of sentiments that pervade the interviews, and they form the essential context for understanding more discrete meanings and functions of the area. There are clearly differences in the details, but the common core lies in a widespread feeling of belonging someplace, of being "at home" in a region that extends out from but well beyond the dwelling unit. Nor is this only because of familiarity, since a very large proportion of the more recent residents (64 per cent of those who moved into the West End during 1950 or after) also showed clearly positive feelings about the area. And 39 per cent of those who moved in during 1950 or after regard the West End as their real home.[4]

[4] It is possible, of course, that we have obtained an exaggerated report of positive feelings about the area because of the threat of re-

Types of Residential "Belonging"

Finer distinctions in the quality and substance of positive feelings about the West End reveal a number of variations. In categorizing the qualitative aspects of responses to two questions which were analyzed together ("How do you feel about living in the West End?" and "What will you miss most about the West End?"), we distinguished three broad differences of emphasis among the positive replies. The three large categories are: (1) *integral belonging:* sense of *exclusive* commitment, taking West End for granted as home, thorough familiarity and security; (2) *global commitment:* sense of profound gratification (rather than familiarity), pleasure in West End and enjoyment; and (3) *discrete satisfaction:* specific satisfying or pleasurable opportunities or atmosphere involving no special commitment to *this* place.

Only a small proportion (13 per cent) express their positive feelings in terms of logically irreplaceable ties to people and places. They do so in often stark and fundamental ways: this is my home; it's all I know; everyone I know is here; I won't leave. A larger group (38 per cent) are less embedded and take the West End less for granted but, nonetheless, express an all-encompassing involvement with the area which few areas are likely to provide them again. Their replies point up a less global but poignant sense of loss: it's one big happy family; I'll be sad; we were happy here; it's so friendly; it's handy to everything and everyone is congenial and friendly. The largest group (40 per cent) are yet further removed from a total commitment but, in spite of the focused and discrete nature of their satisfaction with the interpersonal atmosphere or the convenience of the area, remain largely positive in feeling.

Differences in Foci of Positive Feelings

Thus, there is considerable variability in the depth and type of feeling implied by liking the West End; and the West End as home had different connotations for different people. For a

location. Not only does the consistency of the replies and their internal relationships lead us to believe that this has not caused a major shift in response, but, bearing in mind the relative lack of verbal facility of many of the respondents and their frequent tendencies to give brief replies, we suspect that the interview data often lead to underestimating the strength of sentiment.

large group, the West End as home seems to have implied a comfortable and satisfying base for moving out into the world and back. Among this group, in fact, the largest proportion were more concerned with accessibility to other places than with the locality itself. But for more than half the people, their West End homes formed a far more central feature of their total life space.

There is a difference within this larger group between a small number for whom the West End seems to have been the place *to* which they belonged and a larger number for whom it seems rather to have been the place *in* which they belonged. But for the larger group as a whole the West End occupied a unique status, beyond any of the specific attributes one could list and point to concretely. This sense of uniqueness, of home, was not simply a function of social relationships, for the place in itself was the object of strong positive feelings. Most people (42 per cent) specify both people and places or offer a global, encompassing reason for their positive feelings. But almost an equally small proportion (13 per cent and 10 per cent, respectively) select out people or places as the primary objects of positive experience.

With respect to the discrete foci for positive feelings, similar conclusions can be drawn from another question: "Which places do you mostly expect to miss when you leave the West End?" In spite of the place-orientation of the question, 16 per cent specify some aspect of interpersonal loss as the most prominent issue. But 40 per cent expect to miss one of the places which is completely identified with the area or, minimally, carries a specific local identity. The sense of the West End as a local region, as an area with a spatial identity going beyond (although it may include) the social relationships involved, is a common perception. In response to the question: "Do you think of your home in the West End as part of a local neighborhood?"[5] 81 per cent replied affirmatively. It is this sense of localism as a basic feature of lower-class life and the functional significance of local interpersonal relationships and of local places which have been stressed by a number of studies of the working class[6] and are documented by many aspects of our data.

[5] This question is from the interview designed by Leo Srole and his associates for the Yorkville study in New York.

[6] The importance of localism in working-class areas has been most cogently described by Richard Hoggart, *The Uses of Literacy* (London: Chatto and Windus, 1857), and by Michael Young and Peter Wilmott,

In summary, then, we observe that a number of factors contribute to the special importance that the West End seemed to bear for the large majority of its inhabitants.

1. Residence in the West End was highly stable, with relatively little movement from one dwelling unit to another and with minimal transience into and out of the area. Although residential stability is a fact of importance in itself, it does not wholly account for commitment to the area.

2. For the great majority of the people, the local area was a focus for strongly positive sentiments and was perceived, probably in its multiple meanings, as home. The critical significance of belonging in or to an area has been one of the most consistent findings in working-class communities both in the United States and in England.

3. The importance of localism in the West End, as well as in other working-class areas, can hardly be emphasized enough. This sense of a local spatial identity includes both local social relationships and local places. Although oriented around a common conception of the area as "home," there are a number of specific factors dominating the concrete meaning of the area for different people.

We now turn to a closer consideration of two of these sets of factors: first, the interpersonal networks within which people functioned and, in the subsequent section, the general spatial organization of behavior.

III. Social Relationships in Physical Space

Social relationships and interpersonal ties are not as frequently isolated for special attention in discussing the meaning of the West End as we might have expected. Despite this relative lack of exclusive salience, there is abundant evidence that patterns of social interaction were of great importance in the West End. Certainly for a great number of people, local space, whatever its independent significance, served as a locus for social relationships in much the same way as in other working-class slum areas.[7] In this respect, the urban slum

---

Family and Kinship in East London (Glencoe: The Free Press, 1957). In our own data, the perception of the area as a local neighborhood is largely independent of the individual's own commitment to the area.

[7] Many of the studies of working-class areas make this point quite clear. Cf. Hoggart, *op. cit.;* Young and Wilmott, *op. cit.;* Herbert Gans,

community also has much in common with the communities so frequently observed in folk cultures. Quite consistently, we find a strong association between positive feelings about the West End and either extensive social relationships or positive feelings about other people in the West End.[8] The availability of such interpersonal ties seems to have considerable influence on feelings about the area, but the absence of these ties does not preclude a strongly positive feeling about the West End. That is, despite the prominence of this pattern, there seem to be alternative sources of satisfaction with the area for a minority of the people.

THE PLACE OF KINSHIP TIES

Following some of the earlier studies of membership in formal organizations, which indicated that such organizational ties were infrequent in the working class, increasing attention has been given to the importance of kinship ties in lower-class groups.[9] Despite the paucity of comparative studies, most of the investigations of working-class life have stressed the great importance of the extended-kinship group. But the extended-kinship group, consisting of relationships beyond the immediate family, does not seem to be a primary source of the closest interpersonal ties. Rather, the core of the most active kinship ties seems to be composed of nuclear relatives (parents, siblings, and children) of both spouses.[10] Our data show that the more extensive these available kinship ties are within the local area, the greater the proportion who show strong positive feeling toward the West End. . . . Other relationships point to the same observation: the more frequent the contact . . . with siblings or the more frequent the contact with par-

---

The Urban Villagers (Glencoe: The Free Press, forthcoming); J. M. Mogey, *Family and Neighbourhood* (London: Oxford University Press, 1956); Madeline Kerr, *People of Ship Street* (London: Routledge and Kegan Paul, 1958).

[8] These associations between feelings about the West End and interpersonal variables include interpersonal relationships outside the West End as well. Thus there is the possibility that an interrelated personality variable may be involved. We shall pursue this in subsequent studies.

[9] The importance of kinship ties for working-class people was particularly brought to the fore by Floyd Dotson, "Patterns of Voluntary Association Among Urban Working Class Families," *American Sociological Review*, 1951, Vol. 25, pp. 687–693.

[10] This point is made by Young and Wilmott, *op. cit.* In this regard as in many others, the similarity of the East End of London and the West End of Boston is quite remarkable.

ents or the greater the desire to move near relatives, the greater the proportion who like the West End very well.

THE IMPORTANCE OF THE NEIGHBOR RELATIONSHIP

Important as concrete kinship ties were, however, it is easy to overestimate their significance and the relevance of kinship contacts for positive feelings about the residential area. Studies of the lower class have often neglected the importance of other interpersonal patterns in their concentration on kinship. Not only are other social relationships of considerable significance, but they also seem to influence feelings about the area.

. . . A greater proportion (50 per cent) have a strong preference for relatives, but a large group (31 per cent) indicates a strong preferential orientation to friends. More relevant to our immediate purpose, there is little difference among the three preference groups in the proportions who have strong positive feelings about the West End.

In view of the consistency in the relations between a wide variety of interpersonal variables and feelings about the West End, it seems likely that there are alternative paths to close interpersonal ties of which kinship is only one specific form.[11] In fact, the single most powerful relation between feelings about the West End and an interpersonal variable is provided by feelings about West End neighbors. Although the neighbor relationship may subsume kinship ties (i.e., when the neighbors are kin), the association between feelings about neighbors and feelings about the West End is stronger than the association between feelings about the West End and any of the kinship variables. Beyond this fact, the frequent references to neighbors and the stress on *local* friendships lead us to suggest that the neighbor relationship was one of the most important ties in the West End. And, whether based on prior kinship affiliation or not, it formed one of the critical links between the individual (or family) and the larger area and community.

[11] We do not mean to imply that this exhausts the special importance of kinship in the larger social structure. There is also evidence to suggest that some of the basic patterns of the kinship relationship have influenced the form of interpersonal ties more generally in the urban working class. This issue is discussed in Marc Fried and Erich Lindemann, "Sociocultural Factors in Mental Health and Illness," *American Journal of Orthopsychiatry*, 1961, Vol. 31, pp. 87–101, and will be considered further in subsequent reports.

LOCALISM IN CLOSE INTERPERSONAL TIES

Since the quality of feeling about the West End is associated with so wide a diversity of interpersonal relationships, it is not surprising that the majority of people maintained their closest ties with West Enders. . . . As we would expect on the basis of the previous results, the more exclusively a person's closest relationships are based in the West End, the greater the likelihood that he will have strong positive feelings about the West End.

A few significant factors stand out clearly from this analysis.

1. Although the kinship relationship was of considerable importance in the West End, as in other working-class communities, there were a number of alternative sources of locally based interpersonal ties. Among these, we suggest that the neighbor relationship is of particular importance, both in its own right and in its effect on more general feelings about the area.

2. There is considerable generality to the observation that the greater one's interpersonal commitments in the area, in the form of close contact or strongly positive feelings, the greater the likelihood of highly positive feelings about the area as a whole. This observation holds for all the forms of interpersonal relationship studied.

What is perhaps most striking about the social patterns of the West End is the extent to which all the various forms of interpersonal ties were localized within the residential area. Local physical space seems to have provided a framework within which some of the most important social relationships were embedded. As in many a folk community there was a considerable overlap in the kinds of ties which obtained: kin were often neighbors; there were many interrelated friendship networks; mutual help in household activities was both possible and frequent; many of these relationships had a long and continuous history; and the various ties often became further intertwined through many activities within a common community. But walls are clear-cut barriers between the inside of the dwelling unit and the outer world. And even windows are seldom used for any interchange between the inner world of the dwelling unit and the outside environment (except for sun-

light and air). Most of us take this so much for granted that
we never question it, let alone take account of it for analytic
purposes. It is the value of the "privacy of the home." The
dwelling unit may extend into a zone of lawn or garden which
we tend and for which we pay taxes. But, apart from this, the
space outside the dwelling unit is barely "ours."

As soon as we are in the apartment hallway or on the
street, we are on a wholly *public* way, a path to or from
someplace rather than on a bounded space defined by a subjective sense of belonging.[12] Beyond this is a highly individualized world, with many common properties but great variability in usage and subjective meaning. Distances are very
readily transgressed; friends are dispersed in many directions;
preferred places are frequently quite idiosyncratic. Thus there
are few physical areas which have regular (certainly not
daily) widespread common usage and meaning. And con-
tiguity between the dwelling unit and other significant spaces
is relatively unimportant. It is primarily the channels and
pathways between individualized significant spaces which are
important, familiar, and common to many people. This orientation to the use of space is the very antithesis of that localism
so widely found in the working class.

THE TERRITORIAL SENSE IN THE WORKING CLASS

Localism captures only a gross orientation toward the social use of an area of physical space and does not sufficiently
emphasize its detailed organization. Certainly, most middle-
class observers are overwhelmed at the degree to which the
residents of any working-class district and, most particularly,

---

[12] The comment of one reader to an early draft of this paper is worth
quoting, since it leads into a fascinating series of related problems.
With respect to this passage, Chester Hartman notes: "We tend to think
of this other space as anonymous and public (in the sense of belonging
to everyone, i.e., no one) when it does not specifically belong to us.
The lower-class person is not nearly so alienated from what he does not
own." To what extent is there a relationship between a traditional
expectation (even if occasionally belied by reality) that only *other* people own real property, that one is essentially part of a "property-less
class" and a willingness to treat any property as common? And does
this provide a framework for the close relationship between knowing
and belonging in the working class in contrast to the middle-class relationship between owning and belonging? Does the middle-class acceptance of legal property rights provide a context in which one can *only*
belong if one owns. From a larger psychological view, these questions
are relevant not merely to physical space and physical objects but to
social relationships as well.

the residents of slums are "at home" in the street. But it is not only the frequency of using the street and treating the street outside the house as a place, and not simply as a path, which points up the high degree of permeability of the boundary between the dwelling unit and the immediate environing area. It is also the use of all channels between dwelling unit and environment as a bridge between inside and outside: open windows, closed windows, hallways, even walls and floors serve this purpose. Frequently, even the sense of adjacent human beings carried by noises and smells provides a sense of comfort. . . .

We would like to call this way of structuring the physical space around the actual residential unit a *territorial* space, in contrast to the selective space of the middle class. It is territorial in the sense that physical space is largely defined in terms of relatively bounded regions to which one has freedom or restriction of access, and it does not emphasize the path function of physical space in allowing or encouraging movements to or from other places.[13] There is also evidence, some of which has been presented in an earlier section, that it is territorial in a more profound sense: that individuals feel different spatial regions belong to or do not belong to them and, correspondingly, feel that they belong to (or in) specific spatial regions or do not belong.[14]

[13] These formulations, as previously indicated, refer to modal patterns and do not apply to the total population. Twenty-six per cent do select out the "accessibility" of the area, namely, a path function. The class difference, however, is quite striking since 67 per cent of the highest-status group give this response, but only 19 per cent of the lowest-status group and between 28 per cent and 31 per cent of the middle- (but still low-status) groups select out various types of "accessibility."

[14] Without attempting, in this report, a "depth" psychological analysis of typical patterns of working-class behaviors, we should note the focal importance of being accepted or rejected, of belonging or being an "outsider." Preliminary evidence from the post-relocation interviews reveals this in the frequent references to being unable to obtain an apartment because "they didn't want us" or that the landlord "treated us like dirt." It also emerges in the frequently very acute sensitivity to gross social-class differences, and a sharp sense of not belonging or not fitting in with people of higher status. Clarification of this and related problems seems essential for understanding the psychological and social consequences of social-class distinctions and has considerable implication for urban residential planning generally and urban renewal specifically.

SPATIAL BOUNDARIES IN THE LOCAL AREA

In all the previous discussion, the West End has been treated as a whole. People in the area did, in fact, frequently speak of the area as a whole, as if it were an entity. However, it is clear that the area was differently bounded for different people. Considering only the gross distinction between circumscribing the neighborhood as a very small, localized space in contrast to an expansive conception of the neighborhood to include most of the area, we find that the sample is about equally split. . . . It is apparent, therefore, that the territorial zone may include a very small or a very large part of the entire West End, and for quite a large proportion it is the former. For these people, at least, the boundary between dwelling unit and street may be highly permeable; but this freedom of subjective access does not seem to extend very far beyond the area immediately adjacent to the dwelling unit. It is also surprising how little this subjective sense of neighborhood size is affected by the extensiveness of West End kin or of West End friends. This fact tends to support the view that there is some degree of independence between social relationships and spatial orientations in the area.[15]

Thus, we may say that for almost half the people, there is a subjective barrier surrounding the immediately local area. For this large group, the barrier seems to define the zone of greatest personal significance or comfort from the larger area of the West End. However, it is clearly not an impermeable barrier. Not only does a large proportion of the sample fail to designate this boundary, but even for those who do perceive this distinction, there is frequently a sense of familiarity with the area beyond.[16] Thus, when we use a less severe criterion of boundedness than the local "neighborhood" and ask

[15] The social-class patterning is also of interest. Using the occupation of the head of household as the class criterion, there is almost no difference among the three working-class status levels in the area included as a neighborhood (the percentages who say "much or all of the area" for these three groups are, respectively, 51 per cent, 46 per cent, and 48 per cent). But only 38 per cent of the high-status group include much or all of the West End in their subjective neighborhood.

[16] Of those who include only part of the West End in their designation of their neighborhood, 68 per cent indicate they know a large part or most of the West End well. Naturally, an even higher percentage (87 per cent) of those who include much or all of the West End in their neighborhood are similarly familiar with a large part or all of the area.

people how much of the West End they know well, we find that about two-thirds indicate their familiarity with a large part or most of the area.[17] Although almost half the people consider "home ground" to include only a relatively small local region, the vast majority is easily familiar with a greater part of the West End. The local boundaries within the West End were, thus, boundaries of a semipermeable nature although differently experienced by different people.

THE INNER-OUTER BOUNDARY

These distinctions in the permeability of the boundaries between dwelling unit and street and across various spaces within the larger local region are brought even more sharply into focus when we consider the boundary surrounding the West End as a whole. The large majority may have been easily familiar with most or all of the West End. But it is impressive how frequently such familiarity seems to stop at the boundaries of the West End. . . . A relatively large proportion are familiar with the immediately adjacent areas which are directly or almost directly contiguous with the West End (and are often viewed as extensions of the West End), but only slightly more than a quarter (26 per cent) report familiarity with any other parts of the Boston area. Thus there seems to be a widely experienced subjective boundary surrounding the larger local area and some of its immediate extensions which is virtually impermeable. It is difficult to believe that people literally do not move out of this zone for various activities. Yet, if they do, it apparently does not serve to diminish the psychological (and undoubtedly social) importance of the boundary.[18]

These data provide considerable evidence to support, if they do not thoroughly validate, the view that the working class commonly organizes physical space in terms of a series

[17] We used the term "neighborhood" for want of a better term to designate the immediate local area of greatest significance. On the basis of his ethnographic work, however, Edward Ryan points out that this term is rarely used spontaneously by West Enders.

[18] Unfortunately, we do not have data on the actual frequency of use of the various areas outside the West End. Thus we cannot deal with the problem of the sense of familiarity in relation to actual usage patterns. However, in subsequent reports, we hope to pursue problems related to the bases for defining or experiencing physical-spatial boundaries and the various dimensions which affect the sense of commitment to and belonging in physical areas.

of boundaries. Although we do not mean to imply any sense of a series of concentric boundaries or to suggest that distance alone is the critical dimension, there seems to be a general tendency for the permeability of these boundaries to decrease with increasing distance from the dwelling unit. Significant space is thus subjectively defined as a series of contiguous regions with the dwelling unit and its immediately surrounding local area as the central region. We have referred to this way of organizing physical space as *territorial* to distinguish it from the more highly *selective* and individualized use of space which seems to characterize the middle class. And we suggest that it is the territorial conception and manner of using physical space which provides one of the bases for the kind of localism which is so widely found in working-class areas.

In conjunction with the emphasis upon local social relationships, this conception and use of local physical space gives particular force to the feeling of commitment to, and the sense of belonging in, the residential area. It is clearly not just the dwelling unit that is significant but a larger local region that partakes of these powerful feelings of involvement and identity. It is not surprising, therefore, that "home" is not merely an apartment or a house but a local area in which some of the most meaningful aspects of life are experienced.

V. Conclusions

In studying the reasons for satisfaction that the majority of slum residents experience, two major components have emerged. On the one hand, the residential area is the region in which a vast and interlocking set of social networks is localized. And, on the other, the physical area has considerable meaning as an extension of home, in which various parts are delineated and structured on the basis of a sense of belonging. These two components provide the context in which the residential area may so easily be invested with considerable, multiply determined meaning. Certainly, there are variations both in the importance of various factors for different people and in the total sense which people have of the local area. But the greatest proportion of this working-class group (like other working-class slum residents who have been described) shows a fairly common experience and usage of the residential area. This common experience and usage is dominated by a conception of the local area beyond the dwelling unit as an integral part of home. This view of an area as home and the significance of local people and local places are so profoundly at variance with typical middle-class orientations that it is difficult to appreciate the intensity of meaning, the basic sense of identity involved in living in the particular area. Yet it seems to form the core of the extensive social integration that characterizes this (and other) working-class slum populations.

These observations lead us to question the extent to which, through urban renewal, we relieve a situation of stress or create further damage. If the local spatial area and an orientation toward localism provide the core of social organization and integration for a large proportion of the working class, and if, as current behavioral theories would suggest, social organization and integration are primary factors in providing a base for effective social functioning, what are the consequences of dislocating people from their local areas? Or, assuming that the potentialities of people for adaptation to crisis are great, what deeper damage occurs in the process? And, if there are deleterious effects, are these widespread or do they selectively affect certain predictable parts of the population? We emphasize the negative possibilities because these are closest to the expectations of the population involved and because, so frequently in the past, vague positive effects on slum populations have been arbitrarily assumed. But it is clear that, in lieu of or along with negative consequences, there may be considerable social benefit.

The potential social benefits also require careful, systematic evaluation, since they may manifest themselves in various and sometimes subtle ways. Through a variety of direct and intervening factors, the forced residential shift may lead to changes in orientations toward work, leading to increased satisfaction in the occupational sphere; or, changes may occur in the marital and total familial relationship to compensate for decreased kinship and friendship contacts and, in turn, lead to an alternative (and culturally more syntonic) form of interpersonal satisfaction; or, there may be either widespread or selective decreases in problems such as delinquency, mental illness, and physical malfunctioning.

A realistic understanding of the effects, beneficial and/or deleterious, of dislocation and relocation from an urban slum clearly requires further study and analysis. Our consideration of some of the factors involved in working-class residential satisfaction in the slum provides one basis for evaluating the significance of the changes that take place with a transition to a new geographic and social environment. Only the careful comparison of pre-relocation and post-relocation data can begin to answer these more fundamental questions and, in this way, provide a sound basis for planning urban social change.

THE DEATH AND LIFE OF
GREAT AMERICAN CITIES*

Jane Jacobs

Unslumming and Slumming

Slums and their populations are the victims (and the perpetuators) of seemingly endless troubles that reinforce each other. Slums operate as vicious circles. In time, these vicious circles enmesh the whole operations of cities. Spreading slums require ever greater amounts of public money—and not simply more money for publicly financed improvement or to stay even, but more money to cope with ever widening retreat and regression. As needs grow greater, the wherewithal grows less.

Our present urban renewal laws are an attempt to break this particular linkage in the vicious circles by forthrightly wiping away slums and their populations, and replacing them with projects intended to produce higher tax yields, or to lure back easier populations with less expensive public requirements. The method fails. At best, it merely shifts slums from here to there, adding its own tincture of extra hardship and disruption. At worst, it destroys neighborhoods where constructive and improving communities exist and where the situation calls for encouragement rather than destruction.

Like Fight Blight and Conservation campaigns in neighborhoods declining into slums, slum shifting fails because it tries to overcome causes of trouble by diddling with symptoms. Sometimes even the very symptoms that preoccupy the slum shifters are, in the main, vestiges of former troubles rather than significant indications of current or future ills.

Conventional planning approaches to slums and slum dwellers are thoroughly paternalistic. The trouble with paternalists is that they want to make impossibly profound changes, and they choose impossibly superficial means for doing so. To overcome slums, we must regard slum dwellers as people capable of understanding and acting upon their own self-interests, which they certainly are. We need to discern, respect and build upon the forces for regeneration that exist in slums themselves, and that demonstrably work

* New York: Random House, Inc., 1961, pp. 270–81.

in real cities. This is far from trying to patronize people into a better life, and it is far from what is done today.

Vicious circles, to be sure, are hard to follow. Cause and effect become confused precisely because they do link and relink with one another in such complicated ways.

Yet there is one particular link that is crucial. If it is broken (and to break it is no simple matter of supplying better housing), a slum spontaneously unslums.

The key link in a perpetual slum is that too many people move out of it too fast—and in the meantime dream of getting out. This is the link that has to be broken if any other efforts at overcoming slums or slum life are to be of the least avail. This is the link that actually was broken and has stayed broken in places like the North End, or the Back-of-the-Yards in Chicago, or North Beach in San Francisco, or the unslummed former slum in which I live. If only a handful of American city slums had ever managed to break this link, we might regard it skeptically as grounds for hope. These places might be freaks. More significant are the great number of slum neighborhoods in which unslumming starts, goes unrecognized, and too often is discouraged or destroyed. The portions of East Harlem in New York which had proceeded far along in unslumming were first discouraged by unavailability of necessary money; then where this slowed the unslumming process but still did not bring regression to slum conditions, most of these neighborhoods were destroyed outright—to be replaced by projects which became almost pathological displays of slum troubles. Many areas in the Lower East Side which had started unslumming have been destroyed. My own neighborhood, as recently as the early 1950's, was saved from disastrous amputation only because its citizens were able to fight city hall—and even at that, only because the officials were confronted with embarrassing evidence that the area was drawing in newcomers with money, although this symptom of its unslummed status was possibly the least significant of the constructive changes that had occurred unnoticed.[1]

Herbert Gans, a sociologist at the University of Pennsylvania, has given, in the February 1959 journal of the American Institute of Planners, a sober but poignant portrait of an unrecognized unslumming slum, the West End of Boston, on the eve of its destruction. The West End, he points out,

[1] In 1961, the city is actually trying again for authority and federal funds to "renew" us into an inane pseudosuburb. Of course the neighborhood is fighting this bitterly.

although regarded officially as a "slum," would have been more accurately described as "a stable, low-rent area." If, writes Gans, a slum is defined as an area which "because of the nature of its social environment can be proved to create problems and pathologies," then the West End was not a slum. He speaks of the intense attachment of residents to the district, of its highly developed informal social control, of the fact that many residents had modernized or improved the interiors of their apartments—all typical characteristics of an unslumming slum.

Unslumming hinges, paradoxically, on the retention of a very considerable part of a slum population within a slum. It hinges on whether a considerable number of the residents and businessmen of a slum find it both desirable and practical to make and carry out their own plans right there, or whether they must virtually all move elsewhere.

I shall use the designation "perpetual slums" to describe slums which show no signs of social or economic improvement with time, or which regress after a little improvement. However, if the conditions for generating city diversity can be introduced into a neighborhood while it is a slum, and if any indications of unslumming are encouraged rather than thwarted, I believe there is no reason that any slum need be perpetual.

The inability of a perpetual slum to hold enough of its population for unslumming is a characteristic that starts before the slum itself starts. There is a fiction that slums, in forming, malignantly supplant healthy tissue. Nothing could be farther from the truth.

The first sign of an incipient slum, long before visible blight can be seen, is stagnation and dullness. Dull neighborhoods are inevitably deserted by their more energetic, ambitious or affluent citizens, and also by their young people who can get away. They inevitably fail to draw newcomers by choice. Furthermore, aside from these selective desertions and the selective lack of vigorous new blood, such neighborhoods eventually are apt to undergo rather sudden wholesale desertions by their nonslum populations. The reasons why this is so have already been stated; there is no need to reiterate the sheer impracticality of the Great Blight of Dullness for city life.

Nowadays, the wholesale desertions by nonslum populations which give a slum its initial opportunity to form, are sometimes blamed on the proximity of another slum (especially if it is a Negro slum) or on the presence of a few Negro families, much as in the past slum formation was sometimes blamed on the presence or proximity of Italian or Jewish or Irish families. Sometimes the desertion is blamed on the age and obsolescence of dwellings, or on vague, general disadvantages such as lack of playgrounds or proximity of factories.

However, all such factors are immaterial. In Chicago, you can see neighborhoods only a block and two blocks in from the lake-front parkland, far from the settlements of minority groups, well endowed with greenery, quiet enough to make one's flesh creep, and composed of substantial, even pretentious, buildings. On these neighborhoods are the literal signs of desertion: "For Rent," "To Let," "Vacancy," "Rooms for Permanent and Transient Guests," "Guests Welcome," "Sleeping Rooms," "Furnished Rooms," "Unfurnished Rooms," "Apartments Available." These buildings have trouble drawing occupants in a city where the colored citizens are cruelly overcrowded in their shelter and cruelly overcharged for it. The buildings are going begging because they are being rented or sold only to whites—and whites, who have so much more choice, do not care to live here. The beneficiaries of this particular impasse, at least for the moment, turn out to be the immigrating hillbillies, whose economic choice is small and whose familiarity with city life is still smaller. It is a dubious benefit they receive: inheritance of dull and dangerous neighborhoods whose unfitness for city life finally repelled residents more sophisticated and competent than they.

Sometimes, to be sure, a deliberate conspiracy to turn over the population of a neighborhood does exist—on the part of real estate operators who make a racket of buying houses cheaply from panicked white people and selling them at exorbitant prices to the chronically housing-starved and pushed-around colored population. But even this racket works only in already stagnated and low-vitality neighborhoods. (Sometimes the racket perversely improves a neighborhood's upkeep, when it brings in colored citizens more competent in general and more economically able than the whites they replaced; but the exploitative economics sometimes results instead in replacement of an uncrowded, apathetic neighborhood with an overcrowded neighborhood in considerable turmoil.)

If there were no slum dwellers or poor immigrants to inherit city failures, the problem of low-vitality neighborhoods abandoned by those with choice would still remain and perhaps would be even more troubling. This condition can be found in parts of Philadelphia where "decent, safe and sanitary" dwellings go empty in stagnated neighborhoods, while their former populations move outward into new neighborhoods which are little different, intrinsically, from the old except that they are not yet embedded by the city.

It is easy to see where new slums are spontaneously forming today, and how dull, dark and undiverse are the streets in which they typically form, because the process is happening now. What is harder to realize, because it lies in the past, is the fact that lack of lively urbanity has usually been an original characteristic of slums. The classic reform literature about slums does not tell us this. Such literature—Lincoln Steffens' *Autobiography* is a good example—focused on slums that had already overcome their dull beginnings (but had acquired other troubles in the meantime). A teeming, bustling slum was pinpointed at a moment in time, with the deeply erroneous implication that as a slum is, so it was—and as it is, so it shall be, unless it is wiped away root and branch.

The unslummed former slum in which I live was just such a teeming place by the early decades of this century, and its gang, the Hudson Dusters, was notorious throughout the city, but its career as a slum did not begin in any such bustle. The history of the Episcopal chapel a few blocks down the street tells the tale of the slum's formation, almost a century ago in this case. The neighborhood had been a place of farms, village streets and summer homes which evolved into a semisuburb that became embedded in the rapidly growing city. Colored people and immigrants from Europe were surrounding it; neither physically nor socially was the neighborhood equipped to handle their presence—no more, apparently, than a semisuburb is so equipped today. Out of this quiet residential area—a charming place, from the evidence of old pictures —there were at first many random desertions by congregation families; those of the congregation who remained eventually panicked and departed en masse. The church building was abandoned to Trinity parish, which took it over as a mission chapel to minister to the influx of the poor who inherited the semisuburb. The former congregation reestablished the church far uptown, and colonized in its neighborhood a new quiet residential area of unbelievable dullness;

it is now a part of Harlem. The records do not tell where the next preslum was built by these wanderers.

The reasons for slum formation, and the processes by which it happens, have changed surprisingly little over the decades. What is new is that unfit neighborhoods can be deserted more swiftly, and slums can and do spread thinner and farther, than was the case in the days before automobiles and government-guaranteed mortgages for suburban developments, when it was less practical for families with choice to flee neighborhoods that were displaying some of the normal and inevitable conditions that accompany city life (such as presence of strangers), but none of the natural means for converting these conditions into assets.

At the time a slum first forms, its population may rise spectacularly. This is not a sign of popularity, however. On the contrary, it means the dwellings are becoming overcrowded; this is happening because people with the least choice, forced by poverty or discrimination to overcrowd, are coming into an unpopular area.

The density of the dwelling units themselves may or may not increase. In old slums, they customarily did increase because of the construction of tenements. But the rise in dwelling density typically did not cut down the overcrowding. Total population increased greatly instead, with overcrowding superimposed on the high dwelling densities.

Once a slum has formed, the pattern of emigration that made it is apt to continue. Just as in the case of the preslum emigration, two kinds of movement occur. Successful people, including those who achieve very modest gains indeed, keep moving out. But there are also apt to be periodic wholesale migrations, as a whole population begins to achieve modest gains. Both movements are destructive, the second apparently more so than the first.

Overcrowding, which is one symptom of the population instability, continues. It continues, not because the overcrowded people remain, but because they leave. Too many of those who overcome the economic necessity to overcrowd get out, instead of improving their lot within the neighborhood. They are quickly replaced by others who currently have little economic choice. The buildings, naturally, wear out with disproportionate swiftness under these conditions.

Residents of a perpetual slum constantly change in this fashion. Sometimes the change is considered noteworthy because the economic emigrations and immigrations entail an ethnic change. But the movement occurs in all perpetual slums, even those that remain ethnically constant. For instance, a Negro slum in a big city, such as central Harlem in New York, may remain a Negro slum for a long period, but undergo huge, selective turnovers in population.

The constant departures leave, of course, more than housing vacancies to be filled. They leave a community in a perpetually embryonic stage, or perpetually regressing to helpless infancy. The age of buildings is no index to the age of a community, which is formed by a continuity of people.

In this sense, a perpetual slum is always going backward instead of forward, a circumstance that reinforces most of its other troubles. In some drastic cases of wholesale turnover, it seems that what is getting a start again is hardly a community but a jungle. This happens when the new people flooding in have little in common to begin with, and those who are most ruthless and bitter begin to set what tone there is. Anyone who does not like that jungle—which is evidently nearly everyone, for turnover is tremendous in such places—either gets out as fast as he can or dreams of getting out. Even in such seemingly irreparable milieus, however, if the population can be held, a slow improvement starts. I know one such street in New York where this is true, but it is terribly hard to get sufficient people anchored.

The perpetual slum's progress backward occurs in planned slums, just as it does in unplanned slums. The main difference is that perpetual overcrowding is not one of the symptoms in planned slums, because the number of occupants in dwellings is regulated. Harrison Salisbury, in his series of articles on delinquency in the *New York Times,* has described the crucial link of the vicious circle as it operates, in this case, in low-income projects:

> . . . In only too many instances . . . the slums have been shut up within new brick and steel. The horror and deprivation has been immured behind those cold new walls. In a well-intended effort to solve one social ill, the community succeeded in intensifying other evils and in creating new ones. Admission to low-rent housing projects basically is controlled by income levels . . . Segregation is imposed not by religion or color but by the sharp knife of income or lack of income. What this does to the social fabric of the community must be witnessed to be appreciated. The able, rising families are constantly driven out . . . At the intake end the economic and

social levels tend to drop lower and lower . . . A human catch-pool is formed that breeds social ills and requires endless outside assistance.

It is the constant hope of the builders of these planned slums that they will surely improve as "a community has time to form." But time here, as in an unplanned perpetual slum, is an eternal disrupter instead of a builder. As might be expected, therefore, the worst examples of the immured slums, such as Salisbury was describing, are almost invariably the oldest low-income projects, where the perpetual sliding backward of the perpetual slum has had longest to operate.

However, an ominous modification in this pattern has started to appear. With the increase in planned slum shifting, and the rising proportions of "relocated" people in new projects, these new projects are sometimes starting off today with the sullenness and discouragement typical of old projects or of old perpetual unplanned slums—as if they had already, in their youth, been subjected to the vicissitudes of many disruptions and disintegrations. This is probably because so many of their residents have already lived with such experiences, and of course take them along as emotional baggage. Mrs. Ellen Lurie, of Union Settlement, describing conditions in a new project, comments:

> One observation can easily be made as a result of all the visits with site tenants [families placed in public housing because their old homes were taken for city rebuilding]. As difficult a job as management has in running a large project, a bulk of initially unhappy people, angry at the Housing Authority for forcibly uprooting them, not fully understanding all the reasons for the move, lonely and insecure in a strange new environment—such families must make project management all the more overwhelming a task.

Neither slum shifting nor slum immuring breaks that key link in the perpetuation of slums—the tendency (or necessity) for too many people to leave too fast. Both these devices merely aggravate and intensify the processes of perpetual movement backward. Only unslumming overcomes American city slums, or ever has overcome them. If unslumming did not exist, we would have to invent it. However, since it does exist, and does work, the point is to help it happen faster and in more places.

MANCHILD IN THE PROMISED LAND*

Claude Brown

When I first moved down to Greenwich Village, I didn't know anybody but Tony Albee, who lived next door to me. We used to hang out together whenever there was time. Going to school and working, I didn't have too much time to hang out. For a long time, I just fell into that groove of going to school, hanging out on the weekends, going to work during the day, getting high with Tony and philosophizing at night, peeping the Village scene from the outside, the artists, the quacks, the would-be bohemians.

Most of the time, I would go up to Harlem on the weekends, because this was the only place I knew to go when I wanted some fun. It seemed that if I stayed away two weeks, Harlem had changed a lot. I wasn't certain about how it was changing or what was happening, but I knew it had a lot to do with duji, heroin.

Heroin had just about taken over Harlem. It seemed to be a kind of plague. Every time I went uptown, somebody else was hooked, somebody else was strung out. People talked about them as if they were dead. You'd ask about an old friend, and they'd say, "Oh, well, he's strung out." It wasn't just a comment or an answer to a question. It was a eulogy for someone. He was just dead, through.

At that time, I didn't know anybody who had kicked it. Heroin had been the thing in Harlem for about five years, and I don't think anybody knew anyone who had kicked it. They knew a lot of guys who were going away, getting cures, and coming back, but never kicking it. Cats were even going into the Army or to jail, coming back, and getting strung out again. I guess this was why everybody felt that when somebody was strung out on drugs, he was through. It was almost the same as saying he was dying. And a lot of cats were dying.

I was afraid to ask about somebody I hadn't seen in a while, especially if it was someone who was once a good friend of mine. There was always a chance somebody would say, "Well,

* New York: The Macmillan Company, 1965, pp. 179–85, 188–91 (selected portions).

he died. The cat took an O.D.," an overdose of heroin; or he was pushed out of a window trying to rob somebody's apartment, or shot five times trying to stick up a place to get some money for drugs. Drugs were killing just about everybody off in one way or another. It had taken over the neighborhood, the entire community. I didn't know of one family in Harlem with three or more kids between the ages of fourteen and nineteen in which at least one of them wasn't on drugs. This was just how it was.

It was like a plague and the plague usually afflicted the eldest child of every family, like the one of the firstborn with Pharaoh's people in the Bible. Sometimes it was even worse than the biblical plague. In Danny Rogers family, it had everybody. There were four boys, and it had all of them. It was a disheartening thing for a mother and father to see all their sons strung out on drugs at the same time. It was as though drugs were a ghost, a big ghost, haunting the community.

People were more afraid than they'd ever been before. Everybody was afraid of this drug thing, even the older people who would never use it. They were afraid to go out of their houses with just one lock on the door. They had two, three, and four locks. People had guns in their houses because of the junkies. The junkies were committing almost all the crimes in Harlem. They were snatching pocketbooks. A truck couldn't come into the community to unload anything any more. Even if it was toilet paper or soap powder, the junkies would clean it out if the driver left it for a second.

The cats who weren't strung out couldn't see where they were heading. If they were just snorting some horse, they seemed to feel that it wouldn't get to them. It's as though cats would say, "Well, damn, I'm slicker than everybody else," even though some slick cats and some strong guys had fallen into the clutches of heroin. Everybody could see that nobody was getting away from it once they had started dabbling in it, but still some people seemed to feel, "Shit, I'm not gon get caught. I can use it, and I can use it and not be caught."

Guys who were already strung out were trying to keep their younger brothers away from stuff. They were trying feebly, and necessarily so, because guys who were strung out on drugs didn't have too much time to worry about anybody but themselves. It was practically a twenty-four-hour-a-day job trying to get some money to get some stuff to keep the habit from fucking with you.

There was a time when I'd come uptown on the weekend and cats would say things like, "Man, let's have a drink," or "Let's get some pot," or "Let's get some liquor." But after a while, about 1955, duji became the thing. I'd go uptown and cats would say, "Hey, man, how you doin'? It's nice to see you. Look here, I got some shit," meaning heroin. "Let's get high." They would say it so casually, the way somebody in another community might say, "C'mon, let's have a drink."

I'd tell them, "No, man, I don't dabble in stuff like that." They'd look at me and smile, feeling somewhat superior, more hip than I was because they were into drugs. I just had to accept this, because I couldn't understand why people were still using drugs when they saw that cats were getting strung out day after day after day. It just didn't make too much sense to me, but that was how things were, and it wasn't likely that anybody was going to change it for some time to come.

Then money became more of a temptation. The young people out in the streets were desperate for it. If a cat took out a twenty-dollar bill on Eighth Avenue in broad daylight, he could be killed. Cats were starving for drugs; their habit was down on them, and they were getting sick. They were out of their minds, so money for drugs became the big thing.

I remember that around 1952 and 1953, when cats first started getting strung out good, people were saying, "Damn, man, that cat went and robbed his own family. He stole his father's suits, stole his mother's money," and all this kinda shit. It was still something unusual back then. In some cases, the lack of money had already killed most family life. Miss Jamie and her family, the Willards, were always up tight for money because she spent the food money for playing the numbers and stuff like that. This was the sort of family that had never had any family life to speak of. But now, since drugs demanded so much money and since drugs had afflicted just about every family with young people in it, this desire for money was wrecking almost all family life.

Fathers were picking up guns and saying, "Now, look, if you fuck wit that rent money, I'm gon kill you," and they meant it. Cats were taking butcher knives and going at their fathers because they had to have money to get drugs. Anybody who was standing in the way of a drug addict when his habit was down on him—from mother or father on down—was risking his life.

Harlem was a community that couldn't afford the pressure of this thing, because there weren't many strong family ties anyway. There might have been a few, but they were so few, they were almost insignificant.

There was a nice-looking little dark-skinned girl named Elsie on 146th Street. When she was a little snotty-nosed thing, she used to hang out with my sister Margie. Around 1955, Elsie was thirteen or fourteen. She was a little large for her age, and she'd just gone into junior high school. She wasn't even a real schoolgirl yet. I remember once standing on a stoop on Eighth Avenue, and she came up. I had seen her in a bar, and I had wondered, What the hell is she doin' in a bar as young as she is?

I started talking to her, asking her what she was doing. She told me she was making money, and she sounded as though she was kind of proud of it, as though she thought she was slick.

I asked her, "How much money are you makin', Elsie?"

She said, "Enough for me."

"How much money do you need?" She was thirteen, and it seemed kind of crazy to me for her to be out there tricking.

She wasn't such a beautiful girl. She was just trying to grow old fast, too fast. I had the feeling that this little girl ought to be still reading *True Love* magazines, still dreaming about romance and Prince Charming and all that kind of stuff. Here she was out here acting like a whore.

I wanted to get her to face up to what would happen. I said, "Look, Elsie, what cat's gon want you? The average nigger isn't gonna want to be seen with you in a year or so."

"No, not unless I've got money."

"Look, baby, money's not everything."

She said, no, money wasn't everything, but what money couldn't buy, nobody wanted anyway, so it might as well be everything.

The conversation just went on like this. She had all the answers. She knew that everybody needed money, and she had a good point there. She asked me, "Now, if you ain't got no money and you come uptown, do you think your family would be as happy to see you?"

This stopped me. I knew she was right.

In Harlem, practically everybody I knew had been striving for a long time to make enough money to buy a big car and expensive clothes. They'd always wanted to do these things, and the main way of doing it had been through the numbers.

All the people who had a little more nerve than average or didn't care would take numbers. Numbers was the thing; it sort of ran the community.

Early in the morning, everybody used to put in their numbers before they went to work. I remember that Mama and Dad used to always go up to Miss Rose's house and leave their numbers. Sometimes, if it was getting late, they'd give me the numbers to take up. All day long, they'd be thinking about the numbers. Numbers was like a community institution. Everybody accepted it and respected it. This was the way that the people got to the money. If you were lucky, you hit a number now and then, but very few poor people were lucky enough to hit the number for anything big. A few did, but even if you didn't, you could run numbers. If you could be a numbers runner, you'd make about seventy-five dollars a week, which wasn't that much money, but there wasn't that much work to do. And when people hit, they would give you some.

But then it seemed like drugs were coming in so strong with the younger generation that it was almost overshadowing numbers. A lot of younger cats who were taking numbers would start using drugs, and then they would start fucking with people's money. They couldn't be trusted by numbers bankers any more. A whole lot of things started happening. People started getting shot and things like that over their money because cats needed it to get drugs. A lot of the junkies started sticking up the numbers writers and sticking up the controllers.

Peddling drugs had become a popular vocation in Harlem, and it was accepted by everybody, except the police, and they didn't matter. They didn't count unless you got caught, and, if you didn't get caught, nobody asked where you got your money from. That's why a lot of people went into it.

If there wasn't so much time on a drug bust, I suppose a lot of other people would've gotten into it, some of the more righteous people, who had been controlling the numbers for a long time. I remember once, there used to be a preacher down around Eighth Avenue who preached in Jersey on Sundays and during the week came to Harlem and took numbers. That was all right, but now drugs were the thing. This cat had to move on out because drug dealing was a cold business. Anybody who was dealing drugs now would have to have a gun. There was always somebody trying to stick you up, because they knew how much money you had.

If the plague didn't hit you directly, it hit you indirectly. It seemed as though nobody could really get away from it. There were a lot of guys trying to get young girls started on drugs so that they could put them on the corner. When a chick's habit came down on her, she'd usually end up down in the "marketplace," 125th Street between Third Avenue and St. Nicholas Avenue, where all the whores hung out. They sold cunt out there on the street at night.

If a young girl got strung out on drugs, she wouldn't go around trying to steal. Most girls were afraid they might get caught. Most girls would start selling body. So if a cat was strung out, if there was a young girl he knew who had eyes for him, he would cut her into some drugs to try to get her strung out too. Then he could get the chick to sell cunt for him and get enough money to keep them both high. But it was always just a matter of time before the chick would cut him loose. She'd find somebody else, usually another junkie she dug more than she dug him. She'd go on and pull tight with this cat, and she'd sell body, turn tricks, and make money to support both of their habits. This was usually the way things went.

Many times they were guys who never knew anything about stealing. They were good boys; I mean, they were never into street life. But it seemed as though drugs crawled into all the houses. It even crawled into the churches and pulled some of the nice people right out. It was a plague. You couldn't close all the doors and all the windows and keep everything out. It was getting to everybody. It was getting to cats who went to nice schools, Catholic schools. It was even getting to people whose folks used to live in the Dunbar and up on Edgecombe Avenue in fabulous houses, people who thought cats from Eighth Avenue were dirt.

You'd run into many cats along Eighth Avenue and you'd say, "Look, man, what are you tryin' to do? You tryin' to kick your habit? You want to get yourself together?" A lot of cats just didn't seem to feel that they were in a bad way, being strung out.

They'd say things like, "Man, all I want me is a slick bitch." This was a good thing to have if you were strung out, I suppose, because just about all the young cats, seventeen or eighteen, knew that if you had a slick bitch, you would always have some money. By a slick bitch, they meant chicks who would help you work a Murphy and who would sell some cunt if you got up tight; chicks who would burn other people for you, that is, go into a bar and tell a cat that the Man was on him, or some shit like that, and have him pass his drugs to her. She'd make it out with the drugs, and her man would be waiting outside. Or her man would be playing the police.

Around 1955, everybody wanted a slick bitch; nobody wanted to kick the habit much. They were strung out, and they were really going down. They were ragged and beat-up. Cats who had never come out of the house without a pair of shoes on that didn't cost at least thirty-five dollars, who had never had a wrinkle anyplace on them, who had always worn the best suits from Brooks Brothers or Witty Brothers—these cats were going around greasy and dirty. These were people who had a whole lot of pride. They were people who had had too much pride to put a dirty handkerchief in their pockets at one time. Now they just seemed to be completely unaware of how they looked. They would just be walking around dirty, greasy, looking for things to steal.

The slang was always changing for heroin. They called it duji or shit or stuff or poison. After about 1952, nobody called it horse any more. I always referred to it as the shit plague, because that had more meaning to me.

I ran into Danny in a hallway one night. He was down on his knees crying and holding his stomach. I said, "Danny, what's wrong, baby?"

And he said, "I need some shit. I need some shit."

It just stuck in my mind. I could always see heroin more vividly as shit than anything else, because it was real dirt. They would put it into their veins, and that was the same thing as putting dirt into it.

It was the time and the plague. Everybody knew they had to get away from something and get into something. I guess one of the reasons Tony Albee and I hung out together was that we had to get away from not having a groove. We had to get with somebody and something. We had a lot of expensive clothes, and we would go to parties. We'd party with a lot of the young girls, a lot of the whores. Every Friday and Saturday night, Tony and I would come uptown and go to a party or a dance, or we'd just get high off pot. And we would philosophize about what we were going to do one day, and about the junkies, and about the way the cops were carrying on, the way they were taking target practice on the junkies.

There was a cop up there called Schoolboy. Sometimes

we'd stand on the corner and get high and talk about how the police department planned to let Schoolboy kill off all the junkies. Schoolboy was a white cop who had shot quite a few junkies. It didn't make sense to shoot junkies, because they were sort of harmless people unless you were standing between them and drugs. But Schoolboy shot junkies just for running. I don't know how true it is, but Wally said that when he had been caught on 146th Street, Schoolboy had told him to run. He said he lay down and refused to run, because he knew that Schoolboy liked to shoot junkies. He said when he lay down, Schoolboy shot him in the leg anyway.

I'd heard a lot of cats say they never were going to run from him. Sometimes cats who were stealing stuff would hear him. They'd get up close to a wall or something. He'd say, "Come over here." They'd say, "No, you gon have to shoot me here if you gon shoot me." People in the neighborhood complained about it: "They got this white cop around here killin' all these young boys." The old ladies would say this when the junkies weren't robbing their houses. If the junkies were robbing their houses, the old ladies would say, "They ought to kill all them damn no good junkies." This was the usual story with the junkies and the old ladies.

Nobody in the neighborhood liked Schoolboy, but nobody did anything. This was a sign that the neighborhood had changed. In the old days, somebody would have killed that cat. He couldn't have gone around shooting everybody like that. People said, "Yeah, Schoolboy, he's a nut, and somethin' has to be done about that cat." But right then, nothing was happening.

I heard that one lady said she saw Schoolboy shoot a young boy who was a junkie. Schoolboy had told him to stop, and the boy stopped and was just waiting for him. Schoolboy just walked up to him and shot him. The lady went down to the police station to complain about it. They told her, "Get the hell out of the precinct." There was a big stink about it in the *Amsterdam News*, the colored newspaper, but nothing ever came of it. Everybody just started squawking, "Yeah, they ain't gon do anything to a white cop for shootin' a nigger, even if it is in New York." Perhaps they had something there.

Tony felt that Schoolboy was going to be the one to get rid of all the junkies in Harlem. He was going to shoot them all. He had knocked up a colored girl up the block, and everybody knew he was going around there fucking the young girls and shooting the junkies. I guess a lot of people felt that he should have been killed, because he was no good.

When people got high off pot and philosophized about it, it almost seemed unbelievably funny. But they were right. Nobody seemed to care much about Harlem, not the people who could do something about it, like the mayor or the police.

Some of the cats I knew had gone into the police department. They seemed to be exploiting Harlem too, once they got in there. These were the same cats who had come up in Harlem. They didn't care any more either. They just wanted to go out there and get some of that money too.

Harlem was getting fucked over by everybody, the politicians, the police, the businessmen, everybody. There were a lot of things that we knew about but didn't think about when we weren't high: how nobody cared too much about cleaning up the junkies or making drugs legal so that they'd stop robbing people, since it was just Harlem and East Harlem; how nobody gave a fuck about some niggers and some Puerto Ricans, so that's why nothing was going to be done about it. It seemed that when we got high off pot and stuff and started philosophizing, we really knew things. We understood this whole thing about Harlem, but we didn't mind it too much then. You could get high, sit down, and talk about it, even laugh about it.

We'd laugh about how when the big snowstorms came, they'd have the snowplows out downtown as soon as it stopped, but they'd let it pile up for weeks in Harlem. If the sun didn't come out, it might have been there when April came around. Damn sending snowplows up there just for some niggers and people like that!

Many times we would think we had found the way to get the junkies out, but we could never have taken it down to City Hall and gotten people to listen to it. Especially since we were high. If we'd gone down there and said, "Look, Mr. Mayor, you take a stick-a this, and, baby, when you get up there off this joint, you'll see all this shit out here just the way it is. Like, you get some-a this and come to Harlem and just dig it. You got to be high off some good pot." That's all we needed. They would have said, "These niggers are crazy. Let's call up Bellevue."

We knew we couldn't do that, but we could squawk about the snow. Somebody'd say, "Yeah, this is the last place they git with the snowplows," and somebody else'd say, "Would you listen to that nigger? He must think he's livin' down on

Park Avenue. You better go and take another look in the mirror. Shit, ain't nobody gon be sendin' no damn snowplows up to Eighth Avenue and 145th Street. Shit, they probably ain't got enough people up here who can vote."

There was a lot of sense to this. Even though cats get high off pot, they're not crazy. Most of the men from our community had some kind of bust on them, even if it was just for something petty. The average cat around our neighborhood in Harlem had a sheet on him, so he couldn't vote. Even most of the young cats around there who weren't strung out owed some time for something. A lot of the older people who went to work every day had sheets on them from way back for killing some other nigger in Georgia or running some moonshine.

The women, with their votes, just ran the community. They'd elect the councilmen. They'd elect our same old light, bright, damn-near-white Congressman who was always making those pretty promises that never amounted to anything, those bullshit promises. He was going to keep on doing this, and we knew it even though we were young and high. We could stand around and talk this shit, and we knew we were right, because just about the only people who could vote were the women. So this light, bright, damn-near-white and full of shit cat was going to be in there just as long as women had most of the vote. As Johnny D. once said, a woman's brain is between her legs, and some pretty nigger who was suave, like our good Congressman, could get up there and say, "Look, baby, I'm going to do this and that for you." The women would go right out and vote for him, because the nigger was too pretty for them not to. We kept on getting the same treatment because the women were running Harlem.

Most of the people didn't know it, and this was one of the great truths that we discovered. When you got high, you'd discover a whole lot of answers to many questions. This was one of them. We knew that the women were running Harlem. The women didn't know it themselves, but we knew it. Anyway, we knew it when we got high.

We'd get high, and we'd solve all the problems of Harlem. When it wore off, we would just have to live with them all over again.

III. POLITICS, PLANNING, AND DECISION-MAKING

POLITICS AND RENEWAL

Urban renewal is a political process; the physical structures that rise on a renewal site are the result of political decisions about the allocation of resources and a long journey through many agencies at all levels of government. The vision that stimulated the initiation of the project is subject to an ordeal by politics, and it is the rare vision that emerges unscathed.

In Scott Greer and David W. Minar's paper we are able to see the overarching political structure and the relevant dimensions vitally affecting urban renewal. They emphasize the traditional American distrust of power and commitment to the ideology of the free market, and how the latter are reflected in our political institutions. Broadly speaking, there is a fragmentation of government, with each segment tending toward rigidity. But the fragmentation also offers potentialities and opportunities for flexibility and innovation. The problems of rigidity and flexibility are directly relevant to urban renewal, since renewal needs public planning and intervention into free market processes. Greer and Minar ask whether the necessary innovations can appear, given our ideological convictions and present governmental structure.

Because, as Greer stresses in another selection of these readings, crucial decisions are made at the community level, George Duggar's research was concerned with renewal in context of local governmental structure. He too is concerned with the need for coordination and flexibility, and is interested in discovering whether there is any relation between a particular type of governmental structure, e.g., manager system vs. mayor, and "success" in urban renewal. (We shall refer to one of his findings again in the next section.)

Politics, we said, involves decisions about the allocation of resources, but who makes the decisions and why? A dominant influence is exercised by the "leadership" of a community. Raymond Vernon, who was responsible for a multi-volume report on the New York Metropolitan Region, presents some insights into the sources of their decisions. Most renewal projects have been located in central business districts where land is expensive, and, therefore, the logic of a free market economy dictates how and for what purposes the cleared land will be used. Projects have located in these areas, because for the "elite" of the community the city *is* the central business district. The CBD also contains large numbers of poor people, but they, of course, have less power than the "elite." It is obvious that Vernon's suggestion concerning the poor cannot be thought about without taking account of the political structure of the entire metropolitan region.

Renewal is intimately linked with politics in still another fashion; it can become an issue affecting the fortunes of local politicians. In the many communities where referendums have defeated proposed renewal projects political figures have suffered setbacks. But here we have chosen to present a success story of how a district leader came to power by boldly facing the political dilemmas an urban renewal project posed for him and his adherents.

THE POLITICAL SIDE OF URBAN DEVELOPMENT AND REDEVELOPMENT*

Scott Greer and David W. Minar

In a federal republic, the fate of planned urban development is largely dependent upon the political system. Too many
people have a piece of the polity for any single actor to coerce
all others; thus, however "intrinsically right" our plans may
be, they are only plans until someone harnesses the wild
horses of diverse polities to them. Since, however, any public
development brings real change, on which some will suffer
and some rejoice, this may be appropriate. There is, after all,
no calculus which tells us who should suffer in such a way that
all reasonable men must accept its results. Thus, all urban
development is political in a double sense: it redistributes
wealth by public action, and it is legitimate only when it is
politically supported.

For this reason, our discussion will focus upon the political.
We will describe the present state of the governmental complex in urban areas and the ways in which it influences and
constrains planned urban development. We shall then indicate, briefly, the origins of this complex in the political culture
of United States society. So coercive are the norms of this
culture, so narrowly are they conceived, they probably make
effective planning for urban development nearly impossible in
any direction. Therefore we go on to consider the problem as
one of political redevelopment. In the present impasse of the
local polity lurk certain clues to effective change and experimentation. We select a few of these for examination in the
light of the massive social trends which, willy-nilly, force us
toward political decision.

One of the familiar and fundamental facts of the urban
situation today is its political and governmental fragmentation.
This fragmentation, as we shall try to show, has crucial consequences for redevelopment in the physical, social, and political senses. Before discussing consequences, however, we
might profitably examine the dimensions of the fragmentation

* FROM *The Annals of the American Academy of Political and Social
Science* (March 1964), pp. 63–73.

itself, particularly in the metropolitan complex, which, practically speaking, includes all significant urban phenomena.

The oldest and most fixed dimension of fragmentation is that created by the federal system, written deep into the American political culture and into the nation's constitutional ground rules. Its division of effective operating powers has always been a source of some difficulty, but, with the extension of scale, it has been even more a strait jacket on the processes of political response to social change. Urban problems have become national problems, and metropolitan social space has flowed over all sorts of geographic confinements. Still, the federal system is such that nation, states, and local governments remain as often rival and to some extent independent centers of problem identification and policy-making.

This is not to say, necessarily, that the federal system is obsolete. Many of the geographic, economic, political, and ideological reasons that made it seem a valid schema in an earlier age still pertain. But the point is that the barriers remain to impede accommodation. We do not get the kinds of action we come to want: integrated, unified, co-ordinated, innovative—these are the symbols of desire. They elude us because our problems are generated by relatively autonomous social forces and because our therapeutic techniques labor under the heavy hand of political tradition. And both techniques and problems search vainly for well-defined arenas of responsibility.

Accommodation does often come, of course; the system learns, usually painfully, to handle problems on the level where they occur, but the lag is likely to be long. The national government has a fair repertoire of techniques for dealing with the problems of an urbanized society, derived from the primitive constitutional powers to tax and spend, to regulate commerce, to assure equal protection and due process. But its weapons are still limited and, such as they are, they have been decades in growing. Much the same can be said for the action potential of the states. While their powers in local affairs are supposedly plenary, the traditions of home rule are so strong as to make state efforts to move on urban problems often look ridiculous, and this is to say nothing of the structural and political inhibitions to action built into our state governments.

A second type of fragmentation with similar consequences is that produced by the multiplication of local units of government, particularly evident in the metropolitan area. It takes no special knowledge to realize that the metropolis does not even fit together like a complicated jigsaw puzzle. It is nothing so rational. The very title of Robert Wood's study of government in the New York area, *1400 Governments,* tells a good part of the story of the condition of that metropolitan scene. The spot on which this article is written falls within nine governmental jurisdictions from the county level down. The Chicago standard metropolitan area has nearly a thousand such units. And this picture is duplicated not only in the great centers of population but in most of the smaller ones as well.

Here again the consequences have to do with abilities for action; here again the techniques are incommensurate with the problems. In the sphere of urban redevelopment as in others the difficulties introduced by fragmentation are manifest. Tradition ties action programs to the legal structures of municipalities while problems overrun jurisdictional boundaries. Supplies of leadership and revenue are distributed differently from the stock of urban problems, such as standard housing, crime, and intergroup tensions. Most often, the problems of physical and social decay are seen as the central city's problems, and, even when their broader implications are understood, long-standing legal and ideological boundaries prohibit all but the most feeble of broad-scale remedies. In many places the division of jurisdiction is not only spatial but also functional so that education and recreation and transit and sewage disposal and a host of other aspects of the urban development picture are charged to distinct units of government. Whatever the particular picture for a metropolitan area, its main blank spots are similar: no co-ordination, no power, no responsibility.

Even within jurisdictions fragmentation is a key feature of the political-governmental structure. Here the gross legal picture is one of unity, and, hence, it seems not unreasonable to expect integration of effort. Such integration is much rarer, however, than expectations would indicate. The reasons are several. One of these is simply the organizational difficulties encountered in mobilizing any complex structure for action. Another is the maze of "checks and balances" impressed upon governments at all levels in the interest of limiting authority. A third is the tradition of decision-making through bargaining, probably adopted from the private economy but often assumed to constitute the norm for the public business as well. It is probably accurate to say that our culture is antiauthority; as a result, a good deal of our political energies have gone to invent better ways of inhibiting the exercise of power at its formal and informal operating points.

Thus, mayors and governors have been hedged in with boards and commissions and with other elective officers doing quasi-executive functions. Civil service has been separated from "political" control, often meaning control by responsible administrators. Zoning and planning activities have often been made subject to extensive review procedures in which a variety of interests have their free shots at the "decision-makers'" programs. Even in systems that look symmetrical on organization charts, left hands do not know what right hands are doing and sometimes do not even care.

Out of this diffusion of power and dilution of responsibility comes a curious rigidity, not a rigidity of program but a rigidity of process that enervates program. Most of what we have discussed above involves mechanisms that in themselves or in their interactions make outcomes improbable. It is as though policy must follow an open road full of ruts and chuck-holes, with hairpin curves and false crossroads to confuse the trip. But not only is the road itself difficult, the country is also filled with hostile tribes that may come out of the hills at any step of the way. If one but counts the veto groups that can snipe at public programs or confront them head-on in full battle dress, he may wonder if any program can negotiate the journey successfully. This is the way the system goes. In planning and formulation, in legislation and administration, in the courts and in the phase of popular approval, urban policy is exposed to the conflict of internal and external interests, to competing jurisdictions, competing subbureaucracies, and an endless array of interested private groups. Any one or combination of these may develop the power to revise, delay, obfuscate, or forbid action. This may simply be a way of saying that the urban political world is as complex and sensitive as the urban social world. In any case, its implications for innovation are apparent.

Despite the structural state of metropolitan government today, it has an enormous effect on our possibilities for action. It safeguards stasis. The pattern of delegation, from state to municipality, leaves the local polity as the only legitimate actor on many crucial issues. Though the towns, cities, villages, and special districts of a given metropolis may be completely unable to act effectively, they prevent action by their mere existence. At an extreme, they are governmental reservations, human zoos which keep government out and the animals safe from government.

These existing units of government have a degree of sacredness. This results not only from piety but from the fact that they are the arenas in which citizens may participate and, thus, the grounds for a legitimate delegation of responsibility. The representatives of the local polity, however denigrated in the local press and local gossip, are the only political actors of stature who take as their assignment the affairs of the local area. This dominance rests, in turn, upon a political culture which emphasizes local self-rule, fear of "big government," and the election of local representatives. Thus, consensus is strong on the *forms* of local government; this same consensus, however, prevents agreement on the substantive problems which face that government. Though the central city and suburbs can agree that they should each have their own government, they cannot agree upon the problems of the metropolis as a whole. Urban development, however, is a problem for the metropolis as a whole, and its present status is a result of this contretemps.

PROBLEMS OF URBAN REDEVELOPMENT

The only vigorous efforts to plan the physical development of cities in the United States have been the movement for city planning, the public housing program, and, lately, the urban-renewal program. The latter two are essentially redevelopment programs, aimed at undoing past land uses and creating new, planned uses. City planning, historically separate and preceding the others, has now been so closely linked with urban renewal that it seems useful to include them all under the rubric of "urban redevelopment." Planned development, through county zoning and subdivision control, is at present so new and sporadic that we shall devote most of our attention to efforts at redevelopment.

The redevelopment of our cities depends upon planned public action. The free market in land produces a haphazard order which rarely generates any corrective tendencies; having once developed a given space, the market value moves downward while new investment moves on to other, greener pastures. Planned public action, however, is dependent upon the organization of public powers in the urban area. Competition, conflict, and simple lack of organization characterize this "organization," but it is within such conditions that redevelopment must be carried out.

The present urban-renewal program is, historically, one of our most ambitious efforts to intervene with public power in community development. With its goals of decent housing for all American families, central business district redevelopment, and comprehensive planning for the metropolis, it is a radical program of urban reform. The logic of the program is simple. The police power is used to enforce housing codes, bringing the existing stock up to standard and destroying what cannot be profitably made standard; on the cleared land resulting, new development will replace the lost units. This is modified by the provision that standard structures can be acquired and destroyed if, in the eye of the redeveloper, the surrounding neighborhood is so poor that there is no chance of an upward surge.

The true shape of the program, as it works out in the hundreds of participating cities, is something again. Since the police power and the fisc are used to do the work, limitations upon them are reflected in the outcomes. These limitations include: (1) the dichotomy of public versus private control, (2) the tension between federal and municipal agencies, (3) the division of power among different federal agencies, and (4) the fragmentation of power at the local community level. Each is not so much a problem to solve as a powerful constraint to be "lived with," one that can distort the program beyond recognition in terms of its stated aims.

Although the urban-renewal program can acquire land, by negotiation or eminent domain, displace the present owners and users and destroy existing structures, it cannot build any buildings except public facilities on the cleared land. Thus it is completely dependent upon the private market in real estate for its "renewal" effects. This means that the local public authority must either gamble on its knowledge of the private land market or prenegotiate sales. In either event, renewal occurs not where it might benefit the community directly but where it must do so indirectly through benefiting the private investors. This circumstance greatly limits the areas which can be redeveloped.

Urban renewal is also committed to the government of the local municipality. Because action can be taken only through a local public authority, it must be underwritten in terms of political and fiscal responsibility by the city government. While the federal agency has a veto power on the city's program, the city in turn may refuse to co-operate with the agency. Thus, many of the politically unpalatable aspects of the working program are honored in the breach: housing codes are enforced selectively or not at all, the local contribution in the shape of school buildings, street paving, and the like may be far out of phase with the urban-renewal efforts to improve neighborhoods, and a sudden revolt of the voters through referendum, initiative, or recall may throw out the entire program—in Springfield, Oregon, all three deities of the secular trinity were invoked: the referendum necessary to the program was lost, the housing code was repealed through initiative, and proponents of urban renewal in the city council had to face a recall election. Under the circumstances, the federal agency is notably chary about too rigid an insistence upon the letter of the law.

Many federal programs other than urban renewal have massive impacts on most of the cities where urban-renewal efforts are being made. Co-ordination among the federal agencies affecting a given city is almost nil; this may result from the use of the state as a middleman, as in the case of the federal highway program, or it may result from simple lack of concern, as in the hiatus between the administration of Federal Housing Administration (FHA) mortgage insurance and the planners of urban renewal. In any event, urban renewal may be at the mercy of powerful federal agencies over which it has no control. The federal highway program may site a cloverleaf in the middle of the urban-renewal area, may displace thousands of householders and completely disrupt the urban-renewal relocation operations, and may hold up the sale of urban-renewal land for months while officials decide where access ramps should go. Meanwhile, FHA may co-operate with the highway program in stimulating dispersion to the suburbs while urban renewal struggles to revivify the central city.

At the metropolitan level, the multitude of jurisdictions—cities, towns, suburbs, special districts, counties, even states—makes any over-all planning of the city a farce. Weak as most planning commissions are in effecting development and redevelopment, their power is further curtailed by city boundaries; few of them exercise jurisdiction outside the municipality. And because there is no other local municipal body with power to underwrite the program, urban renewal is similarly limited—usually to a central city and, separately, one or two larger suburbs. The limitation of power is accompanied

by a limitation of vision—the source of the "flight to the suburbs" may be not the declining structures of the central city
but the patterns of development in the suburbs. Few urban-
renewal programers take these matters seriously in their plans.
Yet the governmental log jam at the local level, preventing
metropolitan planning and development, results in serious dis-
tortions of the program. The central city-suburb schisms turn
urban renewal into a holy war to recapture the suburban,
white, middle class—a war the central city is doomed to lose—
and distract attention from the major clientele of the central
city: the working class, the ethnics, the disprivileged.

Thus, the implications of these various divisions of power
for urban development and redevelopment are basic: they
produce the dilemmas of the programs. Destructive as they
seem to those committed to changing the shape of our cities,
they are perfectly understandable in view of the political culture of Americans as it is now translated, through governmental structure, into the local polity. Indeed, many persons
consider both that culture and that structure to be sacred—not
destructive at all.

THE POLITICAL INHERITANCE AND THE REDEVELOPMENT PROCESS

Our problem at this point is twofold: to understand the culture out of which this urban tangle grows and to explore the
alternatives for action it might permit. Both of these jobs are
clearly too big for anything we might attempt here, but a look
at the surface may suggest what lies underneath. Most of what
we have described above rests squarely on a set of commitments that can roughly be equated with the Western liberal
tradition. The commitments are not necessarily active items of
detailed individual belief, but they are part of the cultural
stock from which we draw rationalizations for our habituated
practice. They go to a root individualism which holds (1) that
power is evil and must be contained and (2) that its only
legitimate exercise is based on common participation and
consent.

Such are the themes that lurk in ideology and institution
behind American political development. They may be found
in the early codifications of the political culture, the Declaration of Independence, the federal Constitution, the original
state organic laws. Though there is an element of logical—and
often practical—tension between them, they have gone hand-in-

hand to mold American practice. The interplay between ideology and institution provides mutual reinforcement which gives the entire structure a surprisingly durable quality, a quality the relative richness and isolation of the system have helped to preserve. Each helps to prop the other up, and both give shape to the prospects for public action.

Out of the former theme, the theme of constitutionalism, have come two kinds of political usages with an impact on the urban action potential. One is the simple negative imposed on authority by bills of rights and other abstract statements of limitation of power. In the redevelopment field, perhaps the most pertinent are restrictions on the power of eminent domain, but this, of course, is but one item from a lengthy catalogue. The other aspect of constitutionalism is structural, the aspect that has prompted us to separate, divide, check and countercheck governmental authority. The federal system itself and the idea of home rule are manifestations of this spirit of suspicion of power. Its premises, of course, are simple ones: authority that cannot be used cannot be used for ill, and society does not need much tending anyway. Hence, the unwieldy structures of local government, frequently multiplying the attempt to diffuse power by several times and in several directions, have fed on the main flow of American tradition. Further, the structures themselves—boards, commissions, loosely organized councils, lay administrators—were "natural" organs of authority in a predominantly rural, small-scale society.

The second theme of the tradition is the crux of democracy itself, the idea of consensus. This, too, has been taken as given, and, in effect, it has been interpreted to mean that authority must constantly be refreshed from the wells of popular participation. Its optimal institutional form was, of course, the town meeting, but that device could, over the longer run, serve only as a model to whose merits the representative system might hope to aspire. The career of local democracy in the United States need not be detailed here. We can note, however, that it has imposed burdens in several directions: on the local authority, an obligation to mirror an obscure voice of the people; on the people, an obligation to participate in an often ill-defined game; on the larger system, an obligation to devolve functions as near to the level of the "popular sovereignty" as possible. The principle of responsibility implicit in all this is clear in abstract but difficult in application. "The shame of the cities" has come at least as often from their stumbling over democratic procedures as from their failure to use them.

Two implications of this heritage for urban development merit brief exploration. One is that our classic model of good government supposes a kind of free market place of interests. To use the terms of the philosophical radicals, it assumes that most social conflicts can work themselves out through a natural harmonization and that only a residuum of conflicts must be left to the artificial devices of government. The latter in turn are subject to a similar pull and haul, on a different site; the brawl of interests is moved from the alley to the ring, with some Queensbury rules imposed. The interesting thing about this formulation is that it grants no initiative to the referee, political authority; at its extreme, it does not see the community-as-a-whole as a participant but only as a site, an arena. Innovation in public programs is thus an accident thrown up by the forces of nature. On the national level, practice has seldom conformed to the model; on the local level, it has come much closer. Tradition has thus served as a brake on energetic local public participation in social change.

A second implication lies in the force the tradition has given to localism. The locality, especially the small-scale place, has obvious virtues from the standpoint that would minimize authority and maximize consensus. Its interests are fewer, its life routines more visible, its problems more familiar. Presumably, then, it demands less of authority and knows more about it when it is summoned. So strong is the identification of the local place with the central tenets of the tradition that localism has come to be regarded as a good in itself. Its derivatives include distrust of the big city as an "unnatural," perhaps even an "un-American" place and a "we-they" perspective on national government. Probably to most Americans "the government" means that bunch of people and structures in Washington, D. C., an object of some loyalty and much suspicion. The consequences for innovation, responsibility, and organization in the society of growing scale are evident.

This account has emphasized the rigidity-inducing aspects of the American political culture, the strains that stultify action and inhibit change; yet the system has been a viable one. It has endured the transition from an underdeveloped, small-scale society to the complex society of today, adapting itself to internal socioeconomic revolution and resisting external threats. Certainly part of the reason for the system's persistence may be charged to our capacity for waste. Our endowment of resources has been so rich as to permit us much leeway.

There is, however, another side of our political culture that helps explain what has happened and suggests potentials for the future. This is an ideological capacity for experimentation, an ability to take risks and make bets on the future. Whether this is a unique characteristic of the American culture may be doubted, but that is not the point. Its sources are open to speculation; perhaps it derives from the coincidence of the nation's early development with the bloom of modern science, perhaps it is part of the perspective of a nation of adventurer immigrants. Its manifestations are evident in technological development and economic life, in political organization, even in formal philosophy. The political side is, of course, what chiefly interests us here.

Again we must be content with scattered examples where an exhaustive discussion would serve us better. The history of American politics is full of instances of experimentation, particularly with organizational forms. Often, indeed, the nation has turned with almost mystic faith to tinkering with institutions. The framing of constitutions, federal and state, may be regarded as collective acts of societies willing to try innovation. If their products combined forms and ideas handed to them by tradition, many of the combinations and some of the forms were novel, even brave. Federalism, separation of powers, the presidential institution, judicial review, these are some of the relatively untested devices the nation has committed itself to in spectacular fashion.

The propensity and sometimes the opportunity to experiment have been even more evident at the state and local levels. Because much of what we have been discussing in this section is in some important sense our Jeffersonian heritage, we might remind ourselves of Jefferson's own urgings in the experimental direction, particularly in the local governmental sphere. Jefferson is often and correctly regarded as the patron political saint of the local-self-rule idea, but we are less likely to see his proposals for organizational innovation as pleas for experimentation. Twice when Virginia revised her constitution, however, he suggested extensive revision of the political framework of the locality. It was in this setting that he developed his well-known proposal to divide the country into small nearly autonomous wards, each to be like a "tiny republic unto itself."

Following Jefferson, the nation has continued to try a great variety of local and state organizational modes, to the point where it is possible to see these units as "laboratories for political experimentation." Some devices have succeeded, others have failed. The standards for testing have been undefined and controversial. But the catalogue of attempts is impressive enough to assure us that innovation is a possibility: consider, for example, cumulative voting, proportional representation, initiative, referendum, and recall, various primary nomination systems, unicameralism, commission forms, civil service and merit systems. All of these and others have been put to trial in political practice, and all relate directly to the problem of our political system: How can we make democracy work in the society of expanding scale?

SOME KEYS TO CHANGE

The tradition thus hands us both rigidities and flexibilities. Our problem is to find the workable mix for the urban area. One thing seems certain: we will not be permitted to transgress the culture's long-term image of legitimacy founded on consensus. Whatever paths to action we find, they will be paths that lead through the perils of democratic procedure. To put the point in another way, this means simply that urban redevelopment must continue to do whatever it does in the setting of a politics. The kind of politics, however, is up to us to determine.

Perhaps the answer to our dilemmas lies in further institutional alterations, particularly in the consensus mobilization area and in the matter of fixing responsibility. Innovation for urban action probably needs to take greater account than it has of the functioning of the mediating devices and mechanisms of the society. It needs to decide what its proper publics are and what questions they are asking. And it needs to free some parts of the system—institutions, agencies, people, define them as you will—for the tasks of creation. This implies, at least, the selection of visible and responsible representatives of the major corporate interests—the metropolitan press, the ethnic groups, the business enterprises, and the labor unions. Too frequently, the public for government action is limited before the act, indiscriminately expanded afterward. Equally important, the local polity needs an expansion of competent staff among the interests capable of evaluating change. While genuine conflicts of interest are frequent in the local polity, spurious conflicts are probably more common.

The problem of innovation is not simply a matter of whether there is freedom to do but whether anyone has the time, the insight, and the responsibility for doing. In part, the matter is simply organizational, simply a question of setting aside the slots and filling them with people. In part, too, it is a question of training and recruiting people whose intellectual backgrounds make it possible for them to undertake the rather unique role and functions involved. This is where a live and adventurous social science might come in, for social science can serve not only to show us the conditions and costs of the possible, it can also provide the yeast that can make the organizational loaf ferment. The potential should be a challenge to the academic and practical imagination.

Any change, however, is going to require some adjustments in perspective, some visions of order that transcend those we commonly hold. Perhaps the basic need involves our notion of community, of the fundamental unit for political activity. Much of what we have been saying amounts to propositions about the inadequacy of the community basis for our ongoing political activity. The concept of consensus implies the question of consensus *among whom,* the question of the relevant community public. Our units of community have probably become too small; clearly, they are irrational in terms of patterns of social structure. It is not, however, sufficient to seek community on a broader basis. We should also be prepared to think through the grounds on which community is defined.

Ironically, the cultural heritage itself has given us potentials that we have to a large degree discarded, particularly the repository of state power. The state is seldom a "natural" community, but it affords certain ready opportunities for broader scale planning and action. It is not the paucity of authority but our reluctance to use it that has made of the state a bypassed, neglected unit in the political system. While it may be foolishly optimistic to hope for such development, the state seems to be the most promising organizational lever to break the urban log jam. Among the side effects of vitalizing state power would be the bringing of the hinterlands into proper focus in their relationships with the urban system.

If such vitalization were accomplished, the broader public of the relevant community might be content with exercising its consensual power on such questions as what kind of society it wants to create rather than self-hypnotism with policy details. If so, authority would be freed from its concern with problems that should not be problems, and the state could assume the role of steward for the general interests of the society, including its local components. This may be a dream; as a dream, it suggests ways of harnessing tradition to current needs.

POSSIBILITIES AND LIMITS

Our discussion has emphasized two seemingly contradictory aspects of the situation: the rigidity and massive resistance of our political system to innovation, and the wide range of possible changes in that system. These possibilities do not rest upon basic changes in political norms so much as *experimentation in their application*—experiments appropriate to the changing world of mid-twentieth-century America. This society of enormous and rapidly increasing societal scale *demands* change in the polity appropriate to massive change generated elsewhere. The network of interdependence increases daily, in its extension and its intensity: we are whorled inevitably together in one community, the nation-state. Never before have so many been so interdependent with so many others. This is made both necessary and possible by our enormous energy resources, producing fantastic wealth and possible freedom.

Increasing wealth is evident in real income, in educational levels, and in the phasing out of brute labor. Even the central-city population shows a steady increase in social wealth. This means, for the urban population as a whole, increasing surpluses of money, of time, and of access to communications. No occupational levels of the United States have to be poorly educated or poorly rewarded, when compared to the past or to any other nation on earth.

Freedom from economic anxiety, from intellectual inability, and from parochialism, taken together, amount to major resources for the task of governmental experimentation and change. It should be increasingly possible to educate the people about their public affairs, instead of hypnotizing them with technological vocabularies or bilking them with promises of something for nothing. This is due not only to the mass adult education carried on through the media but also to the flood of new high school and university graduates entering the status of adult and citizen. In a very few decades, half the adult population will have had at least some college experience. This could mean an increasing receptivity to political change as well as a more realistic grasp of our basic political norms and their significance for the quality of our life.

But increasing scale has also meant increasing freedom of location. The space-time ratio, the cost of moving in terms of time and other scarce resources, has shifted radically. With speed of transport and communication, it is possible for us to be a single community in a wide variety of ways. But, while the national order demands such freedom of movement, this freedom is destructive of many older orders: one is the local community. Today the boundaries of all local units are permeable: residents, stores, factories move with ease outside the city—carrying with them all sorts of resources for the municipal corporation. As this occurs, some struggle to reconstitute the city-state; it is a losing struggle, for the nation-state guarantees freedom of movement, and nothing requires continued commitment. Thus, the question arises: Could we, or should we, try to reconstitute the older style of spatially defined community?

Certainly, work on the physical structure of the urban areas, alone, cannot bring it about. The primitive theory of urban renewal, which assumes that land once used will be reused, that centrality equals community, is irrelevant to the broader questions we have raised. Even governmental integration and expanded governmental powers can do no more than refurbish the horizontal and rapidly expanding urban texture.

In truth, community applies to limited, exclusive groups, organized around shared activities. They come together, partially and fortuitously, in the urban scene. And, in that scene, the only encompassing organization is the *political* community —marginal to many, unconsciously accepted by most, an object of passionate striving for a few. It is inescapable, for only the city as a political form guarantees public order and public action. Whether we can make it an arena for significant participation and, in Hannah Arendt's sense, "social action" remains to be seen.

THE MYTH AND REALITY OF OUR URBAN PROBLEMS*

Ray Vernon

REBUILDING THE CITY

Those who have been concerned with transforming our urban areas have not confined their efforts to the use of such feeble tools as zoning and land-use planning. There have been bolder and more spectacular efforts—the rebuilding of downtown New Haven, the rebirth of Pittsburgh's Golden Triangle, the execution of New York's Lincoln Center, and so on. These great schemes of bold and aggressive doers have added hope and cheer to those of us who cherish the vitality of the cities.

In surveying these works, however, there are two debts we must discharge. We have an obligation to the men who conceived and executed these latter-day Herculean labors to express our admiration for their efforts. At the same time, we owe it to ourselves to appraise these results in cold and dispassionate terms, to determine how relevant they may be to the total problem of urban renewal.

To gain this perspective, the best vantage point is a helicopter. Hover motionless over America's major cities and you will shortly be impressed by two facts: As a rule, only minute portions of the older areas of our cities have so far been subjected to rebuilding and renewal in the 20th century. In New York City, for instance—a city whose activities in this field have been more extensive than those of any other in the nation—all of the publicly supported renewal projects undertaken over the past quarter century do not cover as much as three square miles of city surface. Second, the areas of the city which have been the subject of the most intensive renewal activity tend generally to be in or very near the city's central business district. Out beyond the comparatively tiny compact central business districts of our giant urban areas, the gray, monotonous jumble of obsolete structures extends almost uninterruptedly in all directions.

The tiny land coverage of the publicly supported urban re-

* Cambridge, Mass.: Joint Center for Urban Studies of MIT and Harvard, 1962, pp. 40–47.

newal programs is certainly not due to a lack of crying need. By almost anyone's aesthetic or structural standards, literally hundreds of square miles in the urban areas of America should long ago have been torn down. Yet there have been periods of time when uncommitted Federal funds have gone begging for lack of acceptable projects.

Why should acceptable projects have been so hard to find? There are a number of answers to the question. First of all, one has to understand that an urban renewal project is usually a partnership between governmental and private interests; the government procures the site, using its powers of condemnation as necessary, and it turns the site over to private redevelopers at a substantial discount from the acquisition price. The private redeveloper, therefore, must see a possibility for profit; he must see an opportunity to rebuild on the site and to find renters or buyers for the new properties.

At this point, our harassed redeveloper is between the devil and the deep blue sea. Shall he plan to build a little patch of new construction—a small oasis in a sea of decaying structures? If so, though his costs and commitments may be small, his chances of finding renters for his redeveloped properties will be small as well. For who among those capable of paying the $40 or $50 per room for rent would want to wade through the filth and insecurity of the rundown, obsolete neighborhood in order to reach his concrete-and-brick oasis in the city?

Alternatively, then, should our redeveloper cut a wide swath through the city, with a giant redevelopment covering half a square mile or so? But that alternative is just as unprepossessing as the first. It demands the closing of streets, the rerouting of traffic, the reorganization of utilities. It entails staggering financial commitments. And it requires a judgment of market demand for a supply of housing so large as to frighten off the hardiest developer and the most intrepid financier. In a word, the problem seems utterly impossible. Almost impossible, anyway. For there is one place in the built-up portions of the old cities where, with energy and imagination, there is just a chance that a good-sized project may be carried off. That place is in or near the central business district.

The reasons why the central business district should be attractive for redevelopment when the rest of the city usually offers so little attraction are all implicit in what I have said earlier. First, the central business district, unlike the rest of the older portions of the obsolescent cities of America, continues to harbor some elements of vitality and growth. The jobs which demand face-to-face communication in America continue to increase as more of our economic activity is concentrated in financial institutions, central offices, law offices, and the like. Not all cities share in this growth, but many do. As a consequence, a number of large central business districts in America promise to register an increase in jobs. Even those that do not show an absolute increase may experience some upgrading in the jobs they harbor. More executives are likely to appear at the center even if the number of clerks, dishwashers, goods handlers, and factory hands declines. This is one of the forces which explains why it is possible for Pittsburgh's Golden Triangle and Philadelphia's Penn Center to rise out of the ashes and find a basis for survival.

The appearance of a larger number of elite jobs at the center, coupled with the growing remoteness of the exclusive communities and golf courses, stimulates the demand for luxury housing close by the central business district. The amounts involved are not very great, measured in terms of the size of the city as a whole. But the demand is nicely concentrated in a tiny area—in or near the central business district, preferably with a pleasant prospect of river or harbor. When all the elements of demand and subsidy are put together, they sometimes provide the basis for tearing down the structures in the thinned-out slums of the ancient city and building imposing new structures on the site.

There may be another major reason, however, why the central business district tends to capture the lion's share of urban redevelopment projects. If one could plumb the minds of the leadership of any large urban community and look upon the urban area as he sees it, I am confident of the image that would emerge. Instead of seeing the central business district as an area containing one-tenth the city's land and one-twentieth its resident population, the central business district would be seen dominating the image. This is the target of the elite's daily commuting trips. It is the area which contains the city hall, the museums, the theater, the night clubs, and the apartments of friends and associates. It is the area in which the history and the tradition of the city are centered. In short, it is the area that contains almost all that matters in the city for most of its civic leadership. No wonder that there should be a strong bias—unintentional though it may be—in favor of the central business district as a redevelopment site.

Of course, even when the proposed redevelopment is in or

near the central business district, there are difficulties to be overcome. In the usual case, the structures that must be razed have been used to house the very poor. No matter how far an ancient slum may have passed its peak of crowding, it still can shelter a considerable number of families. By a process which we have already described, the families that remain tend to be the most defenseless of the slum dwellers—the oldest, the sickest, or the least able. The others, if my analysis is at all right, have already moved on. Some of the stories which emerge in connection with any account of the problems of relocation, therefore, are calculated to wring the heart of the most callous of observers.

Quite apart from the individual misery occasioned by relocation, one may very well raise questions about the wrecking operation from another point of view. Granting the fact that the situation for the poor is improving, not retrogressing, are we yet prepared to say that it is desirable to cut down the supply of housing available to them? Should we not limit the amount of redevelopment to the amount of low-cost public housing that can be built nearby?

These are the questions that public-spirited groups are prone to ask. Reasonable though these questions may appear upon their face, they seem to me to lead to a public policy which is misdirected, distorted, and unhelpful.

That the poor need housing, I have no doubt. But their housing needs are growing far faster in the suburbs than in the old cities. It is in the suburbs that one finds the growing job markets for unskilled labor. Unless we are prepared to impose on the low-income groups the added burden of commuting outward every day from the older city sections, we are doing them no favor to rebuild housing for them in the city centers.

True, something is better than nothing. But "nothing" is not the alternative here. The poor, I said earlier, tend to create their own housing supply simply by ostentatiously bidding for it in the older suburbs. I would myself be inclined to speed that process. Instead of building low-priced subsidized housing in the old cities, I would bend every effort to speed the movement of the poor to the older suburbs. Two measures in particular could contribute to that end. First, the money spent on low-cost public housing construction and operation could be used instead as a direct subsidy to assist families in the payment of their rent. Second, the poor of the cities, handicapped by ignorance and fright, could be helped by public agencies in the search for suburban space. This kind of assistance need not be limited to those families which may have been dispossessed by urban renewal projects; in fact, such families are less likely to be outstanding candidates for suburban living space than some of the younger and more aggressive breadwinners who have already shown sufficient energy to pull themselves out of the oldest of the slum areas. Help in locating better space, therefore, ought to be more widely available to people who live in areas of substandard housing.

Indeed, my strong inclination would be to provide public help for the poor not only in their search for better housing but in the whole process of adaptation to the urban environment. The case for such assistance is especially strong in areas where the poor consist principally of newly arrived immigrants. In this setting, a little help can go a long way—help in looking for a job, help in finding living space, help in locating the requisite medical assistance or educational facilities. This is no new idea. But now that we have recognized the utility of easing the adaptation process through the manning of an agricultural field service, a depressed areas bill, and an overseas Peace Corps, perhaps we may be moved to apply the principle more broadly.

Finally, it would be worthwhile to experiment with the relaxation of building codes, in order to make a $6,000 or $8,000 structure a possibility once more. Obviously, one would not want to relax provisions which are genuinely essential to health and safety. On the other hand, it is a little ironic to lock the poor into structures in the old city which are both unhealthful and unsafe in the interests of protecting them from lesser risks in a much more healthful and safe setting.

Urban renewal, however, need not be limited to the type of operation we have just discussed. Some of the land uses of our major American cities, whether or not they were appropriate for the 19th and early 20th century, are ludicrously inappropriate today. The placement of the railroad yards in most cities is a striking case in point. In Chicago, Philadelphia, New York, New Orleans, Washington, Pittsburgh, and many other urban areas, the railroad yards preempt some of the choicest and most attractive sites of the metropolis—close inside the urban mass, situated on river banks. The volume of freight passing through the yards goes down each year. The freight that is left can often be much better handled from new locations at the edge of the urban mass.

One day, perhaps, when present patterns of rail freight haulage have gone to join the dodo bird, the giant sites will be abandoned and may revert to other uses, such as river-front recreation or attractive housing. But before that happens in the ordinary course, if it ever does, railroad managements and regulatory bodies will have to be roused from their lethargy or will have to be overrun by some higher authority. And one way or another, the cities and towns involved will have to be persuaded to relinquish their tenacious grip on a tax-paying property, albeit a dying one, before the property is utterly dead as a revenue producer.

The case of the railroad property illustrates a much more general problem of many of America's older cities. Beyond the immediate limits of the central business district, extending deep in every direction, are many miles of structures which will not be recaptured within our lifetimes. In these areas, in the normal course, we can expect the structures to continue to decay, the populations gradually to decline and thin out, the jobs slowly to fall off in number. The wistful anticipation that young middle-class couples or old childless ones may come flocking back to reclaim these obsolescent neighborhoods is, as I have insisted, quite groundless. Of course, we will always be able to identify some cases out of our personal experiences which fit any pattern we seek. But even though there may be a crack or two in the picture window, it will not be sufficient to spark a large-scale return from the suburbs to the central cities.

I can, however, envisage two contingencies which may set this prophecy on its head. One is the possibility that we may simply run out of urban land in America. If I have analyzed the process of spread correctly, however, this is unlikely to occur for a considerable time to come. The second possibility is that of recapturing and redeveloping urban neighborhoods in vast parcels—by the square mile rather than by the acre. Once a piece of real estate has been acquired which is so large as to insulate it utterly from the moldering neighborhoods around it—once it is sufficiently large to be equipped with its own parks, schools, libraries, stores, and social structure—then the possibility of successfully reusing the land for middle-income living increases considerably.

To be sure, such a pattern of redevelopment conjures up an image of the Golden Ghetto set down in surrounding squalor. But until the social values of America's middle-income groups have undergone a revolution, this may be the only pattern on which the middle-income groups would consider reusing the inlying sites of the decaying cities. And if the middle-income groups balk at reusing these sites, there is no other use of which I am aware that has such extensive land-using needs as to offer a real alternative.

THE RELATION OF LOCAL GOVERNMENT
STRUCTURE TO URBAN RENEWAL*

George S. Duggar†

Enthusiasts for a municipal activity which demands wide cooperation from all corners of local government are often likely to favor a clear hierarchy of authority, in which the policy is formulated at the top level of local government—whether it be mayor, council, or city manager—and then is put into effect from above. On the other hand, enthusiasts for a narrowly limited and self-contained activity are likely to favor granting to the organization responsible for the activity a substantial independence from the usual city hall chain of command. Since urban renewal requires both the widespread cooperation of many existing local government departments and agencies and the pursuit of some relatively limited and self-contained new activities, it is understandable that there has been no generally accepted doctrine as to which local government structure is the best for accomplishing urban renewal.

Adding to the complexity of discovering an optimum municipal organization for urban renewal is the fact that the administration of a redevelopment program does not end at the local level. Federally aided local renewal programs involve the close participation of the federal government—as well as that of private organizations, business firms, civic associations, neighborhood groups, and many others. How may all these elements best be coordinated?

Urban renewal is not so narrow and so immediate an objective that renewal enthusiasts dare neglect general local government procedures or authority structure. It is not so broad an objective that whatever contributes to good procedure and executive power, in general, will necessarily be good for urban renewal. Renewal involves "middle-range" objectives which demand both a certain freedom of action in limited fields, and some centralization of responsibility and authority in local

* FROM *Law and Contemporary Problems* Vol. XXVI (Winter 1961), pp. 49–56 (selected portions).

† B.A. 1936, M.A. 1937, University of Wisconsin; A.M. 1944, Ph.D. 1956, Harvard University. Public Administration Analyst, Bureau of Public Administration, University of California (Berkeley), since 1952.

government. In this connection, consider the recent observation of a businessman that "in the past we have generally thought of municipal operations as separate and distinct service functions—police, fire, schools, zoning, sanitation, and so forth . . . the greatest impact of federal programs for urban renewal has been to change completely our purposes and aims of city government. While municipal services continue to be important, we must now look additionally for local governments to think in terms of the economic growth and development of the community."[1]

I. THE URBAN RENEWAL ENTERPRISE

Because of this dual focus of urban renewal, it may be helpful to examine urban renewal as an *enterprise*. An enterprise is defined as "an attempt or project, especially one which involves activity, courage, energy, or the like; an important undertaking."[2] A description of local government organization in urban renewal may appropriately begin with this awareness that widely varying participants engage together in an activity having important substantive goals, demanding a high level of activity, and calling for a forward-looking and venturesome frame of mind in which prospects are weighed and a strategy developed to overcome anticipated obstacles. This is a special type of administration. The activities which the literature of administration illuminates range from routine to innovative, from the largely habitual to the freshly planned.[3] We must be prepared for a large measure of innovative management and freshly planned organization when we attempt to describe the administration of urban renewal.

[1] Palmer, *National Programs Affecting Urban Economic Growth,* in COMMITTEE FOR ECONOMIC DEVELOPMENT, THE LITTLE ECONOMIES: PROBLEMS OF UNITED STATES AREA DEVELOPMENT 48 (1958).

[2] WEBSTER'S NEW INTERNATIONAL DICTIONARY OF THE ENGLISH LANGUAGE 853 (2d ed. unabridged, 1950).

[3] The literature of administrative analysis attempts to formulate general perspectives for understanding local organization. Sometimes the emphasis is on a goal or goal cluster such as "efficiency and economy," sometimes on a method such as "scientific administration," sometimes on realistic analysis of power as in the "pressure group" (or "interest group") and "community power structure" approaches. Sometimes social psychology is stressed in the analytical scheme. Each of the perspectives has added to a general understanding of administration; but at present, we are left with a description which concentrates on one organization at a time and on its "equilibrium" condition, rather than its process of organizing and changing.

The concept of an enterprise is important not only for what it *is*, but also for what it *is not*. An enterprise is not necessarily fully recognized from the start by all its participants; and it may have a structure different from that of any of the formal organizations which participate in it. To be sure, an enterprise's structure may parallel that of a formal organization; but the differences between an enterprise and a formal organization, as well as the rather abstract similarities, are important for our purposes. A formal organization may participate in several enterprises, and an enterprise may depend upon the participation of several formal independent organizations. The most familiar example of an enterprise may be a construction project in which are associated, for the time being, several independent organizations, a client, architects, engineers, contractors, subcontractors, and local building inspectors—all ordinarily independent but all cooperating in one way or another in a project.

All federally aided local urban renewal enterprises draw upon the federal government, some local government or governments, some private firms acting as redevelopers or rehabilitators, some households and firms which own affected property, some civic organizations as supporters or opponents of urban renewal, and the mass media as channels of communication and information. It is difficult to coordinate all of these elements within the framework of a particular local situation. Nonetheless, the relationships, one to the other, of these different participants in the urban renewal enterprise cannot be neglected—nor the import of those relationships in determining which kind of internal organization in local government is most suitable for renewal. What guidance does the enterprise perspective offer toward the optimum form of local government structure for accomplishing urban renewal?

Obviously, not all interested citizen organizations can be lumped together (like a united fund, or community chest) into a single superorganization. And even if this were possible, it would still be necessary to allow for the role of the federal government, mass media, and "the market" for blighted and redeveloped properties. Furthermore, account must be taken of the varying degrees of independence among different local governments—and even among the units nominally within one local government. For instance, the territorial fractionation displayed in metropolitan areas, which contain on the average about 100 local governments each, may affect urban renewal. And surely it is not unimportant to urban renewal in a central city when a ring of suburbs maintains building and subdivision standards which discourage construction of low- and middle-value residential housing, or when a suburban government opposes dispersion of minority ethnic groups.

Overlying government units may also have their effect, favorable or unfavorable. For instance, the actions of the county government may affect solution of the relocation and rehousing problems. And the independent school board or district may be enthusiastic about the opportunity through urban renewal to enlarge school playgrounds and improve the surrounding area as a residential neighborhood. In other words, many activities important to urban renewal lie outside the local government's direct control—irrespective of the internal structure of the local government itself.

Consider also the formally independent municipal bodies politic and corporate, such as the thousand or more housing authorities (many authorized to conduct redevelopment), and the hundreds of similarly constituted redevelopment agencies.[4] Also, bodies within city government—such as planning or zoning commissions, or boards of adjustment—may be possessed of a degree of independence, and often are headed by a board with long, staggered terms or by a directly elected official. Moreover, the units important in urban renewal may be so widely and thinly scattered among major city government departments that no department head would make urban renewal his major responsibility. In this event, which would better accord with renewal administrative needs—superimposing a renewal staff coordinator over all local government renewal activities, or transferring some to a new line "Department for Urban Renewal"?[5]

In practice, many cities do not bother to use either alternative. Among 242 cities of 5,000 or more population which reported on the coordination of renewal in a survey conducted

[4] NAT'L ASS'N OF HOUSING AND REDEVELOPMENT OFFICIALS, HOUSING AND URBAN RENEWAL DIRECTORY 232 (1958).

[5] The literature of administration calls for supplementing the executive model by grouping activities "like" in purpose, process, clientele, or service area. See, e.g., LUTHER GULICK & LYNDALL URWICK (EDS.), PAPERS ON THE SCIENCE OF ADMINISTRATION 15 (1937). The idea that a group of activities are "like" in the sense that they serve renewal purposes, or follow renewal processes, or serve a renewal clientele, or come to bear on renewal areas assumes at least a potential renewal enterprise. That potential enterprise is defined by the opportunities indicated by federal and state legislation and by the local situation and by experience in other localities which have availed themselves of similar opportunities.

in 1958, only 158 reported a central agency or official co-ordinating or administering "a substantial amount of the urban renewal program."[6] The other thirty-five per cent did not claim to have a central agency. Furthermore, some of the central agencies are merely committees; of the 158 cities, only 127 had a full-time director of the central renewal agency. In fifty-three of these 127 cities, the director of the central agency was appointed by a corporately independent redevelopment or renewal agency, which may not have authority over any city department and nowhere exerts police power for enforcement of ordinances governing the conditions or construction of housing.[7] There, in terms of formal organization, the "central" agency was not in a position to insist on coordination among the enforcement agencies and the redevelopment and public housing activities.

Even when the central coordinating agency for urban renewal is itself part of the city government, it ordinarily lacks some of the formal authority to obtain absolute adherence to its decisions. In the survey, this held true of all the full-time directors of central renewal agencies—thirty-one appointed by city managers, twenty-one by mayors, and seven by city councils.

II. HISTORICAL INFLUENCES AND FEDERAL REQUIREMENTS

Certain historical influences are reflected today in the municipal organizational structure within which urban renewal must operate. The professionalization of city government which was accelerated by the reform movement in the second half of the nineteenth century was eventually extended to the chief executive in the form of council-manager government—which also ordinarily strengthened the entire hierarchy of authority in city government. However, even in council-manager cities, there are marked variations today in the extent to which a well-defined hierarchy of authority exists in such local government. Still less hierarchical are some of the cities having mayor-council government and the thirteen per cent of Amer-

[6] Lange, *Housing and Urban Renewal Redevelopments in 1958,* in INTERNATIONAL CITY MANAGERS ASS'N, MUNICIPAL YEAR BOOK 324 (1959).

[7] One model state enabling act circulating in 1953 proposing police powers for Conservation Authorities is reviewed in JACK M. SIEGEL & C. WILLIAM BROOKS, SLUM PREVENTION THROUGH CONSERVATION AND REHABILITATION 139 (1953).

ican cities of 5,000 persons or more which have commission government.[8]

The Great Depression encouraged establishment of municipal tax and debt limitations; and these limitations are, of course, very significant in the allocation of municipal resources for urban renewal. Furthermore, during the Depression, a number of independent authorities were spawned, which in many instances became models for urban renewal commissions or were themselves entrusted with responsibility for the urban renewal enterprise. Under the Housing Act of 1937,[9] annual grants were made to local housing authorities, which were separate corporate bodies and which, on the basis of promised federal grants and anticipated rents from public housing projects, could borrow funds to build the projects. Since the debt was incurred by the housing authority, rather than the city, an escape was provided from debt limits which the downward drift of assessed values during the Depression had made especially onerous. The corporate authority device had obvious relevance as a means for freeing urban renewal enterprises from municipal debt limitations. On the other hand, the relative independence of the corporate authority— due to long, staggered terms of the members of their governing boards[10] and freedom from personnel and budgetary controls—presented problems in coordination.

Federal requirements are relevant for the distribution of authority among private, municipal, and federal participants. The Declaration of National Housing Policy emphasizes private participation and local government responsibility.[11]

[8] See section on governmental data in INT'L CITY MANAGERS ASS'N, MUNICIPAL YEAR BOOK (annually).

[9] 50 Stat. 891, 42 U.S.C. § 1409 (1958).

[10] Typically, a commission of from three to seven members, usually five, heads the local housing authority. Terms ordinarily do not exceed five years, but commissioners may be reappointed. CAL. HEALTH & SAFETY CODE § 34272; ILL. ANN. STATS. ch. 67½, § 3 (1959); MICH. COMP. LAWS ch. 125 (1952); MO. REV. STAT. ch. 99 (1956); OHIO REV. CODE SERVICE ANN. § 3735.01 (1956); PA. STAT. ANN. tit. 35, ch. 18, § 1545 (1956); TENN. CODE ANN. tit. 13, ch. 9 (1956). Note that in Ohio, only two members of five on a metropolitan housing authority are appointed by the mayor. Two are appointed by courts and one by the board of county commissioners.

[11] 63 Stat. 413 (1949), 42 U.S.C. § 1451 (1958). State statutes do not greatly change the breadth of goals, since the statements of purpose in the statutes of the several states conform so closely to national legislation and to each other. Indeed, the state enabling statutes tend to be kept in conformity with federal legislation as it is amended, so that the localities may be in a position to utilize all available federal aid what-

The emphasis on private enterprise is expressed further through project planning procedures which call for evaluation of the project's soundness in terms of market demand. The emphasis on citizen participation is manifested in the workable program requirement with respect to such participation, and through provisions for public hearings. The emphasis on local government responsibility is seen in requirements that each project application have the approval of the local governing body and each workable program bear the signature of the city's chief executive.

Contrasting with these unequivocal procedures is the circumspect federal language concerning the structure within local government. The National Housing Act of 1949 refers to a local public agency as "any State, county, municipality, or other governmental entity or public body, or two or more such entities or public bodies, authorized to undertake the project for which assistance is sought."[12] To apply prior expertise obtained with publicly financed low-rent housing, many states assigned redevelopment to local housing authorities as an additional duty—and sometimes formally redesignated them housing and redevelopment authorities. Other states provided for a new type of authority with its own governing commission, executive director, and staff—a structure similar to the housing authority's. A few states quite early enabled city governments themselves to conduct redevelopment operations or permitted local choice of administrative structure. In federal language, these are all referred to as "local public agencies."

Of key importance has been the broad definition of local public agency (LPA). The federal government contracts with it; but its meaning varies from place to place according to the types permitted by state laws. Under the Housing Act of 1949, few states enabled the city to be its own local public agency;[13] the role of the city government was limited. City Council approval of project plans was, however, required as a condition of federal aids. An early form of model state enabling legislation suggested by the Housing and Home Finance Agency (HHFA) offered no inducement for states to permit local choice of the type of LPA. However, subsequent

ever the current emphasis. In taking property by eminent domain, the use of the taxing power, and so forth, state constitutional restrictions do, however, sometimes hover in the background as a limitation on the objectives which can be pursued under urban renewal.

[12] 63 Stat. 420, 42 U.S.C. § 1460(h) (1958).
[13] Among the early ones were Michigan, New York, and Ohio.

to the Housing Act of 1954, HHFA proposed an enabling statute designed to encourage more local experimentation, and specifically to place the city government and its chief executive in an important role; under this proposal, urban renewal authority would be "conferred on the municipality itself or on one of several other prescribed public bodies selected by the municipality." For states with enabling legislation which followed the earlier model, HHFA stood ready to aid in modifying legislation to permit greater local option. Under the Housing Act of 1949 and related federal regulations, the only city official whose signature had to appear on applications was one "required to sign" under state law or one who served as "recording officer" for the local governing body. The city's chief executive came into a formal role in federal project regulations in 1954:[14]

> When it appears from the initial application for an advance of Federal funds for an urban renewal project that the proposed project will involve activities to be carried out by some entity other than the Local Public Agency submitting the application —such as the municipality—it will be necessary that the application be accompanied by satisfactory evidence that such other entity will actually carry out such activities and has the capacity to do so. Such evidence may consist of an appropriate statement of the chief executive of such entity.

The Local Public Agency Letter outlining this requirement also suggested that "consideration may be given by the community to the desirability of establishing an office for the over-all coordination of urban renewal activities in the community." While there is no requirement that this be a city official, it is noted that, "in some cities, a coordinator for such purposes has been appointed by the mayor, and such coordinator reports directly to the mayor respecting the performance of his functions."[15]

The fourth of the seven elements of the Workable Program requires "a firmly established administrative responsibility and capacity for enforcement of codes and ordinances and for carrying out renewal programs and projects."[16] This has not been used as a springboard for the federal government to leap into the local organization pool. Examination of regional

[14] Urban Renewal Administration, Local Public Agency Letter No. 45, 1954, pp. 1–14.

[15] Ibid.

[16] HOUSING AND HOME FINANCE AGENCY, HOW LOCALITIES CAN DEVELOP A WORKABLE PROGRAM FOR URBAN RENEWAL 8 (1956).

office memoranda on the subject indicates that the requirement has been brought to bear chiefly on code enforcement agencies, and there chiefly to assure that personnel will be adequate. Federal literature suggests that "a local official be assigned the responsibility for preparing for the signature of the chief executive of the local government an application for initial certification of a workable program,"[17] but this official need not be a subordinate of the city executive. Indeed, in many cities, the Workable Program is prepared by the staff of a corporate authority; in some cities, by planning commission staff; in others, by a consulting firm. It is by no means settled that the immediate staff of the chief executive prepares the Workable Program.

III. RELATIONSHIP BETWEEN URBAN RENEWAL ACHIEVEMENT AND FORM OF GOVERNMENT

In pursuit of the broad objectives set forth in federal and state statutes, a renewal program is locally developed which can induce the participation of several formally independent organizations and individuals. Within the generally blighted area, a particular portion is chosen as the first project. It may be chosen not because it is the most blighted portion, but because the market for renewed property there is most assured, or because the owners of property there have the financial credit which most readily permits them to participate, or because in this section there is a local organization which best assures neighborhood communication and cooperation, or because the location is so prominent that its renewal will demonstrate the program to most of the city's citizens.

As urban renewal proceeds into the first project and beyond to later projects, there will be ebbs and flows in active participation and public interest. Of course, the execution of a project will be widely regarded as the single great moment for changing the character of an area, so that public interest will be heightened in this stage. And perhaps the long preparation and planning for the project or the struggles of disposition will be less actively supported by the public. Perhaps, too, one project will attract special attention, and everything later will seem anticlimactic.

Under these circumstances, to achieve both the early accomplishment of statutory objectives and the building of an

[17] *Id.* at 3.

enterprise with assured continuity sufficient to complete the urban renewal task, a strategy is needed which will guide the choices to be made between myriad competing alternatives.[18] The standard for evaluating urban renewal achievement must reflect this variability of strategy and must reckon not only how much *has been* accomplished, but also how much now *appears probable* of accomplishment.

[18] The choices, of course, are limited in many respects by reason of the procedures prescribed in federal and state legislation and regulations. For instance, the federal statutory emphasis on cooperation between public and private participants tends to receive strong local support and itself becomes both a program objective and a determinant of the authority of each urban renewal participant. State laws may determine the form of local government organization. As a consequence of these constraints, the local choices are more in the nature of alternatives for cultivating a given seed, rather than for creating a new product.

URBAN RENEWAL AND THE REFORMER

Jewel Bellush and Murray Hausknecht

This is a story about urban renewal and politics at the neighborhood level. It is an American success story, and as in all such stories, especially those dealing with political success, it represents a fusion of idealism, ambition, and a shrewd eye for the main chance. It highlights a set of problems that renewal presents to an aspiring, young politician, and so brings it into focus as a source of political opportunities and dilemmas. As each problem is met and overcome, we see how a specific project becomes shaped by the political processes of the society.[1]

THE SCENE

The Sixth Assembly District North on the East Side of Manhattan was, during the period of the story, an irregularly shaped district lying between Lexington or Third Avenues and the East River, and stretching as far south as 18th Street and north to 40th Street. Fifty years ago, when Boss Murphy ruled Tammany Hall, it was part of the Gaslight District, and included Murphy's home club located among a dense concentration of Irish residents. The Irish are still highly visible in the district, but by the end of World War II there were also large numbers of Italians; a large concentration of the city's Armenians; Jews; and a scattering of other ethnic groups. The ethnic diversity, however, did not reflect political diversity; as in all low-income neighborhoods dominated by old-law tenements, the population was stanchly Democratic. Except for the Catholic churches and their related organizations, the local Democratic Club was the only association of any consequence.

During the forties the Sixth A.D. North began to interest real estate men. The Metropolitan Life Insurance Company had built Stuyvesant Town just outside the southern boundar-

[1] We wish to thank Mr. Shanley Egeth for allowing us to question him at great length about the politics of the Sixth Assembly District North and the part he played in them. The authors, of course, bear sole responsibility for all descriptions and interpretations of the events related here.

ies of the district, and shortly afterward completed Peter Cooper Village just to the north and within the boundaries of the district. These solidly middle-class projects displaced many previous residents in the area, almost all of whom could not afford the rents of the new housing. One of the attractions was its easy access to the work, cultural, and recreational facilities of the city. The success of Stuyvesant Town and Peter Cooper Village clearly demonstrated that the Sixth A.D. North had an excellent potential as a desirable middle-class residential area. By the early fifties other private builders were beginning to move into the district. Robert Moses, surveying the situation from his position as head of the city's housing and slum clearance program, also saw the possibilities disclosed by Metropolitan Life's venture. He was interested in ridding the area of its old-law tenements, and in the construction of middle-income and luxury housing. Therefore, when New York University suggested a Title I project for area south of Bellevue Hospital, where N.Y.U. had a large medical rehabilitation center, Moses encouraged the plan. But the only part of the proposed redevelopment scheme that survived was a housing development, Kips Bay.

The initial result of the project was a municipal scandal. At that time private developers were responsible for both clearance and relocation, and the city exercised relatively little control over their activities. After taking title to the Kips Bay land the developers neither cleared the land nor maintained the existing housing, and made little effort to assist people in relocating. For many years the developers of Kips Bay engaged in a profitable "slumlord" operation, and when the site was eventually cleared it remained empty for three more years. Finally, Moses arranged for Webb & Knapp, whose president, William Zeckendorf, was one of the pioneers in the profitable use of Title I, to take over Kips Bay and another project afflicted with the same ills.[2] But the long delay plus the new ownership meant a radical change in the nature of the Kips Bay development. Originally conceived as housing renting between twenty-three and twenty-nine dollars a room, at completion it rented at sixty to eighty dollars per room. For the residents of the community Kips Bay became a symbol of redevelopment, a constant reminder that renewal brought them no benefits.

While Kips Bay was still stalled Moses announced another

---

[2] *New York Times*, July 24, 1959.

new development for the Sixth A.D. North, the Gramercy Park North Project. The sponsor was to be a corporation controlled by the family of the wife of the local state assemblyman, and the latter was to be counsel to the corporation. This project had to be abandoned when the Board of Estimate refused to approve it. Thereupon Moses announced, much to the surprise of federal and local officials who said they had not been consulted, that the money the government had earmarked for Gramercy Park North would be transferred to a new project, Bellevue South.[3] The manifest objective of the new plan was to help ease the difficulties of Bellevue Hospital, one of the city's largest, by providing adequate housing for its large staff of internes, nurses, and clerical workers. Over two-thirds of the units of the proposed project were to be efficiency apartments, i.e., sufficient for single adults or, at most, married couples without children. Although approximately 2250 dwelling units would be eliminated by site clearance, the initial plan contained no discussion of relocation procedures.

The announcement of Bellevue South gave a further impetus to real estate speculators and builders to assemble land parcels adjacent to the proposed redevelopment area. All this activity caused much anxiety among the residents of the area who had the history of Kips Bay and Stuyvesant Town behind them. There was particular uneasiness among Catholics; the other projects had meant the loss of many parishioners, and now Bellevue South seemed to threaten the existence of a small Catholic parish whose borders were virtually contiguous with that of the project.

But 1959 was also an important year in local politics, for it was a year when local party leaders came up for re-election. In the Sixth A.D. North the heaviest Democratic enrollment in the district was in the Bellevue South area.

ENTER THE REFORMER

About three months before the announcement of Bellevue South a young lawyer moved into the Sixth A.D. North. Shanley Egeth, like many lawyers, had always been attracted by the thought of a career in politics, and after the war he became active in Democratic Party politics in the Bronx. There he became a precinct captain and vice president of a

[3] *Ibid.*, June 8 and October 1, 1959.

Regular party club, but like many other young Democrats in the early postwar years he was dissatisfied. Even those who experienced no difficulties in staying within the bounds of conventional thought and procedures of the party found that it offered few opportunities for ambitious men. But Egeth and others felt that new ideas and new organizational principles had to be introduced into the party if the ideals of the New Deal and the Fair Deal were to be achieved. In 1948 many of them, including Egeth, formed the Young Democrats, and their organization along with the Lexington Club became the basis of the reform movement in the Democratic Party in the city. Throughout the fifties Egeth, though remaining a resident of the Bronx, participated regularly in Manhattan's reform politics, and he frequently campaigned for friends running under the reform banner. In the course of these activities he became familiar with the Sixth A.D., and the local reform club that was having great difficulties making headway against the regular oganization. In 1958 Egeth became president of the Young Democrats in the city, and the organization that year adopted a policy of encouraging its members to become more actively engaged in grass roots politics. In 1959, therefore, Egeth joined the reform club in the Sixth A.D., and, at the urging of its members, entered the race for leader in the Sixth A.D. North a few weeks before the plan for Bellevue South was made public.

DEFEAT WITH HONOR

The redevelopment plan posed a dilemma for Egeth that, as he puts it, "provided an opportunity to blend various conflicting pressures." A more disinterested observer might say that he was faced less with "opportunity" than cruel necessity. His political base was the support of the middle-class reformers who, as a political type, have been characterized as "amateur politicians" who see "the political world more in terms of ideas and principles than in terms of persons." In contrast, the "professional" is interested in winning elections, and is more likely to adopt a pragmatic position with respect to issues and people.[4] The reformers as a matter of liberal principle favored slum clearance programs, and for Egeth to unconditionally oppose slum clearance would have cost him a significant degree of reform support. On the other

[4] James Q. Wilson, *The Amateur Democrat* (Chicago: University of Chicago Press, 1962), p. 3.

hand, Egeth, sensitive to the political climate of the district, knew that a major portion of the electorate was opposed to Bellevue South. To further complicate matters, in the long run the development was in the interests of reform politics: The new housing would increase the number of middle-class voters who could be expected to be more sympathetic to the reformers than to the old-style clubhouse politicians. While Egeth was aware of this consideration, it was overridden by his feeling that the plan was unfair to the site residents.

For the incumbent leadership, Bellevue South was no problem. Soon after it became public, local business and real estate men plus some residents formed a Bellevue South Preservation Committee (BSPC). The district leader attended its meetings as a representative of the voters, thus openly allying himself with the project's foes. Egeth viewed the Committee with some suspicion, since he believed the real estate men were simply interested in blocking Title I redevelopment so that later they could move in on the land for luxury housing. These suspicions provided him with the cue for his initial tactic. He called a public meeting of site residents at which he attacked the real estate interests who "were merely waiting to take over and evict the tenants when they secured the property for themselves." He also indicted landlords who were already, in anticipation of redevelopment, neglecting proper maintenance of their houses. Several hundred people, including the district leader, turned out for the meeting. There was considerable support in the audience for a plea, voiced by many, for cooperation among all those who were concerning themselves with protecting the interests of those affected by the project.[5] One result of the meeting was the appointment of Egeth to the Executive Board of the BSPC. Since he suspected that the original representatives of the tenants on the Committee were carefully chosen by the real estate interests, he successfully insisted that the Executive Board be enlarged to include additional, legitimate tenant representation. In political terms the meeting gave him wider "exposure," and a chance to identify himself with the working-class population of the district.

He followed his initial move by working out a position enabling him to consolidate his gains, and at the same time retain the support of the reformers. Many of the latter, of course, were fully in accord with Egeth's criticism of the plan.

[5] *New York Times,* August 13, 1959.

But an equally significant number were afraid that Egeth's position would help kill the slum clearance project. His campaign speeches turned on the theme that Bellevue South was not responsive to the needs of the residents of the district. Another prominent theme featured the evils of "the bulldozer"; many buildings in the development area were salvageable, he maintained, and should not be indiscriminately razed. At the same time he approached the head of the city's newly established Rehabilitation and Conservation Program to explore the possibilities of having some of the area designated for rehabilitation rather than clearance. This, of course, was a "constructive approach," though unsuccessful, and helped mollify his uneasy reform supporters. It was also an approach that was adopted by the BSPC as its own position. The strategy and tactics were apparently successful. While he lost the primary, the margin of defeat was three to two; not at all a bad showing for a reformer the first time out in a district like the Sixth A.D. North.[6]

A Narrow Victory

Redevelopment projects involve long delays that usually work to no one's benefit. Egeth's experience with Bellevue South was no exception to the rule; it remained a critical issue that he had to take a stand on through three elections. His management of the issue is testimony to the combination of luck and skill that is the hallmark of the successful politician.

In February 1960 the walls of the pre-Civil War elementary school located within the site collapsed. While officials were still debating whether to repair the school or abandon it, Egeth called a meeting of residents, ministers, and other local leaders to press for its closing. The city decided to close the school. Meanwhile, Egeth continued his attack on the original Bellevue South proposal. He centered his criticisms on the exclusion of public housing from the site; the lack of any thought given to racial and economic integration; and the complete absence of a concern for the future of site residents who were to be displaced. Egeth was impressed by the residents' desire to remain in the neighborhood, and saw the problem as one of replacing the substandard housing without relocating people from the neighborhood. He believed that

[6] New York City Board of Elections, *Annual Report*, 1959.

he had a solution to the problem, and when in the latter part of 1960 the city held a public hearing on the original proposal, Egeth seized the opportunity to present his alternatives to it. At the hearing were three busloads of residents brought there by the district leader.

Egeth concentrated on the issues of public housing and relocation. He proposed vest-pocket housing for tenants to be relocated, and suggested that the site of the closed elementary school and an adjacent parking lot be used for building 267 low-income units. Their construction would involve no relocation, and once built they could be used to receive residents displaced by site clearance. The regular leadership of the district vehemently opposed Bellevue South; they wanted it to be killed completely. Residents at the meeting greeted Egeth's proposals enthusiastically. Once again it was a strategy that paid off. While still identifying Egeth with the working-class residents it did not alienate any of his reform supporters, since he did not oppose the goal of slum clearance. Moreover, he showed by his concern for public housing that he was committed to traditional liberal principles. His lack of intransigence to the idea of Bellevue South also won him the good will of city officials involved with the project. In September 1961 the election for district leader was a three-way race between Egeth and two regular candidates. Riding the coattails of Robert F. Wagner's anti-boss campaign, Egeth won the election by a margin of two hundred votes.[7]

SUCCESS

Given the closeness of the vote and the special circumstances of the election, there were no grounds for optimism about victory in 1963. The new leader threw himself into the traditional round of activities of a professional party leader: attending a variety of social events; visiting neighborhoods to meet his constituents informally; and extending aid to those with personal problems. But redevelopment still remained a crucial issue for the people of the district and a political problem for Egeth. In addition to the impending demolition of the Bellevue South site, private developers were evicting tenement dwellers as they replaced old buildings with luxury housing. In the objective terms of municipal *realpolitik* the influx of middle-class people would be advantageous to the

[7] *Ibid.,* 1960.

reform leadership in the battle with the old-style clubhouse regulars. But it also represented a danger, since the middle-class voter likes to think of himself as "independent." That is, he cannot be relied upon to vote a straight Democratic ticket in an election. From this perspective one can also say that Egeth's insistence on vest-pocket housing—although motivated by a genuine concern with the needs and desires of his constituents—also served the function of retaining a reliable bloc of Democratic voters in the district. In any case, these were long-range considerations that offered no guide to the immediately pressing realities. Sixty per cent of the community were still tenement house residents, and Egeth, even if he was more professional in his outlook than many of the reform club "amateurs," was committed by his own liberal beliefs to fighting for his constituents.

He began to use his position as a leader and his political credit at City Hall to modify the original Bellevue South plan. One of his first successes was to win a commitment from the city to build Nathan Strauss Houses on the site of the abandoned school and parking lot; a suggestion he first made in 1961. After a long series of negotiations the plan was further modified to drastically reduce the number of efficiency apartments and to increase the number of apartments that could accommodate large families. Egeth also fought for another vest-pocket housing project in an area that had been preempted by private real estate interests as a site for luxury housing. Despite the support of city agencies he was unsuccessful: The HHFA would not approve, because the land was too valuable for public housing. However, as a result of this battle another site within the project area, one requiring no tenant relocation, was found for over 200 units of public housing. Finally, the city agreed to a staged demolition of the site area to alleviate the problems of relocation.

While Egeth was busy battling the redevelopment bureaucracies, he was being attacked by local businessmen and real estate interests. The latter, particularly, were opposed to Bellevue South, because they still wanted the area for private redevelopment. Attempting to take advantage of the residents' anxieties and their hostility to the world of officialdom, they charged that Egeth had sold out the residents by supporting Bellevue South. Just before the 1963 primaries the study plan for the project was released by the city, and it incorporated the modifications Egeth had fought for. At a tumultuous public meeting called under his auspices city redevelopment officials explained the plan to residents of the Sixth. At the meeting his opponents took full advantage of the opportunity to renew their charges of a "sellout." The meeting was the climax of that year's campaign.

Once again it was a three-way race, and once again Egeth won. But this time he had an absolute majority of the votes, and carried twenty-two of twenty-nine election districts, including those located in the tenement house areas. Even without the support of the middle class he would have won the election. In 1965 Shanley Egeth ran unopposed for district leader. Bellevue South? Not completed, of course, but it has contributed to an auspicious start to one career in politics.

THE RENEWAL ENTREPRENEURS

One of the interesting results of Duggar's investigation of renewal and local governmental structure is the tendency for the "success" of the renewal "enterprise" to correlate with the emergence of an "executive mode" of leadership. Someone must bridge the multiple fragments of government that constitute the renewal enterprise. Duggar is not the only one to define renewal as an enterprise, and see the need for decisive leadership.

Working from the all-too-few empirical studies of renewal and local political processes we have attempted in our paper to specify the entrepreneurial function in renewal. The entrepreneur "can get things done," because the administrative agency he heads becomes a relatively autonomous force in the political structure, wheeling and dealing with local politicians, federal officials, and private entrepreneurs. A fundamental problem here is whether or not the renewal entrepreneur is an anarchic force in the democratic processes of an advanced industrial society.

Renewal entrepreneurs are not all alike, and whether one emerges in a community is dependent upon the over-all political structure. In New Haven the entrepreneur is the mayor; indeed, as Robert Dahl, Professor of Political Science of Yale, makes clear, the mayor's political success was closely related to his use of urban renewal as a means of attaining office and remaining in power. He could make a success of renewal, because the political structure allowed him to concentrate the necessary powers in his office. Another political scientist, Harold Kaplan, reports a different situation in Newark, for there the renewal effort is concentrated in the housing authority headed by an appointed official. However, the political structure of Newark is such that it permits a great deal of power to flow toward a bureaucratic official. But he must be politically knowledgeable and skillful; he must be aware at all times that one cannot make renewal bricks without political straw. Another kind of situation is illustrated by the work of two academic experts who have written extensively on city planning and urban politics, Martin Meyerson, and Edward G. Banfield's case study of housing in Chicago, where an old-style political machine is strongly entrenched. The political structure severely limits the possibilities for independent maneuvering by an aspiring entrepreneur, and it is interesting to speculate if Louis Danzig of the Newark Housing Authority would have been as successful if he were in Chicago.

At least equally important as the renewal entrepreneur is the private entrepreneur with whom the former must cooperate. Among the private entrepreneurs in urban renewal are large corporations seeking opportunities for corporate profit in renewal investments. Leon Hickman, a vice president of the Aluminum Company of America, helps us survey the renewal scene from the vantage point of a corporation as entrepreneur. It is interesting to note that first among the "problems" he sees is one that has a political dimension.

THE RELATION OF LOCAL GOVERNMENT STRUCTURE TO URBAN RENEWAL*

George S. Duggar

[Based on Professor Duggar's case studies of a number of cities, he tentatively concludes that while form of government—i.e., mayor or manager—is not decisive as to whether urban renewal is successful, someone in the city with power to coordinate and direct the enterprise is of crucial importance.]

With all these factors in mind, we find that form of government is not decisive. From our survey cities we conclude that:

1. Achievement is not consistently associated with form of government, although council-manager cities have a slight "edge."

2. Mayor-council cities slightly more often than council-manager cities display the city's chief executive as the dominant leadership influence, while council-manager cities slightly more often display him as the most committed active leader.

3. The mode of coordination is slightly more executive in council-manager cities.

4. A combination of form of government and population size may affect the leadership of the executive and mode of coordination.

In respect to population size as the "independent variable," the observers found that:

1. Smaller population was accompanied by primacy of the chief executive in committed renewal activity. No difference appears in the totals to indicate that size affects the chief executive's leadership influence. However, the standardized pairs show his influence greater in small cities. The tendency for mayor-council cities to thrust their chief executives ahead as influential leaders may, therefore, somewhat obscure the greater leadership role of small-city executives.

2. Contrast in population appears not to affect mode of coordination.

3. Larger cities had the higher level of achievement, as judged by the observers.

* FROM *Law and Contemporary Problems*, XXVI (Winter 1961), No. 1, pp. 62–69 (selected portions).

Cities were not preselected for similarity or dissimilarity in mode of coordination. The mode was determined only through the field studies. Lack of preselection has both advantages and disadvantages. When not preselected, all eighteen of the pairs instead of twelve are available for comparison, since we have not eliminated any pairs for known lack of contrast. On the other hand, when we do not preselect, we run the risk of finding very little contrast in mode, a contrast which, of course, would have been assured had we preselected for the purpose of displaying that contrast.

Taking the undifferentiated group of eighteen pairs, we find definite tendencies in respect to each of the characteristics studied. More of the cities with the more executive mode are judged by observers to have a higher recent renewal achievement, a higher cumulative renewal achievement, and to display the chief executive as more dominant in committed activity and also in leadership influence. . . .

Where the city is the LPA or where there is a redevelopment agency, "renewal coordinators" or "directors of renewal" tend to be set up for coordinating redevelopment and code enforcement. This is evidenced by the establishment of such offices and by the centralization of power to resolve differences affecting renewal. Where there is a housing and redevelopment authority, the authority itself usually develops from the outset along executive lines; and this does not change much as urban renewal progresses. In that situation, "bridging" is apparently used to coordinate the authority's activities with those of the local government; the bridgers tend to include commission members who govern the authority, councilmen, and even business and civic leaders without public office, as well as full-time officials. In some small cities, the planning commission serves as the chief coordinating group for urban renewal, and so makes unnecessary any other bridging groups.

In general, where there are local government administrative boards or corporate authorities, there is both a greater need for bridging to take place and a tendency for the chairman and the highest subordinates of boards or commissions with urban renewal roles to lead by bridging. On the other hand, where a chief executive leads the local government and there is a clear hierarchy of authority, there is much less need to bridge. Such bridging as there is tends to be performed by the city's chief executive and his chief subordinate for renewal.

In an agency headed by a board, if anyone is to lead in the

coordination of urban renewal activities with other groups, including the local government, then it is reasonable to expect that function to devolve chiefly upon the board's chairman and its primary executive. They are not likely to disagree strongly with the majority opinion of the board, and are likely to know the agency's problems and needs in more detail than other board members and to possess more comprehensive knowledge than other subordinates. Accordingly, their views may receive considerable deference from board members, subordinates of the agency, and others who deal with the agency. In some instances, the authority accorded to a strong board with determined leadership may impair the ability of the city's chief executive to coordinate the urban renewal enterprise; and he may even lose control over the board to outside influences. At the same time, the board, particularly through the chairman, may win considerable additional support and exert added influence beyond the confines of city government owing to the board members' joint status as officials and as occupants of other positions in the civic and business life of the community.

The type of LPA is not easily changed. State law may provide no option. And even when it does, there is reluctance to change type of LPA when the existing one is effective or where new litigation would be required to test its powers. This inflexibility of LPA type tends to limit the trend toward a more executive mode of coordination in cities with corporate LPAs. Similarly, of course, a weak-mayor structure of city government may impede the emergence of an executive mode. Aside from these structural limits, there seems to be an underlying long-term trend toward a more executive mode for the enterprise. At the earliest stages in a renewal enterprise, caution impedes legislative delegation of authority to central management. The lack of central control appears to reassure those who fear that unwanted types of renewal might be imposed by a central executive. Perhaps these elements feel safer as long as the agencies conducting different types of renewal must compromise and curry popular favor. Where rather evenly divided groups in the community intensely disagree on renewal policy, an executive mode is often avoided, or is adopted only in considerable controversy. This may be most important in cities where urban renewal is expected to extend over a wide area and where the exact nature of the future projects is not known. But a number of factors, including the planning process, encourage a more executive mode in the long run.

As ungrounded fears subside, restrictions tend to be withdrawn. State enabling legislation tends to be amended. As a result of this and their greater confidence, local councils become more willing to take responsibility and more willing to delegate authority, and executives more ready to accept it.

More important in the long-run is probably the progressive accomplishment of those renewal projects which are the easiest to achieve without central management. As the areas qualifying for federal aid and appealing strongly to the market are progressively renewed, the remaining areas become administratively more difficult to renew. And market funds may not flow so readily as before. Furthermore, the projects extend closer together and may require coordination of more varied renewal techniques. That is, the need for administrative coordination tends to increase even as the community's disagreements on renewal policy decline.

Neither the support nor the opposition to an executive mode which we noted exists at early stages of the renewal enterprise should be conceived as rooted ordinarily in public opinion. Most people may be unaware or only dimly aware of the issue. The people who participate actively in the enterprise tend to be most important in it. Some accord authority beyond the formal minimum to an executive only as program and procedures are evolved which are acceptable to them. The inspectors who may be chiefly committed to conservation and rehabilitation, but who also make the first contact with property owners in clearance areas, must overcome fear that a centralized operation would neglect conservation and rehabilitation. The housing authority employees who conduct relocation services on contract must overcome fear that a centralized operation might exclude public housing. The organized downtown interests, whose support is necessary in many ways, including, often times, the financing of the work, must overcome fear that a centralized operation would give insufficient emphasis to the surroundings of downtown or would call for public housing on a scale thought by them undesirable. A more executive mode becomes a real possibility as early fears of these kinds are sloughed off by the potential committed active participants.

Contrary to the usual supposition, urban renewal does not tend to conform more closely to the executive mode in large cities. Indeed, it will be recalled that no significant difference was found in this respect among the cities of different size. The level of achievement was higher, however, among the larger cities, while the level of commitment and activity displayed by the city chief executive was higher in the smaller cities. Apparently there is a selection process which attracts small cities to the renewal program only when there is no strong local opposition to renewal, while in large cities, even intense opposition to certain types of renewal does not create a coalition capable of preventing or cutting off the renewal efforts altogether. Possibly a less executive mode has been actually more functional for the renewal enterprise in some large cities by assuring that there will be discussion and compromise before any particular renewal technique is applied in any specific area.

In those cities which enter the program with less than practically unanimous support, the city chief executive is encouraged to take active and committed leadership, but he may not find it necessary to bring much authority to bear. This would explain the greater commitment and activity without greater leadership influence of the chief executives of the smaller cities.

The greater achievement of the larger cities reported by observers appears to reflect, in part, the greater comprehensiveness of their renewal programs and their greater success in resolving policy differences. The smaller cities which entered the program had a less difficult problem to the extent that they, too, generally agreed on a project. But the observers were not confident that they would continue in the program with additional projects.

TYPE OF LOCAL PUBLIC AGENCY

The chief operating agencies within an urban renewal enterprise, the redevelopment, code enforcement and rehousing agencies, present certain problems in organizing for urban renewal which are explainable in the light of their previous purposes. The three types of LPA utilized in urban development projects differ in their advantages and disadvantages for renewal. The differences were most important in the redevelopment period and in the first years of renewal. The housing and redevelopment authorities had staffs experienced in the fields needed in redevelopment, including relocation, while their unfamiliarity with code enforcement and conservation made it difficult for them to develop a program that would give adequate attention to the potentialities of this form of renewal, and local opposition to many of them made it difficult for them to lead.

The availability of the city machinery for coordination and the established relations to the city's political figures have been points favoring the city LPA in renewal, while their lack of familiarity with relocation and housing has made it difficult for them to develop relocation as an important and integral part of the program.

The redevelopment authorities have been free of fixed public attitudes but have lacked experience. Their formal independence of city hall gave them freedom to develop a fresh approach but threatened to leave them "out of the orbit of power and influence."

In actual practice, the disadvantages of each type have tended to be corrected, although not always soon enough to accommodate local opinion. City LPAs have learned renewal methods. Redevelopment authorities in many cities have proved amenable to central management control and have been brought under city government coordinators or administrators much more often than have housing and redevelopment authorities. Many of the housing and redevelopment authorities have learned the value of code enforcement. While the housing and redevelopment authorities have remained formally independent of city government almost everywhere, bridging groups have linked them with the city and have built more confidence on the part of business participants in the authorities. Even the corporate independence of the housing authorities, which, it will be recalled, was originally necessary if housing debt was not to be charged to the city's debt limit, can disappear where the state courts accept segregation of funds as a substitute for corporate separation.

In many large cities, the environmental code enforcement agencies have been scattered through the city government, and such agencies have been only rudimentary in small cities. Often, state regulations have been the only ones enforced in the latter. In cities of all sizes, the most vigorous enforcement program has sometimes been lodged in the health department, sometimes in the building inspector's office, and occasionally in a consolidated inspections department. Under the federally aided renewal program, widespread adoption of local housing ordinances, emphasis on area-wide enforcement, professionalization of the staffs, and consolidation or coordination of the chief enforcement agencies have been stimulated. In many cities, the city organization displays signs of reorganization for urban renewal chiefly in respect to the enforcement activities.

THE URBAN DEVELOPMENT ENTERPRISE

Currently, major new downtown rebuilding projects are taking their places alongside the more established neighborhood renewal efforts, and alongside the projects for construction of major transportation routes as the three major arms of a city program for the reconstruction of the urban environment. The reorganization for urban renewal must, therefore, provide for further evolution to accommodate a new enterprise. Not only is a more executive organization likely to be desirable for renewal in the long run, but the renewal organization must accommodate, at least in the largest cities, to coordinating arrangements for urban development as a whole. Staff, coordinating, and planning agencies will eventually be needed at this level in large and complex cities.

Many small cities in metropolitan areas do not tend to reach that point. They may contain no vast terminal complexes and not even border a major new transportation artery. Their whole area may be the size of a single renewal project. They may organize simply for *renewal* as a sufficient preparation for the emerging metropolitan-area-wide enterprise of urban *development*.

The cycle of adjustment of formal organization to enterprise and of enterprise to formal organization is occurring, then, once again. The tide of reform which swept across municipal government during three-quarters of a century fed on revulsion at the graft and corruption in public works as well as in other forms of boodle. As one result, departments of public works were created under professional engineers. Such departments, ever since, have offered a focus for planning and power to develop an appropriate network of streets and utilities.

As the tide of reform has swept away many of its own sources, and has gradually ebbed, the city governments have continued to evolve under the impact of newer enterprises. Several of these have contributed to the city government structures of today and to the enterprises which now engage the urban communities. To the use of police powers to close or demolish slum buildings was added the public housing enterprise which replaces slum with publicly-financed, low-rent housing. Mortgage insurance was created and freed house-builders to become mass producers and builder-developers who could develop whole "tracts," including the streets and sewers as well as the houses. Redevelopment constituted a new wave, offering to replace slums with any suitable new land use, public or private. Renewal was originated as an-other wave, offering a variety of treatments according to the character of the area. Currently we are in the midst of a new wave of programs for downtown reconstruction which utilize the renewal organizations and also the departments of public works and other agencies concerned with transportation routes. And, if I am correct, we are now entering into another enterprise and a new cycle. This is an ambitious one. It is proposed to harness downtown reconstruction, urban renewal, and freeway construction to a grand strategy for governing the major elements in the over-all physical pattern of urban areas.

Because cities do not completely integrate the institutions for each new enterprise with the inherited institutions, one may trace the several stages of the civic evolution in the or-ganizational structure of local government. The evolution may also be observed by comparing cities which entered upon all the successive enterprises with cities where some or all of these have failed to attract the community's interest. Some cities are just beginning to take urban renewal seriously. They may be the ones for whom the study of renewal experience may be most directly useful. Study of past experience may be equally relevant for those cities which have long since entered into a renewal enterprise and are ready for a newer urban development drama—but more to acquire self-knowledge, to see their past as prologue. They must also recognize the dif-ferences between renewal and the next enterprise. They must recognize, for instance, that the new enterprises envision the metropolitan areas as a whole, and challenge municipal gov-ernment, even impertinently demanding its credentials as more than a pressure group within the urban community.

Our study stops short of these questions concerning organi-zation for future enterprises. On the other hand, it prepares us to see organization for urban renewal as a problem for one of a series of "long waves" in civil life, each dominated by one or more major enterprises. Probably in each of these waves there is a phase when line and staff organization on the cen-tral management model is the most appropriate model. But an important frontier for administrative theory lies in supplying models appropriate for other phases, and in testing the effectiveness of the line and staff and other models for the necessary transitions, from phase to phase and from long wave to wave. The job of organization in those periods when the central management model is not acceptable is not to be dismissed vaguely as "politics" and "compromise." A whole course of organizational change is needed which will keep the structure in accord with political necessities, including the necessity to serve a community's current enterprises.

ENTREPRENEURS AND URBAN RENEWAL:
THE NEW MEN OF POWER*

Jewel Bellush and Murray Hausknecht

In urban renewal, as elsewhere, there is a gap between the idea and the reality, between the conception and the creation: Throughout the country there are communities with renewal programs that show no material indications of their existence, except, perhaps, a hole in the ground. In other communities "something has happened"; their "success" is indicated by the clearance of blighted areas and new construction. But the renewed areas seem to bear little resemblence to the initial visions as they appeared in the blueprints of the planners or the pictures in the glossy brochures. This state of affairs prompts two inevitable questions: Why are so many renewal programs unsuccessful, even in the most simplistic sense of "success"? Why do "successful" programs leave most observers with the feeling that somewhere the spirit and visions underlying the idea of renewal are lost?

There is only one large-scale, detailed study focusing on this first question that provides information for an answer going beyond the most glittering of generalities—Harold Kaplan's important *Urban Renewal Politics.*[1] Two other studies also provide relevant data, although each of them has a different focus from the other, and are not directly concerned with questions we have raised. Robert Dahl's *Who Governs?* examines urban renewal in New Haven only for the light it casts on his primary interest, but it also illuminates the renewal process.[2] The primary interest of Martin Meyerson and Edward Banfield, *Politics, Planning and the Public Interest,* is testing the adequacy of a conceptual scheme.[3] Yet here, too, much pertinent data is reported. But using data from such diverse sources has some grave disadvantages. Since none of the studies share a common analytical perspective there are few comparable observations. Any attempt to generalize on

* FROM *Journal of the American Institute of Planners,* Vol. 32, (September 1966), No. 5., pp. 289–97.
[1] New York: Columbia University Press, 1963.
[2] New Haven: Yale University Press, 1961.
[3] Glencoe, Ill.: Free Press, 1955.

the basis of case study material, even under optimal conditions, is extremely hazardous, because one never knows if any given case is representative of a universe or which universe. But these are hazards and risks endemic to all social research, and one can do no more than grit one's teeth and brave the perils of generalization, fully aware that they may rest on quicksand.[4]

New Haven, Newark, and New York are "successful" examples of urban renewal, and this means nothing more than "something has happened." Our discussion is wholly in terms of this criterion of success, since the introduction of other criteria would take us too far afield. More meaningful criteria are difficult to set up given the profound ambiguities in the stated goals of urban renewal. In these cities the renewal motor, as it were, has started and is running more or less smoothly, while in other cities all one can hear is silence or the sputtering, cranky sounds of a balky engine. This is not surprising, because even in a "successful" city like New Haven there was initially no agency geared to take advantage of the opportunities offered by federal renewal legislation. Typically, as Kaplan notes, community resources necessary for renewal are dispersed; the community is *structurally* unprepared to meet the imperatives of urban renewal. Therefore, in all "successful" instances of renewal we find the emergence of an agency, exercising broad powers, that effectively pulls together and concentrates energies on renewal. Behind the agency, however, the figure of a single individual can clearly be discerned.

Mayor Richard Lee of New Haven is an excellent example. Lee won a decisive victory campaigning on the issue of the city's need for renewal and the failure of the incumbent administration to implement the existing plans. Once in office he vigorously used his powers to activate the renewal process by reorganizing the administrative structure and putting it under the direction of the talented Edwin Logue. Thus with the support of the electorate for renewal and under the leadership of an energetic mayor willing and capable of using his political

[4] Since rehabilitation is a different renewal process from the more usual redevelopment project we have not attempted to use Peter Rossi and Robert Dentler, *The Politics of Urban Renewal* (New York: The Free Press, 1961). Strictly speaking, the Chicago case reported in Meyerson and Banfield also falls outside "redevelopment," but it is close enough for our purposes.

power, New Haven became a prime example of renewal "success."

However, New Haven is not typical of other cities. In most there is a lack of widespread public support for renewal, and the motive or driving force behind renewal is not centered in the mayor's office. In Newark and New York the mobilization of resources is accomplished by a civil servant, a bureaucrat, who emerges as the analogue of Lee in New Haven. What the civil servant and the elected official share is a common role in the renewal process—they are, as Kaplan insightfully observes, *entrepreneurs*. They seem to have such an extraordinary ability to get things done that an observer is tempted to say that if it were not for a Lee and Logue in New Haven, a Louis Danzig in Newark, or a Robert Moses in New York, there would be no renewal in those cities. And to a certain extent this judgment is correct. But buried in this evaluation is an unanswered question, How do they do it? Surely it is not enough simply to say "individual ability," for this comes uncomfortably close to a great man theory of renewal. Nor does it explain why Logue in Boston does not repeat his triumphs of New Haven. The real problem, then, revolves around the meaning of the entrepreneur's role and the consequences of his entrepreneurship for renewal.

The entrepreneurial role embodies three analytically distinct functions.[5] First, there is an investment function or "capitalist" role, i.e., furnishing the necessary money for an enterprise. Second, the function of maintaining the enterprise as an organization involves a managerial role. Finally, there is the role of the entrepreneur proper who "determine[s] the purpose, the spirit, and the place of the enterprise in the market and the national economy".[6] He is a "creative entrepreneur" when he "effects new combinations of the factors of production."[7] In a modern economy of large-scale enterprises the entrepreneurial role is fused with a managerial function, so that the entrepreneur in reality is an entrepreneur-administrator. However, most managerial roles have no entrepreneurial functions—all managers are not entrepreneurs.

Formally, American political structure places the three

[5] Here we follow Fritze Redlich, "The Business Leader in Theory and Reality," *American Journal of Economics and Sociology*, Vol. 8 (1948–49). This work, in turn, is heavily indebted to the ideas of Joseph Schumpeter. See, for example, *Capitalism, Socialism and Democracy* (New York: Harper & Brothers, 1947).

[6] Redlich, p. 224.

[7] *Ibid.*, p. 226.

functions in the elected executive. As the term implies, he is supposed to administer the machinery of government. The office he occupies, the endorsement of the electorate, and his party position give him a fund of "political capital"—power—that can be "invested" in action toward given ends. Finally, a president or mayor is expected to be a "leader," a prime mover in achieving the ends of the community and the society. Among the renewal entrepreneurs Mayor Lee fits this description. Logue, on the other hand, must be excluded from the entrepreneurial category; he tends to be more a manager than an entrepreneur. When we consider a Danzig or a Moses we are looking at a situation analogous to the modern corporation with its divorce of ownership (capital) from control (entrepreneurial and managerial functions). As salaried employees neither Danzig nor Moses has any capital to invest in a renewal enterprise, and so in New York and Newark the "capitalist" function is separated from the entrepreneurial-managerial function. While Lee as an entrepreneur is meeting the formal prescriptions of his role, Danzig, considered as an entrepreneur, is more of a "self-made man," since formally his role is defined in purely managerial terms.[8]

This distinction between the "self-made entrepreneur" and the elected official functioning as an entrepreneur can be misleading. There is always the possibility of the gap between *expectations* and *actual performance* of a role; the contrasting administrations of Dwight D. Eisenhower and Lyndon B. Johnson are cases in point. What is at issue here is the incumbent's definition of his office and role. The importance of this variable is highlighted by the behavior of Lee's predecessor and Mayor Kennelly's behavior in Chicago. The latter succeeded a mayor who had used the political power of his office to the hilt. Kennelly not only dissipated the political capital of the office by allowing power to flow into the hands of the aldermen but also refused to act as a "leader." Therefore, when the Chicago Housing Authority came to the mayor for support for its choice of public housing sites they were leaning on a broken reed.[9] A similar situation was not im-

[8] Moses, as a renewal entrepreneur, we shall see below, represents a third type. Sayre, Wallace and Herbert Kaufman, *Governing New York City* (New York: Russell Sage Foundation, 1960), Chapters IX and X.

[9] The contrast between Kennelly and his predecessor is noted by Meyerson and Banfield: "During his 14 years as Mayor, Edward J. Kelly had been the undisputed boss of the Democratic Party in Chicago and in Cook County. . . . As Mayor and as boss of the machine, Kelly was in full control of the Council. . . . [and] if a Democratic alder-

possible in New Haven: Given a different definition of his role Lee could have allowed power to remain as decentralized as it had been under the old administration. Both in the case of the elected official and the "self-made entrepreneur," then, a necessary condition for future success is a definition of the office as one that permits them to play an entrepreneurial role.

Superficially it would seem that it is easier for an elected official to become an entrepreneur than a salaried administrator, because the expectations concerning "political leadership" provide a basis for entrepreneurial behavior. But, again, appearances may be misleading, especially if the characteristics of the enterprise headed by the administrator are ignored. By its very nature a public authority, the type of organization headed by Danzig in Newark, represents a fragmentation of the leadership functions of government. By law the responsibility and power to achieve an end is removed from the executive and the legislature, and is given to the authority. While the latter is not an absolutely autonomous agency, the control that can be exercised by elected officials is usually so minimal that, for all intents and purposes, the authority represents an autonomous "branch of government." That is to say, for a given area of activity financial resources, entrepreneurial and managerial functions are surrendered to the authority. This means there is not only the institutionalized expectation of creative activity on the part of the agency but also a legitimization of such entrepreneurial action. Therefore, the managerial office of an authority has built into it, just as a mayor's office has, the *potential* for an entrepreneurial role.[10]

Yet an important difference remains between the elected official and the salaried administrator of an authority, and this is related to the difference in degree of *autonomy* allowed to *the individual*. An *elected* official cannot be removed from office until his term has expired; therefore he has more freedom of action than the *appointed* official, who serves at "the pleasure of the mayor." Consequently, before the adminis-

man dared to oppose one of his measures he would call the man's committeeman to demand that he be made to conform. . . . Kennelly is supposed to have accepted the nomination on the explicit understanding that he would not be expected to act as a machine leader or take directions in policy matters from the machine. . . . Whether from expediency, prejudice, or principle, the new Mayor apparently believed that the aldermen should run the city with as little direction from him as possible." Meyerson and Banfield, *op. cit.*, p. 79 ff.

[10] We shall qualify this formulation below, since it will become apparent that it applies to some rather than all authorities.

trator can use his office for entrepreneurial behavior he must bolster his autonomy of action.

Danzig assumed office with the Newark Housing Authority in 1948 at a time when the politicos were threatened by an official investigation of charges of corruption in the Authority, and this deterred them from attempting to continue their usual control over the office.[11] These circumstances also permitted Danzig to demand and receive a five-year contract, thus ensuring himself a minimum kind of security. In sum, then, the astute administrator secures an area of autonomy that goes beyond the formal prescriptions for the office.

It is of some significance that Danzig came into office from a political job rather than a career in planning. Robert Moses, the man who has done more than anyone to transform the physical face of New York City and, possibly, to exacerbate the quality of its life, is a vigorous and acerbic foe of master planning.[12] In the past the planning profession emphasized the necessity of the separation of planning and politics. Today this naïveté has been abandoned, the rhetoric of the profession recognizes their intimate relationship. However, a glance at the curricula of schools of planning suggests, with some notable exceptions, that the professionally trained planner today has only the vaguest notions about the inseparability of politics and planning. This, in turn, suggests that the renewal entrepreneur owes at least part of his success to a career line other than planning. How the latter experience may handicap a potential renewal entrepreneur may be inferred from Meyerson and Banfield's description of Elizabeth Wood.[13] On the other hand, the continuing political inexpe-

---

[11] This is a reminder that if the formal structure permits an authority a great deal of autonomy, it does not mean that an authority will function autonomously. Prior to Danzig's appointment the NHA did not function in this manner.

[12] "The Moses kind find it difficult to accept the framework and the continuing contribution of the professional planner. Nothing, in fact, creates such a fury in the Moses enclave as the suggestion that there is a master plan to which conformance is important. There is a terrible kind of vigilance against potential limitation." Rexford Guy Tugwell, "The Moses Effect" in Edward Banfield (ed.), Urban Government (New York: The Free Press of Glencoe, 1961), p. 468.

[13] Meyerson and Banfield conclude a discussion of the differences between the "style" of Miss Wood and that of the professional politician by noting, "For her part, Miss Wood was apt to think that her opponents comprised a vast conspiracy against good government and against any social reform whatever. Insofar as both sides distrusted each other profoundly, there was no basis for discussion." op. cit., p. 265. For the full discussion see pp. 264–67.

rience of the planner is a condition for the entrepreneur's existence, for it has helped create the dispersal of resources in the community. In addition, the planner's political innocence eliminates him as a potential rival entrepreneur.

As we have already noted, the entrepreneurial role in modern societies includes a managerial function. The interdependence of the two functions appears when we examine another prerequisite of renewal success, building an adequate organization. The immediate problem here is recruiting a technically competent staff. In Newark one of the first things Danzig did was to hire a professional technician, a former federal official with wide experience in the field of housing, and to beef up the staff he inherited. This is less a case of mobilizing existing community resources than of *adding* resources.[14] For a long time the NHA had a monopoly of technical competence in the field of renewal. At a later date, when other groups tried to challenge its control over the redevelopment process in the city, the groups were handicapped by a lack of staff capable of drawing up plans satisfactory to the Urban Renewal Administration. The importance of an adequate staff is illustrated by the Chicago case. In that city, as in Newark, the Authority saw the implication of the 1949 law and acted with commendable speed to take advantage of its provision. But in Chicago new persons had been added to the staff, and it was not yet a smoothly functioning organization. As a result it could not give the problem of site selection the proper attention it deserved; there *organizational* inadequacies contributed to the ultimate disaster.

Technical competence is not the only consideration in building an organization. In New Haven Lee and Logue soon chose a new man, Taylor, for a key office. Unlike his predecessor, Taylor shared Lee and Logue's definition of the way renewal should proceed in New Haven. In other words, the problem is to fashion or refashion an organization so that it will become an instrument for achieving the ends of the entrepreneur. Once again Chicago highlights some of the difficulties. It is quite apparent that Meyerson, one of the key additions to the CHA's staff, had a somewhat different view of the functions of the technical staff than did Elizabeth

---

[14] Formal provision for a Central Planning Board had been made in 1943, but it was not until 1956 that the city hired its first city planning officer.

Wood. It is plausible to assume that this conflict might have become a source of intra-organizational friction hampering the agency if it had ever become actively involved in redevelopment projects.

Of course, the CHA was not designated as the redevelopment agency, but Newark's housing authority did become its redevelopment agency. This points up a crucial aspect of the relationship between the entrepreneur-adminstrator and those who have capital. The successful entrepreneur, or course, is one who takes risks and returns a profit on investment. But when investment and entrepreneurial functions are separated, the financial risks are borne not by the entrepreneur but by the "capitalists." Moreover, since the entrepreneur is a salaried employee, "profit due entrepreneurial activities may go to the capitalists or employees of the corporation who are the superiors of the entrepreneurs."[15] This holds true in the political sphere as well. A renewal agency must have the support of the politicos; projects require some financial aid from the city and its power to condemn land. The investment by the politicos represents a risk, since the electorate will hold them responsible for the results of the entrepreneurial activities of the renewal agency. If the public approves, this is "profit" and may be claimed by the politicos. As long as previous entrepreneurial ventures have been profitable at low risk, further investments are forthcoming. In Newark, then, Danzig was able to have the NHA designated as the redevelopment agency partly as a result of his own acumen, and because at that period his relationships with his investors were good. That is, they saw the move as an opportunity for further profit at little risk to themselves. In Chicago the aldermen (who then possessed the political power), as a result of the fight over the site selections, saw the activity of the CHA as being very risky indeed—the prospect for profits was dim.

But the accumulation of further formal power by the agency does not ensure "success"; after all, what has been granted can easily be taken away. The entrepreneur must strengthen his power to make entrepreneurial decisions by reenforcing his hold upon it. This makes the selection of the first renewal project a strategic decision. In Newark the first choice was a site deep within a slum ghetto, one that would not attract developers and become an ultimately "successful"

[15] *Redlich*, p. 233.

project. Therefore, it was passed over in favor of a potentially "better" site. The criterion for the choice of an initial project, then, was related to *organizational* imperative rather than other criteria.

An initial success is important; it determines, in part, the future career of the entrepreneur. He is dependent upon an investment of political capital, and his needs are most pressing at the outset of his career when his entrepreneurial abilities are still untried. What he desperately requires is a "line of credit"; that is, access to political capital. Now, credit is nothing more than reputation; a man who has proved himself once finds it easier to secure capital a second time at more favorable terms. An elected official, too, needs an initial success, since it maintains the support of the electorate and undermines potential rivals ready to manufacture political capital out of a failure. For the entrepreneur-administrator "success" also re-enforces his autonomy. To the extent that the politicos claim the credit for the "success," they are strengthening their commitment to him and his mode of operation. More simply, perhaps, it is not easy to dispense with a successful man, especially after one has publicly profited from his activity.

An already established line of credit or reputation as an entrepreneur may also be used as a third road to an entrepreneurial career in renewal. Here the case of Robert Moses is instructive. When he became involved in renewal, Moses was already occupying other positions that involved him in dealing with a myriad of political forces, and with the necessity of mobilizing dispersed resources for new construction. Therefore, when Moses was appointed City Construction Coordinator—the formal basis of his entrepreneurial activities—he already had the reputation plus the commitments that allowed him to play an entrepreneurial role. Moses' appointment, unlike Danzig's, carried the implicit if not explicit *assignment* to an entrepreneurial function.[16]

In his relationship with internal community forces, the renewal entrepreneur's primary concern is securing political

[16] On the position of City Construction Coordinator see Wallace Sayre and Herbert Kaufman, *op. cit.*, p. 380 ff. They observed that the past became "one of the important institutionalized expressions of the unusual power exercised in the city's political process by one man, Robert Moses," p. 381. Tugwell comes to a similar conclusion in speaking of Moses' many activities: "They were all public; they were all developmental; they all added to the civic estate; they would all belong to the people; and most of them, or at least many of them, would not

support. But renewal also needs *financial* support, and this means establishing relationships with two other sets of investors. One set consists of the federal urban renewal officials who are probably more interested in local renewal success than many within the community: their *raison d'être* depends upon "something happening" in the community. An initial success facilitates establishing a line of credit with these officials. This line of credit can be converted into an additional resource in the entrepreneur's continuous effort to keep his political backers in line: The claim to "good relations" with the federal officials makes it easier to secure local political support, and is a further prop to his autonomy.

In dealing with Washington the entrepreneur must be sensitive to the problems of the federal officials. The latter must keep a wary eye cocked on Congress and the President: a local project can disturb local political waters that make waves in Washington. Chicago provides an example of one type of situation we have in mind. The nub of the problem there was the relocation of Negroes, and, even in those days before the "Negro Revolution," this represented a delicate political situation. Despite their own commitment to the objectives of the CHA, federal officials could support the Authority only to a limited extent; too strong and unequivocal a support might lead to difficulties with Congress and the President. This suggests that when an entrepreneur, at the beginning of his career, first approaches federal officials, one of the questions they consider is the quality and strength of his internal political position. Thus, the entrepreneur's initial success must demonstrate to the federal officials that his activities will not cause them political difficulties.

The other set of financial investors with whom relations must be established are the developers. Factors that are operative in the other relationships are also present in this one. Success with a developer in an initial project opens up a line of credit to other developers, and can be used in internal relationships the same way the line of credit with federal officials is used. And just as the latter do not like to become involved in local political difficulties, developers, too, shy away from political embroglios. On the surface it may appear that the entrepreneur finds it easier to deal with the federal renewal officials than with developers. The former must have

have come into existence if Moses had not created the circumstances for their beginning and maneuvered them into being." Tugwell, *op. cit.*, p. 463.

results in local communities to justify their existence, and this forces them to take risks the developer does not have to assume. The actual situation, however, is more complicated. What is fundamentally at issue here is the complex relationship between the political order and the economic order in our society.

Until the passage of the Housing Act of 1949 slum clearance programs were in an important sense "non-economic" ventures. The capital invested in housing constructed under the provisions of the older laws was provided wholly by the public sector; that is, the production of a needed commodity did not emanate from its usual source, the market. Second, investment was in a venture *not* designed to return a profit—another departure from the accepted economic rules of the society. Finally, public housing was not expected nor designed to affect the play of forces within the market. This was in contract to TVA, for example, which was supposed to stimulate and aid in the growth of market forces.[17] Title I converted slum clearance into an "economic" enterprise. First, there was the assumption that housing could and should be provided by the usual market forces. Second, government financial investments, e.g., support for the write-down, was a means of stimulating and aiding the market rather than supplanting its traditional functions. Finally, redevelopment projects were to return a profit to private capital investors.[18]

This economic dimension of renewal is important as a source of structural ambivalence affecting the behavior of federal renewal officials.[19] On the one hand, since the end of

[17] To be sure, during the thirties public housing was justified by reference to its stimulating effects on the construction industry, and to this extent the last proposition is not quite accurate. On the other hand, "pump-priming" is an entirely different economic action from the massive flood control and hydroelectric programs of the TVA. The latter is an added economic resource, so to speak, to the economy that allows private industrial enterprise to grow and expand. To use a medical analogy, it is the difference between treating symptoms of disease and curing the disease itself.

[18] What public housing has been produced since 1949 still remains "non-economic" in character as opposed to the "economic" character of redevelopment projects.

[19] Structural ambivalence refers to contradictory patterns of behavior that are normatively expected of a role occupant in a given situation. That is, conformity to the requirements of one norm violates another norm operative in the same situation. Cf. Merton, Robert K. and Elinor Barber, "Structural Ambivalence" in Edward A. Tiryakian (ed.), *So-*

renewal is a "better community," the officials are obliged to encourage and support programs that function toward this end. On the other hand, they must approve projects that meet the economic ends of renewal, e.g., a profit on investments.[20] At least two factors determine how officials will resolve their dilemma. First, there is the relative diffuseness of the norm of a "better community" over against the relative specificity of the requirement for profit—there is little difficulty about deciding the profitability of a venture, but what, after all, produces a "better community"? Second, there is the ready-made, traditionally approved rationale for subordinating one end to another that may be labeled, after one of its latter-day adumbrators, the Charley Wilson Syndrome: What is good for General Motors is good for the country.

In practice this means that any redevelopment project submitted to federal officials must be justified in terms of economic criteria. So, for example, the FHA will not agree to insure necessary mortgages unless it can be shown that the new housing will be profitable. Often the renewal entrepreneur is caught between the cross fire of two economically oriented federal agencies. URA insists that he secure the highest price for the cleared land, because it must provide two-thirds of the cost of the write-down. At the same time, FHA is interested in potential profits, and these will be affected by how much the developer must pay for the cleared land. Placation of these grim official forces, plus the developer's insistent demands for a reasonable chance at a profit, means the continual modification of plans by the entrepreneur. The net consequence is that the goal of a "better community" recedes farther and farther into the background, so that when the project is finally completed one has to search diligently for any indication that it was ever present. However, this problem does not arise for a long time; all dealings with federal officials involve the usual bureaucratic machinery, and this itself becomes another variable in the process. As such, it must be taken into account by the entrepreneur: the time lapse

ciological Theory, Values and Sociocultural Change (New York: The Free Press, 1963), pp. 91–120.

[20] It is, of course, arguable that these are not necessarily incompatible ends; logically speaking, a redevelopment project may result in both profit and a "better community." Yet, when we turn from logic to life, the entire history of renewal shows that as far as housing is concerned these are contradictory demands; standard, low-income housing is too risky a venture to draw capital funds from the market.

between the initiation of a project and its completion affects his search for tangible proofs of his success.

The life of a renewal entrepreneur is obviously a continual round of complex negotiations with politicos, federal officials, and developers, with the demands of each affecting relations with the others. In threading his way among them the entrepreneur uses techniques familiar to all administrators. "Every bureaucrat," Max Weber observed, "seeks to increase the superiority of the professionally informed by keeping their knowledge and intentions secret."[21] One of the operating rules of thumb of NHA's staff was that no one—including politicos, Housing Commissioners, and the public—was informed about plans for a new project until tentative approval had been secured from federal authorities and a developer lined up. In New Haven the Church Street redevelopment plan was drawn "in secrecy." In Chicago the Authority had the alternative of negotiating in private with the aldermen, or of first publicly announcing their site selections. There seems to be a possible correlation between "success" and "secrecy."[22]

The functional consequences of secrecy are readily apparent. Since renewal rather easily stirs up a political hornet's nest, anything that minimizes the possibilities of political difficulties adds to a project's probable success. At the same time secrecy insulates the "outside" investors from those inside the community, and this has two functional consequences for the entrepreneur. First, as Weber noted, it keeps knowledge and skills in his own hands. Second, by presenting the politicos and the public with a *fait accompli,* he makes it difficult for the former to enter into negotiations with federal officials and developers independently of himself. That is, he remains the only channel of communication between those inside the community and those outside it, and this allows him to maintain control of the situation. The insulation of the public from the "outsiders" facilitates the accommodation of renewal projects to the economic criteria of these groups. In other words, the secrecy pattern makes it more difficult for countervailing forces, representing other criteria and ends, to bring their power to bear on the situation.[23]

[21] Gerth, H. H. and C. W. Mills (eds.) *From Max Weber: Essays in Sociology* (New York: Oxford University Press, 1946), pp. 232–33.
[22] Kaplan, *op. cit.,* p. 173 ff.
[23] Local "interest groups" are another internal force the entrepreneur must deal with. Since his relationships with them involve a considera-

If some of the entrepreneur's behavior resembles that of the traditional bureaucrat it is clearly less symptomatic of a bureaucratic psychology than of a highly "realistic," not to say flexible and pragmatic, orientation to the world. This perspective in all probability facilitates his relationship with the developers. Given the American businessman's notoriously negative view of public officials, he does not expect to find one that is as hard-nosed as he fancies himself to be, and after he is pleasantly surprised both can get comfortably down to business. But more is involved here than simply compatibility of orientations or shared perceptions of the world. The developer who participates in renewal projects is himself an entrepreneur, and his situation and problems are similar to that of the renewal entrepreneur. The developer bears relatively little of the financial risks of his enterprise: Major portions of the capital investment are provided by banks, large corporations he is in partnership with, and the federal government by way of guaranteed mortgages and the involutions of the tax laws.[24] As with the renewal entrepreneur, the key to the developer's position is his credit (reputation); once this becomes tarnished his enterprise, no matter how many tons of steel and concrete it has been responsible for in the past, turns into a house of cards. And his lines of credit extend to the same groups that the renewal entrepreneur must deal with: politicos, federal officials, and private investors. The relationship between renewal entrepreneur and developer, then, rests on the similarity of their roles.

The entrepreneurial role and orientation of the developer explains why he so often comes from outside the community. Obviously, one important reason is that the financial investment and skills necessary for participation in renewal projects are beyond the means of local businessmen.[25] Not only are they apt to be small businessmen, but they possess neither the vision nor abilities to be entrepreneurs in a modern economy. Local business in Newark, for example, was unwilling to take the risks of investing in renewal projects and also objected to renewal on *ideological* grounds. Quite anachronistically, they saw renewal as "socialism" and the "destruction of free enter-

---

tion of the whole problem of "citizen participation" we plan to deal with this aspect of the entrepreneur's activity in another publication rather than in the present context.

[24] Anderson, Martin, *The Federal Bulldozer* (Cambridge, Mass: MIT Press, 1964), Chap. 8.

[25] *Ibid.*, Chap. 7.

prise." The *modern* entrepreneur realizes that his opportunities lie precisely at those points at which the economy becomes "mixed," the point at which enterprises draw upon the resources of both the public and private sectors of the total economy. In many local communities, then, one may find the creative entrepreneur not in the private sector but in the public sector; this is, the creative entrepreneur will be a public official. This has some theoretical implications.

We have already noted two points bearing on this problem: The public authority, we said, has an entrepreneurial potential built into it, and, second, since 1949, renewal has acquired an economic dimension. Taken in conjunction these points help specify what kind of authority has the entrepreneurial potential. So, for example, the housing authorities that built and administered public housing under the provisions of the older legislation (and this includes authorities with this as their sole function) cannot perform entrepreneurial functions, since their activities are isolated from the market. Authorities having their origin in legislation designed to aid and stimulate the market clearly possess an entrepreneurial potential. For, if that function is to "determine . . . the place of the enterprise in the market and the national economy," then the social function of those authorities consists precisely of the responsibility for placing public resources into the market and economy as a whole.

We can now see the broader social functions and significance of the renewal entrepreneur's role. The public entrepreneur represents the point of articulation between the political order and the economic order; he is the linchpin connecting the two spheres. The renewal entrepreneur is something more than an individual who mobilizes the dispersed resources of the community for the ends of renewal. In so doing he makes it possible for the political order to achieve the objectives of its intervention into the economic sphere. Therefore, his existence and activities have consequences that transcend the local community. Here, again, he resembles the business entrepreneur whose decisions in a modern economy also vitally affect the total society.

The activities of the private entrepreneur raise a socially important question, and this same question is raised by the activities of the public entrepreneur. In a modern economy entrepreneurial decisions—and, more generally, any action—of a large-scale enterprise like, say, General Motors, has consequences for the entire society, e.g., the decision to expand productive facilities. Control over these decisions in our society, however, cannot be exercised by those who are vitally affected. Even the nominal owners of the enterprise—the shareholders—can do no more than stand helplessly by and cash their dividend checks. To the extent that the entrepreneurial functions of the political order are entrusted to public authorities, there is the same lack of control over their behavior. The question, then, is: How long can a political democracy with a "mixed economy" afford the structure of entrepreneurial activity we have been describing?

URBAN RENEWAL IN NEW HAVEN*

Robert Dahl

Like the distribution of influence on political nominations, influence over redevelopment in New Haven takes a somewhat triangular shape. The people of New Haven acquiesce and approve; they have elected and re-elected a mayoralty candidate whose principal platform has been urban redevelopment. Yet the *direct* influence of the electorate on the key decisions involving redevelopment has been negligible compared with the direct influence of a few leaders. In origins, conception, and execution, it is not too much to say that urban redevelopment has been the direct product of a small handful of leaders.

Origins

Perhaps the most significant element in the modern history of city planning in New Haven is that very little happened until redevelopment became attached to the political fortunes of an ambitious politician. Redevelopment was not produced by a surge of popular demand for a new city nor was it produced by the wants and demands of the Economic Notables, even though many of them believed that changes in the physical pattern of the city were necessary to their own goals. The possibility cannot be ruled out that if the Economic Notables were much more unified, influential, skillful, and dedicated to redevelopment than they are in New Haven, they could provide the dominant leadership and coordination. But in New Haven their support was only a necessary, not a sufficient condition for the aggressive action by city officials required for comprehensive reshaping of the face of the city.[1] This will

* FROM *Who Governs?*, New Haven: Yale University Press, 1961, pp. 115–22, 126–30 (selected portions).

[1] Up to the time of writing, New Haven's redevelopment program has not had many critics. What follows in this chapter, however, is not an appraisal of the desirability of the program but an attempt to understand the political forces that shaped it. Whether the program is eventually judged a brilliant effort or a ghastly mistake is irrelevant to the purposes of this book.

become clear as we examine the origins of the redevelopment program.

Enthusiastic advocates of redevelopment sometimes claim to see its genesis in the first settlement of New Haven in 1638 when the founders, under the leadership of John Davenport, a clergyman, and Theophilus Eaton, a businessman, carefully and deliberately laid out the town in nine squares with the town Green at the center. But we need hardly carry the story to quite so remote a past. For the modern problems of New Haven began after it became an industrial city with slums, run-down areas, and an accretion of man-made features that reflected historical rather than current hopes and needs. In 1907 the mayor of New Haven appointed a New Haven Civic Improvements Committee (at the urging of a distinguished New Haven citizen, George Dudley Seymour) made up of thirteen of the city's most prominent residents, including the governor of the state, some of the most prosperous businessmen, a few of the largest real estate owners, and other worthies. The committee secured the services of Cass Gilbert, architect, and Frederick Law Olmstead, landscape planner, who in 1910 issued the first of several plans and reports that blueprinted a bright future of widened streets, more parks, harbor development, and other changes.[2] But, as was true later on, the net effect of the report was slight. A city plan commission was created in 1913 but was given neither funds nor a professional staff. In the late 1920s and 1930s, James W. Hook, a leading business figure in New Haven, pressed for action on a variety of fronts, but it was 1941 before the City Plan Commission was finally given enough money to hire professional help.

The following year, under the leadership of Angus Fraser, a prominent businessman (in 1943 he was the Republican candidate for mayor), the Commission hired Maurice Rotival, a well-known city planner, as a consultant. Rotival brought out a comprehensive scheme of development, but little was done about his proposals for ten years. In 1953 the Chamber of Commerce produced a "Ten Point Program" that reflected many of the suggestions contained in the earlier plans and reports, including Rotival's.

For three reasons, none of these proposals made headway. First, they were all expensive, and they provided no realistic solution to the problem of costs. Secondly, although they en-

[2] Osterweis, *Three Centuries of New Haven*, pp. 390–92.

visaged comprehensive rather than piecemeal alterations, they did not provide realistically for a political process that would secure agreement on a strategic plan. Thirdly, political officials whose support was necessary if action by the city was to be forthcoming saw no particular political gain and much political loss if they were to push hard on city planning and development.

A partial solution to the first problem was offered for the first time by Title I of the Federal Housing Act of 1949, which authorized the expenditure of one billion dollars in loans to cities for planning redevelopment projects and acquiring property to be cleared. An additional half billion dollars was made available in grants, the cities themselves being required to bear only one-third of the net costs of redevelopment projects. The grants were, in effect, a means of enabling a city to acquire and clear land and then sell it at a loss to redevelopers.

So far as it is now possible to determine, the possibilities created by Title I were first impressed on local political leaders by a man from academia. A young professor of political science at Yale, Henry Wells, who also happened to be the Democratic alderman from the First Ward and the aldermanic member of the City Plan Commission, had carefully studied the new act and concluded that both the city and the Democratic party might gain if the Democrats on the Board of Aldermen seized upon urban redevelopment as a program. Although the Democrats had won a slight majority on the Board of Aldermen in 1949, their candidate for mayor, Richard Lee, had lost to Celentano. To Wells, Title I seemed to offer an issue on which the Democratic majority might take the initiative away from the Republican mayor for the next two years.

Among others, Wells won over Lee and Norton Levine, a new alderman who had succeeded Lee as Democratic floor leader. The state had meanwhile passed a law permitting cities to establish redevelopment agencies. With Lee's approval, Levine talked to Mayor Celentano, who agreed not to veto a resolution establishing the agency if it were presented as a Republican measure. Subsequently, under the stimulus of Lee, Levine, and Wells, the Board of Aldermen passed a resolution in the summer of 1950 authorizing the mayor to create a redevelopment agency and appoint to it a board of unpaid citizens and a paid director.

Thus urban redevelopment in New Haven began, as Wells diagnosed it afterward, as "a power play—to take the ball away from Celentano, the Republican mayor. In other words, urban redevelopment helped solve *our* problem of political rewards—as it did Dick Lee's four years later."

Mayor Celentano's dilemma as Republican leader was serious. The local newspapers would probably oppose redevelopment as costly; along with most political figures in New Haven the mayor attributed to the papers great influence with voters. Many families might have to be displaced; certainly these people would fight the city administration. Redevelopment was untried; mistakes were probably unavoidable; they could be costly; and most voters would probably pin responsibility for mishaps on the mayor rather than on the Democratic majority in the Board of Aldermen. In 1950, redevelopment hardly appeared to possess great electoral appeal. Since the Democrats had only a three-vote majority, they could not override a veto. On the other hand, many members of the business community had long insisted that improvements in the city were indispensable if the downtown business district was to be preserved from decay; most of these businessmen were Republicans and contributors to the party. The Mayor himself personally favored redevelopment. Faced with this uncomfortable dilemma, Celentano chose to support redevelopment; on his urging the Republican minority on the Board regularly voted with the Democrats on redevelopment.

Thus in spite of its partisan origins, urban redevelopment soon acquired a nonpartisan aura that continued to surround it throughout the next decade. Ironically, this aura of nonpartisanship was to serve the political purposes of the Democrats and particularly those of Richard Lee.

Under Mayor Celentano redevelopment moved slowly ahead. In later years, redevelopment in New Haven became so closely fused with the image of Celentano's successor, Lee, that it is difficult now to provide a fair appraisal of Celentano's role. Both friends and critics agree that Celentano was politically somewhat timid and unadventurous. Moreover, though he supported redevelopment he never made it the central policy of his administration; probably only a mayor who did could move redevelopment ahead in the face of all the obstacles to it. The city agencies involved in the numerous aspects of redevelopment were autonomous and uncoordinated; it would require great force and zeal, as well as unusual political skill, to drive these diverse forces as a single team.

Nonetheless, in 1952 with Celentano's backing the Redevelopment Agency secured the approval of the Board of

Aldermen for a proposal to raze fifteen acres of the worst slum area in the city on Oak Street. However, federal funds for the Oak Street project were still a long way off, and before plans proceeded very far the election of 1953 put Lee into the mayor's office.

Only thirty-seven when he was first elected, Lee already had long experience in New Haven politics. He came from a Catholic working-class family of mixed English, Scottish, and Irish origins (in public he chose to emphasize his Irish forebears), went to New Haven public schools, worked as a reporter on the *Journal Courier,* served as an officer in the Junior Chamber of Commerce, had a brief spell in the army, and from 1943 until his election as mayor was in charge of Yale's public relations. He had been a member of the Board of Aldermen, where he quickly became the Democratic minority leader; after an intra-party fight in 1945, in which he supported John Golden, he became a protégé of Golden.

Lee had become a skillful politician. After his two narrow defeats in 1949 and 1951, the last by two votes, he was unusually sensitive to the important consequences of minute shifts in the opinions, habits, or vagaries of voters. Possibly as much by temperament as by his experience of an electoral defeat that could be regarded only as sheer chance, he was prone to worry about the dangers of unexpected and uncontrolled events. For many years he suffered badly from ulcers, which sometimes sent him to the hospital at critical moments. He was a worrier, who spent much of his time laying plans to ward off incipient dangers.

He possessed a large repertoire of political skills and an unusual ability to perform a variety of different roles. His political skills included a talent for public relations that played no small part in developing his national reputation. He had an investment banker's willingness to take risks that held the promise of large long-run payoffs, and a labor mediator's ability to head off controversy by searching out areas for agreement by mutual understanding, compromise, negotiation, and bargaining. He possessed a detailed knowledge of the city and its people, a formidable information-gathering system, and an unceasing, full-time preoccupation with all the aspects of his job. His relentless drive to achieve his goals meant that he could be tough and ruthless. But toughness was not his political style, for his overriding strategy was to rely on persuasion rather than threats.

The Mayor had learned to move with outward ease in

several sharply contrasting worlds. He bought his clothes at the best men's shops in New Haven, customarily wore tweed jackets to work, and with his bow ties, button-down shirts and crew-cut hair, he could pass for any well-dressed Yale alumnus. He was one of the few members of Mory's, Yale's undergraduate eating club, who had never attended Yale; and he was perhaps the only associate fellow in any of Yale's ten residential colleges who had never attended a college or university of any kind. He was on a first name basis with a large proportion of the Yale establishment from the president and deans to the headwaiter at the Faculty Club.

For a poor boy growing up in New Haven, life was not always so congenial, and it is clear that Lee's decade as director of public relations at Yale was an important period in his development. Lee's experiences at Yale extended his horizons and made him receptive to ideas that would have frightened a more run-of-the-mill politician. He learned there how to work easily with professional people and developed a sense of the need for expertness and intelligence in public affairs. He never hesitated, for example, in hiring the best talent the city could buy for redevelopment.

In a city where rancor between town and gown is never far below the surface, the Mayor's Yale associations could have been a severe handicap, but his political opponents found it difficult to change the image that Lee himself carefully cultivated of a local boy in the mayor's office, a home-grown Irishman, a family man, a devoted Catholic, a hard-working mayor and a friend to everyone in the city.

As Lee described it later, by 1953 he had arrived at the conclusion that the problem of "doing something about New Haven" was partly one of coordination. His unsuccessful 1951 campaign had taken him into the worst slums in New Haven:

> I went into the homes on Oak Street and they set up neighborhood meetings for me. I went into block meetings . . . three and four in one night. And I came out from one of those homes on Oak Street, and I sat on the curb and I was just as sick as a puppy. Why, the smell of this building; it had no electricity, it had no gas, it had kerosene lamps, light had never seen those corridors in generations. The smells . . . It was just awful and I got sick. And there, there I really began . . . right there was when I began to tie in all these ideas we'd been practicing in city planning for years in terms of the human benefits that a program like this could reap for a city.

> . . . In the two-year period [before the next election] I began
> to put it together with the practical application. . . . And I
> began to realize that while we had lots of people interested
> in doing something for the city *they were all working at cross
> purposes. There was no unity of approach.*

In the 1953 campaign he emphasized the importance of
doing something about the condition of New Haven. He
promised to appoint a committee of prominent citizens within
sixty days after taking office, to work out a common program for the city. It is impossible to know whether his views
and his promise had any effect on the outcome of the election, which was close. Indeed, in 1953 it was impossible to
foresee the extent to which the emphasis on redevelopment
would turn out to be politically profitable; Lee has since said
that he himself did not anticipate the political harvest he would
ultimately reap. Moreover, it is doubtful whether Lee or anyone else foresaw the kind of organization that was to develop
in New Haven to coordinate the physical transformation of
the city, nor did any one realize how rapidly urban redevelopment would burgeon into a major, perhaps the central activity
of the mayor and his staff.

Lee had difficulty at first in carrying out his campaign
promises. He approached a number of prominent people about
the chairmanship of the citizens committee he had promised;
a few turned him down flatly; others were reluctant. He even
appointed a committee of several well-known citizens to help
him in the search.

Instead of sixty days it was many months after the Mayor
was in office before he got his chairman, a well-known bank
president, Carl Freese, and it was nearly a year after the
election before he was able to announce the creation of the
Citizens Action Commission (CAC). It was not until February
of 1955 that he began to build up a new staff at the Redevelopment Agency. Edward Logue was brought in as Development
Administrator; Logue soon became the Mayor's right-hand
man on redevelopment, a hard-driving, vigorous executive
who coordinated the work of the Redevelopment Agency, the
City Plan Commission, and all other agencies in so far as
they touched on redevelopment. The incumbent director of
the agency was fired, and until the fall of 1955 Logue served
in fact if not in title as the executive director of the Agency.
That fall a Massachusetts man, Ralph Taylor, was named director. The chairman of the Agency resigned and the Mayor

appointed a new man, Frank O'Brion, another banker. Lee now had the core of his redevelopment team: himself, Logue, Taylor, Freese, O'Brion.

Under Lee, the whole pace of redevelopment gradually altered. By the end of his first term Lee had made redevelopment the central policy of his administration. Then the election of 1955 gave him solid grounds for concluding that the political appeal of redevelopment far exceeded any other conceivable issue within his grasp. After having been narrowly defeated twice by Celentano and having won by a margin of less than 2 per cent in 1953, Lee polled 65 per cent of the vote in 1955 against a somewhat inexperienced candidate of Italian extraction (Celentano having decided to bide his time). In the preceding century, no candidate for mayor had ever won that large a percentage; even Roosevelt had carried New Haven with only 63 per cent in 1936. When Lee went on in 1957 to win again with 65 per cent of the vote, the spectacular political appeal of redevelopment seemed proven. At first the unknown mayor of a minor American city Lee (with some help on his part) began to attract national attention. Articles about redevelopment in New Haven, in which Lee featured prominently, appeared in *Harper's*[8] and the *Saturday Evening Post;*[4] Lee became chairman of a Democratic Advisory Committee subcommittee on urban problems; in 1958 he was widely mentioned as a possible candidate for U.S. senator though he declared he would not seek the nomination because he had to see redevelopment through as mayor of New Haven.

For a city of its size, New Haven soon had an urban redevelopment program unmatched in the country. By the end of 1958, New Haven had spent more federal funds per capita for planning its redevelopment projects than any of the country's largest cities, more than any other city in New England, and more than any other city of comparable size except one. Only one city in the country, the nation's capital, had received more per person in capital grants, and no other city had so much reserved for its projects. . . . By 1959 much of the center of the city was razed to the ground.

· · ·

[8] Jeanne R. Lowe, "Lee of New Haven and His Political Jackpot," *Harper's Magazine*, Oct. 1957.

[4] Joe Alex Morris, "He is Saving a 'Dead' City." *The Saturday Evening Post*, Apr. 19, 1958.

THE VARIETIES OF INFLUENCE

Four different though interrelated tasks in the formation and execution of policy had to be shared: (1) setting the general direction of policy, which is partly a matter of determining (explicitly or implicitly, by action or inaction) what kinds of policies would be emphasized and how much in resources would be poured into them; (2) developing specific proposals; (3) negotiating agreements on the specific proposals; and (4) carrying out the policies when enough agreement was negotiated.

Every administration assumes some posture that furnishes participants with clues as to what kinds of policies are most likely to be pushed or opposed and how much of resources in energy, time, skills, and money are likely to be available for different policies. The posture of a "do-nothing," "avoid risk," "save money" administration is soon obvious to all. So is the weakness of an administration that gives away its initiative to all comers. If schools are treated as a favored area, or public works contracts as a protected one, the matter is soon known to all those who need to calculate what they are most likely or least likely to get done in accordance with their own desires and hopes. If an administration publicly favors and privately fears redevelopment, participants soon know it. If an executive lacks energy and drive and his policies wither on the vine, the participants soon adapt their strategies to this particular fact of life.

What Lee did as mayor was to push redevelopment and renewal to the center of focus and to hold it there year after year. He determined that a large share of energy, time, skills, and money would go into redevelopment. He devoted most of his own time and attention to it. He saw the need for a Citizens Action Commission and an extensive system of subcommittees, knew what kind of men he wanted for the CAC, persuaded them to accept membership, brought in Logue, induced him to abandon his attempt to start a law practice in order to work full-time on redevelopment, identified himself fully with redevelopment, and made it into a major issue of his unceasing campaign for re-election. A mere preference for a better city would hardly have been sufficient to maintain his energetic commitment to redevelopment; though he may have been in doubt as to its political payoff during his first term, from his re-election in 1955 onward it was clear that in redevelopment he had managed to identify himself with a program of enormous political potentiality that in time might make him a serious contender for higher office.[5]

No one but the Mayor could have given redevelopment the priority it received. In another administration, the Development Administrator could have been frustrated and helpless. In Lee's, the Development Administrator's furious drive and energy found infinite outlets in redevelopment. Probably more than anyone else, the Development Administrator worked out the proposals that became the policy-goals of the administration and determined the specific forms that redevelopment and renewal were to take.

Edward Logue, the development administrator, graduated in 1942 from Yale, served on seventeen missions as a bombardier with the Fifteenth Air Force in Italy, and returned to New Haven to graduate from the Yale Law School. As a law student, he attracted the attention of the Yale community by organizing the maintenance and service workers of Yale in a CIO union. Shortly after Logue's graduation from law school, Chester Bowles was elected governor, and Logue soon joined the liberal reformer in Hartford as a legal advisor, in which post he began to acquire administrative seasoning. He admired Bowles, in whom he found a political leader congenial to his own strong impulses toward reform, and when Bowles (who was defeated for re-election after a cyclonic single term of innovation in state policies) was appointed ambassador to India by President Truman, Logue accepted an invitation to accompany him as his chief administrative assistant. When Bowles was replaced in 1953 after Eisenhower's victory, Logue came back to New Haven to begin a law practice and at once found himself heavily involved in Lee's political fortunes, first as an active leader of a Citizens for Lee committee and then as the Mayor's chief assistant and counselor on redevelopment. This activity gradually absorbed his entire time, and he gave up the attempt to practice law in order to take over first as acting Director of the Redevelopment Agency and later as Development Administrator.[6]

After determining in a general way where the Mayor

[5] A detailed analysis of the various techniques and relations involved and the parts played by the various participants will be found in the forthcoming companion volume by Raymond Wolfinger, *The Politics of Progress.*

[6] In 1961, Logue left New Haven to head Boston's redevelopment program.

wanted to move next, the Development Administrator usually supervised the development of a specific proposal. In this stage, the Development Administrator served as a stand-in for the Mayor; his word was in effect the Mayor's word. Essentially what he did was to bring the skills of his associates and subordinates to bear on the task of working out a particular proposal. In doing so, he relied heavily on three people and their staffs: Ralph Taylor, the director of the Redevelopment Agency, Norris Andrews of the City Plan Commission, and Maurice Rotival, whose firm of city planners served the city in a consulting capacity. Each of these men, of course, drew in turn on the technical skills of his own staff.

To develop a proposal is not necessarily to invent it. As every historian knows, it is often impossible to determine precisely who first thought of the ideas that shape events. As we have seen, certain general ideas about the city had been floating around New Haven for half a century. In the Oak Street area, the Lee administration carried through an idea already in the planning stage under Mayor Celentano. With Church Street, it was the Development Administrator himself who, after months of consideration, discussion, and preliminary planning, sat down late one night and drew on a city map the boundaries he then proposed and the Mayor accepted—boundaries that in their economic and social implications seemed so bold and daring that for months the exact nature of the proposal was kept in secrecy as the Mayor, the Development Administrator, and the Redevelopment Director tested it for feasibility and acceptability.

In so far as one can ever locate a source of ideas, probably Maurice Rotival was as much the ultimate fount as any living person. As we have noted, Rotival was the author of a master plan for New Haven in 1941. He was an imaginative Frenchman, a professional city planner who spun off ideas as a pin wheel throws off sparks. And, like sparks, his ideas often vanished into the darkness. But his presence in New Haven, where he headed a firm of city planning consultants with a world-wide clientele, insured that his ideas would be heard. In a few places, the sparks fell on tinder, smoldered, and finally burst into flame. Like many inventors, Rotival saw his ideas seized and executed by others in ways he did not altogether approve.

But none of Rotival's proposals, nor those of anyone else, were self-enacting; to pass from idea to reality every proposal required an expenditure of critical resources—money, time, energy, attention, skill, political support. The Development Administrator's influence rested in part on the fact that it was his responsibility to assess the costs and gains—economic, social, political—of the various possible proposals generated by himself, his associates, and his subordinates, to arrive at a judgment about the few that seemed worthwhile, to explore these with the Mayor, and to develop the ones that met with the Mayor's approval to a stage where the Mayor could begin securing the necessary support and approval from others. The Development Administrator could not have discharged this task if he had not had the Mayor's confidence; he could not have retained the Mayor's confidence if he had not been loyal to him and sensitive to his political needs, prospects, and hopes. The Mayor's judgment was final, the Development Administrator's preliminary; but the two men were so close that the Development Administrator's preliminary judgment was unlikely to diverge consistently from the Mayor's final judgment.

The main burden of negotiating support for a proposal was divided among the Mayor, the Development Administrator, and the Director of the Redevelopment Agency. It is only a slight oversimplification to say that it was the Mayor's task to get the support of the major political interests in the community, the Development Administrator's to insure the participation of developers, and the Redevelopment Director's to win the consent of the federal agencies.

The Mayor sought support for his redevelopment proposals from as strange a coalition as had ever existed in New Haven. This coalition included the other leaders of his own party, who were skeptical of redevelopment until the election of 1955 convinced them of its political potency; the DiCenzo-Celentano wing of the Republican party; public utility heads, bankers, manufacturers, and retailers who were Republicans almost to a man; the Yale administration; the liberal Democrats among the Yale faculty; the working-class and lower-middle-class ethnic groups, particularly Negroes and Italians, and their spokesmen; trade union leaders, educators, small merchants, the League of Women Voters, the Chamber of Commerce; and enough voters to win elections by a margin so impressive that it guaranteed not only the continuation of redevelopment but Lee's own long-run political prospects. For the most part, the Mayor met a receptive audience and won the support and acquiescence he needed without serious or prolonged conflict.

The Development Administrator negotiated with potential developers to induce them to come into projects on terms acceptable to the city, and, if they agreed, worked out the specific terms of the understandings and the contracts. At first he also negotiated with the federal authorities, mainly the regional office of the Housing and Home Finance Agency in New York. But after Ralph Taylor became director of the Redevelopment Agency in 1955, he began to take over this function.

Taylor came to New Haven to fill a post made vacant when the Mayor and Logue concluded that the incumbent director lacked the drive and zeal they wanted. Like Logue, Taylor was not a native New Havener; he came from a Jewish family in Somerville, went to Harvard, was in Italy with the army, returned to Harvard to earn his M.A. at the Littauer School of Public Administration, and took over in Somerville as the head of a redevelopment program that proved to be substantially abortive. He had not been in New Haven long before it became clear that he matched Logue in energy, resourcefulness, and dedication, and the two quickly formed a closely knit team. The Director had one great asset the Development Administrator and the Mayor necessarily lacked; he was considered a professional by his peers throughout the country, many of whom he knew well. As the New Haven program began to attract attention, respect for the Director soared among his professional colleagues, including those in the federal agencies. Thus he took on more and more of the task of negotiating with the "Feds"; he knew how to cut through the interminable delays characteristic of bureaucratic agencies, and he exploited statutes and rules to gain concessions for New Haven that cut down the actual cash contribution the city was required to make. Consequently, although the city was supposed to bear one-third of the cost, its actual cash outlay was very much less than this; in one case, even self-liquidating parking garages were included as part of the city's contribution. The city was able to move far partly because its agents moved fast; at a time when most cities were still debating whether to apply for federal funds, New Haven had already secured a disproportionate share of what was available.

If policies are not self-enacting, neither are they self-executing. It is possible to win agreement on a particular proposal and lose it during the execution. The task of driving policies through and securing the coordination needed among a diversity of political officials and city agencies fell chiefly on the Mayor and his Development Administrator. The political structure of the city government was converted from a highly decentralized to an executive-centered order, partly for the purpose of coordinating redevelopment activities. This transformation was largely the work of the Mayor; the day-to-day coordination was largely the responsibility of the Development Administrator.

NHA: THE STRATEGY OF SLUM CLEARANCE*

Harold Kaplan

The ability of any redevelopment agency to realize its goals is circumscribed by the attitudes and responses of local organized interests.[1] Many factors contributing to its success are attributes of the local political environment and are beyond the control of agency officials. As later chapters will document, NHA's [Newark Housing Authority] success can be explained in large part by the permissive character of its local environment.

Environmental factors, however, are a necessary but not sufficient cause of NHA's success in redevelopment. Less adroit agencies might fail to perceive the permissive character of their local environment, and more timorous agencies might fail to exploit it for the benefit of the program. That NHA officials are painstaking strategists, attuned to the problems of successful redevelopment, is highly pertinent to that agency's long-run achievements. This chapter examines the process by which the Authority's staff made its clearance decisions from 1949 to 1959, the substance of its policies, and the strategies it developed for exploiting this permissive environment.

* FROM *Urban Renewal Politics: Slum Clearance in Newark,* New York: Columbia University Press, 1963, pp. 10–15, 28–38, 40–43 (selected portions).

[1] The following account relies heavily on personal interviews and NHA documents. NHA officials kindly permitted the author free access to their files. They also proved most generous with their time. It should not be concluded, however, that they agree with the final product.

The best written sources on NHA are its own documents: NHA Minutes; NHA-Redevel. Minutes; *From the Ground Up* (1958); *Redevelopment Sites in Downtown Newark* (1959); *Construction Report* (1956); *Rebuilding Newark* (1952); *Public Housing in Newark* (1944). In addition: *New Jersey Revised Statutes,* Cum. Supp., 55:14A-3, 4, 6; New Jersey Department of Conservation and Economic Development, Division of Planning and Development, *Directory of Local Housing Authorities and Redevelopment Agencies* (Trenton, N.J., 1959); New Jersey Legislature, *Report of the Legislative Middle Income Housing Study Commission* (Trenton, N.J., 1956).

"Getting the Jump"

Newark was the first city in New Jersey and among the earliest in the nation to begin an urban renewal program.[2] Less than eighteen months intervened between the passage of the 1949 Housing Act and the announcement of Newark's first slum clearance project. Many in the Housing Authority now cite this "jump" as an important contribution to their subsequent success. By submitting a concrete clearance proposal earlier than most other cities in the United States, Newark was able to secure a prior claim to federal funds and to acquire a reputation for competence among federal officials.

Newark could move swiftly in the field of redevelopment because a large municipal organization, the Newark Housing Authority, led by an aggressive Executive Director, Louis Danzig, was poised to act immediately after passage of the 1949 Act. The Housing Authority of the City of Newark had been created in 1938 under the terms of the U.S. Housing Act of 1937 and the New Jersey Local Housing Authorities Act of 1938. Like housing authorities throughout the country, it was an independent public corporation responsible for the construction and management of low-rent housing projects. It was managed by a locally appointed board of six housing authority commissioners and was sustained by federal subsidy, the rent from its projects, and federally guaranteed housing authority bonds. By 1949 NHA was, with the exception of the Board of Education, the largest spender of funds and the largest dispenser of contracts in the city government.

Danzig and his staff had recognized the shortcomings of public housing for some time and had lobbied for legislation on urban redevelopment. Even before Congress and the New Jersey Legislature took final action in 1949, Danzig had his legal staff prepare an ordinance making NHA the city's official redevelopment agency. Immediately after passage of the federal and state legislation, Danzig submitted this ordinance to the city commissioners. The good relations that he had established with the commissioners during the public housing years facilitated rapid approval of the ordinance.

This quick start not only gave NHA the jump on most

[2] *"Getting the Jump":* NHA-Redevel. Minutes, April 12, June 14, Oct. 11, 1950; Newark *News,* Feb. 1, 4, April 27, 1950; City Commissioners' Minutes, July 27, Aug. 10, 24, Sept. 7, 21, 1949, Jan. 11, April 4, May 3, Nov. 8, 1950.

other cities; it also provided the Authority with a strategic edge over most local interests. These local groups failed to recognize the significance of the new program until several clearance projects were under way. By the time these groups were mobilized and prepared to make demands on the Authority, NHA had already established good working relations with the key federal and local officials.

Danzig did not wait for the federal Division of Slum Clearance and Urban Redevelopment to get organized before launching his own survey of potential sites. When federal officials indicated that funds for preliminary surveys would not be available until spring, 1950, Danzig went ahead with staff and funds borrowed from NHA's public housing accounts. Here, once again, Danzig could utilize the resources and organization that NHA had amassed in the 1940s to get a quick start on the new program.

It was during one of his frequent trips to Washington, and one of his frequent attempts to prod federal officials into faster action, that Danzig met Joseph Nevin. Nevin had been an initiator of public housing in New Jersey and had over twenty years of public housing experience behind him. He was recognized as one of the leading housing officials in the nation. Danzig did not succeed in getting federal officials to move faster on the new program, but he did persuade Nevin to leave the Public Housing Administration in order to serve as NHA's Director of Redevelopment. By the close of 1949 NHA had the jump in another sense. It had acquired and retained a staff of housing officials, lawyers, and administrators—a staff which combined experience in housing, sound political instincts, and a strong loyalty to the clearance program.

THE DECISION-MAKING PROCESS

Newark's urban redevelopment policies are products of the interaction of two elements: the goals of NHA's professional staff and the demands of certain nonlocal participants, like the Urban Renewal Administration, the Federal Housing Administration, and the private redevelopers.

NHA officials often say that their clearance decisions are made on the basis of "technical" rather than "political" criteria and that projects are planned in a "nonpolitical" environment. In one sense, those statements are true. NHA's clearance policies have not been the result of open conflict among local interest groups. Such conflict over slum clearance has been rare and has not affected the substance of NHA's decisions. NHA has provided the initiative for all clearance projects. The work of its expert staff has been shielded from random interference by local interests. Though the demands of such interests are often anticipated and taken into account by NHA's staff, decisions on projects are made in a low-temperature atmosphere and are often delegated to middle-rank staff men.

By a nonpolitical environment, Authority officials also mean that the cues of redevelopers and federal officials, rather than those of local interests, necessarily govern NHA's clearance decisions. Negotiations with nonlocal actors are conducted by Nevin and his immediate subordinates; dealing with local interests is deemed political, and this is handled by Danzig. Both are bargaining relations. Since the nonlocal participants largely determine the success or failure of local redevelopment, NHA's negotiations with them have a greater impact on the substance of clearance policy.

The initial goals of NHA's redevelopment officials were derived from their own experiences in public housing, from the values of the housing profession, and from the wording of the 1949 Act. These officials defined Newark's redevelopment problem as a lack of standard housing for middle-income families and an excess of substandard or slum housing. The purpose of the new program was to find the most dilapidated areas in the city, to clear them, and then to sell the areas to private redevelopers who would build moderately priced housing. NHA summed up its goals in one phrase: "Middle-income housing on cleared slum sites."

During Newark's first decade in urban redevelopment NHA discovered that these goals were only partially attainable within the Title I program as it was then defined. From 1949 to 1959 NHA had to learn which portions of its initial program were acceptable to private redevelopers, FHA, and URA, and which parts were not. This, briefly, was the course of redevelopment policy making during the first ten years.

NHA officials also learned that a rigid commitment to the initial goals and a refusal to accept half-victories would foreclose all clearance action. They eventually came to place greater emphasis on winning some kind of clearance than on obtaining clearance strictly in accordance with their initial purpose. As far as NHA officials were concerned, it had to be either pragmatism and flexibility in the planning of projects or no projects at all. . . .

STAGING A PROJECT

The nonpolitical context of NHA's decision making does not insure that agency officials can afford to be oblivious to the problem of securing local acceptance.[3] The Authority's staff, in fact, has developed a conscious strategy for facilitating such acceptance, at the same time protecting its flexibility in dealing with outside parties. This strategy centers around the staging of projects or the sequential order of negotiations. To an extent, the procedures described below have been forced upon NHA by the exigencies of dealing with redevelopers and federal officials. But NHA officials are fully aware of the strategic uses of this procedure.

The keys to NHA's staging process are the elaborate, preliminary negotiations involving NHA, redevelopers, and federal officials, and the low visibility of this preparatory stage. The result of these informal, unpublicized negotiations is a detailed project package. The necessary political support for this package is negotiated in advance in order to avoid public defeats or open skirmishes. Local officials generally must accept the package as is or risk jeopardizing the entire proposal.

NHA's first step in its recent projects has been to find a redeveloper interested in Newark. It is self-evident to NHA officials that decisions on sites and their uses must be adapted to the demands of the investor if projects are to be successful. Such demands, moreover, can best be met if NHA remains the City's sole spokesman in these dealings. No one outside NHA has direct dealings with the redevelopers. Most local participants first learn of a new clearance project when they read the formal announcement by NHA in the newspapers.

It also is self-evident to Authority officials that the formative stages of a project must be protected from excessive public interference. The redevelopers themselves demand secrecy so that they can either back out gracefully or make a dramatic announcement of their plans. In addition, NHA officials feel that the announcement of tentative or alternative plans serves to excite opposition in several neighborhoods, whereas only one area will eventually be cleared. Such a preliminary an-

[3] *Staging a Project:* Since the statements in this and the following subsections are the author's own synthesis of personal interviews and of a large body of written data, the sources of these statements cannot be precisely pinpointed. The generalizations are, to a large extent, documented and illustrated throughout the remainder of the study.

nouncement also gives various local interests the idea that the situation is still fluid and, hence, still amenable to their influence. NHA seldom makes a public announcement until it knows exactly what the project is to be.

NHA's next step, after finding a redeveloper, is to begin discussions with URA in order to secure federal planning funds and a capital grant reservation. Some indication of FHA's willingness to insure a mortgage on the site is also sought. For as long as a year the Director of Redevelopment will shuttle back and forth between the Philadelphia office of URA, the New York office of FHA, and the redeveloper's staff, in search of a plan agreeable to all. From NHA's point of view this is the most crucial stage of a project; it also is the most difficult hurdle to overcome. Once a plan suitable to all interests has been found, the acquiescence of local officials is assured. As one Authority official put it: "There's no point in even talking about a project with the people down at City Hall until Philadelphia [URA] gives the go-ahead." To NHA officials the amazing thing is not that the City backs them fully, but that they ever get URA, FHA, and the redeveloper to agree.

This procedure also has its strategic value. Federal approval of a project makes subsequent local approval extremely likely. If City officials were to try to amend the project, they would disrupt the balanced network of negotiations and probably stop the flow of capital into Newark. When NHA proposals are submitted on the eve of a federal deadline, as they often must be, the pressure on City officials to approve without amendment or delay is even greater.

NHA officials have had good working relations with URA's Philadelphia office from the beginning. The Regional Office has occasionally intervened in local disputes to support NHA's position. When other renewal groups or agencies have tried to deal with URA, they have found that only Danzig and Nevin have good access to the Regional Office. This access has also permitted NHA officials to become the interpreters of federal housing legislation and policies for all others in Newark.

SECURING CITY HALL SUPPORT

NHA's next and final step before a formal announcement is to clear the project with the mayor or, before 1954, with the majority bloc of city commissioners. Even at this early stage the mayor is under pressure to ratify NHA's arrangements with Philadelphia and the redevelopers. If there were any serious political objections to the project, NHA presumably would take them into account. Exactly how far NHA would go in accommodating the mayor is a moot point, for neither Ralph Villani, Mayor from 1949 to 1953, nor Leo Carlin, Mayor after 1953, ever raised any major objections.

The support of municipal agencies involved in public construction related to slum clearance is often as important as the support of the mayor. Any clearance project, but particularly area-wide renewal, requires the widening and repaving of streets, the construction of schools, the relocation of sewers and underground utilities, and other supportive actions by local agencies. To avoid embarrassment after the formal announcement of a project, NHA attempts to extract beforehand a tentative promise of cooperation from the appropriate agencies. Since renewal projects are more palatable to local officials if a large part of the City's one-third share can be defrayed by local construction, NHA has had added incentive for involving public works agencies in its projects.

These agencies have their own good reasons for negotiating with NHA. Most of them find that they can increase their share of the municipal budget and facilitate approval of their projects by linking their activities to an expanding, federally aided program. The Superintendent of Schools, for example, backed NHA's first two projects with public school construction. With URA paying part of the cost of these new schools, approval by the Board of Education was virtually assured, even if it meant slightly increasing the capital budget for those years. This coordination of programs has served, though unintentionally, to weaken whatever control City Hall has over NHA through the City's one-third contribution. The major part of that contribution has been imbedded in the Board of Education's capital budget, where it is less available to manipulation by the mayor or the City Council.

The problem that confronts NHA is how to gain the support of relevant agencies without exposing the project to wholesale intervention by City Hall. How can certain agencies be lined up in advance without accumulating additions or amendments that eventually would make the project unworkable? If the project is ever to get started, the line of participation must be drawn somewhere.

NHA has responded to this problem by distinguishing between those agencies which must be consulted in advance and those agencies whose concurrence usually can be counted upon once the formal announcement has been made. Construction agencies generally fall into the first category; service and regulatory agencies into the second. In the pre-announcement consultations, moreover, NHA tries to extract a pledge of cooperation by outlining the probable effect of the project on the agency concerned and indicating the supportive action required from the agency. Although all questions of the agency will be answered by NHA, the project plans are not made available for general inspection. To minimize potential political interference, NHA's staff members also try, wherever possible, to deal with the corresponding staff official in the agency, not with the top man. Thus, Nevin deals exclusively with the Superintendent of Schools, Edward Kennelly, and lets Kennelly make all presentations to the Board of Education.

The successful nature of these operations was demonstrated in March, 1953, when relevant agency heads were brought together to testify on the proposed redevelopment plan for the North Ward. Commissioner Leo Carlin, who probably expected this meeting to point up NHA's lack of communication with City Hall, found that most of his subordinates in the Department of Public Works already had discussed the project with Nevin and had pledged their support. The agencies indicated that they had been briefed on their role, but they revealed no extensive familiarity with the details of the plan. The agency heads who had not been briefed proved unwilling to stand in the way of the project.

Later, Carlin, as mayor, altered his former position and encouraged negotiations between Nevin and the administrative agencies. Only in those rare cases when NHA and an agency are deadlocked do the negotiations rise to the mayor's office and become visible to the newspaper-reading public. The 1954 City Charter's attempt to centralize authority at City Hall apparently did nothing to disrupt NHA's relations with the administrative agencies. In April, 1955, a meeting of agency heads to discuss the Central Ward project showed the same pattern of support for NHA that had emerged in the 1953 meeting.

THE FORMAL ANNOUNCEMENT

About two years generally intervene between the initial selection of a site and the formal announcement of a project. The proposal is not publicized during this time, in part to protect NHA's negotiations with URA, redevelopers, and City Hall, and in part to secure a maximum impact for the formal announcement. By agreement with the local reporters covering urban renewal, a few discreet hints about a project may be periodically released, but the major announcement is saved for a big spread in the Sunday editions.

Outside of its attempt to stage the announcement of a project, however, NHA does not devote any substantial resources to publicity or public relations. Authority officials have said that too much publicity often stimulates organized interests that otherwise would have remained inert. The public relations staff of the business bloc developed an over-all rationale of the renewal program, which NHA officials have been inclined to let stand. Outside of this, NHA's sole public relations efforts have centered on maintaining good relations with the press.

The Newark *News* has been a major spokesman for the conservative, reform-minded civic leaders and a leading supporter of charter revision, the Carlin administration, and slum clearance. Because of this concern with good government, critics of NHA generally receive short shrift in the editorials of the *News*. In addition, neither the *News* nor Newark's other important daily, the *Star Ledger,* gives significant attention to NHA's negotiations with local parties. These dailies, like many other newspapers, define "news" as dramatic action or conflict. Since overt conflict among the renewal participants is infrequent, press treatment of local renewal is limited largely to formal announcements by NHA.

Reporters covering local renewal often are baffled by the technical questions involved. By seeking clarification of these questions from Authority officials, the reporters help reinforce NHA's position as interpreter of federal policies. Through this symbiotic relationship, moreover, NHA has inadvertently gained considerable influence over the treatment of its activities by the local press. It has had no reason to fear newspaper attacks or attempted exposés.

THE ACCUMULATION OF COMMITMENTS

After the Authority announces a project and the mayor approves an application to URA for survey and planning funds, the pressure on the City Council to add its assent is overwhelming. By this time, to quote one informant, the project is "frozen." The councilmen must consider the proposal

on a "take it or leave it" basis; rarely have they seriously considered "leaving" a proposal approved by NHA and the
mayor.

As the project progresses and the amount of funds and
energy expended by NHA, URA, the redevelopers, and City
Hall agencies accumulates, the commitment of these participants to the project increases proportionately. NHA may begin a project despite some major problem or disagreement
among the participants, confident that the accumulation of
commitments will eventually lead to an agreement or solution.

Such an accumulation of commitments also makes effective
intervention by local interests increasingly difficult. The City
Council must eventually approve an urban renewal plan and
a relocation plan, and the Central Planning Board (CPB)
must declare the entire area blighted, but such action normally has been routine. As members of the Council and CPB
have said, effective local review of clearance proposals can
occur only at the very outset of a proposal.

At the later stages NHA follows the same procedure used in
launching a proposal. The urban renewal plan, for example, is
discussed with the redevelopers, then with URA and FHA,
and finally with the administrative agencies at City Hall. After
further discussion with the mayor it is presented to the City
Council and CPB. At this point the time, energy, and money
already expended preclude serious local review.

MAINTAINING THE PACE

In the post-announcement stage NHA, the redeveloper, and
URA continue to negotiate in order to determine what specific uses are appropriate to the site.[4] In this way it is not
basically different from the pre-announcement stage, although
the bargaining becomes more and more specific. The initial
plan of a project or the public image presented in the formal
announcement may have to be altered substantially as new
problems emerge and the demands of participants change. A
rigid commitment by NHA officials to the initial plan would
strain, if not break, the commitment of other parties to the

[4] *Maintaining the Pace:* For the pyramiding of resources see Robert
A. Dahl, *Who Governs? Democracy and Power in an American City*
(New Haven, Yale University Press, 1961), Chapter 19; for the strategy
of activism as practiced by independent authorities see Wallace S. Sayre
and Herbert Kaufman, *Governing New York City: Politics in the Metropolis* (New York, Russell Sage Foundation, 1960), pp. 337–43.

project. From NHA's point of view the major problem of the post-announcement stage is not to execute the initial plan without alteration but to keep the commitments of outside parties "warm."

One way to maintain such commitments is to maintain a rapid pace throughout the project. Redevelopers and federal officials quickly lose interest in projects that drag on interminably. For this reason, prolonged consideration by the City Council or CPB can prove highly damaging. For the same reason, NHA will hasten to break deadlocks in negotiations, even if it means a further departure from the initial plan.

In October, 1959, when URA told Authority officials that funds for the downtown program would have to be spread over a ten-year period, Danzig and Nevin devised a plan to proceed simultaneously with all projects. Rather than handle each project serially and risk losing some redevelopers who were awaiting their turn, NHA divided the larger projects into stages and sought immediate action on the first stage of all projects. In this way all of the commitments to all of the projects were maintained.

This emphasis on rapid and sustained activity applies not only to particular projects but to the entire program. Since the early 1940s NHA officials have emphasized the importance of keeping active and of always having a few proposals under consideration. Activism draws redevelopers to the city, impresses federal officials, stimulates the morale of the agency's staff, and gives the agency an edge in its negotiations with local interests. In the world of urban renewal, project building seems to yield more project building, and clearance activity seems to acquire a momentum of its own. After a certain point successful agencies can do nothing wrong. They are rarely involved in political skirmishes because they are rarely challenged.

There also seems to be a cycle of failure. Inactivity, a loss of status among redevelopers and federal officials, and increasing vulnerability to local political interference seem to reinforce each other. As some NHA officials see it: "a program either catches fire or it doesn't."

One further comment about NHA's strategies should be made. It may be said that the Authority's rules of thumb provide no help in securing local approval of a ten-year redevelopment plan or a long-range scheme of interrelated projects. In fact, NHA's emphasis on gaining approval of the particular project at hand and on avoiding general policy statements is deliberate. NHA believes that ten-year redevelopment plans are impractical, cannot be realized, and only serve to impede the Authority's negotiations with outside parties. It is also convinced that the difficulty experienced in securing local approval of a proposal increases in direct proportion to the all-encompassing character of that proposal. Agencies should not submit a proposal until they know exactly what they want. Proposals should be worded in the most specific terms possible, and more general questions on "where the program is going" should be avoided. Publicizing long-range policy statements or seeking local approval of a ten-year plan is unnecessary to renewal achievement. More than that, it invites disaster.

THE "CLEAN DEAL"

Ask most Housing Authority officials to explain the success of their redevelopment program, and they will reply that private redevelopers and federal officials know they can get a "clean deal" in Newark. When taking part in a slum clearance project in Newark, these outside participants do not have to make separate arrangements with a variety of local officials, yielding concessions at each step in the negotiations and often getting embroiled in local politics. Instead they conduct all their business with a few men in the Housing Authority. These men have the freedom from local interference to bargain flexibly and are sufficiently confident of their control of local renewal processes to make broad commitments. Having once reached a settlement with Danzig, private redevelopers need not concern themselves with having to amend the agreement or with making political payoffs in order to facilitate its local acceptance. The officials of URA, moreover, need not worry that the project will become a local political football once federal funds have been committed. NHA not only has the autonomy to deal freely with these participants, it also has the capacity to deliver on all its promises in record time.

One observer may have exaggerated NHA's importance, but not by very much, when he said: "They [NHA] own the slums. They can sell any piece of real estate in that area to a redeveloper before it's even acquired. And they don't have to check with anyone [in Newark] before they do it. City Hall has got to back them up." This is another way of saying that the Authority has attained its major goals: a free hand to deal with outside participants and a guarantee of unqualified local acceptance of the resulting clearance proposal. To NHA officials a local redevelopment program stands or falls on whether it attracts the necessary outside commitments. A redevelopment agency that has transformed local renewal processes into a routine operation will have little difficulty in attracting these commitments.

This, in summary, is the pattern of policy formation in Newark's urban redevelopment program. The pattern depends upon the existence of a stable and permissive local environment where organized responses to the agency's decisions can be predicted—and often discounted—in advance. NHA's aggressive procedures would probably backfire if used in a less firmly structured political situation. Exactly how this type of benign environment emerged is a crucial question and one that cannot be answered wholly in terms of NHA's strategies. It is a question which the remainder of this study tries to answer.

At the same time, it would be unwise to overemphasize environmental factors and to underestimate the importance of NHA's personnel and their strategies. The formal organization of urban renewal in all cities tends to be more or less dispersive. Before a project can be launched, a large number of independent actors must be persuaded to participate. Some person or agency must bring all the parties together, negotiate support for the project, and quiet or mediate opposition. Someone must build an organization to provide the dispersed renewal structure with an informal peak. An acquiescent local environment may make the job of the renewal entrepreneur easier, but an acquiescent environment alone is insufficient. There must also exist in the same person or agency both the awareness of the need for this entrepreneurial function and the political skill to carry it out.

In Newark NHA's top staff have the necessary entrepreneurial abilities. In this group (Louis Danzig, Joseph Nevin, Samuel Warrence, Augustine Kelly, and Joseph Reilly) are combined the skills of the housing official, the administrator, the lawyer, and the politician. These men share a strong loyalty to the program and to Newark, a willingness to put in long hours, and an instinctive feeling for the politics of administration. It is true that their task as renewal entrepreneurs has been facilitated by the permissiveness of the local political environment, but it is also true that they had the insight to recognize this permissiveness and to adopt procedures to exploit it. They also had a hand in shaping that environment, as future pages will testify. NHA's responses to the political environment and its efforts to shape that environment are basic concomitants of Newark's success in urban renewal. One member of the business block grudgingly admitted: "Without Lou Danzig and Joe Nevin, there'd be nothing in the city—no clearance, no Jack Parker, no Turner-Galbreath—nothing—just a lot of talk and plans."

. . .

No systematic attempt has been made to determine the exact scope of "political" interference in NHA's decision making during the 1940s, but most informants believe that the scope was broad.[5] In 1948 the Essex County Prosecutor thought he had enough evidence of intervention in site selection to institute a grand jury investigation. Commissioner Ralph Villani, whose department included NHA, was anxious to avoid such an inquiry, particularly since it would occur six months before an election. To avert an investigation, Villani asked for the resignation of NHA's Executive Director and began searching for a new man who would "clean house" at the Authority. He eventually reached into the ranks of his own electoral organization and offered the job to a long-time political aide, Louis Danzig.

Danzig agreed to assume the executive directorship and to clean house in exchange for a set of informal guarantees from Villani and the other city commissioners. First, he insisted that the commissioners help in making the office of executive director the true center of decision and initiative. To meet this requirement, the city commissioners agreed to grant him a five-year contract rather than the single-year agreements heretofore used. They also agreed to transact all their business with NHA through his office and not through the NHA commissioners. Second, Danzig sought full power to take "politics" out of the housing program, that is, to restrict the extent of the politicos' interference in NHA policy making. He insisted on a free hand in matters of policy, along with a guarantee of support for the policies that NHA developed. Danzig made it clear that he wanted no haggling over future projects and that he would make no accommodations or deals to get

---

[5] *Taking NHA out of "Politics":* This account of NHA in the 1940s and of the events in 1948 is based largely on interviews but can be glimpsed in the publications of NHA cited in Note 1. In addition, see: review articles in Newark *News*, Aug. 22, 1952, June 7, 1953, and Sept. 15, 1957; *The Realtor*, 1949, *passim*.

them approved. This understanding was in part explicit, in part tacit, and often ambiguous. Yet, all concerned seemed to agree that some kind of basic accord had been reached.

In 1948 and 1949 NHA embarked on a new set of public housing policies without first consulting the politicos or giving them an opportunity to intervene. First, NHA shifted its emphasis from low-rise projects in outlying areas to mammoth projects in the midst of the Central Ward slums. For the first time, NHA became engaged in the clearance of occupied sites and in the construction of significant new housing in Negro areas. NHA also began racial integration of its existing projects. The pattern of NHA-City Hall relations that has prevailed in the urban renewal program was foreshadowed by the city commissioners' quick approval of all these shifts in public housing policy.

The "Political" and the "Nonpolitical"

While insisting upon this freedom from political interference in matters of policy, Danzig made it clear to the commissioners that he would give fair hearing to all "political" requests that did not affect the substance of general policy.[6] If the Authority could help the politicos on small favors that left over-all policy unaffected, NHA would have been foolish not to do so. Some of NHA's critics among the civic groups disillusioned by the Authority's continuing immersion in "political" practices ignore one important aspect of the change that occurred in 1948. Danzig established large, "political-free" areas of NHA activity and insisted that the politicos respect the line separating "political" and "nonpolitical." In

[6] *The "Political" and the "Nonpolitical":* Statements in this section rely largely on personal interviews. The relevant NHA documents are: Personnel Report (presented by Executive Director at every Board meeting); Annual Report of the Tenant Selection and Relocation Division; Tenancy Report (periodically submitted to the Board), *passim.* The Newark *News* has carefully covered NHA's policies on the hiring of personnel, the awarding of contracts, and the selection and treatment of public housing tenants. Coverage during the 1953–54 change-over in government was particularly good. See: May 6, 10, June 7, 11, 30, July 5, 9, 16, 19, Aug. 2, 25, Sept. 23, Oct. 9, 23, 1953, Jan. 21, 30, March 5, 11, April 17, 30, May 13, 20, June 15, 17, 24, 25, July 22, Aug. 7, 9, 17, 18, 19, 22, 29, Sept. 16, 23, Oct. 21, 1954, Jan. 7, March 2, April 7, May 24, June 2, Sept. 22, Oct. 5, 11, 1955, Jan. 15, June 8, Aug. 9, Nov. 15, Dec. 13, 1956, Jan. 9, 10, March 1, 3, 15, 28, April 11, 26, May 3, 10, 11, 16, 24, June 13, Dec. 19, 1957, April 25, May 9, 31, June 19, July 11, Aug. 6, Sept. 28, Nov. 23, 1958.

short, he continued to deal with the politicos on detailed considerations in return for complete discretion on major policy decisions.

One of Danzig's most important achievements, then, was to eliminate "political" considerations from decisions involving the selection of sites, the awarding of contracts, and the naming of private redevelopers. Another achievement was to remove any taint of wrong-doing or personal profiteering from the program. Even its critics concede that the renewal program is scrupulously run. Through continual negotiations with the politicos, moreover, Danzig has steadily whittled down the size of the remaining "political" area. "Political" considerations, he has argued, must be kept within reasonable limits lest they wreck the program. Excessive "political" interference would destroy the expertise and morale of NHA's staff and could result in another public exposé or grand jury probe.

There probably are limits, however, to how far the Executive Director can curtail this "political" area. He must find an optimal balance between the need to recruit skill, to maintain control over the Authority personnel, and to protect NHA from scandal, on the one hand, and the concomitant necessity of ensuring acceptance of NHA's programs by City Hall, on the other. Thus, both NHA's continuing involvement in "political" considerations and its elimination of such considerations from certain areas are necessary to the Authority's success in slum clearance.

Danzig's practices in hiring NHA personnel illustrate the nature of his arrangements with the politicos. The evidence indicates that appointments to minor positions on NHA's permanent staff and to temporary jobs like real-estate appraisal and day labor have been cleared with the politicos and have often been made on the basis of their recommendations. But Danzig fought to break up the little empires each city commissioner had formed among NHA employees, whose security of tenure fluctuated with the political fortunes of their sponsors on the Board. Under Danzig an employee could not rely on his sponsor for continued employment and would be discouraged from maintaining close ties with that sponsor. Danzig has also sought the freedom to fill the top positions in each division of the Authority by merit and to recruit anywhere in the country. He has occasionally bypassed the politicos on other positions as well. If they insisted upon clearing every NHA appointment, Danzig told them, there would be no program at all.

Next to the hiring and firing of personnel, the activities of the Tenant Selection and Relocation Division are the most important focus of the politicos' demands on NHA. It is here that the Authority comes into direct, persistent contact with the public at large. It is here that the politicos make the most requests and here that NHA can take these requests into account without altering general policy.

A public housing tenant, therefore, may find it easier to secure a public housing unit, prevent eviction from a project, secure a unit in a better project, or have NHA reconsider his rent, if he has the right sponsor at City Hall. In the same way, someone owning property or residing in an area slated for clearance may encourage NHA to give him more information on its plans for his block, to re-examine the appraisal made of his property, to delay an eviction or condemnation proceeding against him, or to give greater attention to his relocation problems. After the Authority has acquired his building, but before it has relocated him elsewhere, he may find it easier to secure more heat and more structural improvements from his new landlord by channeling his requests through certain people at City Hall. Of course, there is no guarantee that he or his sponsor will be successful. A phone call from the politico merely guarantees that the client's folder will be pulled out of the file and re-examined by NHA's staff.

It may be argued, then, that NHA has achieved autonomy in matters of general policy by permitting some degree of "political" intervention in the detailed application of policy. This arrangement has been possible partly because the politicos have appeared less interested in influencing over-all policy than in appearing to help out particular people. It may also be argued that NHA has built the stable relations that sustain its redevelopment ventures by making accommodations in the details of its public housing administration. In one sense, then, vesting redevelopment powers in the public housing agency has contributed greatly to the redevelopment program's success.

POLITICS, PLANNING AND THE PUBLIC INTEREST*

Martin Meyerson and Edward Banfield

The question, therefore, arises why the Council and the Authority engaged in a long struggle rather than in cooperation. We will limit our discussion to the choice of a strategy by the Authority. This strategy was, of course, to some extent a response to that adopted by the Council leadership or, more precisely, to what the heads of the Authority supposed was the strategy of the Council leadership.

The strategy of the Authority was to struggle rather than to bargain. Indeed, the Authority went somewhat out of its way to provoke the leaders of the Council; it did this by refusing to enter into even a *pro forma* discussion with the housing committee of the Council before the sites were formally submitted, by locating a large project in Duffy's ward without giving him any advance notice of it, and by taking a hostile tone in its public appearances before the Council.

It is quite possible that, given the situation that existed in 1949, this was a rational strategy. Certainly it would have been rational if the Authority's ends had been symbolic-ideological, i.e., if it had been interested chiefly in what one public housing supporter called "good ideological education for the thought leaders." But even though its ends were (as we believe) mainly intrinsic-concrete, struggling may nevertheless have been its best strategy under the circumstances. For in 1949 the "Big Boys" were sure they could dictate a settlement; their experience in the relocation program had probably convinced them that the commissioners could be bullied into accepting almost anything and so, although they seemingly were willing to discuss matters with the commissioners, they undoubtedly expected to do most of the talking themselves. If the alternative to a struggle was a dictated settlement, it was better for the Authority to struggle. And if it was necessary to struggle, it was possibly good strategy (although this seems to us very much open to question) to take a hostile posture.

But at an earlier time—say in 1947—the rational strategy might have been very different from that which the Authority

* Glencoe: The Free Press, 1955, pp. 256–67 (selected portions).

actually followed. At that time the heads of the Authority, recognizing that despite the formal independence of their agency they would have to share power with those who controlled the city government, should have tried to reach an understanding on essentials with the new Mayor and with the leaders of the Council. This could not have been done simply on the basis of "good fellowship" of course (although this would have had its place), but it might have been done by making it clear to the politicians that the advantages to them of cooperating with the agency would be greater than the disadvantages. This, in fact, was what Shufro and others had done when they helped persuade Mayor Kelly to make public housing part of his appeal to the liberal, labor, and Negro votes. The Authority's strategy should have been to persuade the "Big Boys" to accept its ends and its view of the situation, of course, but, failing that, it should have made a general compromise which would have defined in broad terms the place that public housing was to occupy in Chicago.[1] Only if it appeared that more could be gained by struggling than by making such a settlement should the Authority have ceased its efforts to negotiate.

A number of reasons can be pointed out why this strategy, which in our opinion was the optimum, was not adopted.

1. During Mayor Kelly's regime the Authority could be independent because Kelly paid its political bills. After Kelly's departure, it had to earn its own political living in a hostile world, but it did not become fully aware of this necessity or its implications for a long time. Until 1948, when the state law was changed to give the Council veto power over sites, the Authority had been free to put projects where it liked. That this freedom existed in part because of the backing of the head of the Democratic machine was lost sight of during the several years Kelly protected it. After his retirement the Authority had only the shell of independence but out of habit it acted as if it had real independence.

2. It was not until late in 1947 or early in 1948 that the heads of the Authority fully realized that Mayor Kennelly

[1] If it could have been sure that the Authority would not go beyond certain agreed-upon bounds, the Council leadership might have been very glad to leave the whole unpleasant business of site selection to the Authority. In that case the Authority could have held its own public hearings on terms favorable to itself (as is done in other cities), and the aldermen could have had the satisfaction of being both for public housing and against disturbance of white neighborhoods without having to take any responsibility for compromising these two ends.

was not going to be a mayor in the same sense that Mayor Kelly had been or, indeed, in any significant sense at all. Until 1948 it was reasonable for them to suppose that the Mayor was the person with whom a general understanding would have to be reached. But when at last it became evident that the city government was to be run by the "Big Boys" of the Council, it would not have been easy for the heads of the Authority, even if they had tried, to reach an understanding with them. The "Big Boys" were not especially interested in public housing except when it was a "hot" issue; for the most part they were occupied with matters such as street lighting and garbage collection which had a more intimate connection with the interests of their wards. It would probably have been hard for the Authority to get the attention of the key aldermen when the housing issue was not especially "hot."

3. The heads of the Authority were, in our judgment, somewhat disposed to underrate the willingness of Duffy and Lancaster to take a reasonable view of things and to make concessions. At the same time they were somewhat disposed to overrate the political power that they and their allies could bring to bear upon the aldermen. This disposition to overrate their power was perhaps, to some extent, an aspect of the "producers' bias" which, in our opinion, caused them to magnify the demand for public housing.

4. Because it interposed a group of part-time amateurs who had no real responsibility for the agency's program between them, the board form of organization made effective contact between the operating heads of the Authority and the political heads of the city government very difficult. Taylor was a conscientious and devoted chairman, but he did not have enough detailed knowledge of the agency's work or a strong enough commitment to its purposes to make him the most effective bargainer on its behalf. The staff could not negotiate with the politicians directly, of course, for the politicians, knowing that Taylor and the other commissioners would be easier to deal with, would have refused to talk with them. Thus, although the situation did not preclude fighting (it was not necessary to be recognized by the politicians in order to fight them of course) it did preclude both cooperation and bargaining, for negotiation could have been carried on only by the board.

5. The Authority was committed to its supporters. During the New Deal era, it was an advantage to be identified with the larger issues of reform and with the liberal-left. Shufro had labored to make the Authority and its leadership a sym-

bol around which believers in good government and, to a lesser degree perhaps, the welfare state would rally. This was good strategy at the time; it was probably in order to have the advantage of such a symbol that Mayor Kelly gave the Authority his protection. But during and after the War the political climate changed so that affiliations which had formerly been an advantage became a decided disadvantage. Assuming as we do that its ends were principally concrete-intrinsic, it would opportunistically have been good strategy for the Authority to have made a break with its old associations and to have emphasized in its public relations line that its ends were purely "practical." However, if it turned its back on its old supporters it might have found no new ones to take their place.

6. The heads of the Authority were lacking in political knowledge (including information, insight, and judgment). Their knowledge may have been good compared to that of most municipal administrators, but, even so, it was not good enough to meet the demands of the situation. They would, we think, have chosen a different and more effective strategy if they had understood the political situation better: if they had realized, for example, how much they owed their independence to Mayor Kelly's protection and how necessary it would be to find some new source of power when that power was withdrawn; if they had seen earlier that it was Duffy, not Kennelly, with whom they had chiefly to deal; and if they had more correctly evaluated the amount of power their allies among the civic organizations could muster and how indifferent some of them—for example, the Negroes—would prove to the public housing site issue.

This lack of knowledge was not an "accidental" feature of the situation. The kind of knowledge that was needed—whether the Mayor would put pressure on Duffy or leave him to manage matters in his own way; how Duffy would evaluate the significance for his own position of pressure from the *Sun-Times* as against opposing pressure from the neighborhood improvement associations in his ward; at what point the residents of Jeffrey Manor would change their registrations from Democratic to Republican; how much importance the Mayor and Duffy would attach to the opinions of 89 pro-public housing Protestant ministers—could not be found in books and could not be obtained by the methods of fact gathering that bureaucracies usually employ. Indeed, some of the information that was most needed could not be obtained by any fact-gathering procedure; it had to be the product of judgment: somebody would have to try to look at matters through the eyes of the Mayor, Duffy, or the residents of Jeffrey Manor and make a guess.

Only people who were more or less constantly occupied with local politics were likely to have the bits and pieces of fact that were needed or to know where and how to get them. People who could think in somewhat the same terms as the Mayor, Duffy, and the residents of Jeffrey Manor—who "spoke their language"—might guess particularly well how they were likely to think. The very fact that their outlook was fundamentally unsympathetic to that of the Mayor, Duffy, and the residents of Jeffrey Manor unfitted most of the supporters of public housing to judge how they would behave. But even if there had not been this difficulty in entering into the others' mental processes, there would still have been few who could have made sound judgments. For making sound judgments under conditions of uncertainty is an art; it cannot be reduced to a technique which one can learn from books.[2]

And, of course, even among people skilled in the art of making political judgments there would probably have been disagreement on some crucial questions. (It is possible, for example, that some astute politicians would have expected the Negro community to give the Authority much more support than it did.) Thus, even with the best information and the best judgment, the Authority might still have made the same mistakes (if mistakes they were); it is, of course, very common for astute politicians to make opposite judgments on the basis of the same facts.

Since there are few objective indicators of political competence except political success (even that is not a very good one, because it is possible to be successful in spite of poor judgment or to be unsuccessful in spite of good judgment), anyone may claim it and whether the claim is warranted or

[2] In his autobiography, *You're the Boss,* Edward J. Flynn has emphasized that a politician's skill lies largely in his ability to "guess right" (p. 228) and that this is something that can be learned only by experience. "It would be rather difficult to put your finger on one particular item or incident that would illustrate just what I learned from Mr. Murphy. It would be like trying to tell what you learned from your childhood nurse. My knowledge was mainly obtained by being with him and observing his political philosophy; by watching situations as they arose and seeing whether his handling of them resulted in success or failure." (p. 131.) Edward J. Flynn, *You're the Boss,* Viking, New York, 1947.

not there is no way to tell for sure.[3] In taking the advice of the Public Housing Association leaders, the heads of the Authority had to make a judgment of these leaders' political competence. And in doing so, they could not help judging their own political judgment.

Since political competence is so hard to gauge, it is easy for a political adviser to be disloyal to his principal. To protect himself against this possibility, the principal must discount the advice he gets from one whose loyalty cannot be counted on absolutely; only the advice of those whose motives are beyond question can be taken at face value. Thus, only the advice of dedicated supporters of public housing was given full weight by the leaders of the Public Housing Association. If someone whom they did not fully trust told them that the Negroes would not support public housing vigorously, this advice would probably have been disregarded. Since the people who were in close touch with the Mayor, Duffy, and the opposition were not dedicated public housing supporters, the advice of many politically well informed people was in general not sought or taken.

Dedicated public housing supporters tend to have what Mannheim termed a "utopian" thought-style: they are systematically biased by virtue of being generally oriented toward changing reality.[4] People who are not biased in this way are

[3] J. S. Mill gives these criteria for distinguishing people of political wisdom: "Actual public services will naturally be the foremost indication: to have filled posts of magnitude, and done important things in them, of which the wisdom has been justified by the results; to have been the author of measures which appear from their effects to have been wisely planned; to have made predictions which have been often verified by the event, seldom or never falsified by it; to have given advice, which when taken has been followed by good consequences, which neglected, by bad. There is doubtless a portion of uncertainty in these signs of wisdom; but we are seeking for such as can be applied by persons of ordinary discernment. They will do well not to rely much on any one indication, unless corroborated by the rest; and, in their estimation of the success or merit of any practical effort, to lay great stress on the general opinion of disinterested persons conversant with the subject matter." *Utilitarianism, Liberty and Representative Government*, J. M. Dent, London, 1910, p. 320.

[4] "The concept of utopian thinking reflects the . . . discovery . . . that certain oppressed groups are intellectually so strongly interested in the destruction and transformation of a given condition of society that they unwittingly see only those elements in the situation which tend to negate it. Their thinking is incapable of correctly diagnosing an existing condition of society. They are not at all concerned with what really exists: rather in their thinking they already seek to change the situation that exists. Their thought is never a diagnosis of the situation; it can be

not likely to be leaders of such groups as the Public Housing Association or even, perhaps, to be dedicated supporters of public housing at all.

A political process which involves negotiation (cooperation or bargaining) necessitates fuller communication among the parties to the issue than does one which involves only struggling. Negotiation must take place through discussion, whereas a struggle, although it involves some exchange of meanings, is primarily a mutual endeavor to apply power. A discussion can be initiated and carried on only if all parties are able and willing to exchange meanings, whereas one party can force others into a struggle simply by attacking them. In our opinion, the choice of struggle rather than negotiation by the leaders of the public housing forces is to be explained in some part by these considerations. The board—and not the CHA staff or the Public Housing Association—was the one body with which the "Big Boys" were willing to negotiate; therefore, the only strategy open to the staff and the Association was struggle. Moreover, none of the public housing leaders—not even the commissioners—was able to communicate effectively with the aldermen, and this was another circumstance which may have inclined them toward struggling as a strategy.

The circumstances which impeded communication between the public housing leaders and the aldermen seem to have been mainly differences in social class, temperament, professional style, and ideology.

The importance as a barrier to communication of differences in social class (along with such empirically related characteristics as education and moral refinement) may be seen in Miss Wood's relations with most of the aldermen. How was she, who had taught English to the girls at Vassar, to do business with Paddy Bauler, a saloon-keeper from a riverward whose way of dealing with a problem might sometimes be to say, "Hell, boys, let's go 'round and have a few drinks?" Even with Duffy, who kept a florist shop instead of a saloon, her communication was not much better. (This was so, although Miss Wood, apparently to overcome the handicap of her class origin, was in the habit of using the word "guy" in place of "person" and even though Duffy, apparently to overcome the handicap of *his* class origin, was in the habit of using

---

used only as a direction for action." Karl Mannheim, *Ideology and Utopia*, Routledge and Kegan Paul, London, 1936, p. 36.

the word "fellow" in place of "guy.") Even with Kelly, who was her strong supporter, she had not been able to communicate effectively. "Kelly respected and admired what I stood for," she once remarked, "but he hated to talk to me. We didn't talk the same language. But communication between us was excellent because Kelly liked to talk to Shufro and Shufro could talk the language of the street."[5]

That Miss Wood was a woman was a further barrier to communication. Some of the aldermen found it very difficult to express themselves in private conversation without resort to profanity.

Miss Wood's militant spirit prevented her from communicating effectively with some people. "She is not a person you can sit down and talk reasonably with," Teninga once complained. What was needed in her position, he went on, was someone who was not emotional and who had experience in the real estate business. This was the point of view of an opponent of public housing, but it was also held by some friends of public housing as well.

In part the difficulty in communication arose out of the difference between the "style" of the efficient professional administrator and that of the professional politician. Miss Wood apparently thought that it was becoming for an administrator to be brisk and businesslike and to give a prompt and highly articulate answer to any question that might be asked. This style seems to have irritated the politicians. They would probably have been more comfortable with someone who appeared ignorant at times, not only factually ignorant but morally ignorant as well. It would not be necessary for Miss Wood actually to be more ignorant—only to appear so. It was, in other words, more a matter of manners than anything else; the politicians seemed to think that to know all of the answers was a sign of arrogance in a bureaucrat—by knowing all of the answers he might mean to convey that he knew more than *they* did and perhaps that he was of higher social standing as well.[6]

---

[5] Interview Document.

[6] "The civil servant," Professor Shils has written, "particularly the civil servant of the level called before Congressional committees, tends to be considerably more educated and probably of a higher social and economic status as regards his origin than the legislator who is requesting a service of him or interrogating him. He is . . . not only more expert in the matter at hand but he usually, either wittingly or unwittingly, is also more the master of the situation than is the legislator. Resentment against those whose fortunate accidents of birth gave them

Finally there were ideological differences, real or imagined, that stood in the way of communication between Miss Wood and most of the aldermen and opponents of public housing. Many of them supposed—wrongly, of course—that she was bent on overturning the social order and, in particular, on building a vast amount of public housing, taxing the middle and upper classes to support the lower classes in comfortable idleness, and all but forcibly mixing the races. For her part, Miss Wood was apt to think that her opponents comprised a vast conspiracy against good government and against any social reform whatever. Insofar as both sides distrusted each other profoundly, there was no basis for discussion.

Many of these same difficulties existed in varying degrees in the relations of the other representatives of the Authority, both the commissioners and staff, with the aldermen and with Finitzo, Stech, Teninga, Sachs, and other small property and neighborhood spokesmen. Taylor was able to talk to the aldermen more easily than was Miss Wood; they knew that he was a businessman who had some influence among Negroes and this won him some respect. The aldermen could see, too, that he was anxious to be a good fellow. But Taylor did not conform to the stereotype of the Negro as a jolly colored man or for that matter to any other stereotype, and he was too dignified, too much a gentleman in his bearing, for most of the aldermen to feel quite at ease with him.

Shufro, Liveright, Alinsky and the many other aggressive spokesmen for the liberal-left were intolerable to many of the aldermen; they were, Duffy once remarked contemptuously, "pinks."[7]

One man who could communicate with the opposition was Commissioner Kruse, the official of the Flat Janitors' Union. Kruse had the vocabulary—the vocabulary of words, intonation, gesture, dress, ethnicity—which made him understood by the aldermen. But Kruse, unfortunately, was not a strong believer in public housing and he could not communicate with Miss Wood or the staff.

---

educational opportunities which were not available to the legislator is heightened—it certainly was heightened during the Roosevelt administration—by an attitude of personal, social and intellectual superiority. This sense of superiority very often does not exist at all but is nonetheless assumed to exist." The animus of the legislator against the bureaucrat is fed, Professor Shils goes on to say, by another cleavage in American life, that between intellectuals and politicians. Edward A. Shils, "The Legislator and his Environment," *op. cit.,* pp. 577 and 579.

[7] Interview Document.

Another who could communicate with the aldermen and the opponents of public housing was Sykes, the Australian-born engineer who had been chairman of the board of the Inland Steel Company. Sykes was not of the same social class as the aldermen, but he had cultivated the art of getting along with the people with whom he had to do business. Once he, Kruse, and McMillen met a group of anti-housing aldermen in the corridors of the City Hall. The aldermen began to attack the Authority. Sykes lifted his hat and pointed to the top of his head in a dramatic way. "Look," he said, "I haven't any horns. Why don't you fellows come over and talk to us?" As a result of this invitation, four aldermen did have an informal discussion with the commissioners, one of the first such discussions to take place.[8]

Miss Wood was aware of these problems. In making certain appointments she acknowledged the need to establish effective communication with the people with whom the agency had to deal: the comptroller, to cite one example, was a man who could talk the language of bankers, accountants, and businessmen. While Kelly was mayor she had used Shufro as a medium of communication with him. But Shufro, a man whom both she and Kelly liked, was a lucky accident, and when it was necessary for her to deal with Duffy and others of the South Side Bloc who did not happen to like Shufro she made no effort to find some new intermediary. Although it was a well understood convention in Chicago that most public jobs went to Catholics (and especially to Irish Catholics) there were very few Catholics on the top policy staff. Many of the top staff were Jews.

One reason why Miss Wood and the public housing supporters did not give more attention to the problem of establishing communication with the City Hall was that they were convinced that nothing short of abject surrender by the Authority would satisfy the politicians. She noted that although Sykes had a friendly conversation with the agency's enemies, they remained its enemies and nothing was changed by the conversation. Communication was valuable only as there was the possibility of reaching agreement and that this possibility existed she very much doubted in 1950.

In our judgment her skepticism was justified then. But a year or two earlier there might have been a possibility of establishing a somewhat more successful relationship with the

[8] Interview Document.

Council, although certainly not one which would have permitted the Authority to do all that its heads believed should be done.

When Mayor Kelly retired and it became evident that the predominant power lay with the South Side Bloc and especially with Duffy, Miss Wood might have done well, we think, to have appointed someone Duffy liked and trusted and for whose appointment to a high-paying job he would be grateful.[9] By making such an appointment, Miss Wood might have relieved herself of certain political tasks for which she was not particularly well qualified, thus freeing herself for long-range planning and for leadership, tasks for which she was preeminently well qualified.

[9] In the Spring of 1953 the board, on the initiative of Sykes, appointed as the Authority's general counsel a young man who was the second cousin of Richard J. Daley, the chairman of the Democratic County Central Committee. Miss Wood publicly protested the appointment, pointing out that a CHA regulation provided that a chief counsel must have eight years legal experience whereas the appointee had only five. The appointee, she told the newspapers, had stood 183rd in a class of 191 in law school and his assistant in the Authority would be a woman who had graduated from the same law school six months before he did standing fifth in a class of 203. "Up to now," Miss Wood said, "the commissioners have taken pride in the fact that the CHA has been untainted by politics. The commissioners do not set a very good example for the staff when they make a political appointment of this nature."

Miss Wood's protest was backed by local and national civic and church leaders. Finally the young man withdrew, hinting that he had been opposed because he was a Catholic. ("As a young American," he wrote, "I thought I would be entitled to the same fair play that any person, regardless of race, color, creed, religion, or nationalistic origin, is entitled to." *Chicago Sun-Times,* April 15 and 17, 1953.)

In our opinion, Miss Wood was wise to oppose this appointment, even though doing so must have created much ill-will. The appointee would have been the board's man, not hers. Moreover, the position of general counsel was too important to take any risks. But we think she would have been wise to have appointed such a man to a major position and to have done so on her own initiative, thus insuring the selection of someone whose loyalty would be to her.

ALCOA LOOKS AT URBAN REDEVELOPMENT*

Leon E. Hickman

THREE THINGS WE HAVE LEARNED

1. *Participation in urban redevelopment is good for Alcoa.*
This for two reasons: (a) The interest of the aluminum industry in the correct and increasing use of architectural aluminum products in high-rise buildings and; (b) our relative financial strength, due in no small part, I hasten to add, to the confidence and support of the banking and insurance fraternities.

Our relative financial stability gives us the strength to carry properties through the construction and fill-up stages when substantial losses are inevitable; and beyond that until an advantageous opportunity to sell is developed. We are also aided by annual earnings in the aluminum business against which we can charge off financing costs during building construction, operating losses during the fill-up period and depreciation once the properties are in operation. This means that the cash drain on a company in Alcoa's position is approximately half what it would be for a developer who had no other business.

2. *Our second conviction is that Alcoa is good for urban redevelopment.* That sounds immodest but I do not mean it in any way singular to Alcoa. The statement would be equally applicable to many well-established, reasonably successful, prideful, industrial companies that had become well enough established to be assured of reasonable permanence, and experienced enough to know that an essential ingredient of success in any business is satisfying the customer.

We know that our properties will only succeed if tenants or lessees get value received. Our reputation being on the line, the properties we develop are of institutional character, by which I mean of a quality at a reasonable midpoint between a speculative development and a monument! In addition to quality properties, we are in a position to furnish continuity of ownership and what we believe to be competent management.

* FROM an address presented at the National Mortgage Banking Conference February 17, 1964, Chicago, Ill., pp. 7–18 (selected portions).

To that end, we are moving toward the concept of being our own managers in all phases of planning, development and operation. Our rather immodest target for ourselves is to develop a real estate management and a rapport with tenants as outstanding as that achieved by the Metropolitan Life Insurance Company in its real estate projects, particularly those in New York City.

3. *The third thing we have learned is that we ought to assume direct responsibility for the planning, construction and management of our projects.* We must build and manage for the long pull. We have got to sell our projects to the communities of which they are a part; and, in terms of specifics, induce individuals to move their homes and businesses into our developments. This we can only do by building well, maintaining adequately and so serving those who pay us that they and their friends will come back for more.

We cannot know if a building is well built unless we supervise its building. We cannot know whether it is properly maintained unless we participate in its maintenance. We can only be sure that our garages are run as service adjuncts for the tenants if we are directly responsible for their operation.

We can only make our 180 acres at Century City a beauty spot that will delight everyone who lives or works there if we make the decisions as to what shall be done and how the property shall be maintained. As owner-managers, we planted 85 acres of it in California poppies and wild flowers; landscaped and planted the railroad right-of-way in front of the property; and boxed and replanted hundreds of priceless trees, reclaimed from the Twentieth Century Fox nursery. Management cannot delegate to others responsibility for deciding whether such investments are an amateur's dream or financially sound. . . .

Now let me mention four doubts, and you will see at once that we have more doubts than answers. These are points on which we have deep concern but no clear answers.

1. *Will local communities complete a redevelopment project?* The answer to this doubt will tell us whether an urban redevelopment is going to roll back the surrounding slums or whether the adjacent distressed areas ultimately will reclaim the island of redevelopment, just as the airstrips of New Guinea ultimately went back to the jungle.

As Alcoa's redevelopment projects come on-stream, we see the battle line forming in every instance. On one side of the street stands our development—new, prideful and hopeful. On the other side of the street—too often literally—stand the slums, waiting to take us over.

In part, it will be an economic battle. Our redevelopment will either so increase property values across the street that the slums no longer make economic sense, or the nearby distressed area will so slow-down or defeat the utilization of our new property that in time we will become discouraged and quit. And, in due course, our property will become indistinguishable from the slums.

The will of the community will be a decisive factor in the battle. This can find expression in a variety of forms, all the way from local aids, both governmental and private, to the initiation of a related series of redevelopment projects, each designed to roll back further the adjacent distressed areas.

The continued participation of the Federal Government is undoubtedly required, both in planning and funds. Certainly it does no good to create an island of redevelopment in an undesirable area if the community, in both public and private sectors, is not organized and determined to clean out the remaining blight. Otherwise, it is too much like removing part of a cancer.

The fight is a worthy one; the character of our urban life may be largely controlled by it. But if private participation like that of Alcoa is to be enlisted and maintained, there must be some assurance that the battle will be fought to a successful conclusion on all sectors.

This is brought home to Alcoa with particular force because its first two projects, Century City, Los Angeles, and our United Nations Plaza building in New York, are not redevelopments at all, but, rather, planning and development of property privately acquired and in neighborhoods entirely harmonious with the improvements we are making. We have to ask ourselves each day whether our shareholders would not be better served if we devoted our real estate efforts to properties in these favorable neighborhoods, rather than participation in the urban redevelopment of slum areas. The latter is the more challenging, probably the more worthwhile to the community, but private capital is only justified in participating if there is reasonable prospect that the battle can be won.

2. *A second doubt concerns the nature of the urban redevelopment programs that are offered for development.* Something is plainly wrong. Of 22,000 acres purchased by cities for redevelopment since the federal program began in 1949, only 6,800 acres have been resold to developers. Of the remaining,

6,000 acres haven't even been cleared of old buildings; while another 3,300 acres have been cleared but no redevelopers located. Some 5,900 acres are cleared and appear close to being sold to redevelopers. Obviously, there are serious gaps between acquisitions, clearing and redevelopment.

Part of the problem is the responsibility of the redevelopment agencies. They ought to choose for development neighborhoods that are capable of total redevelopment in one or a series of programs. Otherwise, you have only an island; or, to change the figure, the cancer is but partly removed.

A private redeveloper has got to have a lot of confidence in his local redevelopment authority to buy one of these programs. The redeveloper needs to know that the authority, and the community behind the authority, are reasonably sure of seeing the total project through to completion. He needs confidence that if he commits for a redevelopment which obligates him to build to a specific program over a substantial number of years, the redevelopment agency will be reasonably flexible in its insistence upon time schedules and in revisions of program, where experience indicates the original concept to be uneconomic.

The community also has a share of the responsibility. Urban redevelopment ought not to be undertaken unless the municipality is organized and dedicated to a total program. Anything short of that means ultimate defeat.

There are quite a number of such aroused communities and they are usually the ones that are staffed with able and dedicated urban renewal officials. I have met many such, but I am pleased to report, with an understandable touch of local pride, that no community is more aroused; no community has done more on its own momentum; and no municipality with which I am acquainted has a better or a more dedicated leadership than my home town of Pittsburgh. That probably had a lot to do with Alcoa's initial interest in this field. Former Governor David L. Lawrence; Mayor Joseph M. Barr; General Richard K. Mellon; Robert B. Pease, the executive director of the local Urban Redevelopment Authority; Theodore L. Hazlett, Jr., its counsel; and a host of others have joined to make urban redevelopment something of a crusade in Pittsburgh. There are many other such cities, but not enough. Short of such total dedication, urban redevelopment is fraught with peril and may be a vast waste of money. This is not a game for halfway measures and weakly-sponsored programs.

3. *Our third doubt goes to the efficacy of F.H.A. financing.*

I mean no criticism by that statement; urban renewal would be lost without the availability of such financing. And yet it has serious limitations.

For one thing, there is the $20,000,000 limit on a project loan. This figure does not fit many excellent redevelopment programs. More and more of such redevelopments are programed in projects several times this maximum figure; and this is highly desirable, for programs ought to be aimed at the removal of blight in an entire neighborhood. But this low ceiling leads to artificial division of many renewal projects into a series of $20,000,000 packages for F.H.A. purposes. When the problem is compounded by combining residential and business properties in a single program—as we must usually do if the residential properties are to be successful—it takes considerable gerrymandering to carve up the development into a series of financial packages that fit Federal Housing Authority requirements. Reflect for a moment on how you would refinance one of those redevelopments when you wanted to sell one of the properties. It ain't easy!

Likewise, feasibility studies, the approvals of plans and inspections of construction, understandably required by F.H.A. —and, in total, very beneficial to the quality of the projects— result in delays and loss of control of the timing of the project under circumstances that are maddening in all instances and financially expensive in most. Rent ceilings are imposed upon the project, understandable from the standpoint of the public, but often very difficult to reconcile with solvency.

All of this poses a dilemma. I grant readily enough that a public agency insuring 90 per cent or more of the construction money is entitled to call the tune; and yet the fact that the developer so largely loses control of his own property, and the timing of its development, is a deterrent to attracting private enterprises such as Alcoa into F.H.A.-financed projects.

Indeed, we are quite uncertain as to whether our Allegheny Center development in Pittsburgh, a choice urban renewal program contracted with the Urban Redevelopment Authority of Pittsburgh and involving some $60,000,000 of building over eight years, should be F.H.A.-financed or completed through regular banking and insurance channels.

It has been our experience with the two developments that we have financed privately—Century City and United Nations Plaza—that banks and other lending institutions have such a variety of lending programs available to a solvent builder of established reputation that it may well be worthwhile to forego the high leverage implicit in a 90 per cent F.H.A.-insured loan in favor of private financing through banks, insurance companies or pension funds.

When I first worked on drafting mortgage indentures nearly 40 years ago, it was the common practice for lenders to impose a great variety of rigid restrictions upon the business to which the money was lent. The indenture was full of them. But all this has long since changed, and today the great beauty of bank and insurance loans is that once the ability and integrity of the borrower are established, the lender takes whatever security is agreed upon but keeps his hands off the management of the business. He wants management to be creative and at its best—not hobbled.

If ways could be found whereby banks, insurance companies and pension trusts could raise their lending limits in qualified situations, I think redevelopers in Alcoa's position would be favorably disposed to financing most redevelopment projects through such private channels.

I want to say again that in making this observation I do not mean to be critical of the Federal Housing Administration. It is doing a grand job. But it could do a better job if it could somehow shorten and simplify its procedures and give the developer a little more leeway to make his own mistakes. However, dealing with public funds and operating under statutory limitations, it is hard to see how the agency can ever develop the flexibility and the constructive features that are available in well-conceived, private financing.

4. *Our fourth doubt concerns real estate taxes.* Our municipalities are so hungry for funds that redeveloped properties are placed on the tax rolls at figures which too often simply kill the attractiveness of the project. This happens before the development is ever filled up with tenants, before it even gets off the ground. In far too many cases a project teeters between red and black ink depending upon the tax assessment.

Real estate taxes that take as much as 27 per cent of the gross rent roll when a building is completely occupied are not unknown in Alcoa's experience. Needful as municipalities are for tax revenue, there ought to be a better understanding than now prevails that the early and heavy imposition of property taxes will in the long run defeat this urban renewal concept and the hoped for improvement of the municipal tax base. If taxes could be imposed at lesser rates in the earlier and more difficult years in recognition of the fact that the developer has got to make a reasonable profit on his development and his management if such programs are to continue, urban renewal would have a much more certain future than is the case today.

IN SUMMARY

There you have it. Alcoa is in urban redevelopment up to its neck. Like most people, we're learning the hard way. We have the conviction that urban renewal is essential if our cities are to survive, and that Alcoa can play a constructive role in that battle and, at the same time, bring home to its shareholders a reasonable return on their investment.

CITIZEN PARTICIPATION

The Economic Opportunity Act of 1965 called for "the maximum feasible participation of the poor" in the war on poverty. Sargent Shriver, testifying before a Congressional committee a year later, reported an extremely low turnout for elections held in poverty areas to select representatives for community action agencies. "We are disappointed in these experiments," he concluded. The experience of the war on poverty is not unique; if Shriver had spoken to members of the Urban Renewal Administration they could have told him of their ambiguous experiences with citizen participation in urban renewal.

The Workable Program requirement of renewal demands that a community demonstrate it has made provision for the participation of citizens in its renewal effort. Our first selection is the federal government's formal definition of citizen participation. It presupposes that all individuals and groups within a community are equally capable of participating in the renewal process. In the editors' contribution we question this assumption, and argue that there are "prerequisities for participation" not possessed by all groups and strata within a community.

A somewhat similar orientation is found in the analysis by James Q. Wilson, Professor of Government at Harvard. He notes that urban renewal typically demands a "public-regarding ethos"; that is, participation by those who are predisposed to view an issue not only in the way it affects themselves but the community as a whole. Participation based on a "private-regarding ethos" will be oriented to purely parochial and particularistic interests. Each ethos tends to be linked to a particular level of education, income, and occupational status. Which ethos is operative in any given situation will affect the degree of cooperation and aid a renewal project will get from a population. What is at issue here transcends the problem of renewal; Wilson contends that the conclusions drawn from an analysis of participation in renewal has important implications for contemporary city politics as a whole.

Wilson's work is based on data drawn from empirical studies of citizen participation in Chicago. The study of participation in New Haven reported in the selection by Robert Dahl illustrates another facet of the problem. There the mayor had established a Citizens Advisory Committee, and Dahl scrutinizes the activities of this group. His conclusion is that its role is merely ritualistic; something that probably can be said of most instances of "citizen participation" in most communities in the nation.

WORKABLE PROGRAM FOR COMMUNITY DEVELOPMENT*

United States Housing and Home Finance Agency

CITIZEN PARTICIPATION

There is some degree of citizen participation in any program a community undertakes. It is evident in expressions of support or opposition in newspapers, in meetings, in conferences, at public hearings, at the ballot box. Ultimate success for the other six elements of a Workable Program depends on the kind of citizen participation a community is able to achieve.

Citizen support and concern for community improvement can be a powerful force. Enlist the finest leadership of every sphere of community life and action—industrial, professional, labor, welfare, religious and educational interests; civic clubs and women's groups. The active support of the business community will be a major asset. Special emphasis should be placed on minority group participation for minorities are often most adversely affected by lack of housing opportunities.

A basic approach to building the kind of citizen participation a Program needs is three-pronged. It must be planned to inform and involve . . .

. . . the community as a whole.

. . . special interest groups, enlisting their assistance in solving particular problems.

. . . residents of areas to be directly affected by various Program activities.

People need to know what is happening to their community; what neighborhoods are going downhill; what is causing blight; what is being done to fight deterioration and what more can be done. They must have every opportunity to take constructive action.

Each community will know from its own experience what means of enlisting citizen participation have proven most successful; what groups and local leaders can provide effective support; the type of information that will promote the understanding and interest of local citizens. Through an officially

* Washington, D.C., revised February 1962, p. 13.

designated citizen advisory committee, work to build the kind of participation that is ready to take action and share responsibility in developing and carrying out a Workable Program for Community Improvement which utilizes the full range of private as well as public resources.

PLANNING, PARTICIPATION, AND URBAN RENEWAL*

Jewel Bellush and Murray Hausknecht

Urban renewal programs have opened a vast complex of activities requiring the skills and knowledge of planners. At the same time that the contributions of planners are called upon, the Urban Renewal Administration calls for the participation of citizens in renewal programs. The law specifies that a community submit a workable program for community improvement which must include provisions for "citizen participation."

> And we mean by that not just a passive acceptance of what is being done, but the active utilization of local leadership and organizations which can profitably assist in the community's efforts.[1]

Admirable as this is as a statement of values, it ignores some inevitable problems of "democratic planning."

For example, if we consider planning as a continuous decision-making process, at the crudest level of analysis we can distinguish three major stages of decision-making. First, there is the decision of a community to embark on urban renewal. Second, there is the formulation of a general plan for a given area which involves decisions as to what kinds of policies are to be emphasized, e.g., a decision to convert a mixed industrial and slum area to all-residential use. Third, the development of specific proposals, e.g., drawing up detailed architectural and engineering plans providing for projected land use and the design of structures in the area. Does the notion of citizen participation mean that members of the community will have a chance to participate in the construction of these designs; have the power to propose revisions; and have the power to approve or reject the final plans?

When the implications of these questions are considered a fundamental difficulty becomes apparent; a difficulty perhaps

* This is a revised version of a paper read at the annual meeting of the American Sociological Association, August 1962.

[1] Address, Robert C. Weaver, Administrator, Federal Housing and Home Finance Agency, at The Family Service Association of America, November 13, 1961.

not as readily perceived if the focus is entirely on the second stage of decision-making. There is an "inarticulate major premise" upon which the notion of citizen participation, as it is currently conceived, rests: *All individuals within a community have the necessary prerequisites or resources for effective participation regardless of their location within the structure of the community.* We intend to analyze the validity of this assumption, and then—to anticipate our conclusions—discuss some implications of the ideology of citizen participation for planners and the planning process.

PARTICIPATION AND SOCIAL STRUCTURE

In our society *effective* political participation requires that an individual be a member of a group or *organization*. This of course is a restatement of the truism that in an industrial society the New England town meeting represents a lost paradise rather than an appropriate model for democracy. Therefore, effective participation requires resources directly related to the formation, maintenance, and use of organized groups. "Resources" suggests a scarcity economics; that is, an unequal distribution of these resources in the community. It also suggests that the distribution of resources will be related to the social location of given populations. Since planning as decision-making is a political process, the findings of social science about the unequal distribution of resources in the community are of strategic importance to planners.

PREREQUISITES FOR PARTICIPATION

Morale-Cohesion. If effective participation implies organization, then a population must have some capacity for becoming a group. We label this capacity "morale," those latent psychological conditions which permit and promote the establishment of the bonds of organization. These psychological conditions are closely linked to a necessary social condition, "cohesion," and therefore we may think of this prerequisite for participation as "morale-cohesion."

The presence of this prerequisite among all populations cannot be assumed. Indeed, for some populations it is safer to assume the contrary. For example, the morale of Negro populations in an urban community tends to be so low that even when a situation is formally structured to facilitate participation, as in urban renewal programs, the opportunity will not be seized by the Negro population.[2] Other populations in a city are also likely to lack minimum morale-cohesion, e.g., residents of "zones of transition" or "gray areas." By pinpointing such groups one of the ironic aspects of the "grass roots" orientation in action becomes apparent. Urban renewal programs, for example, usually affect Negroes and residents of "gray areas," but it is precisely such populations who are least likely to possess the resources for effective participation.

The Capacity for Organizational Behavior. While morale and cohesion may be necessary conditions for effective participation via organization they are not sufficient conditions. "Morale" implies enthusiasm or motivation for organization, but the maintenance of an association requires a capacity for organizational behavior. More simply, perhaps, individuals in the population must have *the capacity to be members,* because, as noted above, effective participation demands the assumption of a role and its attendant obligations within a formally organized group.

The capacity for effective membership is largely a function of *experience.* The more the organizational experience of an individual the greater the likelihood of effective role performance. However, such experience is unequally distributed in the society: The percentage of those who are members of voluntary associations increases as the level of income, education, and occupation increases.[3] In other words, to the extent that participation in any given instance is a function of previous experience in associations, it will be middle-class rather than working-class or lower-class populations which will have the necessary capacity for effective participation. This implies that if indeed the "grass roots" are present in the decision-making process it will be those "grass roots" cultivated in a middle-class environment.[4]

Leadership. An obvious necessary resource for effective participation by any population is a competent leadership. Since

[2] James Q. Wilson, *Negro Politics* (Glencoe, Ill.: The Free Press, 1960). See especially Parts I and II. The above remarks need the qualification that today the level of morale-cohesion in a Negro community can be raised by defining or redefining an issue as one of civil rights.

[3] Murray Hausknecht, *The Joiners* (New York: The Bedminster Press, 1961), pp. 15–30.

[4] Other aspects of the life situation of the lower class affect the capacity for organizational behavior. As one example of the relevant literature see Genevieve Knupfer, "Portrait of the Underdog," in Reinhard Bendix and S. M. Lipset (eds.), *Class, Status, and Power* (Glencoe, Ill: The Free Press, 1953).

there are few populations, if any, which do not have some individuals who are at least potential leaders, one may be tempted to say that leadership is not a scarce resource. But the cry of a "failure of leadership" which perenially echoes through the land should remind us how scarce a resource it really is. Yet the "failure of leadership" is not due to a scarcity of potential leaders but to the very complexity of the leadership phenomenon. We may illustrate the bearing of this complexity on our problem without attempting the full-scale analysis which the subject deserves.

Leadership has many dimensions, but we shall merely single out two of them. Leadership involves an "expressive" function; that is, the leader symbolizes the values and aspirations of the group, and as such serves to maintain morale, reenforce the commitment of the membership, etc. The football coach reanimating his dispirited behemoths at halftime is a good example of expressive leadership. Another dimension of leadership is an "instrumental" one, and this refers to the executive function.[5] It is primarily the instrumental leader, in other words, who is responsible for transforming the action of *individuals* into effective *group* action, and this demands specific skills and knowledge. What this implies may be seen by examining the leadership potential within two populations.

The central institution of a lower-class Negro community is the church, and the leadership for various kinds of action is apt to be drawn from the clergy. But the latter tend to be primarily expressive leaders. Therefore, when the situation calls for instrumental skills and knowledge the clergy are often inadequate for the task. To illustrate: The leadership of a Negro population affected by an urban renewal program, in order to protect its interests, must have some technical knowledge of the mechanics of the program; knowledge of the local political structure; and some knowledge of the complexities of intergovernmental relations. In addition, they must have certain skills relative to the maintenance of an organized group through time with a population whose morale and capacity for organizational behavior is probably extremely limited. Such knowledge and skills are largely a matter of

[5] For the theoretical background of this discussion see Talcott Parsons, *The Social System* (Glencoe, Ill.: The Free Press, 1951), p. 49 *et passim*.

formal education, experience, and occupational roles.[6] Since the education and experience of the clergy tends to be similar to that of their parishioners, there is only a small probability that the lower-class Negro population will have adequate leadership. In any relatively large Negro population there will be middle-class Negroes who have the requisite instrumental skills, but since they are middle class they may have difficulties in performing the expressive functions in this context or will not be sufficiently motivated to assume leadership roles.

However, even if a population has a somewhat higher level of education than that of lower-class Negroes, this in itself does not insure that the pool of instrumental leaders will be larger. A population typically affected by urban renewal programs is a stratum of small shopkeepers and other small entrepreneurs who employ very few people, and who are part of the service economy of the community. A strong tradition of individual entrepreneurship plus the small scale of the enterprises, does not lend itself to the development of those skills necessary for instrumental leadership. An individual in this stratum is not an "organization man" in more than one sense. This is not to say, of course, that small businessmen are not organized in pressure groups, but it is in this stratum that one is apt to find "a failure of leadership"—a failure that is linked to the lack of skills and orientation necessary for effective leadership.[7]

Knowledge. If a leader needs knowledge about the political and economic and social processes in a community, so does the group as a whole. Clearly, a group is more effective when the majority of members know what issues are at stake, and have a good grasp of the most appropriate ways of achieving their ends. Indeed, we suggest that what is often termed a "failure of leadership" is really a "failure of membership."

The necessary knowledge of the environment is largely a function of formal education. On the other hand, a run-of-the-mill ward-heeler or slum-dweller may often have a better grasp of some of the complexities of politics than a college graduate, because such knowledge is, again, often a function

[6] On the national level some of the complexities of Negro leadership can be easily grasped by contrasting the figures of Roy Wilkins of the National Association for the Advancement of Colored People and Martin Luther King.

[7] On the small businessman see John H. Bunzel, *The American Small Businessman* (New York: Alfred A. Knopf, 1962).

of experience and participation.[8] The old, urban political machine may not be what it used to be, but it is still alive enough so that certain parts of the population know more about the realities of politics than do others. Yet such knowledge tends to be limited by the restrictions of the ward-heeler's life situation; the ward-heeler, after all, is just that. Those whose style of life or occupational position is less parochial are in a better situation, formally speaking, for acquiring a more extensive knowledge of the structure. For example, a businessman who is a sub-contractor for a defense industry is more likely to have a better knowledge of the intricacies of the contemporary political and economic processes than a businessman producing for a more restricted market.[9]

Awareness. "Knowledge," as we have been discussing it so far, is a rather meaningless variable in so far as it affects participation. In reality, knowledge of the social structure is part of what Karl Mannheim called "substantive rationality . . . intelligent insight into the interrelation of events in a given situation."[10] In other words, if the ends of a given population are to be achieved, or if their interests are to be protected through participation, there must be an awareness of or an insight into the relationship between these goals and the structure and processes of the society. Knowledge does not automatically lead to awareness.

Awareness too is a function of formal education and experience in participation. Those groups which lack both will be at the greatest disadvantage when they attempt to participate. But again, other aspects of experience must be examined. A stratum of small shopkeepers tends to be highly particularistic in its orientation to the world. The shopkeeper is oriented to a local clientele, often merely a neighborhood clientele, and for all intents and purposes the wider society rarely impinges upon him in the course of his everyday life. His experience puts him at a disadvantage when he must make sense of the relationship between his immediate life situation and the events of the wider society. In other words, it is

[8] Cf. William F. Whyte, *Street Corner Society* (Chicago: University of Chicago Press, 1943), Chapter VI.

[9] The theoretical point here is a generalization of Robert K. Merton's distinction between "locals" and "cosmopolitans." "Patterns of Influence," in Paul F. Lazersfeld and Frank Stanton (eds.), *Communications Research, 1948–1949* (New York: Harper & Brothers, 1949).

[10] *Man and Society in an Age of Reconstruction* (New York: Harcourt, Brace & Company, 1949), p. 52.

not too great an exaggeration to say that this stratum lives in a world it fundamentally does not understand.

If the particularism of the small businessman is a result of an economic and social situation, there are other populations whose orientations to the world are particularistic in a more technical sense, e.g., migrants to the city from the rural South and Puerto Rico. The culture of the communities of origin is antithetical to that of the industrial city. Therefore, their level of awareness and insight tends to be very low. As a result, even if participation is attempted it is often highly ineffective. For example, we may hypothesize that many of the disastrous experiences connected with relocation of residents in urban renewal areas are a result of a lack of awareness on the part of the residents of what could and could not be done. That is, the interests of a group enmeshed in the relocation process cannot be protected by attempting to stop it. A group's interests are protected only if it can gain some measure of control over the process. But a tactics and strategy to gain this degree of power presupposes a high level of substantive rationality.

CITIZEN PARTICIPATION AS AN IDEOLOGY

If the prime assumption underlying the notion of citizen participation, as it is delineated in current rhetoric, is false, then this conception of participation becomes nothing more than an ideology in the worst sense of that term. That is, it functions to subvert and distort the planning process.

As an ideology, uncritically accepted at face value, it can raise unrealistic expectations about the extent of citizen participation, and the inevitable disappointment of these expectations tends to promote cynicism toward democratic processes in planning. When such cynicism is pervasive it raises fundamental problems of value, but the relationship between democratic institutions and planning, despite its importance as a problem, is not the issue here. Our focus is somewhat more "practical." Good planning, by definition, is one which meets the needs of the community and its people, and this entails some communication between planner and community. Citizen participation, properly understood, can be part of a feedback mechanism which allows the planner to meet the needs of the community, and at the same time allows the community to consider new perspectives which imaginative planning can disclose. Clearly, if citizen participation in a meaningful sense is incorporated into the planning process this immediately poses problems of another kind, but solutions to these may be facilitated in the long run by the inherent educational functions served by citizen participation. However, a cynical attitude toward the possibilities of participation blocks, at the root, even the exploration of the functional consequences of grass-roots democracy.

Planners, like other professionals, are susceptible to fads and fashions and to becoming bemused by their own prejudices, preconceptions, and theories. Unlike most other practitioners, however, the planner is part of a highly politicized world in which his work is always the focus of political controversy. It is a world in which groups continually struggle for the satisfaction of their own special interests; in which there is a continual "molding of public opinion" and of abject surrenders to "public opinion"; in which the manipulative misuse of democratic institutions is the order of the day. The problem is *not* that the planner becomes involved in politics; this is both inevitable and necessary. Rather, that the planner becomes involved as a "manipulator" and "molder of public opinion" in pursuit of his own vested interest, i.e., his own prejudices or pet theories. The ideology of citizen participation can serve to mask, both for the community and the planner himself, the distortion of the meaning of planning in a democratic society this kind of political behavior involves.

If the ideology facilitates the planner's manipulative intervention in planning decisions, it also serves the same functions for the many special interest groups in the community. As our analysis shows, some portions of the community are better prepared to exercise their influence and power. Such uses of pressure, especially when they are illegitimate, are effectively cloaked by the ideology of citizen participation—all interventions in the planning process now become legitimated by the magical invocation of "grass-roots democracy." This is of critical concern to the planner, for even under ideal conditions he is the focal point of pressure. But when the illegitimate use of democratic institutions can be disguised by the ideology of citizen participation the planner is placed in an intolerable situation.

CONCLUSION

Given the imperfect nature of the world a planner's experience with grass-roots democracy is apt to be a severely disillusioning one. Even if it does not make him cynical, it certainly tends to promote indifference to the possibilities of citizen participation. But the planner cannot afford this indifference. Citizen participation is as much a technical problem of planning as, say, the allocation of economic resources among alternative transportation systems. It is, to be sure, a problem in another dimension, that of social and political structure, but one which the planner ignores at his peril. For if he is indifferent to the problems of citizen participation he runs the risk of overlooking a vital and functional mechanism of planning, and at the same time falling victim to ideologues hostile to his function in the community.

PLANNING AND POLITICS: CITIZEN
PARTICIPATION IN URBAN RENEWAL*

James Q. Wilson

Few national programs affecting our cities have begun under such favorable auspices as urban renewal. Although public housing was from the very first a bitterly controversial
policy, redevelopment and renewal by contrast were widely
accepted by both Democratic and Republican administrations
and had the backing of both liberals and conservatives, labor
and business, planners and mayors. Yet today, almost fourteen years after urban redevelopment was inaugurated as
Title I of the Housing Act of 1949, the program is beset
with controversy and, what is even more dismaying to its
supporters, lagging far behind its construction goals.

Although there are nearly 944 federally-approved slum
clearance and urban renewal projects scheduled for over
520 different communities, only a little more than half have
proceeded to the point where the cities are authorized to begin assembling and clearing land. And most important, of all
the projects authorized, only 65 have been completed.[1] In
New York, the city which has been the most active in renewal
programs of all kinds, all the publicly-supported projects undertaken over the last quarter century cover less than one
per cent of the city's surface.[2] Further, most of the projects
completed can be found in or near the central business districts of cities rather than in residential areas, and they have
often involved clearing, not slums, but deteriorating commercial and industrial structures.

Some of the reasons for the relatively slight accomplishments of urban renewal are not hard to find. Federally-
sponsored projects such as renewal require dealing success-

* Slightly revised by the author from an article in the *Journal of the
American Institute of Planners,* XXIX, No. 4 (November 1963), pp.
242–49.
[1] Housing and Home Finance Agency, *Housing Statistics: Annual
Data,* April, 1962, p. 76.
[2] See Raymond Vernon, *The Myth and Reality of Our Urban Problems* (Cambridge, Mass.: Joint Center for Urban Studies of MIT and
Harvard, 1962), p. 40.

fully with almost endless amounts of red tape; it has taken a long time for city governments and private developers to acquire the knowledge and experience required for this. Furthermore, even though the federal government pays most of the cost of assembling and clearing the land on which a project is planned, it is not always easy to find a private developer to whom the land can be sold.

An additional reason for slow progress in urban renewal is racial. Blighted areas are often Negro areas. The political and social problems involved in relocating Negroes in other areas of the city are often sufficiently formidable to make opposition to the renewal program as a whole very powerful.

But the most important reason for controversy and slow progress is the mounting disagreement over the methods and even the objectives of urban renewal. The coalition among liberals, planners, mayors, businessmen, and real estate interests which originally made renewal politically so irresistible has begun to fall apart. Liberals, who still see the rehabilitation of the central city as a prime goal for government, have begun to have doubts, particularly about redevelopment that involves wholesale clearance by bulldozers. They are disturbed by charges from many Negro leaders—whom liberals are accustomed to regarding as their natural allies—that liberals have aided and abetted a program which under the guise of slum clearance is really a program of Negro clearance. They have been disturbed and even angered by the elimination of whole neighborhoods, like the Italian West End of Boston; by the reduction in the supply of low-cost housing to make way for high-cost housing built with federal subsidies; and by what they take to be the inhuman, insensitive, and unrealistic designs of some city planners. Jane Jacob's book, *The Death and Life of Great American Cities,* is expressive of one powerful segment of opinion in this regard.[3] The liberals are everywhere demanding that redevelopment (that is, wholesale clearance) be abandoned in favor of rehabilitation—conserving as many existing structures as possible.

Mayors and other city officials in some cities (although not

[3] See also, as an example of liberal objections to renewal, Staughton Lynd, "Urban Renewal—for Whom?" *Commentary,* January, 1961, pp. 34–45. The consequences of urban renewal for the underprivileged in American cities are discussed in Peter Marris, "The Social Implications of Urban Redevelopment," *Journal of the American Institute of Planners,* XXVIII (August, 1962), 180–86.

yet in all) have seen in these debates a sign that a program which began as "good politics" has turned into something which at best is difficult politics. When it seemed possible that a vigorous and ambitious mayor could place himself at the head of an alliance of liberals, planners, businessmen, and newspapers on behalf of restoring the central city, urban renewal became a top priority civic objective. An initial burst of enthusiasm greeted renewal in almost every city where the idea was broached. But after the first few projects were undertaken, the hidden political costs began to become evident. Voters who did not like being called slum-dwellers and who liked even less being forced out of their old neighborhoods began to complain. As the enthusiasm of the civic boosters began to wane, many mayors began to wonder whether they were going to be left alone on the firing line to answer for projects which the boosters had pushed them into in the first place.

What in many ways is the most interesting aspect of the controversy surrounding urban renewal is not the breakup of this coalition, however, but the growing resistance of neighborhoods to clearance and renewal programs. The growth of neighborhood resistance to urban renewal has been gradual and cumulative. Many of the earliest redevelopment projects were completed with little organized opposition. Somehow, however, people have learned from the experience of others, and today, in cities which have been engaged in renewal for several years, the planners often find prospective renewal areas ready and waiting for them, organized to the teeth. In Chicago, for example, the Lake Meadows redevelopment project met with relatively little organized indigenous opposition (although considerable opposition from forces outside the area). The Hyde Park-Kenwood project, undertaken a few years later, was greeted with considerably more opposition. Today, plans for the Woodlawn and Near West Side areas have been met with impassioned opposition from many of the residents of the neighborhoods involved. Similarly, the West End project in Boston had relatively little difficulty in dealing with people in the area; the project planned for Charlestown, begun some time later, has been—at least for the time being— stopped dead in its tracks by organized neighborhood opposition. Today, according to Robert C. Weaver, Administrator of the Housing and Home Finance Agency, "in nearly every major city in the country and many small cities there are heated debates over urban renewal projects that are under-way or under consideration."[4]

Mr. Weaver might well be concerned over these debates, for federal policy requires local citizen participation in the formulation of local renewal plans before federal money can be spent on them. As he himself stressed on another occasion, "We mean [by citizen participation] not just a passive accept-ance of what is being done, but the active utilization of local leadership and organization which can profitably assist in the community's efforts."[5]

Local citizen participation on a city-wide basis is usually not difficult to obtain. "Civic leaders" representing various groups and interests in the community can always be assem-bled for such purposes. But getting the participation, much less the acquiescence, of citizens in the renewal neighborhood is something else again. Although federal law does not require participation at this level, the increased vigor of neighborhood opposition has made such participation expedient if not es-sential—particularly with the new emphasis on rehabilitation and self-help.

THE HYDE PARK-KENWOOD EXPERIENCE

The fullest account we have of such participation is that found in the book, *The Politics of Urban Renewal*, by Peter H. Rossi and Robert A. Dentler. This study dealt with one neighborhood—Hyde Park-Kenwood in Chicago—which in many ways is remarkable if not unique. The site of the Uni-versity of Chicago, it is heavily populated with University professors and business and professional people, all possessing an inordinate amount of education, experience, and skills, and all having a strong commitment to the community. From 1949 on, these people were organized into the Hyde Park-Kenwood Community Conference, a neighborhood group with a professional staff, dedicated to conserving the area against blight. Actual planning for the area was not, of course, done by this organization—that was beyond its resources—but by the planning staff of the University of Chicago and by various city agencies.

The Community Conference took a deep and continuing interest in the $30,000,000 urban renewal plan for the area

---

[4] Quoted in *St. Louis Post-Dispatch*, February 27, 1963.

[5] From an address to the 50th Anniversary of the Family Service Association of America, New York City, November 13, 1961.

and meticulously examined and discussed every part of it. Local and federal authorities judged the Conference to be an excellent example of genuine grass-roots participation in a major renewal effort. After the plan was finally approved by the Chicago City Council, it commanded widespread (although not unanimous) citizen acceptance, even though about 20 per cent of the buildings in the community were to be torn down.

In evaluating the work of this local citizens group, Rossi and Dentler conclude that the Hyde Park-Kenwood Community Conference played two important roles. First, it stimulated public awareness of the necessity and practicability of change and gave people confidence that something could be done to save their neighborhood. Second, the Conference managed to create a climate of opinion in which the actual planning was done, and, although it is impossible to tell exactly what impact this climate had on the planners, it is likely that the general mood of the community as articulated by the neighborhood organization influenced at least the most general goals that were embodied in the final plan.

But it is also important to note what the Conference did not do. According to this study, the organization did not play a crucial part in influencing the specific details of the plan. Instead, it created broad popular acceptance for a plan which was not entirely in keeping with its own objectives. Rossi and Dentler conclude that the "maximum role to be played by a citizen-participation movement in urban renewal is primarily a passive one."[6]

Considering what I have said about the rising opposition of local neighborhoods to urban renewal, the acquiescence of this grass-roots organization seems to require explanation. In the narrowest terms, this support was due to the fact that the Hyde Park-Kenwood Community Conference represented that part of a very heterogeneous community which would ultimately benefit from renewal. The upper-middle-class professors, housewives, and business and professional men (both white and Negro) who made up the bulk of the Conference were mostly people who were going to remain in the community and whose peace, security, cultural life, and property values would probably be enhanced by a successful renewal plan. The persons who were to be moved out of the com-

[6] Peter H. Rossi and Robert A. Dentler, *The Politics of Urban Renewal—The Chicago Findings* (New York: Free Press of Glencoe, 1961), p. 287.

munity and whose apartments and homes were to be torn down were usually lower-income Negroes who, with very few exceptions, were not part of the Community Conference.

But this narrow explanation in terms of self-interest is only partly true, for if low-income Negroes were not directly represented on the Conference they were often represented vicariously—at least in the eyes of the Conference members. Time and again the Conference, or leading members of it, pressed the city to provide middle- and low-income public housing in the renewal area in part to accommodate persons who would be displaced by demolition. The Conference was firmly committed to the idea of a multiracial community; some of its members were committed in addition to the idea of a multiclass community.

I would argue that this broader consideration was equally as important as the narrower one in explaining the positive and constructive role of the Conference. The organization was made up to a large degree of persons who attached a high value to community-wide and neighborhood-wide goals, even (in some cases) when attaining those goals entailed a sacrifice in personal, material satisfactions. They are people who partake to an extraordinary extent of what Edward C. Banfield and I have called in a forthcoming book the "community-regarding" or "public-regarding" political ethos.[7] This ethos, which is most likely to be found among citizens who rank high in income, education, or both, is based on an enlarged view of the community and a sense of obligation toward it. People who display it are likely to have a propensity for looking at and making policy for the community "as a whole" and to have a high sense of personal efficacy, a long time-perspective, a general familiarity with and confidence in city-wide institutions, and a cosmopolitan orientation toward life. In addition, they are likely to possess a disproportionate share of organizational skills and resources.

It is just these attributes, of course, which make such people most likely to participate effectively in organizations whose function—whatever their ostensible purpose—is to create a sense of community and of community confidence and to win consent for community-wide plans. They are, in short, precisely those attributes which are likely to produce "citizen participation in urban renewal" that planners and community

[7] Edward C. Banfield and James Q. Wilson, *City Politics* (Cambridge, Mass.: Harvard University Press, 1963), esp. chap. xvi.

organizers will consider "positive and constructive"—this is, participation which will influence some of the general goals of renewal and modify a few of its details, but allow renewal to proceed.

SOCIAL DIFFERENCES IN CITIZEN PARTICIPATION

Most neighborhoods which planners consider in need of renewal are not, however, like Hyde Park-Kenwood in Chicago and are not heavily populated with citizens like the ones who organized the Hyde Park-Kenwood Community Conference. Most renewal areas are likely to be low-income, often Negro sections, many of whose inhabitants are the opposite in almost every respect from the cosmopolitan elite of Hyde Park-Kenwood. Such people are more likely to have a limited time-perspective, a greater difficulty in abstracting from concrete experience, an unfamiliarity with and lack of confidence in city-wide institutions, a preoccupation with the personal and the immediate, and few (if any) attachments to organizations of any kind, with the possible exception of churches.[8] Lacking experience in and the skills for participation in organized endeavors, they are likely to have a low sense of personal efficacy in organizational situations. By necessity as well as by inclination, such people are likely to have what one might call a "private-regarding" rather than a "public-regarding" political ethos. They are intimately bound up in the day-to-day struggle to sustain themselves and their families.

Such people are usually the objects rather than the subjects of civic action: they are acted upon by others, but rarely do they themselves initiate action. As a result, they often develop a keen sense of the difference between "we" and "they"— "they" being outside, city-wide civic and political forces which seek to police them, vote them, and redevelop them. It is quite natural that the "they" are often regarded with suspicion.

Although such people are not likely spontaneously to form organizations to define and carry out long-range very general

---

[8] Cf. Seymour Martin Lipset, *Political Man* (Garden City, N.Y.: Doubleday & Co., 1960), chap. iv, and Robert Agger, *et al.*, "Political Cynicism: Measurement and Meaning," *Journal of Politics*, XXIII (August, 1961), 477–506. See also the vivid account of the culture of a lower-income Italian section of Boston in Herbert J. Gans, *The Urban Villagers* (New York: Free Press of Glencoe, 1963).

civic tasks, it is wrong to assume that they are not likely to organize—or to allow themselves to be organized—for any purpose. The important thing is not that they are unorganizable, but that they can be organized only under special circumstances and for special purposes. Except for organizations which are in some sense extensions of the family and the church, lower-income neighborhoods are more likely to produce collective action in response to threats (real or imagined) than to create opportunities. Because of the private-regarding nature of their attachment to the community, they are likely to collaborate when each person can see a danger to him or to his family in some proposed change; collective action is a way, not of defining and implementing some broad program for the benefit of all, but of giving force to individual objections by adding them together in a collective protest.

The view which a neighborhood is likely to take of urban renewal, then, is in great part a product of its class composition. Upper- and upper-middle-class people are more likely to think in terms of general plans, the neighborhood or community as a whole, and long-term benefits (even when they might involve immediate costs to themselves); lower- and lower-middle-class people are more likely to see such matters in terms of specific threats and short-term costs. These differences account in great measure for some of the frustrations of the planners, redevelopers, and community organizers who are involved in urban renewal. Whereas it is relatively easy to obtain consent to renewal plans when people are thinking in terms of general goals and community-wide benefits, it is much harder—often impossible—when people see the same set of facts in terms of possible threats and costs.

This interpretation of lower-class behavior applies in its full force only in the extreme case, of course. There are many stable working class neighborhoods where indigenous leadership can be developed and involved in urban renewal programs on a "constructive" basis. The Back of the Yards area of Chicago is an example of one neighborhood of blue-collar families with strong local leadership. But many potential renewal areas, particularly in Negro sections, do not even qualify as "stable working class." Half of all urban Negro families had an income of less than $3,000 a year in 1960. Thus, although the contrast I draw between middle-class and lower-class with respect to their attachment to neighborhood and community is deliberately extreme, it must be remembered that urban renewal is a policy intended in great part to apply to "extreme" areas.

COMMUNITY ORGANIZATION STRATEGIES

Among community organizers, two radically different strategies have been evolved to produce citizen participation under such circumstances. One recognizes the special character of depressed lower-income neighborhoods and seeks to capitalize on it. The most prominent and controversial exponent of this approach is Saul D. Alinsky, executive director of the Industrial Areas Foundation of Chicago. He has created in a lower-income, heavily Negro area near the University of Chicago an organization ("The Woodlawn Organization") built in large part upon the residents' fears of urban renewal. According to a recent account, "Alinsky eschews the usual appeals to homeowners' interests in conserving property values or to a general neighborhood spirit or civic pride—appeals, in his view, that apply only to middle-class neighborhoods." Instead, he "appeals to the self-interest of the local residents and to their resentment and distrust of the the outside world."[9] If residents do not have what I have called a "public-regarding" ethos, Alinsky is perfectly willing to appeal to their "private-regarding" ethos and to capitalize on the fact that collective action among such people is possible only when each person fears some threat to his own interests.

By stimulating and focussing such fears, an organization is created which can then compel other organizations—such as the sponsors of an urban renewal project—to bargain with it. Often the only terms on which such negotiations are acceptable to the neighborhood organization are terms unacceptable to the sponsors of renewal, for they require the drastic modification or even abandonment of the renewal plan. When an organization is built out of accumulated fears and grievances rather than out of community attachments, the cost is usually the tearing up of any plans that call for really fundamental changes in the landscape. On the other hand, such an organization may be very effective in winning special concessions from city hall to remedy specific neighborhood problems.

[9] Charles E. Silberman, "The City and the Negro," *Fortune*, LXV (March, 1962), 88–91. See also Saul D. Alinsky, "Citizen Participation and Community Organization in Planning and Urban Renewal," address before the Chicago chapter of the National Association of Housing and Redevelopment Officials, January 29, 1962.

Many, probably most, planners and community organization specialists reject Alinsky's tactics. To them, his methods produce and even exacerbate conflict rather than prevent it, alienate the neighborhood from the city as a whole rather than bring it into the normal pattern of civic action, and place a premium on power rather than on a co-operative search for the common good.

The alternative strategy of most community organizers is to stimulate the creation of neighborhood organizations which will define "positive" goals for their areas in collaboration with the relevant city agencies and in accord with the time schedule which binds most renewal efforts. In Boston, for example, efforts have been made to stimulate the formation of neighborhood associations which will provide citizen participation in (and citizen consent to) the plans of the Boston Redevelopment Authority (BRA). So far this strategy has had some success, but only in those areas where rehabilitation rather than clearance is to be the principal renewal tactic. In one Negro area, Washington Park-Roxbury, a middle-class Negro organization was given a BRA contract to help organize the neighborhood to discuss renewal plans calling for rehabilitation, spot clearance, and the construction of some lower-middle-income housing. The plans were approved. In Charlestown, an old Irish neighborhood, the original proposals of the BRA were rejected by a citizens' organization created by Action for Boston Community Development (ABCD), a city-wide welfare agency financed in part by the Ford Foundation. The BRA decided to modify the plans and dispense with the services of ABCD; the final plan, developed after protracted discussions between BRA planners and Charlestown residents, emphasized rehabilitation and was approved. In a third area, North Harvard-Allston, the BRA decided to rely on wholesale clearance and redevelopment; there, no effort was made to obtain citizen participation and the plan was approved by the city council without the consent of the neighborhood.

IMPLICATIONS FOR RENEWAL PROGRAMS

If one's goal is urban renewal on any really large scale in our cities, the implications of these observations are disturbing. The higher the level of indigenous organization in a lower-class neighborhood, the poorer the prospects for renewal in that area.

To say that the prospects are poorer does not, of course, mean that renewal will never occur with the consent of strong indigenous organizations in lower-class areas. But the difficulty is substantially increased, and a protracted, subtle, and assiduous wooing of neighborhood sentiment must first take place.[10] Perhaps this explains why, at least until very recently, most local urban renewal directors made no effort to encourage citizen participation except on a city-wide basis—with little or no representation from the affected neighborhood.[11]

In short, while the devotion of some planners today to the concept of "planning with people"—that is, citizen participation in neighborhood rehabilitation—may be an improvement over old-style urban redevelopment which ignored or took little account of neighborhood interests, the enthusiasm with which the new doctrine is being advocated blurs many important problems. The most important of these is that "planning with people" assumes on the part of the people involved a willingness and a capacity to engage in a collaborative search for the common good. The willingness is obviously almost never present when the persons involved will be severely penalized by having their homes and neighborhoods destroyed through wholesale clearance. Nor will that willingness be present when "rehabilitation" means, as it sometimes does, that the residents must at their own expense bring their homes up to standards deemed satisfactory to the renewal agency or have their homes taken from them. But what is less obvious is that it may not be present, even when such clearance is not envisaged, because of important class differences in the capacity to organize for community-wide goals. This means that middle-class persons who are beneficiaries of re-

[10] See the account in Alfred G. Rosenberg, "Baltimore's Harlem Park Finds 'Self-Help' Citizen Participation Is Successful," *Journal of Housing*, XVIII (May, 1961), 204–9. The initial reaction in the neighborhood to a renewal plan was bitter and got worse for three years. Patient community organization managed to overcome some of this resistance after much effort.

[11] See the survey reported in Gerda Lewis, "Citizen Participation in Urban Renewal Surveyed," *Journal of Housing*, XVI (March, 1959), 80–87. Questionnaires returned by about half the local renewal directors in the 91 cities which had approved "workable programs" as of July 31, 1956, showed that "the residents of project areas . . . seem to be relatively uninvolved in urban renewal"; representation from these areas on citizens' committees dealing with renewal was "almost totally absent."

habilitation will be planned with; lower-class persons who are disadvantaged by rehabilitation are likely to be planned *without*.

The fact that some people will be hurt by renewal does not, of course, mean that there should be no renewal. There are scarcely any public policies which do not impose costs on someone. What it does mean is that planners might more frankly take such costs into account, weighing them against the benefits renewal may confer on individuals and the community. There is little except obfuscation to be gained from attempting to maintain, as the slogan "planning with people" implies, that urban renewal and perfect democracy are and always should be compatible; that not only can the city be revitalized, it can be revitalized with the consent of all concerned.

If we decide to try to obtain the consent of those neighborhoods selected for renewal, we had better prepare ourselves for a drastic re-evaluation of the potential impact of that program. Adjusting the goals of renewal to the demands of the lower classes means, among other things, substantially reducing the prospects for assembling sufficiently large tracts of cleared land to make feasible the construction of dwelling units attractive to the middle-class suburbanite whom the city is anxious to woo back into its taxing jurisdiction. This, in turn, means that the central city may have to abandon the goal of recolonizing itself with a tax-paying, culture-loving, free-spending middle class and be content instead with serving as a slightly dilapidated way-station in which lower-income and minority groups find shelter and a minimal level of public services while working toward the day when they, too, can move out to a better life. That, of course, is in great part the function that at least the older central cities of this country have always performed, and until we run out of lower classes (a day unfortunately far in the future), that may be the function they must continue to perform.

POLITICAL EFFECTS

Not only does the question of citizen participation in urban renewal have important implications for the goals of planning and even for one's conception of the function of the central city; it also goes to the heart of a fundamental problem in the urban political process. Resolving this issue is not simply a problem in planning priorities, but in addition a problem in electoral politics.

American mayors today are faced with the problem of governing cities in which to a great extent the traditional sources of political power have been dispersed or eliminated. The old-style political machine is gone except in a very few big cities. Party organization generally is weak. Mayors must still assemble the power to govern but they can rarely do so today by relying on loyal party lieutenants who occupy the lesser city offices and who sit on the council. Instead, the mayor must try to piece together that power out of the support he can receive from city-wide interests, such as newspapers, civic associations, business organizations, and labor unions. Support from such sources, valuable as it is, does not always carry with it the assurance that the support of the rank-and-file voter will also be forthcoming. Average citizens have a way of not sharing (or sometimes not even knowing about) the enthusiasms of the top civic leadership.

To insure against this possibility, many "new-style" mayors are trying to build up new neighborhood associations and enter into relationships with old ones in order to provide themselves with a way of reaching the average voter and of commanding his support. In Boston, for example, it is an open secret that Mayor John Collins is hoping that the support and attention he has given various neighborhood associations will be reciprocated, on election day, by the support of their members for him.

To the extent that these neighborhood associations are courted by mayors, they attempt to extract in return concessions on matters of city policy (such as street sweeping, garbage collection, or playground maintenance) which affect their areas. They see themselves as instruments for adapting the programs of an impersonal city bureaucracy to the various and often conflicting needs of neighborhoods. In a sense, they perform (for entirely different reasons, of course) the same function which the political machine once performed.

The neighborhood civic association is widely regarded as not only a new mechanism for representing citizen wants to the city bureaucracy, but a means of ending the political "alienation" of those citizens. Much has been written of late to suggest that a large and perhaps growing number of people are "alienated" from the American political process, but particularly from the political process in their communities. In

Boston,[12]   Cambridge,[13]   Detroit,[14]   Nashville,[15]   upstate New York,[16] and various other places where studies have been made, the voters—usually (though not always) those with little income or education—feel, we are told, estranged from and even threatened by the political life of their cities. To the extent that this alienation exists (and the studies are not very precise on this), the neighborhood civic association is seen as an important way of giving the citizen a meaningful and satisfactory relationship with his community—a way, in short, of ending his "alienation."[17]

It is not yet clear, however, whether such neighborhood groups will provide a means whereby citizens overcome their "alienation" or whether they will simply provide a forum in which citizens can give expression to it. These groups, after all, are usually concerned about neighborhood, not city-wide, problems, and the member's attachment is often at most only to his immediate family and neighbors, not to the community as a whole. Neighborhood associations seek many goals in their dealings with city hall. Generally speaking, however, they want higher levels of community services but they oppose extensive physical changes in their areas, as would be caused by highway construction or urban renewal programs.

For city-wide officials, such as mayors and planners, the crucial problem is how to make attention to these neighborhood demands compatible with city-wide programs, almost

[12] Murray B. Levin, *The Alienated Voter* (New York: Holt, Rinehart & Winston, 1960), pp. 58–75. See also Murray B. Levin and Murray Eden, "Political Strategy for the Alienated Voter," *Public Opinion Quarterly*, XXVI (Spring, 1962), 47–63.

[13] See William A. Gamson, "The Fluoridation Dialogue: Is It An Ideological Conflict?" *Public Opinion Quarterly*, XXV (Winter, 1961), 526–37, and Arnold Simmel, "A Signpost for Research on Fluoridation Conflicts: The Concept of Relative Deprivation," *Journal of Social Issues*, XVII (1961), 26–36.

[14] Arthur Kornhauser, *Attitudes of People Toward Detroit* (Detroit: Wayne University Press, 1952), p. 28.

[15] E. L. McDill and J. C. Ridley, "Status, Anomia, Political Alienation and Political Participation," *American Journal of Sociology*, LXVIII (September, 1962), 205–13.

[16] Wayne E. Thompson and John E. Horton, "Political Alienation as a Force in Political Action," *Social Forces*, XXXVIII (March, 1960), 190–95 and Horton and Thompson, "Powerlessness and Political Negativism: A Study of Defeated Local Referendums," *American Journal of Sociology*, LXVII (March, 1962), 485–93.

[17] Cf. William C. Loring, Jr., Frank L. Sweetser, and Charles F. Ernst, *Community Organization for Citizen Participation in Urban Renewal* (Boston: Massachusetts Department of Commerce, 1957), pp. 232–38.

all of which will, to some extent, impose hardships on some neighborhoods. The old-style political leaders who were bosses of city machines were not faced to the same degree with this problem. Whenever they could, they avoided the conflict between neighborhood and city by not proposing any extensive programs designed to appeal to city-wide interests. When such programs were politically unavoidable, they resolved the inevitable conflict by "buying off" their neighborhood opponents. The bosses used the jobs, favors, and patronage which they controlled to enforce their wills on neighborhood political leaders and to compensate the neighborhood voters for their distress.

Today's mayor can neither avoid proposing large programs to satisfy city-wide interests nor can he buy off the neighborhood opponents of such projects. Under these circumstances, the mayor must move cautiously between the twin evils of doing so little as to disappoint community-regarding voters and doing so much as to antagonize private-regarding voters.

Citizen participation in urban renewal, then, is not simply (or even most importantly) a way of winning popular consent for controversial programs. It is part and parcel of a more fundamental reorganization of American local politics. It is another illustration—if one more is needed—of how deeply embedded in politics the planning process is.

THE RITUALS OF PARTICIPATION*

Robert Dahl

THE DISTRIBUTION OF INFLUENCE

In its annual report for 1958, the Citizens Action Commission presented a chart showing the organization of city development agencies. Like most charts displaying the formal skeletal features of an organization, this one reveals nothing about the relative influence of the people occupying the various boxes.

Depending on the preconceptions one brings to the matter, a reader of the annual reports of the CAC might reasonably arrive at one of several conclusions. A reader with strongly optimistic and democratic attitudes might draw comfort from the fact that the CAC committees shown on the chart consist of nearly five hundred citizens and from the statement in the 1957 report that

> The CAC and its Action Committees are in the best sense "grass roots" organizations which include a cross section of community life with all its rich and varied character. The knowledge of the program goals and their support by these representative men and women are the democratic foundation on which the success of urban renewal in New Haven depends.[1]

Because the top committee, the twenty-five-man Citizens Action Commission, included the heads of large utilities, manufacturing firms, banks, and other businesses, a reader expecting to find the hidden hand of an economic elite might conclude that his hunch was sound. A reader who noted the extensive responsibilities for coordination placed on Logue, the Development Administrator, might assume that this official was the power behind the throne, and in actual fact some citizens of New Haven evidently decided that the Mayor was a front man for the Development Administrator. A sophisticated reader, observing that the Redevelopment Agency contained

* FROM *Who Governs?*, New Haven: Yale University Press, 1961, pp. 122–26 and 130–37 (selected portions).
[1] New Haven Citizens Action Commission, *Third Annual Report, 1957* (New Haven, 1957), p. 1.

the technicians and experts on redevelopment, might assume that as in many other situations all important decisions were actually made by bureaucrats. Still another line of speculation would move from the fact that the Mayor had been Yale's Director of Public Relations before his election in 1953, to the charge made in the 1955 election that he was Yale's stooge, thence to the fact that Yale's President Griswold had been a vice-chairman of the CAC from its inception, and thus to the natural conclusion that the whole undertaking was essentially Yale's solution to the dangers of living in the very heart of a modern city. An ingenious mind could contrive still other explanations.

Each of these views is plausible enough on the surface. One way to decide the matter is to reconstruct all the important decisions on redevelopment and renewal between 1950–58 and determine which individuals (or in some cases which agencies) most often initiated the proposals that were finally adopted or most often successfully vetoed the proposals of others.

Out of fifty-seven successful actions of this kind, half can be attributed to only two persons: the Mayor and the Development Administrator. The rest of the successes were widely distributed among twenty-three different persons or agencies. . . . The Mayor and his Development Administrator were more often defeated than other participants, but an examination of these defeats is revealing. The seven cases in which the Mayor failed to get some proposal of his adopted were these: in two instances leading business executives declined to serve as chairman of the CAC; in two cases important business firms, one in New Haven and one outside, rejected invitations to participate in redevelopment projects; in the remaining three cases other governmental units (a federal agency, a state agency, and the state courts) made unfavorable decisions. All of these rebuffs reflected not so much a lack of influence over the participants in urban redevelopment as an inability to control certain aspects of the outside environment.

A breakdown of the characteristics of the redevelopment elite also shows that the initiative in the program has lain much more with public officials than with private individuals or groups. . . . However, there were important differences—sometimes gross, sometimes subtle—in the kind of influence exerted by the most important leaders in urban redevelopment. These differences stemmed partly from divergent skills and temperaments and partly from the nature of the offices, skills, and resources available to different leaders. . . .

DEMOCRATIC RITUALS: THE CITIZENS ACTION COMMISSION

What was the function of the Citizens Action Commission? Lee described the CAC this way:

> We've got the biggest muscles, the biggest set of muscles in New Haven on the top C.A.C. . . . They're muscular because they control wealth, they're muscular because they control industries, represent banks. They're muscular because they head up labor. They're muscular because they represent the intellectual portions of the community. They're muscular because they're articulate, because they're respectable, because of their financial power, and because of the accumulation of prestige which they have built up over the years as individuals in all kinds of causes, whether United Fund, Red Cross, or whatever.

The members had been shrewdly selected to represent many of the major centers of influence or status in the community. Its membership included three bankers: Freese, O'Brion, and a third who was president of the New Haven Chamber of Commerce; two men from Yale: President Griswold and Dean Rostow of the Law School; John Golden, the Democratic national committeeman and hitherto the acknowledged leader of the New Haven Democratic party; (Lynch, the aging Republican party leader was approached but refused); the president of the State CIO Council and the secretary-treasurer of the State Federation of Labor; four of the city's most prominent manufacturers; the president of an investment firm; the board chairman of the leading power company; the manager of a large chain store; the Italian-American president of a construction company; an elder statesman of the Jewish community; a partner in one of the leading law firms; and four individuals who had special status in housing, welfare, education, and industrial development. In addition to the Citizens Action Commission itself, there were six special committees; these in turn had nearly thirty subcommittees. Altogether the Commission and the committees had over four hundred members, drawn mainly from the educated, activist, middle-class segments of the community, the very people who ordinarily shunned direct participation in partisan politics.

Except for a few trivial instances, the "muscles" never directly initiated, opposed, vetoed, or altered any proposal brought before them by the Mayor and his Development Administrator. This is what the men on the Citizens Action Commission themselves said:

A banker said:

Well, I think the decisions would be brought up first by the technical staff to the Mayor. The Commission would pass them on the general policy level . . . then the decision would be made by the Board of Aldermen on the recommendation of the Mayor.

Did you have to modify their proposals very often?

Well, they usually came up pretty well developed, but we oftentimes would slant the way we felt the business community would react to certain things and the way we felt the approach should be made. I think that our function was to—*we were a selling organization.*

The president of a large industrial firm said:

The CAC helps set the atmosphere in the community so they're receptive to these things the city administration is trying to do. So, therefore, the city administration is not shoving things down the community's throat. It's selling them to the community, through the CAC.

Have you, for example, done any selling?

Oh yes, oh yes . . . Talking to friends of mine, talking at meetings of the Manufacturers' Association . . .

Do you talk individually or do you give speeches, or what?

Mostly individual. I've never given a speech on the subject.

An executive in a utilities firm:

Have there been any cases where the CAC has modified the proposals that have been put forth since you've been on it?

I can't recall any.

A lawyer:

Who would you say was important in making that decision? [To extend the Oak Street Connector]

Well, the matter was taken up by the Mayor at a meeting of the Citizens Action Commission. It was discussed and debated around and we agreed with the Mayor. He got his information, of course, from the traffic commission, from the engineers, from the Redevelopment Agency and all the others and he passed it on to us. We represent the group through which these decisions are filtered. I've often felt that the group as a group is inadequate in the sense that *we don't really initiate anything as far as I can recall. We haven't yet initiated anything that I know of.* We discuss what has been developed by the Redevelopment Agency or the City Planning Commission or one of the other groups. The Mayor or somebody from one of these groups presents it to us and we discuss it, we analyze it, we modify some of it, we change—

Could you give me an example of some case where you modified or changed some proposal?

Well, I don't think that I can give you an example of anything where I can say that the Commission actually changed a proposal.

A lawyer:

Do you know of any cases where proposals that have been brought forward from the city administration have been altered by the CAC or the people on the redevelopment agency?

No I can't say that I do. I can't think of any that would fall into that description.

The contributions of members of the CAC tended to be minor or, if important, of a technical nature. For example, a leading lawyer, Morris Tyler, whose firm also served as legal counsel to the city on redevelopment matters, discovered in 1955 that under existing state legislation the power of eminent domain permitted the city was wholly inadequate for redevelopment purposes; at the request of redevelopment leaders in New Haven the statute was changed by the state legislature. To see the members of the CAC and its action committees as policy-makers is, however, to miss their real role. The elaborate structure of citizen participation, it must be remembered, did not grow up spontaneously; it was deliberately *created* by Mayor Lee. Its functions in urban redevelopment seem to have been roughly equivalent to those performed by the democratic rituals of the political parties in making nominations for public office; citizen participation gave legitimacy and acceptability to the decisions of the leaders, created a corps of loyal auxiliaries who helped to engender public support for the program and to forestall disputes.

The importance of the CAC in assuring acceptability for the redevelopment program can hardly be overestimated. The mere fact that the CAC existed and regularly endorsed the proposals of the city administration made the program appear nonpartisan, virtually nullified the effectiveness of partisan attacks, presented to the public an appearance of power and responsibility diffused among a representative group of community notables, and inhibited criticisms of even the most daring and ambitious parts of the program as "unrealistic" or "unbusinesslike." Indeed, by creating the CAC the Mayor virtually decapitated the opposition. The presence of leading bankers, industrialists, and businessmen—almost all of whom were Republicans—insured that any project they agreed on would not be attacked by conservatives; the presence of two of the state's most distinguished labor leaders and the participation of well-known liberal Democrats like the Dean of the Yale Law School meant that any proposal they accepted was not likely to be suspect to liberals. To sustain a charge of ethnic or religious discrimination would have required an attack on distinguished representatives of these groups.

A Republican banker on the CAC summed up a prevalent view among the members of the CAC itself: "It [the CAC] has to exist to get the combined community in back of something of this nature. In other words, if the city administration tried to put this over as a political effort it would meet, obviously, right away, serious objections, because it would become a political football." The aura of nonpartisanship helped to gain acceptance for redevelopment and its consequences —not all of which were immediately beneficial—and at the same time did no harm to the political career of Mayor Lee. The leaders of the Republican party were presented with a dilemma which they never quite knew how to meet. Because the Mayor was building his political career on the success of redevelopment, the Republicans could not damage him without attacking either redevelopment or his role in it, but because everything in the redevelopment program was endorsed by Republican notables to attack the Mayor was to alienate established sources of Republican electoral and financial support.

The appointment of over four hundred people to the various action committees gave urban redevelopment a broad and heterogeneous set of subleaders it might otherwise have lacked. The members of these committees initiated no key decisions; they were auxiliaries. They were recruited because they were thought to be favorably predisposed toward certain aspects of redevelopment and renewal; they were counted on to form a group of loyal supporters who would help enlist a community following. Like the main CAC itself, the action committees drew on diverse segments of the community. There was an action committee on industrial and harbor development consisting mainly of businessmen, architects, and lawyers, and a second on the central business district, traffic, and parking, that was drawn from the same sources; there was one on housing, and another on health, welfare, recreation, and human relations, made up in great measure of social workers, liberals, clergymen, Negro leaders, housing officials, and religious leaders; a fourth on education consisted mainly of teachers, members of the Board of Education, school administrators, PTA heads, and housewives; and a small committee on the metropolitan area consisted of leading lawyers, town planners, and architects. Most of the action committees rarely met; many members failed to attend the few meetings there were. The actual effects of membership on the CAC or on action committees is unknown, but it seems reasonable to conclude that many people who might otherwise have been apathetic or even opposed to the program were provided with at least a weak tie of loyalty. One member of the CAC, a lawyer, commented as follows:

Who do you see as the people who are primarily responsible or influential in making these decisions?

Well, I think there that the question indicates to me an error on your part. At least I think it's an error in that it implies the CAC in fact had anything to do with the decision [on Church Street redevelopment]. I think it would be more accurate to say the CAC is again a major stroke of brilliant policy on the part of the regular municipal administration to set up an organization which has its basic function getting so many people that are communally tied to New Haven that once they are sold, their area of influence in the aggregate would be so large that you can get a substantial portion of the thinking public behind these projects, not only the ones we've been discussing, but all the others in mind.

It would be carrying the parallel with political parties too far to say that the democratic ritualism of the CAC and its action committees provided a means for the orderly settlement of conflicts among the leaders for, as we have seen, no significant conflicts ever arose within the CAC or between the CAC and the city administration. Yet the fact that no conflicts appeared is itself significant. For the men on the CAC were too important in their own right, too knowledge-able, and too independent to be merely tools of the Mayor. The interviews leave little doubt that they genuinely believed in the value of redevelopment; they believed in it on grounds that made sense according to their own predispositions. There is no indication in the interviews that the Mayor and the re-development officials significantly altered or even tried to alter the kinds of criteria the men on the CAC brought to their judgments; probably the most the Mayor and redevelopment officials could do was to show how, given these criteria, the proposals made sense. One of the most conservative Republi-cans on the CAC, a banker, evidently saw no inconsistency between redevelopment, which of course depended on federal funds, and his opposition to "giveaway programs," foreign aid, and social security.

> I think there's altogether too much money given away and I don't know where it's going to come from as this thing snow-balls. . . . We are undermining the moral fibre of the whole country. Nobody has to do anything, and I've never seen a country yet, or read of one, that didn't fall apart after they went so far, and that's where I think we're headed.

But as for redevelopment the same respondent said that the Chamber of Commerce

> felt that something had to be done here, it couldn't be done by private interest, it couldn't be done by public entirely, and it couldn't be political. And as a result of that, when Mayor Lee did come into power, he took this over and he's, I think, done a marvelous job with it. . . . I'm thoroughly convinced that if we're going to have a city, and it's going to be a shop-ping area, that something had to be done. Something is being done now. . . . Here's a dream that we've had for a long time and we're very happy to see it be culminated in this final action that's been taken.

Another banker said:

> If taxes are going to remain high and there is going to be a social program in the United States and if . . . there's no other way—if we can't stop it—if personal income taxes can-not be reduced, why there's only one thing to do and that is to devise ways and means so that we can share in it. That's pretty selfish. I'm not interested in building a highway through Montana or . . . a TVA down South, and I'd like to see some

of those dollars come back into Connecticut so that we can enjoy some more benefits.

A labor leader who emphasized the "universal support" of union members and officials for the program was asked whether there had been "any criticism or concern over the large role of the business interests in the program." He replied:

No . . . nobody seems to be bothered by that because I think everybody wants a prosperous community and because in the long run I think everybody feels—that is, most everybody feels —that they benefit in one way or another by a prosperous community, even if it just means a better economic atmosphere. . . . And there's another factor here that's probably important. The building trades, the most conservative element in the labor movement, even more conservative than the teamsters . . . the building trades benefit directly from the program, and so they are enthusiastic towards it and have even made contributions to the CAC committee itself. . . . On the other end of the scale from the conservative building trades, the more sophisticated trade union leaders (and they don't number as many as they did some years ago, when idealism was much stronger than it is today) have been completely taken with the program because of the concern of the program leaders with the human relations aspect of it. So, for different reasons, we have a pretty good cross section of real interest of the labor leadership and of the labor movement in general.

It would be unrealistic in the extreme to assume that these men could have been persuaded to lend their support to just any proposal. The task of the Mayor and the Development Administrator was to persuade them that a particular proposal satisfied their own criteria of judgment, whether these were primarily the criteria of businessmen concerned with traffic and retail sales, trade union leaders concerned with employment and local prosperity, or political liberals concerned with slums, housing, and race relations.

Thus, properly used, the CAC was a mechanism not for *settling* disputes but for *avoiding* them altogether. The Mayor and the Development Administrator believed that whatever received the full assent of the CAC would not be strongly opposed by other elements in the community. Their estimate proved to be correct. And the reason was probably not so much the direct influence over public opinion of the CAC collectively or its members individually, as it was that the CAC *was* public opinion; that is, its members represented and reflected the main sources of articulate opinion in the political stratum of New Haven. The Mayor and the Development Administrator used the CAC to test the acceptability of their proposals to the political stratum; in fact, the very existence of the CAC and the seemingly ritualistic process of justifying all proposals to its members meant that members of the administration shaped their proposals according to what they expected would receive the full support of the CAC and therefore of the political stratum. The Mayor, who once described himself as an "expert in group dynamics," was particularly skillful in estimating what the CAC could be expected to support or reject. If none of the administration's proposals on redevelopment and renewal were ever opposed by the CAC, the explanation probably lies less in the Mayor's skill in the arts of persuasion than in his capacity for judging with considerable precision what the existing beliefs and commitments of the men on the CAC would compel them to agree to if a proposal were presented in the proper way, time, and place.

IV. EXECUTION

RELOCATION

Slum clearance means the displacement of people from homes and neighborhoods. The 1949 law merely stipulated that displaced persons had to be relocated in "safe, decent, and sanitary housing," but left the implementation of the goal entirely in the hands of the local community. It extended little help to the displaced; in New York, for example, relocation was left wholly to the private developers. In 1954, as a result of growing dissatisfaction with relocation practices, the federal government required communities to submit as part of the Workable Program specific plans for relocation, and in 1956 federal money was made available to assist people with moving expenses.

The dimensions of the problem begin to emerge in the debate over what has been accomplished by relocation programs. Critics have charged that relocation has meant moving families from one slum to another. In 1964 Chester W. Hartman as sociologist at the Joint Center for Urban Studies, published an extensive analysis of previous investigations of relocation as well as a report of his own empirical research on relocation in Boston's West End renewal area. He concluded that on a number of crucial counts the evidence shows that relocation has not helped displaced families and individuals to improve their housing situations.

Hartman's work provoked a quick reaction in Washington; Robert Weaver was anxious to show that under the Kennedy and Johnson administrations the relocation situation was not as bleak as Hartman pictured it. Therefore, the Census Bureau was asked to survey those who had been displaced by renewal. The Bureau's findings, reprinted here, do indeed contradict the conclusions of the critics. This, of course, did not conclude the debate. In his rejoinder to the government's report Hartman questions the interpretation of the data and points to some significant problems and questions that were not posed or answered. Clearly the problems of relocation are far from solved; indeed, we are still some distance from an adequate picture of the current situation.

In the final selection the editors have attempted to put the problem of relocation into a broader context. We try to show that the questions raised about relocation are similar to some raised about the war on poverty, and that both phenomena are linked to the problem of social mobility in a complex industrial society.

THE HOUSING OF RELOCATED FAMILIES*

Chester W. Hartman†

Large-scale relocation of families and individuals, such as that occasioned by highway construction and urban renewal, necessarily raises basic questions of social welfare and public policy. Among the more important issues are: how relocation affects the family's ability to meet the society's minimum standards for quality and quantity of living space; the extent to which the family can fulfill its needs and desires in terms of housing and neighborhood characteristics and convenience to employment, community facilities, family, and friends; the costs—financial, social, and emotional—involved in experiencing forced change, and the unintended consequences of such changes; the differential incidence of benefits and costs on various subgroups within the relocation population; the effect of population redistribution on the city's ecological patterns, particularly with respect to racial segregation, and how these more general effects influence the individual family's housing experience.

Obviously, questions such as these can be answered only by a comprehensive investigation of the impact of relocation. A follow-up study of the population dislocated from Boston's West End urban renewal area—a centrally located, 48-acre neighborhood of some 7,500 persons that was demolished in 1958–59 to make way for a luxury apartment-house complex—provides one of the few sources of comprehensive, independently gathered and analyzed data on the effects of slum clearance and relocation on housing welfare. This research has already produced findings which throw light on the psycho-social effects of dislocation and the subsequent adaptation experience.[1] The present paper will be concerned pri-

* FROM *Journal of the American Institute of Planners*, XXX, No. 4 (November 1964), pp. 266–67, 268–75, 278–82 (selected portions).

† Chester W. Hartman is Research Fellow in Sociology at the Harvard Medical School and a Samuel Stouffer doctoral fellow at the M.I.T.—Harvard Joint Center for Urban Studies.

[1] See Marc Fried, "Grieving for a Lost Home," *The Urban Condition*, ed. Leonard J. Duhl, (New York: Basic Books, 1963); Marc Fried, "Social Change and Working Class Orientations: The Case of Forced Relocation," to be published in *Mobility and Mental Health* ed. Mildred Kantor, (New York: D. Van Nostrand, 1964).

marily with housing changes and the financial costs involved for a random sample of more than 500 displaced West End households (approximately 20 percent of the households living in the area at the time of land-taking) who were first interviewed just prior to dislocation and reinterviewed approximately two years thereafter. The central focus will be on changes in several features of housing status: location, housing type and tenure, living space (outdoor and indoor), housing quality, and rent levels.[2] In order to place the West End findings in a broader context and to gain greater perspective on the problem of relocation, some 30 studies which report follow-up assessments of one or more aspects of housing conditions among relocated families are also reviewed here.[3] The overall results of these rehousing studies will be compared with the West End findings . . .

The studies reviewed, which include several reports from the 1930's and 1940's, as well as some more recent reports dealing with relocation caused by programs other than urban renewal, indicate that relocation results vary markedly for different projects and at different points in time. Sufficient information is not available to determine the reasons for these variations, but clearly where there are a great many sound low-rent vacancies available, and where relocation planning and services are competently provided, more satisfactory results are to be expected than under opposite conditions. Despite differences of this kind, inclusion of a range of studies may help to indicate common and persistent features of the relocation process.

[2] Data on location, apartment size, rents, and tenure were gathered in the course of the two interviews. Additional data derive from housing and neighborhood surveys that were undertaken for pre-relocation dwellings by the interviewers, and for post-relocation dwellings by a specially trained crew of housing surveyors. A total of 540 respondents (female household heads between the ages of 20 and 65) answered at least one interview: 432 responded to both interviews, 41 to the pre-relocation interview alone, 67 to the post-relocation interview alone. Through surveys and outside sources, some data are available for the entire sample of 540.

[3] The comparative studies are those located in the libraries of the Harvard Graduate School of Design, the City Planning Departments of the Massachusetts Institute of Technology and the University of Pennsylvania, and the Philadelphia Housing Association. Miss Linda Greenberg of the Philadelphia Housing Association kindly assisted in making available to me materials from the Philadelphia libraries. . . .

WHERE DID THEY GO?

The most striking feature of the redistribution is its "shotgun" pattern—the absence of large-scale clustering in the vicinity of the project area, the relatively weak centripetal pull within roughly a six-mile radius of the West End, and the spread of large numbers of families into virtually every section of Boston and every one of the inner-core suburbs. Approximately the same number of relocated families are found in each of the first five one-mile rings surrounding the West End. Thirty-eight percent relocated outside Boston in other parts of the metropolitan area, and another 6 percent left the metropolitan area entirely.[4]

This dispersion is in sharp contrast with the findings reported in most other studies of the redistribution of relocated families. These studies indicate that most families clustered in the immediate vicinity of the area from which they were dislocated. . . . Reynolds, in his survey of urban renewal and public housing relocation in 41 U. S. cities [33], reported that "a majority of all families . . . took up new addresses not further than about one mile and a half, or 12 city blocks, from their old addresses." . . . The only exceptions to this extreme concentration were found in some areas of New York and Chicago. In these very large cities, a combination of the transportation system (with rapid, cheap, and single-fare transit) and the complex workings of racial ecology frequently resulted in a more widespread distribution of relocatees (although the pattern is polynuclear rather than randomly scattered).

Evidence from these studies and from the West End suggests that a number of factors produced the atypical pattern of wide dispersion from the West End. First, the population was almost entirely white, which meant that families were not subject to the exclusionary pressures that so severely limit the

---

[4] Extrapolation from sample data to the entire West End population indicates that 3,300 persons left the city of Boston as a result of the West End renewal project; of these, roughly 2,800 settled in other parts of the metropolitan area, and 500 left the Boston metropolitan area entirely. Population shifts of this scale may precipitously place major rehousing and welfare burdens on smaller cities and towns, and represent one aspect of the broader implications of renewal policy that should be studied more carefully.

rehousing choices of nonwhite families.[5] Family incomes were relatively high, providing for a fairly wide area of choice and possibility.[6] In addition within a five- to six-mile radius of the West End, residential areas are primarily working-class or lower middle-class. And finally, there was an extremely low rate of sound vacancies throughout this area, so that concentrated relocation would have been difficult, and opportunities for rehousing were especially limited in the area immediately adjacent to the West End.

. . .

How Much Space Did They Secure? Indoor Space

The average number of rooms per household was 4.35 in the West End, and rose to 4.94 in the relocation dwellings. Forty-six percent of the families moved into dwellings containing more rooms than their West End apartment, while 54 percent did not gain space (35 percent moved into dwellings with the same number of rooms, 19 percent moved into apartments with fewer rooms). Gain and loss of household space was closely related to housing type. The greatest gains were secured by those who moved to single-family houses. Substantial, although smaller, gains were achieved by those who moved into two- and three-family houses. Only a minority of those who moved into apartment houses and public housing gained apartment space. If net changes in household space are calculated, taking into account post-relocation changes in household size,[7] 41 percent of all households showed an increase in space, while 59 percent did not (of these, 32 percent maintained the same amount of space and 27 percent experienced a decrease).

[5] As indicated in Chart I, most follow-up studies deal with nonwhite populations. The significance of racial factors will be discussed in greater detail below.

[6] Twenty percent of the pre-relocation sample had weekly family income in excess of $100, 43 percent in excess of $75.

[7] That is, change in number of persons subtracted from change in number of rooms: addition of one room and one person is considered no change; the same number of rooms but loss of a household member is considered a net gain of space.

Forty-one percent of all families responding to both interviews reported a change in household size between the first and second interviews, due to births, departure of grown children, marriage, divorce, and separation, and combining households with friends or relatives. The majority of these changes (59 percent) were increases, rather than decreases, in family size.

Although overcrowding was not a major problem in the West End, overall apartment densities decreased as a result of relocation, and there was a slight drop in the proportion of households living at densities higher than 1.00 persons per room. Nine percent of the families moved from overcrowded conditions into an apartment where household density was 1.00 or less, while 4 percent moved from a previously adequate situation into overcrowded conditions.

A review of household space changes brought about in other rehousing efforts indicates that there has been a general failure to ameliorate overcrowded conditions in the course of relocation. In only 6 of the 18 studies reporting such information was there any significant gain in aggregate living space following relocation, and even in these instances the degree of overcrowding following relocation remained extremely high for the most part. . . . The majority of rehousing studies report no important changes in household densities following relocation and a few even report a considerable *increase* in overcrowding. The report on relocation from the site of Norris Homes in Philadelphia [31] shows that 37 percent of the families were living at densities of 1.01 or more persons per room, both before and after relocation. The average number of rooms per household rose from 3.7 to 4.0 for families displaced from public housing sites in Chicago during 1952–54 [8], but the proportion of families living at densities of 1.01 or more rose from 31 percent to 33 percent, and 36 percent of all households were "doubled up" following relocation. . . . It seems clear that relocation generally does little to improve the overcrowded conditions that existed in the original clearance area.

OUTDOOR SPACE

The West End was a densely populated neighborhood with narrow streets, no building setbacks, and virtually no private or public open space within it. In contrast, a great many relocatees moved into homes which provided them with varying amounts of private or semi-private outdoor space: 6 percent of the relocation sample had extensive yards, 32 percent had small yards, and 26 percent had token yards. While it is clear that relocation resulted in an increase in private open space for many West Enders and more of the amenities of light and air generally considered desirable by planning criteria, at the same time most of the relocated households lost proximity to

(and hence use of) major public recreational areas within
easy walking distance of the West End. City- and even
metropolitan-wide recreational resources such as the Boston
Common, the Public Garden, and the Charles River parks
were utilized intensively by a great many West Enders. Additionally, as other papers on the West End have shown, a considerable portion of West End life took place in the streets,
which were very much a part of the personal living space of
most residents.[8] The question of whether small private yards
are more valuable and desirable than communal and large
public spaces is a matter that must be investigated more carefully, for it raises problems of considerable importance in
evaluating and planning the urban environment.

WHAT WAS THE QUALITY OF THE HOUSING THEY MOVED INTO?

In the aggregate, the physical quality[9] of relocation housing represented an improvement over West End housing conditions, . . . reflecting the physical deterioration of housing
in the West End during the six-year period between the time
that redevelopment plans were first announced and the time of
our interviews, shortly after the city took title to the land.[10]

---

[8] See Marc Fried and Peggy Gleicher, "Some Sources of Residential
Satisfaction in an Urban 'Slum'," *Journal of the American Institute of
Planners,* XXVII (November, 1961), 305–15; Chester W. Hartman,
"Social Values and Housing Orientations," *Journal of Social Issues,*
XIX (April, 1963), 113–31.

[9] Data on pre-relocation housing include ratings of condition and
appearance of both building and dwelling unit. These ratings are available for only 307 of the 473 persons interviewed, since about one-third
of the initial interviews were held after the family had moved from the
West End.

The rating of relocation housing was made as part of a special survey
of the residence and neighborhood for every address at which persons
in the sample had lived from the time of dislocation to the time of the
second interview. Post-relocation housing conditions were judged by
structural condition and maintenance of the respondent's building, plus
interview questions about plumbing facilities. Addresses outside the Boston metropolitan area were not rated, nor were ratings possible for
buildings demolished since the time of the respondent's residence there.

[10] There were wide reports of accelerated deterioration in the West
End as a direct result of the uncertainty and disruption caused by the
rumors and changing plans regarding the fate of the neighborhood:
some families moved out prematurely and few families chose to move
into the area, thereby sharply increasing the vacancy rate and reducing
the normal maintenance which accompanies occupancy; stores lost patronage and owners were forced to abandon their businesses. By the

Hence the data exaggerate somewhat the positive effects of relocation. However, some aggregate improvement in housing quality seems almost certain to have occurred.

The degree of improvement in the quality of the housing may be considered from several vantage points. Two-fifths of the families in the sample were living in sound housing in the West End; after relocation, nearly three-fourths were in sound housing. At the other extreme, more than one-third were in dilapidated housing in the West End, but less than one-fifth were living in such poor housing after relocation. Another way of viewing these data is to compare the pre-relocation and post-relocation housing for each household. Thirty-two percent of the West End population lived in standard housing both before and after relocation; 19 percent lived in substandard housing both before and after. On the other hand, 41 percent moved from substandard pre-relocation housing to standard post-relocation housing; and 8 percent moved from standard pre-relocation to substandard post-relocation housing.

Further improvement in facilities and amenities is indicated by the fact that the proportion of families with central heating rose from 41 percent to 72 percent following relocation.[11] Virtually all families (97 percent) had a private bathroom before and after relocation.

A review of the findings from other studies indicates that in most cases housing quality, measured in terms of structural condition and facilities, improved considerably after relocation.[12] Thus, for families displaced from Chicago public hous-

---

time of land-taking, only 2,555 of the 3,671 units in the project area were occupied, a vacancy rate of over 30 percent. In comparison, the vacancy rate in the project area was only 3.1 percent in 1950, as reported in Housing Census block statistics. For a more comprehensive picture of the effects of redevelopment on the West End community, prior to actual land-taking, see Herbert Gans, *The Urban Villagers* (New York: The Free Press of Glencoe, 1962), pp. 281–335.

[11] Central heating does not necessarily mean more and better heat, however; particularly in working-class areas, it may frequently be (in Herbert Gans' phrase) "central non-heating."

[12] The question of change in housing quality is extremely difficult to assess, for no consistent or standard system of measurement is used by local authorities. Moreover, most reports fail to clarify what standards are used in judging housing condition—census categories, local codes, or special criteria established by the local authority. The limitations of even the most widely accepted single standard for judging housing quality in this country were recently noted by the former Assistant Chief of the Census Bureau's Housing Division, who wrote regarding preparations for the 1960 Housing Census: ". . . All persons familiar with data

ing sites during 1957–58 [9], 83 percent of the families were living in substandard housing before relocation, 42 percent afterwards. In Philadelphia, prior to relocation 83 percent of the households dislocated from the Norris Housing site [31] were living in structures in poor condition, compared with 35 percent following relocation. And the number of families from New York's Manhattantown site [4] living in buildings in poor condition dropped from 39 percent to 18 percent following relocation. While most studies report considerable improvement, significant numbers—in some cases, the majority of families—still live in substandard housing following relocation. The Philadelphia Housing Association reports [30] that 72 percent of the relocated families it studied continued living in substandard housing, and Reynolds' data [33] indicate that for the 41 cities surveyed, roughly 60 percent of the relocated families were still living in substandard conditions.

The few studies that treat separately the housing conditions of those who relocated into public and private housing indicate that families who relocated in private housing as a whole fared considerably worse than those in public projects. The lethargic rate of new public housing construction in recent years and the scant increase in authorizations requested under the Administration's 1964 housing legislation, together with the reluctance of many displaced families to move into public projects, may mean that the growing relocation loads of the next few years will be increasingly dependent on the private stock—a situation which bodes further difficulties for successful relocation.[13]

---

on the condition of housing recognized that the subjective elements entailed in this classification rendered it one of the weakest among all the housing statistics collected." See Frank Kristof, "The Increased Utility of the 1960 Housing Census for Planning," *Journal of the American Institute of Planners,* XXIX (February, 1963), 40–47.

Data on housing condition reported in this section and in Chart I may therefore vary considerably in definition and significance. Questions of standards and reliability of local reports are discussed below in the Postscript.

[13] See Chester W. Hartman, "The Limitations of Public Housing: Relocation Choices in a Working-class Community," *Journal of the American Institute of Planners,* XXIX (November, 1963), 283–96.

Preferential treatment for displaced families in public housing may offset these trends, but whether public housing will in fact be able to accommodate significant numbers of displaced families will in part depend on the economic and social characteristics of the displaced families themselves. This type of preferential treatment, however, provides little net gain to the community, as priority treatment for displaced families serves to deprive other low-income families of needed housing.

WHAT RENTS ARE THEY PAYING?

. . . Relocation resulted in a marked increase in housing costs. In the West End, 88 percent of all households were paying less than $55 per month for their apartments, while only 30 percent were paying similarly low rents[14] after relocation. Conversely, only 2 percent were paying $75 per month or more in the West End, while after relocation 45 percent were paying at least $75 per month, and 20 percent were paying over $95 per month. Median rent rose from $41 to $71, a 73 percent increase. In terms of the incidence of rent change, 86 percent were paying higher rents after relocation, while relocation resulted in decreased rents for only 4 percent. Individual rent increases varied widely, but over half the households were paying at least $30 per month more after relocation, and two-fifths were paying at least $40 more.

Although absolute change in rent level is an important index, perhaps a more relevant consideration for housing welfare is the change in rent level relative to family income. The general effect of relocation was to increase markedly the proportion of income being spent for housing.[15] Expressed as a median, the rent/income ratio rose from 13.6 percent in the West End to 18.6 percent following relocation. To analyze this increase more closely, rent/income ratios were calculated for each household. These data bring out dramatically the impact of increased expenditures for housing following relocation. The proportion of households paying less than 15 percent of their income for housing declined sharply from 64 percent in the West End to only 30 percent after relocation. At the other end of the scale, only 20 percent of the families paid 20 percent or more of their income for rent in the West End, but 43 percent paid this much after relocation.

[14] Unless otherwise indicated, the term "rents" will be used throughout to mean "housing costs," whether for owners or renters.

[15] This increase occurred despite a fairly widespread incidence of higher reported incomes in the post-relocation interviews. Forty-five percent of the families reported post-relocation income in a higher category—and 12 percent in a lower category—than that reported in the West End interview (weekly family income was reported and tabulated in $25 ranges: $0–24, $25–49, and so on). While detailed evaluation and analysis of the implications of these changes is beyond the scope of this article, some evidence from the interviews suggests that the increases are in large part attributable to the addition of secondary income sources as a direct response to increased housing costs. A study of relocation in Indianapolis [15] also reports this phenomenon.

. . . Data indicate that 74 percent of the population were paying a higher proportion of their income for housing after relocation, 11 percent were paying approximately the same proportion, and only 15 percent were paying a smaller proportion. The magnitude of these changes was frequently quite large: following relocation, substantial numbers of households were paying proportions of their income that exceeded by 10, 15, and even 20 percent the proportion they were paying in the West End.[16]

. . . The greater the increase in rent, the better the relocation housing. Among those whose rent increased, the greater the amount of the increase, the lower the proportion of people living in substandard housing.[17] The overall index of housing change also shows that the greater the rent increase, the greater the overall housing improvement. What is perhaps most noteworthy about these data, however, is that a relatively large number of families moved into substandard housing or failed to improve their overall residential status despite increased rents. . . . Among all the families whose rent increased following relocation, fully 27 percent moved into unsound housing and an equal percentage showed no overall improvement on the index of residential change.

The phenomenon of increased housing costs following relocation is characteristic of virtually all the rehousing efforts reviewed. With only one exception,[18] every relocation study,

[16] To make completely clear a point which may be obscured by the limitations of syntax, I am speaking here of absolute changes over time in data which express the relation of two items of information at a given point in time. We are interested in the absolute rent/income ratio before and after relocation, not in the change relative to the original ratio. Changes from 6 percent to 16 percent, 10 percent to 20 percent, 14 percent to 24 percent are all grouped together as increases by 10 percent, even though these are quite different degrees of change in relative terms.

[17] Paradoxically, the results appear to be inconsistent with regard to the condition of the apartments of the few families whose rents decreased. This is no doubt attributable to the fact that this group contains many persons who, upon relocation, combined households with a related individual or family.

[18] The exception is the relocation of a (primarily white) group of elderly individuals and couples in Providence [19]. Sixty-three percent of this group reported lower rents, and only 6 percent reported higher rents. The reason for this is probably the very high vacancy rate in Providence during the 1950's, caused by rapid population loss (Providence lost over 16 percent of its population during the period 1950–60, the largest population decline of any U.S. city with over 200,000 population), which led to a weakened rental market and lower rents.

from the early 1930's until the present, reports increased rents, in some cases relatively small, but in most instances quite substantial. . . .

The sudden and large-scale increase in demand for low-rent housing caused by major renewal projects clearly is a key factor in causing higher rents, particularly in areas of housing shortage. In the words of a Chicago Housing Authority report [9], "city-wide trends in the housing market also contributed to higher rentals, and in a period of rising rents increases were frequently instituted when an apartment is rented to a new tenant." Data from the West End, from Buffalo, and from New York City [4, 6, 26] indicate further that low rents are frequently associated with length of residence, and that upon moving from clearance sites many families are deprived of special advantages which accrue from extended residence (for example, performance of janitorial duties in exchange for reduced rent, and acquaintanceship with the landlord), and which permit these families to pay lower rents.

The increased burden of these higher rents is revealed in the several studies which report rent/income ratios. For example, the San Francisco study [27] indicated that the median rent/income ratio rose from 17 percent to 23 percent following relocation. The 1957–58 Chicago study of families displaced from public housing sites [9] reported an increase in the median rent/income ratio following relocation from 16.6 percent to 26.3 percent. Breaking down changes in rent/income ratio by income level, this same study indicates the degree to which poorer families suffer most from these increases: among those earning less than $3000 per year (35 percent of all households) median rent/income ratio rose from 35.3 percent before relocation to 45.9 percent after relocation; among those in the $3000 to $3999 bracket, the median ratio increased from 18.3 percent to 25.4 percent; and among those earning over $5000, the median ratio increased from 9.1 percent to 17.4 percent.[19]

[10] In his testimony before Congress on February 17, 1964, HHFA Administrator Robert Weaver referred to "a recent survey of 789 families relocated to private housing from urban renewal projects in 9 cities." Forty-three percent of the families interviewed experienced an increase in rent-to-income ratio of more than 5 percentage points. In Baltimore, the median ratio rose from 23 percent to 29 percent following relocation, in Louisville from 28 percent to 31 percent. Fifteen percent of all relocated families in the nine cities had to pay 40 percent or more of their reported income for rent after relocation. (See *Hearings on H.R. 9751, Housing and Community Development Legislation,*

Finally, several other reports indicate the extent to which families must pay increased rents for substandard housing. A 1939 report on the results of relocation from a public housing site in Boston [23] indicated that 23 percent of those paying higher rents relocated in housing inferior to their previous homes. The 1952–54 Chicago Housing Authority report [8] indicated that families who relocated in substandard housing experienced a median monthly rent increase of $27. And the 1957–58 Chicago Housing Authority report [9] indicated that 41 percent of those in substandard housing were paying $80 or more per month gross rent, 19 percent were paying over $90 and 8 percent were paying over $100 per month.

RACIAL FACTORS

Since Negroes constituted only about 1 percent of the West End population, the special relocation difficulties faced by nonwhites are not revealed in our interviews. The majority of other studies deal with totally or predominantly nonwhite populations and provide some indication of the special significance of racial factors in relocation.

Every study of racially mixed relocation areas in which the effects of relocation are analyzed separately for white and nonwhite households indicates that the effects of discrimination make decent relocation housing more difficult and expensive to obtain for nonwhites and force them to pay high rents, even for poor housing . . . the most unsatisfactory relocation results reported, in terms of increased rents and the high percentages of families who relocated into substandard housing, were in predominantly- or all-Negro areas [4, 8, 9, 10, 15, 27, 29, 30, 31, 33, 37].

Reports from Buffalo, San Francisco, and Seattle [6, 27, 35] indicate that the geographical dispersion of displaced nonwhite families was far more limited than that of white families. Chicago experience [8] indicates that for nonwhites, "contrary to the general market, rents did not follow housing quality with any clear consistency" and that "demand held prices generally within the middle range of rents regardless of deficiencies." The report of the Connecticut Civil Rights Advisory Commission [16], while presenting no data on pre-relocation rents or post-relocation housing conditions, indicates

before the Subcommittee on Housing of the Committee on Banking and Currency, House of Representatives, 88th Congress, 2nd Session, pp. 41–42.)

that Negroes and Puerto Ricans were paying considerably higher rents following relocation than were white families. Experience in Chicago and Akron [8, 9, 18] illustrates the severe difficulties faced by Negro home-buyers. The studies indicate minimal use of government-insured loans, a high incidence of purchase through installment contracts (leaving the home-owner without the usual equity protection of a title deed and mortgage loan), and short amortization periods (usually under fifteen years) which, combined with high prices, result in exceedingly high monthly payments. These reports also indicate the difficulties Negro families faced in finding new places to live. In Akron, the time required to find a new home was seven weeks for the average white family, and more than 20 weeks for the average Negro family. In both Chicago and Akron, Negro families were forced to rely primarily on informal sources, such as friends and relatives, in locating a new apartment; in contrast, white families were able to rely on newspaper ads and real estate agencies. The Akron study also reports that the new apartments of Negro families contained fewer and smaller rooms and fewer amenities (private kitchen, private bathroom, hot running water) than did the new apartments of white families. Buffalo's experience [6] likewise documents a significantly higher incidence of overcrowding and doubling-up among nonwhite relocatees.

Relocation may also have an important effect on the overall residential patterns in the city, particularly since the majority of people displaced by renewal have been Negroes. Depending on the goals of the relocation plan and the nature of relocation services offered to displaced families, the process can be one that fosters dissolution of the racial ghetto or one that perpetuates residential segregation and creates further tensions by rapid population shifts. From the few studies in which these broader questions are discussed, it would appear that relocation efforts have gone no further than dealing with the individual family and its housing problems, with the result that existing patterns of racial segregation have either continued or have become intensified. Census tract data from two Chicago studies [8, 9] indicate that that city's huge displacement program during the early 1950's at first sent large numbers of Negro families into predominantly white areas, which shortly thereafter "tipped"; by the late 1950's most of the displaced families were filling vacancies in the predominantly nonwhite neighborhoods. Figures on Buffalo's Ellicott relocation project (an area 80 percent nonwhite) show that 69 per-

cent of the relocated families (and an even higher percentage
of nonwhite families) moved into the seven census tracts
directly north of the redevelopment area, tracts from which
12,000 white families had departed and into which 9,000 non-
white families had moved during the 1950–60 decade [6]. The
report of the Connecticut Advisory Committee to the U. S.
Commission on Civil Rights [16] indicates that although
neighborhood racial composition was relatively unchanged
for nonwhite families before and after relocation, "there
seems to be little doubt about the flight of white families into
all-white neighborhoods after relocation."[20]

RELOCATION AID

Nearly all the studies which examine the quality of assistance in finding housing and the general role of official agencies
in the relocation process emerge with rather negative conclusions. In most instances, the number of families who eventually relocate into housing which they found with agency
aid (other than referrals to public housing) is strikingly small.
Our data indicate that only 15 percent of West End families
(including those who moved into public housing) found their
new apartments with the help of relocation officials.[21] In
Philadelphia, a city with one of the more responsible and
effective renewal programs and one of the first to have a

[20] For a fuller discussion of some of the more general issues con-
cerning the racial aspects of relocation, see George B. Nesbitt, "Relocat-
ing Negroes From Urban Slum Clearance Sites," *Land Economics,*
XXV (August, 1949), 275–88; John B. Collins, "Relocation of Negroes
Displaced by Urban Renewal, with Emphasis on the Philadelphia Ex-
perience" (unpublished Masters thesis, Wharton School, University of
Pennsylvania, 1961); Wolf Von Eckardt, "Bulldozers and Bureaucrats,"
"Black Neck in a White Noose" (Parts I and V of the series "Urban
Renewal and the City"), *New Republic,* September 14, 1963, October
19, 1963.

[21] West End data on attitudes toward relocation officials further indicate that only 13 percent of the families interviewed had positive feelings about the persons whose job it was to help them find housing. In
response to a question asked in the post-relocation interview ("What
kind of contact did you have with the relocation people?") it was not
unusual to receive responses (two years after the time of contact) such
as the following: "They didn't do a damn thing for us"; "They treat
people terribly"; "They didn't even try."

One of the few detailed interview studies of the relocation process
[4] notes that nearly half the tenants interviewed reported receiving
absolutely no help from the site office in locating new quarters and that
(again, two years after relocation) "on balance, feeling among tenants
can conservatively be described as resentful and distrustful."

centralized relocation service, only 0.5 percent of all families displaced during the first two years of this service went into private rental housing on referral from the Rehousing Bureau [30]. In Providence [19], only 15 percent of the families reported using the Family Relocation Service, and only 6 percent reported that they had found their new apartment through this Service. The Chicago Housing Authority studies [8, 9] and the reports on New York City's Manhattantown and West Side Renewal areas [4, 14] indicate similar findings. And in Reynolds' survey [33], local authorities reported that less than one-third of the displaced families relocated into apartments offered by the official agencies, and that "the bulk of the cooperatively relocated clientele consisted of small-sized families . . ."

What is perhaps most disturbing about reports on relocation aid is the high percentage of original site families who are "lost." For example, the New York City Planning Commission [12] reported that 43 percent of the tenants displaced from 39 public housing sites during the 1946–52 period moved to unknown addresses, and in San Francisco [27] approximately 1,600 of the 3,700 households who were enumerated in the original site survey "left the area without seeking the aid of or providing rehousing data to the relocation office." Whether this represents lack of assiduous follow-up techniques on the part of relocation officials, ignorance of available services, or hostility on the part of displaced residents, so high a rate of disappearance would seem to be unacceptable as a by-product of public improvement projects.[22]

Scattered evidence seems to suggest that the quality of relocation help offered by public agencies may be a significant factor in determining the quality and costs of relocation housing. Evidence from several studies [14, 16, 30, 33] indicates

[22] A further group of "lost" families, usually completely overlooked in the relocation operation, are those families who move out of a clearance area between the time of site census and actual land-taking. In the West End, our data show that approximately 8 percent of the population surveyed during the period December, 1957 to January, 1958 were no longer living in the neighborhood by the time of land-taking in April, 1958. A Minneapolis study of a skid-row population [22] showed that 24 percent of the population in the original survey had moved by the time of land-taking. These early movers are not the official responsibility of the public authority and in most cases are not offered the home-seeking services or relocation payments available to those who remain until actual land-taking. Yet their dislocation is clearly caused by the renewal process and their subsequent housing conditions ought to be considered part of the public responsibility.

that where the relocation staff is competent and sensitive in providing lists of available vacancies and in counseling families in need of help, a higher proportion of families relocate in standard and satisfactory housing, at lower rents; more areas of the city are seen as possible relocation destinations, thus widening the family's area of choice; and the tendency to relocate along racial lines into sharply segregated areas is reduced.[23] However, the limited overall benefits reported even in those places where superior relocation services are offered suggest that the problems involved in relocating families require far more fundamental solutions than can be brought about by improvement of relocation services.

CONCLUSION

Although the results of forced relocation appear to vary widely from project to project, on the whole relocation has made a disappointingly small contribution to the attainment of "a decent home in a suitable living environment for every American family." Given the premise that one of the cardinal aims of renewal and rehousing should be the improved housing welfare of those living in substandard conditions, it is questionable whether the limited and inconsistent gains reported in most studies represent an acceptable level of achievement. Not only have the gains been limited, but they have been accompanied by widespread increases in housing costs, often incurred irrespective of an improvement in housing or the ability or desire to absorb these costs. In most clearance areas, some degree of improvement is inevitable, since people are being moved out of marginal or substandard sections.[24] (As the Chicago Housing Authority observed [8],

[23] A major survey research project is currently underway in Topeka, partly under the auspices of the Menninger Foundation, to determine, through use of experimental and control groups, the effects of intensive social and psychological services on the dislocation and adaptation experience.

[24] Many clearance sites (such as the West End), however, contain a considerable amount of decent housing. In all probability, this is true primarily of large sites and of projects where the dominant renewal goals relate to the proposed re-use of the site—such as, civic centers, downtown renewal, and upper-income housing—rather than to efforts at eliminating blighted, unsalvageable structures. In these areas, the number of families living in standard housing prior to relocation should be noted carefully, since ostensibly satisfactory aggregate post-relocation housing conditions may in fact represent only a minor gain.

"It would have been difficult for families leaving the sites to have found a worse segment of the city's housing than the one they had occupied.") The real questions for public policy have to do with the degree of improvement the community should demand from rehousing operations and the nature of the costs imposed.[25]

It is an inescapable conclusion that relocation has been only an ancillary component of the renewal process; were this not the case, the community would find totally unacceptable "slum clearance" projects which leave as many as two-thirds of the displaced families still living in substandard conditions, or which actually increase the incidence of overcrowding. With few exceptions, relocation in this country has not truly been a rehousing effort (in the British sense of the word), a plan which focuses primary attention on the problem of how to insure that people living in substandard housing are resettled into decent homes. In city after city, one sees that the great amount of time and effort spent in investigating and condemning housing conditions in the slums that local authorities wish to tear down is in no sense matched by corresponding public

[25] Clearly, these questions must be placed in the context of housing changes among the population as a whole. A recent H.H.F.A. report shows that in the 1950–60 decade the proportion of occupied substandard units fell from 72 percent to 44 percent among the nation's nonwhite population, and from 32 percent to 13 percent among the white population. (See *Our Nonwhite Population and its Housing*. Washington: Housing and Home Finance Agency, Office of Program Policy, July, 1963.) Since the major portion of this improvement occurred without resort to forced displacement from substandard housing, conclusions about the benefits that flow from relocation must incorporate assumptions about what would have happened to the same population in the absence of forced change.

CHART 1. SELECTED FINDINGS FROM 33 U.S. RELOCATION STUDIES

The chart on the following pages shows these findings in a simple, comparable form. Some data have been recalculated and reformulated from the published figures, and in a few cases outside sources (maps, correspondence) have been used to supplement the information given.

The studies are presented in chronological sequence, together with the name of the author or sponsoring organization. Numbers in brackets refer to the references at the end of this article. Racial composition of the population, where known, is also given in brackets (a question mark indicates that information on race was not given directly, but was either inferred from other materials in the study or from outside sources).

STUDY	DESTINATION	TYPE, TENURE
NEW YORK, 1933, Lavanburg Foundation [white] [26]	86 percent relocated in the "adjoining blocks"	*tenements:* 100 percent pre, 99 percent post
ATLANTIC CITY, 1936, New Jersey State Housing Authority [97 percent nonwhite] [37]	39 percent within ¼ mile; 83 percent within ½ mile; 96 percent within ¾ mile	*1-family/row house:* 70 percent pre, 62 percent post. *2-family:* 15 percent pre, 18 percent post
MINNEAPOLIS, 1938, Chapin [racially mixed] [7]	84 percent within ¾ mile	N.A.
BOSTON, 1939, Housing Association of Metropolitan Boston [primarily nonwhite] [23]	N.A.	N.A.
PHILADELPHIA, 1940, Philadelphia Housing Authority [88 percent nonwhite] [32]	N.A.	6 percent owners pre, 6 percent owners post
DETROIT, 1950, Detroit Housing Commission [17]	N.A.	N.A.
CHICAGO, 1952, Pendelton, Heller [90 percent nonwhite] [29]	36 percent within 1 mile; 59 percent within 2 miles	12 percent owners pre; 9 percent owners post
NEW YORK CITY, 1953, City Planning Commission [12]	N.A.	N.A.

DWELLING SPACE	CONDITION	RENTS
Density 1.01+: 50 percent pre, 47 percent post	*Living in Old Law Tenements:* 96 percent pre, 83 percent post	*Average monthly rent:* $16 pre, $18 post
Average number of rooms: 6.2 pre, 5.1 post; *Density 1.01+:* 10 percent pre, 23 percent post	*Units unfit for use:* 83 percent pre, 34 percent post; *Major repairs needed:* 99 percent pre, 86 percent post	*Median monthly rent:* $12 pre, $15 post 48 percent paying higher rents; 29 percent paying lower rents
Little overcrowding pre- or post-relocation	N.A.	*Average monthly rent:* $16 pre, $18 post
12 percent more space; 34 percent no change; 54 percent less space	78 percent living in "better" apartments	67 percent paying higher rents; (23 percent of those paying higher rents in worse housing)
N.A.	*Needing major repairs or unfit for use:* 90 percent pre, 37 percent post; *Good condition:* 1 percent pre, 20 percent post	*Median monthly rent:* $18 pre, $19 post
Post-relocation: 27 percent doubled-up (no pre-relocation data available)	12 percent moved to substandard housing (no pre-relocation data available)	N.A.
Density 1.51+: 24 percent pre, 27 percent post	*Private bath:* 45 percent pre, 53 percent post; *Central heat:* 83 percent pre, 92 percent post	*$50 or less/month:* 94 percent pre, 62 percent post 46 percent paying at least $16/month more post
N.A.	"73 percent . . . exclusive of those who doubled up or moved into furnished rooms or rooming-houses obtained apartments which appeared to be standard."	N.A.

STUDY	DESTINATION	TYPE, TENURE
CHICAGO, 1952–54, Chicago Housing Authority [primarily nonwhite] [8]	29 percent within 1 mile; 66 percent within 3 miles; 10 percent 5 miles or more	*1-family:* 2 percent pre, 4 percent post; *5+ dwelling units:* 48 percent pre, 46 percent post
SEATTLE, 1954, Seattle Housing Authority [83 percent white] [35]	(Private housing only) 43 percent within 1–1½ miles	0 percent owners pre, 19 percent owners post
AKRON, 1955?, East Akron Community House [52 percent nonwhite] [18]	N.A.	0 percent owners pre; 38 percent owners post
INDIANAPOLIS, 1956, Community Surveys, Inc. [primarily nonwhite] [15]	N.A.	N.A.
NEW YORK CITY, 1956, Women's City Club [4]	59 percent in Manhattan (23 percent within Manhattantown area)	N.A.
NEW YORK CITY, 1957, Morningside Heights Association [primarily nonwhite, Puerto Rican?] [28]	57 percent within Manhattan (19 percent Harlem, 13 percent Washington Heights, 10 percent Upper West Side, 15 percent other); 33 percent other New York City.	N.A.

DWELLING SPACE	CONDITION	RENTS
Median number of rooms: 3.7 pre, 4.0 post; *Density 1.01+:* 31 percent pre, 33 percent post; *Doubled-up households:* 39 percent pre, 36 percent post	*Standard:* 18 percent pre, 53 percent post; *Bldg. 60+ years old:* 89 percent pre, 68 percent post	(Renters only) 85 percent paying higher rents; average increase "about twice" previous rent. *Median monthly rent:* $37 pre, $67 post
N.A.	N.A.	N.A.
Average number of rooms: 4.0 pre, 4.7 post	(Renters only) *Private bath:* 100 percent pre, 62 percent post	*Pre:* $33 (all families paying same rent) *Post:* 70 percent paying over $50 per month, 18 percent over $75
N.A.	Generally improved conditions	(Renters only) ". . . nearly all are paying rents . . . 100 percent–250 percent more than . . . in Area 'A' "
Density 1.01+: 26 percent pre, 10 percent post	*Poor condition:* 39 percent pre, 18 percent post; *Central heating:* 70 percent pre, 97 percent post	*Average monthly rent:* $41 pre, $56 post 53 percent paying higher rents (Private housing only) 51 percent paying one-fifth or more of income for rent, 32 percent one-fourth or more
Average number of rooms: 4.3 pre, 4.0 post; *5+ rooms:* 43 percent pre, 29 percent post	N.A.	*Average monthly rent:* $51 pre, $61 post (relocated by management)

STUDY	DESTINATION	TYPE, TENURE
CHICAGO, 1957–58, Chicago Housing Authority [nonwhite] [9]	"About a third of the households moved to other private dwellings within the vicinity of the clearance site."	19 percent owners pre, 18 percent owners post *1–2 family house:* 16 percent pre, 21 percent post
BOSTON, 1958, Boston Redevelopment Authority [primarily nonwhite?] [5]	29 percent within ½ mile; 45 percent within 1 mile; 73 percent within 3 miles; 16 percent 5+ miles	13 percent owners pre, 9 percent owners post
PORTLAND, 1958?, Slum Clearance and Redevelopment Authority [93 percent white] [36]	74 percent within ½ mile, 86 percent within 1 mile	22 percent owners pre, 21 percent owners post
PHILADELPHIA, 1958, Philadelphia Housing Authority [primarily nonwhite?] [31]	37 percent within 2 blocks, 56 percent within 4 blocks	N.A.
PHILADELPHIA, 1958, Philadelphia Housing Association [95 percent nonwhite] [30]	50 percent within ½ mile, 88 percent within 2 miles, 2 percent 4+ miles	N.A.
CHICAGO, 1958, Land Clearance Commission [43 percent nonwhite] [10]	N.A.	N.A.
U.S. Sample, 1955–59, Reynolds [55 percent nonwhite] [33]	". . . Majority of all families relocated . . . not further than about 1½ miles from their old addresses."	N.A.

DWELLING SPACE	CONDITION	RENTS
Median number of rooms: 4.1 pre, 4.6 post; *Density 1.01+:* 34 percent pre, 30 percent post; *Doubled-up:* 33 percent pre, 34 percent post	*Substandard:* 83 percent pre, 42 percent post; *Central heating:* 56 percent pre, 75 percent post	*Median monthly rent:* $57 pre, $85 post *$100+ month:* 2 percent pre, 27 percent post *Median rent income ratio:* 16.6 percent pre, 26.3 percent post
N.A.	*Post-relocation:* 77 percent standard, 14 percent substandard, 9 percent unreported (no pre-relocation data available)	N.A.
N.A.	N.A.	*Under $20/month:* 50 percent pre, 17 percent post; *under $30/ month:* 90 percent pre, 63 percent post
". . . Extent of over-crowding . . . just about as great." 37 percent living at densities 1.01+ post	*Poor condition:* 83 percent pre, 35 percent post; *Good condition:* 4 percent pre, 17 percent post	Average monthly rent post-relocation 37 percent higher than pre-relocation average *$30+/month:* 23 percent pre, 69 percent post
Density 1.01+: 59 percent pre, 41 percent post	*Unsatisfactory housing:* 100 percent pre, 72 percent post	*Median monthly rent:* $33 pre, $46 post. 72 percent paying higher rents, 19 percent paying lower rents.
N.A.	92 percent relocated into decent, safe housing (no pre-relocation data available)	*Average monthly rent:* $25 pre, $51 post; *$50+/month:* 5 percent pre, 54 percent post
N.A.	Ca. 60 percent relocated in substandard housing (no pre-relocation data available)	". . . Relocatees most often paid more in rents for offsite shelter than they were paying before displacement "

STUDY	DESTINATION	TYPE, TENURE
NEW YORK CITY, 1959, Braislín, Porter and Wheelock [34]	56 percent within Manhattan (33 percent within neighborhood immediately adjacent to site)	N.A.
MORRISTOWN, 1959, Housing Authority of the Town of Morristown [25]	74 percent within 6 blocks	N.A.
BALTIMORE, 1951–60, Baltimore Urban Renewal and Housing Authority [91 percent nonwhite?] [3]	50–82 percent moved within same area *Mount Royal Plaza site:* 43 percent within ½ mile, 68 percent within 1 mile, 89 percent within 2 miles	N.A.
LITTLE ROCK, 1953–60, Housing Authority of the City of Little Rock [primarily nonwhite] [24]	N.A.	48 percent owners pre, 53 percent owners post
PROVIDENCE, 1960, Rhode Island Division of Aging [primarily white?] [19]	65 percent within 4 Census tracts bordering site; of these, most within several blocks of original residence	N.A.
SAN FRANCISCO, 1960, Lichfield, Smith [66 percent nonwhite] [27]	51 percent remained in W. Addition Area (ca. 1 mile radius surrounding site)	9 percent owners pre, 17 percent owners post
PORTLAND, 1961, Citizens Urban Renewal Effort [97 percent white] [11]	N.A.	N.A.

DWELLING SPACE	CONDITION	RENTS
N.A.	N.A.	N.A.
N.A.	100 percent substandard pre, 0 percent substandard post	N.A.
N.A.	N.A.	N.A.
N.A.	86 percent substandard pre, 10 percent substandard post	N.A.
Ca. one-fourth moved to larger units, 7 percent to smaller units	Ca. one-third of the units deteriorated, pre- and post-relocation	6 percent paying higher rents, 63 percent paying lower rents *Less than $45/month:* 15 percent pre, 63 percent post
Density 1.00+: 50 percent pre, 36 percent post	74 percent moved to better area, 23 percent to worse area	*Median monthly rent:* $39 pre, $58 post 83 percent paying higher rents, 12 percent paying lower rents. *Median rent/ income ratio:* 17 percent pre, 23 percent post
N.A.	N.A.	61 percent paying higher rents

STUDY	DESTINATION	TYPE, TENURE
BALTIMORE, 1961, Baltimore Urban Renewal and Housing Authority [2]	(Private housing) 55 percent within ½ mile, 79 percent within 1 mile, 96 percent within 2 miles	11 percent owners pre, 14 percent owners post
BUFFALO, 1961, Buffalo Municipal Housing Authority [80 percent nonwhite] [6]	40 percent within 1 mile, 70 percent within 2 miles	26 percent owners pre, 29 percent owners post
DALLAS, 1961, Texas Transportation Institute [white] [1]	58 percent within 1 mile	100 percent owners pre, 93 percent owners post
NEW YORK CITY, 1962, Community Service Society [85 percent nonwhite, Puerto Rican] [14]	17 percent within renewal area, 63 percent within Manhattan	N.A.
MINNEAPOLIS, 1963, Housing and Redevelopment Authority [96 percent white] [22]	70–80 percent within 1 mile	N.A.

and professional interest in the fate of displaced families once they have been dislodged. It is perhaps revealing to note that only one-half of one percent of the $2.2 billion of gross project costs for all federally-aided urban renewal projects (through 1960) was spent on relocation.[26]

Review of reports and procedures relating to relocation reveals further that environmental considerations are virtually absent in the assignment and evaluation of relocation dwellings. This is in part understandable, since, despite the wording of the 1949 Housing Act, no meaningful criteria have yet been established as to what constitutes a "suitable living en-

[26] See Martin C. Anderson, "The Federal Urban Renewal Program: A Financial and Economic Analysis," (unpublished Doctoral dissertation, M.I.T., 1962).

DWELLING SPACE	RENTS	CONDITION
Average number of rooms: 5.4 pre, 5.1 post; *Density 1.01+:* 19 percent pre, 21 percent post	*Dilapidated structure:* 86 percent pre, 11 percent post; *Central heating:* 22 percent pre, 58 percent post	(Private renters only) *Median monthly rent:* $43 pre, $53 post; *$60+/month:* 13 percent pre, 39 percent post
Median number of rooms: 6.15 pre, 6.19 post; *Density 1.01+:* 13 percent pre, 8 percent post; *Doubled-up:* 18 percent pre, 13 percent post	99+ percent moved to homes in "substantial compliance" with Minimum Standards Housing Ordinance (no pre-relocation data available)	Pre (average): $63 per month, Post (median): $65
Average number of rooms: 5.54 pre, 5.55 post	*Average age:* 29 years pre, 19 years post; *Brick or masonry construction:* 16 percent pre, 51 percent post	*Mortgaged homes:* 29 percent pre, 52 percent post; *Average mortgage:* $3061 pre, $7215 post
N.A.	93 percent moved to standard housing (no pre-relocation data available)	*Average monthly rent (estimate):* $63 pre, $72 post; *$101+/month:* 7 percent pre, 19 percent post
N.A.	*Standard housing:* 17 percent pre, 83 percent post	*Under $20/month:* 44 percent pre, 3 percent post; *$35+/month:* 14 percent pre, 38 percent post

vironment." But at a minimum the local authority should insure that displaced families do not relocate in areas slated for clearance or rehabilitation in the near future, and thereby become part of a population of repeatedly displaced persons. Yet consideration of this factor, which will undoubtedly make the already difficult job of finding decent relocation housing for low-income families even more complex, has rarely been incorporated in the plans and reports of local authorities. (In one of the few reports to consider this factor, the New York City Planning Commission [12] in a sample survey found that of the 709 tenants moving from public housing sites into private housing who reported new addresses, 49 percent moved into housing in areas mapped for future redevelopment.)

Given the realities of the low-income housing market and the impact of public programs, it is likely that, for many families, relocation may mean no more than keeping one step ahead of the bulldozer.

It is clear, too, that relocation results in a somewhat selective incidence of benefits in terms of housing welfare, but imposes a quite unselective incidence of costs, personal as well as financial. These results suggest that far greater attention must be paid to the impact and dynamics of the dislocation and relocation experience on various subgroups within the affected population. Review of the literature on mobility, preparedness for change, and modes of adaptation, as well as preliminary analysis of West End data,[27] suggests that families who relocate satisfactorily are by and large those with adequate financial, personal, and social resources, those who are prepared for upward mobility and who (despite frequent initial resentment about having to leave a satisfying environment) view forced relocation as an opportunity to obtain the kind of housing that they have long desired. On the other hand, those who are least prepared and able to effect a positive change, because of inadequacies in income and personal or social resources, appear to incur heavy costs in terms of severe personal and social disruption, failure to improve housing conditions, and increased housing expenses that are difficult to absorb or unrelated to housing improvement. To a considerable extent, then, the various reports on rehousing suggest that relocation may be resulting in a "rich get richer, poor get poorer" effect. Present renewal operations are, however, highly unselective and do not permit discrimination between families most and least able to profit by the experience. Nor do they provide a variety of aids and programs designed to fit the needs of the different types of families contained in a relocation population. With a greater understanding of the effects of relocation and of the various subgroups within a relocation population, it may be possible to devise more sophisticated programs which will, through incentives, hasten the mobility of those prepared to make changes, and will at the same time be sensitive to the special needs of those who cannot cope with forced change, by providing new services and benefits for them or by obviating the necessity to relocate.

It is of course appropriate to question whether the results of the studies reported here and the conclusions that flow

[27] Fried in Kantor, *op. cit.*

from these findings are applicable to the current housing picture. Over two-thirds of the studies reviewed in this paper report on relocation activities that occurred during the 1950's; only one study is dated as recently as 1963. Thus the data cited here do not permit any definite statements about the results of relocation activity in recent years—more specifically, since 1961 and the change in Administrations. Clearly, there have been new emphases in the federal government's housing policies: the President's executive order on equal opportunity in housing, the moderate-income [Sec. 221(d)(3)] housing program, pilot projects in new ways to house low-income families, a shift away from the bulldozer approach to urban renewal, and increased concern for the problems of relocated families. Nonetheless, it remains unclear whether the shortcomings described in this paper are entirely things of the past. In the first place, reliable data on current relocation experience are not yet available (see the Postscript to this article). Second, it is only through local operating agencies that actual changes will come about, and there still exist wide differences in local conditions and in the aims and personnel of these agencies; these differences make it extremely difficult to translate changes in federal policies and procedures uniformly and rapidly to the local level. Third, the limited supply of low-cost housing continues to make relocation a difficult task. The housing shortage of the early 1950's has been eased considerably, but we do not know whether it has eased sufficiently to provide for current high rates of displacement resulting from urban highway construction, redevelopment projects, and the "financial bulldozer" of rehabilitation. The filtering of housing undoubtedly has helped to create additional vacancies in urban areas, but it is doubtful whether a sufficient number of vacant units are: *one,* in sound condition; *two,* available at prices the poor can afford; *three,* open to nonwhite occupancy; and *four,* suitably located for the social and economic needs of displaced people. The volume of new public housing—another potential resource for relocation—has been small, and the program has been beset by a great many other difficulties. In short, changes have doubtless taken place, and what is happening in 1964 is quite different from what went on in 1954. The question is how much have things changed and how far are we still from acceptable levels of achievement. In view of past experience, the burden of proof must be on the public agencies to produce valid answers to these questions and to demonstrate that satisfactory relocation is now being achieved.

Finally, we must consider how issues of housing welfare relate to the context provided by analysis of the human costs and benefits of relocation. Our findings from the West End, supported by similar studies from other cities, suggest that the deleterious effects of the uprooting experience, the loss of familiar places and persons, and the difficulties of adjusting to and accepting new living envrionments may be far more serious issues than are changes in housing status.[28] If we are to undertake valid cost-benefit analyses of the impact of relocation, it is essential that the investigation of housing change be placed in the larger context of residential change, the various social and psychological aspects of community life, and how they vary among different population groups. During the coming years, thousands of American families will be forcibly dislocated through the workings of governmental programs such as urban renewal, highway construction, and public housing, as well as by the workings of private market mechanisms. It is a serious challenge to the housing and planning professions, as well as to the society as a whole, to clarify and comprehend the effects of relocation and to improve these programs in the light of our increased knowledge.

A POSTSCRIPT

It is evident that relocation presents a serious problem for local public agencies. On the one hand, they have a statutory obligation to relocate all families who so desire in decent, safe, and sanitary housing, convenient to their place of work and at rents they can afford; on the other hand, the agency's rebuilding operations do not provide suitable housing for those

[28] See Fried in Duhl, *op. cit.;* Fried in Kantor, *op. cit.;* Marc Fried, "Effects of Social Change on Mental Health," *American Journal of Orthopsychiatry,* XXXIV (January, 1964), 3–28; Herbert Gans, "The Human Implications of Current Redevelopment and Relocation Planning," *Journal of the American Institute of Planners,* XXV (February, 1959), 15–25; Chester Hartman, "The Limitations of Public Housing: Relocation Choices in a Working-Class Community," *op. cit.;* Vere Hole, "Social Effects of Planned Rehousing," *Town Planning Review,* XXX (July, 1959), 161–73; Peter Marris, *Family and Social Change in an African City* (London: Routledge and Kegan Paul, 1961); Peter Marris, "The Social Implications of Urban Redevelopment," *Journal of the American Institute of Planners,* XXVIII (August, 1962), 180–86; J. M. Mogey, *Family and Neighbourhood* (London: Oxford University Press, 1956); Charles Vereker and John B. Mays, *Urban Redevelopment and Social Change* (Liverpool: Liverpool University Press, 1961); Michael Young and Peter Willmott, *Family and Kinship in East London* (Glencoe, Ill.: The Free Press, 1957).

displaced. The conflict between demands and resources becomes evident when one considers the magnitude of family displacement, the fact that displaced families for the most part have the double disadvantage of being both poor and nonwhite, the shortage of low-rent standard vacancies in most cities, the limited usefulness of public housing as a relocation resource, and the competition for relocation housing from families displaced by the highway program and other forms of public and private construction. The nature of this conflict was eloquently described more than a decade ago by Jack Meltzer, who wrote: ". . . In the final analysis any relocation plan is dependent on an available supply of housing, both public and private. To recognize the fact that relocation must inevitably accelerate competition for an already inadequate supply of housing, particularly for housing at levels that the bulk of relocatees can afford, and then to proceed with the relocation of families without providing for meeting this need is to fly in the face of reason and reality. This becomes doubly serious when Negroes are being relocated, since the competition for housing is most serious for the Negro, and further, a situation is created largely by public action that results in pressures upon the social fabric without an assumption of responsibility for coping with the effects of these pressures."[29]

Given these conflicts, there are bound to be inherent defects in a system that requires the agency executing these programs to evaluate relocation results. Accordingly, one must question whether local authorities are free to judge and report on the results of their relocation operations in an objective and impartial manner. In effect, the local agency may have no choice but to issue extremely positive relocation reports: anything less than this might produce legal, political, and ethical conflicts and could slow up or curtail the entire rebuilding effort, which is the principal goal of the authority and its programs.

Official relocation figures, as reported by local renewal authorities and compiled by the Urban Renewal Administration, indicate that relocation has consistently resulted in an extremely high percentage of families living in standard housing. URA data indicate that through September, 1963, only

[29] Jack Meltzer, "Relocation of Families Displaced in Urban Redevelopment: Experience in Chicago," *Urban Redevelopment: Problems and Practices,* ed. Coleman Woodbury (Chicago: Univ. of Chicago Press, 1953), p. 452.

7.7 percent of the 141,210 families displaced from urban renewal sites for whom post-relocation information is available (87 percent of the total number of families displaced) moved into substandard housing.[30] These reports are widely used by federal and local officials and in planning literature to describe the results of urban renewal, and they contribute significantly to the public's image of the program.[31] Recently, however, responsible persons in the housing and planning field have been questioning the reliability of official figures.[32] Careful study of local housing conditions has led many observers to conclude that in view of the extent of displacement and the income and demographic characteristics of relocation caseloads, it is highly improbable that relocation could have had such consistently beneficial results.

Data collected by the Center for Community Studies on the West End relocation operation—probably the first large-scale, independently-gathered data on the results of relocation —show some marked discrepancies with official Boston Redevelopment Authority data on the West End and furnish support for the prevailing skepticism about official findings. The comparative data, . . . indicate extremely large differences in findings with respect to both condition and tenure (although the proportion going into public housing and the geographical distribution of displaced families—the latter not shown in this presentation—are almost identical in both sets of figures). According to the official data, less than 2 percent of the West End families moved into structurally substandard housing; according to the independently-gathered data, over 25 percent relocated into structurally substandard housing. Whereas the official data indicate that less than 7 percent of West End families bought homes upon leaving the neighborhood, interview data collected by the Center for Community Studies indicate that three times as many families—over 21 percent—moved into their own homes.

Without more detailed investigation, it is impossible to trace

---

[30] Letter from Peter P. Riemer, Director, Program Data and Evaluation Branch, Urban Renewal Administration, May 21, 1964.

[31] See, for example, President Johnson's Message to Congress on Housing and Community Development (*New York Times,* January 28, 1964, p. 16); *Urban Renewal Notes,* March-April, 1964; Robert C. Weaver, "Current Trends in Urban Renewal," *Land Economics,* XXXIX (November, 1963), 325–41; Martin Meyerson, *et al., Housing, People, and Cities* (New York: McGraw-Hill, 1962), p. 311.

[32] See, for example, William G. Grigsby, *Housing Markets and Public Policy* (Philadelphia: Univ. of Pennsylvania Press, 1963), p. 286n.

the source of these discrepancies with any precision.[33] It should be noted, however, that the Center for Community Studies housing surveyors were all well-trained college graduates and made use of criteria approximating those of the U.S. Housing Census. A recent detailed study of the relocation process by Gordon N. Gottsche (coincidentally, also with reference to Boston's West End) offers a critique of the evaluation and data-gathering systems employed by the local authority and suggests one possible source for discrepancies of this sort [20]. Gottsche's principal conclusions are that with respect to post-relocation housing evaluations, "there is no systematic method for the relocation fieldworker to use in the evaluation process" and that a system of "compromised standards" was used in the evaluation process, whereby standards employed in the pre-relocation housing surveys were far more inclusive and detailed than the standards used in evaluating post-relocation housing. Gottsche details and documents these conclusions: lack of recorded inspection specifications, complete freedom of the local authority to establish its own standards and inspection procedures, wholesale but undocumented condemnation of the environment of the renewal site as "uniformly bad," but failure to consider physical or social features of the environment at all in the post-relocation evaluation, and the generally poor level of data recording. Inspection of a (non-random) sample of some 80 relocation dwellings led Gottsche to state that ". . . the governmental standard was compromised in about one-half of the cases, with the structure requiring either demolition or major rehabilitation."

It is not clear whether these critical findings, based on observations of a single operation, can be generalized to other

[33] The Center for Community Studies housing surveys were made approximately two years after relocation, whereas Boston Redevelopment Authority surveys of these same addresses were made at the time of relocation. It is unlikely, however, that this time lag could introduce differences of the magnitude indicated in Table XI. (Furthermore, Gottsche's survey [20] which indicates similar discrepancies, was made at roughly the same time as the B.R.A. surveys.) However, this does raise the issue of "housekeeping," which seems to have attained some prevalence in official circles. Several renewal officials have claimed in conversation that displaced families are relocated into standard homes, but because of poor housekeeping habits and inadequate training turn decent homes into slums within a very short time. Clearly, this argument is applicable only to some aspects of substandard housing: inadequate plumbing or absence of dual egress is not a situation created by a family's behavior. Further, to my knowledge no evidence has ever been offered to support this contention. The matter should be studied, however, since this reasoning appears to have some currency.

cities and to more recent procedures. It is difficult and expensive to obtain independent data, local authorities are frequently reluctant to allow inspection of their records and operating procedures, and until recently few responsible persons have dared express skepticism about the operations of public bodies undertaking renewal. Only a few reports in the above review make reference to this issue. Hollman, in his Philadelphia study [30], reported that the sample he took from Rehousing Bureau files showed results different from the Philadelphia reports to the URA, differences which for the categories "self-relocated to standard private rental housing" and "substandard housing" were statistically significant, although the universe was not entirely the same. In 1962, the U.S. Comptroller General began a series of spot-checks of local renewal operations and reported that federal government inspection of the buildings in Cleveland's Erieview renewal project showed only 20 percent of the buildings to be substandard, although reports of the local authority submitted to the HHFA regional office in Chicago classified 71 percent of the buildings as substandard.[34] This report goes on to recommend that local authorities be more closely supervised by the federal agencies with respect to the standards they employ and the accuracy of data they submit. A great deal of further investigation is needed in order to clarify these matters, but it is clear that as long as relocation remains a secondary interest in the renewal process and the primary impetus for renewal is to replace low-income housing with "higher" uses, there will be strong pressures to use compromised standards and to understate any adverse impact of the relocation process on displaced families.

As a final note, it is difficult to refrain from commenting on the overall quality of relocation reports, as evidenced by the studies reviewed in this article. The most serious shortcoming is the inadequate quantity of relevant post-relocation data. In order to assess the impact of relocation, one must at a minimum have data on geographic dispersion, changes in living space, housing conditions before and after relocation, and changes in housing costs. Yet only 8 of the 33 studies reviewed

---

[34] Comptroller General of the U.S., *Report to the Congress of the U.S.: Premature Approval of Large-Scale Demolition for Erieview Urban Renewal Project I, Cleveland, Ohio*, by the Urban Renewal Administration. *Housing and Home Finance Agency* (Washington, D.C., June, 1963).

contained information on all four of these factors in sufficient quantity to permit the reader to evaluate the impact of relocation. Most studies pay little attention to that part of the relocated population which has "disappeared," and conclusions are made solely on the basis of data on those families for whom information is available. Yet the "lost" families are generally the least stable, most transient group in the area, with fewest resources, and probably fare far worse than those families who receive help and whose post-relocation whereabouts are known. Rarely are conclusions qualified or offered as tentative in view of this unknown factor.[35]

Further, most reports, as evidenced by their style and manner of presentation, apparently are written in order to "sell" relocation, to prove a case; texts are frequently characterized by a roseate tone, stressing achievements and either minimiz-

---

[35] It should be noted that the West End study minimized this skewing tendency markedly. The original sample was drawn randomly from relocation office site occupancy cards. The resultant sample of 585 represented approximately one-fifth of all project area households meeting our sample criteria (the household had to contain a female between the ages of 20–65). Detailed follow-up interview data are available for 499, or 85 percent of the original sample, and some data on housing (including housing type, location, condition of neighborhood and building) are available for 540, or 92 percent of the original sample. This combination of random sampling technique and assiduous follow-up procedure to ensure a high rate of response is virtually unique among studies of this kind and makes the West End data probably the most reliable of all studies reported here.

Of the studies compiled for this article, only one posited various assumptions about the "lost" families and used these assumptions as part of the total analysis and overall findings. (It is perhaps significant to note that this report was done by a private organization rather than a public agency.) In the Philadelphia Housing Association's report on relocation in Philadelphia in 1955–57 [30] nearly half the total caseload was found to have disappeared or refused to cooperate with relocation officials. Of those reporting, 45 percent went into satisfactory housing. However, the Association presents its findings for the entire sample in terms of three assumptions about the unreported group: that the distribution of the unreported sample is identical to the reported sample; that the proportion of the unreported sample relocating into substandard housing is the same as the proportion among the reported sample who relocated into private rental housing without official aid; that the condition of the unreported families is identical to their condition prior to relocation. Under these various assumptions, the proportions of the total caseload relocating in satisfactory housing are, respectively, 45 percent, 28 percent and 21 percent. The report then goes on to explain why it considers the intermediate assumption the most probable of the three and says (realistically) that even this assumption is probably somewhat more positive than the real case; it then makes this preferred assumption the basis for reporting and discussion.

ing or ignoring negative consequences.[36] Even in cases where the tabulated data are comprehensive and objective, texts of official reports are frequently deceptive. Thus, a Chicago Housing Authority report [9] contains the following sentence: "The median rent/income ratio for all households in site dwellings was 16.6%; after relocation this median ratio increased to 26.3%, but was still less than 20% for households with income of $5000 or more"; and the generalization that "all income groups shared in better housing after relocation" (this latter interpretation is based on a table of post-relocation housing condition by income levels, which indicates that among families earning $3000 a year—35% of the population —only 33% relocated into standard housing). Another Chicago Housing Authority study [8] presents detailed data on increases in rent and rent/income ratios following relocation (among the highest reported in any relocation study), which are then described in the following manner: "After moving, most families in each income group still paid less than ¼ of their income for rent, except for those with income under $3000 [over one-third of the population!]. Although the remaining ⅓ paid 25% or more, rents for families in this group usually did not exceed 30% of income." A more objective observer would probably be far less sanguine in describing these findings.[37]

We are still a long way from knowing all that needs to be known about the effects of relocation.[38] Without more de-

[36] Consider, for example, the concluding remarks of the Chicago Land Clearance Commission's *Final Relocation Report, Project No. UR Ill. 6–3* [10]: "Some of the individual householders in the project area required a great deal of help and furnished some of the more complex relocation problems. . . . In each case the relocation staff did wonders through sympathetic, patient and helpful attitudes. . . . The relocation job in project UR Ill. 6–3 proved . . . that redevelopment of a slum and blighted area is advantageous in all its aspects." It would seem that rhapsodic prose of this sort is out of place in any official evaluation report, particularly in one which offers as little information as this one does and in which average monthly rent for the displaced families is shown to have more than doubled following relocation (see the summary of findings in Chart I).

[37] It is interesting to note that the best relocation reports—in terms of clarity, comprehensiveness, and objectivity—are those written by private, rather than public, agencies [see 4, 26, 27, 29, 30].

[38] The introductory words to two of the earliest relocation studies are as applicable today as they were three decades ago. The Lavanburg Foundation's 1933 study of New York's Lower East Side [26] noted: "Housing experts frequently ponder over specific questions in connection with slum clearance without arriving at definite conclusions, because of

tailed knowledge of these effects—in terms of housing, community life and psychosocial reactions—it is impossible to know the ultimate results of our present actions: whether we are improving the living conditions of slum families or merely shifting the slum to another section of the city; whether relocation aids the slum family or whether renewal is merely a device to use urban land for more favored groups in the society. These are questions of vital importance, and there is strong evidence to support a conclusion that the executors of these acts cannot at the same time impartially judge what they have done. In terms of funds, time, and manpower, we allocate far too few resources to feedback analysis of social welfare programs. Not only must we elevate this function to a higher priority, but it must be structured in such a way as to eliminate the possibility of a built-in bias in our evaluations. Given the factors outlined above, one must conclude that this phase of the renewal operation should be placed outside the local renewal authority, either with another government agency or with a non-governmental research group. Only in this way can we be sure that the objective tools and methods of the social scientist will be brought to bear on the reporting and analysis of these critical issues.

REFERENCES

1. Adkins, William G. and Eichman, Frank F. Jr. *Consequences of Displacement by Right of Way to 100 Home Owners, Dallas, Texas.* Bulletin No. 16. College Station, Texas: Texas Transportation Institute, A & M College of Texas, September, 1961.

2. Baltimore Urban Renewal and Housing Agency, Research Division. *The New Locations and Housing Characteristics of Families Displaced from Area 3-C.* Baltimore: Urban Renewal and Housing Agency, March, 1961.

3. Baltimore Urban Renewal and Housing Agency, Research Division. *Ten Years of Relocation Experience in Baltimore, Maryland.* Baltimore: Urban Renewal and Housing Agency, June, 1961.

4. Black, Elinor G. *Manhattantown Two Years Later: A Second Look at Tenant Relocation.* New York: Women's City Club of New York, April, 1956.

5. Boston Redevelopment Authority. *Final Relocation Report, New York Streets Project—UR Mass. 2-1.* March, 1958. (Mimeographed.)

6. Buffalo Municipal Housing Authority. *Ellicott Relocation: Objec-*

the lack of explicit factual information." Chapin's 1936 study of Minneapolis [7] begins with these words: "When a slum is cleared of insanitary dwellings, what becomes of the people who lived in the slum? . . . Answers to these questions have long been sought, but often met in terms of opinion rather than facts. Especially neglected have been the psychological and social aspects of the problem."

tives, Experience, and Appraisal. Buffalo, N.Y.: Municipal Housing Authority, November, 1961.

7. Chapin, F. Stuart. "The Effects of Slum Clearance and Rehousing on Family and Community Relationships in Minneapolis," *American Journal of Sociology,* XLIII (March, 1938), 744–63.

8. Chicago Housing Authority. *Relocation of Site Residents to Private Housing: The Characteristics and Quality of Dwellings Obtained in the Movement from Chicago Housing Authority Slum Clearance Sites, 1952–1954.* Chicago: Housing Authority, November, 1955.

9. Chicago Housing Authority. *Rehousing Residents Displaced from Public Housing Clearance Sites in Chicago, 1957–1958.* Chicago: Chicago Housing Authority, October, 1960.

10. Chicago Land Clearance Commission. *Final Relocation Report, Project No. UR Ill. 6–3, (W. Central Industrial District).* Chicago: Chicago Land Clearance Commission, April, 1958.

11. Citizens Urban Renewal Effort (CURE). *Report of Survey on Relocation of Families in Connection with the Bayside Park Urban Renewal Project.* Memorandum to the Portland, Maine City Council, April, 1961.

12. City Planning Commission, City of New York. *Tenant Relocation Report.* New York: City Planning Commission, January 20, 1954.

13. Cohn, Samuel M. *Report of the Site Survey and Description of the Work of Relocation PA–2–3.* Philadelphia Housing Authority, Department of Research and Information, September, 1940. (Typewritten.)

14. Community Service Society of New York. *A Demonstration Project in Relocation,* New York: Community Service Society, April, 1962.

15. Community Surveys, Inc. *Redevelopment: Some Human Gains and Losses.* Indianapolis, 1956.

16. Connecticut Advisory Committee to the United States Commission on Civil Rights. *Report on Connecticut: Family Relocation under Urban Renewal.* Washington, July, 1963.

17. Detroit Housing Commission. *Monthly Report.* November-December, 1950, pp. 4–9.

18. East Akron Community House. *Where Will They Go?: A Study of 77 Families Forced to Move from the "Mobile Houses,"* East Akron, Ohio, 1955(?).

19. Goldstein, Sidney and Zimmer, Basil. *Residential Displacement and Resettlement of the Aged: A Study of the Problems of Rehousing Aged Residents Displaced by Freeway Construction in Downtown Providence.* Providence: Rhode Island Division on Aging, 1960.

20. Gottsche, Gordon N. "Relocation: Goals, Implementation and Evaluation of the Process, with Reference to the West End Redevelopment Project in Boston, Mass." Unpublished Master's thesis, M.I.T., 1960.

21. H.H.F.A. Urban Renewal Administration. *Relocation from Urban Renewal Areas Through December, 1961.* Washington, 1962(?).

22. The Housing and Redevelopment Authority in and for the City of Minneapolis. *Report on the Relocation of Residents, Businesses and Institutions from the Gateway Center Project Area.* Minneapolis: Housing and Redevelopment Authority, November, 1963.

23. Housing Association of Metropolitan Boston. *Comparative Survey of Present and Former Dwellings of Families Displaced by the Development of a Public Housing Project in Boston.* Boston, Housing Association, October, 1939.

24. Housing Authority of the City of Little Rock, Ark. *Final Relocation Report, Dunbar Redevelopment Project.* 1953(?).

———. *Final Relocation Report, Philander Smith Project Ark. R 1.* January, 1957.

———. *Relocation in the Livestock Show Area of Little Rock, Arkansas.* May, 1960.

———. *Relocation in the Westrock Urban Renewal Project Area.* September, 1960.

25. Housing Authority of the Town of Morristown, New Jersey. *The First Fifty Families: An Analysis of the Relocation Program.* June, 1959. (Mimeographed.)

26. Lavanburg Foundation. *What Happened to 386 Families Who Were Compelled to Vacate Their Slum Dwellings to Make Way For A Large Housing Project.* New York, Lavanburg Foundation, 1933.

27. Lichfield, Nathaniel. "Relocation: The Impact on Housing Welfare," *Journal of the American Institute of Planners,* XXVII (August, 1961), 199–203. See also, Smith, Wallace. "Relocation in San Francisco," *Bay Area Real Estate Report.* 4th quarter, 1960.

28. Morningside Heights, Inc. *Relocation: Critical Phase of Redevelopment: The Experience of Morningside Gardens.* New York, 1957.

29. Pendleton, P. Kathryn and Heller, Howard U. "The Relocation of Families Displaced by an Urban Renewal Project," Master's thesis, Department of Sociology, University of Chicago, 1952.

30. Philadelphia Housing Association. *Relocation in Philadelphia.* Philadelphia: Housing Association, November, 1958.

31. Philadelphia Housing Authority. *Relocation of Families: A Report on the Relocation Operation for the Norris Low-rent Housing Development.* Philadelphia: Housing Authority, 1952.

32. *Report to the Philadelphia Redevelopment Authority on Completion of Morton Relocation Contract by the Germantown Settlement.* Philadelphia, 1961(?). (Mimeographed.)

33. Reynolds, Harry W. Jr. "The Human Element in Urban Renewal," *Public Welfare,* XIX (April, 1961), 71–73, 82.

———. "Population Displacement in Urban Renewal," *American Journal of Economics and Sociology,* XXII (January, 1963), 113–28.

34. Schorr, Philip. *Final Report on Relocation Operations from Fordham University and Lincoln Center Sites.* New York: Braislin, Porter and Wheelock, Inc., November, 1959.

35. Seattle Housing Authority. *Locations and Ownership of Housing Obtained by 1093 Families Moving From Seattle Temporary Public Housing Units—March, 1953 through September, 1954.* 1956(?). (Mimeographed.)

36. Slum Clearance and Redevelopment Authority, and Child and Family Services. *Vine-Deer-Chatham Project Relocation: A Community Effort.* Portland, Maine, 1958(?).

37. State Housing Authority. *Present Dwellings of Former Residents of the Site of Stanley S. Holmes Village, Atlantic City, New Jersey,* Trenton, N.J., June, 1936. (Mimeographed.)

38. Warrence, Samuel. "A Report on Relocation of the Elderly," *Essays on the Problems Faced in the Relocation of Elderly Persons.* Prepared by the Institute for Urban Studies, University of Pennsylvania, and National Association of Housing and Redevelopment Officials, Philadelphia, June, 1963.

THE HOUSING OF RELOCATED FAMILIES*

United States Housing and Home Finance Agency

SUMMARY

The United States Bureau of the Census has released to the Housing and Home Finance Agency the first findings of a nationwide survey of the housing of families displaced from urban renewal sites. The survey consisted of interviews conducted at 2,300 relocation housing units that were occupied by households relocated during June, July, and August of 1964 from urban renewal projects located in 132 cities. Of the households covered, 1,090 were white, 1,210 nonwhite. The interviewing began after Thanksgiving and was completed early in January of this year.

The survey disclosed the following pertinent facts:[1]

—the vast majority—94 percent—of the displaced families were relocated in standard housing;

—median gross rents are higher—$74 compared with $66 prior to relocation—while the median proportion of income spent for rent increased from 25 percent to nearly 28 percent;

—nearly 2 of every 5 relocated families had incomes below $3,000 and almost the same proportion had incomes between $3,000 and $6,000;

—home ownership increased from 33 to 37 percent;

—most relocated families found that work and basic community facilities were at least as conveniently located as before —66 percent finding the convenience of neighborhood shopping about the same or better and 71 percent finding public transportation as satisfactory or better than previously—55 percent reporting their church no farther away than before;

—shifts in jobs following relocation were not substantial, with

* Summary of a Bureau of the Census Survey of Families Recently Displaced from Urban Renewal Sites. Washington, D.C. March 1965 [tables omitted].

[1] As a general rule, throughout this report, percentages relate to the number of cases reporting. For the journey to work and distance to church, however, the percentages relate only to those cases for which the inquiry was applicable. Thus, the unemployed were not queried about their journey to work nor those without religious affiliations about the distance to their place of worship.

only 10 percent of those with a fixed place of employment changing jobs in the period following the move;

—37 percent of the household heads with a fixed place of employment reported a longer journey to work;

—70 percent of the families relocated themselves, although nearly 90 percent of the households received counseling, financial, or other assistance from the local public agency during the relocation process.

HOUSEHOLD INCOME

Poverty was common among the families covered by the survey. Thus, the Census found that 40 percent reported income of less than $3,000 in 1964 and nearly 80 percent had incomes of less than $6,000. The income of half the nonwhites was below the $3,000 level compared with only about one-quarter of the white families. Reflecting the high proportion of families at the lower end of the income scale, the median income for all reporting was only $3,814 compared with $5,631 for all nonfarm families as reported by the Bureau of the Census for 1963.

HOUSEHOLD SIZE AND COMPOSITION

Of the families interviewed in the survey, 47 percent were white, 53 percent nonwhite. The median sized household contained three persons with the nonwhite households tending to run somewhat larger than their white counterparts, 3.2 vs 2.9.

The most predominant sized families contained only two persons. These accounted for 32 percent of the white group, 26 percent of the nonwhite.

There were, however, slightly more than one-third of the households which contained 5 or more persons with nearly 8 or more persons. The typical household, both white and nonwhite, was made up only of related persons. Only 4 percent of the white families, 8 percent of the nonwhite families, contained any nonrelatives.

LENGTH OF TIME AT PREVIOUS ADDRESS

A major portion of those interviewed—59 percent—had lived 5 or more years at their previous address, while an additional 32 percent had been on the urban renewal site for between one and five years. Only a handful—2½ percent—had lived less than 6 months at their pre-relocation address. In other words, the group interviewed had their roots well established in the neighborhood from which they were displaced.

The nonwhite families showed a tendency to have lived a slightly shorter time in their previous neighborhood than whites with roughly 55 percent of them having been five years or more in their previous quarters. Some 63 percent of the whites had lived in their quarters that long.

TYPE OF UNIT

More than half of the families were relocated into one family dwellings. Most of the balance went into apartments in apartment buildings. Only 3 households, all of whom were self-relocated, moved into trailers.

The greater use of public housing by the LPAs is reflected in the fact that 44 percent of the families aided by them in finding housing were placed in apartments in regular apartment buildings. Among the self-relocated, slightly less than one-third went into apartment houses but a higher proportion moved into single family dwellings.

HOUSING QUALITY

With respect to the quality of the housing in which relocated families were found by the Bureau of the Census, the figures show that the vast majority of the displaced families were relocated in standard housing, units which were not dilapidated and which had private bath and toilet facilities. Thus, 94 percent of the relocated families—97 percent of the whites and 91 percent of the nonwhites—were living in standard housing at the time of the survey.

All of these standard units had toilet and bathing facilities for the exclusive use of the families which lived there. Moreover, a very substantial proportion of them were reported by Census as being in sound structures, ones which were well maintained and had few, if any, observable defects. In 9 per cent of the cases, however, the houses were regarded as deteriorating. This means that the units, while still providing adequate shelter for their occupants, were under maintained with the result that there were observable defects, the continued neglect of which could ultimately make the units substandard. Somewhat more of the nonwhite—10 percent—were found to be living in standard, though deteriorating units than was true of white households where only 8 percent were so housed.

Significantly, 70 percent of the displaced families found their own housing accommodations.[2] In the case of white families, 19 percent used LPA help. Among nonwhite families, the proportion who used assistance in finding housing was over 40 percent.

White families did about as well for themselves in finding good housing—96.6 percent—as when they turned to the local public agency for aid—97.1 percent. Nonwhite, in contrast, had less success in finding standard housing than did the LPA. Nearly 95 percent of the nonwhites relocated by the local agencies were found by Census to be in standard housing. Only 89 percent of those who relocated themselves were as well housed.

TYPE OF HOUSING

While the use of public housing was not a major factor in accounting for the high proportion of standard housing into which displaced families as a group were relocated, 13 percent of the group surveyed were rehoused in public housing. Three-fourths of these were nonwhites.

Of the public housing used for displaced families, 90 percent was made available through the relocation efforts of local public agencies. Only 10 percent—6 percent nonwhite, 4 percent—white—of the public units went to families who undertook to find housing for themselves.

RENTS OF RELOCATED HOUSEHOLDS

The process of relocation has led to increases in the rent bill for some of the families moved out of renewal areas, with the median gross rent going from $66 to $74. Contributing to this rise in the median was the increase in the proportion of families paying more than $100 a month. Thus, the Census Bureau found that among present renters, for whom gross rents were reported, 20 percent were now paying that much

[2] While only 30 percent of the households were relocated in housing units to which they were referred by an LPA, 89 percent of all the displaced families reported that they received some type of assistance in the relocation process. This assistance in most instances took the form of financial aid. In addition, some families received counseling and actual assistance in locating suitable housing units.

compared with only 9 percent prior to relocation. The biggest increase came among white families where the percentage paying more than $100 rose from 9 to 24. Among nonwhites the rise was less pronounced, going only from 9 to 17 percent.

At the same time that the proportion of families paying over $100 increased, the portion paying $50 to $75 dropped sharply, from 45 percent to 29 percent. It was only at the bottom of the rent scale that no significant changes occurred. The percent of families paying less than $50 a month remained virtually unchanged—21 percent prior to relocation, 22 percent after.

It would appear that the efforts of local public agencies in finding quarters for displaced families played an important role in holding down rent increases. Thus, among families aided by LPAs, there was a rise from 17 to 29 percent among white families and from 26 to 39 percent among nonwhite families paying less than $50 a month for rent. In contrast, among self-relocated families the proportion paying less than $50 dropped from 14 to 7 percent for whites and from 23 to 14 percent for nonwhites.

The higher proportion of self-relocated families paying over $100 a month for rent is a reflection, in part at least, of the generally higher income of this group.

RENT INCOME RATIOS

Since there was no significant change in the levels of income of relocated households during the period under study, the rise in rent levels led to some increase in the proportion of income being spent for rent. Among a group of identical families who were renters before and after relocation and for whom gross rent information was reported the median proportion of income paid for rent rose from 25 percent to nearly 28 percent.

The most drastic shift which took place was in the proportion of families where rent accounted for less than 20 percent of their income. Here the ratio dropped from 33 to 24. At the other end of the scale there was no significant change in the percentage of families paying 35 percent or more of their income for rent. Here the proportion rose only fractionally from 31.3 to 31.8 percent.

It was among white families that the biggest decline occurred in the proportion whose gross rent was less than 20 percent of their income. There the ratio dropped from 42 to 28. Among nonwhites, in contrast, the decrease was only from 26 to 21 percent. At the upper end of the scale—those whose rents were 35 percent or more of income—the proportion of white families rose fractionally from 24 percent to slightly over 26 percent while the proportion of nonwhites remained virtually unchanged at just under 36 percent. . . .

PLACE OF EMPLOYMENT

The Census survey turned up a significant proportion of household heads—36 percent—who had no fixed place of employment. These were people like laborers, mechanics, and charwomen who customarily shift from job to job or site to site as employment opportunities arise, together with the unemployed and the retired. For this group, it is not possible to gauge the impact of relocation upon their jobs even if they were in the labor force. Among the large group—nearly two-thirds of the household heads in the sample—who did have a fixed place of work at the time of the survey, the Census found that there were only 10 percent who had changed their jobs after their families had been relocated. This would suggest that relocation was not a seriously disruptive factor as far as place of employment was concerned.

Among nonwhite workers there was a slightly lesser incidence of job change after relocation—9.4 percent—than among white household heads—10.3 percent.

JOURNEY TO WORK

Of those workers with a fixed place of employment, more than one-third—37 percent—reported a significant change in their journey to work. On the other hand, 13 percent find that it now takes them less time to get to work. The remaining 50 percent, moreover, believe that there has been no significant increase in travel time to and from their jobs.

Partially, at least, because of their greater tendency to remain in their pre-relocation jobs, somewhat more of the nonwhite workers—38 percent—found it now takes them longer to get to work. Among white workers, only 35 percent found this situation to prevail.

Neighborhood Shopping

Two-thirds of the relocated families found neighborhood shopping at their new location at least as convenient, if not more so than at their previous address. There was very little difference in opinion between white and nonwhite households on this count. Forty-three percent of each race found the stores as conveniently located. Twenty-five percent of the white families and 22 percent of the nonwhites even considered their new shopping facilities more convenient.

There were, however, one-third of the families who found present shopping much less convenient than before they moved. Among white families, 32 percent regarded the situation as such. A slightly larger proportion—35 percent—of nonwhite households shared this view.

Local Public Transportation

Better than 70 percent of the families studied by the Bureau of the Census regarded the local public transportation serving their new home to be either as satisfactory or more satisfactory than what they had had previously.

As a group, nonwhite households appeared to be more satisfied with their present public transportation facilities than whites. Thus, 73 percent regarded the service to their new address as satisfactory if not better than what was available in their old neighborhood. For white households the proportion of this mind was 67 percent.

Among the households who felt that public transportation was much less satisfactory after they relocated, the proportion of dissatisfied households was much higher among the whites—33 percent—than among the nonwhites—27 percent. . . .

A REJOINDER: OMISSIONS IN EVALUATING
RELOCATION EFFECTIVENESS CITED*

Chester W. Hartman

. . . Lest the readers . . . conclude from this report (as
most of the public has) that the relocation problem has been
entirely solved, it is well to highlight some of the shortcomings
of the HHFA study: the questions it does *not* answer, the
meaning of some of the reported data, the problems it indicates still exist. . . .

OMISSIONS

1—The study deals only with the official agency relocation
caseload; hence we have no information on those who leave
impacted areas after announcement of renewal plans, but before actual landtaking. We know from experience that the
number of such families can be considerable and that their
displacement, although technically "voluntary," is nonetheless the result of renewal activities. Where do they move, what
kinds of housing do they secure, and how much are they
paying for their housing? (Also, what about families who
move from areas for which renewal plans have been announced and then subsequently abandoned?)

2—The study omits *individual* householders entirely. While
the proportion of individual householders varies widely from
project to project, on a national basis they average nearly
30 per cent of total caseloads. Since income of individual
householders is usually considerably lower than that of families and since the renewal program itself is reducing the number of available rooming and lodging houses, we can expect
that the relocation problems of these individuals will be far
greater than those of families. Where have they gone, what
sorts of housing did they find and have they been able to find
new quarters within their means?

* FROM *Journal of Housing* (February 1966), Vol. XXIII, No. 2
(slightly abridged).

OVERCROWDING

3—The question of overcrowding is nowhere dealt with in the HHFA report. We know that overcrowding occurs quite extensively in the slum areas that renewal agencies tear down and that of all the evils of the slum, overcrowding is the one most likely to produce disease and emotional stress. If families move from substandard to standard housing at minimal rent increases, it is likely that they must settle for far less space. . . .

MULTIPLE MOVES

4—The multiple displaced family—from one renewal area to another, to a highway route, etc.—is a phenomenon we are all familiar with. One of the primary aims of proper relocation is to ensure that displaced families are not moved to areas slated for clearance in the near future. Yet the HHFA study contains no information on this vital question.

SPECIAL FACTORS

5—What increased housing costs are being paid by home-owners? The HHFA study omits homeowners entirely (nearly two-fifths of the sample) from its presentation of post-relocation housing costs.

6—What differences, if any, exist in the relocation problems of small cities as opposed to large metropolitan areas? The HHFA data, drawn from 132 cities ranging in size from New York and Chicago to cities of 10,000, does not distinguish between areas of different size, although we may expect that relocation problems will be very different in large and small cities. (The HHFA sample was probably weighted toward small cities, since the data show that 53 per cent of the re-located families moved into single-family homes.) One-third of renewal relocation has taken place in just five cities, so it is particularly important to study the problems of large cities separately.

7—What is the impact on the family of paying too high a proportion of income for rent? The HHFA study shows that *median* rent/income ratio is 27.7 per cent after relocation and that 32 per cent of the families are paying 35 per cent or more of their income for rent. Charles Abrams has stated that "paying more rent than a family can afford can do it far more harm than living in a slum, for a family surviving on subsistence level must then buy less food and clothing." For the low-income families being displaced, we must know more about the over-all effects on family life and health of paying these high rents.

8—In this connection, it is also highly important to know the differential impact of relocation on various economic groups. Are those who are most disadvantaged least frequently securing decent relocation housing and most frequently experiencing the biggest rent increases? This information is essential in developing truly adequate relocation services and financial aids, yet the HHFA report offers no help in assessing this issue.

"LOST" FAMILIES

9—What happens to the so-called "lost" families and why are they lost? Of the original Census Bureau sample of 2842 households, almost 20 per cent were not interviewed, for a variety of reasons (and hence we have no information on their fate). Of these, amost half (that is, roughly 10 per cent of the families) could not be found. Why do so many families disappear from case records—and does site census information about these families enable us to say anything about what sorts of families they are? (Many persons think that these "lost" families are the most deprived and alienated of any relocation caseload and fare worst in the relocation process; hence, our statistics on relocation results are skewed toward unrealistically optimistic conclusions, if one considers the displaced population as a whole.)

STANDARDS

10—The question of criteria used in determining "substandard" vs. "standard" housing has long been a vexing one and all who work in housing recognize the largely subjective element involved in making these determinations. The HHFA-Census Bureau study, in asserting that 94 per cent of renewal displacees wind up in standard housing, uses a definition of "standard" that includes units in deteriorating condition, if they have all plumbing facilities; only 85 per cent of the families it rated were living in standard housing, as defined by the more usual Census criteria—in sound condition, with all plumbing facilities. How much truth is there in the charge, made by many responsible persons in the housing and planning field, that "compromised standards" are used in judging post-relocation housing conditions, to arrive at conclusions that overstate the successes of relocation? And what relation do local renewal agency and Census standards bear to the standards set by local housing and sanitary codes (in many areas far more stringent and comprehensive than simple structural and plumbing ratings).

11—Improvement in housing conditions for displaced families must, of course, be related to data on the conditions of these families prior to displacement. We know that not all housing in clearance areas is substandard and in many areas the proportion of sound housing is fairly high. Given the general nature of areas to be cleared, it is inevitable that some improvement in housing conditions will occur for the aggregate of families displaced. The real question is how much improvement and how widespread this improvement is—and this question can be resolved only when we have data on the pre-relocation housing conditions of these same families. (Here, too, the question of standards and criteria is all important: the tendency to regard post-relocation housing conditions with an overly accepting eye may have as its counterpart a tendency to be overly harsh in judging pre-relocation housing conditions in order to justify unquestionably the clearance and redevelopment decision.)

PSYCHOLOGICAL EFFECTS

12—We are learning more and more about the deep attachment many people have for their homes and neighborhoods and about the psychological and social impact of forced uprooting and relocation. In many instances, although housing may improve in physical terms, the loss of familiar places and neighbors may far outweigh any housing benefits and the psychological costs of forced uprooting may be even more severe than added financial costs. This is, of course, a complex issue and one about which it is difficult to collect data. Yet our increasing knowledge of this phenomenon is causing great changes in renewal policy: greater sensitivity to people's housing and community needs and much more restricted use of the bulldozer approach—wherever possible, local agencies are permitting people to remain in their homes and neighborhoods, relying on rehabilitation techniques rather than clearance. The HHFA study of relocation, however, offers virtually no information on this all-important subjective aspect of relocation, on which some light could have been shed by even so simple a question as "How do you like your new home compared with where you were formerly living?" . . .

RELOCATION AND MANAGED MOBILITY*

Jewel Bellush and Murray Hausknecht

The poor in our society are those who have failed to rise from the lowest economic levels, or people who have slipped down to those levels. Therefore, public policy concerned with the poor is in reality directing its attention to the problems of social mobility. More specifically, it is concerned with improving the mobility opportunities of the poor; possible further deterioration of the status of those in poverty; or the prevention of skidding into poverty by those who are not yet "poor." The distinguishing characteristic of all contemporary programs with this focus is their implicit—though rarely explicit—introduction of a new mode of social mobility in the United States.[1] We may grasp what is at issue here if the settlement of the West is taken as a prototypical example of the traditional pattern of American mobility.

Those who seized the opportunity to go West epitomized American "individualism"; people who relied on their own resources in making the move. In other words, mobility was assumed to be a function of "individual initiative"; it did not depend on aid and assistance from others, and particularly not the organized community. In reality, of course, the situation was somewhat more complex. In the post-Civil War period, for example, public policy relative to the disposal of land, the railroads, the activities of private entrepreneurs recruiting labor, and the general expansion of the economy, facilitated social mobility. That is, individual mobility was not unrelated to what was happening to the "opportunity structure," and the latter was being influenced by public policy. Yet it is still accurate to define a mode of traditional mobility as centering about the assumption of individual responsibility for taking advantage of available opportunities for improving one's social status.[2]

---

* Revised version of paper delivered at American Political Science Association, Washington, D.C., September 8–11, 1965.

[1] "Modes of social mobility" as distinguished from *rates* of mobility has previously been discussed by Ralph H. Turner, "Sponsored and Contest Mobility and the School System," *American Sociological Review*, XXV (December 1960), pp. 855–67.

[2] Frederick Jackson Turner, *Frontier and Section* (Englewood Cliffs,

The essence of managed mobility, on the other hand, is the deliberate (purposeful, conscious) extension of aid, by the community and society as a whole, either directly to the individual or indirectly through changes in the structure of opportunities, in order to facilitate his social mobility. Mobility is "managed" when the necessary prerequisites, e.g., vocational training, are deliberately organized for the purpose of aiding mobility. When this requires a restructuring or modification of existing resources or services they are reorganized with this end in view. All this presupposes an institutionalized process—"managing" mobility becomes part of the normal pattern of expectations and action in the community. In the United States as in any modern society the chances for mobility of people at the lower socio-economic levels depend on the existence of the institutions of managed mobility. We may demonstrate the initial plausibility, at least, of this proposition by examining the two patterns of mobility in some historical perspective.

Traditional patterns of mobility are a concomitant of the development of Western industrial societies. That is, this form of mobility is a result of a capitalist economic system and a liberal, democratic political structure. This implies that the pattern arose in situations where it was relatively easy for individuals, regardless of origins, to rise in the class system due to the relative absence (or rapid, progressive breakdown) of formal, legal restraints on mobility. It also implies the existence of a cultural system that provided a set of values allowing individuals to aspire to higher status on their own without aid from others.[3]

In addition to the values motivating individual responsibility for mobility, there must be a complementary set of values that explains mobility *failure* as a fault of the individual and not the institutions and structure of the society. At the same time there must be no progressive "pauperization" of the working class; rather there must be a perceptible improvement in their life situation. When these elements are present they function to weaken any political organization of the "failures," i.e., they undercut any tendencies to "revolution." On the other hand, traditional mobility entails a loss of much potential talent and skill, and the pattern presupposes a society

N.J.: Prentice-Hall, 1961). See Turner's essay, "Social Forces in American History," pp. 154–71.

[3] David M. Potter, *People of Plenty* (Chicago: University of Chicago Press, 1954). Of particular pertinence is Chapter IV.

that can absorb the waste of human resources with a minimum of dysfunctional consequences.

As Western industrial societies mature—the exemplary cases
being England and the United States—changes occur in the
economic and political institutions, making it difficult for traditional mobility to remain a dominant form. A combination
of a growth in power of the working class and the consequences of the dynamics of capitalist development forces
a shift in the assumptions underlying the social structure. In
Great Britain this whole process is symbolized by the growth
in power of the Labour Party, and in the United States by the
successive Roosevelt administrations. It culminates in an explicit avowal of the "Welfare State" (Great Britain) or its
implicit endorsement (the United States).[4]

This ideological tendency and its legal embodiment add up
to the following changes: The dysfunctions of a capitalist
economy for the individual are recognized as consequences of
social forces over which he has minimal control rather than
his own failings. At the same time the state assumes formal
responsibility for mitigating at least some of these dysfunctions through welfare programs. The appearance of the latter
presages the next step, the management of mobility.

As two *examples* of *immediate* stimuli to managed mobility
we may briefly note the following:

1. As an industrial society matures there is an increase in
technological complexity, a decline in the rate of economic
growth, and a consequent increase in the unemployment rate.
In addition to the obvious strains inherent in this situation
there are those a community experiences because of the rise in
welfare costs it is now obligated to provide. The growth of
structural unemployment means that large numbers of people,
particularly young people, may never have the experience of
regular employment. This group, and again particularly the
young, represent a potential latent source of "disorder."
Their life situation makes them both more easily susceptible
to ideologies questioning the legitimacy of the existent social
order and to political action subversive of it.[5]

2. The Negro in the United States represents another type
of stimulus to the management of mobility. In this case a

[4] Robert Dahl and Charles Lindblom, *Politics, Economics and Welfare* (New York: Harper & Row, 1953), pp. 256, 517.

[5] Charles Silberman, *Crisis in Black and White* (New York: Random
House, 1964), p. 351.

minority group that has been in but not of the society demands a change in the situation. As a result of complex historical circumstances their demands and the challenge they present to the established order cannot be ignored further.

Two types of activities illustrate responses to these stimuli that fall into the category of managed mobility.

1. One type centers about the school and the educational process as a means of coping with the problems of unemployment and potentially disaffected youth. Of interest in the present context is the current re-examination of the educational process, e.g., the analysis of the relationship between the structure of the school, its curriculum, and the "dropout" rate. This implies a different way of looking at education. The school has long been dominated by middle-class values and norms, and in the past it has been assumed that all pupils had to adjust to that normative system. This has worked particular hardship on the working class and minority groups, and the school, therefore, has been a cause of mobility failure as well as success.[6] The new perspective asks the school, so to speak, to adapt to the initial situation of the working class and the Negro rather than the other way around.

2. The civil rights movement has been an important element in reorienting thinking about education. The moral here is that improvement of the mobility chances of working-class groups is, in part, a function of *organized political action*. But it is precisely this segment of the population that has the least capacity and resources for political organization and action. This circumstance underpins an important part of the thinking of Mobilization for Youth and HARYOU-ACT in New York. In MFY, partially financed by public funds, working class people are encouraged and helped to form organizations to promote their own economic and political interests vis-à-vis municipal agencies and landlords. This represents another way public policy supports intervention into the social and political processes to aid the mobility opportunities of a segment of the population.

Relocation is still another kind of program that falls squarely into the realm of mobility management. Relocation is an integral part of slum clearance and housing programs,

---

[6] *Ibid.* The materials in Chapter IX are particularly relevant here. For a description of the literature covering this field see Frank Riessman, *The Culturally Deprived Child* (New York: Harper & Row, 1962).

and the latter occupy a strategic position in the life situation and mobility experiences of people: "People frequently see the home as an outer shell of the self. Where a person lives and how he lives determine the view which he has of his place in the community, his role, his status, and his style of life."[7]

RELOCATION AND CONFLICT

"I don't know where to go. If I leave this area I am lost. I have lived here for thirty-seven years. The streets know me." This lament of an elderly woman in a renewal area captures a central aspect of working-class culture and the basis of its attitudes toward relocation.[8] Working-class people are caught up in a network of primary relations based on the local area and revolving mainly about relatives and friends of long standing—they are "locals" rather than "metropolitans."[9] Their basic orientations are particularistic rather than universalistic, with the result that they are less at home, so to speak, than middle-class persons in the abstract, impersonal, bureaucratic environment of the urban community. That environment tends to be an alien one, and the source of mysterious, un-understandable forces afflicting them. Many slum neighborhoods, then, represent social worlds rather than mere aggregates of individuals suggested by the popular mythology of the "disorganized slum." This means that relocation involves not the displacement of individuals alone, but also the displacement of communities. Therefore, the response of slum inhabitants is predictable: a reluctance "to leave their old homes and neighborhoods." The area is symbolic, in short, of the real world of its people, and their resistance to reloca-

[7] Kurt W. Back, *Slums, Projects, and People: Social Psychological Problems of Relocation in Puerto Rico* (Durham, N.C.: Duke University Press, 1962), p. 3. For the strategic significance of the home, see Alvin Schorr, *Slums and Social Insecurity* (Washington, D.C.: Government Printing Office, 1963). Included in this study is a fine bibliography of books and articles relating to housing policies, poverty and security.

[8] For an examination of the empirical data, see Marc Fried, "Grieving for a Lost Home," Leonard J. Duhl (ed.), *The Urban Condition* (New York: Basic Books, 1963), pp. 151–71, and Marc Fried and Peggy Gleicher, "Some Sources of Residential Satisfaction in an Urban 'Slum,' " *Journal of the American Institute of Planners,* XXVII (November 1961), 305–15 [reprinted in this volume].

[9] Robert Merton, *Social Theory and Social Structure* (rev. ed.; Glencoe, Ill.: The Free Press, 1957), Chapter X.

tion is a defense of what is an essential part of their human existence.[10]

The differences between the world of the slum dweller and the middle-class world of the renewal official is a major source of conflict. From the latter's point of view it is necessary that displaced families "understand and accept the goals of the total community," and for them to see renewal as an opportunity for a better life rather than an "oppressant." But this kind of understanding is extremely difficult for the working-class individual accustomed to more concrete and less abstract modes of thought and perception. What follows from the long-range perspective of officialdom can only be apprehended in the working class as a confirmation of the initial assumption that the world of politics and government is stacked against them.

There are matching negative sentiments on the part of relocation officials. The latter tend to see the reluctance of working-class people to move into public housing as irrational, and this leads to a growing sense of exasperation and frustration. Thus the conflict between officials and site residents is heightened and intensified by mutual misunderstandings and misperceptions.

Cross-cutting this conflict is one between dominant and minority groups. Segregation has forced minorities, particularly Negroes, into areas that are prime targets for renewal: Of the 97,509 families living in renewal areas in 1961, 64,425 were non-white.[11] For the Negro, relocation is a double burden. Like all other displaced families he has the task of finding decent quarters in face of a shortage of standard, low-income housing, and a further restriction on the available supply because of discrimination.

[10] For the basis of the description of the working class see, for example, Herbert Gans, *The Urban Villagers* (Glencoe, Ill.: The Free Press, 1962); John Seeley, "The Slum: Its Nature, Use, and Users," *Journal of the American Institute of Planners,* XXV (1959), pp. 7–14 [reprinted in this volume]; S. M. Miller and Frank Riessman, "The Working Class Subculture: A New View," *Social Problems,* IX (1961), pp. 86–97; Albert K. Cohen and Harold M. Hodges, Jr., "Characteristics of the Lower Blue Collar Class," *ibid.,* Chap. X (1963), pp. 303–4. Other relevant papers and further citations to what is a rapidly accumulating literature are conveniently gathered in Arthur B. Shostak and William Gomberg (eds.), *Blue Collar World* (Englewood Cliffs, N.J.: Prentice-Hall, 1964).

[11] Housing and Home Finance Agency, *Relocation from Urban Renewal Project Areas* (through December 1962) (Washington, D.C.: Government Printing Office, 1962).

The racial theme adds another dimension to the conflict between relocation officials and site residents. Typically, renewal means the displacement of Negroes by whites or symbols of the white world. Even when neighborhoods are interracial before relocation they rarely remain so after renewal: "the overwhelming majority of Negroes" from these areas end up "being relocated in neighborhoods having 50 per cent or more Negroes." Thus the Negro tends to see relocation as displacing him because he *is Negro*.[12]

This definition of renewal as "Negro removal" is used by civil rights organizations in their attempts to have renewal and relocation defined as weapons to combat segregation. This complicates life for local governments, since, if they are receptive to these demands, it means potential trouble with white constituencies whose commitment to the American Creed runs noticeably thin where housing is concerned. In cities where working-class Negroes have learned how to use traditional American voting techniques, local politicians can be caught in a cruel squeeze.

Here we should note an interesting paradox. If we assume that slum clearance and relocation in a Negro ghetto represents a real attempt to improve the life situation of the ghetto residents—a not-always-warranted assumption—resistance to these efforts means that managed mobility programs can stir a normally "apathetic" group to political action. That is, the very group that is the object of aid becomes an active political force resisting the program.[13] This suggests that in some communities local governments may not wish to participate in mobility programs, because they may draw new forces into the political arena.

Resolution of many of these conflicts is made more difficult by a material factor, a widespread shortage in the supply of housing. One of the reasons for the shortage is the failure of a "trickle-down" housing market mechanism, i.e., a process in which housing passes down the ladder to different income groups as surpluses of new, better housing are built at each price level. However, since housing surpluses at each level

[12] United States Commission on Civil Rights, Connecticut Advisory Committee, *Family Relocation under Urban Renewal in Connecticut* (Washington, D.C.: July 1963), processed, 74 pp.

[13] In fact Professor James Wilson has suggested that "the higher the level of indigenous organization in a lower-class neighborhood, the poorer the prospects for renewal in that area. . . ." quoted in Silberman, *op. cit.,* p. 343.

rarely occur at a rate to systematically force housing to "trickle down" as it should, the supply of housing open to low-income groups is never sufficient to meet their demand. The demand, already high, is increased whenever a community undertakes a program of slum clearance. The failure of the housing market need not be disastrous if the supply of housing is increased by publicly subsidized housing. However, no more than 20 per cent of the three billion dollars of federal urban renewal funds received by communities "have been earmarked for projects intended to improve the living accommodations of lower income families."[14]

We have already seen that there are negative expectations of clearance and relocation by the working class. The housing shortage means that these expectations are confirmed by the realities of the situation. That is, the displaced persons perceive their initial definitions of the situation as fully justified when they find themselves, as a result of a lack of standard housing, in new quarters no better than the old ones. Even those who do find better homes may be no better off than they were before, since the additional costs of housing entail lesser expenditures for food and clothing.[15]

On a more general level the problem of housing supply shows why relocation represents a rather primitive form of mobility management. Attempting to remove people, as a matter of public policy, from the deleterious effects of the slum is a departure from some of the assumptions underlying the traditional mode of mobility. At the same time, still as a matter of policy, there is a steadfast adherence to other traditional assumptions. That is, there is an unwillingness to manage or control the housing market so that it will produce the standard housing required to satisfy low-income demand. Yet without a proper supply of housing the ends of relocation are defeated.

[14] William Grigsby, "Housing and Slum Clearance: Elusive Goals," *The Annals of the American Academy of Political and Social Science,* March 1964 issue devoted to "Urban Revival: Goals and Standards," p. 110.

[15] See Chester W. Hartman, "The Housing of Relocated Families"; United States Housing and Home Finance Agency, "The Housing of Relocated Families: Summary of a Bureau of the Census Survey of Families Recently Displaced from Urban Renewal Sites"; and Chester W. Hartman, "A Rejoinder: Omissions in Evaluating Relocation Effectiveness Cited"; all reprinted in this volume.

THE PROBLEM OF COMPETENCE

One challenge of managed mobility to a community involves the broader question of municipal competence, the capacity of a community to effectively mobilize its resources to meet the exigencies it faces. One dimension of competence is that of orientation or perspective. A fundamental prerequisite of mobility management is the capacity to see the problems of any segment of the community in terms of broader social, economic, and political contexts. It requires, to use a conventional shorthand, a "metropolitan" orientation rather than a "local" one. Such perspectives have been noticeably lacking in many urban renewal efforts. One large suburban city we have been studying has a renewal project, the construction of a large shopping center, that started in the mid-fifties. It soon became clear that the center was potentially fatal to the Main Street shopping area, already suffering from the competition of other shopping centers in the county. Nothing was done by the local merchants until the owners of Main Street land, large central city real estate interests, entered the picture. Under their prodding and guidance the rather dormant merchants' associations began to think of using urban renewal funds to rehabilitate Main Street so that it could compete with the shopping center.

If competence is lacking in this situation, there is little reason to suppose that the required perspectives will be present in such a relatively new phenomenon as mobility management. In the interests of efficiency and the reduction of the burdens of those living in renewal areas, some groups in the District of Columbia proposed that all relocation services be centralized in one office. An official in charge of redevelopment programs responded that the proposal was nothing more than "hand-holding," and, furthermore, "This city belongs to everybody in the country not just the welfare types."[16]

Here clearly the question of perspective overlaps two other dimensions of community competence: the adequacy of personnel and the adequacy of administration. As Robert Wood notes, there are "variations in political and administrative skill and sophistication at the local level," and the success or failure of large-scale programs often hinges upon the capabilities of

---

[16] Quoted in American Society of Planning Officials, *The Community Renewal Program: The First Years,* prepared by Jerome Kaufman (Chicago: American Society of Planning Officials, 1963), p. 19.

local personnel.[17] So, for example, the relative "success" of cities like New York and Newark in their renewal efforts are, in part, the result of highly professional staffs with a "capacity to act."[18] Therefore, if one thinks of renewal and relocation in terms of its present structure and practices there is today a problem of competent personnel.

But skill is not the only variable. A glance at the administration of city planning reveals a lack of coordination, a lack of over-all purpose, a lack of fiscal support, and a lack of self-confidence that would come from strong community support. As a result what are heralded as "master plans" by city governments are more often than not examples of what may be called municipal fantasies.

There is another aspect to this problem: Are those whom we define as skilled and competent today actually capable of handling the tasks of mobility management? As we have pointed out, "mobility failure" has traditionally been defined in terms of individual responsibility—poverty is a result of a moral flaw in the person—and it's a definition that runs through the administration of most welfare programs today: "Welfare policies tend to cast the recipient in the role of the propertyless shiftless pauper. This implies that he is incompetent and inadequate to meet the demands of competitive life. He is then regarded as if he had little or no feelings, aspirations or normal sensibilities. This process of proving and maintaining eligibility in combination with the literal adherence to regulations and procedures tends to produce a self-perpetuating system of dependency and dehumanization."[19] Mobility management requires another definition of the situation. It is one that, at the very least, suspends moralistic evaluations, and is prepared to contend with the social, psychological, and moral disabilities of the poor as obstacles to improving their chances of mobility. This also implies that we would have to revise the notion prevalent during the Progressive Era—that the voice of the people as spoken through the referendum should be heard. Recent experience with local referenda has shown that

[17] *Suburbia: Its People and Their Politics* (Boston: Houghton Mifflin Co., 1958). See also his *1400 Governments* (Cambridge, Mass.: Harvard University Press, 1961).

[18] Harold Kaplan, *Urban Renewal Politics: Slum Clearance in Newark* (New York: Columbia University Press, 1963).

[19] From a report by Greenleigh Associates submitted to the New York Moreland Commission on Public Welfare. New York State, Moreland Commission, *Public Welfare in the State of New York,* January 15, 1963, p. 53.

the moralistic evaluation determines the results. Elimination of the referendum might, paradoxically enough, improve community competence.

One of the persistent problems of relocation—as with many of the "war on poverty" programs—is getting the "disabled" individuals to accept available services that would help them to escape from their situation, e.g., motivating them to use available free, public health facilities. Mobility management programs would involve these same people in more complex patterns of behavior, and increase the stresses and strains they experience. It is clear that conventional social welfare practices have failed to help this group. An investigation of public welfare in New York State found that some do manage to get off the welfare rolls, but "within a few months, as many as four out of ten recipients were *back* on Public Assistance in one category or another." It was also found that there was a "perpetuation of dependency from one generation to another in one out of four" cases receiving Home Relief, Aid to Dependent Children, and Aid to the Disabled.[20] Obviously new skills and orientations are necessary if the dysfunctional consequences of present practices are to be avoided in the future. Ordinarily this is thought of as a problem for the social work profession, but, in reality, it is a problem that transcends just one profession.

Mobility management by definition involves many different professions: it requires economists as well as social workers, lawyers as well as psychologists, doctors as well as teachers. But if the traditional definitions of the poor and their situation must be abandoned, this will require some reorientation among these professions as well. John Kenneth Galbraith points out that the problems of unemployment and poverty are inextricably linked with the social and cultural characteristics and situation of those caught in these twin catastrophes. "Thus it comes about that the remedy for unemployment and individual privation depends to a very considerable degree on the balance between public and private services— or, more generally, on *measures to improve the quality of life*."[21] However, Galbraith says, the traditional theoretical

[20] From a report by Greenleigh Associates submitted to the New York Moreland Commission on Public Welfare. New York State, Moreland Commission, *Public Welfare in the State of New York*, January 15, 1963, pp. 50, 52.

[21] "On the Quality of Life," *Encounter*, January 1965, p. 37. Emphasis added.

perspectives as well as the structure of economics as a profession make it difficult for its practitioners to acquire this necessary focus on the "quality of life." Mobility management is part of the "measures to improve the quality of life," and a concern with that end is one measure of competence of personnel. What any mobility management program faces, then, in addition to a lack of conventionally trained people, is a clear lack of individuals competent in this sense.

The essence of managed mobility is an intervention into the total life situation of the poor, and a modification of at least some elements of the institutions affecting it. Clearly, today we are still in the process of evolving the adequate means to attain these ends. All that may be said with certainty is that we must adopt a pragmatic approach. To advocate such an approach does not mean a lack of ideological conviction or commitment. The management of mobility, in whatever form it takes, rests on the essential premise that traditional definitions of the situation are inadequate. It assumes, if indeed the goal is the elimination of poverty, that forces previously regarded as being beyond legitimate control by society are now defined as being within the province of public policy and action. It demands that we welcome innovation, and that we are prepared for the modification of traditional social institutions.

PROGRESS: EVIDENCE IN CONCRETE

It is now over fifteen years since the inception of Title I, the basic enabling legislation of urban renewal. What progress has been made? One answer is that there has been a considerable progress as the selections from the Annual Reports of HHFA for 1962 and 1963 document. But it is difficult to think about progress without first raising the prior question of criteria, and it's this question that underlies most of the controversy about the progress of urban renewal. The criteria used by the Urban Renewal Administration must be inferred from the data it presents as evidence of progress. Thus, it reports the number of acres of land that have been acquired for redevelopment; the tax benefits accruing to communities from renewal; the number of projects in the planning and execution stages; the number of cities involved in rehabilitation and conservation projects, etc. The data suggest that one criterion for progress is "something is happening" and "on the way to completion," while another criterion is the size and prevalence of these "renewal events."

The same data, however, can be interpreted as indicating a *lack* of progress when approached differently. The severest critic of urban renewal has been Martin Anderson, who bases his critique on a statistical analysis of the officially reported data. Anderson's strategy is to take the data of, say, the number of acres cleared and acquired; explain that this is but the *preparatory* stage of renewal; and then point to data indicating the agonizing slowness of the execution stage. In effect, then, he says that the criteria for progress should not be "something is happening," but what has actually been produced by all the activity. If one retorts by pointing to the new residential housing on former slum sites, Anderson counters by saying that low-income housing has been destroyed and that the new housing is out of the economic reach of the former slum dwellers. Here the criterion is a measure of what has been built against the stated objectives of renewal.

The controversy involves a major problem in discussions

of any public policy by citizens of a democratic society, and so transcends the specific issue of urban renewal. It is this fact that has guided our choice of selections. Anderson has, of course, been vigorously attacked by partisans of renewal in and out of office. One of the major charges has been that the data of the 1962 FHA report do not reflect the changes and movements since that date. Nonetheless, we have chosen selections from Anderson and the 1962 report he used, because the fundamental problem is how does one think about the "progress" of public programs and use the available evidence.

The problem of evaluation can be illustrated in another, more microcosmic, context. Charles Abrams, unlike Anderson, can discern many benefits from renewal while still maintaining a critical stance. In the selection from his recent book on renewal Abrams argues that renewal offers a community a chance to better its quality of life by an improvement of municipal aesthetics and the opportunity to add cultural facilities. Perhaps the best example of a city attempting to capitalize on these opportunities is New York, where, with the aid of renewal funds, Lincoln Center has been built. There has been general enthusiasm and acclaim for the cultural center, but among the few dissenting voices has been that of Percival Goodman, a well-known architect and city planner. In his satiric essay Goodman reviews the history of the Center, and trenchantly raises the serious question of whether it's indeed a contribution to the cultural life of the community.

REPORT ON URBAN RENEWAL

*William L. Slayton**

By June 30, 1963, over 1,300 urban renewal projects had been initiated. The progressive increase in the number of projects is evident in exhibit 8. For reasons which I will discuss later, there is necessarily a substantial leadtime between the initiation of planning for a project and its actual execution. Therefore, in the early years of this expanding program, the number of projects in planning exceeded those in execution. However, since 1958, the latter group has exceeded the number in planning and is presently increasing very rapidly. Now we are witnessing the same kind of sharp upward trend in project completions, and I expect the number and proportion of completions to rise rapidly from now on. It is worth noting that at the end of the last fiscal year, in addition to the 106 closed out projects, there were 68 others with land disposition over 90 percent completed.

A substantial number of communities are now carrying out more than one project. This is particularly true of the larger communities and those which have been in the program for some time. Usually a community with several projects initiates them progressively so that at any single time they are at various stages of project activity. As a single project moves from one stage to another, it may first occupy primarily the time of the planners, then of the land acquisition people, then of the relocation specialists, and so on. However, as other projects follow, the workload of the entire local agency staff can remain relatively stable with substantial benefits for effectiveness and efficiency in operations.

The increasing number of communities now carrying out several projects suggests the desirability of finding additional ways of administering each local renewal program as an entity, rather than as individual projects. For example, we are now testing methods whereby local public agencies can budget administrative expenditures for all of their projects as a group,

* Commissioner, Urban Renewal Administration, Housing and Home Finance Agency. Statement before the Subcommittee on Housing, Committee on Banking and Currency, United States House of Representatives, November 21, 1963 (pp. 404, 406, 408, 415–17, 426–27).

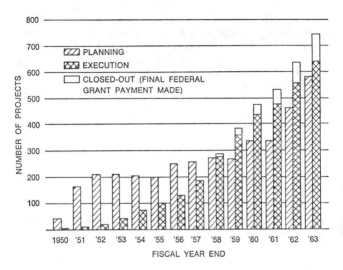

URBAN RENEWAL PROJECTS BY STATUS
1950 — 1963

in order to eliminate unnecessary paperwork and place greater emphasis on the effective administration of the program as a whole. We hope to find ways of extending this principle to other aspects of project operations. . . .

LAND ACQUISITION

In the actual execution of a project the first major step in many cases is the acquisition of the blighted area to be redeveloped. We think the record on land acquisition is a good one, partly because of the scale of the accomplishment but—even more importantly—because of the way in which it has been done.

In recent years the rate at which blighted areas have been purchased has risen very rapidly.

Through June 1963, there were 732 urban renewal projects on which planning had been completed and which had been approved for actual execution. These projects included 29,196 acres of land slated for acquisition and redevelopment.

Over 75 percent of this total area, or 21,970 acres, had been acquired by local public agencies and the balance was in process of acquisition. Perhaps it will help you to visualize this acquired area to think of it as more than 34 square miles.

Although there is necessarily some lag between the purchase of real estate in renewal areas and the actual demolition of the existing buildings, by June 1963 approximately 129,000 structures had been demolished.

In providing financial assistance for this large-scale acquisition of property, we have adopted strong measures to assure that the owners are treated fairly and impartially, and that the public interest is protected against the payment of excessive prices. Our procedures protect both interests.

The principal distinguishing features of property acquisition for urban renewal are: (1) The requirement of two independent appraisals of each parcel, and (2) the practice of making the Federal as well as the local determinations of appropriate acquisition prices before the LPA opens negotiations with property owners.

Obtaining two independent appraisals reduces the risk of error in determining the prices paid for properties. Discrepancies between appraisal reports, whether in the reporting of facts or in the analysis or judgments of the appraisers, highlight matters that otherwise could be easily overlooked.

The LPA initially determines the prices to be paid for properties on the basis of an on-site review of the appraisal reports. The appraisal reports and the LPA's proposed schedule of acquisition prices are then reviewed at the project by HHFA in order to establish the prices the LPA may pay for properties, either by direct purchase from the owners or by stipulations as to value in condemnation proceedings.

We encourage LPA's to make every effort to reach an agreement with each owner on the acquisition price for his property. Condemnation proceedings on the issue of value are thus avoided except in cases where an owner will not accept a price which the LPA, with the concurrence of HHFA, believes to be the fair market value of the property. Condemnation proceedings are of course used where there is faulty title or where such action is a normal local practice.

. . .

THE EXPANDING CONSERVATION PROGRAM

The 1954 act added a most important tool—conservation and rehabilitation—to the urban renewal kit. Vast areas of cities are marked by blight and deterioration that is still susceptible to corrective action short of wholesale clearance. Our success in meeting the challenge offered by these areas while there is still time will determine not only the quality of our communities but also the ultimate extent and cost of slum clearance.

There exist in every city opportunities for the rehabilitation of older and deteriorating homes which are still basically sound in structure and which with proper treatment can have their economic life extended for many years. These homes form one of the best and largest resources for standard housing for lower middle- and middle-income families. The increasing interest of cities throughout the country in this aspect of the urban renewal program has been demonstrated by a steady expansion in the number of projects involving rehabilitation. By the end of the last fiscal year, there were 225 projects which included a significant amount of rehabilitation, often in conjunction with some clearance and redevelopment activity. About three-fifths of these projects had moved from planning into execution.

In a sense, rehabilitation is even more difficult and complex than clearance and redevelopment, primarily because accomplishment depends so much upon the decisions and voluntary actions of many individual owners of a great variety of separate properties. Each individual situation involves its own distinctive combination of owner motivations, physical and financial characteristics of the property, and environmental factors. The process requires a high degree of participation by the local citizenry; skilled guidance for small property owners with respect to design, finance, construction, and other factors; extensive coordination with many city departments; and full participation by local financing institutions.

Lack of experience in this field, on the part of the local and Federal agencies and the construction industry in general, resulted in a slow start. However, in recent years great emphasis has been placed on solving these problems with the result that substantial achievements are beginning to be evident as shown in the following table. By last June 30 over 45,000 structures and 107,000 dwelling units had been identified as requiring rehabilitation in projects which had reached the execution stage. Rehabilitation had been completed or was in process on over 57 percent of the structures in this workload and nearly 44 percent of the dwelling units. Work had been completed on over 17,000 structures, including a total of more than 25,000 dwelling units. Especially gratifying is the fact that the number of dwelling units on which rehabilitation had been completed rose nearly 37 percent during the last fiscal year.

STATUS OF REHABILITATION, JUNE 30, 1963

	Current workload		Completed or in process		Completed	
	Number	Percent	Number	Percent	Number	Percent
Structures	45,444	100	26,004	57.2	17,403	38.3
Residential	40,620	100	24,183	59.5	16,388	40.3
Other	4,824	100	1,821	37.7	1,015	21.0
Dwelling units	107,373	100	46,848	43.6	25,505	23.8

Our experience has shown that even when essential neighborhood improvements are provided, there are still two principal problems which face the typical propertyowner in raising the standards of his own property. One is the difficulty of securing long-term mortgage funds for rehabilitation through conventional financing sources; the other typically is the owner's lack of knowledge of what is needed, of the sources of assistance, and simply of how to go about getting the job done.

We believe that a major breakthrough has been achieved in the rehabilitation program in recent months by our agreement with the Federal Housing Administration on new minimum property standards for rehabilitation in urban renewal areas. With these standards in effect, the way is now open for FHA to play its essential part in financing residential rehabilitation which meets desirable but practical standards. Experience had indicated that FHA regular minimum property standards for new construction could not be applied successfully to rehabilitation. These standards would have required rehabilitation so extensive that the occupants in many cases could not afford the necessary expenditures even with the liberal financing terms provided by FHA mortgage insurance. Moreover, it was physically impossible to alter some of the older buildings enough to conform to the standards. As a result, the FHA mortgage insurance programs have received only limited use in urban renewal projects involving rehabilitation.

The new standards are designed to correct this situation and to provide a basis for a desirable level for rehabilitation with considerable flexibility to meet local situations and needs. They recognize the vast differences that exist among urban renewal areas and the variations in the quality and condition of houses in different locations. Additionally, the standards reflect the fact that the amount of physical improvement that can be achieved in urban renewal conservation areas is limited by the incomes of the persons in these areas and by the fact that the properties to be rehabilitated, although basically sound, generally were built several decades ago.

COMPARISON OF ASSESSED VALUATIONS
BEFORE AND AFTER URBAN RENEWAL

JUNE 30, 1963

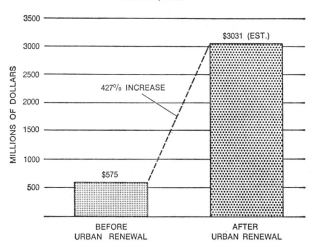

COVERAGE: BASED ON INFORMATION FOR 403 PROJECTS IN WHICH
REDEVELOPMENT WAS STARTED OR IS COMPLETED

There is a great deal of variation in the degree of tax benefit from city to city, depending upon the types of urban renewal projects undertaken. The following examples include several which illustrate the full potential:

The redevelopment of Southwest Washington, D.C., is expected to produce about $4,846,221 annually in taxes after the completion of redevelopment, as compared to about $592,016 previously. This is an increase of about eight times in the yearly tax revenue.

The Gratiot project in Detroit resulted in taxes increasing from $70,000 before redevelopment to $512,000 after, and this occurred despite a 31-percent decrease in the taxable land area.

Mayor Richard J. Daley, of Chicago, has stated that the annual tax revenues from 27 redevelopment projects in his city are expected to increase from $2,321,442 to $4,794,368.

Calexico, Calif., was the first city in that State to complete an urban renewal project (project 1). Before redevelopment, the 21-acre project paid $4,400 annually in property taxes. According to our latest information, the same area is now paying approximately $16,400.

Prior to redevelopment, annual taxes on the properties in the Norfolk, Va., downtown project were $165,650. It is estimated that when redevelopment is completed, the annual taxes will amount to $375,000.

The Clinton Park project in Oakland, Calif., a rehabilitation and conservation project, resulted in nearly $7 million worth of new construction, and tax revenues from the project area rose from $49,000 to $195,000 upon completion.

These tax revenue increases were obtained directly from land and improvements within the urban renewal project areas. It is our experience that urban renewal also generates new investment outside the project area—particularly the fringes—and that this, too, results in higher assessed valuations and tax levies. However, as yet we have no way of measuring this increase. It is also significant that the tax revenue increases occurred despite the fact that in most of these projects urban renewal resulted in an increase in the proportion of tax-exempt land—parks, playgrounds, and so on—in the redeveloped areas.

16TH ANNUAL REPORT*

United States Housing and Home Finance Administration

PROGRAM STATUS, DECEMBER 31, 1962

By the end of 1962, a total of 636 cities were participating in the urban renewal program authorized under Title I of the Housing Act of 1949. More than 66 percent were cities under 50,000 population; about 20 percent had less than 10,000 inhabitants.

A total of 1,210 Title I projects were approved in these 636 cities, involving Federal grants estimated at $3,014 million. Of the 1,210 projects, 588 were in execution, 536 in planning. The loan and grant contracts for the remaining 86 projects had been completed, and redevelopment for private and public purposes was either completed or underway.

Federal grant reservations for urban renewal activities during 1962 amounted to $553 million, as compared to $606 million in 1961. Of the 1962 total, over $309 million was authorized during the last 6 months of the year.

During 1962, 198 urban renewal projects requiring $547 million in Federal grants, were added to the total approved, as compared to 174 projects and $601 million in 1961. The 1962 total included 12 projects, with initial grant reservations of $15 million for project applications under preparation as part of general neighborhood renewal plans. At the end of the year, 80 communities were developing Community Renewal Programs, at a Federal cost of $10.1 million.

Under the urban planning assistance program, a cumulative total of 1,092 grants, totaling over $42 million, had been made, covering the development of plans for 2,605 small communities, 149 regional and metropolitan and other areas, 23 State planning units, and a number of communities in officially designated redevelopment areas.

Twenty-eight approvals for Federal grants totaling $4.5 million were made under the new open-space land program to aid in the acquisition of park and recreation areas.

. . .

* Washington, D.C. Government Printing Office, 1962, pp. 277, 280, 282, 283.

Project Characteristics

At the end of 1962, out of 1,210 urban renewal projects 445 still were in the earlier stages of planning, without definitive information on project content. A total of 765 projects, however, were completed or so far along in planning or execution that their characteristics could be analyzed. (By comparison, 647 projects had reached this stage at the end of 1961.)

Of these 765 "well-advanced" projects, 615 were originally blighted residential areas, 101 were other types of blighted areas, 14 were predominantly open areas, 21 were disaster areas, and 14 were university or college areas. Complete information on all characteristics of all 765 projects was not available at the end of 1962, but reports from 733 indicated total clearance areas of approximately 36,400 acres. In addition to about 10,000 acres retained for or converted to public rights-of-ways, LPA's had made the following land reuse plans for the remaining 26,400 acres:

> *Residential*—13,000 acres
> *Commercial*—4,300 acres
> *Industrial*—6,000 acres
> *Public and semipublic, nonresidential*—3,100 acres.

Individual projects varied greatly in size, from the 0.4-acre "Gates House" project in York, Pa., to the more than 2,500 acres in the "Eastwick" project in Philadelphia.

Reports from 733 projects, originally containing 337,900 dwelling units, showed that 268,000 of these units were substandard. These units housed about 259,504 families, of whom 146,266 were reported to be apparently eligible for public housing.

A total of 492 projects had reached the stage where estimates could be made of the costs of proposed new construction, both public and private. The total reported estimate was $5,813 million, distributed approximately as follows:

> *Private housing*—$2,100 million
> *Public housing*—$83 million
> *Commercial*—$1,286 million
> *Industrial*—$538 million
> *Public and semipublic (including site improvements and facilities)*—$1,806 million.

Cumulative accomplishments on other phases of project activity, as of the end of 1962, included:

Land acquisition—Acquisition of land had been completed in 292 projects and was under way in 331 others. At the end of 1961, this activity had been completed in 248 projects and was under way in 282.

Relocation—Relocation of displaced families had been completed in 315 projects. At the end of 1961, relocation had been completed in 254 projects and was under way in 254.

Site clearance—Demolition and clearance had been completed in 256 projects and were under way in 322 others. At the end of 1961, this work had been completed in 215 projects and was under way in 266.

Site improvements—These had been completed in 130 projects and were under way in 255 others. At the end of 1961, such work had been completed in 105 projects and was under way in 179.

Supporting facilities—Construction of supporting facilities had been completed in 135 projects and was under way in 147 others. At the end of 1961, this construction had been completed in 103 projects and was under way in 133.

Land disposition—Disposition of land had been completed in 132 projects and was under way in 236 others. At the end of 1961, disposition had been completed in 102 projects and was under way in 173.

THE FEDERAL BULLDOZER*

Martin Anderson

THE NEW BUILDINGS

. . . The pleasure of planned construction is one of the most powerful motives in men who combine intelligence with energy; whatever can be constructed according to a plan, such man will endeavor to construct . . . the desire to create is not in itself idealistic since it is a form of the love of power, and while the power to create exists there will be men desirous of using this power even if unaided nature would produce a better result than any that can be brought about by deliberate intention.   BERTRAND RUSSELL

The federal urban renewal program is essentially an attempt to change existing land-use patterns within cities into new, different land-use patterns that some persons feel are more desirable from their viewpoint of the public good. Basically this is accomplished by purchasing real estate, destroying it, and then selling the land to a private developer who erects buildings that meet the approval of the officials of the local renewal agency and others involved in the project. Rehabilitation of existing buildings also occurs although the amount of it to date has been quite small. The construction of the new buildings in former slum areas creates a dramatic effect and is probably the most satisfying part of the whole urban renewal process. These buildings symbolize the progress of the urban renewal program, and in most cases they are the main justification for it. The city planners, the mayors, the urban renewal officials, and others connected with urban renewal can all point their fingers toward the material masses rising skyward and say, "Look, I helped destroy the slum and build that."

All other things being equal, bright, new buildings are preferable to shabby, old buildings, but in urban renewal all other things are not equal. Before we can say unequivocally that these new buildings are desirable, it is necessary to know what kind of buildings are going up and how much they cost. In brief, new buildings are the symbol of urban renewal, and

* Cambridge, Mass.: MIT Press, 1964, pp. 91–105 (selected portions).

they will tell us a great deal about the character of the federal urban renewal program.

The government publishes statistics about the amount of construction that is planned for urban renewal areas, but up to now, they have not published any figures pertaining to the amounts of construction actually started or finished. It is very difficult to evaluate the program by looking at estimates of planned construction because people in charge of programs of this type are often quite optimistic in their predictions of how much will be built and when it will be finished.

The data on the actual amount of construction started that are presented here were developed from the raw files of the Urban Renewal Administration in Washington, D. C. Although reluctant at first, the officials of the Urban Renewal Administration finally agreed to permit the data to be abstracted from the quarterly reports sent in by local renewal agencies all over the country.

The progress reports give the local renewal agencies' best current estimates of the amount of construction that has been started, and of the amount of construction that eventually will be built within the project area. The reports used as the basis for this data were those submitted as of March 31, 1961.[1]

The amount of new construction started within urban renewal areas has been fairly substantial in absolute terms. By the end of March 1961, approximately $824 million of new construction of all types had been started. More than $3 billion worth of new construction was in the planning stage.

Ostensibly the program seeks to provide a better home and living environment for all American citizens. What kind of construction has been started in an attempt to pursue these goals? As of March 31, 1961, approximately 56 per cent of the total value of new construction was devoted to private residential housing. New housing is expensive to build, especially in cities, and, unless other taxpayers pay a substantial part of the rent bill, it is impossible for all but a minute fraction of those people displaced by urban renewal to move back

[1] The author is solely responsible for the compilation and interpretation of the data pertaining to new construction activity. Any views and opinions expressed about new construction activity are the author's and should not be interpreted as being official views and opinions of the Urban Renewal Administration. It should be kept in mind that the figures reported are derived from estimates of local renewal officials, and thus are subject to any uncertainty contained in the original government reports.

into their old neighborhoods. Privately owned housing is not built for altruistic purposes; it is built with the hope of making a profit. Thus, we can reasonably conclude that virtually all of this new, privately owned construction is destined for a completely different group of people than those who originally lived in the urban renewal area.

Six per cent of the total construction started was devoted to publicly subsidized housing. These buildings did not cost much less than the privately owned ones, but the government pays a substantial part of the rent bill, and thus these apartments could be afforded by many of those who were eligible for them.

The remaining 38 per cent of the construction was devoted to nonhousing uses. This means that only 62 per cent of the value of the new construction within urban renewal areas was devoted to housing, and over 90 per cent of the new housing built commanded monthly rents that could be afforded by only the tiniest fraction of those displaced. This conclusively proves that, whereas one of the prime purposes of urban renewal is to improve housing conditions for all income groups, in reality it improves housing conditions for the high-income groups and lowers them for the low-income groups. In effect, the federal urban renewal program makes it possible for local renewal officials to create a new neighborhood of an entirely different "character" than that of the old neighborhood. This is done by evicting people with relatively low incomes and replacing them with people from higher income groups. William Slayton, Commissioner of the Urban Renewal Administration, recently stated:

> In reviewing our wornout slum areas, it is essential to establish a new *character* [my italics] . . . . We must keep in mind what Housing Administrator Robert C. Weaver recently said: "We are concerned not simply with building and investment. It is what we build, where we build, and for whom we build that is important."[2]

The decision as to what is built, where it is built, and for whom it is built must necessarily reside in the hands of thousands of government officials throughout the country. Within the urban renewal area these decisions are made by public

[2] Remarks by William L. Slayton, Commissioner, Urban Renewal Administration, Housing and Home Finance Agency, at the Conference on Urban Renewal and Housing presented by the Practicing Law Institute, Hotel Astor, New York, N.Y., June 21, 1962.

officials, even though most of the construction is privately owned.

A substantial amount of nonhousing construction has also been started. Approximately 24 per cent of the total was devoted to public works, such as parks, schools, libraries, roads, sewerage systems, and other public facilities. Thus, a major segment of urban renewal construction consists of public facilities and other site improvements, most of which will be enjoyed by those who are able and willing to move into the newly redeveloped area.

Private businessmen so far have invested relatively little money in new construction on urban renewal sites in spite of the exhortations of federal and local officials for them to do so. Only 14 per cent of the total construction started was done so by business interests; commercial buildings accounted for 10 per cent, and industrial buildings for only 4 per cent. Perhaps one of the main reasons for this is that federal financing is not available for commercial and industrial ventures, and thus any commercial or industrial building has to justify itself economically on its own merits to a private lender.

The question of who pays for the construction and what type of financing is available has a great deal to do with the kind of construction that is started. Urban renewal construction can be divided into three major categories showing who pays and who provides the financing. The first category is *public construction*—if the entire use of the public facility comes from the urban renewal area, two thirds, or in some cases three fourths, of the total cost is paid for by the federal government. If only a part of its use comes from the urban renewal area, the federal share is scaled down accordingly. The rest of the cost of public construction is paid for by the state and local governments. The second category is *publicly financed private construction*—approximately 43 per cent of all privately owned housing construction in urban renewal areas has been financed by long-term (40 year) loans from the federal government. The third category is *privately financed private construction*—all of this construction, housing, commercial, and industrial is financed by private lending institutions. . . .

So far, most of the construction activity has been concentrated in a few states. New York State alone accounts for 32.4 per cent of all construction activity to date, and virtually all of this has taken place in New York City. Most of the remaining two thirds has taken place in fifteen other states with amounts started ranging from $69 million in Pennsylvania down to $14 million in Alabama. Twenty-three other states had relatively insignificant amounts started; for all twenty-three of these states the total was only $19 million, an average of less than $1 million per state. In the eleven remaining states no construction at all had been started. Thus, less than one third of all the states accounted for 97.6 per cent of the total amount of construction started. As could be expected, urban renewal construction is concentrated in those states which contain large cities.

Construction activity was slow during the first few years of the federal urban renewal program. Virtually no construction was started during 1950 and 1951. As the program evolved, construction activity increased: $36 million of construction was started in 1952, followed by $86 million in 1953. The amount of construction started in 1954 decreased by $19 million, and for the next two years construction activity was relatively small: $49 million in 1955 and $50 million in 1956. Construction activity increased sharply in 1957, as $157 million of new construction was started. Activity moved even higher in 1958 when over $172 million of construction was started. The 1958 figure marked the peak of the annual amount of construction started in urban renewal areas. From 1959 to 1961 construction activity *declined*. In 1959 the value of construction started fell to $118 million, and in 1960, slightly over $17 million of construction was started. Even after making allowances for the fact that these figures are estimates, it is reasonably certain that there was a downward trend in urban renewal construction activity from 1958 to 1961.

However, it does not seem reasonable to assume that this downward trend will continue. The rapidly increasing scope of the program should provide a strong stimulus to new construction in the near future. However, the downward trend from 1958 to 1961 raises some serious questions. Why did the initiation of urban renewal construction decline during one of the most rapid periods of growth of the program? If the same factors that retarded new construction during this period are present in the future, what implications will this have for the course of new construction? Before attempting to answer these questions it will be useful to examine in more detail the types of construction already started.

The estimated annual amounts of urban renewal construction started were broken down into two major categories:

1. The amount of publicly owned construction.
2. The amount of privately owned construction.

Approximately 70 per cent of the estimated total started was privately owned. The remaining 30 per cent was publicly owned.

The trend of public construction differs significantly from the trend of private construction. From 1950 to 1956, public construction in urban renewal areas averaged $8 million per year. In 1957 it was $26 million. From 1958 through 1960, the amount of public construction begun averaged $51 million per year. Based on the amount started in the first quarter of 1961, it is estimated that over $50 million will be started in 1961. Public construction activity in urban renewal areas was characterized by a long initial period of low construction activity up to 1956, a substantial increase from 1956 to 1958, and a relatively high, constant amount of activity from 1958 through 1961.

The time pattern of private construction activity differed considerably. After two years of inactivity during the initial phase of the program, the annual amount of private construction increased rapidly for two years, hitting a peak of $75 million in 1953. It then plunged to $8 million in 1954, picked up to $44 million in 1955 and slipped back slightly to $40 million in 1956. During the next two years there was a burst of private construction activity—$131 million in 1957 and $122 million in 1958. The $131 million of construction started in 1957 was the highest amount for any year to date. In 1959 the amount of private construction begun declined sharply to $68 million, and in 1960 it declined further to $61 million. During the first quarter of 1961 only $5 million was started.

Thus, the decline in over-all construction activity in urban renewal areas throughout the United States from 1958 to March 1961 was due entirely to a decline in private construction activity. Because of the large number of urban renewal projects that appear to be moving forward, this decline will almost surely be reversed in the near future.[8] However,

---

[8] There are indications that the amount of construction activity has increased significantly since the time that this study was made. However, data on new construction activity is not publicly available at present, and it was not feasible to attempt to redo the entire study in order to update the data.

an absolute decline in private construction activity during a period of time when the number of projects was growing rapidly is a clear indication that the program was not moving smoothly.

Most of the sharp increase in private construction activity in 1953 can be attributed to the amount started in New York City. During this time Robert Moses wielded considerable power over the urban renewal program of New York City, and he appears to have been primarily responsible for this burst of private construction activity. He was able to use all the influence, resulting from the important, appointed public offices he held, to persuade private and public interests to proceed rapidly. Usually the disposition of the land was arranged, before it was acquired, by negotiation or eminent domain.

The sharp jump in private construction activity in urban renewal areas throughout the country during 1956 and 1957 probably resulted from the introduction of direct federal financing of private urban renewal construction through the Federal National Mortgage Association (FNMA). A large amount of "potential" private construction was generated by the program from 1950 to 1955, but it appears that it did not materialize because of the lack of available financing. Financing appears not to have been available because the lending institutions felt there was a high degree of risk attached to this type of construction. FNMA remedied this in late 1955, thus releasing the backlog of private residential construction.

During the period from 1958 to 1960, it appears that the Eisenhower Administration was becoming dissatisfied with the program and was scrutinizing each project carefully.[4] During this period the Commissioner of the Urban Renewal Administration, Mr. David Walker, made the following statement to a group of housing and redevelopment officials:

> If urban renewal becomes a program with public housing down at one end and luxury and semi-luxury housing down at the other, leaving out a whole gray area between, this program can go no place but into disrepute—and there it belongs.[5]

[4] Interview with Professor Chester Rapkin, University of Pennsylvania, April 1962.

[5] Mr. David Walker, Commissioner, Urban Renewal Administration, before the Potomac Chapter of the National Association of Housing and Redevelopment Officials, October 1, 1959.

Practically all of the housing started under the federal urban renewal program has been of just the type specified by Mr. Walker. The fact that the federal urban renewal program produces small amounts of public housing and large amounts of luxury and semiluxury housing casts doubt on the validity of the program. Is this the purpose of urban renewal?

The apparent disenchantment of the Eisenhower Administration with the urban renewal program led to a tightening up of urban renewal regulations. During this time the private redevelopers encountered many delays primarily caused by the slow processing of applications. At the same time it appears that some of the private developers themselves were becoming dissatisfied with the operation of the program. New Haven, Connecticut has often been called one of the outstanding examples of urban renewal in the United States. Mayor Lee of New Haven has made urban renewal the key plank in his campaign platform and up to now has achieved considerable success by doing so. The primary private developer is Roger Stevens, probably better known for his successful Broadway shows. However, in early 1962 both of them seemed to be entertaining some doubts about the program:

> Although Lee foresees a "spanking new and exciting" New Haven by 1965, he isn't planning to run again. Nor is Roger Stevens planning new redevelopment ventures (*"I'll never go into another one of these things."*)[6] [My italics.]

This lack of desire for urban renewal arises from many sources. First, financial institutions have been reluctant to lend money for projects in these areas, and understandably so— as of December 1962, over 27 per cent of the urban renewal apartment building mortgages in FNMA's portfolio were delinquent from one to six months. . . . Political pressures and red tape have also slowed down the construction process in urban renewal areas.

> Developer Stevens . . . admits that political maneuvering caused costly delays. *"Some decisions about the Church Street project didn't make economic sense from the beginning,* but they were politically necessary."[7] [My italics.]

Generally speaking, urban renewal has not turned out to be

---

[6] "City Face-Lifting—New Haven [Connecticut] Points Up the Problems of Redevelopment," *Wall Street Journal*, January 17, 1962.
[7] *Ibid.*

as lucrative as was first believed—and redevelopers have been re-evaluating the program.

New York City alone has accounted for roughly 32 per cent of the urban renewal construction started. Because of the large effect that New York has on the total figures of the country, it was decided to eliminate New York City from the total summary in order to get a clearer idea of what has been happening in the rest of the nation. In general, the experience of the rest of the United States is comparable to New York City's. The same pattern of increasing construction activity up to 1958 and then a sharp decline that was characteristic of the entire United States is also evident when New York City is omitted from the totals.[8]

According to the reports of 369 local renewal agencies on March 31, 1961, it was estimated that about $3,964 million of new construction would be built in these urban renewal areas.[9] The composition of planned construction differs significantly from the composition of construction already started. If the past record of actual construction activity in urban renewal areas can be considered indicative of the future course of the program, these construction plans may have to be drastically revised. . . .

The estimated value of all new construction includes the amount of construction already started. Of the $3,964 million of estimated new construction, $824 million or about 21 per cent has already been started, leaving 79 per cent still in the planning stage. Therefore, as of March 31, 1961, about $3,140 million of construction was in planning. The relative amounts of the different kinds of construction planned are quite different from the relative amounts of the type of construction that has been started.

So far (March 1961), 56 per cent of the construction started has been privately owned housing, yet only 33 per cent of the planned construction is expected to be in this category. Public works has accounted for 24 per cent of the amount started, but only 19 per cent of the planned construc-

[8] It is interesting to note that there appears to be an upturn in urban renewal construction activity just before each presidential election—see 1952, 1956, and 1960.

[9] These reports reflect the estimates of the local urban renewal officials. For 191 of the 369 local renewal agencies reporting, the amount of planned construction reported also includes the amount of construction that had already been started as of the reporting date.

tion is in this category. The discrepancy in the commercial construction category is very large; over three times as much is planned as was actually started. Commercial construction accounted for 10 per cent of the total started and is expected to constitute almost one third, or 32 per cent, of the planned construction. The same type of relationship holds for industrial construction. This category accounted for only 4 per cent of the amount started yet it is expected to take care of 15 per cent of the planned construction.

The public housing category has some interesting implications for the future course the federal urban renewal program is apt to take. It only accounted for 6 per cent of the actual amount started, but future plans indicate that it is expected to account for less than 1 per cent of the construction to be built.

There are two future possibilities: either the plans for new urban renewal construction will have to change or the past pattern of construction will be altered significantly. According to the plans of the urban renewal experts, a great deal more commercial and industrial construction will be forthcoming, with a corresponding relative reduction in the amounts of privately owned housing, public works, and public housing. It is possible that approximately 47 per cent of future urban renewal construction will be devoted to commercial industrial use, but the past record of the program indicates strongly that business interests will be slow to respond to the blandishments of proposed urban renewal sites. It seems more likely that local urban renewal officials, in their desire to "revitalize" their cities, have become overly optimistic in their projections.

THE CITY IS THE FRONTIER*

Charles Abrams

ENCOURAGEMENT TO AESTHETICS

The exercise of public power to enforce aesthetics as well as safety, comfort, health, morale, and welfare had long been restricted by the courts.[1] Now, since the Supreme Court's decision in *Berman* v *Parker* (1954), official agencies no longer need show that a slum is a slum with all the abominations ascribed to it by criminologists and slumsisters. In this respect, it may ultimately induce fewer projects that displace the poor. Like patriotism, however, which George Jean Nathan once described as the arbitrary veneration of real estate over principles, the aesthetics of some renewal operations venerate profit above honor.[2] Under a system in which every investment dollar over the 90 per cent mortgage is held to a minimum, a renewer may see beauty as costing too much and yielding too little. So too, some officials with the new power over beauty may in beauty's name condemn a Negro settlement for a park or a project.

Yet not all officialdom is devoid of moral and aesthetic sensibilities, and some have given their architects and planners the latitude to design something seemly. Others have become concerned about losing their old architectural landmarks and have called upon urban renewal to preserve them. With more than 1,500 projects approved for more than 740 communities and only 118 completed by 1964, an over-all appraisal is premature. But if there are projects that are not much better than the run-of-the-mill speculation, there are also those with

---

* New York: Harper & Row, 1965, pp. 157–63 (selected portions).

[1] *Haller Sign Works* v. *Physical Culture Training School*, 249 Ill. 436 (1911): "The courts of this country have with great unanimity held that the police power cannot interfere with private property rights for purely aesthetic purposes."

[2] Alexis de Tocqueville reflected that the people of a democratic nation "will habitually prefer the useful to the beautiful, and they will require that the beautiful be useful" (*Democracy in America,* Century, 1898, II, 56). After de Tocqueville, however, America became more interested in what was salable or rentable, rather than beautiful. The architect who can produce something that is profitable as well as beautiful is the still-undiscovered genius.

merit. When profit is the motive, the influence of better design may be subordinated, for it is not easy to effect a good compromise between design and dollars. But since William Slayton took over the Urban Renewal Administration, a serious effort has at last been made to make design a major factor.

One now sees plazas and pedestrian malls, underground parking, and a better relationship between buildings. The manufacturers who were to build plants in New Haven had always relied on stock plans pulled out of a file by an industrial engineer—today they have been induced to employ architects. Elsewhere builders have been shown preliminary models of new designs which had never been within their contemplations and they have begun to accept them. The combination of rehabilitation and new building as part of a single project now makes for a project unity which could never have been achieved before. The use of landscaping interspersed in a project (as in Hartford Plaza), more spacing between buildings, and the placing of schools as part of the project (as in New Haven), are other gains.

Thus there are bright spots in the total picture as well as dismal ones, but without the pressure for something better, all or most would have been the routine speculation or stock plan. Washington, D.C.'s Southwest project, New Haven's contributions, Philadelphia's Society Hill, San Francisco's Western Addition, and Detroit's Lafayette Square are among the program's better contributions. There will doubtless be others and one of the most hopeful signs is that the more prominent architects have been brought into the picture—I. M. Pei in Pittsburgh, New York, Boston, and Philadelphia; Mies van der Rohe in Detroit and Baltimore; Paul Rudolph in Boston and New Haven; William W. Wurster in San Francisco; Minoru Yamasaki in Honolulu—while others are being given the chance for the first time to add design to profit criteria. "By slow degrees, we are learning a new technique," says the architectural critic, Douglas Haskell, and urban renewal is supplying the occasion. How much of the product will be better in the end will depend not only on the architects but on a more enlightened federal policy, on whether the market in a city justifies the additional investment, and on whether more cities will subordinate their yearning for higher tax receipts to better architecture and planning.

SPUR TO CIVIC INTEREST

If the patterns of cities are chaotic, the interest of citizens has been inert. If the slumberers have been occasionally aroused to protest, it has usually been because of the threatened destruction of a landmark they were accustomed to pass but never look at. Rarely has civic exertion been expressed in a passion for the creative.

Recently, however, the central city's loss of population and the departure of chain stores has brought out a kind of last ditch, never-say-die gallantry among the good-citizen residuum. They have been joined by the real estate men and department store owners as well as by leaders of the threatened institutions. The Charles Street Center in Baltimore was initiated and planned largely by a group of downtown businessmen who saw both the handwriting on the wall and the figures on their balance sheets. In Washington, D.C., and Providence, Rhode Island, similar groups helped with the new plans for the downtown area. In Boston, the Chamber of Commerce put up the initial planning funds for studying the city's waterfront area, and businessmen have also sparked interest in New Haven, Hartford, Philadelphia, Cincinnati, Norfolk, St. Louis, Denver, Pittsburgh, and Cleveland. The renewal program has aroused a keener interest in urban disorders. Outside specialists have often been called in to take a look and prescribe. The interest of David Rockefeller in the redevelopment of New York City's downtown is one of the hopeful examples.

In 1948, when I was a housing columnist for the *New York Post* and tried to plug city planning, the city editor would tell me to get back to the subject of rats biting babies.[3] City planning now makes the front page if for no other reason than that the suburban threat to the department store has alerted the paper's business department to the link between downtown sales and newspaper profits. The *Washington Post* or the *Louisville Courier* will publicize, serialize, and editorialize anything on urban renewal, and the *New York Times* will give a tome on city or regional planning more attention than the fight over Fanny Hill.

---

[3] This wasn't such a good idea either for an evening paper. The editor soon discovered that people stopped buying it because it spoiled their appetites for supper.

IMPETUS TO CIVIC AND CULTURAL IMPROVEMENTS

Cities are perennially in need of new courthouses, parks, schools, administrative buildings, and other improvements which growing financial embarrassments have forced them to shelve. Urban renewal is far from being the wand that waves such improvements in, but it has sometimes been the persuader that goads officials into taking a second look at some of the fading blueprints in their pigeonholes.

One of the most important contributions has been the large number of public schools that have been generated by the credits the renewal program allows against the city's contribution to the write-down of land cost. While it is hard to determine precisely how many of these schools would have been built without the renewal inducement, there is little question that the program has been responsible for a good proportion.

Good civic and cultural centers (if there were a federal program that helped finance them) would be a gain for cities. Our own centers are far from rivaling the Forum and the Acropolis, nor do they compare with the examples of Venice and Stockholm, but some have won the plaudits of architectural critics.[4] Norfolk's $15 million Civic Center will have a thirteen-story municipal building and four other structures as part of an extensive downtown development. Boston has started a government center with an estimated cost of $185 million. If more centers were properly located and if they included some skillful focuses of interest to which people would be drawn, civic spirit would get a sizable lift.

So with cultural improvements. Culture in the United States has depended largely on private support, and less than 4 per cent of all corporate contributions go to the arts. In contrast to Europe, even public museums depend on hard-won gifts and on membership dues for survival, and the city's penchant has therefore been for the stadium, paying coliseum, and big auditorium. Less than a third of the cultural centers being built or on the drawing boards can accommodate more than one of the performing arts and many are little more than sports arenas or convention halls. A small town will build a costly swimming pool and do without a library. The promotion of the "progress of science and useful arts" encompassed

[4] Lewis Mumford, "Civic Art," *Encyclopedia of the Social Sciences,* Macmillan, 1942, II, 493.

in the federal constitution was only to protect copyrights, and not until the 1960s did the President designate a special consultant on the arts. His role, however, seemed to have been confined to making public statements, one of which was: "The American people have been slow to recognize that artistic and cultural expression is closely related to the vitality of institutions."[5] Federal interest in culture, meanwhile, has been confined mostly to agriculture.

The most dramatic cultural example is Lincoln Center in New York City. The project originated when Carnegie Hall was scheduled for demolition and the Metropolitan Opera decided to move. A site was available under the urban renewal program which "answered the real estate riddle of an adequate site at a reasonable price in the heart of skyscraper-crowded Manhattan."[6] Lincoln Center of the Performing Arts was born. "For me," said John D. Rockefeller, "new horizons began to open. Since the war my work had been concentrated in the international area. I had begun to think more seriously of my responsibilities as a citizen of New York."[7] His assumption of responsibility led to an investment by him and other sources of $170 million for the housing of the performing arts and a seating capacity for 12,000 patrons in six new buildings.

While urban renewal spurred both this citizen activity in New York and its new cultural center, the site for Lincoln Center was acquired not because culture was a public use authorizing the taking of $7.5 million in private land, but because the site was called a slum. To comply with the statute, high-rent housing had to be built on the site though it had no logical place in a cultural scheme. The statute also led to the building of a single center when a few smaller centers strategically placed in several sections of Manhattan—on the East Side, West Side, and lower Manhattan—would have reinforced existing entertainment clusters.

Lincoln Centers or at least their smaller cultural equivalents are needed in many cities. They should be authorized by state laws, and the power of eminent domain should be granted. Their fulfillment should depend neither on the provision of housing on the site nor on the selection of a slum area as a

[5] August Heckscher, *New York Times Magazine*, September 23, 1962, p. 39.

[6] *New York Times*, Supplement, September 23, 1962.

[7] *Ibid.*, p. 14.

prerequisite. They are more within the range of public use than slum razing for high-rental project building. That urban renewal has spurred civic and cultural improvements that might have been stillborn is a big plus for the program.

LINCOLN CENTER, EMPORIUM OF THE ARTS*

Percival Goodman†

*"Lincoln Center will be great theatre, great music—and great
fun."*—(Ad in N. Y. *Times,* January 11, 1960)

John D. Rockefeller III, President of the Lincoln Center
of Performing Arts, says, "Lincoln Center is a story in the
American tradition of voluntary private initiative and of what
it means in service to the public. . . . It can be one means of
helping to meet a paramount need of our time: the need of
modern man for creative fulfillment—his striving for self-
expression and the emotional and aesthetic satisfactions that
set him above the animal . . . The task ahead [raising money]
can be accomplished only with the interest, understanding and
cooperation of all the segments of our society who have a
stake in Lincoln Center—Government, business, labor, phi-
lanthropy and above all, the individual American citizen."

The President of the United States, at the ground-breaking
ceremony, said of Lincoln Center, "Here will develop a mighty
influence for Peace and Understanding."‡

It is curious that, in the face of such inspiring statements,
the building of this huge civic project has not aroused an enthusiastic response on the part of the citizenry. Even enlightened people are strangely apathetic. Indeed, despite the fact
that individual American citizens are making a substantial
money contribution to Lincoln Center, there is a general be-

* FROM *Dissent,* VIII (Summer 1961), pp. 333–38.

† I owe this title to Jacques Barzun (*Columbia University Forum,*
Winter 1960).

‡ (This article was written about a year ago. Some things have
changed—the General is no longer the President of our country, the
Park Commissioner is no longer Park Commissioner nor is he Slum
Clearance Chairman, yet just as influential withal. As head of the
World's Fair 1964 he has convinced the city fathers that Lincoln Center
is part of the Fair and so gotten the Center a substantial money gift by
this feat. The architects' plans have been "finalized." The Philharmonic
Building stands roughed out on its site and it, as well as a building for
Fordham, blend perfectly into the existing street scene of automobile
showrooms and old hotels. In spite of the fact that a professional survey showed "as many people know about Lincoln Center as know about
the pyramids," money is still short and citizens still inert.)

lief that the project is a private enterprise like Woolworth's or the A & P.

Perhaps Lincoln Center is an idea that average people cannot grasp: it is too big and new; only minds that have been molded by great organizations can appreciate works of this sort. And perhaps intellectuals cannot appreciate the simple principle that if one thing is good, then ten of them is ten times as good. Furthermore, it is apparently necessary to explain the essential correctness of using public funds without consulting the public or their elected representatives—even when it is for a project obviously in the public interest. My purpose in writing this article, then, is to help towards a better understanding of Lincoln Center.

Let us first consider how the conception of Lincoln Center arose. The Metropolitan Opera and the Philharmonic wanted new buildings. Their difficulty was in finding land that they could afford, raising funds, etc. Juilliard needed a new campus; Fordham University wanted a downtown branch. No one could deny that a repertory theater was desirable in principle. No one would be so philistine as to question the importance of a dance theater. By lumping all the performing groups together, adding Fordham University and certain special housing, a project big enough for a proper public-relations approach was conceived. The directors of this promotion are distinguished men: the old salt. They include a vice-president of Abraham & Straus, a director of Union Carbide, the former president of General Foods, the president of Steuben Glass, the chairman of Cuban-American Sugar, the rector of Fordham University, a former chairman of U. S. Steel, and John D. Rockefeller III. These men have had the vision to foster the arts by geographical concentration.

Robert Moses, in his capacity as Chairman of the Slum Clearance Committee, had the *modus operandi*. He had already shown that if the sponsor of a project was personally acceptable, he could construe the rather loose wording of Title I of the Urban Renewal Law to suit the sponsor's purpose. The Urban Renewal Law itself was enacted to tear down slums and build housing at rents people could afford to pay; briefly stated, slums were to be bought and sold to private developers at marked-down prices. Mr. Moses had brilliantly interpreted this law to allow the building of such a monument as the Coliseum Exhibition Hall and Office Building, whose architecture forms an ideal background for the National Hardware Show and similar spectacles.

The path to Lincoln Center was therefore clear: its sponsorship was of the best and it presented an extraordinary opportunity for civic improvement and "long-term investment at modest profit." Not only could there be a substantial contribution through the Title I land grant, but "grants-in-aid" could be secured for such appurtenances as plazas and parking garages. Not least important, other contributions would be tax-exempt. There would be a partnership between an organization trained in big enterprise which would make the decisions and spend the money, and the public, the ideal partner, not only silent but unaware. Finally, the biggest contribution might well turn out to be the perpetual tax-exemption of fourteen acres of prime, improved property: a notable gesture towards the better life by a city government plagued by financial difficulties.

Why, then, have most New Yorkers been so apathetic to this project? By way of an answer, let us discuss the development of Lincoln Center.

First, the City Planning aspects of the project. Section 197 of The New York City Charter instructed the City Planning Commission to prepare a master plan. In 1940, the City Planning Commission stated, "A Master Plan can only be conceived and developed by first striving for the most comprehensive view and clearest understanding of a Master Plan by the citizens . . . It can be as good and effective as they make it." The fact that in the last twenty years there has been no master plan simply demonstrates that our people will not be coerced: New Yorkers believe in laissez faire and the planning of Lincoln Center is the proof.

In the site planning, the architects (of whom we shall speak later) turned for advice to other, less well-organized men, notably Alvar Aalto of Finland and Sven Markelius of Sweden. Yet, as it turned out, it was neither an American architect nor these foreign authorities who made the crucial site-planning decision—it was Robert Moses himself. Mr. Moses, in his capacity as Park Commissioner, decided that there had been enough shilly-shallying. "The park," he said, and pointed with his pencil, "will be there."

The Center has the charm, then, of being located by architectural hazard—not, of course, economic hazard—a method planners call "spot development" (an American invention). The architects, at one period in the designing, seem to have felt that this was a fault, for they proposed an enclosing arcade, to create as they said, its own environment. Fortunately, this idea was discarded because of the expense.

It is true that the streets around Lincoln Center will be congested; the surrounding streets and avenues cannot be redesigned to handle the traffic. But imagine the excitement of that great crowd of taxis and people converging at curtain time! Some 11,000 people will be fighting to get to their seats at 2:30 or at 8:40. It will be the kind of battle that we all love, a true test of American initiative. Then, cooled in the air-conditioned halls, 11,000 people will relax in comfort and plan the strategy of getting home.

The Progress Report calls some of the contiguous projects "neighbors." These include Fordham, Princess Gardens (420 "middle income" cooperative apartments at $900.00 down plus $30.00 a room), and 4200 "Luxury" apartments sponsored by Webb and Knapp. The new housing at Lincoln Center was perhaps cannily planned to create a convenient audience. The approximately 2000 families displaced by the project were surely not concert-goers.

Fordham University, with 9000 students, will add to the importance of the area. Unlike New York University, which had to acquire its campus at private developers' prices, block by block and sometimes house by house, Fordham has been given a campus at a bargain price by the government, with an adjacent public park kept up at city expense, and a group of plazas and gathering places kept up by Lincoln Center. That all this is done for a private denominational college, shows the basic concern for education in New York City.

Lincoln Center, as planned, has the benefits of centralization. Here will be found fourteen whole acres of culture, practically under one roof. It is as grand as a suburban shopping center. Contrast this with the old-world city planning idea of dispersing public buildings as points of interest in neutral surroundings. The whole thing would lose its impact. It would not be *big*.

But we must not neglect the buildings and architectural scheme of the Center. For a big job like this you need a top organizer and Wallace Harrison was the inevitable choice. He was the main architect for the UN Complex and the Socony building, had been the consulting architect for The Metropolitan Opera Company and is the architect for the new opera house. His partner, Max Abramovitz, was selected by the Philharmonic. The design of the other buildings was entrusted to some of our most prominent architects: Philip Johnson,

Pietro Belluschi, Eero Saarinen, Skidmore, Owings & Merrill, Walker, Foley, Smith & Smith. This is a roster of distinguished men and yet some of our younger architects are disgruntled. They complain that just one hundred years ago, when the Paris Opera construction was started, it was designed by a then unknown architect, Charles Garnier, and that he (under a monarchy) won this job through a public competition. But these youngsters do not realize that instead of employing the wasteful method of public competition used in less organized countries such as Switzerland, Sweden, Israel, and England, we have the largest and busiest firms do the work. Young men who might otherwise be wasting their time competing against each other, instead, collaborate with the efficiency of an auto assembly line. Such a method may not lead to buildings quite so original as those of Le Corbusier, Nervi, or Candela, and our opera house may not have the striking quality of the competition-winning design of the opera in Sydney, Australia. But our buildings will also not have the gross defect of being novel; their designs will be tried and true.

Of course, it is difficult to evaluate what is being done at Lincoln Center. What has been shown publicly is rather sketchy, though the Hugh Ferriss sketches are wonderfully nostalgic of the Chicago 1934 World's Fair. We may rest assured, however, of the caliber of the teams. To indicate the boldness of the Opera House design, let us quote the words of the *Architectural Forum:* "The new exterior design is simpler, less flamboyant . . . The former design had the appearance of a mammoth foot . . . In the new we have a ten story high vaulted arcade . . ." Here, then, is a building bold in scale! (Consider the comparatively small scale of the Doge's Palace in Venice or the Baptistry at Pisa where the arcades are only a single story high.) The stage house will be twenty stories high, to house the elephants of *Aida,* the swan of *Lohengrin,* and the dragon of *Siegfried.* (If only the walls were of glass!)

"In seeking to meet the expanding need for the arts, Lincoln Center is a pioneer," says a Lincoln Center fund-raising brochure. Such men as Mr. Norman Cousins and Mr. Kolodin of *The Saturday Review,* Mr. Paul Henry Lang of *The Herald Tribune,* and a few others, surely are ill-informed in their criticisms of the reduction of seating at the new Philharmonic. The architects and acousticians of Lincoln Center are creating in the Philharmonic Hall "a perfect musical instrument." Critics make statements such as "the needs of the community should dictate the size of the Hall" (*The Herald Tribune*), or, "As for the standees, they are out in the cold . . . perhaps there was something inartistic and untidy about people breathing hard as they crowded around the back and sides of an otherwise majestic auditorium" (*The Saturday Review*). Let LaScala in Milan or the Opera in Paris have their *piccionaia,* their *paradis,* their peanut gallery; the new Philharmonic is dedicated to quality.

These criticisms suggest a certain petty jealousy. For example, Mr. Newbold Morris, when asked why the City Center was not included, said, "We were not invited." We grant that the City Center has consistently large audiences, good programs and popular prices, despite the fact that it "plays in a warehouse so ugly and unsatisfactory from every point of view that no self-respecting community one-tenth the size of New York would put up with it" (Paul Henry Lang). But are those audiences of the quality that Lincoln Center is trying to attract? Do those audiences contain "potential givers"?

According to the Lincoln Center Public Relations Office no one will be left out in the cold: "The Buildings are designed to facilitate broadcasting. For every person who attends the performances, thousands will see and hear them in living rooms across the country." In this country even the poorest citizen has his television set, and certainly he is better off at home in a comfortable armchair. Why should he struggle through the subway crush only to suffer the feeling of inferiority common to those who peer dizzily down from the uppermost balcony at the glittering tiers below.

It has been suggested that "what is needed is a larger concert and opera hall with reduced prices." Impresarios like Sol Hurok have even said that the size of the potential audience is 5 per cent of the metropolitan area population of 600,000 people. Such statements, however, reflect nothing more than crass commercialism.

Another critic suggests that it might be better to develop a repertory group of significance before building a special repertory theater, that it is more important to have dancers of artistic merit than a dance theater. Anyone familiar with show business, however, knows that there are plenty of artists and no one would dare to suggest that we do not have great plays. The only shortage lies in jobs.

Most of the objections urged against Lincoln Center have already been answered. But allow me for a moment to be the devil's advocate in order to indicate the absurdity of the arguments against the Center.

1. There is no point in having a center at all. Reason: The buildings have no necessary connection with one another.

2. Gigantism is a disease: fourteen acres stuffed with "culture" is a syndrome.

3. The planning of Lincoln Center is insular: it takes no account of the city plan.

4. Lincoln Center will include the Met, the Philharmonic, a repertory and dance theater, a library, a museum, a bandshell, Fordham and Juilliard: nine buildings or groups which are each potentially interesting. If these buildings were established as focal points in groupings of housing, office buildings, even non-nuisance factories spread through the city, would not the city as a whole be more interesting? Would it not be of advantage to have eight or nine plazas each with its own character, each located to avoid congesting the streets? Would it not, in some cases, bring interest to an otherwise quiet neighborhood, or an evening excitement to a district busy only in the daytime?

5. Supposing each one of these nine projects had designs selected through a public competition. Would the work be less competent than what is being done? Aren't the chances good that established architects, under the spur of competition, or perhaps some totally unknown young men, would produce designs of even greater merit?

Our response to such remarks must be sharp. First: every society gets the kind of architecture it deserves, and Lincoln Center when built will be expressive of our moment in history. Second: Lincoln Center must be big, for anything less than a hundred million dollar deal isn't worth the trouble of the great financial and civic leaders who are backing "this great cultural adventure" (to again quote our President). Third: the public idea of "creative fulfillment" *means* the usual great American norm, but more so.

Lincoln Center will be all of these and in addition "great theater, great music and great fun," a tribute to and fulfillment of the American dream.

PUBLIC HOUSING: IT WAS MEANT TO FAIL

Urban renewal emerged from the New Deal's efforts to improve the housing conditions of the poor through slum clearance and public housing. But urban renewal has moved away from a concern with public housing; renewal now means redevelopment. Yet, as Scott Greer remarks in his recent study of renewal, one must remember "the basic importance" of the public housing program "for any over-all effort at 'rebuilding the cities.'" Moreover, the public makes no distinction between public housing and redevelopment. For historical, theoretical, and practical reasons, therefore, one must examine public housing in looking at the results of urban renewal.

The results have been distinctly disappointing. In the selection by Alvin Schorr, a government researcher, we can see the multitude of problems besetting public housing in the United States, and how housing policy has attempted to cope with them. His conclusion that the policy has served "only some" of the poor seems to be a realistic one. Many might agree with Schorr and still take an even more pessimistic view of the results. What Harrison Salisbury, now an editor of *The New York Times,* sees in Fort Greene Houses, one of the oldest public housing projects in New York City, is what most citizens can see for themselves or hear about all too easily from others: Public housing has become the site of new ghettos and a place where all the conditions of the stereotypical slum have been re-created. Not all projects are like this, of course, but there can be no blinking of the fact that many are—or worse. Why hasn't public housing lived up to the high hopes that many have held for it from the Progressive Era to the present?

Some of the reasons have to do with the unrealistic nature of those hopes, and some have to do with certain practical difficulties examined by Schorr. One major reason for the failure of public housing is explored by the sociologist, Lee Rainwater. His thesis, in broad terms, is that the poor are thought of in monolithic terms; that is, differences among the poor are ignored. If one distinguishes, as Rainwater and other sociologists now do, between the "lower class" and the "working class," one finds that each has a particular life style and distinctive needs and desires. Public housing projects do not fit the life styles nor meet the social and psychological needs of the people who live in them. The dysfunctional nature of public housing is due, in part, to our past lack of knowledge about the poor. However, something more basic than sheer ignorance is involved. We argue in our contribution that the very nature of our society and culture leads to a lack of attention to the housing problems of the poor, and an unwillingness to evolve a public housing policy that can aid the poor and society as a whole.

SLUMS AND SOCIAL SECURITY*

Alvin Schorr

Public Housing.—Public housing is not a single program, historically; it is a single vessel that has been used for diverse public purposes. In the 1930's, public housing was intended for families who voluntarily sought to improve their housing but could not afford private rentals. This group was not regarded as dependent. Indeed, some housing authorities limited the number of public assistance recipients they would accept and others would not admit any. In the 1940's, the program was redirected to provide housing for war workers. Following the Housing Act of 1949, public housing was oriented again to poor families—with a difference. Partly because postwar amendments gave priority to families having the most urgent housing need, to the aged, and to those displaced by urban renewal, this third generation in public housing contains a high concentration of depressed, untutored, and dependent families.

It would be misleading to speak of the development of the program as if all the crucial changes were made by Congress. If public housing is the vessel, perhaps Congress is the vintner, but one must ask about the grape and the palate of the taster. The recipe for populating a city, of which we have spoken, concentrates Negroes in public housing as in slums. Segregation is not entirely new, of course, but since 1954 it has become a more open insult. To the extent that public housing found its sites chiefly in land cleared for renewal, large areas were devoted exclusively to public housing (St. Louis is an example). To the extent that the growing suburbs successfully resisted public housing, they confined it to the city core. Meanwhile, as between 1935 and 1960, there was a greater proportion of Americans who had never experienced poverty personally or were trying to forget it. They contributed to a more critical, if not pious, public view of public housing. Thus, a conjunction of social and economic trends leads to the setting apart of families in public housing.

* Washington, D.C.: Government Printing Office, Department of Health, Education, and Welfare, 1963, pp. 110–20; 135–37 (selected portions).

As is so often the case, internal problems of policy and administration aggravate a difficult situation. Authorities have been widely criticized for poor housing design—too much standardization, too high densities, lack of imagination, and disregard of informal social patterns. The Commissioner of Public Housing took note of the criticism in a letter to local authorities.

> What the localities need [she said in part] is a loosening of regulations by Washington, and that we will do. There are so many regulations about square footage and the space between buildings, for example, that the result is the same housing in Maine and in southern California.

Housing that was tending to be concentrated in terms of people had taken on, as well, an institutional appearance. Further, tenants must leave public housing if their income exceeds a permissible maximum.[1] In effect, those families must leave who achieve at least limited success and who might provide variety and leadership in the housing developments. The struggle of housing authorities to find remedies may itself create a problem. As a number of tenants have the most primitive understanding of housing, regulations and penalties proliferate: Windows must be shut in the winter . . . a fine if drains are plugged without good reason . . . eviction for an illegitimate pregnancy . . . and so forth. Some tenants find this to be precisely a confirmation of their greatest anxiety, that they were being offered decent housing in exchange for their independence. The stage is set for mutual suspicion between tenant and manager, with relationships inside a housing development diverging increasingly from those that are typical in private housing.[2]

The alteration in its population also leads to a financial problem for public housing. Tenants' income (in constant dollars) has remained level in the past decade, but each year the tenants' income falls further below the median for the country. That is, in 1955 the median net income of families admitted to public housing was 46.5 percent of the median income of all families in the United States. In 1961, it was less

[1] The Housing Act of 1961 permits local housing authorities to retain over-income families for a limited period if it can be shown that standard private housing is not available to them.

[2] A study of management policies in public housing concludes that ". . . the imposing of numerous controls on tenant behavior has tended to intensify the misunderstandings which arise between tenants and managers."

than 40 percent. Consequently, the rents that may be collected from tenants do not rise as rapidly as maintenance costs. Between 1950 and 1958 monthly receipts from rent increased by 25 percent (from $28.93 to $36.50 per unit per month), but expenditures increased by 52 percent (from $21.32 to $32.50). Not unexpectedly, then, the Federal contribution to local housing authorities has been moving steadily toward its permissible maximum. With the overall Federal contribution reaching 87 percent of the maximum in fiscal year 1961, some local housing authorities would find themselves still with substantial leeway and others with rather little.

Public housing is faced with grave problems which go to the heart of its ability to remain solvent and shape the kind of housing, in the sense of total social and physical environment, that it is able to provide.[8] What are the consequences for tenants? The first and perhaps the most serious consequence is that public housing is not available to more than a small proportion of the low-income families. Though the Housing Act of 1949 authorized 810,000 units, that authorization is as yet far from exhausted. There are in all something over half a million units—roughly 1 percent of the housing supply. If public housing were limited to the lowest incomes, with current resources it could house 2 million of the 32 million we have defined as poor. As it reaches above the very lowest incomes, it houses even a smaller percentage of the poor than these figures indicate. Consequently there are waiting lists of people eligible for public housing. In the District of Columbia, the number of families awaiting admission has at times exceeded the total number of housing units.

Since public housing must look to its receipts, it tends to exclude families with the lowest incomes who cannot pay minimum rents. That is, the bulk of families entering public housing have incomes under $4,000 a year. Among the families having less than $4,000, in the total population roughly one in four has under $1,500 income. But only one in eight of those who move into public housing has less than $1,500.[4] Families

---

[8] Not all of the problems have been touched on here. For a careful description of policy and financial developments, see the "working paper" by Warren Jay Vinton for the Conference of Housing the Economically and Socially Disadvantaged Groups in the Population. For a development of the meaning of the change in tenant population, see "Public Housing and Mrs. McGee."

[4] Perhaps half of the families with less than $1,500 income who move into public housing are public assistance recipients. The nonrecipient

may be excluded as undesirable, too. Though such exclusions would doubtless diminish if there were more public housing, they represent an effort to maintain a degree of acceptability among tenants. On the other hand, when careful study was made of 82 families excluded as undesirables in New York City, the decision was reversed for 33 of the families. Other reviews have produced higher percentages of reversal. In addition to the limited capacity of the program, we have already noted that many presumably eligible families are not willing to live in public housing. Their reluctance must arise, to some degree, from the program's current difficulties, but it also represents a feeling about living in a managed—particularly, in a Government-managed—community. As early as 1946, a local study reported that only a third of those eligible were willing to live in public housing. In sum, public housing is limited by its quantity, its fixity upon the middle range of low incomes, and by management and tenant views of acceptability.

Americans are often more attentive to the tempo and direction of a trend than to the underlying facts. Because we are preoccupied with the problems and movement of public housing, we may conceivably overlook the function it is performing. When they are asked, the majority of families who live in public housing say that they like it. They appreciate its facilities; their general morale is higher than it was in substandard housing. One must, of course, take into account that those who would object most to public housing never enter it, or they leave.[5] Nevertheless, for those who take up tenancy, public housing represents a considerable improvement in physical surroundings. Moreover, the aspects of the environment which are offensive to some families may be secondary or even functional for others. Kurt W. Back finds that two types of people move into public housing, those who seek to use it as a vehicle for change and those who see it as an end in itself. Of the latter, he writes:

> In general, the tenants form the weaker and more vulnerable part of the [public housing] population. They have less income, less secure income, and are more likely to represent broken homes. In a very real way they need the protection afforded by government action, and many of them received

---

with very low income is therefore represented in a very small proportion indeed.

[5] The rate of moveouts, though it signals difficulty in some places, is not strikingly high compared with general population mobility. It is lower overall than the moveout rate for rental housing insured by FHA.

some government aid. These people apparently look on government housing as a type of institutional support, which they need.

Thus, public housing performs at least acceptably for those poor families who see it as an improved, somewhat protected environment. Presumably, it offers their children a better start than they might otherwise have had. Analysis of turnover statistics suggests that others use public housing as a way station to improved housing. In this sense, too, public housing serves the prevention of poverty.

Thus, strictly managed housing may suit one family—or at least not trouble it—and trouble others very much. Public housing is pressed, if it is going to serve families with any precision, to define its objectives and to alter policies to further these objectives. At least three choices are open: (1) A real estate operation for the respectable poor—the purely poor. (2) A rehabilitative program for the seriously dependent and troubled poor. (3) A greatly enlarged and altered program, at least in part deinstitutionalized, with a variety of kinds of housing opportunities. In the absence of a settled decision to seek the third course and of the legislation that would make it possible, local housing authorities are moving slowly, in most cases with pronounced reluctance, toward rehabilitative programs.[6] Under present circumstances the families who are entering public housing make such a course inevitable. Not only are the families isolated and segregated; increasing numbers are aged, many receive public assistance, and many are in broken families. They cannot be abandoned to their problems; they must be served. Moreover, when they are not served, buildings deteriorate, delinquencies occur, and deprived youngsters grow into disabled adults. It becomes plain that neglect is expensive.

Ambivalence about what course to take is reflected in the development of practices concerning the provision of health and social services. During most of its postwar third stage, public housing has been a real estate operation in theory if not in fact. Health and social services, except as they contributed directly to management, have been regarded by the Public

[6] At one extreme, a rehabilitative program suggests therapeutic housing communities, planned to protect and teach families. Tried in a number of European countries, these smack of regimentation to Americans. Though it may seem inconsistent with observations about management tendencies, distaste for excessive management responsibility is probably one factor that leads local authorities to resist the rehabilitative trend.

Housing Administration as an inappropriate cost. At most, housing authorities might provide space to community agencies and employ staff members to direct tenants to appropriate community services. The rationale for this point of view has been clearly expressed by social welfare and housing organizations:

> Public housing management is not equipped either by training, personnel, structure, or financing to assume full responsibility and direction of the social aspects of the program—nor would it be desirable to supplant the traditional reliance of management on public and voluntary organizations sustained by citizen support. United funds, community chests, welfare planning councils, public welfare agencies: these are the organizations through which the total community conscience is motivated and applied. . . .

The quotation implies another important argument for relying upon community services. That is, services offered internally might add to the degree of isolation that tenants feel.

This statement of principles was not intended simply to limit the services that public housing might offer. Rather, it was intended as an affirmation that would move public housing and community services at least to the point of full collaboration. There have been some encouraging demonstrations of what might be achieved by such a partnership. But generally speaking, services have not been available—frequently not sought and, when sought, only sometimes provided. The principle of community provision of services offers only a temporary resting place and appearance of consensus. Those who wish to continue a real estate operation but perceive that they must take a new approach to new tenants, are hoping to do both at once. Those who perceive the need for a rehabilitative development see the opportunity to take a step forward. If we reflect upon the problems that were enumerated in the section on "community services," we shall appreciate the magnitude of the problem in bringing community services to bear. For, in fact, the need of families in public housing has become critical in the very period that community health and welfare services were tending to lose touch with the neighborhoods in which public housing is located, and the professionals helping with this type of client. The problems of public housing are not the only reasons for seeking to direct services back to neighborhoods and there is little doubt that special efforts will have some result. It may be questioned whether they will have adequate result. If public housing is to deal with the troubled families whom it assembles, it may have to provide its own direct services to supplement and bring more effectively to bear those that must come from community agencies.

The provision of direct services by public housing would, necessarily, raise the question whether the Federal subsidy is adequate to the current task of public housing. Generally speaking, the subsidy covers capital costs and debt service; operating cost must be met out of income. In effect, additional costs mean tenants must pay higher rent. Other considerations than providing health and social services suggest that the subsidy requires reexamination. We have noted, first, that management costs have risen more sharply than the income of tenants. Second, the lowest of the low-income families are finding it doubly hard to get into public housing. Third, almost half the families in public housing are paying 20 percent or more of their income for rent. Some are paying over 30 percent. We have suggested that this is too much. Recent legislation provides a special additional subsidy for housing very low-income, aged persons. Thus, the problem has been recognized, but the problem is by no means limited to the aged.

Health and social services are a significant element of a rehabilitative program, but they are undermined if the structure of the program is, in other significant respects, antirehabilitative. (Services are undermined too, to be sure, if larger community forces are antirehabilitative—if, for example, there are no jobs for the public housing tenant who has been retrained.) A number of policy and legislative changes that are required for a rehabilitative program have been the subject of public discussion and are fairly well understood.

There have been attempts to develop "vest pocket" or "scattered" sites for public housing—that is, small units wherever opportunity and cost permit. Vest pocket housing may be built new or existing housing rehabilitated. On a reasonably large scale, such a development would help to dissolve tenants' feeling of isolation. It would allow housing to be assigned because it is particularly suited to a family's size or housekeeping competence. Scattered sites might also be a solution to the increasingly serious problem of finding space for public housing. On the other hand, many neighborhoods show considerable resistance to public housing of any sort or size. Similar in purposes is another proposal to establish statewide housing authorities which would be able to distribute public housing more widely and rationally than municipal authorities can.

Various devices are offered to secure a more representative cross section of tenants in public housing. Special efforts may be made to provide housing developments with a sufficiently high proportion of white occupants to assure continuing integrated tenancy. In at least some places, a percentage of apartments is reserved for white tenancy. (The proposition that a "benign quota" is constructive or is discriminatory provides the basis for a highly sophisticated controversy in race relations.) A legislative change might permit over-income tenants to remain, perhaps with some limitation as to their maximum numbers. In addition to diversifying tenancy, this would meet the problem that, at a particular income level, additional earnings may mean having to move out. Apart from the intrinsic merits of the proposal, it may be difficult to visualize taking such a step while eligible low-income families await admission.

It may conceivably be possible to work out a method for tenants to purchase their living units as their income rises. The idea is not entirely novel; war housing was disposed of to tenant cooperatives. Vest pocket public housing might readily be sold to occupants, and the money turned over into new rental dwellings. The caution has been offered that, in individual ownership of public housing, "there is a danger of crystallizing minimum standards." That is, once people purchase, they may tend to stay even though they are able to afford improved housing. As a practical matter, it is probably a more serious difficulty that, on however small a scale, the Government would be building for eventual low-income ownership. On the other hand, the possibility of ownership offers an attractive method of combating feelings of isolation and encouraging families to strive for higher income.

Such proposals may be viewed discretely, taking each one on its merits and balancing its cost against its contribution to a rehabilitative program. Providing a thoroughly constructive environment for a group of seriously dependent and troubled poor families is not a mean task. If the proposals are taken together, however, it is possible to make out the shape of a program that meets a larger objective. It would provide standard housing to all who are too poor to buy it in the private market; provide housing in a fashion that is open ended, tends to move families up the income scale, and leaves them in time able to pay for private housing; and would be sufficiently flexible and diversified to have room for those who are both poor and require protection or rehabilitation. Within this context, one sees proposals in a somewhat different light.

The magnitude of the larger objective provides, by contrast with the present program, part of the answer to the question—How does public housing serve the poor? It serves some of them, a small minority of them. Those it serves, does it serve them well? Some of them, only some of them.

. . .

CAN POOR FAMILIES BE HOUSED?

If one reflects upon the ways in which poor families pay for housing in their private lives and upon the ways in which public policies assist them, it is possible to perceive a discrepancy. The private and the public dimensions are out of balance. Poor people pay for housing as a total effort, out of their food and out of the fabric of their lives together. The effects of the struggle are experienced without Sabbath and without holiday. But public efforts to assist them are directed only to a minority. Out of those who are reached, many are helped meagerly, subject to conditions that may be relevant, irrelevant, or even self-defeating.

In public efforts to provide housing we have so far relied chiefly upon stimulation and subsidy of private industry. The results, for those with incomes over $5,000 or $6,000, have been respectable. Recent legislation attempts to extend the impact of such activity to lower incomes. The problem has so far appeared to be one of interesting builders and developers in such a market. It appears likely that some gains will be made. But it must be evident that the problem of the poor will not be met in this manner. We have referred to the reasons; they require only to be brought together.

First, though special incentives for low-income building and contraction of demand in the middle-income market may lead to more builder interest in low-cost housing than heretofore, it is unlikely that interest will reach down to the families with $2,500 incomes. High risks, limited profits, and other difficulties that have discouraged business from building for families with $5,000 incomes will seem insuperable at half those incomes.

Second, it is not unreasonable that builders and banks should take pause. A family of four with less than $2,500 income is not able to buy a house or pay a rent that provides a profit on it, no matter how low the interest rate on the mortgage. The family's income is not adequate to its need for food, clothing, and other necessary items—even if it were paying no rent at all.

Third, inducing low-income families to pay 25 or 30 percent of their incomes carries a heavy risk of its own and is not sound public policy. The housing that is bought at the expense of food or medical care is dearly bought.

This is not to say that we are unable to provide decent housing for all American families. Public housing and public assistance provide avenues for decent housing, providing that the serious limitations of these programs are corrected. Small-scale experiments of other sorts are being tried. A number involve public subsidy to those who provide housing for low-income families, with purchasers or tenants making such payments as they can afford. There has been recurrent consideration of the possibility of providing a direct subsidy to low-income families to be used for purchasing or renting standard housing. Such a proposal was considered by the Senate Subcommittee on Housing and Urban Redevelopment headed by Senator Robert A. Taft. Reporting in 1945, the subcommittee rejected direct subsidies, mainly because they might flow to substandard housing. There was also objection to channeling such funds through public assistance agencies. After more than a decade of experience with urban renewal, attention has been turning again to the possibility of providing a direct subsidy to poor families. A number of schemes have been put forward that provide protections against misuse; nor would subsidies necessarily be furnished through public assistance agencies.

We can indeed shape a program that will provide "a decent home and a suitable living environment for every American family." Such a program need not appear to be favoritism. On the contrary, aids that have so far been devised (income tax advantages, mortgage insurance) reach middle- and upper-income families with special effect. Resources and techniques are available to right the balance.

THE SHOOK-UP GENERATION*

Harrison Salisbury

THE NEW GHETTOS

Many Americans have a comfortable feeling that city slums are a thing of the past. Slums are something we associate with the Triangle Shirtwaist fire, the "melting pot," the crowded and colorful life of the lower East Side at the turn of the century.

Most New Yorkers share that feeling. The city's slums, they believe, were eliminated in the days of the New Deal and Mayor LaGuardia. They speed down East River Drive and marvel at the phalanxes of new structures. They congratulate themselves upon the elimination of the squalor against which Jacob Riis crusaded so long ago.

New brick towers rise along the right-of-way of the New York Central and the New Haven as the commuting trains sweep down from Connecticut and Westchester. The men from Wall Street sometimes talk about it as they fold away the *Times* and the *Tribune* and prepare to get off at Grand Central. It is remarkable, they say, the progress which is being made in the city. You can hardly recognize Harlem. The East Side has been transformed.

Driving out the Gowanus Super-Highway they admire the rectangular patterns of Fort Greene Houses, Gowanus Houses, Red Hook Houses, Queensbridge Houses. It makes you feel good, they say, to live in a country where progress happens almost overnight. Of course, they do not agree with some of the things that are being done in Washington but you have to admit that people are better taken care of than in the old days. Maybe they are treated too well. It just encourages more of them to come up from Puerto Rico and the Deep South.

This is how the people talk. I know because this is the way I talked until recently. I have been away from the United States a good deal since the war. When I came back to New York and drove the expressway around the island I hardly recognized parts of the city. The great experiment in public

* New York: Harper & Brothers, 1958, pp. 73–88.

housing launched during the Roosevelt administration seemed to have paid off. I was amazed at the changes. Whole areas of the city had given way to fine new construction. I wished that I could take a delegation of Russians around and show them what a magnificent job we were doing in the field of public housing.

Then, last winter I visited Fort Greene Houses, Brooklyn. I was warned that most visitors preferred to walk up three or four flights instead of taking the elevator. I quickly understood why they chose the steep, cold staircases rather than face the stench of stale urine that pervades the elevators.

Until my nostrils ferreted out the fetid story of Fort Greene and until I had seen the inside of Marcy Houses and St. Nicholas Houses I was not aware that in too many instances we have merely institutionalized our slums. We have immured old horror and new deprivation behind these cold walls.

I saw shoddy housing in Moscow. Many Soviet apartment houses are built so cheaply and maintained so badly that you cannot guess from looking whether they are two years old or twenty. I have seen Moscow elevators that don't work and Moscow plumbing that stinks. But until I visited Fort Greene I had never seen elevators used by children as public toilets. I never imagined that I could find the equivalent of Moscow's newly built slums in the United States. But I have made that unfortunate discovery at Fort Greene and other places. The same shoddy shiftlessness, the broken windows, the missing light bulbs, the plaster cracking from the walls, the pilfered hardware, the cold, drafty corridors, the doors on sagging hinges, the acid smell of sweat and cabbage, the ragged children, the plaintive women, the playgrounds that are seas of muddy clay, the bruised and battered trees, the ragged clumps of grass, the planned absence of art, beauty or taste, the gigantic masses of brick, of concrete, of asphalt, the inhuman genius with which our know-how has been perverted to create human cesspools worse than those of yesterday.

If these words seem strong, visit these massive barracks for the destitute yourself. Visit Fort Greene with its thirty-four hundred families—possibly seventeen thousand people. It is described as the world's largest housing project. It is better described as a $20,000,000 slum.

Fort Greene and projects like it are forcing centers of juvenile delinquency. They spawn teen-age gangs. They incubate crime. They are fiendishly contrived institutions for the debasing of family and community life to the lowest common mean. They are worse than anything George Orwell ever conceived.

These are strong words also. But go talk to the despairing people immured in Fort Greene. See for yourself if the words are exaggerated.

This situation would be bad if it were unavoidable and irremediable. It is neither. It was created by the perversion, part accidental, part deliberate, of a well-intended effort to eliminate a sordid social evil, the old slum. Many of these conditions are caused by blind enforcement of bureaucratic rules. Others stem from inadequate concepts; bad administration and, often, deliberate sabotage by cruel, stupid and heartless men. Some projects seem more like Golgothas designed to twist, torture and destroy the hapless people condemned to their dismal precincts than new homes for misfortunates. None of this is necessary. All of it could have been avoided.

There is a pleasant view from the window of Mrs. Angus's apartment at Fort Greene. It looks out on the one island which has been carved into the uniform rectangles of the project. On this island stands St. Edward's Church, a gray stone structure, neo-Byzantine in concept, possessing both character and strength. It is a quiet view, a relief from the planned stereotypy of the Fort Greene scheme.

"The things I have seen from this window!" Mrs. Angus sighs as she pulls aside the ragged lace curtain to look out. "You'd never guess. Terrible things."

Terrible, indeed. On a Christmas Eve two years ago a group of Italian sailors were walking through Fort Greene. They had been celebrating at a bar. How they came to enter Fort Greene is not important. Perhaps they noticed the church and thought to attend the Mass of Christmas Eve. Perhaps not. In any event they halted in the little triangle outside the church to speak to a passing boy. Exactly what followed has never been exactly clear. But the results are well known. Within St. Edward's the choir sang the immortal strains of the Christmas Oratorio. A golden glow from the great stained glass windows illuminated the Christmas dusk. A thousand red and green and blue lights winked from a thousand holiday homes. And a teen-age gang boy stealthily drew his switchblade knife, thrust it into the back of a sailor and ran off, leaving the man to die in a bloody pool beside the white statue of the Virgin in the churchyard.

Nor is this the only terror which has been seen from the windows looking down on St. Edward's. Here one evening there was a swift rush of children in the street, the shout of young voices, the flash of steel, the crunch of heavy boots in soft flesh. It was over in a minute. But when the youngsters fled down the street they left a boy behind them, stomped to death on St. Edward's steps.

Must these things happen? Is there some vicious, ingrained trait inherent in the people who live at Fort Greene? Not by any means.

None of the residents of these houses were born to crime— unless you count poverty, illiteracy and cultural deprivation as crimes.

The only real criminals are the men who turn Fort Greene and its sister projects into evil things.

Not all low-cost housing projects are like Fort Greene. Some are as good as you could wish. All have been founded in noble and high intent. But in practice Fort Greene and some others have been turned into monsters, devouring their residents, polluting the areas around them, spewing out a social excrescence which infects the whole of our society. The damage is not confined to New York. The violence loosed by Fort Greene sets in motion a wave of adolescent conflict which is borne from one end of the nation to the other.

Admission to low-rent projects, in New York City, basically is determined by income levels. The lower the income the higher the priority. Charity, welfare and relief cases get first choice. No discrimination for color, creed, or race is permitted. Or such is the pleasant theory. Actually, the sharp knife of poverty discriminates far more effectively than a *numerus clausus*. The rules tend to make ghettos of color and race out of the huge aggregates in which one family out of twenty in New York City now lives.

In the last seven years 300,000 Puerto Ricans have migrated to New York. In the same period perhaps 300,000 Negroes have come in. A high percentage of these people are in the bottom income category. Many are jobless. They go on welfare. The transition from the barrios of Puerto Rico to the factories of New York is not always so easy.

Because of their social and economic need these people receive preference in public housing. There is nothing wrong about this. Public housing is subsidized by the state for the specific purpose of helping low-income groups. But indiscriminate application of this means test populates Fort Greene or Red Hook almost exclusively with that segment of the population which is least capable of caring for itself—economically, socially, culturally.

The concentration of the ill, the halt and the crippled (socially or physically) increases constantly because when a family's income rises to a minimum figure it must leave the project. The able, rising families are driven out month after month as their wages cross the ceiling mark. At the intake end economic and social levels drop lower and lower as inflation waters down the fixed-income limit and depression bites away at employment. It is the new unskilled immigrant from Mississippi or San Juan who first loses his job, goes on relief and is put at the top of the waiting list for low-cost housing.

In some New York housing projects the majority of the families are welfare cases. At Red Hook Houses relief cases constitute 25 per cent of the twenty-nine hundred families in the project. By screening the applicants to eliminate those with even modest wages the project community is systematically deprived of the normal quota of human talents needed for self-organization, self-discipline and self-improvement. It becomes a catch basin for the dregs of society. It lacks capability to help itself. It breeds endless social ills. It constitutes an ever-replenishing vessel for trouble. It is a built-in consumer of limitless social assistance.

The trouble starts long before the prisonlike towers and blocks of Fort Greene or Marcy Houses begin to fill up with socially deprived people. It starts when slum clearance begins.

The stated objective of slum clearance is to clean out a section of the city which has decayed, to tear down dilapidated, rat-infested tenements, to wipe out the debris-filled "home" workshops, obliterate the dives, the dens, the cribs and the blind pigs.

The concept is a little like that of a dentist. Drill out the infected cavity and fill it with nice new wholesome cement. It may hurt a little at first but the end justifies the pain. However, the slum clearer is not a dentist. His drill uproots all the people in the neighborhood, good as well as bad. He tears down the churches. He destroys local business. He sends the neighborhood lawyer to new offices downtown. The clinic and the synagogue move to the Bronx.

Bulldozers do not understand that a community is more than broken-down buildings and dirty storefronts. It is a tight skein of human relations. It has a life all its own. The wreckers tear this human fabric to ribbons. The old-timers are driven from their run-down flats and their ancient brick houses. They cannot wait three years for the new houses to open. Nothing more than a passing effort is made to give them a place in the new building anyway. They need a place to live here and now. So they drift away. They find a worse flat in a tumble-down on the edge of the new ghetto-to-be. They go their way, resentful, bitter, lives twisted out of joint. The new neighborhood can never be as good as the old, or so they think.

The trucks begin to bring in the steel girders and the cheap brick. The new barracks go up and up. Perhaps twenty stories. (Our new slums are skyscraper slums complete with elevators.) No more old-fashioned six-flight walkups. The old-timers watch the towers rise.

"The first thing that happens," a housing man told me, "is the kids begin to destroy the property. Even before it is built. They steal the place blind. As soon as the windows go in they smash them. They smash them again and again. What difference does it make, it's public, ain't it? That's what they say."

Maybe this is just kid hooliganism. Maybe it is the kids acting out the real feelings of the neighborhood against the new Goliath erected in their midst.

Before a single family has moved into the project the lines of community warfare have been drawn. The stage is set for hatred, feuds, gangs, rumbles, street fighting and killings.

Into this neighborhood where nerves are still raw and bleeding pour hundreds and thousands of new faces, often of a race and nationality different from that which lived there before.

This is a human revolution. But seldom are the social effects recognized. No effort is made to orient the new people. Nothing is done with the old residents. Institutions which might have been bridges between new and old have been ruthlessly ripped out.

"Wherever you have great population mobility and disrupted population areas," according to Hugh Johnson of the Youth Board, "gangs spring up to replace the broken stability of the group. Wherever the pattern of life breaks down kids form gangs to give themselves a feeling of protection and stability."

Before East Harlem began to resound to the deadly plong of the wreckers' ball and the tattoo of new steel work it was a slum. But it had many institutions that gave stability. There were the Neapolitan blocks, the street fiestas, the interwoven relationship of stores and neighbors. Out it all went. In came the gangs.

The new project may permit a church to survive on a small island like St. Edward's. But an absence of churches and an absence of religious influence is notable among project youngsters. The Negro children seldom go to church. The same is true of the Puerto Ricans. The Irish and Italian gang youngsters are usually described by their priests as "bad Catholics," irregular in church observance.

The projects are political deserts. The precinct bosses have been wiped out with the slum. They do not seem to come back. No one cares whether the new residents vote or not. There is no basket at Thanksgiving. No boss to fix it up when Jerry gets into trouble with the police. The residents have no organization of their own and are discouraged from having any.

"We don't want none of them organizers in here," one manager of a project told me. "All they do is stir up trouble. Used to be some organizers around here. But we cleaned them out good. Lotsa Communists. That's what they were."

Lack of political and social organization was not characteristic of low-rent projects when they first started going up in the late 1930's. Housing specialists understood that if you simply built barracks for the poor you were only creating a new ghetto. In the early days the housing projects had good social components.

Long before the old slum was torn down social service teams went in to prepare the people for what lay ahead. They arranged to give displaced persons priority in the new buildings. Care was taken to provide social facilities to replace those torn out. Community centers, child care centers, playgrounds and other facilities were built. (But never as many as were needed because of shortage of money.) It was recognized that families of low cultural background would have to be helped to adjust or they might turn their new surroundings into a replica of the old.

One simple and effective device used in the early days was the "rent girl." The young woman was, in fact, a social service worker or student. Each month she went from door to door and collected the rent. She stopped in for a cup of coffee or tea. She knew all the women. She knew their troubles. She was regarded as a friend—not an inquisitive social worker. She was able to help new families get started and stop trouble before it became serious. She could tell the manager what his tenants were up to. It was an effective device. It was cheap. It was simple.

But bureaucratization set in, economy waves, reduction of everything to the lowest possible denominator. It was always easy to cut the social services. They weren't essential. They were the "frills" seized on by real estate interests, stupid congressmen, sensation-mongering tabloid newspapers. The "rent girls" quickly vanished. Now, the tenant is required to come to the manager's office to pay his rent. The relationship is strictly impersonal. No one sets foot in the apartment until after the trouble starts. No one has any way of learning what is happening to the people. No one really cares.

In the early days the projects had tenants' associations. They were lively affairs, full of politics, sprouting with good works, enthusiasm and argument. They were training grounds in democracy. Then the Communists moved in on them. Soon the associations were devoting more time to the party line than to the lives of the people.

Now they have been destroyed, root and branch. Most of them found their way onto the Attorney General's subversive list. They were harassed and harried out of existence. But the destruction of the associations created a vacuum. We threw the baby out with the bath water. The big low-cost projects have no organizations, no political interests. Their community structure has been turned into social mush by stupidity and bureaucracy. . . .

The residents of some projects even find the neighborhood centers supposedly installed for their benefit closed to their use. It is usually the children who are barred from these facilities. Some centers close their doors to all youngsters except members of one designated gang. I was told of one center where until recently no children of the project it was intended to serve were being admitted. Too destructive. We must protect our property, the director insisted.

The manager of a project spoke to me in similar terms.

"My first concern is to run the project and maintain it as well as possible," he said. "I must protect the property and concern myself with vandalism, which results when youngsters don't behave. Delinquency, as I see it, is primarily vandalism. As far as the gangs are concerned they should be broken up by the Police Department at every opportunity."

I asked him what he thought was the cause of gangs.

"Well," he said, thinking a bit. "I suppose it is a feeling of wanting to belong. Some of them join to protect themselves. Yes. Protection and wanting to belong. These are the main things."

It was his ironclad practice that the family of any boy found to be a gang member was given an eviction notice. Kick 'em out! That was his rule.

It does not require much insight to see that when housing projects are conducted in this atmosphere they contribute to the development of gang delinquency. Ralph Whelan, director of the New York City Youth Board, reports that his experience shows an invariable rise in delinquency rates in the first six to eighteen months of any new housing project.

The Chicago sociologist, Frederic M. Thrasher, attributes this to the creation of what he calls "interstitial areas," lacings of different ethnic and social groups which generate conflict and the emergence of gangs.

Color seems to play only a secondary role in these conflicts. The experience of the Riis Community Center in Red Hook demonstrates this. Walter J. Weinert has been director there for many years. He has watched the changing ethnic character of the neighborhood and the shifting lines of conflict.

Before Red Hook Houses were built about twenty years ago this was an Irish-Italian neighborhood with a long record of combat among street gangs of the same ethnic composition. The first tenants of Red Hook Houses were mostly Jewish. Conflict broke out between the native Irish and Italians and the incoming Jewish residents. Hostility was common among adults. There was gang fighting between the adolescents.

The population of Red Hook Houses today is two-thirds Negro and Puerto Rican. The hostility between project and neighborhood has not lessened. Ethnic lines have changed. Lines of combat have not. From the social standpoint the Red Hook neighborhood is more fortunate than others. It has a well-run community center, street club workers provided by the Youth Board and a Catholic Youth Center. But today, twenty years after the establishment of the Housing Project, there are only rudimentary beginnings of an organization designed to integrate the project and the community. Even this effort to lessen hostility would not have been made but for the initiative of the Youth Board.

The mere fact that a housing project has existed in a community for many years is no guarantee of lack of tension. The population within the project shifts constantly. Residents are forced out because their income goes over the permitted maximum or because of misconduct, usually gang activity by the children. The evictees often find slum housing in the same area. Their bitterness at eviction adds to the cumulative total of bitterness.

Yet, none of this need be.

There are excellent examples of low-cost housing in many parts of the United States—housing accompanied by thoughtful, effective social planning which gets the best results from the expenditure of public funds. Such planning strengthens the community rather than weakens it. In a real sense this is urban renewal so badly needed by our many blighted cities. Such good projects can be found in Stamford and New Haven, Connecticut. They can be seen in Newark, New Jersey, just across the Hudson River from New York in a city which has the same Metropolitan problems as Manhattan. But in Newark there are intelligent and sensitive officials, interested not just in payrolls but in the improvement of the community. They demonstrate clearly that it is not the system but the way it is run which makes the difference.

Indeed, New York itself has some good low-income housing. One of the best projects exists in Chelsea on the lower West Side. Credit for this goes mostly to the social understanding and vigor of the Hudson Guild, a settlement house founded by the late Dr. John Lovejoy Elliott in 1895.

Until just before World War II Chelsea had been a comfortable lower-middle-class and workingman's residential neighborhood, largely Irish and Italian. Many men drove trucks or worked on the nearby docks. It was a close-knit community. Everyone knew whose boy married whose girl. It was a good place for kids to grow up in. There was credit at the grocery store when a man had to lay off work with a strained back. Rents were cheap, housing not too bad, the schools were good and there was a hospital nearby.

But the housing began to run down and a project was built in the area, opening in 1947. Veterans were given preference. The income requirements were low and few of the displaced residents of Chelsea were able to get flats in the new houses. Hostility to the project ran high. It mounted higher when it was learned that Negroes would be admitted to Elliott Houses. There was talk of going into the streets to prevent the Negro invasion.

At this point Hudson Guild went into action. It undertook to explain to every family in the whole community just what the Project was and what it would do for the area and why the new residents should be welcomed. The job was done well. One of the first Negro families was refused admission to Elliott Houses after the moving truck with their furniture had arrived. It was a technical difficulty of some kind. But Chelsea didn't know that. The whole community stormed over to the project office, demanding that the Negro family be permitted to move in.

Dan Carpenter and Tom Wolfe, leaders of Hudson Guild, knew that this was only one side of the coin. The other was the task of fitting the newcomers into the community. Six hundred and seven families moved in, forty-seven of them Negro.

"We set up a model apartment," Wolfe recalls. "We showed the new people how to furnish their apartments. We explained about time payments and how they could buy second-hand furniture much cheaper and fix it up with a little paint. We visited every family as it came in. We told them all about their new community."

The results can be imagined. Elliott Houses became part of the Chelsea community. There was no dividing line between new and old. Rather, a firm new bond was created and one which was quickly needed. Without the sound early work at Elliott Houses, Chelsea would have become a street battleground when hundreds of Puerto Rican families began to pour into the area. Chelsea had absorbed some three thousand Negroes without undue tension but the flood of Puerto Ricans caused trouble. It shifted the population balance radically. There are perhaps twenty-five thousand Puerto Ricans now in a total of sixty-five thousand population. Most of the Puerto Ricans have come in the last five years.

Street gangs appeared in Chelsea, but by strenuous work the Hudson Guild contained the situation. It put a large Spanish-language program into action. It managed to prevent the development of chronic street war and, instead, channeled the clubs into social activities.

Meantime, the ethnic composition of Elliott Houses has shifted. It is now roughly one-third Negro, one-third Puerto Rican, and one-third white.

"And that is the way we want it to stay," the Hudson Guild people say. They are tough about this point. They won't listen to the arguments of purists who insist that they must not tamper with "natural" selection.

"We believe in this neighborhood," Mr. Wolfe says. "We believe in it being a good place for people to live. If we can maintain the housing project on its present balance we can hold the line of the community."

A big union co-op housing project is coming into the area. This will bring in about twenty-six hundred middle-income families. It will balance the middle-income loss that has been suffered due to the Puerto Rican influx. (For example, St. Columba parish lost two hundred of its sixteen hundred families, mostly middle-income, last year. They moved out of the parish.)

"We don't want any ghettos here," Mr. Wolfe says. "We want a comfortable neighborhood in which everyone can live his own life decently. There is no bopping here. Our boys are growing up as good boys. And we are going to see that they have a chance to go on growing up that way."

I walked away from Hudson Guild in the bright sunshine of a brilliant New York day. The Guild is located in the center of the housing project. Sunning themselves in a tree-lined courtyard were old men reading their papers and young mothers with their perambulators. On the street leading away from Elliott Houses a half-dozen teen-agers were playing bounce ball against a wall. Two were Negro, two Puerto Rican and two white. They seemed to be having a good time. No shifty glances from the corners of their eyes, no telltale movements of hands toward switchblades hidden in trousers pockets. They didn't even bother to look up when I went past. I thought they seemed relaxed and secure. It was a good sight to see on the streets of New York City—the kind of a sight which with some expenditure of thought, energy and money could be made too common to be worthy of mention.

FEAR AND THE HOUSE-AS-HAVEN
IN THE LOWER CLASS*

Lee Rainwater†

Men live in a world which presents them with many threats to their security as well as with opportunities for gratification of their needs. The cultures that men create represent ways of adapting to these threats to security as well as maximizing the opportunities for certain kinds of gratifications. Housing as an element of material culture has as its prime purpose the provision of shelter, which is protection from potentially damaging or unpleasant trauma or other stimuli. The most primitive level of evaluation of housing, therefore, has to do with the question of how adequately it shelters the individuals who abide in it from threats in their environment. Because the house is a refuge from noxious elements in the outside world, it serves people as a locale where they can regroup their energies for interaction with that outside world. There is in our culture a long history of the development of the house as a place of safety from both nonhuman and human threats, a history which culminates in guaranteeing the house, a man's castle, against unreasonable search and seizure. The house becomes the place of maximum exercise of individual autonomy, minimum conformity to the formal and complex rules of public demeanor. The house acquires a sacred character from its complex intertwining with the self and from the symbolic character it has as a representation of the family.[1]

These conceptions of the house are readily generalized to the area around it, to the neighborhood. This fact is most readily perceived in the romanticized views people have about suburban living.[2] The suburb, just as the village or the farm

* FROM *Journal of the American Institute of Planners*, XXXII, No. 1 (January 1966), pp. 23–31 (selected portions).

† Lee Rainwater is Professor of Sociology and Anthropology at Washington University, St. Louis. He is currently directing a five year study of social and community problems in the Pruitt-Igoe housing projects of St. Louis, and has previously carried out several studies of working and lower class life styles.

[1] Lord Raglan, *The Temple and the House* (London: Routledge & Kegan Paul Limited, 1964).

[2] Bennett M. Berger, *Working-Class Suburb* (Berkeley: University of California Press, 1960) and Herbert Gans, "Effect of the Move From

homestead, can be conceptualized as one large protecting and gratifying home. But the same can also be said of the city neighborhood, at least as a potentiality and as a wish, tenuously held in some situations, firmly established in others.[3] Indeed, the physical barriers between inside and outside are not maintained when people talk of their attitudes and desires with respect to housing. Rather, they talk of the outside as an inevitable extension of the inside and of the inside as deeply affected by what goes on immediately outside.

When, as in the middle class, the battle to make the home a safe place has long been won, the home then has more central to its definition other functions which have to do with self-expression and self-realization. There is an elaboration of both the material culture within the home and of interpersonal relationships in the form of more complex rituals of behavior and more variegated kinds of interaction. Studies of the relationship between social class status and both numbers of friends and acquaintances as well as kinds of entertaining in the home indicate that as social status increases the home becomes a locale for a wider range of interactions. Whether the ritualized behavior be the informality of the lower middle class family room, or the formality of the upper middle class cocktail party and buffet, the requisite housing standards of the middle class reflect a more complex and varied set of demands on the physical structure and its equipment.

The poverty and cultural milieu of the lower class make the prime concern that of the home as a place of security, and the accomplishment of this goal is generally a very tenuous and incomplete one. (I use the term "lower class" here to refer to the bottom 15 to 20 percent of the population in terms of social status. This is the group characterized by unskilled occupations, a high frequency of unstable work histories, slum dwellings, and the like. I refer to the group of more stable blue-collar workers which in status stands just above this lower class as the "working class" to avoid the awkwardness of terms like "lower-lower" and "upper-lower" class.) In the established working class there is generally a somewhat greater degree of confidence in the house as providing shelter and security, although the hangovers of concern with a threat-

---

the City to Suburb" in Leonard J. Duhl (ed.), *The Urban Condition* (New York: Free Press, 1963).

[3] Anselm L. Strauss, *Images of the American City* (New York: Free Press, 1961).

ening lower class environment often are still operating in the ways working class people think about housing.[4] . . .

ATTITUDES TOWARD HOUSING

. . . let us look briefly at some of the characteristics of two working class groups. These observations come from a series of studies of the working class carried out by Social Research, Inc. over the past ten years. The studies have involved some 2,000 open-ended conversational interviews with working class men and women dealing with various life style areas from child rearing to religion, food habits to furniture preferences. In all of this work, the importance of the home and its location has appeared as a constant theme. These studies, while not based on nationally representative samples, have been carried out in such a way as to represent the geographical range of the country, including such cities as Seattle, Camden, Louisville, Chicago, Atlanta, as well as a balanced distribution of central city and suburban dwellers, apartment renters, and home owners. In these studies, one central focus concerned the feelings working class people have about their present homes, their plans for changes in housing, their attitudes toward their neighborhoods, and the relation of these to personal and familial goals. In addition, because the interviews were open-ended and conversational, much information of relevance to housing appeared in the context of other discussions because of the importance of housing to so many other areas of living.[5] In our studies and in those of Herbert Gans

[4] In this paper I am pulling together observations from a number of different studies. What I have to say about working class attitudes toward housing comes primarily from studies of working class life style carried out in collaboration with Richard Coleman, Gerald Handel, W. Lloyd Warner, and Burleigh Gardner. What I have to say about lower class life comes from two more recent studies dealing with family life and family planning in the lower class and a study currently in progress of social life in a large public housing project in St. Louis (being conducted in collaboration with Alvin W. Gouldner and David J. Pittman).

[5] These studies are reported in the following unpublished Social Research, Inc. reports: *Prosperity and Changing Working Class Life Style* (1960) and *Urban Working Class Identity and World View* (1965). The following publications are based on this series of studies: Lee Rainwater, Richard P. Coleman, and Gerald Handel, *Workingman's Wife: Her Personality, World and Life Style* (New York: Oceana Publications, 1959); Gerald Handel and Lee Rainwater, "Persistence and Change in Working Class Life Style," and Lee Rainwater and Gerald Handel, "Changing Family Roles in the Working Class," both in Arthur

and others of Boston's West End, we find one type of working class life style where families are content with much about their housing—even though it is "below standard" in the eyes of housing professionals—if the housing does provide security against the most blatant of threats.[6] This traditional working class is likely to want to economize on housing in order to have money available to pursue other interests and needs. There will be efforts at the maintenance of the house or apartment, but not much interest in improvement of housing level. Instead there is an effort to create a pleasant and cozy home, where housework can be carried out conveniently. Thus, families in this group tend to acquire a good many of the major appliances, to center their social life in the kitchen, to be relatively unconcerned with adding taste in furnishings to comfort. With respect to the immediate outside world the main emphasis is on a concern with the availability of a satisfying peer group life, with having neighbors who are similar, and with maintaining an easy access back and forth among people who are very well known. There is also a concern that the neighborhood be respectable enough—with respectability defined mainly in the negative, by the absence of "crumbs and bums." An emphasis on comfort and contentment ties together meanings having to do with both the inside and the outside.

Out of the increasing prosperity of the working class has grown a different orientation toward housing on the part of the second group which we can characterize as modern instead of traditional. Here there is a great emphasis on owning one's home rather than enriching a landlord. Along with the acquisition of a home and yard goes an elaboration of the inside of the house in such a way as not only to further develop the idea of a pleasant and cozy home, but also to add new elements with emphasis on having a nicely decorated living room or family room, a home which more closely approximates a standard of all-American affluence. Similarly there is a greater emphasis on maintenance of the yard outside and on the use of the yard as a place where both adults and children can relax and enjoy themselves. With this can come also the development of a more intense pattern of neigh-

---

B. Shostak and William Gomberg, *Blue-Collar World* (New York: Prentice-Hall, 1964).

[6] Marc Fried, "Grieving for a Lost Home," and Edward J. Ryan, "Personal Identity in an Urban Slum," in Leonard J. Duhl (ed.), *The Urban Condition* (New York: Free Press, 1963); and Herbert Gans, *Urban Villagers* (New York: Free Press of Glencoe, Inc., 1962).

borhood socializing. In these suburbs the demand grows for good community services as opposed to simply adequate ones, so that there tends to be greater involvement in the schools than is the case with traditional working class men and women. One of the dominant themes of the modern working class life style is that of having arrived in the mainstream of American life, of no longer being simply "poor-but-honest" workers. It is in the service of this goal that we find these elaborations in the meaning of the house and its environs.

In both working class groups, as the interior of the home more closely approximates notions of a decent standard, we find a decline in concerns expressed by inhabitants with sources of threat from within and a shift toward concerns about a threatening outside world—a desire to make the neighborhood secure against the incursions of lower class people who might rob or perpetrate violence of one kind or another.

As we shift our focus from the stable working class to the lower class, the currently popular poor, we find a very different picture. In addition to the large and growing literature, I will draw on data from three studies of this group with which I have been involved. Two studies deal with family attitudes and family planning behavior on the part of lower class, in contrast to working class couples. In these studies, based on some 450 intensive conversational interviews with men and women living in Chicago, Cincinnati, and Oklahoma City housing was not a subject of direct inquiry. Nevertheless we gained considerable insight into the ways lower class people think about their physical and social environment, and their anxieties, goals, and coping mechanisms that operate in connection with their housing arrangements.[7]

The third study, currently on-going, involves a five year investigation of social and community problems in the Pruitt-Igoe Project of St. Louis. This public housing project consists of 33 11-story buildings near downtown St. Louis. The project was opened in 1954, has 2,762 apartments, of which only some 2,000 are currently occupied, and has as tenants a very high proportion (over 50 percent) of female-headed households on one kind or another of public assistance. Though originally integrated, the project is now all Negro. The project community is plagued by petty crimes, vandalism, much

---

[7] Lee Rainwater, *And the Poor Get Children* (Chicago: Quadrangle Books, 1960), and Lee Rainwater, *Family Design: Marital Sexuality, Family Size and Family Planning* (Chicago: Aldine Publishing Company, 1964).

destruction of the physical plant, and a very bad reputation in both the Negro and white communities.[8] For the past two years a staff of ten research assistants has been carrying out participant observation and conversational interviewing among project residents. In order to obtain a comparative focus on problems of living in public housing, we have also interviewed in projects in Chicago (Stateway Gardens), New York (St. Nicholas), and San Francisco (Yerba Buena Plaza and Westside Courts). Many of the concrete examples which follow come from these interviews, since in the course of observation and interviewing with project tenants we have had the opportunity to learn a great deal about both their experiences in the projects and about the private slum housing in which they previously lived. While our interviews in St. Louis provide us with insight into what it is like to live in one of the most disorganized public housing communities in the United States, the interviews in the other cities provide the contrast of much more average public housing experiences.[9] Similarly, the retrospective accounts that respondents in different cities give of their previous private housing experience provides a wide sampling in the slum communities of four different cities.

In the lower class we find a great many very real threats to security, although these threats often do seem to be somewhat exaggerated by lower class women. The threatening world of the lower class comes to be absorbed into a world view which generalizes the belief that the environment is threatening more than it is rewarding—that rewards reflect the infrequent working of good luck and that danger is endemic.[10] Any close acquaintance with the ongoing life of lower class people impresses one with their anxious alienation from the larger world, from the middle class to be sure, but from the majority of their peers as well. Lower class people often seem isolated and to have but tenuous participation in a community of known and valued peers. They are ever aware of the presence of strangers who tend to be seen as potentially dangerous. While they do seek to create a gratifying peer group society, these groups tend to be unstable and readily fragmented. Even

---

[8] Nicholas J. Demerath, "St. Louis Public Housing Study Sets Off Community Development to Meet Social Needs," *Journal of Housing*, XIX (October, 1962).

[9] See, D. M. Wilner, *et al.*, *The Housing Environment and Family Life* (Baltimore: Johns Hopkins University Press, 1962).

[10] Allison Davis, *Social Class Influences on Learning* (Cambridge: Harvard University Press, 1948).

the heavy reliance on relatives as the core of a personal community does not do away with the dangers which others may bring. As Walter Miller has perceptively noted, "trouble" is one of the major focal concerns in the lower class world view.[11] A home to which one could retreat from such an insecure world would be of great value, but our data indicate that for lower class people such a home is not easy to come by. In part, this is due to the fact that one's own family members themselves often make trouble or bring it into the home, but even more important it is because it seems very difficult to create a home and an immediate environment that actually does shut out danger.[12]

DANGERS IN THE ENVIRONMENT

From our data it is possible to abstract a great many dangers that have some relation to housing and its location. The location or the immediate environment is as important as the house itself, since lower class people are aware that life inside is much affected by the life just outside.

In the following table I have summarized the main kinds of danger which seem to be related to housing one way or another. It is apparent that these dangers have two immediate sources, human and non-human, and that the consequences that are feared from these sources usually represent a complex amalgam of physical, interpersonal, and mortal damage to the individual and his family. Let us look first at the various sources of danger and then at the overlapping consequences feared from these dangers.

There is nothing unfamiliar about the non-human sources of danger. They represent a sad catalogue of threats apparent in any journalist's account of slum living.[13] That we become used to the catalogue, however, should not obscure the fact that these dangers are very real to many lower class families. Rats and other vermin are ever present companions in most big city slums. From the sense of relief which residents in public housing often experience on this score, it is apparent

---

[11] Walter Miller, "Lower Class Culture as a Generating Milieu of Gang Delinquency," in Marvin E. Wolfgang, Leonard Savitz, and Norman Johnson (eds.), *The Sociology of Crime and Delinquency* (New York: John Wiley Company, 1962).

[12] Alvin W. Schorr, *Slums and Social Insecurity* (Washington, D.C.: Department of Health, Education and Welfare, 1963).

[13] Michael Harrington, *The Other America* (New York: Macmillan Co., 1962).

A Taxonomy of Dangers in the Lower Class Home and Environs:
Each of These Can Involve Physical, Interpersonal,
and Moral Consequences

Source of Danger

Non-Human	*Human*
Rats and other vermin	Violence to self and possessions
Poisons	Assault
Fire and burning	Fighting and beating
Freezing and cold	Rape
Poor plumbing	Objects thrown or dropped
Dangerous electrical wiring	Stealing
Trash (broken glass, cans, etc.)	Verbal Hostility, Shaming,
Insufficiently protected heights	Exploitation
Other aspects of poorly designed	Own family
or deteriorated structures (e.g.	Neighbors
thin walls)	Caretakers
Cost of dwelling	Outsiders
	Attractive alternatives that wean
	oneself or valued others away
	from a stable life

that slum dwellers are not indifferent to the presence of rats
in their homes. Poisons may be a danger, sometimes from
lead-base paints used on surfaces which slum toddlers may
chew. Fires in slum areas are not uncommon, and even in a
supposedly well designed public housing project children may
repeatedly burn themselves on uncovered steampipe risers. In
slums where the tenant supplies his own heating there is always the possibility of a very cold apartment because of no
money, or, indeed, of freezing to death (as we were told by
one respondent whose friend fell into an alcoholic sleep without turning on the heater). Insufficiently protected heights, as
in one public housing project, may lead to deaths when children fall out windows or adults fall down elevator shafts. Thin
walls in the apartment may expose a family to more of its
neighbor's goings-on than comfortable to hear. Finally, the
very cost of the dwelling itself can represent a danger in that
it leaves too little money for other things needed to keep body
and soul together.

That lower class people grow up in a world like this and
live in it does not mean that they are indifferent to it—nor that
its toll is only that of possible physical damage in injury, illness, incapacity, or death. Because these potentialities and
events are interpreted and take on symbolic significance, and

because lower class people make some efforts to cope with them, inevitably there are also effects on their interpersonal relationships and on their moral conceptions of themselves and their worlds.

The most obvious human source of danger has to do with violence directed by others against oneself and one's possessions. Lower class people are concerned with being assaulted, being damaged, being drawn into fights, being beaten, being raped. In public housing projects in particular, it is always possible for juveniles to throw or drop things from windows which can hurt or kill, and if this pattern takes hold it is a constant source of potential danger. Similarly, people may rob anywhere—apartment, laundry room, corridor.

Aside from this kind of direct violence, there is the more pervasive ever-present potentiality for symbolic violence to the self and that which is identified with the self—by verbal hostility, the shaming and exploitation expressed by the others who make up one's world. A source of such violence, shaming, or exploitation may be within one's own family—from children, spouse, siblings, parents—and often is. It seems very likely that crowding tends to encourage such symbolic violence to the self but certainly crowding is not the only factor since we also find this kind of threat in uncrowded public housing quarters.[14] Most real and immediate to lower class people, however, seems to be the potentiality for symbolic destructiveness by their neighbors. Lower class people seem ever on guard toward their neighbors, even ones with whom they become well-acquainted and would count as their friends. This suspiciousness is directed often at juveniles and young adults whom older people tend to regard as almost uncontrollable. It is important to note that while one may and does engage in this kind of behavior oneself, this is no guarantee that the individual does not fear and condemn the behavior when engaged in by others. For example, one woman whose family was evicted from a public housing project because her children were troublemakers thought, before she knew that her family was included among the twenty families thus evicted, that the evictions were a good thing because there were too many people around who cause trouble.

Symbolic violence on the part of caretakers (all those whose occupations bring them into contact with lower class people

[14] Edward S. Deevey, "The Hare and the Haruspex: A Cautionary Tale," in Eric and Mary Josephson, *Man Alone* (New York: Dell Publishing Company, 1962).

as purveyors of some private or public service) seems also endemic in slum and public housing areas. Students of the interactions between caretakers and their lower class clients have suggested that there is a great deal of punitiveness and shaming commonly expressed by the caretakers in an effort to control and direct the activities of their clients.[15]

The defense of the client is generally one of avoidance, or sullenness and feigned stupidity, when contact cannot be avoided. As David Caplovitz has shown so well, lower class people are subjected to considerable exploitation by the commercial services with which they deal, and exploitation for money, sexual favors, and sadistic impulses is not unknown on the part of public servants either.[16]

Finally, outsiders present in two ways the dangers of symbolic violence as well as of physical violence. Using the anonymity of geographical mobility, outsiders may come into slum areas to con and exploit for their own ends and, by virtue of the attitudes they maintain toward slum dwellers or public housing residents, they may demean and derogate them. Here we would have to include also the mass media which can and do behave in irresponsibly punitive ways toward people who live in lower class areas, a fact most dramatically illustrated in the customary treatment of the Pruitt-Igoe Project in St. Louis. From the point of view of the residents, the unusual interest shown in their world by a research team can also fit into this pattern.

Finally, the lower class person's world contains many attractive alternatives to the pursuit of a stable life. He can fear for himself that he will be caught up in these attractive alternatives and thus damage his life chances, and he may fear even more that those whom he values, particularly in his family, will be seduced away from him. Thus, wives fear their husbands will be attracted to the life outside the family, husbands fear the same of their wives, and parents always fear that their children will somehow turn out badly. Again, the fact that you may yourself be involved in such seductive pursuits does not lessen the fear that these valued others will be won away while your back is turned. In short, both the push and

[15] A. B. Hollingshead and L. H. Rogler, "Attitudes Toward Slums and Private Housing in Puerto Rico," in Leonard J. Duhl, *The Urban Condition* (New York: Free Press, 1963).

[16] David Caplovitz, *The Poor Pay More* (New York: Free Press of Glencoe, 1963).

the pull of the human world in which lower class people live can be seen as a source of danger.

Having looked at the sources of danger, let us look at the consequences which lower class people fear from these dangers. The physical consequences are fairly obvious in connection with the non-human threats and the threats of violence from others. They are real and they are ever present: One can become the victim of injury, incapacitation, illness, and death from both nonhuman and human sources. Even the physical consequences of the symbolic violence of hostility, shaming, and exploitation, to say nothing of seduction, can be great if they lead one to retaliate in a physical way and in turn be damaged. Similarly there are physical consequences to being caught up in alternatives such as participation in alcohol and drug subcultures.

There are three interrelated interpersonal consequences of living in a world characterized by these human and nonhuman sources of danger. The first relates to the need to form satisfying interpersonal relationships, the second to the need to exercise responsibility as a family member, and the third to the need to formulate an explanation for the unpleasant state of affairs in your world.

The consequences which endanger the need to maintain satisfying interpersonal relations flow primarily from the human sources of danger. That is, to the extent that the world seems made up of dangerous others, at a very basic level the choice of friends carries risks. There is always the possibility that a friend may turn out to be an enemy or that his friends will. The result is a generalized watchfulness and touchiness in interpersonal relationships. Because other individuals represent not only themselves but also their families, the matter is further complicated since interactions with, let us say, neighbors' children, can have repercussions on the relationship with the neighbor. Because there are human agents behind most of the non-human dangers, one's relationships with others—family members, neighbors, caretakers—are subject to potential disruptions because of those others' involvement in creating trash, throwing objects, causing fires, or carrying on within thin walls.

With respect to the exercise of responsibility, we find that parents feel they must bring their children safely through childhood in a world which both poses great physical and moral dangers, and which seeks constantly to seduce them into a way of life which the parent wishes them to avoid. Thus, childrearing becomes an anxious and uncertain process. Two of the most common results are a pervasive repressiveness in child discipline and training, and, when that seems to fail or is no longer possible, a fatalistic abdication of efforts to protect the children. From the child's point of view, because his parents are not able to protect him from many unpleasantnesses and even from himself, he loses faith in them and comes to regard them as persons of relatively little consequence.

The third area of effect on interpersonal relations has to do with the search for causes of the prevalence of threat and violence in their world. We have suggested that to lower class people the major causes stem from the nature of their own peers. Thus, a great deal of blaming others goes on and reinforces the process of isolation, suspiciousness, and touchiness about blame and shaming. Similarly, landlords and tenants tend to develop patterns of mutual recrimination and blaming, making it very difficult for them to cooperate with each other in doing something about either the human or nonhuman sources of difficulty.

Finally, the consequences for conceptions of the moral order of one's world, of one's self, and of others, are very great. Although lower class people may not adhere in action to many middle class values about neatness, cleanliness, order, and proper decorum, it is apparent that they are often aware of their deviance, wishing that their world could be a nicer place, physically and socially. The presence of nonhuman threats conveys in devastating terms a sense that they live in an immoral and uncontrolled world. The physical evidence of trash, poor plumbing and the stink that goes with it, rats and other vermin, deepens their feeling of being moral outcasts. Their physical world is telling them they are inferior and bad just as effectively perhaps as do their human interactions. Their inability to control the depredation of rats, hot steam pipes, balky stoves, and poorly fused electrical circuits tells them that they are failures as autonomous individuals. The physical and social disorder of their world presents a constant temptation to give up or retaliate in kind. And when lower class people try to do something about some of these dangers, they are generally exposed in their interactions with caretakers and outsiders to further moral punitiveness by being told that their troubles are their own fault.

IMPLICATIONS FOR HOUSING DESIGN

It would be asking too much to insist that design per se can solve or even seriously mitigate these threats. On the other hand, it is obvious that almost all the non-human threats can be pretty well done away with where the resources are available to design decent housing for lower class people. No matter what criticisms are made of public housing projects, there is no doubt that the structures themselves are infinitely preferable to slum housing. In our interviews in public housing projects we have found very few people who complain about design aspects of the insides of their apartments. Though they may not see their apartments as perfect, there is a dramatic drop in anxiety about nonhuman threats within. Similarly, reasonable foresight in the design of other elements can eliminate the threat of falling from windows or into elevator shafts, and can provide adequate outside toilet facilities for children at play. Money and a reasonable exercise of architectural skill go a long way toward providing lower class families with the really safe place of retreat from the outside world that they desire.

There is no such straightforward design solution to the potentiality of human threat. However, to the extent that lower class people do have a place they can go that is not so dangerous as the typical slum dwelling, there is at least the gain of a haven. Thus, at the cost perhaps of increased isolation, lower class people in public housing sometimes place a great deal of value on privacy and on living a quiet life behind the locked doors of their apartments. When the apartment itself seems safe it allows the family to begin to elaborate a home to maximize coziness, comfortable enclosure, and lack of exposure. Where, as in St. Louis, the laundry rooms seem unsafe places, tenants tend to prefer to do their laundry in their homes, sacrificing the possibility of neighborly interactions to gain a greater sense of security of person and property.

Once the home can be seen as a relatively safe place, lower class men and women express a desire to push out the boundaries of safety further into the larger world. There is the constantly expressed desire for a little bit of outside space that is one's own or at least semiprivate. Buildings that have galleries are much preferred by their tenants to those that have no such immediate access to the outside. Where, as in the New York public housing project we studied, it was possible to lock the outside doors of the buildings at night, tenants felt more secure.

A measured degree of publicness within buildings can also contribute to a greater sense of security. In buildings where there are several families whose doors open onto a common hallway there is a greater sense of the availability of help should trouble come than there is in buildings where only two or three apartments open onto a small hallway in a stairwell. While tenants do not necessarily develop close neighborly relations when more neighbors are available, they can develop a sense of making common cause in dealing with common problems. And they feel less at the mercy of gangs or individuals intent on doing them harm.

As with the most immediate outside, lower class people express the desire to have their immediate neighborhood or the housing project grounds a more controlled and safe place. In public housing projects, for example, tenants want project police who function efficiently and quickly; they would like some play areas supervised so that children are not allowed to prey on each other; they want to be able to move about freely themselves and at the same time discourage outsiders who might come to exploit.

A real complication is that the very control which these desires imply can seem a threat to the lower class resident. To the extent that caretakers seem to demand and damn more than they help, this cure to the problem of human threat seems worse than the disease. The crux of the caretaking task in connection with lower class people is to provide and encourage security and order within the lower class world without at the same time extracting from it a heavy price in self-esteem, dignity, and autonomy.

Author's Note: This paper is based in part on research aided by a grant from the National Institute of Mental Health, Grant No: MH–09189 "Social and Community Problems in Public Housing Areas." Many of the ideas presented stem from discussions with the senior members of the Pruitt-Igoe Research Staff—Alvin W. Gouldner, David J. Pittman, and Jules Henry—and with the research associates and research assistants on the project.

PUBLIC HOUSING: THE CONTEXTS OF FAILURE

Jewel Bellush and Murray Hausknecht

In 1965 Congress passed the Economic Opportunities Act, two aid to education bills, and the Medicare program. The same Congress passed the rent subsidy provision of a housing bill by the barest possible margin, and concluded its session by refusing to appropriate funds for the program. The behavior of Congress is symptomatic of the status of public housing in the United States: while there is an increasing willingness to extend and implement public welfare policies in many new directions, there is no similar willingness to extend and support public housing programs.

The preamble to the Housing Act of 1949 stated:

> To establish a national housing objective and the policy to be followed in the attainment thereof, to provide Federal aid to assist slum-clearance projects and low rent public housing projects initiated by local agencies, to provide for financial assistance by the Secretary of Agriculture for farm housing, and for other purposes.

Despite the clear emphasis on housing, the passage of the act and subsequent ones has had very little effect on the housing situation of the poor. The 1960 Census found one-eighth of all urban households living in dwellings that were dilapidated or lacking in sanitary facilities.[1] Indeed, one housing specialist concludes that:

> . . . the housing problem of the disadvantaged has gradually ceased to be of major concern to those responsible for public policy. Faced with declining ratables and rising costs for municipal services, cities have used federal renewal funds for projects that would shore up local finances.[2]

There is an irony here. Today, as never before in our history, there is a consciousness of the urgency of urban prob-

[1] Conference on Economic Progress, *Poverty and Deprivation in the United States* (Washington, D.C.: Conference on Economic Progress, April 1962), Chap. X.

[2] William Grigsby, "Housing and Slum Clearance: Elusive Goals," *The Annals of the American Academy of Political and Social Science* (March 1964), Volume 352, p. 109.

lems, a consciousness that represents a belated triumph for the long line of urban reformers. One of their focal interests was the deplorable state of housing in our cities, and now that we have caught up with their awareness we slight one of their central concerns. This underlines the main problem of explaining the strange neglect of public housing in an era of innovation in welfare policies.

Conventionally public housing is placed in the broad category of "welfare," and so Medicare is assumed to be basically similar to housing as public programs. To the extent that Medicare and public housing represent a recognition of material needs that can only be filled by some sort of government intervention, these are similar programs. But when we ask whom do these programs affect, what proportion of the total population, and which strata of the society, a critical difference emerges. Medicare is designed to meet the needs of the aged, and everyone is destined to age. Given the increasing costs of medical care, few people can look forward without anxiety to meeting future health costs from their own resources. Thus Medicare affects almost the entire society and cuts across class lines; almost everyone has either a present or future stake in the program. Public housing, on the other hand, affects only one class and a much smaller proportion of the total population. Equally important, unlike the problem of health and old age, few people see public housing as being important to them in the future.

When we contrast the scholarship aid provisions of the education acts of 1965 with public housing, still another difference among welfare programs emerges. The fundamental premise of the scholarship programs is that no one who can qualify for a college education should miss the opportunity through lack of money, and this applies to the "poor" as well as to those solidly ensconced in the middle class. Once again, then, it is a program that crosscuts class lines. More to the present point is the premise that those who *deserve* it ought to receive aid. In a society that evaluates individuals on performance criteria a distinction is always drawn between the *deserving* and the *undeserving* as measured in terms of individual achievement. Public housing seems to ignore this principle, since it benefits the poor, those who have failed to achieve, i.e., the *undeserving*.

Obviously, other welfare programs, notably those included in the war on poverty, also benefit the poor. But these are related to performance and achievement. The typical poverty program tries to aid the poor to achieve in a society governed by universalistic norms; the program is designed to improve the *performance* of the individual. Public housing has no such apparent instrumental relevance to performance. Moreover, job retraining programs, for example, are self-limiting; that is, once the individual is "retrained," aid stops, and he is once again on his own. Public housing does not have this kind of self-limiting mechanism for the lower class; if a family's income remains below a certain level it still retains its apartment. In other words, if family income is an index of achievement, then public aid continues even after lack of achievement has been demonstrated. In this sense, public housing aids the undeserving poor, as do home relief and aid to dependent children. It is precisely these programs that focus on the undeserving poor that become the targets for public criticism and legislative hostility.[3]

The importance of the distinction between the deserving and the undeserving can be seen from another perspective when we contrast general housing policy in our society with public housing policy. Such programs as FHA insured mortgages, GI Bill home loans, and state-aided cooperative housing, assist individuals who ordinarily could not purchase homes in the open market. However, the programs aid only the deserving, i.e., those who have accumulated some resources through their own efforts. At the other extreme, the *most* undeserving poor are denied admission to public housing: In almost all communities multi-problem families, for example, are ineligible for public housing. In sum, then, we may say that public housing differs from other welfare programs in that it allocates resources in a manner that ignores performance criteria.

But a home is something more than a "resource"; it has a symbolic significance. Home ownership in our society is a symbol of civic virtue—it is regarded as a prerequisite for the integrity of the social system. It is not surprising to learn that Herbert Hoover once intoned, "The present large proportion of families that own their own homes is both the foundation of a sound economic and social system, and a guarantee that our society will continue to develop rationally as changing conditions demand." Some, however, may be disconcerted to hear this echoed in Franklin D. Roosevelt's assertion that "a

---

[3] See the stimulating paper by S. M. Miller and Martin Rein, "The War on Poverty: Perspectives and Prospects" (February 1965) (mimeographed).

nation of homeowners, of people who own a real share in their own land, is unconquerable."[4] But the sentiments will not surprise those who recall Thomas Jefferson's exaltation of the yeoman farmer or the ideological underpinnings of the Homestead Act of 1862. In the twentieth century, the virtues of the yeoman farmer and the sterling pioneer are embodied in "the homeowner."

In addition to its civic significance, home ownership also symbolizes individual worth. In our culture the ownership of one's own home is an important symbol of achievement, whether it be a castle at San Simeon, a town house on New York's East Side, or a mass-produced, split-level, or ranch house of the suburban subdivision. It is, in short, a visible sign of individual success, and an important reassurance that the American Dream is not a nightmare. Thus, from a sociological perspective, the home is also a *reward*. But rewards in our society are supposed to be distributed on the basis of achievement, and we have seen that public housing is allocated to those who have failed to achieve.

Public housing, then, runs counter to the implications of traditional notions about virtue. The tradition wraps up home ownership, individual achievement, and "the foundations of a sound economic and social system" into one tightly knit whole, and in this ball of cultural yarn there is no room for public housing. In addition, to provide public housing for the undeserving poor subverts the significance of owning one's own home, be it ever so humble or substandard. This is to say nothing, as yet, of the willingness, in practical political terms, of the latter-day descendants of yeoman farmers and sturdy pioneers to see their taxes go to those so clearly undeserving in comparison with themselves.

Our cultural traditions play into the situation in yet another way. The Jeffersonian idealization of the yeoman farmer is an integral part of the anti-urban bias of our society. The yeoman farmer embodies civic virtue because he is a rural man; urban man, by definition, is corrupt. It does not matter that the contemporary homeowner is highly urbanized, or that he may live in the densest part of the metropolitan area. Home ownership makes him the heir to all the rural virtues, or at least a rural bastion against the vice-filled streets of the city. Public housing has historically been provided for the urban mass

[4] Both statements quoted in Glenn Beyer, *Housing: A Factual Analysis* (New York: The Macmillan Company, 1958), p. 249.

whose present state and historical antecedents both exemplify and contribute to urban sin. Thus, public housing does not crosscut another great divide of American society, the rural-urban division. And so, by being so securely identified with Sodom and Gomorrah, it manages to mobilize all the traditional negative perceptions of the city and its inhabitants.

Despite their concern for the urban masses, the urban reformers' ideas were not at odds with the cultural tradition we have been describing. Adequate homes for the urban, immigrant masses was a necessary condition for dealing with their poverty; that is, housing reform and the elimination of the slums went hand in hand with education as an instrument or means of social mobility. By 1950, however, it was apparent that the beliefs of the champions of public housing were based on myths rather than facts.[5] It was not simply that the occupants of public housing remained among the poor and that the social ills of the city were not abated as public housing rose in the former slum areas—although this would have been bad enough. During the fifties observers were also pointing out that the huge public housing projects, while still physically decent, showed all the other characteristics of the slums they had replaced. It was difficult to escape the conclusion that housing made little difference to the situation it was supposed to remedy. Thus, the traditional rationale for public housing was destroyed, and its liberal proponents were thrown into ideological disarray.[6]

Consequently, the liberals were left at a considerable disadvantage on the level of practical politics. But another factor must be noted as well. The decade of the fifties represented for most American liberals "the end of ideology"; it was an era in which one was forced to recognize old beliefs, commitments, and political theories as shibboleths that had no relevance to the world of the "cold war" and the "affluent society." As one shucked off "ideological" orientations one became more "pragmatic," and by 1960 this became central to the "style" of a new Democratic Administration. The new political style was fateful for public housing, because it further weakened and drained off commitment to the program. The basic argument for public housing had been, in any case, a pragmatic one, i.e., it had always been justified in terms of its

[5] James B. Conant, *Slums and Suburbs* (New York: McGraw-Hill Book Company, 1961), p. 33.

[6] See the reading selections in this book by Harrison Salisbury, Jane Jacobs, and Lee Rainwater.

instrumental functions for alleviating poverty and civic immorality. To continue to advocate a policy and a program that could not be justified pragmatically meant that one was still in the grip of "ideology." Realism demanded that one seek other means of combating poverty and other social ills.

The suspicion of "ideology" and the celebration of a pragmatic politics turned political energies toward other programs, but this was not an inevitable consequence. A pragmatic orientation in these circumstances could lead to a rethinking of the role of public housing. The rent subsidy program shows that, in fact, no attempt was made to seriously re-examine the problem, and it serves as a central clue to another cause of the decline of effective political commitment to public housing.

Public housing programs failed to meet the expectations of their proponents because the programs did not link housing as physical structure with the social and cultural components of a neighborhood. A "slum" is a community as well as a site of substandard housing, and the amelioration of the conditions of life of its inhabitants depends upon dealing with the community as well as the physical dwellings. From this perspective the object of aid is not the individual but the community; the lot of the individual changes with a change in the community. There are two prerequisites that must be met before this perspective can be meaningfully implemented. First, there must be the acceptance of the proposition that the social ills and problems of the slum—where these are empirically correlated—are phenomena linked to the class status of the community rather than to individuals *qua* individuals. That is, the phenomena are the result of structural conditions rather than purely individual problems. Secondly, there must be a recognition that "class" means something more than low income; it means a distinctive sub-culture and distinctive styles of life related to social position. A total program of aid, of which public housing would be one component, would have to, then, be based on the potentialities and limitations of a specific class community. This orientation would also mean, to revert to an earlier point, overlooking the differences between the deserving and undeserving poor.

It is a perspective, however, that is extraordinarily difficult to achieve in American society. A unique combination of historical circumstances has produced relatively high standards of living for all strata, and these have produced, in turn, a blurring of class lines and distinctions. Consequently, in the public sphere Americans, liberals and non-liberals alike, show little consciousness of class, and they are prone to the myth of classlessness, i.e., that the United States is not "really" a class society—"we are all really middle class." (This does not mean that in the private sphere, e.g., choosing whom one marries or where one lives, Americans are not sensitive to class differences, and do not act on their knowledge of the differences.) The myth is not totally unrelated to reality; from a political perspective, at least, class phenomena in the United States often have a different significance than in comparable European countries. At the same time the myth obscures an important aspect of the American reality, that there are class communities with distinctive sub-cultures and styles of life to which the assumption and implications that "we are all middle class" do not apply.

In the rent subsidy program we can still see the myth at work and the way the class realities of American life are ignored. The program implicitly assumes that the poor are distinguished from others *only* by a lack of money; that their values, aspirations, and styles of life are not meaningfully different from others; that once the lack of money has been compensated for they will merge relatively easily into their new surroundings. Our class system does produce many individuals for whom these assumptions are appropriate. The rent subsidy proposal, therefore, is quite conventional in its approach, since it concerns itself with individuals and the deserving poor. It demonstrates a failure to see public housing in relation to the poor as members of a community, and to see the community in terms of its class characteristics. Thus, the inability to come to terms with the class dimensions of urban ills leaves the champions of public housing pursuing traditional paths that lead to defeats in the political arena, and to a further weakening of commitment to public housing. For it is in the political arena that the factors of American history and society we have been discussing take on practical significance.

In practical political terms there are powerful forces arrayed against public housing. In the forefront of the battle are such imposing organizations as the National Association of Real Estate Boards, the National Association of Home Builders, the United States Home Building League, and the U. S. Chamber of Commerce. Behind them are such dependable supporters as the National Retail Lumber Dealers Association and other commercial and industrial groups linked to the construction industries. While on many other issues of public policy, e.g., government-insured mortgages and interest rates, these organizations are in opposition to one another, on the issue of public housing they can sink their differences and present a united front with no fear of defections. Opposition to public housing serves for each of the groups a common material interest, but the unity is also founded on their sharing the common values and perceptions toward housing and the poor we have surveyed.[7]

The strength that comes from unity is re-enforced by financial means and organizational strength. Each organization has a long history as a trade association, and each has developed a permanent staff in Washington that keeps a close and continuous watch on all legislation affecting its interests. The staffs have established lines of communication with influential legislators and key Congressional committeemen. When national and local officers of the organizations come before these committees the staffs coordinate their appearances and prepare the briefs for maximum effect. The financial resources necessary for these operations are always present. During the last eight months of 1949, when urban renewal was being debated in Congress, the anti-public housing forces spent two hundred thousand dollars on their efforts in Washington alone. That same year, the Realtor's Washington Committee, one segment of the total effort, had a budget twice as large as all the proponents of public housing put together.

A good deal of the strength of an organization like the National Association of Real Estate Boards rests on its representation of locally potent political forces. A congressman buttonholed by its Washington lobbyist knows that he is speaking for real estate men and home builders in his district and state; men who are reliable contributors to campaign funds. The anti-public housing lobbies, then, represent real and strategic local political forces that a legislator cannot afford to ignore. But if mundane self-interest plays an important role, we should not forget that the legislator is already favorably predisposed to the blandishments of the lobbyist. The latter represents the biases, values, and sentiments shared by the legislator himself; the lobbyist is not converting the heathen but preaching to the faithful. Thus, the success of the anti-

[7] See the hearings of Congress on public housing for any session since 1937, *Congressional Quarterly Almanac* (1955), p. 254.

public housing forces is the result of a happy conjunction of self-interest and personal values and attitudes.

The opponents of public housing, of course, do not have the field to themselves. It has even been suggested that "effective political power" is "evenly balanced" between the forces ranged on opposing sides of the public housing question.[8] Yet the consistent defeat of public housing programs indicates that a critical imbalance of power exists. On the surface the forces supporting public housing seem to be equal to their opponents. The largest group of supporters—a loose coalition of labor unions, welfare, and civic associations— was organized during the thirties as the Public Housing Conference. In terms of numbers the total membership of these organizations easily outweighs those against public housing, but numbers alone do not make for effective political power. The primary difficulty has been, and continues to be, that none of the organizations has public housing as its primary focus of concern, and the issue itself tends to be a divisive one within and among organizations nominally committed to it.

The organizations with the most political leverage are those based on organized labor. But American labor has always been oriented to bread-and-butter issues: laws affecting the unions themselves, wages and hours, etc. Public housing has never been part of such traditional interests and issues. This is not to say that labor is not interested in housing policy, but the interest has been shaped by the nature and situation of their membership. Those manual workers most in need of the decent homes provided by public housing are unorganized. The semi-skilled and skilled union members, because they are organized, have incomes that make them ineligible for public housing and allow them to share the dominant ideologies about the meaning and significance of the house. Consequently, the unions have concentrated their attention and energies on housing programs appropriate to the needs of their membership. In the main these have been programs that provide subsidies for middle-income cooperative housing projects. The peripheral status of public housing as a programatic issue is also found in other organizations counted as supporters of public housing. These groups are usually organized around ethnic and religious affiliations—Na-

[8] Martin Meyerson, Barbara Terrett, and William Wheaton, *Housing, People, and Cities* (New York: McGraw-Hill Book Company, 1962), p. 278.

tional Catholic Welfare Council, B'nai B'rith, National Council of Churches of Christ—that also have bread-and-butter issues that do not include public housing, e.g., birth control, federal aid to education, religious discrimination in employment. Moreover, the membership of the organizations are even further removed than are union members from the needs satisfied by public housing. The goad of direct self-interest is removed from the efforts of these supporters of public housing legislation.

When self-interest was operative among the memberships it was dysfunctional for the cause of public housing. In the larger northern cities, especially, public housing means a high proportion of Negro residents and a change in the complexion of neighborhoods in which projects appear. In 1950, for example, when the Chicago Housing Authority was embroiled in a controversy with the Board of Aldermen over housing sites, the Authority was supported by the CIO's Chicago Office, in line with the CIO's official support of public housing, but local unions within the city played a distinctly "minor role." Prejudice among rank-and-file union members, who have the typical white American stake in residential segregation, does not make public housing an issue that commands their support. Nor does it commend itself, for the same reasons, to the middle-class member of "liberal" organizations who officially support public housing legislation.

Compared to their opponents the public housing coalition is at a great financial disadvantage. Many of the organizations maintain staffs that watch their interests in Washington, but at no time can the coalition mobilize resources that match those of their opponents. The housing forces cannot even mobilize a body of imposing "experts" and "professionals" capable of impressing legislators. Among those claiming expert and professional status are representatives of the National Association of Housing and Redevelopment Officials. Even from a purely objective perspective their claim to "professional" status, in view of their training and recruitment, is hardly tenable. Moreover, they are civil servants, the living embodiments of "red tape bureaucracy," and, as such, automatically suspect of inefficiency and incompetence. Finally, they are vulnerable to attacks on the grounds that they are merely defending their own crass, material self-interests, and unlike the representatives of the American Medical Association, for example, they have developed no rhetoric that effectively masks these interests.

Yet even if the public housing supporters could spend more money for a more elaborate lobbying effort it is doubtful whether this would be sufficient to overcome their critical handicap. The very same factors that realistically prevent a powerful presentation of their case in the halls and committee rooms of Congress deprives them of the ultimate weapon that makes a lobbying effort effective. The public housing forces represent no political force "back home" that a legislator as a political animal must attend to. He knows that no matter what a George Meany or a Walter Reuther says in Washington, the union members in his district couldn't care less about how he voted on public housing. He also knows that the representatives of the other groups testifying and trying to influence his vote for public housing have higher priorities than housing; as long as he votes "right" on these issues he is "safe" as far as those groups are concerned. In short, what precisely defines the proponents of public housing in the rough-and-tumble fight of the political arena is a *lack* of effective political power.[9]

The United States today is committed to a broad program of welfare policies. It is not as advanced in this respect as England or Sweden, but, nonetheless, it is clearly a welfare state. Yet, as the case of public housing shows, there is not so strong a commitment to welfare policies that it can overcome the inertia of forces emanating from the social and cultural traditions of the society. These forces not only make us reluctant to deal effectively with a range of problems but also weaken the power of those who feel a sense of urgency about the neglected problem areas. We shall not catch up with the more advanced welfare states until there is a greater sophistication and self-consciousness about the nature of our society and the politics it spawns.

[9] In fact, in November 1965 New York voters in referendum turned down, for the first time, housing propositions for low-income families. See the analysis of this vote in Citizens' Housing and Planning Council, *Housing and Planning News* (November–December 1965), Vol. 24, Nos. 3, 4.

V. OVERVIEW: SUCCESS OR FAILURE?

Previous parts of these readings have been concerned with many facets of renewal. In this section we turn to over-all assessments of where renewal now stands, and, as ought to be expected, certain themes come to the surface again. And, as also might be expected, there is controversy.

Herbert Gans is a research sociologist who has investigated newly established suburban communities, and he has written a study of Boston's West End slum community before it was cleared for an urban renewal project. He is particularly sensitive, therefore, to the impact of public policy on communities and groups within the larger city. His theme is the failure of renewal to aid the urban poor; Gans seems to imply, with his emphasis on how much housing renewal has destroyed and how many neighborhoods have broken up, that it may have done more harm than good. The housing situation of the poor is the major problem that has to be solved by urban renewal, and he urges the transformation of urban renewal into an urban rehousing program that would take as its focus the entire metropolitan area.

George M. Raymond's rejoinder to Gans contains a considerably more favorable view of renewal. He is a city planner and a member of a firm that has served as consultants to many communities with renewal projects. His tendency is to view renewal in terms of its actual and potential impact on the city as a whole. Therefore, Raymond discounts Gans' stress on housing. He maintains that Gans ignores the most recent advances made by renewal in this problem area. Of more importance, perhaps, is his argument that a community needs facilities other than housing, important as the latter may be. If the cities are to remain viable entities there must be improvements, and urban renewal is the means for making cities better communities.

Malcolm Rivkin is an economic specialist connected with a firm that has acted as a consultant for area redevelopment work in underdeveloped countries, and, perhaps, this is what makes him sensitive to an important political dimension. Rivkin takes Gans to task for overemphasizing the importance of the federal government in renewal: The primary source of the difficulties of renewal is "the ruling elites of the cities." Where community leadership is good, renewal projects meet the needs of the community; where it is bad, renewal fails. The fate of renewal in communities, he concludes, will be closely related to the future course of Negro political activity.

THE FAILURE OF URBAN RENEWAL:
A CRITIQUE AND SOME PROPOSALS*

Herbert J. Gans†

Suppose that the government decided that jalopies were a menace to public safety and a blight on the beauty of our highways, and therefore took them away from their drivers. Suppose, then, that to replenish the supply of automobiles, it gave these drivers a hundred dollars each to buy a good used car and also made special grants to General Motors, Ford, and Chrysler to lower the cost—although not necessarily the price—of Cadillacs, Lincolns, and Imperials by a few hundred dollars. Absurd as this may sound, change the jalopies to slum housing, and I have described, with only slight poetic license, the first fifteen years of a federal program called urban renewal.

Since 1949, this program has provided local renewal agencies with federal funds and the power of eminent domain to condemn slum neighborhoods, tear down the buildings, and re-sell the cleared land to private developers at a reduced price. In addition to relocating the slum dwellers in "decent, safe, and sanitary" housing, the program was intended to stimulate large-scale private rebuilding, add new tax revenues to the dwindling coffers of the cities, revitalize their downtown areas, and halt the exodus of middle-class whites to the suburbs.

For some time now, a few city planners and housing experts have been pointing out that urban renewal was not achieving its general aims, and social scientists have produced a number of critical studies of individual renewal projects. These critiques, however, have mostly appeared in academic books and journals; otherwise there has been remarkably little public discussion of the federal program. Slum-dwellers whose homes were to be torn down have indeed protested bitterly, but their outcries have been limited to particular projects; and because such outcries have rarely been supported by the local press, they have been easily brushed aside by the

* FROM *Commentary* (April 1965), pp. 29–37.

† HERBERT J. GANS is an associate professor of sociology at Teachers College, Columbia University. A sociologist and planner, Mr. Gans is the author of *The Urban Villagers*—a study of Boston's West End community—and is completing a book on one of the Levittowns.

political power of the supporters of the projects in question. In the last few years, the civil rights movement has backed protesting slum-dwellers, though again only at the local level, while rightists have opposed the use of eminent domain to take private property from one owner in order to give it to another (especially when the new one is likely to be from out-of-town and financed by New York capital).

Slum clearance has also come under fire from several prominent architectural and social critics, led by Jane Jacobs, who have been struggling to preserve neighborhoods like Greenwich Village, with their brownstones, lofts, and small apartment houses, against the encroachment of the large, high-rise projects built for the luxury market and the poor alike. But these efforts have been directed mainly at private clearance outside the federal program, and their intent has been to save the city for people (intellectuals and artists, for example) who, like tourists, want jumbled diversity, antique "charm," and narrow streets for visual adventure and aesthetic pleasure. (Norman Mailer carried such thinking to its farthest point in his recent attack in the *New York Times Magazine* on the physical and social sterility of high-rise housing; Mailer's attack was also accompanied by an entirely reasonable suggestion—in fact the only viable one that could be made in this context—that the advantages of brownstone living be incorporated into skyscraper projects.)

But if criticism of the urban renewal program has in the past been spotty and sporadic, there are signs that the program as a whole is now beginning to be seriously and tellingly evaluated. At least two comprehensive studies, by Charles Abrams and Scott Greer, are nearing publication, and one highly negative analysis—by an ultra-conservative economist and often irresponsible polemicist—has already appeared: Martin Anderson's *The Federal Bulldozer*.[1] Ironically enough, Anderson's data are based largely on statistics collected by the Urban Renewal Administration. What, according to these and other data, has the program accomplished? It has cleared slums to make room for many luxury-housing and a few middle-income projects, and it has also provided inexpensive land for the expansion of colleges, hospitals, libraries, shopping areas, and other such institutions located in slum areas. As of March 1961, 126,000 dwelling units had been demolished and about 28,000 new ones built. The median monthly rental of all those erected

[1] M.I.T. Press, 272 pp., $5.95.

during 1960 came to $158, and in 1962, to $192—a staggering figure for any area outside of Manhattan.

Needless to say, none of the slum-dwellers who were dispossessed in the process could afford to move into these new apartments. Local renewal agencies were supposed to relocate the dispossessed tenants in "standard" housing within their means before demolition began, but such vacant housing is scarce in most cities, and altogether unavailable in some. And since the agencies were under strong pressure to clear the land and get renewal projects going, the relocation of the tenants was impatiently, if not ruthlessly, handled. Thus, a 1961 study of renewal projects in 41 cities showed that 60 per cent of the dispossessed tenants were merely relocated in other slums; and in big cities, the proportion was even higher (over 70 per cent in Philadelphia, according to a 1958 study). Renewal sometimes even created new slums by pushing relocatees into areas and buildings which then became overcrowded and deteriorated rapidly. This has principally been the case with Negroes who, both for economic and racial reasons, have been forced to double up in other ghettos. Indeed, because almost two-thirds of the cleared slum units have been occupied by Negroes, the urban renewal program has often been characterized as Negro clearance, and in too many cities, this has been its intent.

Moreover, those dispossessed tenants who found better housing usually had to pay more rent than they could afford. In his careful study of relocation in Boston's heavily Italian West End,[2] Chester Hartman shows that 41 per cent of the West Enders lived in good housing in this so-called slum (thus suggesting that much of it should not have been torn down) and that 73 per cent were relocated in good housing—thanks in part to the fact that the West Enders were white. This improvement was achieved at a heavy price, however, for median rents rose from $41 to $71 per month after the move.

According to renewal officials, 80 per cent of all persons relocated now live in good housing, and rent increases were justified because many had been paying unduly low rent before. Hartman's study was the first to compare these official statistics with housing realities, and his figure of 73 per cent challenges the official claim that 97 per cent of the Boston

---

[2] See the November 1964 issue of the *Journal of the American Institute of Planners.* The article also reviews all other relocation research and is a more reliable study of the consequences of renewal than Anderson's.

West Enders were properly re-housed. This discrepancy may arise from the fact that renewal officials collected their data after the poorest of the uprooted tenants had fled in panic to other slums, and that officials also tended toward a rather lenient evaluation of the relocation housing of those actually studied in order to make a good record for their agency. (On the other hand, when they were certifying areas for clearance, these officials often exaggerated the degree of "blight" in order to prove their case.)

As for the substandard rents paid by slum-dwellers, this is true in only a small proportion of cases, and then mostly among whites. Real-estate economists argue that families should pay at least 20 per cent of their income for housing, but what is manageable for middle-income people is a burden to those with low incomes who pay a higher share of their earnings for food and other necessities. Yet even so, low-income Negroes generally have to devote about 30 per cent of their income to housing, and a Chicago study cited by Hartman reports that among non-white families earning less than $3,000 a year, median rent rose from 35 per cent of income before relocation to 46 per cent afterward.

To compound the failure of urban renewal to help the poor, many clearance areas (Boston's West End is an example) were chosen, as Anderson points out, not because they had the worst slums, but because they offered the best sites for luxury housing—housing which would have been built whether the urban renewal program existed or not. Since public funds were used to clear the slums and to make the land available to private builders at reduced costs, the low-income population was in effect subsidizing its own removal for the benefit of the wealthy. What was done for the slum-dwellers in return is starkly suggested by the following statistic: *only one-half of one per cent* of all federal expenditures for urban renewal between 1949 and 1964 was spent on relocation of families and individuals; and 2 per cent if payments to businesses are included.

Finally, because the policy has been to clear a district of all slums at once in order to assemble large sites to attract private developers, entire neighborhoods have frequently been destroyed, uprooting people who had lived there for decades, closing down their institutions, ruining small businesses by the hundreds, and scattering families and friends all over the city. By removing the structure of social and emotional support provided by the neighborhood, and by forcing people to rebuild their lives separately and amid strangers elsewhere, slum clearance has often come at a serious psychological as well as financial cost to its supposed beneficiaries. Marc Fried, a clinical psychologist who studied the West Enders after relocation, reported that 46 per cent of the women and 38 per cent of the men "give evidence of a fairly severe grief reaction or worse" in response to questions about leaving their tight-knit community. Far from "adjusting" eventually to this trauma, 26 per cent of the women remained sad or depressed even two years after they had been pushed out of the West End.[3]

People like the Italians or the Puerto Ricans who live in an intensely group-centered way among three-generation "extended families" and ethnic peers have naturally suffered greatly from the clearance of entire neighborhoods. It may well be, however, that slum clearance has inflicted yet graver emotional burdens on Negroes, despite the fact that they generally live in less cohesive and often disorganized neighborhoods. In fact, I suspect that Negroes who lack a stable family life and have trouble finding neighbors, shopkeepers, and institutions they can trust may have been hurt even more by forcible removal to new areas. This suspicion is supported by another of Fried's findings—that the socially marginal West Enders were more injured by relocation than those who had been integral members of the old neighborhood. Admittedly, some Negroes move very often on their own, but then they at least do so voluntarily, and not in consequence of a public policy which is supposed to help them in the first place. Admittedly also, relocation has made it possible for social workers to help slum-dwellers whom they could not reach until renewal brought them out in the open, so to speak. But then only a few cities have so far used social workers to make relocation a more humane process.

These high financial, social, and emotional costs paid by the slum-dwellers have generally been written off as an unavoidable by-product of "progress," the price of helping cities to collect more taxes, bring back the middle class, make better use of downtown land, stimulate private investment, and restore civic pride. But as Anderson shows, urban renewal has hardly justified these claims either. For one thing, urban renewal is a slow process: the average project has taken twelve

[3] See "Grieving for a Lost Home," in *The Urban Condition*, edited by Leonard Duhl.

years to complete. Moreover, while the few areas suitable
for luxury housing were quickly rebuilt, less desirable cleared
land might lie vacant for many years because developers were
—and are—unwilling to risk putting up high- and middle-
income housing in areas still surrounded by slums. Frequently,
they can be attracted only by promises of tax write-offs, which
absorb the increased revenues that renewal is supposed to
create for the city. Anderson reports that, instead of the anticipated four dollars for every public dollar, private investments have only just matched the public subsidies, and even
the money for luxury housing has come forth largely because
of federal subsidies. Thus, all too few of the new projects have
produced tax gains and returned suburbanites, or generated
the magic rebuilding boom.

Anderson goes on to argue that during the fifteen years of
the federal urban renewal program, the private housing
market has achieved what urban renewal has failed to do. Between 1950 and 1960, twelve million new dwelling units were
built, and fully six million substandard ones disappeared—all
without government action. The proportion of substandard
housing in the total housing supply was reduced from 37 to
19 per cent, and even among the dwelling units occupied by
non-whites, the proportion of substandard units has dropped
from 72 to 44 per cent. This comparison leads Anderson to
the conclusion that the private market is much more effective
than government action in removing slums and supplying new
housing, and that the urban renewal program ought to be
repealed.

It would appear that Anderson's findings and those of the
other studies I have cited make an excellent case for doing
so. However, a less biased analysis of the figures and a less
tendentious mode of evaluating them than Anderson's leads
to a different conclusion. To begin with, Anderson's use of
nationwide statistics misses the few good renewal projects,
those which have helped both the slum-dwellers and the cities,
or those which brought in enough new taxes to finance other
city services for the poor. Such projects can be found in small
cities and especially in those where high vacancy rates assured
sufficient relocation housing of standard quality. More important, all the studies I have mentioned deal with projects carried out during the 1950's, and fail to take account of the improvements in urban renewal practice under the Kennedy and
Johnson administrations. Although Anderson's study suppos-

edly covers the period up to 1963, many of his data go no further than 1960. Since then, the federal bulldozer has moved into fewer neighborhoods, and the concept of rehabilitating rather than clearing blighted neighborhoods is more and more being underwritten by subsidized loans. A new housing subsidy program—known as 221(d) (3)—for families above the income ceiling for public housing has also been launched, and in 1964, Congress passed legislation for assistance to relocatees who cannot afford their new rents.

None of this is to say that Anderson would have had to revise his findings drastically if he had taken the pains to update them. These recent innovations have so far been small in scope—only 13,000 units were financed under 221(d) (3) in the first two years—and they still do not provide subsidies sufficient to bring better housing within the price range of the slum residents. In addition, rehabilitation unaccompanied by new construction is nearly useless because it does not eliminate overcrowding. And finally, some cities are still scheduling projects to clear away the non-white poor who stand in the path of the progress of private enterprise. Unfortunately, many cities pay little attention to federal pleas to improve the program, using the local initiative granted them by urban renewal legislation to perpetuate the practices of the 1950's. Yet even with the legislation of the 1960's, the basic error in the original design of urban renewal remains: it is still a method for eliminating the slums in order to "renew" the city, rather than a program for properly rehousing slum-dwellers.

Before going into this crucial distinction, we first need to be clear that private housing is not going to solve our slum problems. In the first place, Anderson conveniently ignores the fact that if urban renewal has benefited anyone, it is private enterprise. Bending to the pressure of the real-estate lobby, the legislation that launched urban renewal in effect required that private developers do the rebuilding, and most projects could therefore get off the drawing board only if they appeared to be financially attractive to a developer. Thus, his choice of a site and his rebuilding plans inevitably took priority over the needs of the slum-dwellers.

It is true that Anderson is not defending private enterprise *per se* but the free market, although he forgets that it only exists today as a concept in reactionary minds and dated economics texts. The costs of land, capital, and construction have long since made it impossible for private developers to build for anyone but the rich, and some form of subsidy is needed to house everyone else. The building boom of the 1950's which Anderson credits to the free market was subsidized by income-tax deductions to homeowners and by F.H.A. and V.A. mortgage insurance, not to mention the federal highway programs that have made the suburbs possible.

To be sure, these supports enabled private builders to put up a great deal of housing for middle-class whites. This in turn permitted well-employed workers, including some non-whites, to improve their own situation by moving into the vacated neighborhoods. Anderson is quite right in arguing that if people earn good wages, they can obtain better housing more easily and cheaply in the not-quite-private market than through urban renewal. But this market is of little help to those employed at low or even factory wages, or the unemployed, or most Negroes who, whatever their earnings, cannot live in the suburbs. In consequence, 44 per cent of all housing occupied by non-whites in 1960 was still substandard, and even with present subsidies, private enterprise can do nothing for these people. As for laissez faire, it played a major role in creating the slums in the first place.

The solution, then, is not to repeal urban renewal, but to transform it from a program of slum clearance and rehabilitation into a program of urban rehousing. This means, first, building low- and moderate-cost housing on vacant land in cities, suburbs, and new towns beyond the suburbs, and also helping slum-dwellers to move into existing housing outside the slums; and then, *after* a portion of the urban low-income population has left the slums, clearing and rehabilitating them through urban renewal. This approach is commonplace in many European countries, which have long since realized that private enterprise can no more house the population and eliminate slums than it can run the post office.

Of course, governments in Europe have a much easier task than ours in developing decent low-income projects. Because they take it for granted that housing is a national rather than a local responsibility, the government agencies are not hampered by the kind of real-estate and construction lobbies which can defeat or subvert American programs by charges of socialism. Moreover, their municipalities own a great deal of the vacant land, and have greater control over the use of private land than do American cities. But perhaps their main advantage is the lack of popular opposition to moving the poor out of the slums and into the midst of the more affluent residents. Not only is housing desperately short for all income groups, but the European class structure, even in Western socialist countries, is still rigid enough so that low- and middle-income groups can live near each other if not next to each other, and still "know their place."

In America, on the other hand, one's house and address are major signs of social status, and no one who has any say in the matter wants people of lower income or status in his neighborhood. Middle-class homeowners use zoning as a way of keeping out cheaper or less prestigious housing, while working-class communities employ less subtle forms of exclusion. Consequently, low-income groups, whatever their creed or color, have been forced to live in slums or near-slums, and to wait until they could acquire the means to move as a group, taking over better neighborhoods when the older occupants were ready to move on themselves.

For many years now, the only source of new housing for such people, and their only hope of escaping the worst slums, has been public housing. But this is no longer a practical alternative. Initiated during the Depression, public housing has always been a politically embattled program; its opponents, among whom the real-estate lobby looms large, first saddled it with restrictions and then effectively crippled it. Congress now permits only 35,000 units a year to be built in the entire country.

The irony is that public housing has declined because, intended only for the poor, it faithfully carried out its mandate. Originally, sites were obtained by slum clearance; after the war, however, in order to increase the supply of low-cost housing, cities sought to build public housing on vacant land. But limited as it was to low-income tenants and thus labeled and stigmatized as an institution of the dependent poor, public housing was kept out of vacant land in the better neighborhoods. This, plus the high cost of land and construction, left housing officials with no other choice but to build high-rise projects on whatever vacant land they could obtain, often next to factories or along railroad yards. Because tenants of public housing are ruled by a set of strict regulations—sometimes necessary, sometimes politically inspired, but always degrading—anyone who could afford housing in the private market shunned the public projects. During the early years of the program, when fewer citizens had that choice, public housing became respectable shelter for the working class and even for the unemployed middle class. After the war, federal officials decided, and rightly so, that public housing ought to be reserved for those who had no other alternative, and therefore set income limits that admitted only the really poor. Today, public housing is home for the underclass—families who earn less than $3000-$4000 annually, many with unstable jobs or none at all, and most of them non-white.

Meanwhile the enthusiasm for public housing has been steadily dwindling and with it, badly needed political support. Newspaper reports reinforce the popular image of public-housing projects as huge nests of crime and delinquency—despite clear evidence to the contrary—and as the domicile of unregenerate and undeserving families whose children urinate only in the elevators. The position of public housing, particularly among liberal intellectuals, has also been weakened by the slurs of the social and architectural aesthetes who condemn the projects' poor exterior designs as "sterile," "monotonous," and "dehumanizing," often in ignorance of the fact that the tightly restricted funds have been allocated mainly to make the apartments themselves as spacious and livable as possible, and that the waiting lists among slum-dwellers who want these apartments remain long. Be that as it may, suburban communities and urban neighborhoods with vacant land are as hostile to public housing as ever, and their opposition is partly responsible for the program's having been cut down to its present minuscule size.

The net result is that low-income people today cannot get out of the slums, either because they cannot afford the subsidized private market, or because the project they could afford cannot be built on vacant land. There is only one way to break through this impasse, and that is to permit them equal access to new subsidized, privately built housing by adding another subsidy to make up the difference between the actual rent and what they can reasonably be expected to pay. Such a plan, giving them a chance to choose housing like all other citizens, would help to remove the stigma of poverty and inferiority placed on them by public housing. Many forms of rent subsidy have been proposed, but the best one, now being tried in New York, is to put low- and middle-income people in the same middle-income project with the former getting the same apartments at smaller rentals.

Admittedly, this approach assumes that the poor can live with the middle class and that their presence and behavior will not threaten their neighbors' security or status. No one knows whether this is really possible, but experiments in education, job training, and social-welfare programs do show that many low-income people, when once offered *genuine* opportunities to improve their lives and given help in making use of them, are able to shake off the hold of the culture of poverty. Despite the popular stereotype, the proportion of those whom Hylan Lewis calls the clinical poor, too ravaged emotionally by poverty and deprivation to adapt to new opportunities, seems to be small. As for the rest, they only reject programs offering spurious opportunities, like job-training schemes for non-existent jobs. Further, anyone who has lived in a slum neighborhood can testify that whatever the condition of the building, most women keep their apartments clean by expenditures of time and effort inconceivable to the middle-class housewife. Moving to a better apartment would require little basic cultural change from these women, and rehousing is thus a type of new opportunity that stands a better chance of succeeding than, say, a program to inculcate new child-rearing techniques.

We have no way of telling how many slum-dwellers would be willing to participate in such a plan. However poor the condition of the flat, the slum is home, and for many it provides the support of neighboring relatives and friends, and a cultural milieu in which everyone has the same problems and is therefore willing to overlook occasional disreputable behavior. A middle-income project cannot help but have a middle-class ethos, and some lower-class people may be fearful of risking what little stability they have achieved where they are now in exchange for something new, strange, demanding, and potentially hostile. It would be hard to imagine an unwed Negro mother moving her household to a middle-income project full of married couples and far removed from the mother, sisters, and aunts who play such an important role in the female-centered life of lower-class Negroes. However, there are today a large number of stable two-parent families who live in the slums only because income and race exclude them from the better housing that is available. Families like these would surely be only too willing to leave the Harlems and Black Belts. They would have to be helped with loans to make the move, and perhaps even with grants to buy new furniture so as not to feel ashamed in their new surroundings. They might be further encouraged by being offered income-tax relief for giving up the slums, just as we now offer such relief to people who give up being renters to become homeowners.

Undoubtedly there would be friction between the classes, and the more affluent residents would likely want to segregate themselves and their children from neighbors who did not toe the middle-class line, especially with respect to child-rearing. The new housing would therefore have to be planned to allow some voluntary social segregation for both groups, if only to make sure that enough middle-income families would move in (especially in cities where there was no shortage of housing for them). The proportion of middle- and low-income tenants would have to be regulated not only to minimize the status fears of the former, but also to give the latter enough peers to keep them from feeling socially isolated and without emotional support when problems arise. Fortunately, non-profit and limited dividend institutions, which do not have to worry about showing an immediate profit, are now being encouraged to build moderate-income housing; they can do a more careful job of planning the physical and social details of this approach than speculative private builders.

If the slums are really to be emptied and their residents properly housed elsewhere, the rehousing program will have to be extended beyond the city limits, for the simple reason that that is where most of the vacant land is located. This means admitting the low-income population to the suburbs; it also means creating new towns—self-contained communities with their own industry which would not, like the suburbs, be dependent on the city for employment opportunities, and could therefore be situated in presently rural areas. Federal support for the construction of new towns was requested as part of the 1964 Housing Act, and although Congress refused to pass it, the legislation will come up again in 1965.[4]

To be sure, white middle-class suburbanites and rural residents are not likely to welcome non-white low-income people into their communities even if the latter are no longer clearly labeled as poor. The opposition to be expected in city neighborhoods chosen for mixed-income projects would be multiplied a hundredfold in outlying areas. Being politically autonomous, and having constituencies who are not about to support

[4] Meanwhile, several private developers are planning new towns (for example, James Rouse who is building Columbia near Baltimore, and Robert Simon who has already begun Reston, outside Washington) in which they propose to house some low-income people.

measures that will threaten their security or status in the slightest, the suburbs possess the political power to keep the rehousing program out of their own vacant lots, even if they cannot stop the federal legislation that would initiate it. On the other hand, experience with the federal highway program and with urban renewal itself has demonstrated that few communities can afford to turn down large amounts of federal money. For instance, New York City is likely to build a Lower Manhattan Expressway in the teeth of considerable local opposition, if only because the federal government will pay 90 per cent of the cost and thus bring a huge sum into the city coffers. If the rehousing program were sufficiently large to put a sizable mixed-income project in every community, and if the federal government were to pick up at least 90 per cent of the tab, while also strengthening the appeal of the program by helping to solve present transportation, school, and tax problems in the suburbs, enough political support might be generated to overcome the objections of segregationist and class-conscious whites.

Yet even if the outlying areas could be persuaded to cooperate, it is not at all certain that slum-dwellers would leave the city. Urban renewal experience has shown that for many slum-dwellers, there are more urgent needs than good housing. One is employment, and most of the opportunities for unskilled or semi-skilled work are in the city. Another is money, and some New York City slum residents recently refused to let the government inspect—much less repair their buildings because they would lose the rent reductions they had received previously. If leaving the city meant higher rents, more limited access to job possibilities, and also separation from people and institutions which give them stability, some slum residents might very well choose overcrowding and dilapidation as the lesser of two evils.

These problems would have to be considered in planning a rehousing program beyond the city limits. The current exodus of industry from the city would of course make jobs available to the new suburbanites. The trouble is that the industries now going into the suburbs, or those that would probably be attracted to the new towns, are often precisely the ones which use the most modern machinery and the fewest unskilled workers. Thus, our rehousing plan comes up against the same obstacle—the shortage of jobs—that has frustrated other pro-

grams to help the low-income population and that will surely
defeat the War on Poverty in its present form. Like so many
other programs, rehousing is finally seen to depend on a step
that American society is as yet unwilling to take: the deliberate
creation of new jobs by government action. The building of
new towns especially would have to be coordinated with measures aimed at attracting private industry to employ the prospective residents, at creating other job opportunities, and at
offering intensive training for the unskilled after they have
been hired. If they are not sure of a job before they leave the
city, they simply will not leave.

The same social and cultural inhibitions that make slum
residents hesitant to move into a mixed-income project in the
city would, of course, be even stronger when it came to moving out of the city. These inhibitions might be relaxed by moving small groups of slum residents en masse, or by getting
those who move first to encourage their neighbors to follow.
In any case, new social institutions and community facilities
would have to be developed to help the erstwhile slum-dweller
feel comfortable in his new community, yet without labeling
him as poor.

Despite its many virtues, a rehousing program based on the
use of vacant land on either side of the city limits would not
immediately clear the slums. Given suburban opposition and
the occupational and social restraints on the slum-dwellers
themselves, it can be predicted that if such a program were set
into motion it would be small in size, and that it would pull
out only the upwardly mobile—particularly the young people
with stable families and incomes—who are at best a sizable
minority among the poor. What can be done now to help the
rest leave the slums?

The best solution is a public effort to encourage their moving into existing neighborhoods within the city and in older
suburbs just beyond the city limits. Indeed, a direct rent subsidy like that now given to relocatees could enable people to
obtain decent housing in these areas. This approach has several advantages. It would allow low-income people to be close
to jobs and to move in groups, and it would probably attract
the unwed mother who wanted to give her children a better
chance in life. It would also be cheaper than building new
housing, although the subsidies would have to be large enough
to discourage low-income families from overcrowding—and
thus deteriorating—the units in order to save on rent.

There are, however, some obvious disadvantages as well. For one thing, because non-white low-income people would be moving into presently white or partially integrated areas, the government would in effect be encouraging racial invasion. This approach would thus have the effect of pushing the white and middle-income people further toward the outer edge of the city or into the suburbs. Although some whites might decide to stay, many would surely want to move, and not all would be able to afford to do so. It would be necessary to help them with rent subsidies as well; indeed, they might become prospective middle-income tenants for rehousing projects on vacant land.

Undoubtedly, all this would bring us closer to the all-black city that has already been predicted. For this reason alone, a scheme that pushes the whites further out can only be justified when combined with a rehousing program on vacant land that would begin to integrate the suburbs. But even that could not prevent a further racial imbalance between cities and suburbs.

Yet would the predominantly non-white city really be so bad? It might be for the middle class which needs the jobs, shops, and culture that the city provides. Of course, the greater the suburban exodus, the more likely it would become that middle-class culture would also move to the suburbs. This is already happening in most American cities—obvious testimony to the fact that culture (at least of the middlebrow kind represented by tent theaters and art movie-houses) does not need the city in order to flourish; and the artists who create high culture seem not to mind living among the poor even now.

Non-white low-income people might feel more positive about a city in which they were the majority, for if they had the votes, municipal services would be more attuned to their priorities than is now the case. To be sure, if poor people (of any color) were to dominate the city, its tax revenues would decrease even further, and cities would be less able than ever to supply the high quality public services that the low-income population needs so much more urgently than the middle class. Consequently, new sources of municipal income not dependent on the property tax would have to be found; federal and state grants to cities (like those already paying half the public-school costs in several states) would probably be the principal form. Even under present conditions, in fact, new sources of municipal income must soon be located if the cities are not to collapse financially.

If non-whites were to leave the slums en masse, new ghettos

would eventually form in the areas to which they would move. Although this is undesirable by conventional liberal standards, the fact is that many low-income Negroes are not yet very enthusiastic about living among white neighbors. They do not favor segregation, of course; what they want is a free choice and then the ability to select predominantly non-white areas that are in better shape than the ones they live in now. If the suburbs were opened to non-whites—to the upwardly mobile ones who want integration now—free choice would become available. If the new ghettos were decent neighborhoods with good schools, and if their occupants had jobs and other opportunities to bring stability into their lives, they would be training their children to want integration a generation hence.

In short, then, a workable rehousing scheme must provide new housing on both sides of the city limits for the upwardly mobile minority, and encouragement to move into older areas for the remainder. If, in these ways, enough slum-dwellers could be enabled and induced to leave the slums, it would then be possible to clear or rehabilitate the remaining slums. Once slum areas were less crowded, and empty apartments were going begging, their profitability and market value would be reduced, and urban renewal could take place far more cheaply, and far more quickly. Relocation would be less of a problem, and with land values down, rebuilding and rehabilitation could be carried out to fit the resources of the low-income people who needed or wanted to remain in the city. A semi-suburban style of living that would be attractive to the upper-middle class could also be provided.

At this point, it would be possible to begin to remake the inner city into what it must eventually become—the hub of a vast metropolitan complex of urban neighborhoods, suburbs, and new towns, in which those institutions and functions that have to be at the center—the specialized business districts, the civil and cultural facilities, and the great hospital complexes and university campuses—would be located.

Even in such a city, there would be slums—for people who wanted to live in them, for the clinical poor who would be unable to make it elsewhere, and for rural newcomers who would become urbanized in them before moving on. But it might also be possible to relocate many of these in a new kind of public housing in which quasi-communities would be established to help those whose problems were soluble and to provide at least decent shelter for those who cannot be helped except by letting them live without harassment until we learn how to cure mental illness, addiction, and other forms of self-destructive behavior.

This massive program has much to recommend it, but we must clearly understand that moving the low-income population out of the slums would not eliminate poverty or the other problems that stem from it. A standard dwelling unit can make life more comfortable, and a decent neighborhood can discourage some anti-social behavior, but by themselves, neither can effect radical transformations. What poor people need most are decent incomes, proper jobs, better schools, and freedom from racial and class discrimination. Indeed, if the choice were between a program solely dedicated to rehousing, and a program that kept the low-income population in the city slums for another generation but provided for these needs, the latter would be preferable, for it would produce people who were able to leave the slums under their own steam. Obviously, the ideal approach is one that coordinates the elimination of slums with the reduction of poverty.

As I have been indicating, an adequate rehousing program would be extremely costly and very difficult to carry out. Both its complexity and expense can be justified, however, on several grounds. Morally, it can be argued that no one in the Great Society should have to live in a slum, at least not involuntarily.

From a political point of view, it is urgently necessary to begin integrating the suburbs and to improve housing conditions in the city before the latter becomes an ominous ghetto of poor and increasingly angry Negroes and Puerto Ricans, and the suburbs become enclaves of affluent whites who commute fearfully to a downtown bastion of stores and offices. If the visible group tensions of recent years are allowed to expand and sharpen, another decade may very well see the beginning of open and often violent class and race warfare.

But the most persuasive argument for a rehousing program is economic. Between 50 and 60 per cent of building costs go into wages and create work for the unskilled who are now increasingly unemployable elsewhere. A dwelling unit that costs $15,000 would thus provide as much as $9000 in wages—one-and-a-half years of respectably paid employment for a single worker. Adding four-and-a-half million new low-cost housing units to rehouse half of those in substandard units in 1960 would provide almost seven million man-years of work, and the subsequent renewal of these and other substandard units yet more. Many additional jobs would also be created by the construction and operation of new shopping centers, schools, and other community facilities, as well as the highways and public transit systems that would be needed to serve the new suburbs and towns. If precedent must be cited for using a housing program to create jobs, it should be recalled that public housing was started in the Depression for precisely this reason.

The residential building industry (and the real-estate lobby) would have to be persuaded to give up their stubborn resistance to government housing programs, but the danger of future underemployment, and the opportunity of participating profitably in the rehousing scheme, should either convert present builders or attract new ones into the industry. As for the building trades unions, they have always supported government housing programs, but they have been unwilling to admit non-whites to membership. If, however, the rehousing effort were sizable enough to require many more workers than are now in the unions, the sheer demand for labor—and the enforcement of federal non-discriminatory hiring policies for public works—would probably break down the color barriers without much difficulty.

While the federal government is tooling up to change the urban renewal program into a rehousing scheme, it should also make immediate changes in current renewal practices to remove their economic and social cost from the shoulders of the slum-dwellers. Future projects should be directed at the clearance of *really harmful* slums, instead of taking units that are *run down but not demonstrably harmful* out of the supply of low-cost housing, especially for downtown revitalization and other less pressing community improvement schemes. Occupants of harmful slums, moreover, ought to be rehoused in decent units they can afford. For this purpose, more public housing and 221(d) (3) projects must be built, and relocation and rent assistance payments should be increased to eliminate the expense of moving for the slum-dweller. Indeed, the simplest way out of the relocation impasse is to give every relocatee a sizable grant, like the five-hundred dollars to one thousand dollars paid by private builders in New York City to get tenants out of existing structures quickly and painlessly. Such a grant is not only a real incentive to relocatees but a means of reducing opposition to urban renewal. By itself, however, it cannot reduce the shortage of relocation housing. Where such housing now exists in plentiful supply, renewal ought to move ahead more quickly, but where there is a shortage that cannot be appreciably reduced, it would be wise to eliminate or postpone clearance and rehabilitation projects that require a large amount of relocation.

Nothing is easier than to suggest radical new programs to the overworked and relatively powerless officials of federal and local renewal agencies who must carry out the present law, badly written or not, and who are constantly pressured by influential private interests to make decisions in their favor. Many of these officials are as unhappy with what urban renewal has wrought as their armchair critics and would change the program if they could—that is, if they received encouragement from the White House, effective support in getting new legislation through Congress, and, equally important, political help at city halls to incorporate these innovations into local programs. But it should be noted that little of what I have suggested is very radical, for none of the proposals involves conflict with the entrenched American practice of subsidizing private enterprise to carry out public works at a reasonable profit. The proposals are radical only in demanding an end to our no less entrenched practice of punishing the poor. Yet they also make sure that middle-class communities are rewarded financially for whatever discomfort they may have to endure.

Nor are these suggestions very new. Indeed, only last month President Johnson sent a housing message to Congress which proposes the payment of rent subsidies as the principal method for improving housing conditions. It also requests federal financing of municipal services for tax-starved communities, and aid toward the building of new towns. These represent bold and desirable steps toward the evolution of a federal rehousing program. Unfortunately, however, the message offers little help to those who need it most. Slum-dwellers may be pleased that there will be no increase in urban renewal activity, and that relocation housing subsidies and other grants are being stepped up. But no expansion of public housing is being requested, and to make matters worse, the new rent subsidies will be available only to households above the income limits for public housing. Thus, the President's message offers no escape for the mass of the non-white low-income population from the ghetto slums; in fact it threatens to widen the gap between such people and the lower-

middle-income population which will be eligible for rent
subsidies.

On the other hand, as in the case of the War on Poverty, a
new principle of government responsibility in housing is being
established, and evidently the President's strategy is to obtain
legislative approval for the principle by combining it with a
minimal and a minimally controversial program for the first
year. Once the principle has been accepted, however, the program must change quickly. It may have taken fifteen years
for urban renewal even to begin providing some relief to the
mass of slum-dwellers, but it cannot take that long again to
become a rehousing scheme that will give them significant
help. The evolution of federal policies can no longer proceed
in the leisurely fashion to which politicians, bureaucrats, and
middle-class voters have become accustomed, for unemployment, racial discrimination, and the condition of our cities are
becoming ever more critical problems, and those who suffer
from them are now considerably less patient than they have
been in the past.

URBAN RENEWAL: CONTROVERSY*

George M. Raymond, Malcolm D. Rivkin, Herbert J. Gans

GEORGE M. RAYMOND

Recognizing that all urban slums should not necessarily be replaced by low-rent or subsidized middle-income housing in the same location (which is all that the Housing Act of 1937 permitted localities to do), Congress in 1949 enacted a statute designed to make it economically feasible for cities and private enterprise to re-use the cleared land for whatever purpose local governments felt to be in the best interest of their communities. Since it was clear that many relatively disadvantaged families would be displaced in this process, the new law required them to be rehoused in decent, safe, and sanitary dwellings within their means, anywhere in the locality within convenient distance of their places of employment.

The above describes those aspects of the federal urban renewal program that concern clearance and redevelopment. It is difficult to find any similarity between what this program actually is and what Herbert J. Gans has made it seem to be in his astoundingly ill-considered attack.

Mr. Gans begins by berating urban renewal for not having built as many dwelling units as it has demolished. As a close observer of urban renewal projects, however, he must be fully aware that any comparison between the number of apartments demolished and the number subsequently erected in the same areas is totally invalid and irrelevant. Let us see why:

(1) Many areas now occupied by slum housing are unfit for continued residential use (for reasons such as their being surrounded by industry, subject to flooding, etc.).

(2) Other areas are peculiarly suited to that expansion of schools and hospitals which is so essential to their ability to supply the services demanded by our growing population.

(3) Many slum areas tightly surround our cities' obsolete business districts, and are badly needed to facilitate the expansion of the latter.

(4) Slum housing frequently needs to be removed to make

* FROM *Commentary* (July 1965), pp. 72–80 (selected portions).

way for the new schools, parks, and playgrounds that are so essential to the upgrading of our cities' vast "gray areas."

As a result of such factors, the public interest more often than not requires that less land be devoted to residential use after rebuilding than before. Furthermore, existing housing has to be demolished at least two years before new housing becomes available for occupancy. Thus, any comparison between the number of units demolished and the number built at the time of any survey will necessarily *underestimate the program's potential for creating new housing.* Any fair observer, therefore, knows that the only valid comparison between the housing supply antedating renewal and that in existence subsequently, is one that includes all housing built in the community during that period, regardless of location, as well as *all housing that has become available to people in the same income bracket as those displaced, from whatever source* (such as the migration to the suburbs of upwardly mobile white families). In Brooklyn alone, it has been estimated that between 1950 and 1960 half-a-million white persons were replaced by an equal number of generally lower-income non-whites and Puerto Ricans. The units into which these newcomers moved represented a net addition to the housing supply available to lower-income minority families. Mr. Gans has failed to take any of these well-known facts into consideration.

Strangely enough, Mr. Gans admits that the data on which he relied were supplied by Martin Anderson, author of *The Federal Bulldozer,* and characterized by Mr. Gans as "an ultra-conservative economist and often irresponsible polemicist." How, then, can he defend his use of the slanted, incomplete, and poorly digested data from such a discredited source? The answer to this question is quite clear: were Mr. Gans to use reliable data, his case against urban renewal would collapse. Let me illustrate.

An incredibly large proportion of all families displaced by urban renewal are being relocated in decent, safe, and sanitary dwellings. (Admittedly, this was not the case with many families displaced by previous programs, which were not required by law to provide relocation housing.) While local public agencies had claimed that some 84 per cent of all families had been adequately rehoused, the studies cited by Mr. Gans maintained that as many as 70 per cent were merely rehoused in other slums. However, a recently completed impartial survey by the Bureau of the Census found that 94 per cent of those displaced families whose move could be traced (or more than 75 per cent of the total sample) were relocated in standard dwellings. This was accomplished even though 40 per cent of these families had an income of under $3,000! Thus it appears that the claims of local agencies were much closer to the truth than those of the detractors of urban renewal.

Mr. Gans cites a Chicago study to the effect that rents rose from 35 per cent of family income before relocation, to 46 per cent afterward. The above-mentioned Census survey, however, reported that the median proportion of income spent for rent rose by only 3 per cent, from 25 to 28 per cent. It must be noted that the Chicago study dealt with public housing, rather than urban renewal and relocation; in any event it was made in 1957, eight years ago, and long before the improved housing programs and relocation procedures—which Mr. Gans himself cites—could possibly have taken effect.

Mr. Gans accuses the program of having spent only *one-half of one per cent* (the italics are his) of all federal expenditures for urban renewal between 1949 and 1964 on the relocation of families and individuals, but he admits that the proportion rises to 2 per cent if direct relocation payments are included. One must question the basic relevance of these figures. The one-half of one per cent represents only the cost of the local public agencies' administration of relocation programs. It does not include any of the federal subsidies involved either in the construction and operation of low-rent public housing into which many families were relocated, or in the advance of below-market interest rate loans to private builders of middle-income housing. It also omits the non-federal subsidies offered by local communities in the form of tax abatement, social services, relocation bonuses, etc. In the aggregate, these expenditures represent many times the amount claimed by Mr. Gans to be the only public assistance extended to relocated families.

Urban renewal is of no assistance to cities, Mr. Gans suggests, because "the average project has taken twelve years to complete." What he fails to point out is that a project can be 99 per cent finished, and yet be carried on the books for years as incomplete. In New York City, this is the case with such projects as Lincoln Square or Penn Station South, which have been paying taxes for years. Furthermore, in many projects, the first building erected returns many times the taxes paid by the entire project area before renewal. (A recent example is the Medical Tower office building *which occupies only 2.5 acres* of a 35-acre renewal project in Norfolk, Virginia, *and which returns twice the amount of taxes previously paid by the entire area.*) Thus, even though only partially completed, a renewal project can begin to help the city meet not only the remaining cost of the project itself, but also its many other pressing obligations.

Mr. Gans accuses urban renewal of falling short of expectations because private investments, which were to exceed public expenditures by four times, have barely matched the latter. But here again, we are confronted with a comparison made at a time when the major portion of all public expenditures designed to prepare the site for private development has already been committed, while private investment in the new buildings is only beginning to be made. For an accurate picture of the position of private vs. public investment, one has to look at individual projects. Thus, in New Haven's Oak Street Project, *assessments* (which represent only a fraction of actual construction costs) have increased from $2 million to $16.6 million, while the total public cost has been only $5 million. (Incidentally, this project, which now pays eight times the taxes collected from the area before renewal, is still listed as "incomplete.") In Hartford, Connecticut, Constitution Plaza will be assessed at $46 million as against the previous $9 million; the total public cost is $10.4 million. Since these figures are very easy to obtain, it is strange that Mr. Gans relies on Anderson's admittedly biased data.

Between 1950 and 1960, Mr. Gans claims, "six million substandard dwellings disappeared—all without government action." The sad fact is that the decade began, and ended, with 4.1 million dilapidated units, and that some 15 million Americans continue to live in them. As a sociologist and planner, Mr. Gans should know full well that during this period the Bureau of the Census adopted a fundamental change in definitions relating to substandard housing, and that therefore his startling statistic is due to what can most charitably be described as mere sleight-of-hand, rather than to a dramatic conversion to the paths of righteousness by the nation's slum landlords.

So much for the shaky and sometimes obviously biased foundations of Mr. Gans's case against urban renewal. It is strange that he continues to beat the dead horse of the program as it was run in the 1950's, even though he recognizes that the many changes effected under the Kennedy and Johnson administrations have given it a new direction. He must surely know that the effect of new legislation on a program that takes years to mature will not be felt for four or five years. And yet, he makes no effort either to project the effect of these changes into the future, or to understand the extent to which they may vitiate much of his criticism. His constant use of data which, given his own questioning of the source, he must know to be untrue, disqualifies him as a dispassionate observer or objective scientist. For the true marks of a scientist are his ability to survive that "great tragedy of Science—the slaying of a beautiful hypothesis by an ugly fact" (T. H. Huxley), and his readiness to build a more advanced hypothesis upon its ruins. By contrast, Mr. Gans seems to be unable to abandon discredited theories, even if he has to resort to outright distortion of facts in order to hold on to them.

Before turning to Mr. Gans's proposed solution to some of the most complex and danger-laden social problems of our time, let us examine the reasons for the difficulties in the path of urban renewal. Anyone who has ever tried to set an urban renewal project in motion knows that the main reason for its bogging down is the relocation problem. By this is meant not the absence of housing or of means to develop needed housing, but the totally unbending refusal of the white community to accept any Negro settlement in its midst. The task is further complicated by the fact that many sites which are proposed for the construction of new housing are not acceptable to the Negro leadership because these sites fail to further racial integration. Under these circumstances, the only dynamic force for at least some integration in housing is a community desire to undertake urban renewal. The community is motivated by the very reasons at which Mr. Gans is so prepared to sneer, including the addition of new tax revenues to its dwindling coffers, the revitalization of its downtown areas, and the halting of the exodus of middle-class whites to the suburbs. Many early projects, begun shortly after the enactment of the basic legislation in 1949, actually did concentrate on the worst slums, as Mr. Gans would have all of them do. But instead of achieving the results he desires, these projects remained vacant for years because sites still surrounded by slums do not attract private developers.

The second major source of opposition to urban renewal

are the slumlords, who frequently hide behind the arguments so generously supplied by Gans, Anderson, et al. In many communities, large and small, the poor are now exploited to the point where the shacks in which they live bring 25 to 30 per cent net profit to the owners. No wonder, therefore, that these "real-estate investors" oppose the cities' efforts at slum-clearance.

In the light of these serious difficulties, how relevant are Mr. Gans's proposals? He would like all slum-clearance efforts to be stopped until the suburbs are ready to accept in their midst "groups of slum residents en masse," together with all the "new social institutions and community facilities [needed] to help the erstwhile slum-dweller feel comfortable in his new community." Somehow, he also expects to make it possible for these "erstwhile slum-dwellers" to be moved into their new environments without being labeled as poor—which can only be interpreted to mean that they will be discreetly provided with not only housing and furniture on a par with their middle-income neighbors, but also with a continuing income equal to theirs. Given this country's traditional economic stance, it is quite doubtful that our government is about to embrace the doctrine of "from each according to his ability, to each according to his needs," which would have to provide the basis for any income policy whereby erstwhile slum-dwellers could be supplied with an instant middle-income. As for the chance of moving low-income Negroes into the suburbs, Mr. Gans himself recognizes that this would be a hundredfold more difficult than moving them into middle-income, white, city neighborhoods. Since even this, less difficult, objective has proven well-nigh impossible to accomplish, Mr. Gans's vision has all the marks of an unattainable utopia.

But the most incredible of Mr. Gans's proposals is that the federal government should accelerate the transformation of our cities into predominantly, or even exclusively, Negro enclaves. He even goes so far as to suggest that poor whites who wish to move from areas inhabited by Negroes should be given a subsidy to enable them to move to new housing on the city's outskirts! This proposal is based on the romantic notion that "non-white low-income people might feel more positive about a city in which they were the majority, for if they had the votes, municipal services would be more attuned to their priorities than is now the case." This presupposes that the City of the Poor will be governed by philosopher-kings, rather than by the kind of politician who usually rises to rule the poor and ignorant. After all, venal leadership of cities in which the poor or near-poor, of whatever color, are a majority is not a novelty on our political scene: Jersey City produced not Woodrow Wilson, but Frank Hague. The priorities under the latter's enlightened leadership did little for the poor—except, of course, for the well-publicized turkey on Thanksgiving.

Cities deprived of their upper and middle classes, and thus composed chiefly of the poor, would inevitably entail a serious deterioration in the quality of our entire civilization, since it is the *cities*, not the suburbs, that have always carried and nurtured this precious, complex heritage. Mr. Gans's failure to grasp such a fundamental point leads him to proposals which are truly subversive, in the best sense of that word. In his legitimate concern with the problems of the poor, he is much too ready to sacrifice the city.

Furthermore, he himself admits that cities inhabited exclusively by the poor will not be able to raise the huge amounts of money required for necessary services. How realistic is it to believe that the federal government will then be ready to provide massive aid, considering that even now what is forthcoming from that source is a mere pittance when compared with the vastness of the need?

In Mr. Gans's vision of America's future city, the low-income Negroes will be able to occupy the housing in better neighborhoods vacated by all the whites and a large number of the "upwardly mobile," highly educated, and highly skilled Negroes, who will have moved to the suburbs. This process, he says, will leave so many vacant units in the old slum areas as to make it relatively easy and inexpensive to tear them down, and to turn these areas into "the hub[s] of . . . vast metropolitan complex[es] of urban neighborhoods, suburbs, and new towns. . . ." In theory, perhaps: but in real life one needs to ask a few additional questions. What would happen if the rate of new construction were to fail to keep pace with population growth? Or if the migration of the unassimilated poor to the city continued, or even increased? Would these factors not tend to keep the slums, by then fully segregated, occupied indefinitely? And at the end of the decades it would take for this process to consummate itself, what is to guarantee that the centers of cities would still be there to be salvaged? What assurance is there that the middle class, by then totally suburbanized, would continue to brave the daily trip across the angry, seething, indigent "black belt," rather than decentralize those functions which now make that trip, already excessively difficult, necessary?

As for the "hard-core," multi-problem families and socially deviant, self-destructive individuals—whose presence frequently holds up completion of renewal projects for many months, if not years, and which is, in part, responsible for the poor image of much public housing—Mr. Gans has an easy answer. For the mentally ill, the dope addict, the habitual prostitute, etc., he would either leave the existing slums, or set up "a new kind of public housing . . . quasi-communities . . . to provide at least decent shelter for those who cannot be helped . . . until we learn how to cure" their ills. This has often been advanced as the "halfway house": a settlement saturated with social services, from which families might be able to move to normal public housing if they could overcome their anti-social or self-destructive behavior. Up to now it has been rejected by those in positions of responsibility, not for lack of thought, but because it runs counter to our democratic ethos and because it much resembles the idea of "caring" for undesirables in concentration camps.

No reasonable person will resist any possible improvement of the renewal program. But notwithstanding the misleading appeal of Mr. Gans's oversimplified, hollow, and totally impractical arguments, his proposals do not amount to any program of action which lies in the realm of the possible. A clue to the nature of his confusion is furnished by his statement that "what poor people need most are decent incomes, proper jobs, better schools, and freedom from racial and class discrimination." "Indeed," he continues, "if the choice were between a program solely dedicated to rehousing, and a program that kept the low-income population in the city slums for another generation but provided for these needs, the latter would be preferable, for it would produce people who were able to leave the slums under their own steam." But unfortunately, the only choice open to us is between leaving the poor in their slums, and supplying some of them with decent housing in good neighborhoods. Dr. Robert C. Weaver, the nation's Housing Administrator and one of its foremost urban scholars, has observed that while it is true that good housing "is not itself a remedy for a family's ills . . . [it] does offer the environment in which many . . . family problems can be successfully treated." Besides, as Mr. Gans recognizes, the renewal program constantly brings problems out in the open which our society has previously been content to sweep under the rug. For example, much of the impetus for the war on poverty can be attributed to the difficulties discovered in the path of urban renewal. Also, as Mr. Gans himself points out, the construction activity which can be generated by housing and urban-renewal programs could well contribute to creating a level of employment which would include jobs for many of the unemployed poor.

Most tragically, Mr. Gans either does not know, or has forgotten, what slums are like, and what cruel effects they have on those who live in them. While doing his research for *The Urban Villagers,* he acted as a "participant observer." He may or may not have done the same in a New York City slum neighborhood. Dan Wakefield did, and this is how he described the vast gulf between the meaning of the slum to a participant observer and to a slum-dweller:

> I cannot know the slums or hate them as profoundly as Alicia does because I wasn't born there. I am able to hate them and know them in some small way because of the brief time I lived in Alicia's neighborhood. I cannot approach the abyss of her understanding because no matter what happened I knew I could always escape; I was only a visitor. There were times, though, when I tried with an effort of imagination to extend my experience to that of my neighbors. There were times when I came home tired, late at night, on 100th Street, and climbed the stairs and opened the door of my room and turned the light on and watched the sudden scurry of the cockroaches that moved on the paint-chipped kitchen wall like the scattered filings of a magnet controlled by some invisible force. I would close the door and take a deep breath of the stale, heavy air, and then suddenly I would remember that after all, this wasn't my real home—I would later move on to some clean, well-lighted place like the ones I had lived in before. But then I would close my eyes and concentrate and try to imagine that this was my home and would always be my home and that the clean, well-lighted places of the world were forever closed to me. Most of the time I could not believe it; I could feel nothing. Sometimes, though, for the briefest instant, I could catch a flicker of the nightmare that was the only reality for every other human being beneath that roof. I could feel the enclosure of the flaking walls and see through the window the blackened reflection of the tenement across the street that blocked out the world beyond. But it was only a glimpse.

The participant observer can afford to wait for the elimination of slums. For him there is less urgency about that than about trying to make the world fit his preconceptions. Unhappily, Mr. Gans's vision of a world where poor Negroes are welcomed to the suburbs is a mirage. Thousands of years ago, a world was envisioned in which "the wolf shall dwell with the lamb, and the leopard shall lie down with the kid," but it has not yet come to pass.

Must we, then, have the slums always with us, as we seem fated to have the poor?

I do not mean to suggest that we should resign ourselves to the status quo, nor do I mean to deny that Mr. Gans is clearly motivated by a deep dedication to the cause of the downtrodden. As is well known from several millennia of experience, however, it takes more than dedication to help improve the condition of the poor. Certainly, two basic prerequisites are an ability to distinguish reality from wishful thinking, and a willingness—in the words of President Johnson—to "deal with the world as it is, if it is ever to be as we wish." That may be more difficult than spinning dreams of utopias, but it is essential if the necessary job is to be done.

MALCOLM D. RIVKIN

Herbert J. Gans is probably the most sensitive critic of urban renewal writing today. His measured analysis in COMMENTARY reflects intimate familiarity with the program and its problems. Unlike those critics who would scrap urban renewal, Mr. Gans sees a prospect for adapting the present machinery—with significant changes—in order to ameliorate severe social problems of contemporary urban society. His proposals for federal action are sound and realistic enough to be enacted by our urban-minded President and a cooperative Congress.

But Mr. Gans has oversimplified the solutions by seeking too hard for a *deus ex machina* in the form of federal intervention. Overstating the possibilities of the federal role in urban renewal, he diverts our attention from the real source of difficulty: the ruling elite of individual American cities. Basically, the city councils, planning boards, renewal authorities, and social institutions of our urban communities determine the kind of renewal that is effected. And regardless of any new federal legislation, these local authorities will continue to dominate the field. Mr. Gans, of course, recognizes local leadership as a problem, but he fails to emphasize the prime responsibility it bears. The following points must therefore be noted:

(1) The present urban-renewal legislation, even as it stands, is not bad legislation. It does not encourage segregation or the destruction of salvable minority-group housing. It may indeed place insufficient emphasis on rehabilitation, on combining better housing with better employment opportunities, and on other socially-motivated programs which I join Mr. Gans in desiring. But such projects can today be undertaken as part of the regular renewal activity, as special demonstration programs, or in combination with other federal and state aid programs that are already available to local municipalities. Renewal depends mainly on what the *community* wants. The present legislation is broad in concept. It does set guidelines, and its accompanying administrative regulations (often cumbersome, to be sure) do establish detailed technical criteria and standards, but these guidelines and standards are applied to projects initiated by the local communities themselves. HHFA has respected the existing division between federal and local powers to a degree not commonly appreciated by the critics of "growing federal control." Before a project even comes to the federal authorities for approval and allocation of funds, it has been drafted by local planners, approved by the City Council after public hearings, and endorsed as harmonious with community interests by a "representative" advisory committee of civic leaders. It is difficult if not impossible for the federal authorities to reject out of hand a technically sound proposal that has received full support from the official and articulate elements of the community—especially when the project violates no civil-rights or other law.

I remember the genesis of one particular project in a middle-sized New England city. A small three-acre parcel of land near a well-to-do residential area had been scheduled for clearance. The renewal planners and the City Council considered a number of alternative uses for the land. It could be employed for public housing, or a limited-dividend project for middle-income families, or a high-rise, high-rent development that would bring significant revenues to the city by way of property taxes and tenant purchasing power. The federal authorities would have approved any of the feasible projects. Much citizen activity was generated, and a heated debate ensued. Finally, the local planners and the City Council (after a public hearing) opted for the high-rent, high tax-paying alternative. As this was the local decision, endorsed by the community leadership, the project (which met all the necessary technical specifications) was approved by HHFA.

(2) Excellent, socially-motivated projects—stemming from local initiative and community leadership, not federal decree —have been accomplished under the present urban-renewal program. I am thinking particularly of New Haven, which— under the forceful guidance of Mayor Richard Lee—has both increased its tax base and provided stable middle- and lower-income housing. New Haven's techniques have included rehabilitation as well as new construction. It has pioneered in the use of rent subsidies under a demonstration grant from HHFA, and it has gone far toward using urban renewal as a means of fostering integrated neighborhoods. New Haven's success, although not complete, has occurred under the same federal legislation that has elsewhere led to excesses of clearance and luxury housing. But New Haven's leaders wanted something better for their city.

(3) Current federal activity (in the poverty program and area redevelopment) is placing more rather than less emphasis on local responsibility. This is a harbinger of things to come. The Office of Economic Opportunity requires locally staffed and planned Community Action Programs as the prerequisite for much of its assistance. Although it tries to secure the "involvement of the poor" in the framing of such programs, OEO can act only on plans produced by local agencies. Area development assistance efforts in Appalachia and elsewhere are based on the premise that the states or areas in question will themselves decide on what is needed. I do not believe that we can realistically expect any "new look" in urban renewal—no matter how enlightened it is at the federal level—to diverge from this increasing emphasis on local and state decision-making.

Nor can I agree with Mr. Gans that the carrot of heavy federal financial assistance will be so tempting that communities will lightly do away with long-held prejudices in order to collect large sums of "free" money. We must recognize that the alacrity with which local communities seize 90-10 federal highway funds for expressways is not due to the money's being there for the having, but rather to powerful pressure groups within these communities—from the average auto owner to the trucking associations—who want to drive on good roads. There must be such pressure from within. I agree completely with Mr. Gans on the need for new federal legislation and on its content, but unless community attitudes change, this legislation will not be worth the paper on which it is printed.

The difficulty of producing this change constitutes the real roadblock to effective renewal, and leadership by federal example is at best a partial answer. At present, the fear of Negro movement into white neighborhoods is deep-rooted and strong among both suburbanites and well-to-do central city residents. Moreover, the continuing erosion of downtown tax bases and the crazy-quilt system of municipal revenue, make high tax-producing renewal projects of particular—and understandable—importance to city authorities. Until, however, integrated neighborhoods and good housing for the poor become local political issues of equal or greater significance than the tax base, very little change will occur—regardless of new federal laws. This does not mean the situation is hopeless. There are signs of growing articulateness in the Negro communities of Chicago, Washington, and other cities where Negro population and Negro incomes are both rising. This expression of concern will, one hopes, be channeled into a constructive force. The growing number of foundations and OEO-supported community action organizations, such as Community Progress in New Haven and the United Planning Organization in Washington, can certainly contribute to this process. By helping the poor to define their own needs and desires, these organizations can begin to express demands which political leaders will be unable to ignore. But the process will be slow and arduous.

HERBERT J. GANS

Professor Raymond's argument in support of present urban renewal policies is an extremely complex one, but it may be summarized as follows. Slums ought to be cleared to meet the need for new schools, hospitals, recreational facilities, and expanded business districts. On the one hand, urban renewal can proceed without replacing the cleared units, because of the white exodus to the suburbs, and because improved relocation procedures are providing enough better housing for displaced poor non-whites. On the other hand, urban renewal cannot proceed, because whites refuse to let non-whites move into their neighborhoods and relocation is therefore impossible. It is, however, subversive to help non-whites move into such neighborhoods, nor does the answer lie in public-housing projects, which are too much like concentration camps. Nevertheless, something ought to be done, for slums are extremely harmful to their occupants. The solution consists of "supplying some of [the slum-dwellers] with decent housing in good neighborhoods" which requires "the ability to distinguish reality from wishful thinking and a willingness . . . 'to deal with the world as it is' "—or as President Johnson says it is.

Since it is impossible to deal with such an argument, I will confine myself to comments on some of Mr. Raymond's individual charges. I did not say that urban renewal had to replace demolished low-cost housing in the same area; I merely said that in cities where such housing is in short supply, renewal ought to be halted—regardless of how many whites leave Brooklyn. Even though Mr. Raymond thinks it is more important to provide community facilities for gray areas and to build stores in downtown districts that already have too many vacancies, than it is to provide housing for displaced slum-dwellers, the latter do have to live somewhere.

Perhaps they could build shacks out of all the government reports which demonstrate the high quality of relocation procedures. The latest such document, just issued by the Bureau of the Census and cited by Mr. Raymond, may be impartial but it is also inconclusive. Unlike the studies I drew on, which describe what happened to *all* the residents of an urban renewal area after their displacement, the Census study only dealt with people who had actually been relocated by 132 local agencies during a three-month period in 1964. However, anyone who has ever worked in an urban-renewal agency knows that many slum-dwellers flee from a project area when renewal is announced; others leave before they can be interviewed by renewal officials; and yet others depart before they can be offered relocation aid. A high proportion of all these premature movers go to other slums. According to a report of the New York City Department of Relocation, for example, 47 per cent of the slum-dwellers in the urban-renewal area of the Upper West Side left between the early months of 1963, when the city took title to the area, and at the end of the same year, when it started relocation activities. The Census report, in other words, covers only a portion of those displaced. The premature flight of so many slum-dwellers is not entirely the fault of urban-renewal procedures, but it must be taken into account in any honest evaluation of relocation.

I did not—and still do not—question the possibility that in cities where inexpensive housing is plentiful, humane relocation is taking place. But we still need reliable studies to prove this, especially in the case of big cities. Moreover, there is a similar lack of evidence concerning the amount of rent increase paid by the relocatees.

If relocation is as beneficial as local and federal officials are constantly trying to prove, why are slum-dwellers—who live in blight and misery and who want better housing—so opposed to urban renewal? Is it because they are participant observers "who can afford to wait for the elimination of slums," or "socially deviant, self-destructive individuals" who enjoy holding up the completion of renewal projects? Or is it possibly because they have too many relatives and friends who have suffered from urban renewal?

And, indeed, how could it be otherwise, given the meager public-housing program, the shortage of other relocation housing, and the niggardly sums spent for relocation? Mr. Raymond seems pleased that fully 2 per cent of all federal renewal funds are allocated for relocation payments, but the fact is that 1.5 per cent of these funds is spent for payments to relocated *businesses*. Displaced residents, therefore, receive only one-half of one per cent, which is what I indicated in my article. Moreover, this figure refers to actual relocation payments by the federal government, and not to local administrative costs, as Mr. Raymond claims. The other benefits he mentions accrue to middle-income relocatees, and, according to the Census report cited above, the "many families" who move into public housing turn out to be exactly 13 per cent of all those people actually relocated by local agencies.

There have, of course, been some projects which have brought higher taxes to their cities, and I said as much. I also said that federal renewal and relocation policies had improved immeasurably since the end of the Eisenhower administration. But in too many cities local agencies are still proposing renewal projects which call for the displacement of large numbers of slum-dwellers into non-existent relocation housing, and—as Mr. Rivkin points out—the federal government cannot seem to stop them. I know of one Eastern city in which a luxury apartment house, built as part of an urban-renewal program, still stands almost half empty; nevertheless, there has recently been a proposal for a huge new upper-income project that will consume much of that city's federal quota of renewal funds for the next decade. In another city, rehabilitation is being used to help a Negro middle-class area oust its poor neighbors; and Columbia University has just persuaded New York City to approve a plan for the removal of many Negro and Puerto Rican residents—without adequate provision for their relocation.

If Mr. Raymond had read my article properly, he would have realized that I am quite aware of the obstacles to renewal created by white opposition to racial integration. If anything is to be done, then, about the slums occupied by non-whites, there are three possible courses of action: to rebuild within the present ghettos; to enable slum residents to move into better neighborhoods outside the ghetto, and into the suburbs as quickly as possible; or to continue the present renewal policy, which does nothing about the ghetto slums, and only lets a few upper-middle-income Negroes move into a handful of integrated projects built on renewal sites.

Mr. Raymond opts for the third solution, and this suggests how much he is really concerned about the slum-dwellers, notwithstanding his quotation from Dan Wakefield. The first solution is bitterly opposed by many Negro leaders, and is in any case impossible at present because new housing cannot be built for ghetto residents until a massive rent subsidy scheme is created for the lowest-income groups, or until the public-housing program, now virtually moribund, is expanded. Since the ghetto's principal blight is overcrowding, new housing cannot be built there without relocation, and many of its occupants will have to be helped to move into other neighborhoods.

Not only does this solution require less rent subsidy than the plan to build new housing within old ghettos, but is also practical, for it merely assists the natural ecological process by which poor people have always bettered their housing conditions. If it entails a further white exodus to the suburbs, many cities will, to be sure, become increasingly non-white, just as a century ago, they became increasingly non-Protestant —and without resulting in the end of democracy or any of the other catastrophes predicted at the time by Mr. Raymond's ideological ancestors. I am not, then, as skeptical as he is of the ability of the poor to choose their own political leaders if they have the power to do so. They will not choose philosopher-kings any more frequently than affluent voters will, and they will rarely choose patricians like Woodrow Wilson. Their politicians might be corrupt, but even corrupt politicians respond to their constituents' demands in order to get re-elected. And since federal politicians are similarly responsive to their constituents, I am sure that the federal government will not stop funneling funds into a city merely because its voters are predominantly poor.

This brings me to the real meaning of Mr. Raymond's solution. In proposing that slum clearance continue despite the difficulties of relocation, he is really maintaining that the most important task is to provide more urban facilities for the upper and middle classes, and that we should not worry too much about the poor since they have always been with us anyway. If the city is not rebuilt for the higher income groups, he argues, there will be "a serious deterioration in the quality of our entire civilization." In short, if the choice is between eliminating poverty and saving civilization, the latter comes first.

Now if this were really the choice, Mr. Raymond might have a point, although one could still argue that a civilization which allows poverty to continue in the midst of affluence is not the "precious heritage" he believes it to be. But this is *not* the choice, and Mr. Raymond is merely repeating another hoary 19th-century cliché. Culture (which is what Professor Raymond seems to mean by civilization) is not intrinsic to cities; it existed there in past centuries because the upper-income groups who supported it—and still support it—happened to live almost entirely in cities. Today this is no longer the case, for the affluent have been living in the suburbs for more than a generation. Thus, if Mr. Raymond were correct, we should now be in the midst of a serious cultural decline, but all evidence suggests the contrary. The only change I can see is that some culture is moving into the suburbs in order to be near its major supporters, and we are now witnessing the emergence of art galleries, theaters, and the like beyond the city limits. Yet no urban concert halls or museums have closed down, though their audiences are heavily suburban too.

Many of those who create culture also live in the suburbs, and there is no evidence that their creativity is thereby impaired. Moreover, the artists who live in the handful of American cities where culture is actually being created (Manhattan, Boston, Chicago, and a few others) seem to be highly productive even though their neighbors are poor and non-white in an increasing number of cases. Manhattan, a world capital rather than the typical American city I was considering, is in no danger of becoming a community of poverty-stricken non-whites. Yet even if it were, I would wager that culture would continue to flourish there, partly because the creators of culture are often poor themselves, but mainly because culture is not as fragile as to be destroyed by residential change. Moreover, if we decided to give poor non-whites an even break, they might even contribute to the creation of better culture and a better civilization.

Mr. Raymond's difficulty is that of the city planner who thinks of the city as a collection of buildings, facilities, and gray areas, but not as a place where people live. What is worse, he only wants to plan for buildings and facilities that are used by upper- and middle-income groups; ignoring the needs of the poor, he is ready to support plans that perpetuate, in Michael Harrington's inimitable phrase, "socialism for the rich and private enterprise for the poor."

One could, of course, simply attribute my disagreement with Mr. Raymond to our opposing views of priorities for governmental action; he favors the rich, and I the poor in what is for all practical purposes a latter-day class struggle. Ironically enough, however, since poverty and discrimination are the primary causes of what is wrong with our cities even by Mr. Raymond's city-planning standards, his proposal to build for the affluent cannot even achieve his own goals. After all, slums exist because too many people cannot afford or cannot get into decent housing. Urban facilities and services are so unsatisfactory because the cities must spend huge sums for welfare and for the protection of property and people against the crime, addiction, and mental illness which are ultimately also produced by poverty and discrimination. Replacing the buildings of the city without solving the problems of their present occupants is thus a spurious proposal. This is why a serious poverty program not only has priority over urban renewal, but why it is also the most effective method of achieving the civilized and beautiful cities that Mr. Raymond, and I, and everyone else desire.

Consequently, his petulant rejection of my proposals as at best utopian and romantic is self-defeating. So, too, is his unwillingness to accept criticism of urban renewal: if it had not been for earlier critics, we might still be saddled with the urban-renewal procedures of the 1950's. His argument is also ultimately irrelevant, for whether he likes it or not, the federal government will eventually have to adopt a rehousing program. I thought I had made it perfectly clear that the change of policy will be difficult and slow, but this does not mean that our facing up to the problem now is either impractical or subversive. Rather, it is the indispensable prerequisite of proper planning.

This is also the crux of my answer to Mr. Rivkin's thoughtful remarks. He is absolutely right, of course, to suggest that the current inadequacies of urban renewal stem principally from local community decisions, and more specifically, from the failure of downtown business and real-estate interests to realize that they must use their power to improve the lot—and the purchasing power—of the low-income population, instead of continuing with useless attempts to lure the middle class back to the city.

It is also true that local autonomy in the expenditure of federal funds is not likely to decrease, although I am not as content with this trend as Mr. Rivkin seems to be. The "downtown influentials" are seldom wise enough to plan beyond their own immediate interests, and until a systematic benefit-cost analysis is made of the New Haven renewal and poverty programs, I am not sure that we can use even that city as a model of local enlightenment. Although its programs are probably the best in the country, there is some evidence that they do not provide much help to the poverty-stricken, and that they are not good enough to cope with New Haven's basic problems.

I believe that the only solution to the present impasse is more federal intervention, and since this cannot be achieved by federal control of local programs, it must be effected by the expenditure of more federal funds. Of course, federal subsidies are now accepted because of local demands and pressures for them, but the availability of new funds would create new local demands. For example, a major impetus for New York's Lower Manhattan Expressway came from the unions who want the jobs that new construction will generate. If a massive federal rehousing program were instituted, and if it were to include proper incentives for both urban and suburban demands, local support for the program would be created. Such support would not develop overnight, but if there is no new federal spending it will not develop at all.

I agree with Mr. Rivkin that local urban-renewal decisions

will improve as Negro voters become more influential in city
politics; even now they have exercised their power to bring
the program to a virtual standstill in some cities. This is of no
help either to themselves or to the cities in which they live,
but only a rehousing program will enroll their support in the
future. I am not as sanguine as Mr. Rivkin, however, about
the contribution of the urban universities. They are, among
other things, real-estate operations, and when it comes to moving poor residents out of university neighborhoods, they act
with the same ruthlessness as other real-estate operations.
They are justifiably concerned with expanding their campuses,
but they also believe, and unjustifiably so, that crime and
blight can be dealt with by moving out as many low-income
residents as possible, however law-abiding they may be. In
this process, they pay little attention to relocation needs.

Nor am I as hopeful as Mr. Rivkin that the urban university will train the next generation of urban politicians and
officials to be aware of the real problems of the cities. They
will do a much better job than in the past, because they did
almost nothing in the past. But up to now, much of the improvement in urban planning and research programs has been
generated by funds from federal agencies and foundations,
and by the greater concern with social justice and social science among the new generation of students in the field of
city planning. Meanwhile, too many professors are still advocat-
ing architectural solutions that benefit mainly the upper-
income groups, and Professor Raymond's remarks provide
depressing evidence that progress is likely to be slow.

VI. NEW DIRECTIONS

Even the most enthusiastic partisans of urban renewal concede the program could benefit from improvements and new ideas, and recently some innovations have been suggested.

The idea receiving the greatest attention is the rent subsidy or rent supplement program. Ever since the first public housing act Congress has been reluctant to appropriate enough money to supply the demand for low-rent housing. As we have seen, housing projects have come under criticism as "new slums" and for their tendency to become racially segregated. Rent subsidies, in theory at least, seem to offer opportunities for putting more people into standard housing and meeting the goal of residential desegregation. The basic notion is simple: Low-income families will rent homes and apartments on the private housing market, and government subsidies to the families will make up the difference between what they can afford to pay and the rent charged. Another variant of the same idea is the rehabilitation of deteriorated housing by a municipality, and the renting of apartments to families with rent subsidies.

The 1961 housing act authorized funds for a demonstration program, and Joel Cogen and Kathryn Feidelson report the experience to date with the New Haven project. One of the conclusions they reach is the necessity for the "careful selection of families to live in scattered housing." Since there seems to be almost universal agreement on the need for selection, a fundamental question arises: To what extent can the rent subsidy program make a meaningful dent in the problem of 12.5 million people who cannot afford the rents of private housing? Moreover, the relative success of the New Haven program is no indication that the same type of program would succeed elsewhere, if only because demonstration programs tend to operate under optimal conditions almost ensuring their success.

The lack of coordination in urban renewal has been a persistent focus of criticism. The Demonstration Cities Program recently suggested by President Johnson is designed to bring some order out of a chaotic situation. He proposes that a city set up one agency to bring all the tools of redevelopment together; administer current services; and coordinate all types of development grants to cities. The concentration of the renewal effort in one agency would allow for a "creative" use of energies and resources. Any city that participates will receive, in addition to the grants it now receives, a further grant of 80 per cent of the cost of the matching funds cities must normally make to receive federal grants. The suggested six-year appropriation amounts to four hundred million dollars a year. In the excerpt we have selected from the testimony of Mayor John V. Lindsay of New York, he dramatically points to the gap between the magnitude of the tasks and the proposed financial support. Lindsay might have added that there is no evidence to support the notion that creativity thrives on economic deprivation.

The Demonstration Cities Program is not the only mechanism aimed at improving coordination. The Urban Renewal Administration now grants money to a community for establishing a Community Renewal Program. "CRP is a method for assessing in broad terms the community's over-all needs for urban renewal and developing a staged program for action to meet these needs, commensurate with the resources available to the community." New York City recently published its Community Renewal Program, which blueprints the "over-all strategy" to be pursued by its renewal program. Neither Richard May, Jr., a city planner, nor Walter Thabit, an architect, are exactly enchanted by the proposals. Their comments would probably apply to any similar document.

At the turn of the century the Englishman, Ebenezer Howard, introduced the idea of the New Town, a planned community to be built outside already established cities. The New Town concept has been very influential in England, and today a significant part of its urban development activities center about the planning and building of New Towns. The idea has had an impact on this country as well; communities like Radburn built during the twenties and the Greenbelt towns of the New Deal era owe their inspiration to the New Town concept. In the past few years there has been a resurgence of interest in New Towns as one means of dealing with some of the problems of urban areas. Several private developers are actively engaged in building New Towns, and perhaps the best known, Reston, Virginia, has already received its first inhabitants.

A bill has been introduced in Congress that would authorize the government to assist in the development of New Towns.

It is interesting to note in Robert Weaver's testimony and in Senator John G. Tower's questioning of Weaver the reappearance of the traditional American ideologies and anxieties. Thus, Weaver, in order to make sure that no one will think the Administration is supporting a program smacking of "socialism," talks of "new communities" rather than New Towns. And, of course, these "new communities" will be built by private enterprise with a minimum of government assistance. Robert Gladstone, in another selection, says a primary advantage of a New Town is the opportunity to plan a community that is designed to be functionally integrated into the structure of a metropolitan area. He also goes beyond Weaver in his anticipations of the role of government. While Weaver sees the role as being minor, Gladstone suggests, on the other extreme, it might be useful for a level of government to build New Towns under its own auspices.

RENTAL ASSISTANCE FOR LARGE FAMILIES:
AN INTERIM REPORT*

Joel Cogen and Kathryn Feidelson

Rental assistance by the government for low-income families in privately owned housing is proving successful in a year-and-a-half old demonstration program in New Haven, Connecticut. The principal conclusion to emerge from New Haven's experimental effort with unusually large families is that the program is administratively feasible, socially sound, financially responsible, and politically acceptable, but that it is not without difficulties. It is a practical supplement to conventional public housing for selected families under prescribed conditions. The New Haven experience thus offers concrete support for major innovations proposed in President Johnson's now-pending housing bill.

STATUTORY PERSPECTIVE

A revitalized and expanded program of publicly assisted housing will have to be among the array of weapons in the new national assault on poverty. 12½ million American families who now live in substandard housing cannot afford to purchase or rent a decent home without public financial assistance. In the words of Housing and Home Finance Administrator Robert C. Weaver, the federal government must "help bring to the impoverished and disadvantaged the kind of homes and physical environment in which the full range of remedial efforts can be successfully applied and achieve lasting results."

To explore means to achieve this objective, Congress, in Section 207 of the Housing Act of 1961, authorized the Housing and Home Finance Administrator to enter into contracts to make grants to public or private bodies or agencies "for the purposes of developing and demonstrating new or improved means of providing housing for low-income persons and families." The amount of grants authorized was $5,000,-

* FROM *Pratt Planning Papers*, June 1964, Vol. 3, No. 1, pp. 9–11, 13–17, 19–21 (selected portions).

000. To date 23 such demonstration grant contracts have been awarded in 18 cities across the nation.

One of the most challenging experiments, utilizing existing housing scattered throughout the community for large families, is being undertaken in four variant forms in Philadelphia, Washington, New York, and New Haven. The Philadelphia Housing Authority is expanding its program of purchase and rehabilitation of existing structures, with special approaches being tried to create units for large families from smaller existing units. Privately-owned single-family dwellings are being leased by the Washington Housing Authority, which then subleases them to eligible large low-income families. The New York Housing Authority is purchasing, rehabilitating, and converting 3-story buildings, with two of the stories being used to create large duplex apartments for families of 10 or more members. The principal distinguishing characteristic of the New Haven experiment is a lease agreement directly between the low-income tenant and his private landlord, with the Housing Authority guaranteeing the lease and paying the difference between the contract rent and a stated percentage of the family's income.

Results of these demonstrations, which have fulfilled many of the theoretical expectations, buttress President Johnson's call for acquisition and lease by local housing authorities of 100,000 existing housing units in the next four years.[1] Since New Haven's demonstration has also wrestled with the long-advocated technique of rental assistance, it supports at the same time the administration's proposal for monthly rental assistance to low-income families displaced by urban renewal for whom no public housing is available.[2]

THE PROBLEM

Large low-income families are one of America's principal "poverty groups" and the most difficult to house. Decent housing units of sufficient size simply do not exist for these families in any significant number and those that do exist are unobtainable at low rents. The high cost of producing such units precludes their construction in the private market and militates strongly against their construction in public housing projects.

---

[1] Secs. 404 and 405 of the proposed Housing and Community Development Act of 1964.

[2] Sec. 101 of the proposed Housing Act would authorize payments to these families for up to 2 years following their displacement.

The difficulties of housing this segment of our population are so great that new approaches to solve the problem must receive wide attention.

NEW HAVEN'S DEMONSTRATION

New Haven is a fitting scene for such an experiment. There, under the vigorous and imaginative leadership of Mayor Richard C. Lee, one of the most ambitious urban renewal programs in the country has for ten years drawn national attention for innovation and achievement, and recent emphasis upon human renewal has made New Haven a fore-runner in the war on poverty. Its rapid progress toward the objective of becoming a slumless city helped focus New Haven's concern on the particular plight of its large low-income families.

The demonstration aimed to alleviate the critical shortage of standard housing suitable for the relocation of low-income families with 5 or more children. A drastic reduction in the number of remaining substandard housing units through redevelopment, highway construction, and code enforcement, made urgent the need to provide quickly a substantial number of large units of public housing.

Aware that it was impossible to build new apartments fast enough and in sufficient number to meet the need, and believing that in any event a choice of housing opportunities—not just conventional projects—should be available to large low-income families who had to relocate, New Haven proposed to house such families in non-project neighborhood environments through a rental assistance plan. The plan was designed to test a flexible technique for rapidly providing low-income housing. The units to be selected would be dispersed throughout the city, would include different types of structures, and would have environmental characteristics which varied according to the particular neighborhood. The leased units could be made available on either a long- or short-term basis, and in either case the housing supply available to low-income families could be expanded quickly without a long-range capital commitment.

To this end the City proposed that 40 low-income families with 5 or more children, meeting Housing Authority standards of eligibility, be housed in privately owned homes or apartments. Each of the families would be provided with a rental supplement in the amount of the difference between the actual cost of rent, including utilities, and the amount the family was considered able to pay according to Housing Authority standards.[3]

Housing units in proper environmental settings were to be screened to assure compliance with the New Haven Housing Code, and wherever necessary, arrangements would be made for the owner to make the improvements needed to conform to these standards.[4] The Housing Authority would negotiate with the landlord to establish the rent, which could not exceed fair rental value. The terms of occupancy were to be established by a lease between tenant and landlord, with rental assistance provisions to be contained in supplementary contracts between the Authority and the tenant and between the Authority and the landlord. Social services, including homemaking assistance, would be provided to each family to the extent necessary. The project was to be fully evaluated in a research program. As first proposed in 1962, the demonstration was to last three years. . . .

With the initial term at its midpoint, 227 people in 26 families have been relocated to decent homes in 9 different neighborhoods (11 different census tracts). The full 40 have not yet been subscribed because it has been extremely difficult to obtain enough large units. Of the 26 families, 14 have 9 or more members and the remainder have 7 or 8 members. Gross family incomes range from $2,678 to $7,295, per capita incomes from $334 to $891. Average gross income is $4,784 per family and $554 per capita. All but 3 of the families are Negro; 1 is Puerto Rican.[5]

The housing units are of varying types: 10 are single-family houses; 3 are halves of duplexes; 12 are located in 2- or 3-family houses, and 1 is in a 5-family dwelling; 13 have 4 bedrooms, 10 have 5 bedrooms, and 3 have 6 bedrooms. In 5 cases larger units were provided by combining formerly separate apartments or adapting formerly unused areas. Pri-

---

[3] 21.8 per cent of adjusted income, as in the Authority's conventional low-rent projects.

[4] The Housing Code conforms to FHA's minimum property standards for rehabilitation mortgages under Sections 220 of the Housing Act of 1949 as amended.

[5] In selecting families for the units, priority has been given to those longest in need of relocation. This fact tends to eliminate certain families who have more ability to find quarters for themselves; it also tends to make the group predominantly non-white. Assignment merely on the basis of relocation priority, without sufficient consideration of the families' varying capacities to adjust to the requirements of the program and to the housing itself, has had a bearing on the results of the program, discussed below.

vate landlords have spent an estimated $43,000 in rehabilitation to meet the program's requirements. A housing "project" has been virtually "built" and integrated into the community in a short time with no public capital expenditure.

In the process lessons have been learned, expectations confirmed, and myths exploded.

In the first place, rehousing randomly selected large low-income families in middle-class neighborhoods does not necessarily arouse ill feeling, provoke hostility, or create community tensions.

Nor, for the other side, does relocation to widely scattered rental units, which meet recognized criteria of physical and environmental excellence and which are totally devoid of institutionality, together with provision of supportive social services, completely eliminate rent delinquency, poor maintenance, or antisocial behavior by such families.

Although a definitive evaluation must await completion of the demonstration and the accompanying research program, it is possible now to draw some preliminary conclusions.

SCATTERED SITES

The social advantages of scattered sites for public housing have been widely considered in theoretical discussion: Institutionalization is avoided. Dispersion of the ghetto helps achieve socio-economic and racial integration. The loss of easy identification with a chronically underprivileged class provides an opportunity for human improvement and growth. Ineffective patterns of living can be altered under the influence of others which present greater strengths. Concentrated social services may have a greater chance to succeed in such a setting. Distribution of low-income families among many school districts is an effective tool for reducing racial and socio-economic imbalance in the public schools. Finally, use of scattered sites can maximize public housing's potential as a step toward housing independence. This would be particularly true if tenants in single-family houses could be given an option to purchase if their incomes rise sufficiently.[6]

[6] This would be facilitated by making available to individual homeowners with low and moderate incomes FHA-insured mortgages at below-market interest rates such as are now available for multi-family housing under Section 221(d) (3) of the Housing Act of 1949 as amended.

RENTAL OF PRIVATE HOUSING

In an era of great mobility of population and much displacement due to urban renewal and public construction, it is important for a community to be able to absorb the impact of demographic changes it cannot stop and physical changes it cannot afford to stop. Fast construction of needed relocation housing, even if it were possible, would be only a partial answer. As a practical matter, local and national politics and administrative red tape being what they are, we are never going to see a volume of public housing construction sufficient to serve all the low-income families who are now inadequately housed. We need a device which can respond quickly to immediate needs without requiring a permanent investment which the community either does not want, or cannot afford, to make. Rental of privately owned housing units for public housing purposes is just such a device; because it is fast (most of the time-consuming processes which precede public construction are bypassed) and there is no public capital outlay or other long-term commitment, the use of private rentals is a practical adjunct to conventional public housing projects, particularly for a community's short-term needs. In the New Haven demonstration, 26 large low-income families displaced by highways, urban renewal, and housing code enforcement, have been rehoused in private units with rental assistance while the community has been wrestling with the proper location and design for the first large units to be built or rehabilitated for public ownership.

Rents, of course, are only half of the subsidy picture, the other half being the families' incomes; in the demonstration the government makes up the difference between the rent (fair rental value) and the portion paid by the family (21.8 per cent of its adjusted income). Given any rent, the lower the family income, the greater the subsidy. Subsidies in the demonstration average $96 for 4 bedrooms, $112 for 5 bedrooms, and $137 for 6 bedrooms, with $106 the overall average. . . .

ADMINISTRATION OF THE PROGRAM

Scattered sites and the use of private rentals inevitably impose upon the Housing Authority an administrative burden of some proportions. Long-standing operating procedures, applicable to consolidated projects, do not all work in the new context. Distance and diversity among units add to overhead. A single project manager can efficiently handle far fewer units when they are not physically connected. The opportunities of bulk purchasing are minimized (an experiment in bulk purchasing of fuel for all the demonstration units in New Haven may be tried next fall). Numerous landlords must be dealt with in a variety of circumstances during the contract period—a landlord's failure to maintain a unit adequately and another's desire to evict a tenant for apparently insufficient cause are but two of the situations which confront the Authority here and not in the conventional project. Above all looms the formidable task of obtaining the housing units, establishing the rehabilitation standards and seeing that they are met, determining the fair rental value and negotiating to obtain the unit at not more than that price, and finally matching up the unit with a family currently in the relocation workload.

INDUCEMENTS TO LANDLORDS

To induce landlords to enroll their units in the demonstration at reasonable rents, despite a shortage of suitable units and antipathies to the kinds of families involved,[7] the Authority has had a number of incentives to offer. Most effective has been the program's central feature, whereby full payment of rent each month for the duration of the program is guaranteed by the Authority by contract with the landlord. If the tenant fails to pay his share on time in any month, the Authority makes good to the landlord and assumes the burden of going after the tenant. Similarly, if a unit has become vacant through no fault of the landlord, the Authority continues to pay the full rent until a new tenant moves in. Another important inducement to property owners is assistance—technical and financial—in properly rehabilitating the property. To help the landlord plan the best and cheapest way to meet the required standards, the Authority's inspection team includes a rehabilitation specialist and, where appropriate, an architect. A mortgage specialist is available to help the landlord obtain FHA or conventional financing, and the prospect of the rental guarantee may make the loan easier to obtain. Indeed, the financial mechanism of the rental assistance con-

[7] Landlords feared most that property would be destroyed and rent not paid on time.

tract offers a supplemental means of stimulating compliance with the housing code, particularly outside of urban renewal areas where substantial improvements of substandard housing are often difficult to finance. Where a landlord has inadequate capital to finance the necessary improvements, the Authority may advance a portion of the cost to pay for the specified work. This sum is then treated as partial prepayment of the subsidy portion of the rent, to be repaid by applying it against the rent in equal installments over a given number of months. This plan has been used in 8 of the 26 units leased to date, and in several was crucial in assuring that the property would be available to the program.

AUTHORITY–TENANT RELATIONSHIP

Simply by obtaining a housing unit for a large low-income family, the Housing Authority performs a positive function, for it is quite obvious that none of the families placed would have had the skill or resources to obtain decent housing on their own.

After the family moves into the housing unit, however, the Housing Authority's responsibilities continue as counselor, arbiter, and occasionally, policeman. The landlord-tenant relationship is between the property owner and the family. The Authority is tied to each by separate agreements, the essence of its role being to assure the continued availability of the housing unit for the duration of the demonstration period and the continued fulfillment of the landlord's and tenant's duties to each other. Landlord and tenant have all the customary rights and obligations of that relationship, and only in the event of specific stresses does the Authority come into the picture. Tenants are encouraged to deal directly with landlords and vice versa, but the Authority is the umpire and may be called in by either side when a problem cannot be resolved. The demonstration project staff has been particularly active with those tenants who have never learned to deal successfully and independently with landlords, and with those landlords who have corresponding difficulties with particular tenants.

Interesting and significant is the fact that many families have preferred to deal with the Authority rather than with the landlord when difficulties arise. Ordinarily public housing tenants regard the Housing Authority primarily as a landlord, but here another party fills that role; the Authority and its staff seem to be regarded by the family as its partners and counselors rather than as authoritarian figures. This may have facilitated the delivery of social services, which are offered to each family to the extent necessary. . . .

Indeed, the demonstration program's social service arm has played a key role in helping the families adapt to their new circumstances. From the outset it was recognized that sudden introduction of large low-income families into good neighborhoods without sufficient preparation might be disastrous to families, housing, and neighborhoods alike. Each family, therefore, has received continuing assistance from trained homemaking advisors, in most cases before its move as well as in its new home. The homemaking advisors give instructions in household routines, child care, and budgeting, and their support has been well received by the families. Frequency of visits ranges from every few days to once a month, depending upon the need. In addition, the advisors have been helpful in response to the families' crises, particularly financial ones. The homemaking advisors receive guidance and supervision from the director of the Homemaking Program and a trained social service coordinator on the project staff, who have also been responsible for trying to develop relationships with public and voluntary social agencies for family-oriented rather than individual crisis-oriented social work. The limited success in getting voluntary agencies to devote their energies and resources to multi-problem low-income families points to the necessity of adequately budgeting and staffing public welfare and housing agencies to provide the necessary supportive services.

SOCIAL EVALUATION

What effect has all this had upon the individual families? Generally speaking, the record of the families has been good. In most instances, payment of rent has been prompt and maintenance adequate. Although the Authority has had to cover the rent in some cases, the delinquent families have usually caught up within a month; in only two instances has there been chronic non-payment.[8] There has been evidence of

[8] To date, in 20 months, the Housing Authority has had to cover the tenant's share of the rent in the case of 7 of the 26 families on a total of 26 monthly occasions out of a possible 294. Over half of these payments were made on behalf of 2 families. The Authority has had to pay the full rent on 1 occasion because of vacancy due to a family's sudden

dramatic improvement of morale, and virtually all families have shown some degree of improvement. On the other hand, some habit patterns have been difficult to dislodge—for instance, it is difficult to convince a family which has never had central heating that the best method is not to turn up the thermostat and regulate the heat by raising and lowering the windows—and rental assistance and coordinated social services cannot help a desperately poor family fill a 9-room apartment with more than a few pieces of dingy furniture.[9] Furthermore, the multiple problems which some families face—educational, psychological and medical in addition to the financial one—are much too serious and deep-seated to be quickly resolved by short-term treatment. Some families simply are not ready to live in this kind of housing, and it may well be detrimental to them as well as to the community to deal so radically with their housing situation before some of their other problems have been alleviated. Such families may gain greater benefit from living in a housing project, with the greater opportunities it presents for imposition of constructive social controls.

For these reasons, careful selection of families to live in scattered housing, be it publicly owned or rental assisted, is a necessity. Management and social service personnel must carefully assess the strengths and weaknesses of income-eligible families. Evidence of a family's past performance must be evaluated in an attempt to arrive at judgments as to future capabilities.[10]

COMMUNITY RELATIONS

Community reaction to the families' presence has for the most part been heartening: generally, acceptance with no undue notice. Although there have been some complaints from

---

departure from New Haven. The Authority's payments terminated as soon as another demonstration family moved into the unit.

[9] Some families have wondered what they were supposed to do with all the space, and occasionally project personnel have wondered, too. Minimum standards of the housing code may compound the difficulties of providing adequate housing for low-income families. Modification of standards may be desirable under carefully defined circumstances within prescribed limits, e.g. dormitory sleeping arrangements where there is adequate light and ventilation.

[10] Such a method of tenant selection has already been used successfully in the Used House public housing program in Philadelphia, and New Haven's demonstration has made attempts at such screening.

immediate neighbors, particularly in one neighborhood which
had not previously been integrated, there has been little evidence of any substantial negative reaction to the families.[11]
In most cases, no distinction seems to have been made between families in demonstration units and other families on
the block.[12] In one instance a neighbor greeted the new
arrivals with a cake. In another there has been a curious reversal: an especially capable mother in a demonstration unit
has helped a neighbor improve low standards of housekeeping
and child care. Individual examples aside, from the viewpoint
of community relations the program seems to have succeeded.

CONCLUSION

Many details of the demonstration have been altered in the
year and a half since its inception. As a "demonstration," it
has been possible to adapt the program to realities encountered in the field, and the accumulated experience will result
in a stronger program. For example, under the original format
the subsidy check was mailed to the tenant for him to turn
over to the landlord, on the theory that this would encourage
responsibility on his part; in practice, delays in forwarding
some checks to landlords suggested that a more direct route
would have certain advantages, and it became apparent that
the development of strengths in the family did not depend
upon such esoteric administrative details.

Other departures, some much more substantive, have been
suggested but not yet followed up. For instance, it may be
possible to obtain relatively many housing units through cooperation of non-profit local institutions which acquire them
expressly for the purpose of renting at a low rate of return
to low-income families. During the remainder of the demonstration's term and a proposed extension period, procedures
will be refined further. A second demonstration proposed for
New Haven would provide rental assistance to low income
families of normal size, in part to permit costs, landlord at-

[11] The only public furor was by the predominantly Negro community
association in a predominantly Negro neighborhood, which objected to
locating demonstration units in the neighborhood and, it said, further
crowding the schools.
[12] Legal arrangements for the demonstration were devised to avoid
the necessity of public hearings; as a result, neighbors, in many instances at least, are unaware that a family is receiving rental assistance.

titudes, and administrative procedures to be studied without the aberrant complications of large families.

One thing is quite clear: 26 large low-income families who have been rehoused in demonstration units would not otherwise have been adequately rehoused.

The results to date of New Haven's demonstration program encourage further exploration of rental assistance as a means to rapidly expand the supply of housing for low-income families in a fashion consistent with current notions of individual and community improvement.

SPECIAL MESSAGE TO CONGRESS ON IMPROVING NATION'S CITIES*

President Lyndon B. Johnson

A DEMONSTRATION CITIES PROGRAM

I propose a demonstration cities program that will offer qualifying cities of all sizes the promise of a new life for their people.

I propose that we make massive additions to the supply of low and moderate-cost housing.

I propose that we combine physical reconstruction and rehabilitation with effective social programs throughout the rebuilding process.

I propose that we achieve new flexibility in administrative procedures.

I propose that we focus all the techniques and talents within our society on the crisis of the American city.

We intend to help only those cities who help themselves.

I propose these guidelines for determining a city's qualifications for the benefits—and achievements—of this program.

[1] The demonstration should be of sufficient magnitude both in its physical and social dimensions to arrest blight and decay in entire neighborhoods. It must make a substantial impact within the coming few years on the development of the entire city.

[2] The demonstration should bring about a change in the total environment of the area affected. It must provide schools, parks, playgrounds, community centers, and access to all necessary community facilities.

[3] The demonstration—from its beginning—should make use of every available social program. The human cost of reconstruction and relocation must be reduced. New opportunities for work and training must be offered.

[4] The demonstration should contribute to narrowing the housing gap between the deprived and the rest of the community. Major additions must be made to the supply of sound dwellings. Equal opportunity in the choice of housing must be assured to every race.

* January 26, 1966 (selected portions).

[5] The demonstration should offer maximum occasions for employing residents of the demonstration area in all phases of the program.

[6] The demonstration should foster the development of local and private initiative and widespread citizen participation—especially from the demonstration area—in planning and execution of the program.

[7] The demonstration should take advantage of modern cost-reducing technologies without reducing the quality of the work. Neither the structure of real estate taxation, cumbersome building codes, nor inefficient building practices should deter rehabilitation or inflate project costs.

[8] The demonstration should make major improvements in the quality of the environment. There must be a high quality of design in new buildings, and attention to man's need for open spaces and attractive landscaping.

[9] The demonstration should make relocation housing available at costs commensurate with the incomes of those displaced by the project. Counseling services, moving expenses, and small business loans should be provided, together with assistance in job placement and retraining.

[10] The demonstration should be managed in each demonstration city by a single authority with adequate powers to carry out and coordinate all phases of the program. There must be a serious commitment to the project on the part of local, and, where appropriate, state authorities. Where required to carry out the plan, agreements should be reached with neighboring communities.

[11] The demonstration proposal should offer proof that adequate municipal appropriations and services are available and will be sustained throughout the demonstration period.

[12] The demonstration should maintain or establish a residential character in the area.

[13] The demonstration should be consistent with existing development plans for the metropolitan areas involved. Transportation plans should coordinate every appropriate mode of city and regional transportation.

[14] The demonstration should extend for an initial six-year period. It should maintain a schedule for the expeditious completion of the project.

These guidelines will demand the full cooperation of government at every level and of private citizens in each area. I believe our Federal system is creative enough to inspire that cooperative effort. I know it must be so creative if it is to prosper and flourish.

SIZE OF THE PROGRAM

The program I recommend is intended to eliminate blight in the entire demonstration area. Through efficient rebuilding it must replace that blight with attractive and economic housing, social services, and community facilities.

There are many ways by which this can be done, once the commitment has been made to do it. Total clearance and reconstruction; partial clearance and rehabilitation; rehabilitation alone—any of these methods may be chosen by local citizens.

There are few cities or towns in America which could not participate in the Demonstration Cities Program. We shall take special care to see that urban communities of all sizes are included. For each such community, the impact of the program will be significant, involving as much as 15 to 20 per cent of the existing substandard structures.

For the largest qualifying cities a relatively modest program could provide decent housing for approximately 5,000 families now living in substandard dwelling units. It could rehabilitate other marginal housing sufficient to affect 50,000 people. A typical program could well involve a total of 35,000 units or 100,000 people.

For cities of approximately 100,000 people, 1,000 families could be rehoused, and 3,000 units rehabilitated, affecting a total of 10,000 people.

BENEFITS OF THE PROGRAM

I recommend that participating cities receive two types of Federal assistance:

First, the complete array of all available grants and urban aids in the fields of housing, renewal, transportation, education, welfare economic opportunity and related programs.

Second, special grants amounting to 80 per cent of the non-Federal cost of our grant-in-aid programs included in the demonstration. These grants are to supplement the efforts of local communities. They are not to be substituted for those efforts.

In every qualifying city, a Federal coordinator would be

assigned to assist local officials in bringing together all the relevant Federal resources.

Once authorized, the supplemental funds would be made available in a common account. They would be drawn at the discretion of the community to support the program. They would be certified by the Federal coordinator.

It is vital that incentives be granted for cost reductions achieved during the performance of the program.

At least as vital as the dollar commitment for rebuilding and rehabilitation is the social program commitment. We must link our concern for the total welfare of the person, with our desire to improve the physical city in which he lives. For the first time, social and construction agencies would be joined in a massive common effort, responsive to a common local authority.

FEDERAL COST

Funds are required in the first year to assist our cities in the preparation of demonstration plans. We should not underestimate the problems involved in achieving such a plan. The very scale of the demonstration, its widespread and profound effects on the social and physical structure of the city, calls for marshaling the city's planning and administrative resources on an unprecedented scale.

I estimate the appropriate Federal contribution to this planning effort at $12-million.

For the supplemental demonstration grants I will recommend appropriations, over a six-year period, totalling over $2.3-billion, or an average of some $400-million per year.

It is impossible to estimate exactly—but it is necessary to consider—the rising cost of welfare services, crime prevention, unemployment and declining property values that will plague all governments, local, state, and Federal, if we do not move quickly to heal and revitalize our cities.

TESTIMONY BEFORE THE HOUSING SUB-COMMITTEE OF THE HOUSE BANKING AND CURRENCY COMMITTEE ON H.R. 12341, THE PROPOSED "DEMONSTRATION CITIES ACT OF 1966"*

John V. Lindsay
Mayor of New York City

The President's message and budget call for $2.3 billion to be made available over a five-year period beginning in fiscal 1968. In fiscal 1967, a total of $17 million is to be made available for planning the demonstration.

These sums will limit sharply both the number of cities that may participate in the program and the scale and impact it can have on the individual communities which do, in fact, participate. It is of the utmost importance that the program be large enough and so apparent that our people will readily perceive its value.

I would urge that you amend the survey and planning provisions of the urban renewal program to have funds available as planning grants from that source. This would mean that a much larger amount of money could be made available and that the number of demonstration cities could be enlarged. A competition among America's cities with the fate of the poor at stake, is not a very attractive prospect for local officials.

In the past, in urban renewal and other programs, quotas have been set to limit the amount of aid given to New York City. While the concern of others that New York not gobble up entire programs is understandable, it seems fairer to me that the Congress provide programs as large as the problems—and in the case of New York City, the problems are of unparalleled magnitude.

It might be useful if I sketched for you the dimensions of our problem. We have a population of 8 million people. Twenty-four per cent of our City's 2,655,000 households have an annual income under $3,000 making them eligible for consideration for poverty program activities. One million, six

* Washington, D.C.: March 2, 1966 (selected portions).

hundred thousand people live in these poverty-stricken households. New York City has 2,758,000 housing units, of which 276,000 are to a significant degree substandard. Over half a million people receive various forms of public welfare at an annual cost to the federal, state and local governments of more than half a billion dollars.

If Manhattan, Brooklyn, and the Bronx were separate cities, they would constitute three of the five largest cities in the nation and you would not hesitate to provide for them accordingly. The blighted areas of each of our boroughs are tragically large and unhappily famous. Central Harlem, and East Harlem, the Lower East Side in Manhattan. Bedford-Stuyvesant, Brownsville, and East New York in Brooklyn. The South Bronx and South Jamaica.

A massive demonstration program would be a major impetus to our efforts to revitalize these areas. The President appears to contemplate demonstration projects involving 10% of the total population of a city. Such a program, adequately funded, would have a profound impact on our City, though it would be far short of reaching all the areas of critical need.

It would be a disaster for the morale of New Yorkers if, after all the publicity, we were to learn suddenly that New York City would again be restricted to a relatively modest program. The President's Message refers to programs in our largest cities that would provide decent housing for approximately 5,000 families, rehabilitate other marginal housing for 50,000 people, and involve a total of 35,000 units or 100,000 people. If this were to be taken as a limit on a demonstration for New York City, it would involve little more than 1% of our population and little more than 1% of our housing stock.

Such a limitation would be an outright discrimination against our City solely because of its size. It would mean that a vast number of the poor, the badly housed and the socially disadvantaged of New York would be denied the opportunity to participate in this and other federal programs merely because they live in the largest city in the nation.

I hope that you will make clear in the legislation and in the committee report that these illustrations in the President's Message are not to be taken as applying a ceiling for New York City.

The Demonstration Cities Program must offer solutions to New York on the same relative scale as they are offered to any other community in this nation. We should not be put in the position of choosing Harlem over Bedford-Stuyvesant over South Bronx. It must be clear that the largest cities, certainly New York, may have more than one demonstration area. . . .

PLAN REVIEWS: NEW YORK CITY'S
RENEWAL STRATEGY, 1965*

Richard May, Jr., Walter Thabit

REVIEW, *Richard May, Jr.*

It is perhaps best to describe this report, which has been heralded in *The New York Times* as the most significant study of the City's housing problems ever undertaken, in terms of what it is not, rather than what it is or purports to be. Unfortunately, in spite of repeated use of the words "strategy," "policy," and "priorities," no strategy, policy or priorities which can serve as a guide for public action are presented for consideration.

The bulk of the report consists of a comprehensive and detailed inventory of city-wide housing demand and supply based on the 1960 Census and a description of the types of State and Federal housing and renewal programs and aids now available. This is followed by a map of the City delineating areas for "major action, renovation, and neighborhood conservation" and those which are predominantly sound but differ in having older or newer housing stock. This overall statement should more properly have served as the point of departure rather than the conclusion or summary, because the reader looking for guidance or new insights on renewal programming is left with the same difficult questions he had before reading this report—particularly if he has been struggling with renewal and housing problems as a professional.

The report therefore has little to offer to anyone who has given thought to the planning and programming of urban renewal activities. One can only conjecture that possibly the five years of study and three and a half million dollars or more expended have served largely to educate the CRP staff in the fundamentals of a problem which is already voluminously covered by official documents, books, and articles currently available. In fact, one is struck by the staff's amazing innocence of the imaginative use of renewal as a comprehensive planning tool for effective city rebuilding in such nearby cities

* FROM *Journal of the American Institute of Planners,* Vol. XXXII (March 1966), No. 2, pp. 122–26.

as New Haven, Philadelphia, and Boston. New Yorkers have always been guilty of provincialism, but never has it been so blatantly expressed in the terms found here: New York City is "a world." One cannot but suspect that the awe with which the authors approached their assignment indicated a lack of conviction as to anyone's ability to comprehend the City, much less deal with it. The result of this attitude is a report so resplendent in generalities and "overallness" that the reader cannot but be left with the impression that New York will never solve its housing problems. Indeed if the City's programmers were to be guided by all the requirements and restraints enumerated, it is likely that little if any progress would be made in this direction.

Inherent in the approach to this study is the assumption that it was possible to assemble a set of criteria and determinants which, matched with a detailed analysis of housing demand and area characteristics, could mechanistically produce not only an overall City-wide renewal program, but also the guidance for policy determination within each area of the City. The report effectively demonstrates the inherent fallacies of this "Brave New World" theory, because it leaves us with only the vaguest generalities to guide the decision making process.

Renewal remains one of the most complex undertakings of contemporary society. It must be undertaken within the context of a number of general policy directives, many of which inevitably contradict or overlap each other, no matter how one may try to organize them into a manageable system. Renewal activities are a reflection in microcosm of the complexities of urban life and its political and economic institutions, which are continuously engaged in struggle and resultant change. Within this context there can only be general policies and no overall "strategy" in the true sense of a synthesis of policies providing for effective action toward a defined goal. Within each local area some goals will have to be given precedence over others. One can never know with complete certainty what the effect of a selected set of criteria will have on city-wide objectives. The test of the veracity of a project's objectives lies not in an intellectual or mechanical evaluation, but in its political acceptability. It is in the determination of not only what is desirable, but also what is feasible; and indeed it is in engaging in the process of making solutions feasible and acceptable that renewal planning merges from science to art.

The above is in no way intended to indicate there is no need for city-wide policies. They are desperately needed and in greater detail and explicitness than as set forth in this CRP report. But they are distinct from strategy which can only be developed for a locality at a point in time and is meaningless on a city-wide basis. Fortunately, the city is a dynamic organism and physical changes in housing and the environment take time to accomplish. This makes possible the revision of plans and their adjustment to changes as they occur, regardless of how fixed they may seem in the eyes of some planners.

One would have hoped that this report could not only have set forth policies and dealt with their interrelationships, but also that it might have defined the resources needed for an effective renewal program in New York City. For it was the aim of Congress in authorizing such studies that some dimensions in terms of resource requirements be defined for its guidance. It is only by setting forth the dimensions of the job that progress can be made toward making the necessary resources available.

An evaluation of the resources needed for effective renewal would inevitably have shown that efforts to date, though impressive, leave the City far from any minimal goal in improvement of its environment. It would have taken courage to state this, but it might have been effective at this moment of a change in City administration and a threatened curtailment in domestic expenditures by Congress. This same tendency to timidity may account for the omission of any recommendations in the report for bringing about more effective administration of existing programs and may perhaps also explain the penchant for generalities. One could accept this had the report not made such vociferous promises to present specific strategies.

Clearly, renewal programming in New York has only begun, in spite of the tremendous effort and expenditure to date. When it becomes clear that this emperor presented by the New York Times has no clothes, one hopes that New York will undertake moves toward effective renewal programming.

REVIEW, *Walter Thabit*

For a city in which 1,000,000 families have critical housing needs, in which 500,000 families cannot find suitable dwellings, in which areas containing 800,000 dwelling units need government aids to restore a sound residential environment, *New York City's Renewal Strategy, 1965,* is disappointing at best, an alarming example of political bankruptcy at worst.

The report starts off with some welcome candor about the need for more public housing (a 20,000- to 25,000-unit yearly program is recommended) and some needed changes in the city's manifold programs. It suggests mixing low- and middle-income families, group maintenance of tenements, gradual rebuilding rather than mass action in small renewal projects, the establishment of a major rehabilitation industry, and major subsidies if the poor are to be rehoused at rents they can afford.

It is when the report comes to central issues and hard programming facts that it bursts at the seams. It slams the door on open occupancy by refusing to rehouse the poor on large vacant tracts because ". . . it would be necessary to provide improved access to jobs in the core of the City." Such tracts should be developed for "families whose breadwinners work in neighboring industrial sections, or who are able to take a car to work." This is an expression of indifference to or ignorance of the racial and income discrimination implicit in this policy. Similarly, the report rejects rehousing the poor on non-residential slum land, rejects rent supplements in existing housing (except for relocation), and rejects slum clearance and rebuilding in stages, the only method by which poor people can be rehoused in their own neighborhoods. Staging, the report suggests, "ignores the fundamental renewal objective of providing households with a variety of housing choice." Housing choice is not increased by ignoring people's preference for remaining in their own neighborhoods.

How busily the blue pencils have been wielded by politicians and appointed officials is also seen in the total absence of the real program components: numbers, timetables, and costs. Why doesn't the report point out that the proposed approach would cost in excess of $1 billion in Harlem? Why doesn't it contrast the City's current $200,000 receivership program with the $200,000,000 needed in receivership-level improvements? Why doesn't it recommend definite programs for definite areas, to which specific costs and recommended timetables are attached? This material exists. Why hasn't it been made public?

One does not have to seek far for the answers. Our leaders do not wish to call attention to the magnitude of their failures.

They prefer to avoid commitment to real programs. Perhaps it is well not to provide the poor with a real assessment of their needs. Who knows? The poor might want some of them satisfied.

EXCHANGE OF TESTIMONY, SUB-COMMITTEE OF THE COMMITTEE ON BANKING AND CURRENCY OF THE U.S. SENATE, HEARINGS, 88TH CONGRESS, SECOND SESSION ON S.2468*

Robert Weaver and John Tower

. . . Senator TOWER. Under title X, do you really comprehend here the planning of actual new towns, perhaps new municipal corporations even?

Dr. WEAVER. No, sir. I purposefully did not call them new towns, because "new towns" carries with it the connotation of what has happened in many parts of Western Europe.

In Great Britain, for example, the new towns are developed by the Government.

Senator TOWER. Yes.

Dr. WEAVER. The Central Government goes out, picks the site, and it does all the planning.

Here in this country we already have some 75 new communities in various stages of conception, about 20 of them in planning and execution. And these are all being developed by private developers.

Two examples here locally are Reston in Virginia, in Fairfax County, and Columbia in Howard County in Maryland.

The private developers have gone in and decided the location. They are doing the planning. They are doing the site planning. They are doing it, however, in coordination—they have to—with local units of government.

So this is going to be a privately developed program and not one in which the Government is going to come in, as we did, say, in the Greenbelt towns during the New Deal. This is not going to be another Greenbelt program. It is not going to be the counterpart of the European new towns. It is going to be an American variation.

Senator TOWER. In other words, it will not be comparable to the British new towns?

Dr. WEAVER. No, sir. I hope it will be much more attractive than many of them. Many of them are very dreary, despite the fact they have good site planning.

* February 19, 20, 24, 25, 26, 27, 28, and March 3, 1964, pp. 404–7, 417–19.

Senator TOWER. Would the primary difference be that, whereas in Great Britain the Central Government plans new towns or new communities, whatever you want to call them, although they call them new towns there, here they would be local planning bodies but the aegis would come from the housing agency?

Dr. WEAVER. Well, it would be not exactly that. As a matter of fact, in many of the British new towns not only does the Central Government plan them but the Central Government executes them. Here the initiative would come usually through a private developer. The private developer would then hire planners to do the site planning and to do all of the other things.

This is not academic. This is now actually happening in Reston and in Columbia, the two that are close by, and in some 20 others.

The planning that might be done by any governmental agency obviously would be done by a local governmental agency, and this would be not the detailed site planning of the areas themselves but planning of a comprehensive nature.

For example, it would be to see that the carrying out of a particular community would not conflict with where a highway was going to come or where there is going to be a right-of-way for some other purpose subsequently, and to see that it would be tied in with a communications system that would be necessary.

So that one of the requirements would be that this would be consistent with an areawide plan. This plan would be done locally. The Federal Government participation in this as far as the planning is concerned would be financial assistance but not carrying out the plan.

Senator TOWER. I am glad that nothing like the British new towns is contemplated. I have seen some of those new towns, and they are pretty dreary looking affairs.

Now, there is another question here, and that is when we talk about a local public body doing the planning, are local public bodies competent to do that in every State?

For example, do county commissioners in some States or your county supervisors, or whatever they might be, always have this authority to make plans?

Dr. WEAVER. Some of them lack the authority, but many of them have more authority I think than they have staff and experience. Lack of authority is certainly not widespread. If it were, we would not be in this field at all.

Senator TOWER. But conceivably if such a community were contemplated outside the corporate limits of any town ——

Dr. WEAVER. I beg your pardon. I did not get that.

Senator TOWER. I say if a new community were contemplated outside the corporate limits of a town or a city, then it would probably be up to county authorities to do the planning, and in some States it is my understanding that county authorities do not have, or county public bodies do not have, such authority.

Dr. WEAVER. There are two things here, I think, that we have to differentiate.

First, I would like to say that because of the very nature of our economy I think that it is fairly safe to assume these are going to be removed from the centers of cities. Otherwise you are not going to be able to get land reasonably enough to carry them out.

Secondly, as far as the planning, you have to differentiate the planning, the overall planning, of an area and the detailed planning of a particular new community.

The detailed planning of the new community is going to be done by private developers, and they or a local governmental agency might do the general plan for the new community. The planning in which the governmental agency would necessarily be involved would be an areawide plan, or planning process, and, as I said before, about two-thirds of our communities already have these, and more will have them, because the Highway Act requires that this planning be underway by 1965 to be able to qualify for that. . . .

Senator TOWER. Are we to understand the planning authority will try to predetermine what proportion of the houses must be low-income housing, and what should be middle-income housing, and what should be high-income housing, and approximately how many old people would have to be housed?

Will the planning authority have to do all of this?

Dr. WEAVER. The planning authority would not have to do this. The situation there would be this: In the first place, again I do not think maybe I have made my point clear. The planning authority, insofar as it is a governmental agency, will primarily be concerned with an overall area plan in which this new community may be located and which will cover a great deal larger area. It will be concerned with how the highway system is going to move in there. It is going to be concerned with whether or not, if there is a countywide or if there are local types of water and sewer, these can be extended and how this will fit into an overall area of which it is a part.

Because no matter how large the new community is, it is part of a larger area obviously.

Although the preliminary general plan for the new community might be done by a local governmental body, the actual detailed planning of the particular development will not be done by these governmental bodies. It will be done by the developer. And he will then make his decisions as to how he is going to plan this, where he is going to locate various types of land use, and so forth.

The HHFA will be concerned in the new communities, if these assistances which are set forth in this bill are provided to him, that he do several things: First, that he conform with this wider plan I have mentioned.

Secondly, that he provide within that community the facilities that are necessary for a good life. And this would be adequate schools, adequate recreation, adequate communications, adequate transportation. And that he have employment opportunities there. That there be adequate commercial, adequate cultural, adequate recreational facilities.

We would also insist that there be an economic mix in that community. This is something that would vary from community to community, reflecting in many instances the employment opportunities that would exist there and reflecting the peculiar attributes of that particular community.

There is no formula that we could establish, and there is no formula in my opinion that can be established as to what the proportions would be in each area. . . .

"NEW TOWNS" ROLE IN
URBAN GROWTH EXPLORED*

Robert Gladstone

New communities program proposals have been controversial for a number of years, failing twice to gain Congressional acceptance, although changed in substance—and even in name—from "new towns" initially to "extensive development" in the 1965 attempt. . . .

CENTRAL CITY, NEW COMMUNITIES

Perhaps the single most critical issue is the relationship between central city development and redevelopment and the creation of new communities in the metropolitan orbit. Key questions are: Do new communities compete with central cities for development, sapping the vitality of the central city? Is suburban "sprawl" actually an advantage to central cities? Would new communities compete for federal urban development funds, drawing them away from central cities?

Fundamental to resolution of these questions are the trends, scale, and location of urban gains in United States metropolitan areas. Analysis of these trends and patterns—to be discussed in further detail below—points up a number of important factors that would hold whether or not a new communities policy were to operate for the nation. These factors include the following:

—The fact of urban growth is not arguable in terms of the past record, as well as the indicated future pattern.
—The location of new growth within metropolitan areas has been and must continue to be dominantly peripheral, even though redevelopment and intensification in central city locations may occur. We are familiar with the pace of urbanization dramatically expressed by the reminder that one million acres of new land moves into urban development each year. And indeed, the function of the metropolitan periphery—where open land is available—is to absorb much of the new growth occurring in urban locations.

* FROM *Journal of Housing*, XXIII (January 1966), pp. 29–35 (selected portions).

—The largest share of urban gains is focused to a remarkably high degree on a selected group of United States metropolitan areas. These limited, maximum impact areas are the most seriously affected by growth and extension problems and, of course, would potentially be the most directly affected by new communities policies. I would estimate that only one-third of our 200-plus metropolitan areas would be substantially affected, based on present pace and scale factors in the marketplace.

Given the pattern of continuing, substantial, fast-paced urban gains, the key issues as they relate to city development patterns then become:

—*First,* not whether metropolitan growth and extension *will* occur, but, rather, *how, where,* and *when* it will occur, and

—*Second*, whether suburban development patterns typical of postwar USA are to continue—and make no mistake here, because the outlook is for a continuation into the future—or whether improved patterns based on specific program and policy intervention can be introduced to better this pattern.

In this context, the role of the central city would remain strong, although dynamically changing. The task of central city development is to identify existing as well as new strengths and support them fully and creatively by appropriate action. Rather than competing with central cities, in a rational distribution of the region's activities, new communities would complement them.

NEW COMMUNITY CONCEPTS

A new communities policy and effective programs for their development are potential basic ingredients in a new pattern of urban growth for the nation. The prime objective in a new communities program would be to accommodate the nation's urban gains on an improved basis. Critical to this concept would be a full response in the new communities to urban growth needs. To do this, they would need to be an integral part of the metropolitan regional system, directly relating to the metropolitan social and cultural structure: its economy, its transportation system, its open space and land development patterns, and the full range of its market systems.

Although some relatively isolated, semi-autonomous, or economically specialized new communities might continue to be built, as in the past, the overwhelming orientation of new communities would be toward metropolitan locations, where the major population gains of the nation and its primary economic growth are taking place. Los Alamos, Kitamat, and other "Shangri-La" communities are not relevant to the mainstream issues of urban and metropolitan problems in the nation today.

No hard and fast definition of new towns is applicable to all situations in various parts of the country. This is especially true at the present time, even though a more sophisticated definition might evolve with further new community building in the years ahead. However, criteria relating both to scale and features of such development can be established now. Specifically, the following items are of key importance:

1—*Features.* A planned new community should program for multi-purpose development, providing living choices in a full variety of housing types for a range of socio-economic levels within the limits of available demand and available housing programs. In addition, as broad a complex of job types, economic activities, and ancillary functions as can be appropriately accommodated and attracted to the community should be included. Jobs, based on population-serving activities could, of course, be a major source of community employment. In addition, other job types—"basic" to the new community as well as to the surrounding region—might also be provided, insofar as they relate to a functional pattern of job distribution in the region.

The new community should be reasonably autonomous in terms of the facilities it provides, yet physically and functionally related to the surrounding region and central city. Although providing selected economic and cultural activities, the new community should also rely on facilities and institutions that serve the entire region from a central city location.

NEW COMMUNITY VALUES

Apart from underlying forces that establish new community potential, there is the basic question of *why* new communities. What advantages do they offer? Conversely, what problems might they eliminate? How do they compare in these points to the present pattern of urban development?

Principal benefits from new community development have traditionally been argued in physical terms. The origin of new community thinking goes back more than half a century. The "garden city" idea and the planning ideal of the "city beauti-ful" were early goals in urban design.

The potential of new communities today, however, is more than a sentimental recall of these earlier designed-motivated, even Utopian concepts. The new building opportunities today generate directly from hard realities of urban expansion in the nation. Similarly, potential meaning of new communities needs to be assessed in terms of economics, governmental organiza-tion, and fiscal benefits as well as social considerations. The potential for realization of these benefits in new communities as against present suburban development patterns—discussed further below—is the specific focus for this analysis.

Before going on to governmental and social issues, an over-view of the development values potentially attainable in new communities can be set forth:

—Shorter work-to-home trips for a sizable portion of commu-nity residents, based on balanced community development and the appropriate location of economic activity.

—Greater ease of internal movement, based on limited com-munity size.

—Elimination of "sprawl" and continuous urbanization with-out interruption, achieved by a variety of development types and open space.

—Better proximity to open space and accessibility to major recreational areas.

—Improved visual environment.

—Economies in land development and utilization.

—Potential for a full variety of housing types and choices.

—Reduced pressure for irrational rezoning and development patterns.

—Opportunity to create rational service areas for local gov-ernment.

—Greater potential for fiscal viability based on balanced de-velopment patterns.

GOVERNMENT AND SOCIAL ISSUES

Given a new communities policy as an appropriate response to urban growth problems, then issues of government; public interests and finance; segregation and social balance can be analyzed in comparative terms—the effects of new commu-nities in these matters as against typical metropolitan develop-ment patterns.

Within the over-all issue of local government and public interest in new communities, a wide range of specific problems is involved. These include the following items:

1—How to achieve short- and long-term fiscal stability for new communities within the constraints of suitable tax rates, high early costs, and initially "slim" tax base.
2—How to provide adequate urban services including necessary utilities, schools, public safety, welfare and recreation services, given the local tax base.
3—How to introduce a local government apparatus responsible for providing urban services and representing public interests in relation to private interests.

These questions are difficult—and thoughtful public administrators tell us that no final blanket answers as they relate to new communities are available. The key issue here is the degree to which new communities inherently add to the present complexity of local government issues or simplify them in contrast to current patterns of outlying development. The full range of local government problems just listed are now applicable to typical suburban developments and new communities would not alter the nature or extent of these problems. Accordingly, this becomes a neutral issue with respect to a new communities policy.

Social issues—segregation and diverse population characteristics—simply must be examined in terms of comparative effects of alternate development policies. I would emphasize that problems of segregation and social balance—although manifest in outlying and central city area development patterns—must be dealt with in the larger context of programs aimed at eliminating poverty; narrowing income gaps; stimulating economic development; providing equal access to jobs based on equal educational opportunity; adjusting social attitudes; eliminating discrimination in housing; and broadening the reach and effectiveness of new housing programs oriented to low-income demand sectors.

The need for action within this broader framework, however, should not preclude the recognition of such specific issues related to metropolitan development patterns as:

1—The ghettoization of low-income, minority groups within central city areas as a result of traditional patterns of job location; discrimination; and supply of dilapidated, second-hand housing stock.

2—Major impediments presently operate against suburbanization of these minority groups, despite the increasing potential for such a shift based on expansion of suitable jobs and growing incomes of minority group members.

3—Major impediments notwithstanding, some factors are now operating to alter these patterns including specific housing programs with suburban location potential; non-discriminatory requirements of law; and the efforts of fair housing groups and others of good will.

It is unrealistic to expect that new communities are inherently capable of changing this pattern without energetic application in a variety of other programs. The following factors, however, could operate to help improve social balance under a new communities program:

—Financial constraints on new community developers to maximize sales, makes it advantageous to reach the full range of housing types and markets. Balanced against these constraints, however, are the "classic" concerns, whether real or imagined, of prejudice among suburban residents and possible loss of community acceptance as a result.

—In comprehensive new community programs seeking a full range of economic activities, the need for diversified labor skills to meet requirements of varied enterprises creates another constraint for socially balanced population.

—To the extent that federal, state, and local government agencies in selected areas become involved in new community programs, realistic efforts for social balance could be promoted or, alternatively, required as a condition of involvement.

POSSIBLE APPROACH

Many proposals have been advanced for implementing new communities policy in metropolitan regions. Approaches include:

1—Substantially independent private operations, with minimum government involvement. Essentially this is a status quo approach. Further "encouragement," as appropriate, by use of government powers to control and spend—including zoning, utilities and municipal services extension, highway and access development, open space acquisition—might also be involved.

2—Land development insurance programs for large-scale

building and land development operations. The beginnings of this program have been incorporated into the '65 act. This approach would involve private land acquisition and the development of sites with back-up support in the form of credit risk insurance through standard Federal Housing Administration sources.

3—Eminent domain procedure involving public acquisition by local authority and improvement, followed by subsequent disposition to developers for final construction operations. Fundamentally, this is an urban renewal type of operation. Precursor of this approach is the open land-arrested development feature in earlier acts.

4—Direct action by state agency to undertake new communities development, with or without eminent domain procedures. A variant of this approach would be direct action by another specially created public or quasi-public development corporation, which would perform similar new community development tasks.

In addition to the approaches outlined, one other can be added. This would be to involve the central city actively in the new community process. This approach could reverse central city concern for compatibility of its interests with new community development. In some senses, this would adapt the "mother city" concept from Greek city-states to a modern urban situation.

The central city has both capabilities and needs that could be effectively served under this approach. Capabilities include substantial know-how in the "business" of city operation derived directly from experience with municipal activities. Specific capabilities related to new community requirements include financial resources and financial know-how; experienced staff in the operation and construction of utilities distribution and treatment facilities; design, construction, and maintenance of street and highway facilities; an array of services in general administration, planning and zoning, urban renewal and redevelopment, public housing and community economic development.